Contents

Study and examination skills

- Differences between GCSE and Sixth Form History
- Extended writing: the structured question and the essay
- How to handle sources in Sixth Form History
- Historical interpretation
- Progression in Sixth Form History
- Examination technique

This chapter of the book is designed to aid Sixth Form students in their preparation for public examinations in History.

Differences between GCSE and Sixth Form History

- **The amount of factual knowledge required for answers to Sixth Form History** questions is more detailed than at GCSE. Factual knowledge in the Sixth Form is used as supporting evidence to help answer historical questions. Knowing the facts is important, but not as important as knowing that factual knowledge supports historical analysis.
- **Extended writing is more important in Sixth Form History.** Students will be expected to answer either structured questions or essays.

Structured questions require students to answer more than one question on a given topic. For example:

1. In what ways did Disraeli try to improve social conditions between 1874 and 1880?

2. To what extent was Disraeli 'a genuine social reformer'?

Each part of the structured question demands a different approach.

Essay questions require students to produce one answer to a given question. For example:

How successful was Gladstone in dealing with Irish problems between 1868 and 1886?

Similarities with GCSE

- **Source analysis and evaluation**

The skills in handling historical sources, which were acquired at GCSE, are developed in Sixth Form History. In the Sixth Form, sources have to be analysed in their historical context, so a good factual knowledge of the subject is important.

- **Historical interpretations**

Skills in historical interpretation at GCSE are also developed in Sixth Form History. The ability to put forward different historical interpretations is important. Students will also be expected to explain why different historical interpretations have occurred.

Extended writing: the structured question and the essay

When faced with extended writing in Sixth Form History students can improve their performance by following a simple routine that attempts to ensure they achieve their best performance.

Answering the question

What are the command instructions?
Different questions require different types of response. For instance, 'In what ways' requires students to point out the various ways something took place in History; 'Why' questions expect students to deal with the causes or consequences of an historical event.

'How far' or 'To what extent' questions require students to produce a balanced, analytical answer. Usually, this will take the form of the case for and case against an historical question.

Are there key words or phrases that require definition or explanation?
It is important for students to show that they understand the meaning of the question. To do this, certain historical terms or words require explanation. For instance, if a question asked 'how far' a politician was an 'innovator', an explanation of the word 'innovator' would be required.

Does the question have specific dates or issues that require coverage?
If the question mentions specific dates, these must be adhered to. For instance, if you are asked to answer a question on Gladstone and the Irish Question it may state clear date limits, such as 1868 to 1886. Also questions may mention a specific aspect such as 'domestic policy' or 'foreign affairs'.

Planning your answer

Once you have decided on what the question requires, write a brief plan. For structured questions this may be brief. This is a useful procedure to make sure that you have ordered the information you require for your answer in the most effective way. For instance, in a balanced, analytical answer this may take the form of jotting down the main points for and against an historical issue raised in the question.

Writing the answer

Communication skills
The quality of written English is important in Sixth Form History. The way you present your ideas on paper can affect the quality of your answer. Since 1996 the Government (through SCAA and QCA) have placed emphasis on the quality of written English in the Sixth Form. Therefore, punctuation, spelling and grammar, which were awarded marks at GCSE, require close attention. Use a dictionary if you are unsure of a word's meaning or spelling. Use the glossary of terms you will find in this book to help you.

The introduction
For structured questions you may wish to dispense with an introduction altogether and begin writing reasons to support an answer straight away. However, essay answers should begin with an introduction. These should be both concise and precise. Introductions help 'concentrate the mind' on the question you are about to answer. Remember, do not try to write a conclusion as your opening sentence. Instead, outline briefly the areas you intend to discuss in your answer.

Balancing analysis with factual evidence
It is important to remember that factual knowledge should be used to

support analysis. Merely 'telling the story' of an historical event is not enough. A structured question or essay should contain separate paragraphs, each addressing an analytical point that helps to answer the question. If, for example, the question asks for reasons why the Boer War began in 1899, each paragraph should provide a reason for the outbreak of the Boer War. In order to support and sustain the analysis evidence is required. Therefore, your factual knowledge should be used to substantiate analysis. Good structured question and essay answers integrate analysis and factual knowledge.

Seeing connections between reasons
In dealing with 'why'-type questions it is important to remember that the reasons for an historical event might be interconnected. Therefore, it is important to mention the connections between reasons. Also, it might be important to identify a hierarchy or reasons – that is, are some reasons more important than others in explaining an historical event?

Using quotations and statistical data
One aspect of supporting evidence that sustains analysis is the use of quotations. These can be from either a historian or a contemporary. However, unless these quotations are linked with analysis and supporting evidence, they tend to be of little value.

It can also be useful to support analysis with statistical data. In questions that deal with social and economic change, precise statistics that support your argument can be very persuasive.

The conclusion
All structured questions and essays require conclusions. If, for example, a question requires a discussion of 'how far' you agree with a question, you should offer a judgement in your conclusion. Don't be afraid of this – say what you think. Students who write analytical answer, ably supported by factual evidence, under-perform because they fail to provide a conclusion that deals directly with the question.

Source analysis

Assessment Objectives
1 knowledge and understanding of history
2 evaluation and analysis skills
3 a) source analysis in historical context
b) historical interpretation

Source analysis forms an integral part of the study of History. In Sixth Form History source analysis is identified as an important skill in Assessment Objective 3.

In dealing with sources you should be aware that historical sources must be used 'in historical context' in Sixth Form History. Therefore, in this book sources are used with the factual information in each chapter. Also, a specific source analysis question is included.

How to handle sources in Sixth Form History

In dealing with sources, a number of basic hints will allow you to deal effectively with source-based questions and to build on your knowledge and skill in using sources at GCSE.

Written sources

Attribution and date
It is important to identify who has written the source and when it was written. This information can be very important. If, for instance, a source was written by Benjamin Disraeli during the General Election campaign of 1874, this information will be of considerable importance if you are asked about the usefulness (utility) or reliability of the source as evidence of Conservative election policy in 1874.

It is important to note that just because a source is a primary source does not mean it is more useful or less reliable than a secondary source. Both primary and secondary sources need to be analysed to decide how useful and reliable they are. This can be determined by studying other issues.

Is the content factual or opinionated?
Once you have identified the author and date of the source, it is important to study its content. The content may be factual, stating what has happened or what may happen. On the other hand, it may contain opinions that should be handled with caution. These may contain bias. Even if a source is mainly factual, there might be important and deliberate gaps in factual evidence that can make a source biased and unreliable. Usually, written sources contain elements of both opinion and factual evidence. It is important to judge the balance between these two parts.

Has the source been written for a particular audience?
To determine the reliability of a source it is important to know to whom it is directed. For instance, a public speech may be made to achieve a particular purpose and may not contain the author's true beliefs or feelings. In contrast, a private diary entry may be much more reliable in this respect.

Corroborative evidence
To test whether or not a source is reliable, the use of other evidence to support or corroborate the information it contains is important. Cross-referencing with other sources is a way of achieving this; so is cross-referencing with historical information contained within a chapter.

Visual sources

Cartoons
Cartoons are a popular form of source used at both GCSE and in Sixth Form History. However, analysing cartoons can be a demanding exercise. Not only will you be expected to understand the content of the cartoon, you may also have to explain a written caption – which appears usually at the bottom of the cartoon. In addition, cartoons will need placing in historical context. Therefore, a good knowledge of the subject matter of the topic of the cartoon will be important. To test your ability to analyse cartoons successfully use the *Punch* cartoon on page 151.

Photographs
'The camera never lies'! This phrase is not always true. When analysing photographs, study the attribution and date. Photographs can be changed so they are not always an accurate visual representation of events. Also, to test whether or not a photograph is a good representation of events you will need corroborative evidence.

Maps
Maps which appear in Sixth Form History are predominantly secondary sources. These are used to support factual coverage in the text by providing information in a different medium. Therefore, to assess whether or not information contained in maps is accurate or useful, reference should be made to other information. It is also important with line written sources to check the attribution and date. These could be significant.

Statistical data and graphs
It is important when dealing with this type of source to check carefully the nature of the information contained in data or in a graph. It might state that the information is in tons (tonnes) or another measurement. Be careful to check if the information is in index numbers. These are a statistical device where a base year is chosen and given the figure 100. All other

figures are based on a percentage difference from that base year. For instance, if 1850 is taken as a base year for iron production it is given the figure of 100. If the index number for iron production in 1860 is 117 it means that iron production has increased by 17% above the 1850 figure.

An important point to remember when dealing with data and graphs over a period of time is to identify trends and patterns in the information. Merely describing the information in written form is not enough.

Historical interpretation

An important feature of both GCSE and Sixth Form History is the issue of historical interpretation. In Sixth Form History it is important for students to be able to explain why historians differ, or have differed, in their interpretation of the past.

Availability of evidence

An important reason is the availability of evidence on which to base historical judgements. As new evidence comes to light, an historian today may have more information on which to base judgements than historians in the past. For instance, a major source of information about 19th-century political history is the Public Record Office (PRO) in Kew, London. Some of the information held at the PRO has remained confidential, in some cases for 50 to 100 years. Therefore, it is only recently that historians have been able to analyse and assess this evidence.

'A philosophy of history?'

Many historians have a specific view of history that will affect the way they make their historical judgements. For instance, Marxist historians – who take the view from the writings of Karl Marx the founder of modern socialism – believe that society has been made up of competing economic and social classes. They also place considerable importance on economic reasons in human decision making. Therefore, a Marxist historian of Chartism may take a completely different viewpoint to a non-Marxist historian.

The role of the individual

Some historians have seen past history as being moulded by the acts of specific individuals who have changed history. Gladstone, Disraeli and Lord Palmerston are seen as individuals whose personality and beliefs changed the course of 19th-century British history. Other historians have tended to 'downplay' the role of individuals; instead, they highlight the importance of more general social, economic and political change. Rather than seeing Joseph Chamberlain as an individual who changed the course of political history, these historians tend to see him as representing the views of a broader group of individuals, such as the industrial middle class of late Victorian Britain.

Placing different emphasis on the same historical evidence

Even if historians do not possess different philosophies of history or place different emphasis on the role of the individual, it is still possible for them to disagree because they place different emphases on aspects of the same factual evidence. As a result, Sixth Form History should be seen as a subject that encourages debate about the past based on historical evidence.

Progression in Sixth Form History

The ability to achieve high standards in Sixth Form History involves the acquisition of a number of skills:

- Good written communication skills
- Acquiring a sound factual knowledge
- Evaluating factual evidence and making historical conclusions based on that evidence
- Source analysis
- Understanding the nature of historical interpretation
- Understanding the causes and consequences of historical events
- Understanding themes in history which will involve a study of a specific topic over a long period of time
- Understanding the ideas of change and continuity associated with themes.

Students should be aware that the acquisition of these skills will take place gradually over the time spent in the Sixth Form. At the beginning of the course, the main emphasis may be on the acquisition of factual knowledge, particularly when the body of knowledge studied at GCSE was different.

When dealing with causation, students will have to build on their skills from GCSE. They will not only be expected to identify reasons for an historical event but also to provide a hierarchy of causes. They should identify the main causes and less important causes. They may also identify that causes may be interconnected and linked. Progression in Sixth Form History will come with answering the questions at the end of each sub-section in this book and practising the skills outlined through the use of the factual knowledge contained in the book.

Examination technique

The ultimate challenge for any Sixth Form historian is the ability to produce quality work under examination conditions. Examinations will take the form of either modular examinations taken in January and June or an 'end of course' set of examinations.

Here is some advice on how to improve your performance in an examination.

- **Read the whole examination paper thoroughly**
  Make sure that the questions you choose are those for which you can produce a good answer. Don't rush – allow time to decide which questions to choose. It is probably too late to change your mind half way through answering a question.

- **Read the question very carefully**
  Once you have made the decision to answer a specific question, read it very carefully. Make sure you understand the precise demands of the question. Think about what is required in your answer. It is much better to think about this before you start writing, rather than trying to steer your essay in a different direction half way through.

- **Make a brief plan**
  Sketch out what you intend to include in your answer. Order the points

you want to make. Examiners are not impressed with additional information included at the end of the essay, with indicators such as arrows or asterisks.

- **Pace yourself as you write**
  Success in examinations has a lot to do with successful time management. If, for instance, you have to answer an essay question in approximately 45 minutes, then you should be one-third of the way through after 15 minutes. With 30 minutes gone, you should start writing the last third of your answer.

Where a question is divided into sub-questions, make sure you look at the mark tariff for each question. If in a 20-mark question a sub-question is worth a maximum of 5 marks, then you should spend approximately one-quarter of the time allocated for the whole question on this sub-question.

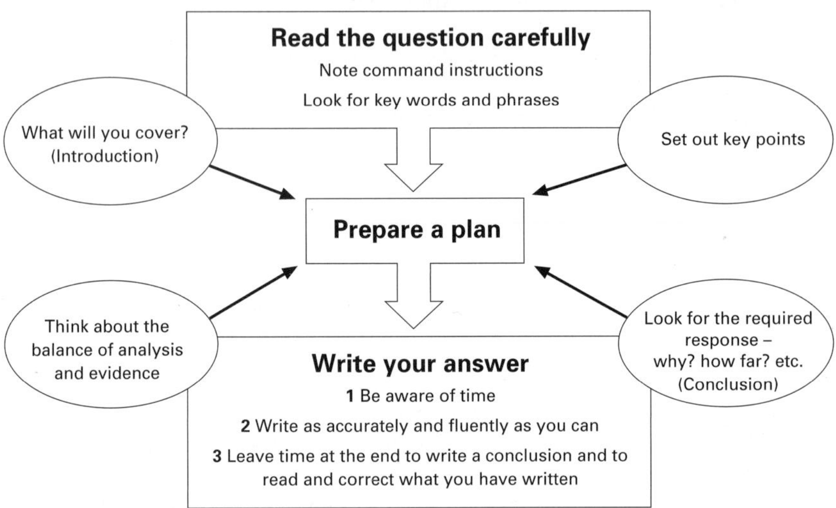

Britain 1783–1918: a synoptic assessment

1.1 How did British society change in the years 1783–1918?
1.2 Why was the extension of the right to vote an important issue in the British political system between 1783 and 1918?
1.3 How did political parties develop in the years 1783–1918?
1.4 Why did Britain experience rapid economic growth between 1783 and 1873?
1.5 What impact did relative economic decline have on Britain in the years 1873 to 1918 ?
1.6 What were the main aims of British foreign policy 1783–1918?
1.7 Were the British 'reluctant imperialists'?

Key Issues

- *Why did the British political system change from rule by the monarchy and aristocracy in 1783 to a parliamentary democracy by 1918?*
- *Why did Britain experience rapid economic growth and then relative economic decline in the years 1783–1918?*
- *Why did Britain become the world's major imperial power in the years 1783–1918?*

Overview

BRITAIN underwent considerable political, social and economic change in the period 1783 to 1918. It began and ended with a major war. In 1783, Britain had just lost the American War of Independence. For much of the period 1793 to 1815 Britain was at war with Revolutionary and Napoleonic France. Victories at Trafalgar, in 1805, and Waterloo, in 1815, confirmed Britain's position as a European Great Power. In fact, Nelson's naval victories, culminating in Trafalgar, ensured that Britain also became the world's major naval power throughout the 19th century.

In political terms, Britain was a constitutional monarchy in 1783 where the monarch, George III, could exercise considerable political influence. In 1800, George III intervened to prevent Catholic emancipation. In 1834 William IV was able to dismiss the Prime Minister, Lord Melbourne. By 1918, however, the role of the monarchy had changed considerably. In 1918, George V reigned but did not rule. The monarchy had become the ceremonial head of nation and Empire.

This change took place alongside the growth and development of political parties as the real power base in the formation and dismissal of governments. Although political parties had existed in Britain since the reign of Charles II (1649–85), their growth as nationwide institutions capable of gaining electoral support in their quest for government office only occurred during the 19th century. The need to become national organisations was a response to the extension of the right to vote. In 1800, only 3% of adult males could vote. Through parliamentary reform acts in 1832, 1867, 1884 and 1918 the right to vote was extended to include, by 1918, all adult males over the age of 21 and women over the age of 30. The British political system had been transformed from rule by a few to a democracy.

This political transformation had taken place during a period of dramatic social and economic change. In 1783, Britain had already undergone the early stages of an **industrial revolution**. Britain was alone in the world as the only country to have experienced such economic and social change. In the years 1783 to 1873 the British economy grew rapidly, making Britain 'the workshop of the world', the centre for world manufacturing, finance and trade. After 1873, however, Britain's position as the world's major economic power came under threat. The growth in economic power of the United States and Germany led many in Britain to question why Britain had lost its economic lead. Although Britain was able to defeat one of its major economic rivals, Germany, in the First World War, by 1918 Britain had lost its economic supremacy to the United States of America.

Industrial revolution: A term meaning that the majority of the working population became involved in manufacturing industry (the secondary sector of the economy) rather than agriculture (the primary sector of the economy). This took place relatively rapidly from the mid-18th century onwards. It also involved the idea of 'self-sustaining growth', an idea associated with the American economist Walt Rostow. This meant the economy was able to grow using wealth it had created through manufacturing. Such a change would then be irreversible.

Britain's economic development was accompanied by major social change. Although new industrial towns had been created by the Industrial Revolution, Britain was still a predominantly agricultural country in 1783 with most of the population living and working in the countryside. By 1918, Britain had a predominantly urban population with the majority of the population employed in manufacturing and commerce rather than farming. With the rise of industry and commerce came the rise in number and importance of new social classes: the industrial middle class and the industrial working class. The traditional wealthy élite, the **aristocracy**, was now faced with an economic and a political challenge from these groups. The campaigns for the extension of the right to vote are interconnected with these social developments. The rise in political power of the House of Commons and the decline in power of the House of Lords reflected the decline in political power of the aristocracy.

Aristocracy: A Greek word meaning, literally, 'the government of a state by its best citizens'. In the period covered by this book, the aristocracy comprised titled families whose wealth passed down the generations by inheritance. About 200 or so families controlled most of the nation's land and dominated the political and social leadership.

While British economic power was under challenge in the years after 1873, Britain's imperial power reached its height. Although Britain had acquired a large empire in the 18th century, the loss of the American colonies in 1783 marked the end of this first empire. However, during the 19th century, and in particular after 1880, Britain acquired the largest empire in world history. By 1918 the British Empire covered one-quarter of the world's land area and encompassed one-third of the world's population. The centre of British imperial power throughout the period 1815 to 1918 was India. The focus of British foreign policy throughout the period was to preserve Britain's economic and imperial position. For this reason, Britain was an enthusiastic supporter of the preservation of European peace through the balance of power.

On three occasions between 1783 and 1918 Britain went to war with another Great Power, 1793–1815, 1854 and 1914. On these occasions, the prime concern was to maintain the European balance of power.

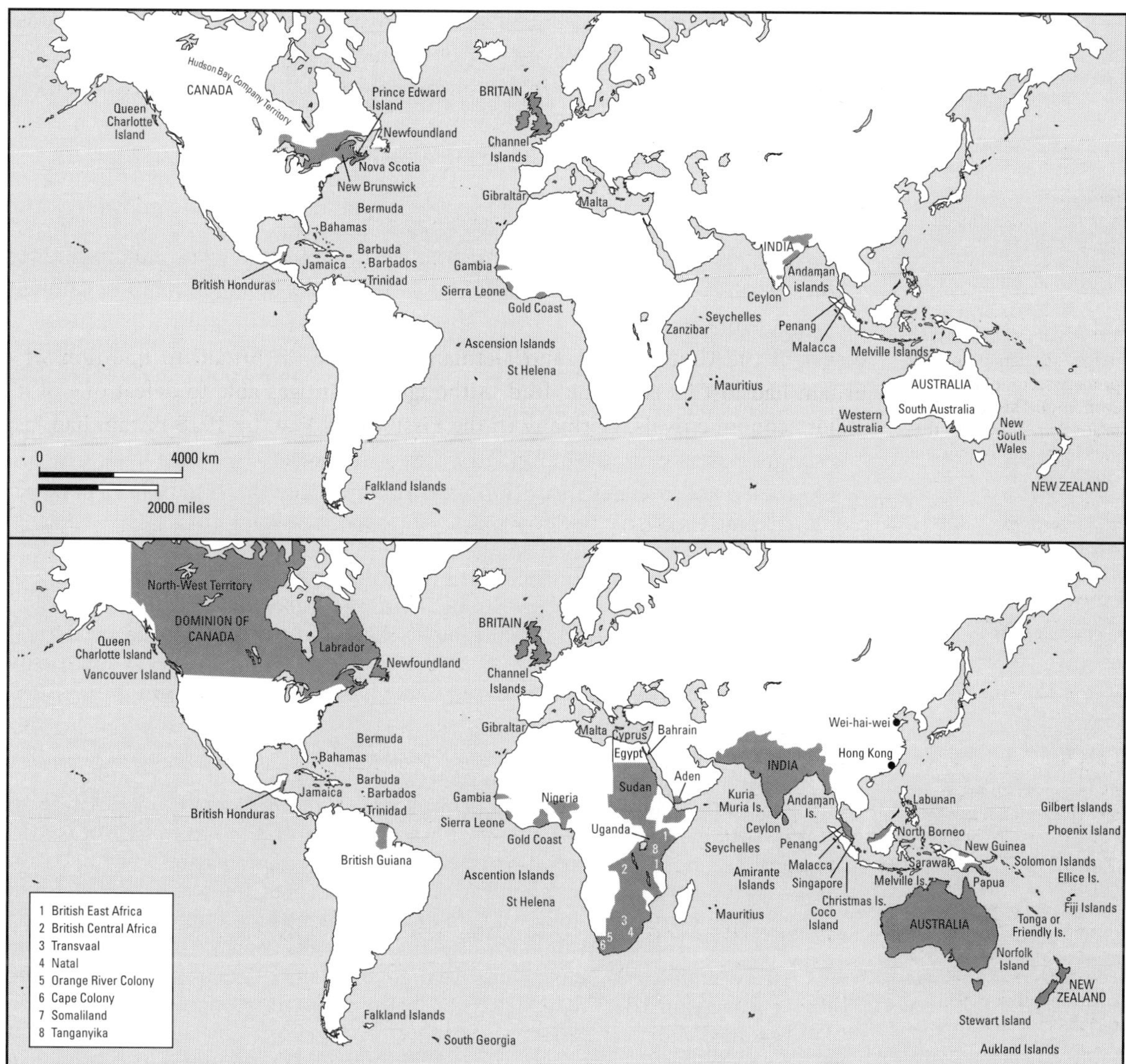

The British Empire in 1783 (top) and 1918 (bottom)

1.1 *How did British society change in the years 1783–1918?*

In 1783, British society was dominated by the monarchy, the landowning class (in particular the aristocracy), and the Established Church. In England, Ireland and Wales, the **Established Church** was the Anglican Church. In Scotland, it was the Presbyterian Church of Scotland. These institutions formed the ruling élite of the State. They dominated the House of Lords which, until 1911, possessed an absolute veto on all legislation passed by Parliament. They also dominated government. Nearly every prime minister between 1783 and 1918 came from this group. The most notable exceptions were Benjamin Disraeli and David Lloyd George. It was not until 1868 that the first non-Anglican Cabinet minister was appointed, John Bright, a Quaker.

Established Church: The Anglican Church in England, Wales and Ireland and the Church of Scotland in Scotland. This was the religion recognised officially as the State religion. The monarch was Supreme Governor and the religion had special privileges and received financial support from the government.

In England, Wales and Ireland, education was also dominated by the Anglican establishment. Oxford, Cambridge and Trinity College, Dublin were all Anglican foundations. So were the major public schools: Eton, Harrow and Winchester.

Religion and the Established Church

Nonconformity: Religious groups who were Protestant but not Anglican. These included Quakers, Methodists, Baptists and Unitarians. They wished to have political, social and religious equality with Anglicans.

In the years after 1783, however, the Anglican landowning establishment came under attack. Firstly, within England and Wales, the Church of England was challenged by the rise in popularity of **Nonconformity**. The development of Methodism in the 18th century and the growth of churches such as the Baptists, Unitarians and Congregationalists meant that 19th-century Britain was affected by intense religious rivalry between nonconformist and Anglican. This rivalry was given a boost when, in 1851, the American Horace Mann took the only religious census in British history. The census revealed that the nonconformist and Anglican churches had approximately the same number of followers. (According to the census, of the 6.3 million who attended church on Easter Sunday 49% were nonconformists, 47% were Anglicans and 4% were Catholics.) This religious rivalry took place in many areas. In politics, the repeal of the Test and Corporation Acts in 1828 gave the nonconfomists equal political rights with Anglicans. The rise of political nonconformity was an important factor in the formation of the Liberal Party during the 1850s. Conflict also took place in education, which proved to be a major issue dividing Anglicans from nonconformists throughout the period. Finally, many nonconformists wished to see an end to the Anglican Church's established status. In this, they were partly successful. In 1869, the Anglican Church was disestablished in Ireland and, in 1914, in Wales.

The other major religious group in the United Kingdom was Roman Catholics. Although they comprised a small minority of the populations of England, Wales and Scotland, they constituted 80% of the population of Ireland in 1783. Before 1829, Catholics were prevented from sitting as MPs and getting this situation reversed – **Catholic emancipation** – was a dominant issue in British politics from 1801 to 1829, when it was achieved. From 1829 onwards, the House of Commons contained a group of Irish Catholic MPs who supported the idea of greater self-government for Ireland. In the 1830s and 1840s, this group was led by Daniel O'Connell. Later in the century, after 1870, many Irish MPs belonged to the Home Rule Party, which became Britain's third largest party.

Catholic emancipation: The right of Catholics to sit as Members of Parliament (MPs). Although before 1829 Catholics could vote in elections, if they possessed the necessary voting qualifications, the oath of allegiance all MPs had to take before sitting in the House of Commons was anti-catholic. After the passage of the Catholic Relief Act in 1829, the oath was altered.

Although Catholics formed a small part of the population of Britain in 1783, this situation changed dramatically after 1845 with the onset of the Great Irish Potato Famine. Over 1.5 million Irish emigrated, many going to Britain. Regions such as Clydeside in Scotland and South Lancashire in England received large numbers of Irish Catholic immigrants. In fact, so large were the numbers that the Liverpool Scotland Road Division constituency returned an Irish Home Rule MP from 1885 to 1924.

Catholicism also had an important impact on the Church of England. Beginning in Oxford in the 1830s and 1840s, many Anglican academics supported the idea that the Anglican church should adopt Roman Catholic religious practices while maintaining the Church of England's independence from Rome. The Oxford Movement, led by Henry Newman and John Keble, established Anglo-Catholicism which became an important and divisive force with the 19th-century Anglican Church. Newman eventually left the Anglican Church and became a Roman Catholic cardinal.

The decline of the landowning class

Perhaps the most important challenge to the Anglican-landowning establishment were the social changes brought about by the Industrial Revolution. The growth in size and economic importance of the industrial middle class meant that wealth was no longer centred on the land. The most dramatic examples of this challenge to the landowning class came in 1830 to 1832 and in 1846. In 1830–32 middle-class agitation was an important factor in the extension of the **franchise** which broke the landowning monopoly on political power. In 1846, partly as a result of agitation by the Anti-Corn Law League, the economic basis of landowning power was threatened with the repeal of the Corn Laws. Although landowners did not face financial ruin immediately after the repeal of the Corn Law in 1846, this event marked a turning point in the decline of landowner power in Britain. It was not until the 1870s that agricultural Britain faced a major economic depression that lasted until the outbreak of the First World War.

Franchise: The right to vote. Also known as suffrage.

Although the landowning classes' dominant position in politics and the economy declined during the 19th century, it did not disappear. Aristocrats continued to be important members of every government, including prime minister. The last aristocrat to hold the position of Prime Minister was Lord Salisbury, who retired in 1902.

However, in 1911, following a major constitutional crisis over the Budget, the House of Lords lost its absolute right to **veto** legislation. As if to confirm the decline in the political power of the aristocracy it has been a convention of Parliament that all Prime Ministers since Lord Salisbury must be MPs.

Veto (Latin – 'I forbid'): A negative vote exercised constitutionally by an individual, an institution or a state. It has the effect of automatically defeating the motion against which it is cast.

By the early 20th century, the aristocracy may have lost political and economic power but they maintained their social prestige. Many members of the industrial middle class wished to emulate the aristocracy by sending their sons to Eton and Harrow, and Oxford and Cambridge. Even at the end of the First World War many a 'captain of industry' was willing to part with a large sum of money to buy a noble title from Lloyd George, the Prime Minister.

The decline of the monarchy's political power

The decline in the political power of the aristocracy was mirrored by a decline in the political power of the monarchy. In 1783, the monarchy still possessed considerable political power. The monarch could create peers and had considerable influence over many parliamentary constituencies. Up until 1867, a general election had to be held on the occasion of a monarch's death. With the reform of the electoral system and the decline in power of the aristocracy, monarchic power was almost inevitably going to decline as well. However, the decline was accelerated by the nature of the monarchy. In 1815, George III was regarded as insane and his son acted as **regent**. His successor, George IV, was deeply unpopular and in 1837 an 18-year-old girl, Victoria, occupied the throne.

Regent: Person who is given royal authority on behalf of another. It usually applies when the monarch is a minor (under age).

William IV, in 1834, may have been the last monarch to dismiss a prime minister but it did not mean the monarch was without political influence. Victoria's consort, Prince Albert, worked closely with many prime ministers, in particular Robert Peel. In 1861, his intervention in the Trent Incident helped prevent war breaking out between Britain and the United States. In 1880, Victoria refused to read out in the Queen's Speech that British troops were to be withdrawn from Afghanistan. But this did not prevent Gladstone from doing so. However, in 1894, Victoria ignored Gladstone's advice concerning his successor as Liberal Prime Minister and chose Lord Rosebery instead.

George V also tried to play an advisory role when he hosted the Buckingham Palace Conference on Ulster, in June 1914. He too was aware of the need to sustain the monarchy's popularity by changing the family name in 1917, at the height of the Great War, from Saxe-Coburg to Windsor.

The changing role of women

An important social change that occurred during the 19th century was the position of women within society. The Industrial Revolution had brought about new opportunities for women in the economy. Women were able to obtain employment in textile mills and factories. But the most likely occupation for a woman in Victorian Britain was in domestic service. The change in the economic position of women acted as a catalyst to the move for women's political rights. Votes for women was discussed seriously for the first time during the Reform Bill debates of 1867. However, it was not until 1894 that women could vote for parochial councils and in 1907 for county councils. In 1870, 1882 and 1884, Married Women's Acts gave married women considerable financial independence. However, it took until 1918 for women to gain the right to vote in national elections and to become MPs. These developments took place following a concerted political campaign by women's groups – the most notable being the Suffragettes and Suffragists (see Chapter 22) – but also due to the major role women played in the war economy during the Great War.

1.2 Why was the extension of the right to vote an important issue in the British political system between 1783 and 1918?

One of the most significant political developments between 1783 and 1918 is the transformation of Britain from a state ruled by the monarchy and aristocracy into a parliamentary democracy. This transformation occurred through the passage of a number of Acts of Parliament in 1832, 1867, 1884 and 1918. Although the passage of the first two acts was associated with rioting and demonstrations, the process took place relatively peacefully.

TABLE 1: *The population and electorate of the UK, 1831–1918*

	Population	Electorate
1831	24 million	435,000*
1833	24 million	813,000 (1 in 7 adult males)
1865	30 million	1,430,000
1868	30 million	2,500,000 (1 in 3 adult males)
1883	35 million	3,000,000
1885	36 million	4,900,000 (2 in 3 adult males)
1918	42 million	21,394,000 (61% adult males; 40% adult females)

* = estimate

Why did the aristocracy, who dominated the political system and Parliament, allow the extension of the right to vote? One major factor was the tremendous social and economic change that occurred in Britain during the Industrial Revolution. Before the beginning of the Industrial Revolution (about 1760–1914), the main source of economic wealth in Britain had been land and agriculture. As the largest landowners, the aristocracy were the wealthiest members of society. They dominated the House of Lords. They also dominated the electoral system: without the secret ballot, and with very small electorates, the landowning class were able to 'buy' seats, and thus have a dominant role in the House of Commons. According to Patrick Colquhoun's estimate, in 1815, the aristocracy and nobility comprised only 53,000 out of an estimated population of 20 million.

Artisans: A term to describe members of the working class. They usually acquired a trade after a lengthy period of apprenticeship (e.g. carpenters, mechanics and boilermakers).

With the Industrial Revolution the industrial middle class (factory owners and merchants) and the industrial working class (factory workers and **artisans**) grew rapidly in number. As these social classes gained increased economic wealth, they also wished to gain political power through securing access to the political system through the electoral system and, thence, to the House of Commons.

By 1783 the electoral system, which had been based on a pre-industrial society, was out of date. Although attempts to change the electoral system were made in 1785, the French **Revolution** (1789–1815) prevented any attempts at parliamentary reform. Throughout the period 1815–30, parliamentary reform was an important political issue among radical elements in society. By 1830, it was also an important issue within the Whig Party, which regarded the unreformed electoral system as favouring the Tory Party. Thanks to a split in the Tory Party and fear of rioting and unrest, the Whig Government was able to pass the Great Reform Act of 1832. Although regarded at the time as a final settlement in the electoral system, it in fact paved the way for moves towards further reform. In 1835, the electoral system for local government in towns was reformed and the size of the electorate was increased dramatically. (Further reform in 1888 and 1894 brought **democracy** to local government.) It also provided the unifying focus for the world's first working-class political movement, Chartism, which from 1836 to 1850 demanded major parliamentary reform.

Revolution: A complete change in society usually accompanied by violence. The French Revolution set an example for others to follow due to the execution of the King and his replacement by a republic (see page 206).

Democracy: A system of running organisations, businesses, government etc. in which each member is entitled to vote and participate in management decisions.

Between 1865 and 1867, extra-parliamentary agitation, again, helped force an extension of the franchise. The 1867 Reform Act gave the franchise to artisans. In 1884, agricultural labourers were added and, in 1918, most adult males and women over 30 joined the electoral system.

These changes meant that Britain was able to modernise its electoral system peacefully. The terms of the 1832, 1867 and 1884 Reform Acts were phrased in such a way as to allow a specific social class to enter the political process. In 1832 it was the industrial middle class, in 1867 the skilled working class and in 1884 the agricultural worker. It was not until 1918 that universal male suffrage (one of the Chartist demands of the 1830s and 1840s) was achieved. Even then, those men who had been conscientious objectors during the First World War lost their right to vote.

TABLE 2: Parliamentary and electoral reform, 1832–1918

1832	Reform Act
1835	Municipal Corporations Act created elected town government
1858	Abolition of Property Qualification for MPs
1867	Second Reform Act
1872	Secret Ballot Act
1883	Corrupt and Illegal Practices Act aimed at preventing corruption at elections
1884	Third Reform Act
1885	Redistribution of Seats Act creates equal electoral districts and single-member constituencies
1888	County Councils Act creates elected county government
1894	Parish Councils Act creates elected village government
1911	Payment for MPs
1918	Reform Act creates universal male suffrage and gives women the right to vote and become MPs for the first time.

1.3 How did political parties develop in the years 1783–1918?

The evolution of a parliamentary democracy by 1918 is closely associated with the development of political parties. As the 19th century progressed, these institutions became the base for political power. In the 18th century, it was unlikely that any prime minister would survive in office if he lacked the support of the monarch. In the 19th century, prime ministers had to ensure they had majority support in the House of Commons. Although many MPs were independent of party allegiance in 1815, by the end of the century the political system was in the hands of political parties.

The 19th-century political system was dominated by the Whig/Liberal Party and the Tory/Conservative Party. The change in name of these political groupings reflects a change in aims, composition and organisation, which was associated with the extension of the franchise. Throughout the century, the Tory/Conservative Party was associated with defending the Anglican landowning establishment. The Whig/Liberal Party was associated with gaining religious and political equality for nonconformists and free trade.

In organisational terms, the parliamentary reform acts were important milestones. Until 1832, political parties were organised as groups within parliament. Outside parliament, party organisation was limited to a number of select gentlemen's clubs in London, such as Whites and Boodles. After 1832, both major parties began to set up registration associations to gain support from the newly enfranchised electorate. After the 1867 Reform Act, first the Conservatives and then the Liberals set up a nationwide network of party organisations. In 1867, the National Union of Conservative Associations was formed, followed three years later by the creation of Conservative Central Office. In 1877, the National Liberal Federation was formed. As the electorate became ever larger, leading politicians realised they had to engage in nationwide campaigning to gain votes. Peel's 'Tamworth Manifesto' in 1835 was the first example of this development. For the general election campaign of that year, the party's name was officially changed from Tory to Conservative. Later in the century, Disraeli's speeches at Manchester and the Crystal Palace in 1872, and Gladstone's Midlothian campaigns of 1879 and 1880 are further examples.

The development of political parties in the years 1783 to 1918 was far from smooth. Between 1828 and 1830 and, again, in 1846 the Tory/Conservative Party split. In 1846, the landowning and industrial middle-class wings of the party split over the repeal of the Corn Laws. The industrial middle-class wing became known as 'Peelites', and subsequently joined the Liberal Party in 1859. Between 1903 and 1905, the Conservatives again suffered a major split over economic policy – this time on the issue of tariff reform.

The Whig/Liberal Party was also prone to splits and divisions. The Whigs, along with Peelites and Radicals, formed the Liberal Party in 1859. However, from its creation the party was in danger of splitting apart. In 1866, the Party split over parliamentary reform, Robert Lowe leading an 'Adullamite' faction against the Liberal plan for reform. In 1874, the Liberal Party's internal divisions led to its electoral defeat. However, the most spectacular split was in 1886 over Irish Home Rule. The party split between Gladstonian Liberals and Liberal Unionists, the latter joining the Conservatives in 1895. Although the Liberals recovered in 1905–15 to win three successive general elections, another split between the Liberal leaders Asquith and Lloyd George, in December 1916, proved to be a blow from which the party never recovered.

Although the period is dominated by these parties, two other political parties did make a significant impact. Between 1870 and 1918, the Irish Home Rule Party acted as a third party. From the mid-1880s to 1918, it consistently won three-quarters of the Irish seats and, between 1892 and 1895 and between 1910 and 1915, Irish Home Rule support kept the Liberal Party in power. Yet in the years 1916 to 1918 the Party declined rapidly, being replaced as the main voice for Irish nationalism by Sinn Fein.

The other political party was the Labour Party. Founded in 1900 as the Labour Representation Committee, it did not change its name to the Labour Party until 1906. The Party remained a relatively minor political force until 1917–18 when it benefited from reorganisation and the split in the Liberal

Party to gain 22.2% of the vote and 63 seats in the December 1918 general election.

The influence of pressure groups

Pressure groups: Organisations that wish to influence political decision making but do not wish to gain political power. (See also page 235.)

Apart from political parties, **pressure groups** were another major force for change. These organisations did not want to win political power. Instead, they wished to influence government in favour of a particular issue or group in society. In Ireland, in 1823, Daniel O'Connell helped create the Catholic Association which supported the idea of Catholic emancipation. It was this pressure group that forced the Government to pass the Catholic Relief Act of 1829. In parliamentary reform, the Birmingham Political Union in 1830–32 and the Reform League and Reform Union in 1865–67 kept up pressure on Parliament to push through electoral reform.

Perhaps the most famous early Victorian pressure group was the Anti-Corn Law League. Under the leadership of Richard Cobden, John Bright and Wilson, this group pressured Sir Robert Peel into repealing the Corn Law. When repeal came in 1846, this development not only split the Conservative Party but also was a milestone on Britain's road to becoming a free trade nation.

The political party most closely associated with pressure groups was the Liberal Party. In fact, the party could be regarded as a coalition of pressure groups. The United Kingdom Alliance and the Band of Hope Union wished to see changes in laws relating to alcohol drinking. The Liberation Society wanted to disestablish the Church of England while the National Education League wanted free, compulsory state elementary education. These competing interests were one of the reasons why it was difficult to keep the Liberal Party united.

A set of pressure groups which represent a section of society was trade unions. Throughout the period 1783 to 1918 trade unions attempted to improve the pay and working conditions of their members. Groups of workers were formed in the 18th century for this purpose. However, with the passing of the Combination Acts of 1799 and 1800, trade unions were made illegal. These Acts were passed because the Government feared links between trade unions and ideas associated with the French Revolution. Although legalised in 1824, trade unions found it difficult to organise and develop due to opposition from Parliament and the courts. The Tolpuddle Martyrs and the collapse of the Grand National Consolidated Trades Union, both in 1834, are examples of this problem. It was not until the formation of New Model Unions after 1850 that trade unions began to wield some economic and political power. However, trade unions were limited to only the skilled element of the workforce. Only between 1871 and 1875 did trade unions gain full legal protection and the right to picket peacefully.

Although closely associated with the Liberal Party from the 1850s to the 1890s, the trade unions eventually decided in 1900 to found their own political party, the Labour Representation Committee, which became the Labour Party.

?

1. In what ways was the organisation of political parties different by 1918 from 1783?

2. The period 1783–1918 saw many turning points in the development of political parties.

Using the information contained above, find out when these turning points occurred.

3. Which turning points in the development of political parties do you regard as the most important?

Give reasons for your answer.

1.4 Why did Britain experience rapid economic growth between 1783 and 1873?

The political changes that occurred during the 19th century took place against a background of major economic change. In the period 1783 to 1873, Britain could rightly claim to be the 'workshop of the world'. Britain was the leading country in the manufacture of textiles, in particular cotton, iron and coal. In addition, Britain was the world's major shipbuilding nation with British merchant shipping dominating world trade. To help finance these developments the **City of London** was the world's financial centre for banking, insurance and financial trading in shares and commodities. Why was Britain so prosperous compared to other countries at this time?

City of London: General name given to the banks, insurance companies and financial institutions in the centre of London.

- Firstly, Britain had acquired sufficient financial wealth during the 18th century to finance industrial and commercial growth. The growth of the British Empire in the Caribbean and North America and the development of the Atlantic slave trade had provided the wealth that could then be invested in the development of industries such as cotton textile production.
- Secondly, this acquisition of wealth took place at a time of rapid population growth. In 1711, the population of England and Wales was estimated at 6 million. By 1791, it had risen to 8.3 million and by 1821 to 13.9 million. This increased population provided both a source of labour and a market for manufactured goods.
- Thirdly, **technological innovation** enabled manufacturing production to increase rapidly. In cotton textile production Hargreaves' 'spinning jenny' in 1764, Crompton's mule in 1779 and Cartwright's power loom in 1785 all helped to increase the output per worker. These changes also took place at a time when manufacturing was being relocated from cottage-based domestic industry to factories located near sources of power, such as rivers for water power or coalfields for steam power. Therefore, in the years after 1760 to the mid-19th century industrial towns in east Lancashire and west Yorkshire – such as Blackburn, Manchester, Leeds and Bradford – developed rapidly. The two latter towns were involved in woollen textile production. In Scotland the Clyde valley towns of Coatbridge, Hamilton and Motherwell developed due to the coal and iron industries.

Technological innovation: The practical application of inventions that improve the production process.

To allow the easy movement of raw materials and finished goods, a cheap and extensive transportation system was required. Canals provided the basis of the late 18th-century transport network linking industrial towns like Birmingham to seaports and sources of raw materials. However, from 1830 onwards, railways had superseded canals. By 1870, Britain had the most

The port of Liverpool in the late 19th century

extensive railway system in the world. In that year, it carried 490 million passengers on 13,500 miles of track.

A stimulus to economic growth in the late 18th and early 19th centuries was the demand for goods associated with warfare. From 1793 to 1815, Britain was almost continually at war with France. This led to government demand for shipping, uniforms and armaments.

After 1815, economic growth was sustained by the gradual adoption of a free trade policy. In the years 1823–63, Britain abolished virtually all taxes on imported and exported goods. As Britain had the most advanced, competitive economy in the world, British businessmen were able to acquire new markets for their goods. The British Indian Empire and China provided huge potential markets in Asia, while a free trade treaty with the Turkish Empire in 1838, and with France in 1860 (the Cobden Treaty) allowed the economic exploitation of European middle-eastern markets.

Government policy also aided the development of the economy internally. Acts passed in the 1830s and 1840s allowed the creation of joint stock, limited liability companies. In 1844, the Bank Charter Act placed British banking on a sound financial footing. Low taxation and the avoidance of major war, except in 1854–56, provided economic stability. Britain's political stability in the years 1815–73 stood in marked contrast to some of its potential economic rivals in Europe. For example, France was affected by revolution in 1830 and 1848, followed by a political coup in 1851 and military defeat in 1870–71 by Prussia.

1. What were the main reasons for the rapid economic growth of the period 1783–1873?

2. How far was government policy responsible for this growth?

TABLE 3: Output of selected British industries (in thousands of tonnes)

	1800	**1880**
coal	10,000 tonnes	147,000 tonnes
iron	200 tonnes	7,700 tonnes
cotton imported	22 tonnes	650 tonnes
shipping launched	50 tonnes	660 tonnes

1.5 What impact did relative economic decline have on Britain in the years 1873 to 1918?

Some historians have regarded the years after 1873 as the 'Great Depression'. Although the British economy continued to grow each year, the rate of growth was smaller. What was more worrying was the increased economic rivalry Britain was facing from other countries, in particular the United States of America and Germany. Table 4 below shows the share of the world's manufacturing output in the years 1870–1900.

TABLE 4: Percentage share of the world's manufacturing output

	Britain	**USA**	**Germany**
1870	31.8	23.3	13.2
1881–85	26.6	28.6	13.9
1896–1900	19.5	30.12	16.6

The relative decline of Britain's economic position in the world had several important repercussions. Firstly, the need to maintain markets for British goods helps to explain why Britain obtained colonies during the last quarter of the 19th century. In west Africa, the need to defend British markets was the main reason for the growth of the Empire.

Secondly, as the Great Depression developed, all of Britain's main economic rivals placed taxes (tariffs) on imported goods in order to protect their own industries. This meant that by 1900 Britain was the only major economic power which still had a free trade policy. Demands for Britain to abandon free trade had begun to grow in the 1880s. A Fair Trade League pressured the government to introduce tariffs. The most significant supporter of fair trade was Joseph Chamberlain, the Birmingham businessman and politician. In 1897, as Colonial Secretary, he attempted to establish an imperial free trade area (Imperial *Zollverein*) within the Empire protected from outside competition by tariffs. However, his ideas were not supported by Canada and the Australian colonies.

In 1903, Chamberlain resigned from the Government to lead a campaign for tariff reform. The campaign split the Conservative Government and led to a major electoral defeat in the General Election of 1906. Although the Conservative Party were in favour of tariff reform, Britain remained a free trade country until 1931.

Britain's relative economic decline also prompted the development of the idea of 'national efficiency' in the years after 1900. If Britain was to maintain its economic position in the world then it had to become a more efficient nation. Supporters of national efficiency were found in both the Liberal and Conservative parties. In the Liberal Party they were most closely associated with Liberal Imperialists such as Lord Rosebery. The demand for national efficiency was an important reason behind the Liberal welfare reforms of 1906 to 1914. It was also an important idea behind plans by Lloyd George in 1910 to form a national government, and the desire to bring successful businessmen into government in the years before 1914.

Reparations: Payments made by a defeated state to compensate the victorious state(s) for damage or expenses caused by the war.

In what ways did Britain's relative economic decline after 1873 affect British politics and British political parties?

The First World War had a mixed effect on Britain's economic position in the world. In the first two years of war, Britain was able to replace Germany in many of its overseas markets. In addition, Germany's defeat in 1918, its loss of territory and the **reparations** it was forced to pay all helped reduce the German economic threat. However, the war also helped boost American economic growth. By 1918, the USA had become the world's largest economy.

1.6 What were Britain's aims in foreign policy in the years 1783 to 1918?

In 1783, Britain had just lost the American War of Independence and with it a large amount of territory in North America. Although Britain began to recover rapidly from the war in the years 1783–92, it was again involved in major war against Revolutionary and Napoleonic France from 1793.

War with France dominated British foreign and imperial policy from 1793 to 1815. In 1815, Britain, along with its European allies such as Prussia, Russia and Austria, had defeated the French. Britain was one of the major European countries that produced the Treaty of Vienna which redrew the map of Europe in 1814–15.

Great Power: A term used to describe the major military powers of Europe. Between 1815 and 1846 there were five Great Powers: Britain, France, Russia, Austria and Prussia.

Throughout the period 1815–1918, Britain was regarded as a European **Great Power**. The other Great Powers were Russia, France, Austria and Prussia (after 1871 Prussia was absorbed into the German Empire). Britain's claim to be a Great Power rested on British sea power, trade and industry, and its imperial possessions across the globe. Although British foreign policy was conducted by a large number of individuals from several different political parties in the years 1815–1918, there were a number of aims that remained constant for much of the period.

The Concert of Europe

One of the most important aims in foreign policy was the need to maintain the European balance of power. Following the defeat of Napoleon, the peacemakers at Vienna tried to prevent future European war through an international system where no one European power had sufficient military strength to dominate the rest of Europe. From 1815 to 1918, Britain supported this idea. The main method used by the Great Powers to solve international disputes was the 'Concert of Europe'. This idea involved the Great Powers working together (in concert) to solve disputes. Between 1815 and 1823, the Concert of Europe took the form of the Congress System. After 1823, when international disputes occurred, meetings of the Great Powers helped to maintain European peace. The issues of Greek and Belgian independence (1820s and 1830s), the issue of the Straits (1841) and the Great Balkan Crisis (1878) were all solved by this method.

However, on a number of occasions the Concert of Europe failed to maintain European peace. In 1853–54, a crisis in south-eastern Europe led to a Great Power war involving Britain – the Crimean War. Again, in July–August 1914, another major European war occurred involving Britain. On both occasions, Britain went to war to preserve the European balance of power. In the Crimean War the Great Power which threatened European peace was Russia and in 1914 it was Germany.

The defence and promotion of trade

De facto: This term refers to governments in actual control of a country. Sometimes governments which are legally recognised but have lost control are termed *de jure* governments.

Another aim of most British foreign secretaries was support for British trade across the globe. This involved the recognition of ***de facto*** governments. For instance, in the 1820s Canning recognised the new republics of Latin America. In December 1851, Palmerston recognised Louis Napoleon's *coup d'état* in France. On both occasions, decisions were made with the aim of furthering British trading opportunities. From 1880 to 1914, Britain was involved in the partition of Africa. This was due, at least in part, to the desire to assist British trade.

In some cases, British foreign secretaries actively promoted the growth of British trade. The most notable was Lord Palmerston, who had considerable influence on British foreign policy from 1830 until his death in 1865. In China in 1839–42, and again in 1857–60, Palmerston helped to force the Chinese government to open up their Empire to British trade. Palmerston was also able to aid British trade in the Anglo-Turkish Convention of 1838. On several occasions, he came to the defence of British subjects abroad when they faced problems with foreign governments. In 1850, he came to the aid of Don Pacifico in his dispute with the Greek government. In 1863, he used the Navy to bombard the Japanese town of Kagoshima after a conflict between the local ruler and British traders.

In the period 1815 to the 1860s, another aim followed by successive foreign secretaries was the opposition to the Atlantic slave trade. Britain had abolished the slave trade in 1807 and for the next 50 years attempted to prevent any other country participating in the trade. The main method used was the 'right of search', where British warships searched any foreign ship on the high seas for slaves. In addition, Palmerston's recognition of the Texas Republic in 1836, as an independent state, was only on the basis that Texas accepted the end of the Atlantic slave trade.

'Splendid isolation'

Another feature of foreign policy during this period was the desire of Britain not to be allied to other countries, if at all possible. Between 1815 and 1823, Britain was a part of the Congress System. Again from 1904 to 1914, Britain became closely associated with France. However, for much of the century Britain stayed isolated from the other European powers. Britain did make some agreements, but these were for specific reasons and for a short period of time. In 1834, Britain signed the Quadruple Alliance with France, Spain and Portugal as a counter to the Holy Alliance of Russia, Prussia and Austria. In 1854, Britain signed an alliance with France against Russia in the Crimean War. Then in 1878 Disraeli signed secret agreements with Austria and Turkey shortly before the Congress of Berlin.

Britain was able to remain aloof from European alliances partly because of the success of the Concert of Europe but also because Britain's main foreign policy interest lay outside Europe. Throughout the 19th century, Britain possessed the largest Empire of any European state. In particular, Britain had major interests in India. Up to 1858, the East India Company handled British interests in India. After that date, the British Indian Empire was proclaimed under the responsibility of a cabinet minister.

Foreign affairs were not an isolated aspect of government policy. On a number of occasions there was a direct link between political developments in Britain and the foreign policy pursued by the Government. On several occasions, George Canning (Foreign Secretary 1822–27) and Lord Palmerston used foreign policy issues to gain political popularity at home. Canning's opposition to the Congress System in 1822–23, and the Don Pacifico Affair of 1850 were two examples. In 1868, Disraeli sought popular support with his expedition to Abyssinia. In 1876, Gladstone came out of retirement to lead a campaign against Disraeli's handling of the Eastern Question. Perhaps the most important example of the interaction of domestic with foreign policy came in the late 1890s with policy towards southern Africa. Joseph Chamberlain's desire to make imperialism an issue with the electorate led to a confrontation with Transvaal over the voting rights of British citizens in that country. The Transvaal refusal to accept British claims led to the outbreak of the Boer War in 1899.

During the period 1815–1918, the Great Power most distrusted by Britain was Russia. From 1815 to 1848, Russia acted as a force for conservatism and reaction in Europe, which was opposed by foreign ministers such as Canning and Palmerston. However, the main reason for hostility towards Russia was fear of Russian ambitions in south-eastern Europe. The danger of Russian expansion at the expense of the Ottoman Empire and the possibility of Russian warships entering the Mediterranean Sea were major worries for British governments from the 1820s to the 1880s. Britain's involvement in the Crimean War was associated with these issues. After 1860, Russia posed a threat to British interests in Central Asia and India. From 1880 to 1905, Russia posed a threat to British interests in China and the Far East.

In contrast, Britain's relations with the German powers, Prussia and Austria, were more cordial. Hostility with the German Empire began as economic rivalry from the 1870s but, most importantly, with naval rivalry in the first decade of the 20th century.

Relations with France varied considerably during the period 1815 to 1918. On occasion Britain and France came close to war, in 1840 over the Eastern Question, in 1859 over a fear of French invasion and in 1898 over Fashoda in the Sudan. However, for large parts of the century Britain and France were on good terms. In the 1830s Britain and France stood together against the Holy Alliance Powers and between 1854 and 1856 Britain and France fought together against Russia in the Crimea. Perhaps the most significant period of Anglo–French friendship began in 1904 with the Entente Cordiale. Through mutual suspicion of Germany, Britain and France worked closely together in foreign affairs between 1904 and 1914. In 1914, Britain decided to support France against Germany, thereby involving itself in the First World War.

1. In what ways did British foreign policy change during the years 1783–1918?

2. In what ways did British foreign policy remain the same during the years 1783–1918?

3. How far do you think British foreign policy changed during the years 1783–1918? Give reasons for your answer.

The Irish Question

The Irish Question is the name given to the series of issues which affected British–Irish relations. It involved political, economic, religious and strategic issues. On several occasions, Irish issues caused the resignation of prime ministers. In 1801, Pitt the Younger resigned because of George III's opposition to Catholic emancipation. Peel fell from power in 1846 over the repeal of the Corn Laws. Gladstone split the Liberal Party in 1886 with his conversion to Irish Home Rule. The Liberal governments from 1912 to 1914 faced a serious crisis over Ulster which was brought to a temporary conclusion by the outbreak of the First World War. Finally, Lloyd George's fall from power, in 1922, was due at least in part to his handling of the Irish Question in 1921.

Therefore, as a theme the Irish Question must be regarded as an important, if not the most important, aspect of British domestic history (see Chapter 5).

1.7 Were the British 'reluctant imperialists'?

During the 19th and early 20th centuries, Britain expanded its political control across the world. By the conclusion of the First World War, the British Empire covered 25% of the world's land surface and included one-third of the world's population. British imperial possessions could be found on every continent.

However, British imperial expansion was not an even process. For much of the period 1815 to 1880, Britain seemed to be uninterested in acquiring colonial possessions. Then, from 1880 to 1914, Britain expanded its empire rapidly, mainly in Africa.

Was there a sudden change in thinking in government circles around 1880 towards the Empire or was there a continuity of approach?

Although the first half of the 19th century was not noted for imperial expansion, Britain did acquire colonial possessions: Hong Kong in 1842, British Columbia in 1846 and, most notably, in India where the East India Company expanded its control over northern India from the River Indus to the Ganges.

However, for most of this period British governments did not feel the need to acquire overseas territory formally. This period was seen as an era of 'informal' empire where Britain controlled the trade of overseas areas without the need to control regions politically. In south America and much of Africa, British traders dominated international trade.

It has been claimed that Britain's decision to acquire colonies after 1880 had a lot to do with the increasing economic challenge of other countries in a period of economic depression. Britain's acquisition of territories in west Africa had much to do with the protection of British trade.

Also of importance in the acquisition of colonies was the desire to protect Britain's position in India, the 'jewel in the Crown' of the British Empire. The decision to expand colonial control in southern Africa from 1870 to the end of the century and the decision to invade and occupy Egypt in 1882 had a lot to do with protecting the sea routes to India. In order to protect these areas British governments, reluctantly, were forced to take control of other parts of Africa, such as the Sudan and Uganda, to protect the River Nile and

Why did Britain abandon informal control and replace it with formal political control, in areas such as Africa, after 1880?

1. 'Britain went through a period of major political, social and economic change in the years 1783–1918.'

Using the information from this synoptic assessment, explain why this statement could be regarded as accurate.

2. In what ways can it be argued that in spite of considerable change there were elements of continuity in Britain's political, social and economic development and Britain's relations with Europe and the world?

Egypt, and the Transvaal and Orange Free State, to protect the Cape of Good Hope.

The main instrument British governments possessed to defend this large empire was the Royal Navy. Throughout the 19th century, Britain possessed the world's largest navy. To maintain a naval presence around the globe, harbours and coaling stations were required. Territories such as Malta, Labuan and Mauritius were acquired as strategically placed naval bases to defend the world's sea routes.

There were many reasons for the expansion of the British Empire. Trade, strategic reasons and the defence of India were the most important. Throughout the 19th century Britain acquired colonies, with the most rapid expansion taking place during the 1880s in Africa.

William Pitt the Younger, 1783–1801

Key Issues

- *Why did William Pitt the Younger dominate politics from 1783 to 1801?*
- *How successfully did William Pitt the Younger face the challenge of the French Revolution 1789–1801?*
- *Why did William Pitt the Younger fall from power in 1801?*

Framework of Events

1759	William Pitt the Younger born in South London
1773	Pitt the Younger attends Pembroke College, Cambridge
1780	Elected MP for Appleby, aged 21
1782	Appointed Chancellor of the Exchequer in Shelbourne's Ministry
1783	Appointed Prime Minister, aged 24 years and 7 months
1784	March: wins the general election and remains in power until 1801 with the support of George III; begins his reform programme with Commutation Act; Passage of India Act
1786	Establishment of the Sinking Fund; Eden Treaty with France
1788	Regency crisis threatens Pitt's position as Prime Minister
1789	French Revolution breaks out; King George III recovers his health
1790	Burke's *Reflections on the Revolution in France* is published
1791	Thomas Paine's *The Rights of Man* is published
1793	Britain declares war on Revolutionary France
1794	Pitt suspends *Habeas Corpus*; Duke of Portland and other leading Whigs join Pitt's Administration
1795	The 'Two Acts' introduced
1797	Year of economic crisis as debts increase
1798	United Irishmen Rebellion in Ireland with French support
1799	Income tax is introduced; trade unions are banned under the Combination Act
1800	Act of Union creates the United Kingdom of Great Britain and Ireland
1801	Pitt resigns as Prime Minister after George III refuses to grant Catholic emancipation
1804	Pitt returns as Prime Minister
1806	Pitt dies at the age of 47.

Overview

Pittites: Young Tory politicians who were supporters of William Pitt the Younger. Many were 'placemen' – MPs who owed their parliamentary seats to the support of King George III.

THE career of William Pitt the Younger (1783–1801) is one of the most remarkable in British political history. Many of the leading politicians of the early 19th century, such as Lord Liverpool, George Canning and Sir Robert Peel, often referred to themselves as **Pittites**. They saw in the Younger Pitt a role model for success. From an early age, Pitt the Younger possessed many political virtues and it was no surprise that his meteoric rise to power occurred. He had experience and ability beyond his years and, as one contemporary remarked, 'He is not the chip off the old block; he is the old block itself.' Pitt's career coincided with some of the greatest and most turbulent events of this country's history, such as the Industrial Revolution and the French Revolution.

Pitt the Younger's harsh response to the latter event won him few friends among his radical opponents. However, modern historians mostly accept the necessity for harsh legislation at a time of full-scale war with France and a severe economic crisis at the end of the 1790s. Many of the modern methods which present-day governments use to regulate their economies can be traced to this period, namely financial and administrative efficiency and the curbing of corruption. Pitt was, in many ways, his country's greatest servant during this period. He sacrificed a family life for duty to his country and pledged (often at a cost to his health) to do all that he could to ensure that Great Britain prospered. His strength as a domestic politician is often contrasted with his rather ineffective role as a war leader. This weakness often haunted Pitt the Younger, especially during the later period of his ministry when he faced the strength of Napoleonic France and opposition in Ireland.

His workmanlike relationship with the monarch, George III, was to prove most useful especially in the unstable early years of his career. However, it was also the cause of his resignation in 1801. Ireland's acceptance of the Act of Union of 1800 should, in Pitt's mind, have been accompanied by Catholic emancipation but the King refused to accept this and the relationship between the two men ended. Although briefly returning as Prime Minister in 1804, Pitt's failing health and the precarious nature of the war against France meant he could never recapture earlier success. His death, in 1806, tragically cut short the life of a great benefactor of modern Britain.

2.1 Why did Pitt rise to the position of Prime Minister by 1783?

Pitt was the youngest Prime Minister this country has ever had, at 24. He had gained some knowledge of political matters whilst an undergraduate at Cambridge and entered Parliament as MP for Appleby, in Westmorland (now in Cumbria), in 1780. From 1780–83, he accumulated ministerial experience and served as Chancellor of the Exchequer in 1782 under a ministry led by the Earl of Shelbourne. Pitt the Younger was also well trained in the art of politics by his father, William Pitt the Elder (later the Earl of Chatham).

Pitt the Younger was an extraordinary politician. He soon began to impress his contemporaries with the quality of his parliamentary speaking and his mastery of complex political issues. Pitt aroused much jealousy, however, because of his ability and his tender years. It was during this early stage in his career that one of the greatest rivalries in British political history was born, namely between William Pitt and Charles James Fox (soon to be leader of the Whig opposition). Both men were highly ambitious, but ultimately it was Pitt who would dominate.

William Pitt the Younger (1759–1806)

Son of William Pitt the Elder (1708–1778), he entered Cambridge University at the age of 14 and became an MP at 22. He served as Chancellor of the Exchequer (1782–83) under the Earl of Shelbourne, before becoming England's youngest Prime Minister at the age of 24. During his first spell as PM (1783–1801), he reorganised the country's finances and negotiated tariff reductions with France. However, England fared badly under the new French republic. Also, Pitt the Younger's policy in Ireland led to the 1798 revolt, and he tried to resolve the Irish Question by Act of Union in 1800, but George III rejected the Catholic emancipation that Pitt had promised as a condition. This led to Pitt resigning in 1801. On his return to office in 1804, he organised an alliance with Austria, Russia and Sweden against Napoleon, which was shattered at Austerlitz. On hearing the news of this defeat in 1806, Pitt died.

Pitt also possessed a remarkable ability for financial skill and administration. He was to need these qualities as the situation he inherited as Prime Minister, in December 1783, was far from secure. The disastrous American War of Independence (1775–83) had drained the country's finances and led to a humiliating loss of face for George III, the Hanoverian monarch. The opposition party, the **Whigs**, labelled the new regime 'the mince pie administration' because it was unlikely to survive beyond Christmas 1783. Yet Pitt had several advantages, the most important of which was the support of the King, who decided when the next general election should be called. As it turned out, Pitt was able to survive until the election of March 1784, when he achieved a remarkable victory. This triumph formed the basis of support for the 17 years of Pitt's first administration, whilst during the same period the Whigs lost a great deal of support and public sympathy. This was due primarily to their opposition to war with France and their support for parliamentary reform. The King now had a stable ministry and, in the early years of his relationship with Pitt, a trusted confidant. Pitt was now in a position to embark on an ambitious reforming programme, up to 1793.

Whigs: Members of an English political party in the 19th century that represented people who were eager for political and social reforms.

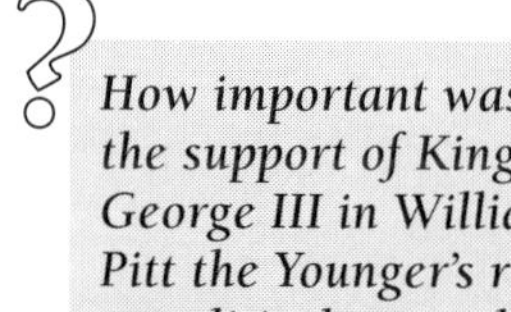

How important was the support of King George III in William Pitt the Younger's rise to political power by 1783?

2.2 Why was Pitt able to dominate domestic politics between 1783 and 1789?

Britain was in crisis when William Pitt took over as Prime Minister in 1783. Defeat in the American War of Independence (1775–83) had created a major financial crisis for the English Government. The value of exports declined as a result of the difficulties in trading during the war and the **National Debt** had risen dramatically to £242 million by 1784. Pitt had to think of how to cut expenditure whilst raising taxes to meet the deficit. This was especially unpopular because the war had been lost. He was also very keen to introduce a more efficient method of collecting these new taxes. This was to be the cornerstone of his success as Prime Minister during this period. Pitt's financial policies in this period reveal his genius. Although many of his policies had been tried before, it was the determination and ruthlessness that contrasted Pitt with previous governments.

National Debt: The amount of money the Government owed as a consequence of the massive expenditure required by the war.

Financial policy

Stopping the smuggling trade

In 1784, Pitt the Younger introduced two measures aimed at cutting the growing smuggling trade. Smuggling had become a highly profitable business, especially in more remote areas of the country such as Cornwall. It was costing the country thousands of pounds in lost revenue.

1. Pitt introduced the Commutation Act, which was designed to lower the import duty on tea and therefore make smuggling less profitable.
2. The introduction of a Hovering Act allowed smugglers' vessels to be searched up to 12 miles out to sea.

Significantly, Pitt and his Ministers, from 1785–87, reduced duties on items such as brandy. This led to an increase in the value of food and raw material imports, exactly as Pitt wanted.

Raising taxes

Higher taxes have always been unpopular. Pitt realised that the best way of raising new revenue would be through indirect taxes on the rich. He therefore embarked on taxing the strangest of pleasures enjoyed by the upper classes, such as horses, wigs and hair powder. He even took the liberty of taxing windows! Many people responded by bricking up their windows to avoid having to pay this particular tax.

Pitt also hit the lower orders with taxes on candles. However, his taxation policy was generally successful. The amount of tax reaching the Treasury improved dramatically and, in some cases, almost doubled. Pitt created much-needed money to wage war against France after 1793.

Introducing the Sinking Fund

Sinking Fund: A fund of money kept by the Treasury to meet any emergency payments the Government might have to make in the future.

In 1786, Pitt introduced the **Sinking Fund**. This was a way of reducing government debt by accumulating money. There was nothing original about such a venture but, as in all his financial dealings, Pitt ensured it was placed on a sure footing. Commissioners were appointed to ensure the Sinking Fund ran efficiently and that it was not subject to crisis management normally used to overcome a government revenue shortfall. In peacetime, it worked well and, by 1793, the National Debt had been reduced by around £10 million. The outbreak of war with France, in 1793, naturally meant that the national debt rose and with it the idea of the Sinking Fund became less attractive. By 1820, Lord Liverpool abandoned the idea of the Sinking Fund.

Administrative policy

William Pitt the Younger was a great believer in making government more accountable for its actions. Administrative policies were introduced to cut out waste and to improve efficiency in the running of government. Pitt was also a great believer in a career based on talent and ability, rather than on birth, background and inheritance. There were two key areas where improvements in government administration were made.

1. In 1784, Pitt passed the India Act. This was designed primarily to remove the exclusive rights the East India Trading Company had in the financial administration of this ever-growing and profitable area of the empire. A Board of Control was set up to scrutinise the administration of the East India Company. Pitt himself was one of its members. It did not solve all the problems it was intended to. The East India Company still retained a large financial and political stake in the running of British India's administration. The East India Company continued to administer British India until the Indian Mutiny of 1857 forced the British Government to take direct control in 1858.
2. Cutting out government waste was another Pittite preoccupation. In particular, there was an excessive amount of patronage (see page 41) exercised by the King. Yet Pitt the Younger was in a tricky situation. George III was an immensely powerful political patron, as Pitt himself was only too aware. As a result of Pitt's reforms, government control over the Excise Board (the government department responsible for tax

and import duty collection) was strengthened and government financial accountability was increased. Patronage was still in existence way into the 19th century, but Pitt's reforms in this period sowed seeds for future administrations to cultivate.

Trading policy

The development of trade was an equally important Pittite obsession. The disruption of trade as a result of the American War of Independence (1775–83) forced Pitt's Government to widen Britain's trading horizons. Britain began to trade more with Europe in order to make up the revenue and trading shortfall left by the loss of the United States of America.

Pitt was also a supporter of freer trade. Much of the trade policy of 18th-century Britain was associated with mercantilism. This idea suggested that the world's economic wealth was limited. For one country to become richer, it could do so only at the expense of other countries. To protect a country's trade, large taxes (tariffs) were charged on goods from other countries. In contrast, the idea of 'free trade' suggested that greater trade between countries would lead to greater economic wealth all round. Such trade could be aided by lowering, rather than increasing, tariffs. This was an idea that Pitt began to support after reading *The Wealth of Nations* by the Scottish economist Adam Smith (published in 1776). In addition to the economic benefits of free trade, Pitt passionately believed that trade barriers between countries were politically dangerous and caused wars.

The most famous trade treaty signed by Pitt's Government was the Eden Treaty with France, in 1786. This was an important agreement which gave citizens of Britain and France free access to the goods produced by each other's countries, as well as reducing the number of tariffs on selected items. British manufacturers were especially grateful to the Government for finding new areas for their products, and tended to do better out of the arrangement than their French counterparts. The outbreak of war in 1793, however, proved the Treaty's undoing and it was abandoned soon after.

The support of the King

The support of the King was of central importance in ensuring that Pitt dominated politics in this period. The monarch at this time, George III (King 1760–1821), was an extremely influential politician who could make or break a ministry. A Prime Minister who failed to realise this crucial fact was not likely to last long. Although Pitt and George III did not always get along, they did rely on one another for support during this period, especially during the first few difficult years of the 1780s when Pitt was hanging on for his political future.

The two worked well with one another on a variety of issues and a mutual respect (if not friendliness) developed. Events during the Regency Crisis, in 1788, convinced Pitt of the need for George III's support. The King, for his part, was only too happy to cooperate with Pitt even if the only reason for this was to keep his harshest critic, Charles James Fox, out of office. Fox did not possess Pitt's political tact. In fact, it was Fox who called for the power of Parliament to increase at the monarch's expense.

George III had another more important reason for hating Fox. This was because of his close political relationship with the King's son, the Prince of Wales, whom he openly despised. Fox and the Prince were always looking to undermine the King. Ultimately, this played into Pitt's hands.

1. In what ways did Pitt's financial and economic reforms help make Britain more prosperous during the period 1783 to 1789?

2. Why did King George III support Pitt's Government during the 1780s?

2.3 How successfully did Pitt deal with the threat of the French Revolution 1789–1801?

Charles James Fox (1749–1806)
Son of the leading Whig politician, Henry Fox. At the age of 21, Charles Fox was appointed Junior Lord of the Admiralty in the administration of Frederick North but was dismissed in 1774. He was a staunch supporter of the American Colonists and, after 1780, took up the cause of parliamentary reform. Fox was appointed Foreign Secretary in the Marquis of Rockingham's ministry in 1782 but left after being unwilling the serve under the new Prime Minister, Lord Shelborne. In 1789, he embraced the ideas of the French Revolution and opposed the war with France which broke out in 1793. A lifelong rival of William Pitt, Fox was briefly to serve as Foreign Secretary in 1806. Ill-health unfortunately led to his premature death in the same year.

The outbreak of the French Revolution, in the summer of 1789, was arguably the most important event in modern history. It cast a shadow over British politics well beyond 1801. The overthrow of the French King, Louis XVI, and the subsequent terror against Church and aristocracy had a devastating impact on the ruling classes in Europe as a whole. The Whig opposition leader, Charles James Fox, claimed that the French Revolution was 'the greatest event ... that ever happened in the world'. Initially, Fox and the Whigs welcomed the revolution. This enthusiasm saw the establishment of a number of radical working-class organisations committed to their own 'English Revolution', such as the Sheffield Society for Constitutional Information and the more influential London Corresponding Society (LCS). The Radicals' main inspiration was Thomas Paine's *The Rights of Man* (published in 1791). Paine supported the right of the people to overthrow hated aristocratic government and even talked about the establishment of an English republic.

How did the French Revolution help to restructure British party politics during the 1790s?

The French Revolution could not have come at a worse time for Pitt the Younger. Between 1788–89, his position was undermined by the first outbreak of George III's mental illness, which modern scientists have identified as Porphyria. The prospect of the King stepping aside for the pro-Whig Prince of Wales was a real concern for Pitt as Prime Minister. In the event, the recovery of the King by 1789 and Whig divisions over how to approach the French Revolution played into Pitt's hands. Fox was extremely enthusiastic about the French Revolution. Yet fellow Whigs, such as Edmund Burke, did not share his enthusiasm. Burke's *Reflections on the Revolution in France* (published in 1791) proved to be the mouthpiece of those who supported the monarchy and opposed violent change. In his book, Burke condemned the bloodshed, anarchy and executions occurring in France. This and Burke's *Appeal from the New to the Old Whigs*, in which he condemned Fox for supporting the revolution, furthered the split.

1. Describe how British and French liberty are shown to be different.

2. How useful is a cartoon like this as evidence of contemporary British views of the French Revolution?

A British political cartoon of 1792, showing the contrast between Britain and France.

In addition, two of Fox's closest political allies – Earl Grey and Samuel Whitbread – demanded parliamentary reform just at the time when events in France were becoming more extreme. This alienated Whig landowners, who feared for their lands and property. Pitt saw an opportunity to win over moderate Whigs who were upset by Fox's extreme views in supporting the French Revolution, Fox's opposition to the war with France and his enthusiasm in taking up the cause of parliamentary reform.

As a result, moderate Whigs, led by the Duke of Portland, joined Pitt's Tory administration in 1794. This created the first broad-based aristocratic Conservative administration in British history. This government or 'law and order' was the foundation of what became the Conservative Party of the 19th and 20th centuries.

What did Pitt do to prevent the threat of revolution in Britain during the 1790s?

Pitt the Younger was determined to stamp out the radical threat that seemed to be strongest in the cities and was dominated by skilled artisans and craftsmen. Fearful of the effect Thomas Paine was having on an increasingly literate and educated working class, two royal proclamations were passed in 1792 against what were labelled as 'seditious writings'. Using spies and secret agents, Pitt exaggerated the nature of the radical threat and established a committee of secrecy to monitor their activity. During the period 1792–1801, a number of laws were passed aimed at undermining the radical movement:

1. The Habeas Corpus Amendment Act was suspended from May 1794 to July 1795 and again from 1798 to 1801. This meant that anyone could be arrested and held indefinitely, merely on suspicion of having committed a crime. This may seem extreme to modern observers, but we must not forget the fact that Pitt the Younger was very concerned about the security of the state at the height of war. In reality, this Act was used sparingly during this period and few radicals were tried.

2. The stoning of the King's coach by an unruly London mob, in 1795, and the return of a difficult economic situation mainly as a result of the war produced a fresh batch of anti-radical legislation: the Seditious Meetings Act and the Treasonable Practices Acts – best known as the 'Two Acts'. These banned meetings that had not been approved of by the local magistrate. These Acts attempted to keep an eye on illegal gatherings and broadened the definition of treason (or crimes against the State) to allow more arrests of known radicals.

3. In 1797, following a mutiny in the Navy at Spithead and the Nore, a law was passed which increased the penalty for undermining authority. This was especially important to ensure loyalty among the armed forces. The Navy was, in many respects, the strength of the British response to France. Anyone caught inciting mutiny and unrest was dealt with severely by the authorities.

4. In 1798, a Defence of the Realm Act was introduced, which required information and numbers ready to fight for King and Country. It was a typically Pittite administrative response. This Act was especially important as a failed French invasion had just taken place in Pembrokeshire the previous year. The French were also known to support radical republican organisations in Ireland. In 1798, the United Irishmen failed in their attempt at a rising to remove English rule.

5. In 1799, trade unions were effectively abolished, when Pitt banned the 'combination' of men. This hit the radical movement especially, as the trade union was the only method working men had of redressing

Republicans: A loyalist term of abuse to describe the 17th-century radical group who were known to support working-class radical demands.

Levellers: Radicals during the English Civil Wars (1642–49) who wanted to redistribute wealth from rich to poor.

Propaganda: Information, often exaggerated or false, which is spread by political parties in order to influence the general public

grievances with an unscrupulous employer. The Government usually saw trade unions as centres of unrest and, by many, this was seen as a sensible measure.

The Radicals claimed that England was living under a harsh regime that ignored individual liberty. Strange as it may seem, most people welcomed this harsh legislation to root out dangerous 'Jacobins' (i.e. supporters of the French Revolution in England). Furthermore, the 1790s witnessed the creation of many loyalist, pro-monarchy associations, such as that founded in 1792 by John Reeves 'for the preservation of property against **Republicans** and **Levellers**', in support of the King and country. They attacked Radical meetings knowing that the local magistrates would turn a blind eye to their activities.

Pitt the Younger was successfully winning a **propaganda** war, where 'Jacobinism' meant disloyalty and pro-French sympathy. The sacred institution of monarchy, under the much-loved George III, was now much more respected by the people. Support for the King also increased as a result of the French execution of their King Louis XVI in 1793 and the patriotic feeling created by the declaration of war between France and England a year later.

1. How did the French Revolution affect the Whig Party?

2. 'Pitt's measures against Radicals were harsh but necessary.' Do you agree or disagree with this statement?

Explain your answer.

2.4 *How close did Britain come to revolution in the 1790s?*

A CASE STUDY IN HISTORICAL INTERPRETATION

The aftermath of the French Revolution caused massive upheaval all over Europe. It was indirectly responsible for the outbreak of the French Revolutionary Wars from 1792. In Britain, opinion was divided over its importance. The Radicals, supported by the Foxite Whigs and leading writers such as Thomas Paine, argued that the principles of 'liberty, equality and fraternity' were as appropriate to the English as they were to the French. The established orders, which included the Government of William Pitt, argued with equal passion that the Revolution was an attack on liberty and especially the sacred concept of property rights. The majority of the population generally supported this view and a brand of conservative loyalism emerged in support of the King by the end of the period. The question we need to ask is whether the passions aroused by the Revolution created a situation, in the 1790s, where the ruling orders felt under threat from a French-style revolution.

Radicals: A term used to describe those who wished for a fundamental change in the political system and wanted a government based on the principles of liberty and equality.

The case for

The **Radicals** – who advocated the extension of the franchise, the curbing of royal power and the enhanced role of Parliament – were delighted at the prospect of the revolutionary ideas spreading across the channel from France. Radicalism was not new as a concept, but events in France had given it a sharp and sustained focus. The major thrust, initially, came in the form of the Corresponding Societies. An increasingly literate working class joined, for example, the Sheffield Corresponding Society in 1791 or the

London Corresponding Society in 1792, in their thousands. They read and enjoyed the works of Thomas Paine and questioned their own position in English society. Many advocated violence to achieve their goals, although the more moderate elements were content with parliamentary reform.

As the war with France and economic hardship caused by harvest failure took hold, the radical message seemed to carry more weight. In 1795, for example, the anti-monarchy/revolutionary feeling was shown when the King's coach was attacked by a mob in London on his way to open a new session of Parliament. The Government was alarmed by what it saw as a rising tide of violence. One contemporary said of the Prime Minister: 'I see that he expects a civil broil (war). Never was a time when so loudly called on to expect the worst.'

The Government's response was severe, as we have seen already. Many historians have claimed that the harsh legislation amounted to a Pittite reign of terror and a reaction to a potentially revolutionary climate. The situation was at crisis point in 1797 when radical elements of the Navy mutinied at Spithead and the Nore. In the same year, an attempted French landing in Fishguard and the dangerous situation in Ireland convinced Pitt the Younger that more severe legislation was needed to crush the revolutionary spirit of his opponents. Pitt also employed an increasingly sophisticated spy network to root out radical tendencies and used the full resources of the State to undermine a dangerous opposition. Historians such as E.P. Thompson see this period as potentially revolutionary and a crucial stage in the development of the English working classes.

The case against

The revolutionary threat posed by the French Revolution stretched the resources of the State to breaking point in this period. Yet, through a combination of strong anti-radical legislation as well as the support of the people in loyalist associations throughout the country in this period, Britain managed to weather the storm. The Radicals' threat, although potentially strong, did not possess the resources to overcome the institutions of the State. Any successful revolution requires a number of preconditions to be satisfied:

1. **A genuine public desire to overthrow a hated regime**
   This was certainly not the case in Britain in the 1790s. The King, George III, had come through a difficult period of illness during the period 1788–89 and this event seemed to make him more popular with the public at large. Loyalist propaganda portrayed the monarchy as a focal point for unity during the war against the French. In addition, Loyalist associations grew up in this period to act as a counterweight to Radical propaganda. In 1792, John Reeves founded a society whose aim was to protect property from republicans. Throughout England, authorities recruited ordinary men into **militias** to protect the country from the internal threat.

Militias: Part-time, untrained military forces, one based in each county – a sort of Home Guard.

2. **A serious economic crisis**
   Although the years 1795 and 1797 were very difficult in terms of high bread prices and unemployment, they did not have the severity one would look for to act as a catalyst for revolutionary ideas to take hold. The **standard of living** of most people at this time had improved as a result of the Industrial Revolution and they were not prepared to jeopardise the gains made by a change of regime.

Standard of living: A measurement of economic prosperity; a minimum standard refers to what was regarded as the lowest level of economic prosperity required for members of society not to starve.

3. **A strong and united revolutionary opposition**
   The Radical movement was potentially a threat, but in the final analysis did not have the support it needed. The movement was split along a

A British cartoon of 1796, during a period of inflation (rising prices). On the butcher's slab (table) are prices. 'D' refers to pence.

1. According to the information on the butcher's table, why is it difficult for bakers, gardeners, smiths and husbandmen (those who look after livestock) to afford to buy meat?

2. How reliable is this cartoon as evidence of the economic problems facing Britain in 1795?

North–South divide and was also split over aims. Some radicals argued that parliamentary reform went far enough, while others maintained that a republic was the only solution to their problems. In addition, they did not possess the arms or weaponry to start the whole process. The war with France, which broke out in 1793, did not help the cause either. Charles James Fox's opposition to the war was an act of stupidity and Radicals in general were portrayed as traitors to the cause.

4. **The weakness of the existing government**
   If a revolution is to be a success, the existing regime has to collapse. As we have seen, the Government of William Pitt the Younger did exactly the opposite. A number of harsh pieces of legislation during the 1790s may have been unpopular with the Radicals, but the general public (despite some reservations over the loss of their individual liberty) supported these measures. In many cases, the threat of their use was enough to deter the Radical movement.

Thus, there seems to be an overwhelming case against the view that England was on the verge of revolution in the 1790s. The preconditions

1. Why do you think historians have disagreed about the likelihood of revolution in Britain in the 1790s?

2. Which case do you think is the stronger: the case for or the case against the idea that a revolution was likely in the 1790s? Explain your answer.

for a successful revolutionary climate failed to exist and the Government was adept at countering any potential threat, either through harsh legislation or by encouraging and manipulating loyalist conservative propaganda. However, to dismiss the opposition at this time would be foolish. The impact of the French Revolution cannot be ignored and the Radical movement was to learn many lessons as regards future strategy. Many of the Radicals and their ideas of the 1790s were to be incorporated into the strategies employed by the Chartists in the 1830s and well into the next century.

2.5 Why did William Pitt the Younger fall from power in 1801?

The strong political alliance that existed between William Pitt and George III was ended over Irish affairs at the turn of the century. The Act of Union, signed between Ireland and England in 1800, was an important turning point in relations between the two men. A violent uprising against British rule, led by the Irish patriot Wolfe Tone, had preceded it. The French had also been involved in this attempt to undermine British rule but the strength of British forces ensured that the rising failed. The savage reprisals of the British soldiers towards the conspirators were very unpopular with the Irish in general, but Pitt realised a more permanent arrangement between the countries was needed if history was not going to repeat itself.

The Act of Union was signed in 1800. It created the United Kingdom of Great Britain and Ireland. As a result, Ireland lost many of the privileges it had once taken for granted. However, it also gained from being part of the British State. Pitt the Younger realised that an incentive was needed in order for the Irish to feel more at home with their British masters. He therefore took up the cause of Catholic emancipation and argued that Catholics should be allowed to become MPs and take up their seats in the Parliament at Westminster. George III refused to agree to this Catholic emancipation because he felt that he would be undermining his coronation oath, in which he promised to uphold the Church of England as the State religion. All Hanoverian monarchs had a deep suspicion of the loyalty of Catholics towards their rule. This left Pitt and his followers no option but to leave office. The special relationship on which Pitt had relied on throughout his career was now officially over. Pitt returned as Prime Minister in 1804, but his new ministry was cut short by ill-health. He died in 1806, claiming on his deathbed 'Oh, my country! How I leave my country.'

1. Why was Catholic emancipation a controversial issue in British politics at the beginning of the 19th century?

2. On balance, do you think Pitt was a successful Prime Minister? Give reasons to support your case.

2.6 Pitt's career: an assessment

William Pitt the Younger is an important figure in British politics for a variety of reasons. Firstly, his career shows the importance of the monarch in British politics. Pitt became Prime Minister because George III chose him. He won the 1784 general election because the King used his control over a large number of constituencies to win Pitt the House of Commons majority required to keep office. Pitt's position as Prime Minister only became vulnerable when the King's support was in doubt. This occurred during the

Regency Crisis of 1788 when George III suffered the first of his major illnesses, which ultimately prevented him from acting as king from 1811 to 1821. Pitt's fall from power, in 1801, was due to his conflict with the King over the issue of Catholic emancipation.

In another way, Pitt's career paves the way to the 19th century. From 1794, when the Portland Whigs joined his administration, Pitt developed a power base in Parliament that formed the basis for Tory Party dominance until 1830. Although many claim the title of founder of the Conservative Party, Pitt's claim is very strong.

Pitt was the first major politician to consider parliamentary reform, in 1785. His wish to modernise the electoral system was a forerunner for the demands for parliamentary reform from the early 19th century. It could be argued that without the outbreak of the French Revolution some parliamentary reform might have taken place during Pitt's Administration.

In financial and economic affairs, Pitt's Administration made considerable changes. He is regarded as an innovator in financial administration. This suggests that Pitt not only introduced new ideas to financial administration and economic matters, but also used old practices in new ways. As a result, Pitt can be credited with helping Britain recover economically from the American War of Independence.

The most controversial part of Pitt's career involved the French Revolution. Pitt's repressive policies were seen as necessary at the time to deal with the potential threat of a 'French-type' revolution occurring in Britain. Although England, Wales and Scotland had limited support for French revolutionary ideas and actions, Pitt the Younger did face a major rebellion in Ireland in 1798. The most important consequence of the Irish Rebellion was the Union of Great Britain and Ireland in 1800.

Pitt's career also suffered from his role as war leader between 1793 and 1801. The Royal Navy played an important part in limiting French influence and expansion outside Europe. The most important act was Nelson's naval victory over the French at Aboukir Bay, in 1798, known as the Battle of the Nile. Nelson's action thwarted Napoleon's attempt to conquer Egypt. In Europe, however, Pitt achieved little in terms of limiting French influence. Napoleon's Italian campaign of 1796–97 brought virtually all northern Italy under French influence and threatened Britain's position in the Mediterranean. Shortly after Pitt's resignation in 1801, the Peace of Amiens was signed between Britain and France. This brought only a temporary respite in the conflict between the two sides. When Pitt returned to power in 1804, Britain was again at war with France. In Pitt's short second period in office, Britain achieved its greatest ever naval victory over France in the battle of Trafalgar, off southern Spain. Yet even with the victory of Trafalgar, Napoleon dominated the European continent from the Atlantic Ocean to Russia.

Overall, Pitt the Younger can be regarded as a politician who bridged the political world of the 18th and 19th centuries. His Administration of 1783–1801 brought stability and recovery after the defeat in the American War of Independence. After Pitt's death, in 1806, another period of ministerial instability occurred. It was not until 1812, with the appointment of Lord Liverpool as Prime Minister (following the assassination of Spencer Perceval), that a comparable period of ministerial stability returned.

1. Using information contained within this chapter, what do you regard as Pitt the Younger's greatest political achievement? Give reasons to support your answer.

2. 'Pitt the Younger's most successful period in office was before 1789.' Using information in this chapter, how far do you agree with this statement?

The Tory Party, 1815–1830

Key Issues

- *What problems did the government face in this period?*
- *How successfully did the government deal with the difficulties it faced?*
- *Did the government change its policies during this period?*

3.1 What was British society like in 1815?
3.2 What problem faced Lord Liverpool's Government in 1815?
3.3 How close did Britain come to revolution between 1815 and 1821?
3.4 Why did the Tory Government survive between 1815 and 1821?
3.5 How enlightened or liberal were the Tories between 1815 and 1827?
3.6 What were the features of Enlightened Toryism between 1821 and 1827?
3.7 Historical interpretation: To what extent did the Cabinet changes of 1821–23 bring about a change in government policy?
3.8 Why did the Tory Party collapse between 1827 and 1830?

Framework of Events

1812	Lord Liverpool becomes Prime Minister
1815	The Battle of Waterloo marks the end of the Napoleonic War
1815	The introduction of the Corn Law
1816	Income Tax repeal; Game Laws introduced; Spa Fields meeting takes place in London
1817	Suspension of *Habeas Corpus*; Seditious Meetings Act; Pentrich Rising; March of the Blanketeers
1819	Peterloo Massacre in Manchester; Six Acts; return to Gold Standard
1820	Cato Street conspiracy takes place; death of George III
1820–21	The Queen Caroline Affair
1821	George IV is crowned King
1822–23	Cabinet changes bring in new younger Tories, such as Canning, Peel, Huskisson and Robinson
1823	Reciprocity of Duties Act passed; Gales Act passed; relaxation of Navigation Laws
1824	Repeal of the Combination Laws
1825	Amending Act
1825–28	Remodelling of the Penal Code
1827	Resignation of Lord Liverpool after a stroke; replaced by George Canning who dies in same year
1827–28	Frederick Robinson, now known as Lord Goderich, is appointed the new Prime Minister; his ministry lasts until January 1828
1828	Duke of Wellington is appointed Prime Minister; Daniel O'Connell is elected MP
1829	Roman Catholic Emancipation is passed; Roman Catholics now permitted to become MPs
1830	Wellington's ministry loses the general election; Lord Grey forms a Whig government.

Overview

Reactionary: A person opposed to political change.

THE Tory Party dominated politics from 1815 to 1830 to such an extent that the Whig opposition failed to occupy office at all during the period. The Prime Minister from 1812 to 1827 was Lord Liverpool and he presided over a number of important developments, such as the defeat of Napoleonic France in 1815. There is considerable controversy over Liverpool's administration and the place it occupies in history. People at the time tended to dismiss it as being **reactionary**. Recently however, historians such as John Derry have produced a far more positive view of his achievements. By comparison his successors – George Canning, Lord Goderich and the Duke of Wellington – proved to be much less successful. The collapse of Tory rule in 1830 meant a period in the political wilderness that would eventually come to an end in 1841 under Peel.

Britain in 1815 was a society undergoing considerable change as a result of the Industrial Revolution. The urbanisation of society led to the growth of major industrial cities such as Manchester, Leeds and Sheffield which all experienced massive population growth that required a change in working patterns and living conditions. The predominantly rural society that had been a major feature of the 18th century was now changing at a rapid rate, but the agricultural changes that had been a major feature of the Agricultural Revolution helped feed a growing population.

Since 1793, Britain had been almost continuously at war with France. The eventual victory in 1815 should have led to celebration, but the aftermath of the war caused many problems as Britain failed to come to terms. For example, around 400,000 demobilised soldiers and sailors entered an already depressed labour market. The resentment and sense of not belonging to this new society produced radical movements that threatened to undermine it and increase demands for a republic and an extension of the right to vote. Up to 1821, the Tory Government was forced to introduce some drastic measures in order to maintain law and order. However, once economic conditions improved, from 1821, the Tories were able to govern more sympathetically and introduce a series of measures that some have labelled Enlightened Tory.

Politics in the latter half of the 1820s was dominated by the issues of Catholic emancipation (see Chapter 6) and the demands of the Radicals and the Whig opposition for more people to have the vote. It was these two issues, and the splits within the party they revealed, that led to the collapse of Tory rule in 1830.

3.1 What was British society like in 1815?

How did the political system work?

Parliamentary democracy: Term used to describe today's political system in Britain with its emphasis on the use of elections, a free press and full participation in the political process by anyone over the age of 18 who possesses the vote.

At the end of the Napoleonic War the political system in Britain had changed little from the 17th century. Our modern political system is based on **parliamentary democracy**. The main features of our modern political system are contrasted with that of the early 19th century system in the following table:

Today	*1815*
Adults over 18 have the right to vote	The electorate is very small. One in 24 adults over 21 have the right to vote
Elections every 5 years	Elections every 7 years
Secret ballot	Open ballot (which allows bribery, corruption and intimidation)
Party competition	Parties are factions of one small social group – the upper class
Even distribution of seats	Towns under-represented
Monarch acts as a figurehead	Monarch possesses political power

The system in place in the early 19th century had lasted a long time because it served a useful purpose. It had reflected the social and economic system of pre-industrial Britain. Most power lay with the majority in Parliament and the men who controlled it, but it was never seriously understood that this body represented the people. Those who defended the system stated that it defended the landowning majority. In 1815, the authority of the Cabinet was a recent development and the principle of collective responsibility was not yet accepted. The office of Prime Minister was undefined, for all ministers were servants of the King and his support was vital if any government was to survive. Political parties as we understand them today did not exist, as there was no party discipline or organisation on voting. Many Independents (non-party MPs) were quick to change sides over issues that affected their personal interests, regardless of political loyalties. At the beginning of the period, the position of Lord Liverpool's ministry was made even more difficult by the monarchy's weaknesses. George III ceased to be important as a king after 1810 due to mental illness and George IV was unable to support or strengthen the position of his ministers. Yet to underestimate the power of the monarchy was fatal as it had the power to bring down a government. Up to 1830, the King was the most important political figure.

British society in 1815

Most British institutions had been operated for, and on behalf of, the landowning class, headed by the aristocracy. The basis of their social power was the amount of land they owned. These leading landowners dominated the House of Lords and the Commons was filled with their supporters. It was claimed that men who had no property were unfit to govern and could be indirectly represented by these men of property on whose behalf they were elected. As Anthony Wood has written, in *Nineteenth-Century Britain* (1981), 'whether Whig or Tory, either would be likely to uphold the interests of landowners and farmer'. Government service, the Church and the powerful positions in the armed forces helped to provide for their families. In the 18th century, **patronage** and corruption were natural, and acceptable, as the central government's role in life was so limited.

It was local government that affected people more directly and not surprisingly the bulk of this was left to the nobility in the counties. The key people were the **Justices of the Peace (JPs)**, appointed from the prominent landowners in the district on the recommendation of the Lord Lieutenant of the county (normally the greatest landowner).

Patronage: The right of giving offices and privileges on the basis of favour and not as a result of merit. The monarch at this time was said to be a great political patron.

Justices of the Peace (JPs): Officials who bore the brunt of English local government. JPs were the key officials responsible for maintaining law and order and for exercising criminal jurisdiction. In addition, JPs were responsible for carrying out much of the legislation concerning poor relief, vagrancy, apprenticeship and other social laws.

How far did the Agricultural Revolution change Britain?

Agrarian: Relating to the ownership and use of land, especially farmland.

Society was predominantly rural, **agrarian** and based on 18th-century values but there were dramatic forces at work. These threatened not only to change the economic system but, as a result, would have serious political consequences.

The massive scale and pace of agrarian and industrial change brought painful consequences. The countryside faced an agrarian revolution. This resulted in a more efficient use of the land but, by around 1780, it also created a new class of landless agricultural workers. Cottagers lost their old rights to the common land and the fuel they once gathered from the wastelands. This compact society was under siege from increased commercialisation: farming for profit rather than just making a living. These trends increased pressure on the land to feed a growing population and these difficulties were made even worse by the Game Laws of 1816.

Why was the Industrial Revolution so important?

Together with great changes in the countryside, there were even bigger developments in the scale of the workplace. The historian Anthony Wood describes it, in *Nineteenth-Century Britain*, as 'A momentous change from an agrarian to an industrial society'. What is meant by this? The demands to feed and clothe a growing population led the pressure to move from a predominantly domestic (cottage based) industry. Cottage industry was carried out usually at home on a small scale for a small market. With a growing population, industry moved to a larger site usually in an urban area and for a larger market. Urban growth and the Industrial Revolution went hand in hand (e.g. Manchester, Sheffield). There were many positive aspects such as large-scale production; but equally there were as many drawbacks:

Luddites: Those who objected to the machines needed to equip the new factories during the Industrial Revolution. They developed as a movement between 1811 and 1817 as a reaction against what they saw as a threat to their livelihood and what was obviously an inferior product mass produced by workers in the factories who did not have their technical skill.

- Manual skills – work carried out by hand in the home was replaced by the new machines located in factories. Eric Hobsbawm, a well-respected left-wing historian, writing in support of the new working classes, has described the machine breaking carried out by the **Luddites** as 'collective bargaining by riot'. Serious outbreaks of machine breaking in the East Midlands were commonplace because of the resentment produced.
- The social consequences of industrialisation tended to widen the differences between rich and poor and to create 'slum' conditions. This produced a group of workers who felt hatred towards the establishment which they blamed for their distress. Added to this were:
  - the discipline and rigour of factory work;
  - the physical conditions and long hours;
  - the employment of young women and children denied legal protection against industrial exploitation and banned from joining trade unions (which had been the case from 1799).

  Now you can begin to get the picture. Wage reductions and the threat of imprisonment hung over them if they refused rates of pay.

What were the effects of a rising population at this time?

To make these massive socio-economic changes seem worse, add a rising population. This process had begun in the middle of the 18th century but reached its height at the start of our period.

Population growth in Britain 1801–1821

1801	10.5 million	an increase of 25.5%
1811	12 million	
1821	14.1 million	

It was the speed of this change more than anything else that destabilised society. A rising population had a number of implications for Britain after 1815:

- There was a need to feed more mouths, therefore greater pressure on the land. The system of farming in the early 19th century was unable to cope with that increased demand.
- A rising population placed greater strain on the system of poor relief, especially the **Speenhamland system**. It was always assumed that these payments were in proportion to family size and it was argued that a large family made one idle and employers knew they could underpay because the difference would be made up by the poor rate. The historian John Plowright argues that the burden on taxpayers increased fourfold between 1775 and 1817 as a result of these developments.

Speenhamland system: A system of poor relief devised in 1795 that attempted to help the large numbers of unemployed. Extra money was made available to the needy from parish funds depending on the size of the recipient's family and the price of bread. Initially used in the south of England, it became more widespread as the 19th century progressed. This was the 19th-century equivalent to a welfare system.

Ancien régime: A term first used to describe the regime in France that was overthrown by the French Revolution. It is now used more generally to describe any regime that has been replaced by another.

What were the consequences of the French Revolution for Britain?

Arguably the most important political event in modern history, the French Revolution broke out in July 1789 and was a protest against privilege, patronage and inequality. The ***ancien régime*** (old order) collapsed quickly as a result of the pressures imposed by the 'have nots' in French society. The ultimate expression of their hatred was the execution of the French king, Louis XVI, in 1793. The shock waves of these events soon spread across the Channel and divided political opinion. These events also helped to intensify existing radical grievances and produced an extreme reaction on the part of the Government. The leading writer supporting the rights of the French revolutionaries was Thomas Paine, in his book *The Rights of Man* (published in 1791). Paine advocated an impassioned defence of people in France displaying their natural rights to freedom, equality and brotherhood. The conservative response to the French Revolution was voiced by Edmund Burke in his *Reflections on the Revolution in France* (1790) – a strong critic of the violence, bloodshed and disregard for property. Burke argued that the gradual and peaceful nature of the British political system was its greatest defence. Radicalism developed at first among skilled artisan groups in London but spread rapidly during the Napoleonic Wars, centring on the northern industrial towns. An increasingly literate workforce read the latest publications with enthusiasm and formed their own political organisations. They were demanding a more open debate on the existing political and social system, which deprived them of their rights.

1. What do you regard as the main features of British society in 1815?

2. How far was Britain a society undergoing major social and economic change?

3.2 What problems faced Lord Liverpool's Government in 1815?

How did war affect Britain between 1793 and 1815?

Britain declared war on France in 1793. The war was to last almost continually until Napoleon's defeat at Waterloo in June 1815. How did war speed up change in society?

- The war gave a boost to the enclosure movement in the countryside as pressure on the land grew to feed a growing population. More land was needed for cultivation at a time of great national crisis.

- The demand for more industrial (heavy) goods brought more squalor to the working classes, especially in the major cities, as working conditions worsened and ruthless employers were able to get away with lower pay rates. The terrible social consequences of industrialisation were felt by those in society unable to defend themselves against its worst effects.
- The war brought dear food as farmers benefited from inflated prices (which workers' wages never matched). War kept prices high due to the breakdown of trade between nations in Europe, helping home producers make large profits at the expense of those for whom bread was their staple diet.
- More expensive timber, bricks and glass meant inferior housing which further deteriorated the social living conditions of the poor.
- Despite the introduction of **income tax** in 1797 (from which the poor were exempt), two-thirds of total tax revenue came from indirect tax on goods (beer, for example). The 'lower orders' in society bore the burden of the continuation of the war effort at a time when they were least able to afford it.
- In 1806, Napoleon, Emperor of France, introduced the Continental System. This was an attempt to starve Britain into submission by preventing other countries trading with it. Britain's response was the Orders in Council in 1807 which restricted a neutral country's ability to trade with France. This was a direct cause of war between Great Britain and the United States of America between 1812 and 1814. This unstable situation caused bankruptcy and unemployment and was made worse by harvest failures of 1809–11.
- As a result of these developments and the demands of fighting a war for over a quarter of a century, Great Britain's national debt – the amount the Government owed – rose from £238 million in 1793 to £902 million in 1816.

Income tax: A tax introduced in 1797 at the height of the Napoleonic War. It was based on how much a person earned and, therefore, was bound to fall more heavily on the richer sections of British society, namely the aristocracy. It was a means of financing the war but it was always regarded as a temporary measure!

What difficulties did the end of war bring for the country?

In June 1815, Napoleon was defeated at Waterloo, war came to an end and British prestige had never stood higher. Britain was the only European power not to have been defeated by Napoleon Bonaparte, the French ruler since 1799 and its chief military genius. It was British finance that had sustained the **coalition** of powers against France and its navy and goods that had defeated the Continental System. Norman Gash, a leading historian of this period, argues that 'war was an abnormal stimulus to the economy'. Levels of demand for example in those industries associated with the war effort, such as the armaments industry, enjoyed a boom period that lasted only as long as the war did and it was 'almost inevitable that it should be followed by acute depression'. It was the combination of full-blooded industrialisation together with postwar circumstances that made 'peace without plenty' so painful.

Coalition: A term used to describe the cooperation of the Great Powers such as Britain, Russia, Prussia and Austria in their common fight against France during the Napoleonic Wars.

In the countryside, crisis conditions had been developing since 1813. Generally, wheat prices fell due to good harvests and the influx of more foreign corn, but the position of farmers had changed during the inflated period of the war. When boom conditions prevailed, they had borrowed heavily to cultivate marginal land. They now had to repay the interest on their loans at a time of falling prices. The farmers eventually received some protection with the passing of the Corn Law in 1815 but even then the positive effects were debatable. Those who survived did so by reducing wages. This made matters worse for the already poor, landless agricultural

Aggregate: A term used to describe something when taken together; in this case all the problems Liverpool's Government faced came at the same time.

1. How severe were the problems facing Lord Liverpool's Government in 1815?

2. You might highlight the difficulties associated with agriculture, politics, industry and the problems linked to the end of the war.

labourers who were forced to seek poor relief from the Speenhamland system.

In industry, the end of the war and a return to peace meant no substantial improvement either. The Corn Law and the abolition of income tax, in 1816, were used as examples of class legislation. This means that laws were passed to help the landowning class. New changes had to be made by the Government to cope with the reduction in demand for products associated with war (e.g. iron, clothing etc. and the substantial problem of 400,000 demobilised soldiers on an already depressed labour market). The historian Norman Gash, in *Aristocracy and People, Britain 1815–1865* (1987), summarises the problems facing the Government in 1815: 'Any one of these would have caused difficulty for the government of the day. Together they created an **aggregate** of social evils which took 50 years to bring under control.' Perhaps a little exaggerated, but it is certainly worth bearing in mind the sheer scale of the forces undermining society.

3.3 How close did Britain come to revolution between 1815 and 1821?

It has been alleged that this period was the closest that Britain ever came to an internal revolution in its history, with the possible exception of the civil war in the 17th century. The Tory Government of Lord Liverpool, which had been in office since 1812, faced massive problems that, for the most part, it inherited. The poet Percy Shelley's famous description of the Government at this time as 'Rulers who neither see, nor feel nor know' has been passed down to generations of students as an acceptable opinion. To make matters worse, the period 1815–21 saw an intensification of the Radical movement which went out of its way to try to win over a working class by the use of an extensive radical press and a reliance on open-air mass meetings. Despite the threats the Radical movement posed, the reality was that the Government survived some pretty difficult times relatively unscathed.

How was the Radical threat expressed between 1815 and 1821?

Origins

Those who opposed the policies of the Tory Government in this period had to have an effective platform to voice their opposition. The most persistent and conspicuous opponents of the regime came mostly from outside Parliament. This opposition took many shapes and forms. These Radicals, as they were known, had grown out of a reaction to the American and French Revolutions at the end of the 18th century, where new ideas such as liberty, equality and brotherhood developed. Their demands were:

- *A more representative parliamentary system* whereby the wishes and opinions of the nation would be better served than in the present situation which represented the narrow interest of the landed aristocracy.
- *Annual elections*. This would make sure MPs would always act in the interests of their constituents.
- *The use of a secret ballot in elections*. This would avoid the common practice at election time of intimidation and bribery. For example, a farmer faced the threat of eviction from his land if he did not vote for the landowner or his appointed candidate.

It would be wrong to see Radicalism as the result of economic depression. The historian Walt Rostow's famous 'social tensions chart' identifies political unrest coinciding most sharply with economic hardship. Certainly this is the case, especially in the immediate post-Napoleonic war period after 1815, when wheat prices were at their highest levels for the whole of the century. This opinion, however, tends to take a largely negative view of the ability of the working class to act independently of economic unrest. The historian E.P. Thompson, in his study *The Making of the English Working Class* (1980), argues that working-class political awareness was apparent before these crises occurred. J.R. Dinwiddy, in an article in *The Modern History Review* (November 1990), also maintains that the Radical programme revived after 1815 not only because of economic hardship and the demands of reform, but also because radicals had been deprived of displaying their grievances in a lawful manner during wartime (1793–1815).

What role did the different personalities in the Radical movement play?

The British Radical message was spread in a number of ways during this period.

Major Cartwright's political clubs
Major John Cartwright led a colourful political existence and was prominent in the development of the Radical movement in the 18th century. His major contribution to the movement was to establish over a hundred debating societies known as Hampden Clubs. They held a national convention in London in 1817 and part of their programme was the presentation of their grievances in the form of a petition to Parliament.

The development of a radical press
William Cobbett was the leading Radical journalist of this period. He had spent his formative years studying the American system of government, which left a lasting impression on him. He hoped to make the British system more democratic, like the USA. His famous *Political Register* was published from 1802 to 1835. Unfairly labelled the 'Twopenny trash' by its conservative critics, the paper was important in the development of working-class political education. Other papers, such as Thomas Wooler's *Black Dwarf*, continued in the *Register*'s footsteps and in J.R. Dinwiddy's opinion 'A radical press … did much to give coherence and unity of purpose to the popular reform movement'.

Henry 'Orator' Hunt's 'platforming' or open-air meetings
Henry 'Orator' Hunt was the most recognisable spokesperson of working-class Radicalism in the postwar years. Yet his background, like that of William Cobbett and John Cartwright, was hardly typical for a radical politician (he owned 3,000 acres of land in the south-west of England). Hunt's claim to radical fame was his ability to stir up protest and feelings among the masses at another key feature of postwar radical development – the open-air meeting.

How effective was the Radical threat between 1811 and 1817?

Luddism 1811–1816
The first major and open display of Radical discontent was machine breaking in the form of the Luddite riots which occurred in the East Midlands and the North of England. The protesters were expressing their hostility towards the increasing use of machines in the textile industry and the resultant unemployment of handloom weavers, shearers and croppers. These difficulties were made worse by a series of bad harvests between 1809

and 1812. Rising prices, unapprenticed and, in most cases, cheap labour together with the refusal of the employers to set a minimum wage, led to the rise of Luddism. There were isolated incidents of open violence, such as the Horsfall incident (where a leading opponent of Luddism was murdered in April 1812), but in reality the movement had peaked by 1812.

Spa Field Riots, December 1816

The emphasis on open-air meetings as a form of protest was first illustrated as a more serious threat to the Government in a series of three meetings at Spa Fields, in London, at the end of 1816. It was organised by a revolutionary political movement known as the Spenceans. Well-known Spenceans included Arthur Thistlewood and the father and son Doctors Watson. At the second such meeting in 1816 a breakaway group attacked a gunsmith and made plans to take over the Bank of England, as well as other leading establishment institutions. Yet as John Plowright contends, in his book *Regency England* (1996), 'strong ale and the prospect of loot, rather than strong words and the prospect of liberty' seem to have influenced those who carried out the disturbances.

The March of the Blanketeers, 10 March 1817

As a direct result of the Seditious Meetings Act of the same month – where large-scale gatherings for political purposes were banned – a small, disorganised band of workers planned a march from Manchester to London to present their grievances to the **Prince Regent** in person. The marchers themselves were predominantly cotton weavers who decided to make their protests more visible by draping themselves in blankets (hence the name). The protest was mainly peaceful and carried out in a legal fashion in defiance of government legislation. The March ended in failure and tragedy when one marcher was killed in a heavyhanded and needless display of brutality by the authorities in Stockport, Cheshire.

Prince Regent: A prince who is regent of a country, during a minority, or in the absence or disability of the monarch (e.g. title given to George Prince of Wales during the mental incapacity of George III (1811–20)).

Pentrich Rising, 8–9 June 1817

On 8 June 1817, the local **yeomanry** easily suppressed a disturbance in Huddersfield. On the following day, the focal point was to be the East Midlands – always a heartland of postwar Radicalism. Approximately 500 disaffected workers from a variety of occupations set out from villages with the intent of attacking Nottingham Castle as a prelude to a wider national rising moving south towards London. The 'Rising' was a farce and the ease with which the Government suppressed it was in no small part due to the use of government spies, such as the discharged debt collector W.J. Richards (known in radical circles as 'Oliver the spy'). The response of the local authorities was severe and went far beyond the perceived threat. Jeremiah Brandreth, one of the leaders, was executed on 7 November 1817 for his involvement.

Yeomanry: A term used at this time to describe wealthy working farmers below the rank of gentlemen. Whether they were owner-occupiers or tenants was unimportant. The main feature the yeomen had in common was moderate wealth.

Did the Radical threat intensify between 1818 and 1821?

The year 1818 was a relatively quiet time for the Radical movement due primarily to the return of more prosperous conditions and a successful harvest. The Tory Party increased its majority in Parliament as a result of the general election of that year. It seemed that whatever radical 'threat' existed had declined and the 'eye of the radical storm' had passed over Britain with relatively little damage being inflicted. Yet over the next four years the threat to Lord Liverpool's Government was greater than at any time and reached its peak during the Queen Caroline Affair of 1820.

The Peterloo Massacre, 1819

On 16 August 1819, a crowd estimated at around 60,000 gathered at St Peter's Fields in Manchester to support the cause of parliamentary reform.

The crowd came to hear the main speaker, Henry Hunt, launch into a determined attack on the corrupt parliamentary system. The Manchester local authorities were alarmed at the prospect of what they saw as an invasion of undesirables on their own doorstep at a time when they lacked the ability to administer peaceful and effective law and order. The Home Secretary, Lord Sidmouth, had urged the authorities to let the protest go ahead, fearing the consequences if it was prohibited. The events of that fateful day have gone down in working-class history as an example of an 'over-the-top' reaction by a repressive government to peaceful and legitimate protest. When the authorities unleashed the local yeomanry (the effective police force of the time) the result was 11 deaths and the injured put at over 400. The response in the country at large was riot in support of what now were working-class martyrs. The Government's reaction was, on the face of it, far more extreme legislation in the shape of the Six Acts or Gagging Acts.

The Cato Street Conspiracy, 1820

The following year arguably the most bold and daring Radical act emerged with the exposure of a plan to assassinate the entire Tory Cabinet. Arthur Thistlewood, a leading Spencean, was believed to be the motive force behind the attempt but the authorities were aware of the plot months in advance – due again to the spying activities of W.J. Richards. An element of farce underpins the whole episode but the fact that a small but dedicated band of revolutionaries dared the ultimate act of terror is evidence of the contempt that the Government was held in by 1820. Thistlewood and four other conspirators were tried and executed.

The Queen Caroline Affair, 1820–1821

The background to the next threat was the marriage in 1794 of the Prince Regent (later George IV) and a German princess, Caroline of Brunswick. They were two wasteful individuals and the sham marriage was ended in 1796 when Caroline fled abroad, eventually settling in Italy by 1815. The separation was far from friendly and this affected the popularity of the monarchy at the time when the Prince's father, George III, was unfit to govern due to a severe mental illness. The Prince was despised by the public and was regarded as a waster of public money at a time of acute crisis. By 1820, the Prince was fed up with his marital situation and demanded a divorce.

The responsibility was to be handed over to the Prime Minister who attempted to pass a bill through Parliament known as the Bill of Pains and Penalties. The Queen Caroline Affair now took on a more serious turn of events. Caroline was determined to return to Britain and claim what was rightfully hers, namely the title 'Queen of England'. She was also determined that maximum publicity should be given to her case. To a lesser extent, she was used by the Radicals to discredit the Government, and William Cobbett acted as her unofficial adviser. The potential was there for serious embarrassment for both Government and future King. By November 1820, Lord Liverpool came to the conclusion that the Bill of Pains and Penalties would not pass and he abandoned it, thus worsening an already difficult relationship with the Prince.

Rioting and criticism were widespread. Things were made worse by the actions of George IV and Caroline. The whole sorry episode continued into 1821, much to the Government's embarrassment. When it was announced that the King would be crowned in the summer of 1821, the prospect of Caroline appearing at the Coronation was too worrying to contemplate. The crisis was resolved with the offer of a £50,000 settlement, which was accepted. Caroline, however, did not live long enough to spend her newly acquired fortune, dying two months later.

The political consequences for the Government were serious enough to justify the resignation of Lord Sidmouth as Home Secretary, who was blamed for the London mob rioting, and George Canning as President of the Board of Trade amid allegations that he was having an affair with the Queen. Was the crisis worth the resignations of two members of the Cabinet? Definitely not, but they must be seen in the context of the time; namely, that the Government was regarded as being so out of touch with public opinion and from that point of view both ministers were understandable scapegoats.

We now turn to the Government's response to such threats in more detail.

Did the policies of the Tory Party make matters worse between 1815 and 1821?

The Prime Minister of Britain since 1812 had been Robert Banks Jenkinson, Lord Liverpool, whose family had been ennobled as a result of loyal service to George III. Lord Liverpool had served in a variety of important ministerial offices. He had been Foreign Secretary (1801–03) and held office as Secretary for War and Colonies (1809–12). He was also Leader of the House of Lords and a gifted debater. Liverpool was aware of the rising tide of discontent after the war but was hampered by the fact that he was, in many ways, a prisoner of his own party's beliefs and outlook. Most of the Tory Party supporters were aristocrats who felt that their Prime Minister had a duty to protect their interests and save them from the Radical threat outlined above.

The Corn Law, 1815

Laissez-faire: Minimum government intervention in economic matters.

Personally, Lord Liverpool was very much a liberal in economic terms and believed in the philosophy of ***laissez-faire***. So it is hard to justify why a law was introduced in 1815 which went against these principles.

The Corn Law guaranteed protection for wheat prices for the agricultural or landowning interest from foreign imports of grain. The concept was not new. A similar law had been introduced in 1804, but to guarantee 80 shillings a quarter (£4.00 per quarter tonne or £16 per tonne) for producers before foreign grain was permitted to enter the British market seemed to government critics a little excessive. The whole point of the Bill, as far as the government was concerned, was to guarantee landowner profits at a level to which they had become accustomed during the war. Naturally, opponents of the regime – both inside and especially outside Parliament – saw it as a piece of class legislation in that it saved the landowners from cheaper foreign grain, stabilised prices and made it more expensive for the consumer. The consequences for the Government were riots, petitions and demonstrations.

Income Tax Repeal, 1816

Income tax had been introduced at the height of the Napoleonic War, in 1797, by the then Prime Minister William Pitt. It was a tax based on how much you earned and, therefore, bound to fall more heavily on the richer sections of British society, namely the aristocracy. It was a means of financing the war but it was always regarded as a temporary measure, because of its unpopularity with Tory MPs, which would end as soon as the fighting was over. Not surprisingly, an aristocratically dominated Parliament who had taken the brunt of the tax needed no excuse to abolish it. In 1816, they voted by a majority of 37 to repeal or abolish income tax. The problem for the Government was how to fill the gap in revenue left by such a departure. The obvious conclusion they drew was to increase indirect taxation on popular items such as beer, sugar etc. The harm done to the common people by this measure would be greater than the potential damage inflicted by the Corn Law because the lower orders were more likely to suffer as a result of the abolition of income tax as they used these items on a regular basis.

The Game Laws, 1816

These were toughened up in 1816, making poaching against a landowner punishable by up to seven years' imprisonment or transportation, usually to Australia. In a predominantly rural society, where this pastime was considered to be a legitimate way of supplementing income and feeding one's own family at a time of marked economic difficulty, these laws were as unpopular as the two previously mentioned. They were, according to historian E.P. Thompson, 'as much a sign of the continued ascendancy of the landowners as was the protection of the Corn Law itself'.

Habeas Corpus: This Act protected people from being kept in prison for long periods without being charged.

The suspension of Habeas Corpus, *March 1817*

Following the Spa Fields meetings in December 1816, the Government reacted by suspending ***Habeas Corpus***. If this Act was suspended, the Government could hold someone suspected of radical or anti-government behaviour without trial for an indefinite period. The Act's critics saw it as a severe measure introduced at a time of potential revolution and as a denial of basic human rights. Recent historical writing – such as John Plowright in *Regency England* (1996) and Eric Evans in *Britain Before the Reform Act* (1989) – however, have been more kind, pointing to its temporary nature during a period when difficult decisions had to be made in the interests of State security. The Act only lasted a year and the small numbers held under its terms were released when it was repealed in 1818. Norman Gash, in *Aristocracy and People* (1987), sums up its impact by claiming it was 'not exactly a reign of terror'. However, the Seditious Meetings Act of March 1817, which forbade the unlawful assembly of more than 50 people and imposed the death penalty for mutiny in the armed forces, must again be seen as temporary. It was used sparingly by the authorities.

1. How serious was the threat posed by the Radical movement between 1815 and 1821?

2. Did the Government's response make matters worse? Explain your answer with reference to the legislation of the period.

The Six Acts, December 1819

'They were a commentary on recent disturbances' as John Plowright claims in *Regency England*, introduced as a response to events in Manchester in 1819. The Six Acts were an attack on any possible threat to the State – ranging from

1. How useful is the cartoon as evidence of popular feeling towards the Tory regime at this time?

2. What images does Cruikshank use to convey the unpopularity of the Tory regime?

This cartoon by George Cruikshank was published in January 1820. It is meant to convey a criticism of the consequences of the Six Acts. Castlereagh is seen tearing up a well-known radical newspaper, the *Twopenny Trash*, while John Bull, representing the public, is imprisoned under the pressure of Lord Liverpool's legislation. The symbol of English liberty, the Magna Carta, has a dagger thrust through it; the musket and cannon show the threat of violence the Government is willing to use to enforce the Act.

an attempt to restrict the activities of the Radical press, through the speeding up of the judicial process, as well as defining the rights of assembly restricting radical activity by outlawing large-scale protest meetings such as Peterloo. Critics point to the fact that these Acts amounted to the harshest example of the reaction of the Government after 1815. Norman Gash, in *Aristocracy and People*, claims that the 'sinister reputation of the Six Acts is not borne out by the facts'. The measures introduced were a commonsense reaction to a dangerous situation and deserve to be looked at in a more positive light in terms of their supposed severity on the radical threat to the regime.

Source-based questions: The Peterloo Massacre, August 1819

SOURCE A

This meeting was no sooner assembled to 150,000 persons, young and old of both sexes, in the most peaceable and orderly manner, than they were assailed [attacked] by the Manchester yeomanry cavalry who charged the multitude, sword in hand, and without the slightest provocation or resistance on the part of the people, aided by two troops of the Cheshire yeomanry, the 15th Hussars, the 8th Regiment of Foot, and two pieces of flying artillery, sabred, trampled on, and dispersed the offending and unresisting people when 14 persons were killed and upwards of 600 wounded.

A primary source from one of the leaders of the Radical movement, Henry 'Orator' Hunt, who was present at the meeting in St Peter's Fields. It is from Memoirs of Henry Hunt, *written in 1820 while in Ilchester Jail.*

SOURCE B

I saw the main body proceeding towards St Peter's Fields, and never saw a gayer spectacle ... The 'marching order' of which so much was said afterwards was what we often see now in the procession of Sunday School children ... Our company laughed at the fears of the magistrates and the remark was, that if the men intended mischief they would not have brought their wives, their sisters or their children with them.

A primary source, although published in 1851. It is from Historical Sketches of Manchester *by A. Prentice who was there at the meeting when the alleged disturbance took place.*

SOURCE C

A contemporary drawing of the Peterloo Massacre, published in August 1819. The Captain on the left is saying: 'Down with 'em! Chop 'em down, my brave boys! Give them no quarter. They want to take our Beef and Pudding from us – and remember the more you kill the less poor rates you'll have to pay so go it lads, show your courage and your loyalty!'

Source-based questions: The Peterloo Massacre, August 1819

SOURCE D

When on 16 August thousands of workers from Manchester and the surrounding cotton districts gathered peacefully in St Peter's Fields to listen to Orator Hunt – their injunctions [demands] were 'cleanliness, sobriety, order and peace', and among their slogans was 'No Corn Laws' – the magistrates, scared of an uprising, employed the local yeomanry to arrest him. When the forces of the yeomanry proved inadequate, they called in regular cavalry to disperse the crowds. A savage struggle followed in which 11 people were killed and over 400 wounded. Within a few days the damaging term 'Peterloo' had been coined.

A secondary source from a modern historian, describing events at Peterloo. It is from The Age of Improvement 1783–1867 *by Asa Briggs, published in 1979.*

SOURCE E

Peterloo was a blunder; it was hardly a massacre. Possibly half the deaths, probably even more of the non-fatal injuries, were among those who were trampled underfoot by horses and the crowd in the panic that ensued. The public indignation was a mark both of the strong liberal feeling in the country and of the general restraint normally exercised by the authorities in dealing with large political assemblies. It was because Peterloo was uncharacteristic that it achieved notoriety.

A secondary source from a modern historian who takes a different view of events at Peterloo. It is from Aristocracy and People, Britain 1815–1865 *by Norman Gash, published in 1987.*

1. Study Source A.

Describe the mood of the meeting at St Peter's Fields in August 1819.

How reliable is Henry Hunt's speech as evidence of popular attitudes at Peterloo?

2. Study Sources C and E.

How do these sources differ in their interpretation of Peterloo?

3. Study Sources C, D and E.

Does Source C agree with either Source D or E in its interpretation of Peterloo?

4. 'Peterloo was a blunder … it was hardly a massacre.' Using the sources and your own knowledge, explain whether you agree or disagree with this statement.

3.4 Why did the Tory Government survive between 1815 and 1821?

So how close was Britain to a French style revolution in this postwar period up to 1821?

The weakness of postwar Radicalism

- The Radical movement was divided between those who advocated a more violent programme of change, such as the Spenceans, and the majority of the Radical movement – those advocating a non-violent response. Hunt, Cartwright and Cobbett all believed in non-violent protest. This division was to weaken the development of a united working-class response. Part of this division is also apparent in the regional differences of the movement's outlook. Hunt tended to represent the northern radicals, while the two other major personalities took a more southern outlook.
- The Radical movement was severely weakened by a lack of weaponry. The success of any revolutionary organisation depends on a successful

use of arms to overpower a government. Radicalism lacked the military teeth to make such a possibility realistic.

- It could also be argued that the outbreaks of unrest amounted to nothing more than a local expression of grievances carried out by hopeful protesters and not hardheaded revolutionaries. Luddism was more an expression of dissatisfaction against the new machines themselves rather than part of a serious political threat to the establishment. The March of the Blanketeers and the Pentrich Rising, although claiming to be part of a national uprising, both have elements of comedy. Spa Fields and Peterloo – seen as massive protest meetings at the time – were predominantly peaceful and legal and taken over by a tiny minority of extremists who took the law into their own hands.

Henry Addington, first Viscount Sidmouth (1757–1844)
An example of the reactionary wing of the Tory Party, Addington had served with distinction as Prime Minister (1801–03) and was appointed Viscount Sidmouth in 1805. During the premiership of Lord Liverpool after 1812, Sidmouth served as Home Secretary and was responsible for the passage of much of the unpopular legislation after 1815; for example, the Gagging or Six Acts of 1819.

Anarchy: Situation where nobody seems to pay attention to any rules or laws.

How effective were the Tory Party policies in dealing with postwar problems?

In response to these threats, the Tory Government was a major factor in preventing the spread of revolution. There are instances when legislation was not really defensible – for example, the introduction of the Corn Laws in 1815 and the repeal of Income Tax in 1816 are nothing more than pieces of class legislation directed against the working classes. Yet the Government acted firmly and decisively:

1. At a time when the forces of law and order were basic, to say the least, the Government had to rely on the local yeomanry and the armed forces to uphold the law in the areas where the threat was greatest. Twenty-three thousand troops were posted to these areas in the North and East Midlands in an effective show of strength at a time of great difficulty.
2. The use of undercover government agents and spies has been the subject of much criticism especially among those critical of Liverpool's Government. It was alleged that the Government invented plots and exaggerated the threat in order to justify what was regarded as harsh legislation afterwards. The reality was that the use of spies in undermining disorder was a fact of life at this time. In order to understand their use we must appreciate that there were no precedents for this type of potential unrest and that the Government acted as it saw fit to try to stop it. The Spenceans, for example, were a small but dedicated band of revolutionaries.
3. The legislation introduced by the Government in this period has been criticised as an attack on basic civil liberties. They made the Government the most unpopular in living memory, lacking any sensitivity at a difficult period in Britain's historical development. Once again, the condemnation can be dismissed if the legislation is to be understood in its context. The French Revolution hung over the whole period and the Government did not wish to see the **anarchy** of the 1790s being transported across the Channel. The suspension of *Habeas Corpus* and the Seditious Meetings Act were both temporary measures at a time when the radical threat was believed to be at its greatest. Although their sinister reputation suggests a denial of freedom, the Acts were in reality used sparingly and removed once conditions were suitable. The Six Acts, or Gagging Acts as they have become known, represent a commonsense approach by a government firmly in control of the situation.
4. It has also been alleged that the members of the Government were out of touch with proceedings and took a great delight in imposing

1. What were the main problems facing Lord Liverpool's Government in the years 1815–1821?

2. How successful was Lord Liverpool's Government in dealing with the domestic problems it faced in the years 1815–1821?

3. What do you regard as the most serious threat to the Government in the years 1815–1821? Give reasons to support your answer.

unpopular decisions. Historians such as John Derry have put forward a more positive image of Lord Liverpool, but the Home Secretary Lord Sidmouth and Castlereagh the Foreign Secretary were seized upon by radical poets, such as Byron and Shelley, as symbolising this reaction. Sidmouth deserves some re-appraisal because as Home Secretary he was at the forefront of the fight against Radicalism. In 1819, for example, before the Peterloo massacre took place, he had urged the Manchester authorities to allow the meeting to go ahead and begged restraint in dealing with it.

At what point was the threat to the Government at its greatest? The Queen Caroline Affair, or 'Carol-loo' as Eric Evans has described it in *Britain Before the Reform Act* (1989), deserves greater attention because at the height of the affair Lord Liverpool lost both Sidmouth and Canning and, perhaps more importantly, the support of the new monarch George IV. The whole episode was neither the creation of difficult postwar circumstances nor a persistent radical threat. Although the Radicals liked to use the scandal for their own gain, they were reacting to, rather than initiating, the political agenda and therefore had little chance of overthrowing the Government.

3.5 How enlightened or liberal were the Tories between 1821 and 1827?

Following the upheavals of the period 1815–21, the country needed a period of calm and prosperity to recover its economic status and soothe the political situation. The Queen Caroline episode revealed to the Prime Minister, Lord Liverpool, how unpopular the Government had become. It, allegedly, provided the spark for a change of direction in policy. This is the traditional view put forward by a generation of historians, such as W.R. Brock and Derek Beales, who argue that Liverpool's Ministry can be conveniently divided into two parts. The first they claim ran from about 1815 to 1821 and was characterised by an intolerant attitude towards any opposition. It was dominated by harsh legislation such as the Six Acts. The second period was completely different and has been described as 'Enlightened Tory' in outlook. This suggests a far more tolerant and sympathetic government attitude towards economic and political change.

This traditional view has now been challenged by a generation of modern historians, such as Norman Gash, J.E. Cookson and Eric Evans, who reject the idea that the period falls into two convenient divides. Continuity is the idea which they stress, both in personnel and policy.

What does the term 'Enlightened', or 'Liberal', mean?

It can be used to describe a number of different views.

- *Freedom of religion*
  'Enlightened' or 'Liberal' could mean the ability to worship free from interference from the authorities. Remember that nonconformists – those Protestants that were not members of the official Church of England and Roman Catholics – were denied these freedoms. Most of the Tory Party at this time were committed to maintain this situation and were especially suspicious of Catholicism.
- *Political rights*
  It could also mean someone committed to a more representative

political system. This could mean giving the vote to a wider section of the community and extending their ability to participate in the political process. Remember that, at this time, the landed aristocracy dominated the Tory Party and they did not want an extension of the right to vote.

- *The right to free expression*
  It could also mean a commitment to the idea that any individual has the right to express their opinions without fear or restraint, even if these views are unpopular with the government of the day. In the period up to 1821, the Tory Government of Lord Liverpool had attempted to prevent this freedom from taking place with the introduction of various laws such as the Gagging Acts (Six Acts).
- *Free trade*
  This is the idea that there should be no government interference in economic matters and that countries should participate in 'free trade' as a sign of the goodwill that existed between them. Remember that in 1815 the Tories had introduced the Corn Laws to protect the agricultural community, preventing free trade taking place.

What do you understand by the term 'Enlightened or Liberal' as applied to the 1820s?

These characteristics of being Enlightened or Liberal seem to stand in stark contrast to the government record up to 1821. However, the Enlightened Tories will deserve their name if their policies seem to be informed by Liberal ideas and if these ideas seem new to the administration after 1821.

3.6 What were the features of Enlightened Toryism between 1821 and 1827?

The Cabinet changes that occurred between August 1822 and January 1823 do seem to suggest a change of direction of the Liverpool Government. The new 'so-called Liberal Tories' had a younger and more middle-class outlook than those they replaced. From an examination of their policies, one can detect an attitude that bears a closer resemblance to that definition of an 'Enlightened' or 'Liberal' Tory. The so-called Liberal Tories were:

- George Canning who replaced Viscount Castlereagh as Foreign Secretary between 1822 and 1827.
- Sir Robert Peel who became Home Secretary 1822–27, taking over from Lord Sidmouth.
- Frederick Robinson occupied the vital office of Chancellor of the Exchequer from 1823 to1827, taking over from Nicholas Vansittart.
- William Huskisson who became President of the Board of Trade 1823–27.

It would be a mistake to assume that these new men were fully Liberal in their outlook, but they shared a desire for greater efficiency in the running of the government. Also, they were all influenced by the **utilitarian** philosopher Jeremy Bentham who believed that the 'greatest happiness of the greatest number' should be the aim of any successful government. The key to this success was the improvement of economic conditions which took away the reasons for criticising government policy.

Utilitarian: Followers of the political philosopher Jeremy Bentham (1748–1832) argued that government should be efficient and accountable, based on the idea of the 'greatest happiness of the greatest number'. Many of the Whig reforms in the 1830s were based on this concept. (See also 'Benthamites' on page 124.)

Economic policy

The main emphasis was on the attempt to improve Britain's trading position with the rest of the world, based on the philosophy of free trade. The Prime Minster, Lord Liverpool, was known to be a supporter of this idea. In a famous speech, in 1820, he argued a need to reduce tariffs or taxes imposed on imports from abroad. Apart from the wishes of the Prime Minister, there were powerful sections among the business community that shared these beliefs in 1820. For example, the merchants of Manchester, Glasgow and London had all petitioned the Government for free trade. They were affected by tariffs which had been imposed to protect the home market from cheaper goods from abroad. Contemporary economists, such as David Ricardo, saw free trade as part of a moral crusade to improve the economic condition of Britain. They followed in the footsteps of the most influential free trade philosopher Adam Smith who argued, in *The Wealth of Nations* (1776), that the fewer restrictions there are on the development of an economy, the more successful it would become. William Huskisson, in his position at the Board of Trade, was especially keen to take up the challenge in the following ways:

1 The Reciprocity of Duties Act 1823

This attempted to change the navigation laws, passed in the 17th century. These were designed to protect British ships from competition from the Dutch at that time by stating that any goods or materials entering Britain or its colonies had to be carried by British ships or the ship of the country of origin of the goods. By the early 19th century, these restrictions were unnecessary and they were doing more harm than good because other countries were responding by excluding British ships from their ports. The Reciprocity Act of 1823 overcame these obstacles by allowing free entry of foreign ships into Britain on the same basis as their British counterparts. The aim was clear, as far as Huskisson was concerned. It would it be seen as a gesture of goodwill abroad, while attempting to reduce the costs of imports to British manufacturers.

2 Relaxing of trade restrictions

The next logical step was to relax the restrictions on trade with Britain's colonies which had previously been subject to strict control. As a result of Huskisson's influence, the colonies could now trade with foreign countries for the first time. He also attempted to retain their support by ensuring that duties were lower on goods trading between Britain and the colonies than non-Imperial trade.

3 The Chancellor's reputation

Frederick Robinson's liberal reputation as Chancellor of the Exchequer was based on his desire to reduce the domestic duties. This tended to complement Huskisson's strategy of promoting free trade. Robinson's main focus was the reduction of import duties on a variety of raw materials and customs and excise duties. For example duties on wool, silk, linen, tea, coffee and rum were reduced to encourage demand and improve economic stability. In addition, in a series of far-sighted Budgets between 1821 and 1827 Robinson managed to reduce indirect taxation on a variety of goods.

Frederick Robinson, first Earl of Nocton, Viscount Goderich (1784–1859)
Chancellor of the Exchequer during the Enlightened Tory period after 1823. 'Prosperity Robinson', as he was known, had previously held office as President of the Board of Trade, and was responsible for a series of Budgets that reduced import duties on a variety of goods such as rum and silk.

Social reform

While improvements in the economy were intended to increase the standard of living, there also had to be an improvement in the living and working conditions as well as an attempt to improve the legal system for the Government to be labelled 'Enlightened Tory'. The minister given the responsibility of supervising these improvements was the Home Secretary, Sir Robert Peel. According to the historian Eric Evans, Peel was suited to the task because of his organisational and administrative skills. His policies can be seen as Liberal or Enlightened in the following ways:

1. Trade unions had been banned in Britain since 1799 because it was felt that they posed a threat to the stability of the state, especially when unity was needed during the middle of the Napoleonic Wars. Trade

unions were created to protect the interests of the workers against exploitation by the employer. Every member of the trade union paid a weekly contribution to safeguard them against injury and illness. In order to escape fines and punishment, the unions merely changed their names and became known as 'friendly societies'. Radical MPs such as Joseph Hume and Sir Francis Burdett had campaigned for repeal of the Combination Acts of 1799 and 1800. They argued quite correctly that once workers' rights were reinstated, there would be an improvement in the relationship between employer and employee. Finally, common sense gave way and in 1824 the Combination laws were repealed.

Penal Code: The list containing punishment for the different crimes.

2. The inefficiencies of the English legal system were self evident in an age that liked to see itself as civilised. The **Penal Code** was ripe for reform: over 200 offences carried the death penalty and some were so innocent as to be laughable, such as stealing a loaf of bread. Inter-related to these problems was the condition of prisons. They were filthy and unkempt, and in need of improvement. Peel was determined to improve the system. Although he came under the influence of humanitarian reformers committed to improving the system, such as John Howard and Elizabeth Fry, there is little doubt that matters of efficiency, rather than a genuine concern for the welfare of the criminals and prisoners, dominated Peel's work. As Home Secretary, Peel passed a whole series of reforms, between 1823 and 1830, that transformed the rather outdated system he inherited:

   - Between 1825 and 1828, 278 legal reforms were passed which completely changed the practice of justice in England. The Penal Code was improved and the death penalty abolished for over 180 offences. The Juries Regulation Act made the jury aware of its responsibilities during a trial, and the whole system seemed more humane and tolerant.
   - In 1823, the Gaols [Jails] Act was passed. It represented an attempt by Peel to streamline the foul conditions inmates had to endure, as well as trying to improve the system that gaolers themselves laboured under. Gaolers were now to be paid and all inmates were to receive a basic education. Policy would, from this point, be conducted on a national basis – as all county and large towns were required by law to possess a gaol or house of correction.
   - Peel is perhaps best remembered for the establishment of the Metropolitan Police Force during his second period as Home Secretary, under Wellington in 1829. The creation of a police force to patrol the capital was a unique experiment that was later to be applied to the rest of the country. The 'Bobbies' or 'Peelers', as they were known, attempted to stem the alarming rise in crime that the capital suffered from at this time. The Metropolitan Police Act created 3,000 paid police officers, to be financed by the ratepayers of the city whose livelihoods and interests they were trying to protect. Despite some misgivings that the police were an attack on English liberties, the gradual respect the police enjoyed and a reduction in the crime rate seem to confirm that such a measure was necessary.

1. What changes took place in government policy as a result of the Cabinet reshuffle between 1822 and 1823?

2. Were the changes forced upon the Government or were they a genuine attempt to relive distress? Give reasons to support your answer.

The differences in government policy outlined above seem to confirm the view that there was a change of direction after 1821. The new men were responsible for a new attitude, if nothing else. This view has come in for criticism recently, and new ideas have emerged.

3.7 *To what extent did the Cabinet changes of 1821–1823 bring about a change in government policy?*

A CASE STUDY IN HISTORICAL INTERPRETATION

The dividing line between a reactionary period before 1821 and a more liberal period after is too convenient for many modern historians to accept. J.E. Cookson was the first to question the term 'Enlightened Tory' in his *Lord Liverpool's Administration, The Crucial Years 1815–1822* (1975). He argued that the term was an invention of modern historians. Norman Gash and Eric Evans continued this theme, pointing to the fact that most of the groundwork for change had been completed before the so-called Liberal or Enlightened Tory administration began. The revisionist or modern explanation is based on four important ideas:

1. The new men were not new in the sense that they had all occupied ministerial office during the so-called reactionary phase before 1821. George Canning, the Foreign Secretary, had a long history of ministerial service that originated during the premiership of Pitt the Younger. He had served as President of the Board of Trade before his resignation in 1820 at the height of the Queen Caroline Affair. Frederick Robinson was known to be a close follower of the supposedly reactionary Viscount Castlereagh and followed in Canning's footsteps at the Board of Trade between 1818 and 1823, before becoming Chancellor of the Exchequer. William Huskisson had served in the rather obscure position of Commissioner for Forests since 1814. He was regarded as an important economic adviser before he became President of the Board of Trade. Finally, Peel had held office in Ireland since 1812 as Chief Secretary and was aware of the difficult situation the Government had to face in the years 1815 to 1821.

   These new Enlightened Tories were merely completing work that had been started in the reactionary phase of the administration. An analysis of Canning's foreign policy appears in Chapter 4, but the clear-cut divide that allegedly exists between Castlereagh the Reactionary and Canning as Enlightened or Liberal has been questioned on the grounds that the similarities in policy outweigh the differences. Robinson, according to historian Norman Gash, took the credit for economic prosperity in the 1820s that should have been given to his predecessor at the Treasury, Nicholas Vansittart. It was Vansittart who had taken Britain back to the Gold Standard in 1819, returning the economy to sound money and thereby stabilising the currency. By 1823, Robinson inherited a budget surplus. Huskisson, and to a lesser extent Robinson, owed a great debt to the unsung hero of the move toward free trade: Thomas Wallace, who as Vice President of the Board of Trade in the so-called reactionary period, recommended many of the changes, including the relaxation of the Navigation Laws. Peel was also instrumental in proposing a return to the Gold Standard in 1819, being a member of the influential committee that investigated the matter.

2. A new interpretation of this period questions the view that the period up to 1821 was not as reactionary and repressive as historians would have us believe. The Government's response to a series of unprecedented circumstances in 1815–21 represented a commonsense reaction on the part of a government that was at least trying to survive the difficulties of post-Napoleonic War Britain. The abolition of income tax in 1816 – often seen as an example of reaction that eagerly shifted the burden of taxation from the aristocracy – was opposed by Lord Liverpool, but he was forced to accept it under pressure from influential

backbench opinion. There are other examples of so-called Enlightened laws passed during the reactionary period: for example, the Factory Act 1819 which prevented children under the age of nine from working in the mills and regulated the working hours of other children up to 16. The Truck Act of 1820 attempted to prevent employers from paying wages in goods rather than money and to safeguard the rights of the workers. In addition, a number of important committees were set up to investigate known problems such as the legal system. Why did these policies not come in sooner and assume the more official tone that they seemed to after 1821? The answer lies probably in the circumstances of the time that were not suitable for reform. It is also probably correct to assume that the Government was giving these more liberal proposals serious consideration before the Queen Caroline Affair broke and distracted the attention of Lord Liverpool from the issue of reform.

3. There is also some truth in the allegation that the Enlightened Tory legislation passed after 1821 was not as liberal as would first appear. The **social policy** of Peel seems to be the most obvious area of concern. The repeal of the Combination Law in 1824 seems on paper to herald a new relationship between the Government and the trade union movement, but following repeal the country witnessed numerous disputes as workers demanded wage increases. The Government response could hardly be described as 'Enlightened' when, in 1825, they introduced the Amending Act. This allowed trade unions to exist only for the purpose of negotiating wages. The reform of the legal system was not carried out from any humanitarian perspective but from a desire to improve the efficiency of the way in which justice was administered. The motivation behind the Gaols Act was being considered by the so-called reactionary Home Secretary, Lord Sidmouth, before Peel took office. Again, the credit and the groundwork was already well in advance of the Enlightened era.

Social policy: A term used to describe the ways in which the Government tries to deal with issues such as poor housing and prisons and, at the same time, attempt to increase prosperity.

Why have historians of the Tory Party (1815–27) differed in their explanations of a possible change of policy after 1821?

4. The two most controversial issues of the age were parliamentary reform and the emancipation or equality of Roman Catholics. Lord Liverpool's Government made a conscious effort to avoid both of these potentially divisive issues. Tories avoided the issue of electoral reform, or an extension of those able to vote, because ultimately they felt threatened by the prospect of those they regarded as inferior being allowed to vote and determine their own future. The detailed arguments over this issue are dealt with in Chapter 6. However, if the Government regarded itself as Enlightened then it should have at least attempted to change what was obviously an unfair system. The question of giving political rights to Roman Catholics was another controversial issue. It is dealt with in the next section in relation to the collapse of the Tory Party. Liberals such as Canning favoured emancipation, but **Ultras** such as Wellington and Peel refused even to tolerate it until circumstances forced their hand. Lord Liverpool was in an extremely difficult position because the issue of Roman Catholic rights was potentially explosive. He was determined to avoid this issue at all costs in order to keep the different factions within the Government together. This may be regarded as another commonsense approach by a Prime Minister wanting to avoid potential catastrophe for his party, but it cannot be regarded as the most Liberal of actions.

Ultras: A term used to describe those members of the Tory Party who opposed giving any concessions to dissenters or Roman Catholics. They regarded any concessions as a direct attack on the Church of England.

Continuity seems to be the key in understanding the premiership of Lord Liverpool, both in personnel and policy. As Norman Gash has pointed out in *Aristocracy and People* (1987), 'the mythical transformation of the ministry from reactionary Tory before 1822 to Liberal Tory afterwards was the invention of subsequent historians. Liverpool's objective was not to alter course but to reorganise his crew for a voyage that had already started.' The real changes had begun long before the Cabinet reshuffle took place and the economic situation began to improve, but were only postponed by the Queen Caroline Affair. Yet it does seem, at first glance, that there was something different about the government attitude in the 1820s that separated it from the dangerous period up to 1821. The real difference lies in the political and economic climate that allowed the government to introduce these changes in the more prosperous 1820s.

The Premiership of Lord Liverpool – arch mediocrity or effective politician?

Robert Banks Jenkinson, second Earl of Liverpool (1770–1828)
Lord Liverpool was Prime Minister between 1821 and 1827. He was the longest single-serving PM of the 19th century. He presided over enormous changes at a time when the Government had little idea how to cope with them. Strangely, he was accused by his critics of an intolerant and unsympathetic attitude towards the plight of the working class, especially before 1821.

Write a brief account of the premiership of Lord Liverpool. Do you think he was an effective politician or an arch mediocrity? Give reasons to support your answer.

Arch mediocrity?

Contemporaries of Lord Liverpool were very critical of his policies. They accused him of creating unrest by such measures as the introduction of the Corn Laws and the repeal of income tax. Radical poets such as Byron and Shelley were scathing in their treatment of a government that ignored the wishes of the people, describing them as 'rulers who neither see nor feel nor know'. Personally, Liverpool lacked the intellectual qualities of Peel and the charisma and popular appeal of Canning. He refused to tolerate the major issue of parliamentary reform and even less so Catholic emancipation, which he knew would split the party. This rather negative reputation continued after his death when his fellow Tory, the future Prime Minister Benjamin Disraeli, writing in his political novel *Conningsby* in 1844, described Liverpool as the 'Arch Mediocrity' or someone who lacked the charisma that the author so admired in his public figures. This rather dismissive comment tended to illustrate the career of Robert Banks Jenkinson until recently when an effective defence was put forward.

Effective politician?

Historian John Derry described Lord Liverpool as the 'unobtrusive Prime Minister', meaning that here was a modest and unassuming man carrying out his work with quiet efficiency. There is a lot to be said for modesty in a politician. Lord Liverpool had a talent for moderation and reconciling more hotheaded colleagues, keeping them under the broad umbrella of the Tory Party. This modest efficiency drew great devotion from Cabinet colleagues who were prepared to 'go down with their captain' over issues such as the Queen Caroline Affair, when the King threatened to introduce a Whig ministry.

Lord Liverpool's policies now draw much more applause than they did from contemporaries. Income tax repeal was forced on him by influential backbenchers in the Commons and the Six Acts have been re-assessed as hardly amounting to a reign of terror. Lord Liverpool presided over the prosperity of the 1820s and was a firm and enthusiastic supporter of free trade. You must also remember that it was during Liverpool's ministry that the Napoleonic Wars were finally won. As Prime Minister, he was ultimately responsible for all elements of government policy. Also, although there were more able and indeed popular colleagues, it was Liverpool who acted as the continuous link throughout his premiership. As you will note in the next section, his death in 1828 split the Party and ensured a considerable period in the political wilderness.

3.8 Why did the Tory Party collapse between 1827 and 1830?

The death of Lord Liverpool and the disputes over the succession

These events led to party disunity. In February 1827, Lord Liverpool suffered a stroke from which he never recovered. His death the following year robbed the country of one of its most underrated prime ministers. He had held the position since 1812 and had guided the country and his own party through some very difficult times. The quality of his leadership would be demonstrated when, over the next three years, the different factions within the Tory Party argued over policy and major differences appeared between the various personalities contesting the leadership. The succession question was solved temporarily, in the spring of 1827, when George IV appointed George Canning as the new Prime Minister.

Canning was an extremely popular choice in the country at large and he was determined to follow his own agenda. Undoubtedly a brilliant politician with experience of a number of important offices, such as Foreign Secretary, Canning was equally unpopular with large sections of his own party. Wellington and Peel both resigned and refused to serve under him. The major area of dispute between them was Canning's known support for Roman Catholic emancipation, which was completely unacceptable to the Ultras. There was also the issue of his personality, which was generally considered as being vain and overbearing.

William Huskisson (1770–1830)
One of the leading Enlightened Tories after 1822. Huskisson was heavily influenced by George Canning. His appointment as President of the Board of Trade in 1823 ensured that government economic policy became more enlightened – for example, the passage of the Reciprocity of Duties Act 1823. He died after falling under the train making the first run from Liverpool to Manchester – the first railway line built primarily to carry passengers.

The survival of Canning's ministry depended on an alliance of Enlightened Tories such as Huskisson and Palmerston and members of the other main political party, the Whigs. Unfortunately, the ministry was only to last a few short months until Canning's premature death in the autumn of 1827. The new Prime Minister, Frederick Robinson – created Lord Goderich at the time of the formation of Canning's ministry – was to be one of the worst of the whole century, remaining in office as it did until January 1828. The only realistic alternative as Prime Minister was the Duke of Wellington, the great hero of the Napoleonic Wars but completely unsuited to the position because of his brutal honesty and lack of tact. His appointment split the Party even further. The supporters of Canning – Canningites as they were known – were extremely uneasy at the prospect of a known Ultra at the helm. The ministry of Wellington would finally condemn the Tories to a period in the political wilderness, but in 1828–30 it was policy, as much as personality difference, that would dominate the Party.

Why were there differences within the Tory Party over Catholic emancipation?

Ever since the post-1689 penal laws, passed by William III, Catholics had been treated badly by Britain's Protestant rulers. For a long time, there was a fear of an invasion by foreign Catholic powers, such as France and Spain, and this was used as justification for persecution. By the early 19th century, the only serious threat to the stability of the Protestant dominance came from Irish Catholics. In Ireland, growing conflict threatened the stability of the state. Here, Catholics formed a large majority, yet they were regarded by the British ruling class as second-class subjects. Economically, Ireland was underdeveloped compared with Britain. Agriculture was barely advanced enough to feed a growing population. All land and wealth in Ireland was concentrated in the hands of a small group of Protestants, **absentee landlords**. The wealth and status of the Anglican Church stood in stark contrast to the position of the Catholic Church, which relied on the contribution of its congregation. While Catholics had the vote if they held enough land, they were prohibited from holding any public office – the important offices

Absentee landlords: Those not living on their estates but still taking in the profits at the expense of their poor peasant tenants. They charged high rents and were only interested in profit.

Arthur Wellesley, later Duke of Wellington (1769–1852)
Most famously remembered for his military victories against Napoleon, especially at Waterloo in 1815. Less successful as a politician, he was involved in foreign policy during the 1820s and became Prime Minister 1828–30 after Lord Liverpool's resignation. Known for his anti-Reform and anti-Catholic prejudices, he served briefly as Foreign Secretary and minister without portfolio in Peel's two governments.

of state that could change the existing situation. 'Emancipation' would involve the removal of these restrictions and, its supporters claimed, solve all the problems of Ireland.

Violence had been a common feature in Irish politics since the Act of Union of 1800 – when Ireland was made a part of the United Kingdom. The governments of both Pitt and Liverpool had used various measures to contain the situation, but little or nothing had been done to tackle the causes of unrest. There were two major reasons for this:

1. Both George III and his son George IV were hostile to the idea of conceding any ground to the Catholics in Ireland because they were of the belief that Irish Catholics were not loyal subjects.
2. There was a great majority within the Tory Party that shared these ideas. Religious bigotry or hatred was rife and any discussion of the issue threatened the fragile unity of the Party. Under Lord Liverpool, the issue had always been an 'open question', but once he went the disputes between the various factions came out into the open. The ultra-Protestant group, led by Wellington and Peel, were strongly opposed to emancipation; the Canningites were far more open in their support.

The events of the late 1820s forced the Tories to abandon their open policy and to make some firm commitments. The political situation in Ireland had been changing since 1823 when agitation from Daniel O'Connell's 'Catholic Association' grew, until it was banned in 1825. O'Connell was a brilliant barrister who managed, through non-violent means, to convince the Irish people that emancipation was worth pursuing. His crusade touched a raw nerve with the Whig opposition who sponsored a bill that many Tories such as Canning and Huskisson supported. The bill passed the House of Commons, but was defeated in the Lords. In May 1828, O'Connell saw his opportunity when a by-election was held in County Clare. O'Connell stood against Vesey Fitzgerald, a pro-emancipation Protestant and a popular MP. Fitzgerald was forced to call a by-election because he had become a junior minister in the Government. Here, O'Connell argued, would be an opportunity to test the Government's resolve and to challenge the restrictions against Catholics entering Parliament.

O'Connell was elected with a large majority. Wellington and Peel now realised that unless O'Connell was allowed to occupy his seat, Ireland would be plunged into civil war. In February 1829, both Wellington and his Home Secretary Peel announced their conversion to Catholic emancipation in the interests of law and order. The Ultras were outraged by what they saw as the most humiliating of political U-turns and a denial of one of the most fundamental principles of Tory Party policy. The law was formally proclaimed in April 1829 when Parliament agreed to admit Catholics to its benches and all but a few offices. The 142 Tories who voted against the bill were determined to discredit the ministry up to its conclusion in November 1830. Peel, in particular, never regained his reputation with the Tory Ultras amid accusations of betrayal.

How did the question of parliamentary reform lead to the final collapse of Tory rule in 1830?

The more detailed arguments regarding the issue of reform will be dealt with in Chapter 6. This section will refer mainly to the issue of reform as a factor in the collapse of the Tory Party. Most Tories were staunch supporters of the existing electoral system because it represented their interests as landowners and was a safeguard against revolution on the French model of 1789. Wellington, Peel and the Ultras were firmly against the extension of the franchise (vote) for precisely these reasons. The more

Liberal wing of the party – the Canningites – were more enthusiastic. However, George Canning himself was less open about the issue of parliamentary reform than he was about Catholic emancipation. The Whigs, the other main political party, were committed to the idea but had been unable to command a majority in Parliament. The divisions in the Tory Party had been partially exposed in 1828 when an opportunity arose to enfranchise the under-represented cities of Manchester and Leeds. Wellington was opposed to the idea and this led to the resignation of the leading Canningite, Huskisson.

The issue of Catholic emancipation had a knock-on effect on parliamentary reform because peaceful protest had ensured the abolition of what was regarded as one of the fundamental pillars of the Tory Party. Ironically, a small minority of the 142 members who voted against emancipation now became unlikely converts to the idea of electoral reform. They felt a wider franchise would have ensured a rejection of emancipation on the grounds that the people were more trustworthy than Parliament! In a speech on 11 November 1830, Wellington continued his opposition to reform, which forced the Whigs and Canningites into open opposition.

1. What do you regard as the most important reason for the collapse of the Tory Party in 1830?

2. Why do you think that the two issues of emancipation and parliamentary reform proved to be such difficult issues for the Tory Government?

The death of George IV in 1830 and the accession of William IV were another blow to those that opposed parliamentary reform. The new king was known to be more tolerant towards the Whig position than his brother had ever been. Economic and political conditions were worsening, highlighting the need for change. Wellington's Government managed to stutter along until the end of 1830 when it was defeated over an investigation into the Civil List accounts – the annual amount the royal family is awarded by Parliament. The Tories had survived worse crises since 1815, but the Duke of Wellington commanded little loyalty among his own party and was confronted by a resurgent Whig Party led by Earl Grey. The end of Tory rule was now a certainty.

4 British foreign policy, 1815–1846

4.1 What were the principles governing British foreign policy?
4.2 How successful was Castlereagh as Foreign Secretary?
4.3 What problems faced Canning as Foreign Secretary in the years 1822–1827?
4.4 Historical interpretation: Change or continuity? A comparison of the foreign policies of Castlereagh and Canning
4.5 To what extent did Palmerston uphold British interests abroad in the years 1830–1841?
4.6 How successful was the Earl of Aberdeen as Foreign Secretary between 1841 and 1846?

Key Issues

- *What were the main aims of British foreign policy?*
- *How far was there continuity in foreign policy in this period?*
- *How successfully were British interests defended in this period?*

Framework of Events

1793–1815	Wars with France
1812–15	Britain at war with USA
1812	Castlereagh is appointed Foreign Secretary
1814	Congress of Vienna opens. Bourbon Monarchy is restored to France
1815	Napoleon is defeated at Waterloo
	Holy Alliance signed between Russia, Prussia and Austria
	Quadruple Alliance signed between Russia, Prussia, Austria and Britain
1818	Congress of Aix-La-Chapelle
	France admitted into the Quadruple Alliance
1820	Castlereagh issues the State Paper
	Revolutions break out in Spain, Italy and Portugal
	Congress of Troppau (reconvened at Laibach 1821)
1821	Congress of Laibach; outbreak of Greek Revolt
1822	Castlereagh commits suicide; Canning is appointed Foreign Secretary
1823	French troops invade Spain. Monroe Doctrine issued
1824	Britain recognises the independence of Spain's former colonies of Columbia, Mexico and La Plata (Argentina)
1826	Britain intervenes in Portugal. Protocol of St Petersburg
1827	Treaty of London signed by Britain, France and Russia recognising Greek independence but under Turkish control
	Death of Canning
1828	War breaks out between Russia and Turkey
	Earl of Aberdeen is appointed Foreign Secretary
1829	Treaty of Adrianople
1830	July: Revolution in France; the Belgian and Polish revolts
1833	Treaty of Unkiar Skelessi
1834	Signing of the Quadruple Alliance
1839	Treaty of London recognises an independent Belgium
1841	Straits Convention signed. Earl of Aberdeen becomes Foreign Secretary again
	Opium War with China
1844	France acquires Tahiti and the Society Islands
1846	Spanish marriages question begins.

Overview

FOREIGN policy in this period was dominated by four larger-than-life characters: Viscount Castlereagh (Foreign Secretary 1821–22), George Canning (1822–27), Lord Palmerston (1830–34, 1834–41) and the Earl of Aberdeen (1841–46). Each had strong views on the role that Britain should play in Europe. Castlereagh, as Foreign Secretary, had played a leading role in the defeat of Napoleon Bonaparte and was especially keen to restore peace to Europe based on the concept of the Congress System. Yet his separation from the idea of collective diplomacy was confirmed at the Troppau Congress in 1820. Up to Castlereagh's suicide in 1822, Britain became increasingly distanced from the other Great Powers.

George Canning, Castlereagh's successor from 1822, had enjoyed a colourful political career up to that point and was determined to make politics more appealing to a wider audience. His attitude to the Congress System was more hostile, bearing in mind his belief that Britain's real interests lay outside Europe. In addition, he had no special relationship with those statesmen who had worked with Castlereagh, such as the Austrian Chancellor, Metternich. Canning attempted to safeguard Britain's interests in Spain, Portugal and Greece. By the time of his death in 1827, he had succeeded in maintaining British interests while playing a leading role in the collapse of the Congress System.

Wellington's brief ministry of 1828–30 was dominated by the issue of the Greek revolt in which he attempted to reverse some of Canning's forward policies regarding Greek independence. Ultimately, Wellington was unable to contain the inevitable and an independent Greek state was declared in 1830. Palmerston's foreign policy between 1830 and 1841 was, in many ways, directed by Canning's legacy. His emphasis in his policies regarding the Eastern Crisis, France and the USA was always to put British interests at the top of the agenda. As Palmerston stated in a speech in the House of Commons in March 1848: 'The furtherance of British interests is the only object of a British Foreign Secretary and that Britain has no permanent friends or enemies.' He was generally successful but left many problems for his successor, the Earl of Aberdeen. Aberdeen's approach to foreign affairs, in the period 1841–46, differed from Palmerston's as he always aimed to avoid war if at all possible and to settle disputes peacefully.

4.1 What were the principles governing British foreign policy?

British foreign policy in this period operated on a number of clear principles. Although each Foreign Secretary manipulated these principles to suit their own policies, there was a high degree of continuity between them.

Britain's foreign policy and its relations with other European powers should be seen in the context of the wars with France. From 1793 to 1815, Britain was almost continuously at war, first against the French Revolutionary government and then against Napoleon I. Throughout the period of the French Wars, Britain had played a major diplomatic and military role. In the formation of coalitions of countries against France, Britain was a leading player. In 1812 Castlereagh was an important force in the creation of the Fourth Coalition between Britain, Russia, Austria, Prussia and Sweden against Napoleon. It was this coalition which finally brought Napoleon's first abdication in 1814 and his final defeat at Waterloo in June 1815. In addition, British armed forces played a major role: the Royal Navy prevented the French invasion of Britain with Nelson's victory at Trafalgar in October 1805, while land forces, under the Duke of Wellington, helped defeat the French in the Peninsular War (1808–1814) and led the Allied army that defeated Napoleon at Waterloo.

When the French Wars came to an end, Britain was the world's major naval power. It possessed colonies across the world and was regarded as a European Great Power (see page 22). So what were the main principles governing British foreign policy after 1815?

The maintenance of British naval power

The historian James Joll declares, in his book *Britain and Europe 1793 to 1940* (1961), that 'British interests are those arising out of Britain's position as a maritime and commercial power'. In the implementation of this policy, Britain aimed to keep command of the sea lanes of the world and to prevent any other power from threatening this position.

At the Congress of Vienna (1814–15), Castlereagh acquired a number of strategically important colonial possessions which aimed to maintain Britain's naval position. For instance, in the Mediterranean Sea Britain controlled Gibraltar before 1815. As a result of the treaty, Malta and the Ionian Islands were added to the Empire which helped to reinforce British naval control.

Associated with this principle was the policy of preventing Great Powers threatening British naval supremacy. In the Straits Convention of 1841, Palmerston succeeded in preventing the Russian navy entering the Mediterranean Sea through the Bosphorus and Dardanelles.

Britain's position as the world's major naval power was reinforced by the British claim, up to 1858, to the right of 'visit and search' of any ship on the high seas. This claim was used mainly to intercept ships in the north Atlantic which the British suspected of participating in the Atlantic slave trade. It was a constant cause of tension between Britain and other European states, such as France, Spain and Portugal.

Furthering British trading interests

Lord Granville once remarked that 'one of the first duties of a British government must always be to obtain for our foreign trade the security which is essential to its success'. This was to be achieved not only through the maintenance of Britain's naval supremacy, but also through other policies. The recognition of *de facto* governments (see page 23) was an important feature of foreign policy throughout this period. Castlereagh's State Paper of 5 May 1820 implied it, while Canning's recognition of the Greeks as co-belligerents in their revolt against Turkey had more to do with trade than any attachment to the Greek cause. Perhaps the best example of this principle is the recognition of the Latin American republics which had declared independence from Spain during the Napoleonic Wars.

This principle was taken one step further with the Government's active promotion of British trade. In 1838, Palmerston negotiated a free trade convention with the Turkish Empire. Then, in the following year, the outbreak of the Opium War with China was a blatant attempt to open up the Chinese Empire to British trade.

Maintaining the European balance of power

Peace and political stability on the European continent was essential in order to ensure Britain remained the world's major trading and commercial power. Therefore, throughout the period, successive foreign secretaries actively supported the concept of a European **balance of power** as the best means of maintaining this peace.

Balance of power: Within the context of European history this was the concept that peace would best be preserved if just one Great Power had the military might to threaten the rest of Europe. It was hoped that a 'just equilibrium' would be established. This was clearly not the case with Napoleonic France.

Concert of Europe: The practical application of maintaining the European balance of power. When international crises occurred, the Great Powers would meet and provide a peaceful solution to the problem. The Congress System could be regarded as a formal version of this idea. (See also pages 22–23.)

Viscount Castlereagh, in association with Prince Metternich of Austria, ensured that this principle was enshrined in the terms of the Treaty of Vienna in 1815. To maintain the balance of power, British foreign secretaries used a number of policies. Between 1815 and 1822, Castlereagh was willing to work closely with the European Great Powers through the Congress System. After 1822, foreign secretaries adopted a more detached position but continued to use the **Concert of Europe** to resolve disputes peacefully.

Between 1825 and 1827, Canning worked with Russia and France to solve the Greek problem. After 1830, Palmerston worked through the Concert of Europe to establish independent Greek and Belgian kingdoms and to provide an international agreement over the Straits.

The two Great Powers which Britain regarded as having the potential to disrupt the European balance of power were France and Russia. Britain's relations with France, in particular, went through many phases of friendship and hostility between 1815 and 1846. One of the main aims of the Congress of Vienna was to prevent France again threatening European peace. Yet in the period 1818–22 Britain worked with France through the Congress System. This relationship was maintained by Canning over the Greek Revolt in the 1820s. In 1834 and again in 1844, Britain signed agreements of friendship with the French state.

However, on occasion fear of France did emerge: during the Belgian revolt Palmerston aimed to prevent the French gaining control over the Channel coast; in 1840 both countries faced the threat of war over Mehemet Ali, the Pasha of Egypt, and his war with the Sultan of Turkey.

Although Britain had allied with Russia to defeat Napoleon, after 1815 Britain became suspicious of Russian policy in Europe and the Middle East. The Tsar's creation of the Holy Alliance in 1815, and its re-affirmation in the Munchengratz Agreement of 1833, raised British fears that Russia wished to extend its influence in Europe to the detriment of Britain. Castlereagh's State Paper of May 1820 and Palmerston's conclusion of the Quadruple Alliance of 1834 with France, Spain and Portugal were attempts to counter Russia. The most important area of conflict between Britain and Russia came in the Middle East over the Turkish Empire in the period 1833–41. A secret clause of the Treaty of Unkiar Skelessi of 1833 between Turkey and Russia gave the Russian navy access to the Mediterranean Sea. From that date onwards, Britain aimed to remove Russian influence from Turkey and to replace it with British support.

Barbary pirates: Superb seamen, based in Algiers in northern Africa, who made their living from piracy. They often attacked shipping in the Mediterranean.

Opposition to the Atlantic slave trade

In 1807, Parliament abolished the slave trade, although slavery still existed in the British Empire until 1833. Throughout the period 1815–46, Britain attempted to enforce the abolition of the slave trade. Firstly, a west African naval squadron was created which used the right of search to intercept any merchant ship on the high seas. If slaves were found, they were confiscated and returned to the British west African colony of Sierra Leone where they were freed. This policy caused friction with those European states still engaged in the slave trade, such as France, Spain and Portugal.

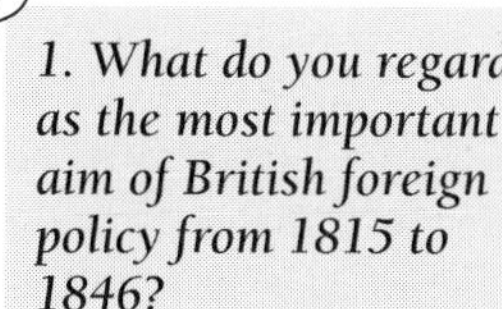

1. What do you regard as the most important aim of British foreign policy from 1815 to 1846?

2. How consistently was this aim followed in this period?

Secondly, at the Congress of Vienna Castlereagh was able to gain international opposition to the **Barbary pirates** of North Africa who engaged in the slave trade. Finally, in 1836, Palmerston was willing to recognise the independence of the Republic of Texas in return for the acceptance of an end to the slave trade.

4.2 How successful was Castlereagh as Foreign Secretary?

Contemporaries were highly critical of the policies pursued by the Foreign Secretary between 1812 and 1822 – Robert Stewart, Viscount Castlereagh, who was made the second Marquis of Londonderry in 1821. Ten years at the Foreign Office saw him become the subject of a smear campaign that was without parallel in its severity. The modern historian and American statesman Henry Kissinger stated: 'Castlereagh walked his solitary path as humanly unapproachable as his policy came to be incomprehensible to the majority of his comtemporaries.' A more flattering view was put forward by the historian Sir Charles Webster, who argued that the reputation Castlereagh enjoyed was primarily a reaction to his involvement in Irish politics at the turn of the century and his membership of Lord Liverpool's Cabinet during the so-called 'reactionary period' – 1815–21. Modern historians, such as John Derry in the *Modern History Review*, have gone as far as to suggest that 'in his defence of British interests he [Castlereagh] set the course for British foreign policy continued by Canning, Palmerston and Salisbury throughout the next century'.

Robert Stewart, Viscount Castlereagh (1769–1822)
He took the courtesy title Viscount Castlereagh when his father, an Ulster landowner, was made an earl in 1796. Sat in Parliament from 1790 until his death in 1822. As Chief Secretary for Ireland (1797–1801), Castlereagh suppressed the rebellion of 1798 and helped Pitt the Younger secure the union of England, Scotland and Ireland three years later. It was as Secretary for War and the Colonies (1805–06 and 1807–08) that he had to resign after a duel with the Foreign Secretary, George Canning. As Foreign Secretary himself (1812–22), Castlereagh coordinated the European opposition to Napoleon and then represented Britain at the Congress of Vienna (1814–15). At home, he repressed the Reform movement, and popular opinion held him responsible for the 1819 Peterloo massacre.

How far did Castlereagh's early career affect his later policy?

Robert Stewart (Viscount Castlereagh) was born in Dublin, in 1769, of Ulster stock. He spent his early career rejecting the excesses of the French Revolution. Castlereagh's Irish background was important, according to historian John Derry, because 'it gave him an insight which perhaps an Englishman lacked, into the problems of peacemaking or cajoling different communities to co-exist together'. In 1797, Castlereagh was heavily involved in thwarting an intended French invasion of Britain. He used his position as Irish Secretary to warn the authorities of the potential support the invasion would receive in Ireland. His ministerial experience increased when he became President of the Board of Trade in 1802. From 1812, Castlereagh occupied the Foreign Office under the then Prime Minister, Spencer Perceval. Almost immediately, Castlereagh played a vital role in negotiating the Fourth Coalition against Napoleonic France and showed considerable skill in holding it together between 1812 and 1815.

When Britain found itself at war with the United States of America (USA) in 1812, Castlereagh attempted to resolve the disputes over the slave trade and the position of Canada as quickly as possible in order to concentrate on matters in Europe. Although there were still issues to resolve between the two countries, the peace negotiations at Ghent in 1814, which brought the conflict to an end, resulted in an acceptable compromise for all concerned.

The Congress of Vienna (1814–1815)

Having played a major diplomatic role in the defeat of Napoleon, Castlereagh represented Britain at the European Congress, which concluded peace after almost 25 years of continuous war and revolution. Although virtually all European governments were represented, the proceedings were dominated by the representatives of the five Great Powers. Apart from Castlereagh, Prince Metternich represented Austria, Charles Talleyrand France and Karl Hardenburg Prussia, while Tsar Alexander I led the Russian delegation. Castlereagh's personal attitude to the policy was clear when he stated 'it is not our business to collect trophies, but to try, if we can, to bring the world back to peaceful habits'. How accurate is Castlereagh's statement concerning the Congress of Vienna?

Creation of a European balance of power

At Vienna, Castlereagh broke with the instructions of a cautious government in London and signed a secret treaty in January 1815 with Austria and

France. The treaty aimed to prevent Russia and Prussia gaining too much territory at the expense of Poland and Saxony, which could prevent the establishment of a balance of power. In general terms, it must rank as one of Castlereagh's triumphs that a balance of power was created at Vienna which remained largely intact until the outbreak of the First World War.

To ensure that the balance of power would be maintained, Castlereagh was the main force behind Article VI of the Second Treaty of Paris, 1815, which created the Quadruple Alliance between Britain, Russia, Prussia and Austria. It suggested that from time to time the European Great Powers should meet to discuss the affairs of Europe. This treaty and other agreements made in the closing stages of the Napoleonic Wars laid the foundation for the establishment of the Congress System which operated between 1815 and 1823.

The containment of France

In order to prevent France threatening the peace of Europe again it was forced to give up all the territory it had acquired since 1790. In addition, the border areas surrounding France were strengthened. Holland and Belgium were united, with the Great Powers paying for the construction of defensive fortification on the Franco–Belgian frontier. Prussia was given Rhineland/Westphalia, Austria was given Venetia in order to strengthen its hold on north Italy and Piedmont received Genoa.

Legitimacy: A term used to describe the rightful rulers of any given country based on their hereditary rights. In 1815, the restoration of these legitimate rulers was regarded by the peacemakers at Vienna as the best way of maintaining peace and stability in Europe after the upheavals of the Napoleonic Wars.

The principle of ***legitimacy***

In order to offer international support for the restoration of the Bourbon monarchy to France, it was proclaimed at the Congress of Vienna that those monarchs who lost their thrones during the Napoleonic era would regain them. Although there is some evidence to suggest that this was implemented in Germany and France, it did not prevent the Great Powers ignoring the idea when other issues such as the balance of power, the containment of France and their own self-importance were concerned.

Rewarding the victors

All the victorious powers gained extra territory as a result of the Congress:

- Russia gained Finland, the kingdom of Poland and Bessarabia.
- Prussia gained two-fifths of Saxony and Rhineland/Westphalia.
- Austria gained Salzburg and Venetia, though it lost Belgium.
- Territorial acquisitions reinforced Britain's position as the world's premier trading and naval power. Malta, the Ionian Islands and Heligoland provided important naval bases in the Mediterranean and the North Sea. The acquisition of Ceylon (Sri Lanka) and Mauritius gave Britain a major naval presence in the Indian Ocean, while the acquisition of the Cape of Good Hope (purchased from the King of Holland for £6 million) gave Britain strategic control of the seas between the south Atlantic and Indian oceans. The acquistion of Tobago and St Lucia, in the West Indies, increased British control of the sugar trade.

Punishing France

The representatives at Vienna agreed that France should suffer punishment not only for plunging Europe into nearly 25 years of warfare, but also for allowing Napoleon to return for the '100 days' in 1815. France's borders were reduced to those of 1790 and art treasures taken from other states were to be returned. In addition, France had to pay a **war indemnity** and suffer an army of occupation, which was withdrawn in 1818.

War indemnity: A payment made by a defeated side in order to pay the costs incurred by the victors in the war.

What was Castlereagh's policy towards the Congress System 1815–1822?

The first meeting of the Great Powers following Vienna took place at Aix-la-Chapelle (Aachen) in 1818. France was readmitted to the Concert of Europe and the Quadruple Alliance was extended to become the Quintuple Alliance. Although generally regarded as successful, the Congress did witness the beginnings of a future split when Tsar Alexander I proposed an agreement whereby the Great Powers would have the right to intervene in other states. This seemed to be a re-affirmation of the Holy Alliance of 1815 which was also put forward by the Tsar and signed by most European states except Britain, the Vatican (Pope's residences in Rome) and Turkey.

This problem came to a head at the next congress held at Troppau, in Austrian Silesia, in 1820 in the wake of revolutions in Spain and Naples and disturbances in Piedmont-Sardinia. Although Castlereagh agreed that Austria had the right to suppress revolution in Naples (in its capacity as the dominant Great Power in Italy), the British Foreign Secretary opposed intervention in Spain especially if this involved Russian intervention. The Congress's main conclusion was the signing of the Troppau Protocol by the other Great Powers. This accepted the principle that the Great Powers had the right to intervene in any European state where revolution occurred. Castlereagh refused to sign. His counter to this policy had been the State Paper of 5 May 1820. This was a rejection of the idea of intervention, as he told a packed House of Commons:

> 'The [Quadruple] alliance … was never intended as a union for the government of the world … such a scheme was only legitimate where a power or combination of powers were threatening the peace of Europe by threatening to mount aggression against a neighbour.'

From this point on, Britain became less involved in the Congress System. When the Congress at Troppau reconvened, at Laibach early in 1821, Castlereagh did not attend. The cracks that had begun to appear at Troppau widened with the outbreak of the Greek Revolt in 1821 against Turkey. Although Castlereagh sympathised with the Greeks, as did much of educated Britain, he was worried that Russia would intervene on the side of the Greeks who were also Orthodox Christians. Britain's detachment from the other Great Powers of the Congress System seemed to be complete when Castlereagh committed suicide in August 1822.

How successful was Castlereagh in dealing with the USA?

American historian Bradford Perkins has claimed that Castlereagh was the first British minister to accept American independence and its implications for the conduct of future British foreign policy. Castlereagh, although a strong opponent of the slave trade, realised that it was foolish for the two countries to go on fighting. Following the Peace of Ghent in 1814, Castlereagh attempted to improve relations between the two countries even further. Firstly, in 1818, he accepted that the 49th Parallel should form the basis of the border between Canada and the United States west of the Great Lakes. Although not formally agreed until Palmerston was Foreign Secretary in 1840, this compromise agreement was primarily the result of Castlereagh's cautious diplomacy in this period.

Also in 1818, Castlereagh prevented deterioration in Anglo–American relations following General Jackson's invasion of Spanish Florida and his execution of two British subjects accused of organising Indian raids into US territory. As Castlereagh's biographer Sir Charles Webster notes: 'All that he did was done so unobtrusively and with such little desire to enhance his own reputation that it obtained the obscurity necessary for success.'

Study the two maps. Explain how the political make-up of Europe changed between 1810 and 1815.

Europe in 1810

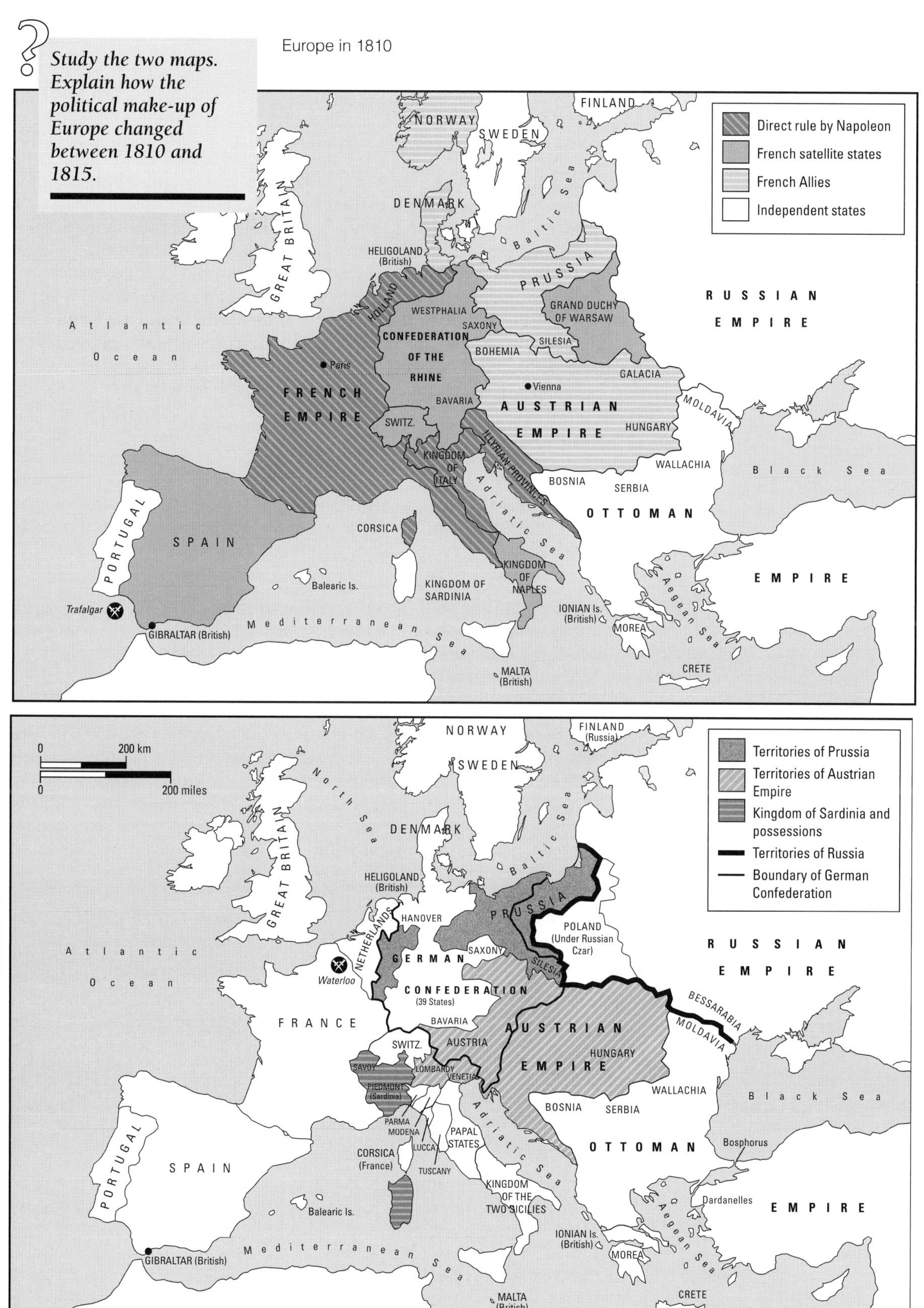

Europe after the Congress of Vienna 1815

In 1819, Britain and the United States concluded the Rush–Bagot Agreement, which aimed at reducing military and naval forces in the Great Lakes area. In addition, potential flash points between the two states over such issues as fishing rights off Newfoundland were resolved amicably, confirming Castlereagh's cautious approach to Anglo–American relations.

Castlereagh's foreign policy: an assessment

The reasons behind Viscount Castlereagh's suicide can be explained partly by a nervous breakdown, and partly by a smear campaign by radical opponents who accused him of homosexuality. Whilst running the Foreign Office in this period, Castlereagh was also leader of the House of Commons and the Government's chief spokesman – bearing in mind that the Prime Minister, Lord Liverpool, sat in the Lords. Castlereagh unfortunately occupied this position at the precise time when the Government's popularity was at an all-time low as a result of its repressive policies.

In addition, Castlereagh felt no need to justify his position to satisfy public opinion. As the historian Muriel Chamberlain states in *'Pax Britannica?' British Foreign Policy 1789–1914* (1988): 'Castlereagh felt no obligation to try and explain his policy to a wider public. International diplomacy he saw as a highly skilled, very technical, entirely confidential profession.' With such an arrogant attitude, Castlereagh became the focus of reaction. Unfortunately for him, those most capable of literary genius were the most critical. Lord Byron's poem 'Don Juan' was written with Castlereagh in mind, as this extract shows:

> States to be curbed, and thought to be confined,
> Conspiracy or congress to be made –
> Cobbling at manacles for all mankind –
> A tinkering slave-maker who mends old chains,
> With God and man's abhorrence for its gains.

Castlereagh's reputation never fully recovered. During the course of the 19th and early part of the 20th century, he was not regarded as a hero by those Nationalist historians, and his close attachment to Europe alienated those who advocated the policy of splendid isolation. He was, according to Muriel Chamberlain, 'left singularly friendless among historians as well as contemporaries'. Yet Castlereagh's reputation has recently been the subject of re-assessment. Few would now argue that, between 1812 and 1822, he played a main part in the defeat of Napoleon, safeguarded Britain's vital interests in Europe and overseas, created a system of diplomacy that attempted to deal with the contemporary issues, and was associated with a peace treaty at Vienna that lasted at least 25 years after the war ended.

Source-based questions: Castlereagh – an appraisal

SOURCE A

I believe that he was seduced by his vanity, that his head was turned by emperors, kings and congresses, and that he was resolved that the country which he represented should play as conspicuous a part as any other in the political dramas which were acted on the Continent. The result of his policy is this … that we have associated ourselves with members of the Holy Alliance along with the acts of ambition and despotism [ruling/acting in unfair manner without the consent of the majority] in such a manner as to have drawn upon us the hatred of the nations of the Continent.

From the diary of Charles Greville, August 1822 – a primary source from a respected political diarist.

SOURCE B

I met Murder on the way –
He had a mask like Castlereagh –
Very smooth he looked, yet grim;
Seven bloodhounds followed him.

All were fat; and well they might
Be in admirable plight.
For one by one, and two by two,
He tossed them human hearts to chew
Which from his wide cloak he drew.

'The Masque of Anarchy' by Percy Bysshe Shelley, 1819. Shelley was a contemporary British poet and a close colleague of Lord Byron. He wrote the poem after hearing of the Peterloo Massacre of which Castlereagh approved.

SOURCE C

Castlereagh's death, in so far as it is possible for an individual to influence the course of history was a matter of profound international significance. In foreign affairs his suicide marked the end of an era, especially in foreign policy.

From Castlereagh *by C. Bartlett, 1966 – a secondary source from a modern biography.*

SOURCE D

There was a vigorous debate in Parliament when the Whigs strongly criticised Castlereagh's surrender to European 'reaction', not knowing that Castlereagh in private was referring to the Holy Alliance (September 1815) between the absolute monarchs of Russia, Prussia and Austria as a *'piece of sublime mysticism and nonsense'* … In fact, during these years Castlereagh managed to stear clear of the Holy Alliance and refused to identify Britain too closely with the policies of the European powers … Before he committed suicide in 1822 Britain had begun to part company with the other Great Powers on the question of intervention to maintain autocratic government in Spain, Portugal and Sicily.

From The Age of Improvement 1783–1867 *by Asa Briggs, published in 1979.*

---

1. Study Source A.

What is the 'Holy Alliance' mentioned in this source?

2. Study Sources A and B.

How similar are the criticisms made of Castlereagh as Foreign Secretary in these sources?

3. Study Source B.

How useful is this source to an historian writing about Castlereagh as Foreign Secretary?

4. Study Source B.

How does Shelley, by the use of language and style, portray Castlereagh in an unfavourable way?

5. 'Castlereagh was one of the greatest British foreign secretaries.' Using information in the sources and from this chapter, do you agree with this statement?

4.3 What problems faced Canning as Foreign Secretary in the years 1822–1827?

George Canning (1770–1827)
Entered Parliament at the age of 23, as a Tory. Served as Foreign Secretary 1807–10. Was forced to resign after a clash with Castlereagh, in which Canning blamed the Secretary of War for two British defeats. The two men fought a duel on Wimbledon Common to settle the matter, during which Canning was wounded in the thigh. Canning was President of the Board of Control 1816–20. On Castlereagh's death in 1822, Canning again became Foreign Secretary. He supported the national movements in Greece and South America. Appointed Prime Minister in 1827 and when Wellington, Peel and other Tories refused to serve under him, Canning formed a coalition with the Whigs. Died after a sudden illness, whilst in office.

George Canning was one of the most able and brilliant politicians of his day. Like Castlereagh, he had grown up politically under the influence of William Pitt the Younger. He had also occupied a variety of ministerial positions that ranged from Paymaster General in 1800 to a brief occupation of the foreign secretaryship under the Duke of Portland's ministry in 1807. These different positions gave him an insight into the workings of government, but he was regarded as a flamboyant character who had made many enemies along the way, especially within his own party. His appointment as Foreign Secretary in 1822, for a second period, appeared to herald a change of direction, from the pro-European stance that Castlereagh adopted to an international policy that paid little attention to cooperation in Europe.

What was Canning's policy towards Spain?

George Canning inherited the problem of a revolution in Spain. At the Congress of Verona in 1822, Wellington, the British observer, was out on a limb in his refusal to support French intervention. Each of the Great Powers argued that legitimacy should be restored, but differed as to who should take the initiative. Tsar Alexander I of Russia wanted a joint European force, but had to agree finally to French intervention in April 1823. The French easily overcame the rebels and the former King Ferdinand VII was restored to the throne in an aggressive display of French power. Canning knew that the danger now lay with the possibility of France intervening in Spain's former South American colonies who had broken away from Spanish control. He was prepared to tolerate what was a diplomatic defeat in Europe, but was determined that French influence should not spread into Spain's former Latin American colonies. In 1823, Canning managed to negotiate the **Polignac Memorandum** with the French ambassador in London forcing France into a position of neutrality over the issue. Canning was determined that Britain's trading rights would be maintained in the area and warned that he was prepared to use force to achieve his objectives.

The whole situation was complicated by the presence of the USA who had enjoyed a frosty relationship with Britain since the war of 1812. The USA had warned of the danger of European intervention and President Monroe had taken the bold step of issuing a doctrine to the same effect in 1823. Britain took the next step and, in 1824, recognised the independence of Columbia, Mexico and La Plata (Argentina). Canning's hostile attitude towards France over the issue of the former Spanish colonies won him much praise from a supportive public. As he told the House of Commons in December 1826: 'I resolved that if France had Spain, it should be not Spain "with the Indies". I called the New World into existence to redress the balance of the old.'

Although the whole affair had been a defeat because he had failed to stop French intervention in Spain, Canning's public anti-French stance hid this fact from most people. The one positive element for Canning was that the crisis had revealed Britain's ability to take successful action independent of other Congress powers. This was an important milestone and ultimately doomed the Congress System to almost inevitable failure.

Polignac Memorandum: An agreement signed between Britain and France in 1823. France agreed not to intervene in British attempts to reach trading agreements with Spain's former colonies. It was an attempt by George Canning to warn off France from taking advantage of Spain's precarious position in Europe at this time by attempting to intervene in its colonial affairs.

A new policy towards Portugal?

One of the major successes of Canning's foreign policy occurred in Portugal which had long been an important trading partner as well as enjoying a strong sense of cooperation with the British monarchy. A revolution in 1820 had forced King John VI to accept a liberal constitution, which his son

Miguel had attempted to overthrow in 1823. Canning was in a difficult position, initially sympathising with Miguel but realising that there were many similarities with the situation he had squandered in Spain. He was again worried at the prospect of French intervention in what was a traditional British sphere of influence. In the summer of 1823, the Royal Navy was sent to monitor the situation but the counter-revolutionary activity fizzled out and the spirit of liberalism was retained.

This initial success was once again threatened in 1826 when the young Queen Donna Maria Gloria was given the throne. The Portuguese conservatives saw this as an opportunity of restoring Miguel and replacing any liberal sympathies. When Canning found out that Miguel had many Spanish supporters in his entourage, he was again worried at the prospect of a Spanish puppet placed on the Portuguese throne. On 9 December 1826, British troops were sent to protect the young queen and to safeguard the liberal constitution. On the face of it, Canning had intervened to defend constitutional government against conservative reaction. He was again the darling of public opinion fighting the corner of innocence against oppression. Yet Canning was merely doing what he felt to be right, as he told the Commons on 12 December 1826: 'We go to Portugal not to rule, not to dictate, not to prescribe constitutions, but to defend and preserve the independence of an ally.' On this occasion, his policy was a triumph.

The Greek Revolt: a success or failure for Canning's policy?

The decline of the Turkish Empire was viewed with much suspicion in Britain especially as the Russians would be the obvious beneficiary of any such event. British foreign policy strongly advocated maintaining the independence of the Empire and thwarting the many potential forces of **nationalism** in the area. Canning was concerned when the Greeks rose up against the Turks in an attempt to assert their nationalist rights. Russia was particularly concerned at the plight of fellow Orthodox Christians fighting to free themselves from Muslim rule. Initially, Tsar Alexander I had shown much sympathy towards the Greeks but was restrained from intervening by Metternich who argued against supporting nationalist causes.

Nationalism: The idea that an individual country had the right to look after its own interests free from influence by a foreign power. The 19th century has been labelled the 'Age of Nationalism' with the unification of Italy and Germany being two of the most significant developments.

Canning was in a difficult position as there was much sympathy for the Greek cause in Britain especially among the influential educated élite. The romantic poet Lord Byron was keen to fight and eventually die for the cause. This sympathy increased when the Turks conducted a wholesale massacre of Greek Christians and murdered the Patriarch of Constantinople on Easter Sunday 1821. Canning, having recognised the Greeks as **co-belligerents** in 1823, was now faced with the prospect of Russian intervention in an area of obvious economic and strategic interest. If Canning viewed events from the sidelines, then the Russian influence in the area would increase and threaten these vital interests. The crisis intensified following the Sultan's decision to use his **vassal**, Mehemet Ali of Egypt, to crush the revolt. Between 1826 and 1827, an Egyptian army under Mehemet Ali's son, Ibrahim Pasha, gained the upper hand over the Greek rebels.

Co-belligerents: An attempt to recognise a country's right to defend its interests against aggression. In this instance, Canning realised the rights of the Greeks to take up arms against an unpopular Turkish regime.

Vassal: Someone who holds land as a direct favour from a superior. In this case, Mehemet Ali held land in Egypt directly as a result of a favour from the Turkish Sultan. He was also obliged to help the Sultan if his interests were threatened.

The situation took a fresh turn in 1825 when the new Tsar, Nicholas I, openly expressed his desire for direct intervention with or without international cooperation. Wellington was dispatched to St Petersburg to offer the new Tsar the possibility of joint mediation to solve the dispute. The outcome was the **Protocol** of St Petersburg of April 1826, by which the British and Russians offered mediation to the Turks as long as Greece retained some form of self-government. The international flavour of the negotiations was confirmed in July 1827: Britain, Russia and France signed the Treaty of London confirming the previous year's arrangements. The difference between the two agreements was that the latter was more strongly

Protocol: An original draft of a diplomatic document agreed to in a conference and signed by all parties.

worded and implied the use of force if necessary. The rejection of international diplomacy by the Turks led to the sending of a joint British/Russian fleet, which destroyed the Turkish/Egyptian fleet at Navarino Bay on 26 October 1827. The fact that the whole issue was resolved by conflict can be interpreted as a failure on the part of the Great Powers and Canning in particular. Yet by the time the fleet was dispatched, Canning's career had been tragically cut short when he died after a sudden illness, in August 1827.

Wellington as Prime Minister and Aberdeen as Foreign Secretary aimed to reverse many of the policies towards the Turks between 1828 and 1830. Wellington was far more positive in his attitude and understood their importance as a strong presence against Russian influence far more than Canning ever did. Between 1828 and 1829, Russia was at war with Turkey and Wellington felt he was losing the initiative in the area. The Treaty of Adrianople in September 1829 saw Russia make gains on the Black Sea and the Danubian principalities. Greek independence was now a formality, but an acceptable settlement was not reached until November 1830 when Prince Otto of Bavaria became the new king. In 1832, in the Treaty of London, the five Great Powers accepted Greece as an independent kingdom.

How successful was Canning's foreign policy?

George Canning's career as Foreign Secretary in 1822–27 was a mixture of success and failure. His biggest failure was his inability to prevent a French invasion of Spain in 1823, but he had managed to balance these changes in Europe with a more successful strategy in the Americas. His Portuguese policy was a great success and he managed to retain Britain's special relationship with the Portuguese.

1. What do you regard as the most significant development in the conduct of foreign policy under George Canning in this period?

2. Why do you think Canning's foreign policy was so popular with the British public?

Canning's biggest problem was in relation to the Greek Revolt. Working through the Concert of Europe, he devised a policy which would involve cooperation between Britain, France and Russia. However, Canning followed a risky policy that always had the potential of leading to an outbreak of fighting. If Canning had not died prematurely, perhaps his diplomatic skill would have prevented the outbreak of war. As it was, British policy lacked direction after Canning's death in August 1827. This resulted in the battle of Navarino Bay and the outbreak in the following year of the Russo–Turkish War.

Canning's special talent for self-publicity had made British foreign policy more intelligible to the mass of the British public. In addition, he had taken great satisfaction in undermining the Congress System. In the Greek Revolt it was Canning, not Metternich, who acted as the major player in European diplomacy.

4.4 Change or continuity? A comparison of the foreign policies of Castlereagh and Canning

A CASE STUDY IN HISTORICAL INTERPRETATION

The case for change

The conduct of British foreign policy between 1815 and 1830 has caused great debate among historians. The traditional view is that 1822 marks a dividing line similar to the division noted in domestic policy. The period before represents one of repression and an extreme reaction to the principles of liberty and equality. The peacemakers of Vienna were accused of redrawing the map of Europe without taking any account of the wishes of popular opinion.

The restoration of unpopular legitimate rulers was a classic example of this attitude. In Britain, Foreign Secretary Castlereagh bore the brunt of public criticism especially as he was known to support repressive measures in domestic policy – such as the Peterloo Massacre in 1819. Shelley, the romantic poet, summed up opinion in 'The Masque of Anarchy':

> I met Murder on the way –
> He had a mask like Castlereagh.

Whilst Castlereagh was heavily criticised for his policies and conduct, his successor Canning stood in stark contrast. Canning's arrival at the Foreign Office marked the transition from a conservative foreign policy aimed primarily at preserving the Congress System, to one that attempted to destroy it and move Britain out of a European context into a more global policy. Canning tried at all times to justify his actions to a wider public.

The case for continuity

This rather simplistic dividing line has been the subject of much re-appraisal by historians in recent years. John Derry claims: 'It is a simplistic misrepresentation to regard Castlereagh as a conservative and Canning a liberal.' This has led historians to identify possible areas of continuity in policy between the two men:

- Both men agreed that collective intervention in any state's internal government was morally wrong. Castlereagh had stated his objections in the State Paper of 1820. Canning did nothing to change this basic policy after 1822, acknowledging the debt his policies owed to those outlined in the State Paper.
- Castlereagh and Canning were in agreement over their mistrust of Russia. They were eager to defend Portuguese independence especially against Spanish intervention. Also, both had been anxious to stop French intervention in Spain.
- Their Eastern policy also showed remarkable similarities. Both men realised that the Greek Revolt had to be restrained in order to maintain the balance of power in the area. Turkey's independence had to be maintained to prevent Russian expansion in a traditional sphere of influence.
- Castlereagh had started the process in 1808 of recognising the struggle of Latin American republics in their desire for independence against Spain. Formal recognition, he claimed, would allow British business to break into hitherto untapped trading markets. Canning had 'called … the New World into existence …', but had only been continuing a policy initiated by his predecessor.
- Both foreign secretaries supported the policy of stopping the Atlantic slave trade. They were committed to the idea of the right of search of international shipping.
- Both believed in the maintenance of the European balance of power through the operation of the Concert of Europe. Castlereagh, through Article VI of the Second Treaty of Paris, was instrumental in establishing the Congress System, which was a continuation into peacetime of the Fourth Coalition against Napoleon. Although Canning was suspicious of close cooperation on a general basis with conservative European politicians such as Metternich and the Tsar, he was prepared to work through the Concert of Europe on specific issues – such as the Greek Revolt. The St Petersburg Protocol and the Treaty of London, 1827, are examples of this.

There were, however, a number of differences.

- Although both men realised the limitations of the Congress System (especially after the Troppau Protocol in 1820), they did so with different emotions. As John Derry has stated, 'Castlereagh contemplated disengagement from Europe with sorrow and regret ... Canning did so with enthusiasm and in the invincible conviction that events had proved him right all along.'
- Castlereagh saw international politics as a highly selective occupation that did not have to be justified or explained to a wider audience. He disagreed with other European statesmen over the conduct of policy but the public were unaware of these differences. Canning, on the other hand, was an expert at self-publicity who used the press and the House of Commons to justify his hostility to Europe. He made it his duty to convince the public of the direction of his policy – even if on occasions he was wrong! According to the historian H. Temperley, 'In Canning's view it was essential that future foreign policy should be both intelligible and popular.' Mrs Arbuthnot, one of Canning's contemporaries, noted that he was 'going round the country speechifying and discussing the acts and intentions of the government'.
- The context of Castlereagh's conduct of foreign policy was different to Canning's. From 1812 to 1822, Castlereagh had been a key figure in maintaining an alliance against Napoleon Bonaparte and saw it as a natural consequence that this postwar cooperation should continue based on the idea of creating a 'just equilibrium', or balance of power. Canning, on the other hand, was under no such pressure. He saw the future rather as 'Every nation for itself and God for us all'. He was more of an opportunist than Castlereagh who had done a great deal to create the structure of postwar cooperation.
- As regards policy towards the USA there was a sharp departure over tactics and policy. Although Britain and America had been at war between 1812 and 1815, Castlereagh felt peace should come at all costs to safeguard the border between the USA and British-controlled Canada. Canning felt less respect towards the USA and was only concerned with using any opportunity to discredit American influence in the area. The Monroe Doctrine of 1823 is an example of how frosty relations had become.
- Castlereagh's personal relations with European statesmen were on a more friendly footing than Canning's. The two men's respective attitudes to Prince Metternich of Austria are a clear illustration of this difference. Castlereagh and the Austrian Chancellor had enjoyed a fruitful and successful working relationship that mirrored their respective political attitudes; Canning was less keen to follow Metternich's ultra-conservative policies and a genuine hatred developed between the two men. Metternich is once said to have described Canning as 'the greatest rogue and liar on the continent, perhaps in the civilised world'.

1. Which issue do you regard as the most important which faced both Castlereagh and Canning? Give reasons to support your answer.

2. 'Differences in style rather than policy.' Using the information in this section, assess the validity of this statement in relation to the foreign policies of Castlereagh and Canning.

4.5 To what extent did Palmerston uphold British interests between 1830 and 1841?

John Henry Temple, third Viscount Palmerston (1784–1865)
John Henry Temple succeeded to his Irish peerage at the age of 18. As a Tory he became an MP in 1807, and was Secretary at War (1809–28). Palmerston broke with the Tories in 1830 and sat in the Whig Cabinets of 1830–34, 1835–41, and 1846–51 as Foreign Secretary. His foreign policy was marked by distrust of France and Russia. He was Home Secretary in the coalition government of 1852, before becoming Prime Minister for two spells: in 1855–58, he put right Aberdeen's mismanagement of the Crimean War, suppressed the Indian Mutiny and carried through the Second Opium War; in 1859–65, he was involved in the American Civil War on the side of the South. Although he was popular with the people and made good use of the press, his high-handed attitude annoyed Queen Victoria and other ministers.

Viscount Palmerston enjoyed a remarkable political career that lasted from 1807 to 1865, most of which was spent in the House of Commons. Initially, he began his career as a Tory MP, but became heavily influenced by the 'Enlightened Tories' and by 1830 had joined the Whigs under Earl Grey. In this period, 1830–41, he became very popular with the public because he was determined to stand up for British rights throughout the world. In his conduct of foreign policy a number of 'Palmerstonian' principles can be identified.

Like his two predecessors, Palmerston was a supporter of the European balance of power and believed in using the Concert of Europe to maintain European peace. On a number of occasions – over Greece in 1832, during the Belgian Revolt of 1830–39 and in the Straits Convention – Palmerston worked with the other Great Powers to maintain European peace.

Palmerston was also a supporter of stopping the slave trade. Throughout his period as Foreign Secretary, he maintained the west African naval squadron and was able to persuade the Republic of Texas to abandon the trade.

During the 1830s, Europe seemed to be facing an ideological split between the forces of conservatism, led by Russia and Austria, and the demand for liberal reform. On a number of occasions, liberal-inspired revolutions occurred: in France in 1830 and in the Italian states in 1830–32. Palmerston wanted to follow a middle course between these two extremes. He believed an important stabilising factor in European relations would be 'the export of the English constitution'. He hoped to achieve this with the creation of a constitutional monarchy in Belgium and Britain's support for the same through the Quadruple Alliance of 1834 with France, Spain and Portugal.

Palmerston was also an active supporter of British trading interests. In 1838, he concluded a free trade convention with the Turkish Empire, providing much needed markets for British manufacturers. In 1839, using the pretext of the seizure of an illegal opium shipment by the Chinese authorities, he launched a military campaign against the Chinese Empire.

Although willing to uphold European peace, Palmerston was not against threatening war if he felt it would benefit British interests. In the Belgian Revolt, he threatened both France and Holland with military action. He did so again against France in 1840 over the Eastern Question. In the same year, he threatened the USA over the McLeod Case. However, all of these policies had one goal: maintaining British interests.

Palmerston was influenced by both Castlereagh and Canning, but it is most likely that the latter's influence was the stronger. As the historian H. Bell claims in his biography of Palmerston: 'In his desire that England should stand upon her own feet, his appreciation of the great force of public sentiment, and his taste for constitutional government as the proper medium between autocracy and democracy, he was a natural born Canningite.'

How successful was Palmerston in dealing with the Belgian Revolt of 1830–1839?

The Belgian Revolt was inspired by the overthrow of the hated Charles X in France during the summer of 1830. Yet there were deeper economic, religious and social reasons why the Belgians wanted to overthrow their Dutch masters. These included the fact that Belgian claims for independence had been ignored at Vienna in 1815 and that there were deep religious divisions between the Catholic Belgians and Protestant Dutch. In addition, the Kingdom was no more than an artificial creation that had been used at Vienna in 1815 and was thus deeply resented by the Belgians. The Revolt was a major challenge to the success of theVienna settlement and gradually involved all the Great Powers in one way or another.

Palmerston viewed the prospect of Belgian independence favourably, thus reversing previous British policy, but equally he was worried at the prospect of French involvement. He feared the French might try to revive their old claim to control the economy of Belgium, which would be to Britain's disadvantage. The three Great Powers – Prussia, Austria and Russia – using the Troppau Protocol of 1820 as their guideline, tended to support legitimacy in the form of Dutch King William I. They were warned that liberal revolution would ultimately be a blow against their own monarchies. Palmerston had to walk a diplomatic tightrope by showing his anger at possible French intervention whilst preventing the Great Powers becoming involved, leading to the risk of a general war. The Belgians themselves complicated the issue by choosing Louis Philippe's second son, the Duc de Nemours, as their new king.

Palmerston objected strongly and managed to secure the appointment of the German Prince Leopold of Saxe-Coburg, the uncle of the future British Queen Victoria, as their new monarch. The Dutch refused to accept the new arrangements and began instead to regain their lands. Palmerston was in a dilemma: he did not want to allow the French to support the Belgians alone because he knew the Eastern powers would intervene. A combination of luck and political skill solved the situation. The luck came with the news that a revolt had broken out in Poland conveniently distracting Russia, Prussia and Austria from events in Western Europe.

The political wisdom was shown when Palmerston made sure that when the French intervened it was always part of joint cooperation with Britain. This was clearly shown when a joint force expelled the Dutch from the important economic centre of Antwerp in 1830. The whole episode dragged on until 1839, when the Dutch finally accepted the new Belgian state in the Treaty of London. In addition, all of the Great Powers guaranteed to honour Belgian neutrality (a fact that was eventually to drag Britain into the First World War in 1914 when Germany violated it). This episode was a spectacular success for Palmerston as he had displayed a consistent and firm line towards Belgian independence whilst preventing unilateral French intervention, yet at the same time protecting Britain's interests. He had also used the Concert of Europe to solve a potentially dangerous flash point.

Portugal and Spain

Since the Treaty of Utrecht in 1713, which had confirmed British control of Gibraltar and given Britain significant influence in the Mediterranean, British policy had always been to ensure the independence of Portugal and Spain from any French intervention. Canning had continued this trend especially with regard to Portuguese policy. The continuity in policy is emphasised by historian Muriel Chamberlain in *'Pax Britannica?' – British Foreign Policy 1789–1914* (1988): 'Palmerston's priorities were the same as Canning's, to stop another power, especially France, from taking advantage of the situation.' The situation had produced a crisis whereby the two constitutional sovereigns of Spain and Portugal – Isabella and Maria – were challenged by **despots**, Don Carlos and Don Miguel. Support for the young queens was very popular, but how would Palmerston overcome the difficulty of preventing France intervening alone? The solution lay in the creation of the 1834 Quadruple Alliance of Britain, France, Portugal and Spain. This had a twofold purpose: namely to retain Anglo–French cooperation which would, in addition, act as a counterweight to the alliance between Russia, Austria and Prussia signed at

Despots: Rulers who have a lot of power and use it unfairly or cruelly.

Münchengrätz in 1833. The result was a successful resolution to both crises. British naval power was used to support the constitutional parties. In Portugal, Don Miguel was expelled in 1834 but Don Carlos' removal from Spain proved more difficult and it was not until 1839 that the situation was resolved. Once again, Palmerston had played a decisive hand in Europe while preserving Britain's strategic interests and had successfully exported the British constitution to both Spain and Portugal.

Palmerston and the Eastern Question: Mehemet Ali and the Straits, 1831–1841

The Near Eastern Crisis, 1831–1833

The problems of the Turkish Empire and the need to maintain British naval supremacy in the Mediterranean involved Europe in two major international crises. Between 1831 and 1833, a war between Mehemet Ali, Pasha of Egypt, and the Sultan of Turkey threatened the stability of the Middle East. Unfortunately, as this crisis developed Palmerston was involved in issues nearer home: as a member of the Whig Government he was entangled in the Reform Bill crisis; and as Foreign Secretary he was heavily involved in resolving the Belgian dispute. With Britain distracted elsewhere, it was the Russians not the British who made political capital out of the Sultan's misfortune.

Having been promised the island of Crete and the Morea (see map) as reward for his participation in subduing the Greek Revolt, Mehemet Ali was not content to acquire this island possession, he also had ambitions of replacing the Sultan as ruler of the Turkish Empire. In 1832, an Egyptian army overran Palestine and Syria and defeated the Turks at Konieh (in modern-day Turkey). This left the Egyptian army with the opportunity of attacking Constantinople, the Turkish capital.

The Middle East in 1821

With Britain distracted elsewhere, the Sultan was forced to appeal to Russia for military assistance. He asked for 30,000 troops and four ships. In return for military aid, the Sultan signed the Treaty of Unkiar Skelessi, in July 1833. The Treaty let Mehemet Ali retain Syria and, in a secret clause, allowed the Russian navy to enter the Mediterranean through the Straits.

This development dealt a potential double blow to British interests. Firstly, Egypt had received considerable military assistance from France and Palmerston feared a French client state developing. Of more immediate importance, Palmerston feared the growth of Russian influence over the Turkish Empire. The Treaty of Unkiar Skelessi marked a turning point in British policy towards Turkey. Up to 1833, Britain had recognised the importance of Turkish independence but had not developed a consistent policy. After the treaty, Britain followed a policy that aimed at removing Russian influence in Turkey, replacing it with British influence and then defending Turkish independence. As part of this policy, Palmerston concluded the Anglo–Turkish Trade Convention in 1838. This opened up the Turkish market for British manufacturers.

The Near Eastern Crisis of 1830–1841

The second Near Eastern Crisis opened when the Turks launched an invasion to recapture Syria in 1839. However, with the help of French officers, Mehemet Ali's forces managed to inflict a crushing defeat on the Turks. The French Prime Minister, Adolphe Thiers, was even talking about taking parts of Syria as a reward for French intervention. Palmerston was determined to prevent the extension of French influence and to stop Russia from intervening alone on the Turkish side. Furthermore, Palmerston regarded Mehemet Ali as nothing more than a criminal, so a personal dislike was combined with these other motives.

As far as Palmerston was concerned, the solution lay with multilateral diplomacy. The Convention of London in 1840 was signed by Britain, Russia, Austria and Prussia (France was furious at being excluded). It demanded that Mehemet Ali withdraw his forces from Syria. Not surprisingly, Ali refused to accept the terms. He had changed his mind by December 1840 when Acre on the Syrian coast was captured and Alexandria was bombarded by a British fleet. France, and Thiers in particular, talked the language of war, but Louis Philippe was not in a position to back up any threat.

Fortunately, the pro-British François Guizot replaced Thiers as Prime Minister and joined with the other powers, in July 1841, in signing the Straits Convention. This international agreement forbade the passage of warships through the Bosphorus and Dardanelles, thus cancelling the privileges of Unkiar Skelessi. Also, Palmerston used the Concert of Europe to discredit the French, as he had done successfully over Belgium.

Palmerston emerged from the crisis with enormous credit, managing to preserve British interests; at the same time discrediting France and Russia without resorting to a major war. Turkish independence was guaranteed and both Syria and Crete returned to the Empire. At home, his policies won him acclaim, apart from the members of his own party with French sympathies. As the historian D. Judd claims, 'Palmerston had won a tricky game hands down'.

The Opium War with China, 1839–1842

Perhaps the most blatant example of Palmerston promoting British trading interests abroad was the Opium War. The East India Company, which controlled British territory in India, grew opium which was then exported to China. The issue which sparked off the war was the seizure of East India Company opium in the southern Chinese port of Canton (now Guandong).

However, as the historian Muriel Chamberlain notes, 'Opium smuggling was the trigger point but the issues were wider than that'. To Palmerston and British traders, China seemed to offer a huge, untapped market for British goods. The Chinese government though prevented foreign states from trading in China. The war ended successfully for Britain. In the Treaty of Nanking, which was signed after Palmerston had left office, Britain received the island of Hong Kong, at the mouth of the Canton river. This island was to act as a base for British trade in the South China Sea. Of equal importance was the opening up to British trade of six Chinese ports, including Canton, Shanghai, Amoy and Foochow. In addition, the Chinese government agreed to pay £6 million compensation for British losses in seizures and embargoes on trading.

Relations with the USA

Palmerston's quarrels with the United States of America in this period related directly to two key issues: the slave trade and Canada's borders with America. Palmerston had consistently campaigned against the slave trade throughout his career and was determined that American merchants would not get away with flouting the terms of an agreement the US government had signed in 1807 to outlaw the slave trade. In addition, Palmerston had agreed, in 1836, to recognise an independent Texas but only if the state government was willing to renounce the slave trade. Palmerston concluded that the only way to check and regulate the transportation of slaves would be through what he described as a 'right of search'. This allowed British warships to board and, if needed, impound ships carrying slaves to and from Africa. Not surprisingly, the US government was not prepared to tolerate this 'right of search', which they saw as violation of **sovereignty**.

Sovereignty: The complete political power that a country possesses to govern itself or another country or state.

1. How successfully did Palmerston uphold British interests abroad between 1830 and 1841?

2. Can you detect any continuity in policy between Palmerston and any other Foreign Secretary you have studied in this period?

The situation in Canada was just as tense. It was made worse by the outbreak of rebellion against British rule in 1837. Palmerston correctly suspected that official American aid was given to the rebels and fully supported the efforts of the Canadian authorities to pursue them. This led to a highly publicised incident when an American citizen was killed following the sinking of a gun-running vessel, the 'Caroline'. The Americans were furious, but Palmerston publicly supported the Canadian government, thus making relations between the two even more strained.

In 1841, Palmerston complained to the American authorities over the McLeod Case: a Canadian militiaman was put on trial by the New York state authorities for supposedly shooting a US citizen during the 1837 rebellion. Fortunately, Palmerston lost office before the matter became too intense.

4.6 How successful was the Earl of Aberdeen as Foreign Secretary between 1841 and 1846?

The Conservative victory under Sir Robert Peel in 1841 led to the appointment of George Hamilton Gordon, the fourth Earl of Aberdeen, as Foreign Secretary. He had previously held the same position in the ill-fated Wellington ministry between 1828 and 1830, but this new opportunity heralded his greatest opportunity thus far. His style and temperament were completely different to the sabre-rattling of Palmerston. The Earl of Aberdeen developed a system of diplomacy that relied on caution and avoiding war at all costs.

Historians have largely ignored the Earl of Aberdeen's career. His inheritance could hardly have been worse. The situations in China, the USA and Afghanistan were very tense, and relations with France were cool to say the least. Britain needed a calm hand in charge of foreign affairs to avoid complete humiliation.

George Hamilton Gordon, fourth Earl of Aberdeen (1784–1860)
Aberdeen entered the House of Lords in 1806 and enjoyed a successful political career, serving as Foreign Secretary under Wellington in 1828 and most famously under Peel 1841–46. His approach to foreign policy was less aggressive than that of Palmerston but equally successful. The climax of his career came when he was appointed Prime Minister of a Whig/Peelite ministry. He resigned in 1855 at the height of the Crimean War and died in 1860.

Relations with the USA

Aberdeen's relations with the United States of America initially owed much to Palmerstonian policy. Yet, during the period, he managed to resolve the border disputes that had been such a feature of the previous administration. The signing of the Webster–Ashburton Treaty in 1842 resolved the disputed territory between Maine and New Brunswick. In 1845, Aberdeen sensibly approved the US annexation of Texas, which had gone contrary to Palmerston's policy of 1836. In addition, the prospect of a war between Mexico and the USA had opened the possibility of Britain being offered territory in California, which was part of the Mexican Empire. Aberdeen again refused to upset the Americans and politely turned down the offer.

The main Anglo–American problem at this time was the Oregon boundary dispute. Both Britain and the USA had claim to territory on the west coast and the Americans, in particular, were very keen to acquire a harbour in the area. The disputed territory was all land north of the Columbia river and south of latitude 44°40′ North (the 49th Parallel). The election of the anti-British James Polk as President in 1844 made matters worse, especially as he was committed to the idea of the maximum purchase of land available. Aberdeen was faced with an awkward situation that required a great deal of political skill. Compromise was again achieved as the dispute was settled along latitude 44°40′ North. Although Palmerston was critical of Aberdeen's policy – he claimed it was too weak on Britain's key interests – the policy found favour with the majority of the British public.

This 1846 cartoon shows John Bull, representing Britain, and a scruffy looking American trying to patch up their differences. The caption at the bottom begs the Americans not to resort to violence to solve territorial disputes.

Relations with France

The Earl of Aberdeen's close personal relationship with Guizot, the French Prime Minister, initially set the tone for relations between Britain and France. Aberdeen trusted Guizot and attempted to resolve any differences between the two sides. Closer relations were forged between the British and French royal families and the idea of an *entente cordiale* (friendly understanding) was even suggested. Yet by 1844, the situation had deteriorated to the point of war. The starting point was the French decision to annex Tahiti and imprison a number of leading British missionaries. This caused uproar in Britain and at the same time it was announced that France intended to annex Morocco. Britain again felt its interests were being threatened, especially bearing in mind its strategic importance to the Mediterranean. Again Aberdeen defused a potential crisis when he gained assurances that France was not going to proceed with its claims on Morocco.

1. What were the problems facing Aberdeen as Foreign Secretary?

2. What were the main differences between the foreign policies of Palmerston and Aberdeen? Were there any similarities? Use the information from the whole chapter.

3. Was Britain's international position stronger in 1846 than it was in 1815? Give reasons to support your answer.

Relations had reached a tolerable level once again, but were soon to be upset when the question of the Spanish marriages (see page 205) came to the fore. Aberdeen and Guizot could have solved the dispute amicably but, as Palmerston's provocative policies revealed, the crisis was far from over. As the historian Muriel Chamberlain claims, 'In 1846 Aberdeen was regarded as a sound statesman, who had extricated Britain from potentially dangerous quarrels with France and the United States, kept the Eastern Question quiet, safeguarded Britain's trading interests from China to South America and ... retained the support of Wellington and Peel, neither usually judged to be weak men.' This is indeed a fitting tribute to a much under-rated Foreign Secretary.

Ireland 1798 to 1921: a thematic study

Overview

THE 'Irish Question' is the name given to the set of issues which affected British–Irish relations. It involved political, economic, religious and strategic issues.

Irish issues caused the resignation of British Prime Ministers on several occasions. In 1801, William Pitt the Younger resigned because of King George III's opposition to Catholic emancipation. Robert Peel fell from power, in 1846, over the repeal of the Corn Laws. William Gladstone split the Liberal Party, in 1886, with his conversion to Irish Home Rule. The Liberal Government from 1912 to 1914 faced a serious crisis over Ulster, which was brought to a temporary conclusion by the outbreak of the First World War. Finally, David Lloyd George's fall from office, in 1922, was due in part to his handling of the Irish Question in 1921.

Therefore, as a theme, the 'Irish Question' must be regarded as an important – if not the most important – aspect of British domestic history.

5.1 Theme 1: Who opposed the Union?

5.1.1 What was the situation in Ireland in 1798?
5.1.2 Why was the Act of Union passed in 1800? Why did opposition to the Union start almost immediately?
5.1.3 What were the next stages of opposition to the Union?
5.1.4 Why did opposition to Union grow after 1900 and culminate in war and final independence?

Key Issues

- *Why did opposition to the Union develop in the 19th century?*
- *What form did opposition to the Union take?*
- *What were the reasons for the initial failure, and final success, of the Irish nationalists?*

Framework of Events

1798	Wolfe Tone or United Irish Rebellion
1800	Act of Union
1824	Formation of Catholic Association
1828	Country Clare Election
1845–49	Great Famine
1848	Young Ireland Rising

1858	Irish Republican Brotherhood (Fenians) founded in USA
1866–67	Fenian outrages in Britain, Ireland and Canada
1870	Butt forms Irish Home Government Association
1871	Obstruction process starts in House of Commons
1879	Formation of Irish Land League
1880	Parnell leads Irish Nationalist Party
1882	The Phoenix Park Murders
1885	Irish Home Rule Party hold balance of power in Commons following June 1885 general elections
1886	Gladstone converts to Irish Home Rule
1888	Parnell falsely accused of involvement with Phoenix Park Murders of 1882
1890	Parnell falls from leadership of Irish Home Rule Party; Party splits into pro- and anti-Parnell factions
1891	Parnell dies
1900	Irish Home Rule Party re-united under John Redmond
1905	Creation of United Ulster Unionist Council
1912	Passage of Third Home Rule Bill starts Ulster Crisis. Creation of Ulster Volunteer Force
1913	Irish Volunteers is formed
1916	The Easter Rising
1917	de Valera is elected leader of Sinn Fein
1917–18	Meeting of Irish Convention
1918	Sinn Fein wins majority of Irish seats in UK general election
1919–21	The Anglo–Irish War
1920	Government of Ireland Act gives Home Rule to Northern Ireland; rejected in southern Ireland
1920	Bloody Sunday in Dublin
1921	Anglo–Irish Treaty creates Irish Free State with dominion status within British Empire
	Anglo–Irish Treaty accepted by Dail. Civil war breaks out in Irish Free State over the Treaty.

5.1.1 What was the situation in Ireland in 1798?

The majority of the Irish population viewed the English as alien colonisers there to exploit them. There were profound differences between the mass of the population and the ruling minority. The mass (about 6 million) tended to be Roman Catholic, illiterate, landless and usually extremely poor. The ruling minority was Protestant, wealthy and landed. They controlled the political system and owned more than 95% of the land and much of the limited industrial wealth.

The history of Ireland in the 18th century is marked by:

- poor social conditions
- frequent food shortages
- a rising population
- very limited economic progress
- a growing sense of anger against trade restrictions, which seemed to benefit English manufacturers.

Tithes: A tax payable to the Church based on one-tenth of your property; usually paid in kind with animals from the land. This was a very unpopular system.

The official 'State' religion was the Protestant Church of Ireland, yet the vast majority of the population was Roman Catholic. They were forced to pay **tithes** to support a Protestant church they hated. Roman Catholics were discriminated against by law, and not allowed to hold official positions, or to become Members of Parliament. However, the Roman Catholic religion was officially tolerated and was growing in influence over the majority of the population. Protestant nonconformists, who were not members of the Church of Ireland, were another important religious minority. These included Quakers and Presbyterians. Most lived in north-east Ireland.

Agrarian violence: Trouble in rural areas, usually caused by problems relating to agriculture.

Agrarian violence was a regular feature of Irish history in the 18th century, particularly between 1760 and 1780. A group known as the Whiteboys made some particularly savage attacks against landlords. The Government in London reacted with a series of Acts of Parliament, which ordered the death penalty for most forms of protest.

However, the British Government – perhaps frightened that their Irish colony might go the same way as the American colonies, towards independence – began to relax some of the stronger restrictions. Some Roman Catholics were allowed to vote, for example, and it became easier for Roman Catholics to purchase land by the end of the 18th century. It is worth remembering that the bulk of the population were Roman Catholic and that they might feel resentful of being 'allowed' by the English to vote and purchase land in Ireland – their own land.

Why did a serious rebellion break out in 1798?

The concessions made by London over voting and land purchase were inadequate for many Irishmen. The French Revolution, which had broken out in 1789, inspired many Irish to seek their freedom. The ideals of the French Revolution – liberty and equality – inspired many Irishmen. Hatred of rule by aliens, with a strong flavour of Roman Catholic versus Protestant and the poor Irish against the rich English, led to open rebellion in 1798. The leader of the revolt was Wolfe Tone (1763–98), a Protestant Irish lawyer inspired by the examples of both the American and the French Revolution. He took advantage of the simmering hatred between many Irish people and their English rulers to try to get the French to invade Ireland as part of their war against England.

The French fleet failed to land troops and weapons, mainly due to bad weather and poor seamanship, and the armed rising largely died out, after a brief skirmish in 1798 known as the 'battle' of Vinegar Hill. The British Government passed laws that allowed imprisonment without trial. Tone was captured, but he committed suicide before he could be executed. Many English people felt that the Irish had behaved treasonably in helping the French. They failed to realise that they, the English, were seen as an 'enemy' by the Irish people – in the same way that the English viewed the French as an enemy. In fact, many Irishmen saw the French as potential liberators, just as the Germans were to be seen in 1916.

5.1.2 Why was the Act of Union passed in 1800? Why did opposition to the Union start almost immediately?

One reaction by the British Government in London to the revolt of 1798 was strong coercive (repressive) measures. Although these were measures designed to punish and deter, it was not the only reaction. The Prime Minister, William Pitt the Younger, adopted a more positive and proactive role. His suggestion, backed by Lord Castlereagh, the Minister responsible for Ireland, was the Act of Union.

This Act would end the Parliament in Dublin (Protestant dominated and with limited powers), and replace it with a system whereby MPs and peers were elected or chosen in Ireland and then represented Ireland in the UK Parliament in London. These MPs would have the same power and status as 'normal' UK MPs. A number of Irish peers were allowed to sit in the House of Lords. Other Irish peers had to seek election to the House of Commons. Lord Palmerston was an example.

This was designed to end all Irish problems, as the Irish would have the same rights as any other UK citizen. Pitt and Castlereagh felt that this would end opposition to English rule. They hoped it would make the Irish feel and react in the same way as any other UK citizen. Union would lead to peace and integration.

Castlereagh, sometimes using corrupt methods, persuaded the Irish Parliament to vote itself out of existence. The Act of Union was passed in 1800. The first Irish MPs and peers arrived in the UK Parliament in London in that year.

However, there were major flaws in the Act of Union. The first was that Pitt and Castlereagh indicated that Catholic emancipation would follow the Act of Union, and implied it in the negotiations. It did not follow. Some historians argue that this was because the King, George III, refused to sign the Bill as it might break his coronation oath. Others suggest that Pitt and Castlereagh never intended it to happen. It was unlikely that the House of Lords in London would ever pass an Act giving Roman Catholics a seat in Parliament.

The Union of Britain and Ireland therefore got off to a bad start. Many Catholics felt betrayed and conned into a deal. Only 20% of all the MPs in London were Irish, and anger was felt at Irish problems now being looked at from a 'London' perspective. In addition, Roman Catholics were now a minority in the whole of the UK.

However, Ireland remained reasonably quiet and loyal for the rest of the Napoleonic Wars, so England benefited from not having to worry about potential treason coming from the West.

The end of the Napoleonic Wars, in 1815, brought major economic problems to the whole of the UK, but they were felt particularly keenly in Ireland. There was no welfare system at all in Ireland, so poverty was more extreme. Roman Catholics still had to pay the hated tithe to support what they felt was an alien religion based in London. Irish local government was dominated by Protestant (and frequently absent) British landlords and was corrupt and inefficient. It was still felt that 'London' deprived Ireland of its fair share of wealth and trade.

The overwhelming feeling in Ireland, by 1820, was that Union had been an elaborate trick to keep Ireland quiet. It was solely to benefit the United Kingdom.

How was emancipation for Roman Catholics gained?

The first signs of protest against London's 'rule', and its methods, started in 1804 with the formation of the Catholic Committee. This was designed to protect and advance Irish interests in general, and to gain full citizenship rights for Catholics in particular. The Government repressed this in 1811, but the idea of united action by both Catholic and Protestant Irishmen against 'British' rule was born again.

In 1823, a more powerful pressure group was created. This was the Catholic Association. Its objective was to end all discrimination against Roman Catholics. Its leader was Daniel O'Connell. He was one of the first Roman Catholics to be allowed to practise law in Ireland, after the Catholic Relief Acts of the 1790s. What was different about the Catholic Association was that not only did it have O'Connell's charismatic leadership, but also the Roman Catholic Church enthusiastically supported it. In addition, its membership was not just middle-class merchants and lawyers, but by being cheap to join it attracted a mass membership among the working class. The Catholic Association became remarkable in that it was probably the first truly national mass-membership pressure group in modern British history. It was also successful. Although the British

Daniel O'Connell (1775–1847) O'Connell was a Catholic lawyer and landowner. He led the campaign for Catholic emancipation in the 1820s and was elected MP for County Clare in 1828. O'Connell established the Irish Party at Westminster, which successfully campaigned for tariff reform and brought down Peel's Government in 1835 after the Lichfield House Compact (see page 124). He was extremely important in maintaining the Whigs in power after 1835. O'Connell also led the campaign for the Repeal of the Act of Union in the 1840s. This resulted in his arrest in 1844, which was quashed on appeal to the House of Lords.

Government tried to suppress it in 1825, it re-formed and still attained its objective. Emancipation cleared the House of Commons in 1825, but failed in a House of Lords dominated by Tories and members of the Church of England.

In a by-election in 1828, Daniel O'Connell stood as a candidate for Parliament. Technically speaking, this was impossible, as he was a Roman Catholic. He was duly elected, but was unable to take his seat, until Peel and Wellington (the Tory leaders in London), frightened of a possible uprising in Ireland, passed Roman Catholic emancipation. This allowed Roman Catholics to become MPs in the House of Commons.

What was the impact of emancipation and the Catholic Association?

Emancipation made O'Connell into a national hero in Ireland. It also gave Ireland a leader, which it had not really possessed before. This enabled O'Connell to get the London Government to focus on further reforms, such as reforming Irish local government and ending the tithes paid to the Church of Ireland. O'Connell was also anxious to increase the number of those entitled to vote. He raised the political consciousness of Catholics and Irishman, particularly among the poorer sections of society. Pressure politics had clearly worked, mass protest had attained difficult objectives, and that lesson was not forgotten. O'Connell fanned Irish nationalism and set the issue of an independent Ireland very much on the agenda of Ireland, if not England. He wanted a separate Irish parliament to deal with Irish issues. Another product of his success was that he raised huge fears among the Protestant population of the North of Ireland, and they started to organise to defend their ideas and values.

5.1.3 What were the next stages of opposition to the Union?

By 1840, O'Connell had founded the Repeal Association. This was openly committed to ending the Act of Union and setting up a separate Irish parliament. He organised huge mass meetings, some with over 100,000 present. With the Roman Catholic Church supportive of his movement, O'Connell looked like making as much progress towards independence as he had towards Catholic emancipation. However, Sir Robert Peel (Prime Minister 1841–46) refused to consider such a proposal. The attitude of both the Conservative Government and the Liberal Opposition was that much had been done for Ireland in recent decades, and that the Act of Union was of considerable benefit to Ireland. This huge misunderstanding, that Union had in some ways been a favour to Ireland, was to be a key reason for the growth of an Irish 'problem' in the coming decades.

Peel's reaction to the agitation of O'Connell was twofold. O'Connell was imprisoned in 1844. On the other hand, Peel put forward reforms in an attempt to pacify the growing Irish Catholic middle class. These reforms were in areas such as landlord–tenant relations, Catholic education and the education of Roman Catholic priests. Peel was not totally successful, as the Young Ireland movement was to demonstrate.

O'Connell addressing a Repeal meeting in September 1843

Young Ireland was a radical group of nationalists, founded in 1842. They were less inclined to accept the moderate separation looked for by O'Connell. They founded a paper called the *Nation*. They achieved little as the movement was split between those who wished to work with O'Connell and those who did not, and those who were prepared to use violence to attain separation and those who were not. An armed rebellion failed in 1848, when the famine and strong coercion brought to an end most protest. Internal division was often a reason why Irish opposition to 'English' rule could be unsuccessful.

What was the impact of famine on the opposition to the Union?

In many ways the Great Famine of 1845–49 was a turning point in the history of opposition to the Union. It accelerated the move towards Home Rule for an independent Ireland. O'Connell had helped to create modern Irish politics, a political machine capable to taking the issue forwards, with a strong sense of a national identity.

The Great Famine created a sense of anger and injustice. It also raised social tensions to a much higher level. Many died and more emigrated. It was easy to blame the richest country in the world, with its huge resources, for the human, social and economic devastation of Ireland in the late 1840s.

Most Irish people felt bitterly they had been betrayed and abandoned by the English. There was huge anger at the perceived treatment of the Irish masses by an incompetent and uncaring 'English' Government.

The general election of 1852 led to at least 40 of the Irish MPs backing major social and economic change. This group formed the Independent Irish Party, from 1850 to 1859. As often happened with such Irish MPs, they were divided between those who were prepared to work under British rule to improve things and those who were not. This became apparent with two Irish MPs, Keogh and Sadlier, joined the Whig–Peelite Coalition of 1852–55 as junior ministers. However, unity among opponents grew when the Irish Tenant League, founded by Charles Gavan Duffy in 1850, determined to gain for Irish tenants in the (Catholic) South the same sort of tenure rights that England and the North (Protestant) of Ireland got. The Catholic Defence Association, founded in 1851, allied with it to form another powerful anti-Union pressure group. It was this linking of different pressure groups that gave anti-Union sentiment such force.

With Ireland devastated by famine, and politically divided, opposition could attain little in the 1850s. It was clear that the peaceful methods inherited from O'Connell had failed, and Young Ireland had been too badly organised to succeed.

In 1858, a more radical group – the Irish Republican Brotherhood (IRB), nicknamed the 'Fenians' – was formed in the USA. Many of the key figures in the IRB had been involved in the Young Ireland Rising of 1848. The key figure was James Stephens (1824–1901), and it aimed to overthrow English rule, by violence if necessary. It had no social or economic programme, its members just wished to create an Irish Republic free from English rule.

The IRB embarked on a programme of violence, in Ireland, Britain and Canada. This led to persecution and executions of Fenian leaders. The movement began to decline by 1867. Many opponents of the Union were bitterly divided over both the objectives and the methods of attaining them.

Why did opposition to the Union grow in intensity after 1870?

Several factors combined to start a process, which led finally to Home Rule. Economic conditions in the South of Ireland grew particularly bad after 1870. This led to social distress. This naturally encouraged support for a break from England, which was seen as the cause of their economic distress. There was growing hatred of the system of land tenure in the South of Ireland, which gave the landlords (frequently Protestant, English and absent) much greater control of their tenants than was the case elsewhere.

Again a powerful social and economic pressure group, the Land League, fanned by hunger and poverty, joined forces with another pressure group, the Home Rulers, who were led by a highly charismatic and able leader, Charles Parnell.

Although Gladstone's legislation had removed some of the worst grievances of the Irish between 1868 and 1874, the feeling in Ireland was that this was totally insufficient. While official opinion in England felt that by 1874 Ireland had been 'sorted', opinion in much of Ireland was that the Union had failed and that Home Rule, in some form, was the only way forward for Ireland.

The Act that was perhaps to have most effect on Irish opposition to Union was the 1872 Ballot Act. This enabled Irish voters to vote freely for nationalist MPs without fear of eviction by their pro-Union landlords. The result was that, in 1874, a large group of MPs from Ireland committed to Home Rule was elected. The Home Rule Party grew, initially under the leadership of Isaac Butt, who favoured a federal solution to the Irish problem, with substantial devolved power to a Parliament in Dublin. A more dynamic and charismatic leader, Charles Parnell, replaced him by 1880. William Shaw was the leader between Butt and Parnell.

Parnell gave a huge boost to the movement to end British rule over Ireland. Using obstructionist tactics to force the Irish issue to the attention of the House of Commons, he worked closely with the leaders of the Land League to ensure that every method was used, from peaceful protest,

Charles Stewart Parnell (1846–1891)
Parnell was elected MP for Meath in 1875. He supported a policy of obstruction and violence in order to attain Home Rule for Ireland. Became President of Nationalist Party in 1877. In 1879, he approved the Land League, and his involvement led to imprisonment in 1881. Parnell welcomed Gladstone's Home Rule Bill, and continued his agitation after its defeat in 1886. A year later, however, his reputation suffered from an unfounded accusation in *The Times* of involvement in the murder of Lord Frederick Cavendish, Chief Secretary to the Lord Lieutenant of Ireland. Parnell's career was ruined when he was cited as co-respondent in a divorce case in 1890. For fear of losing Gladstone's support, Parnell's party deposed him. He died of rheumatic fever at the age of 45.

Boycotting: A term now used to describe people who are shunning, or organisations that are ignoring. Its origins lie in the nationalist agitation in Ireland in the late 1870s and early 1880s led by Parnell. Tenants were frequently evicted during the Great Famine of the late 1870s and their land taken over by others. Those who took over the land from evicted tenants were often treated with extreme hostility and given no help to farm their land. This fate befell Captain Charles Boycott (1832–97), in County Mayo. The Government had to come to his aid, spending far more on protecting him and getting his crops harvested than the crops were worth.

through '**boycotting**' landlords, to violence to ensure that land reform was successful. Gladstone put through a major land reform act, in 1881, where most of the objectives were attained. Again, strong pressure had attained the needed objectives. The Roman Catholic Church backed Parnell fully.

After the June 1885 general election, Parnell was in a position where he held the balance of power in British politics and a committed Nationalist held nearly every Irish seat in the House of Commons.

Gladstone produced his first Home Rule Bill for Ireland, in 1886. This was partly in response to the powerful and growing pressure in Ireland. Some historians, such as J.L. Hammond and G. Steele, believe that Gladstone had come to the view that this was the only solution to the Irish problem. Other historians have a more cynical view of Gladstone's motives. A. Cooke and John Vincent, in *The Governing Passion*, and D.A. Hamer, in *Liberal Politics in the Age of Gladstone and Rosebery,* believe Gladstone converted to Home Rule to re-assert his control over a divided Liberal Party. As a result of the introduction of the Home Rule Bill in 1886, Gladstone split the Liberal Party. The action did re-assert Gladstone's leadership over the larger part of the Liberal Party. It also forced Liberal Unionists, led by Joseph Chamberlain and Lord Hartington, to support the Conservatives.

Opposition in Ireland suffered a further blow when Parnell became implicated in a divorce case, in 1890. The case alienated the Roman Catholic Church and weakened its support for Home Rule. Gladstone's refusal to work with the Home Rule Party as long as Parnell remained leader, split the Home Rule party in two in 1890. For the whole of the 1890s, the Home Rule party remained divided into pro- and anti-Parnell factions.

How useful is this photograph as evidence of poverty in Ireland in the 1890s?

A one-roomed peasant's cabin in Donegal, in the 1890s. The large basket is a creel for carrying turf.

Opposition to Home Rule was further weakened in the late 1890s by a series of Conservative reforms, nicknamed 'killing Home Rule by kindness'. Inefficient and corrupt local government was reformed, giving cheaper and better local services. Arthur Balfour, the Irish Secretary, pushed through a decent poor relief system. There was agrarian reform as well. Balfour's nickname was 'Bloody Balfour' on account of his willingness to use **coercion** to deal with any opposition in Ireland. Huge numbers of Irish emigrated to the USA. Taxpayers' money was pumped into education and railways – the former providing opportunity and the latter employment. In Wyndham's Land Act of 1903, the UK Government pumped in over £86 million to help farmers and, indirectly, their labourers. **Cottage industries** were subsidised by the State, and public money was spent on roads and bridges, generating more wealth and employment. The mix of coercion and reform eased opposition to the idea of Union.

Coercion: Term given to government policy usually involving the removal of civil rights and can include imprisonment without trial.

Cottage industries: Small manufacturing enterprises carried out in the workers' own homes, such as weaving or bootmaking.

The supporters of Home Rule were divided in the late 1890s, and with the Liberals uninterested and the Conservatives following a policy of generosity, backed by ruthless firmness to any disorder, opposition to Union lost steam.

5.1.4 Why did opposition to Union grow after 1900 and culminate in war and final independence?

A sense of Irish nationalism continued to grow from 1900 onwards. Some Irish people had sympathised with the Boers in the South African War (1899–1902). The Irish nationalists saw the Boers as another nationalist group that wanted independence from Britain.

In 1905, Arthur Griffith founded the **Sinn Fein Party**. It supported the idea of a dual monarchy between Britain and Ireland, similar to the Empire of Austria-Hungary. Both Britain and Ireland would be self-governing but would share defence and foreign policy. Also at this time, the Irish Republican Brotherhood began to gain support. This was due in part to the nationalist enthusiasm created by the centenary celebrations in 1898 of the 1798 Rebellion.

Sinn Fein Party: A radical political party committed to Irish independence and unity.

In addition, a working-class movement with socialist ideas allied with the nationalist groups. They saw the British Liberal and Conservative parties as unlikely to bring about the social reforms they desired.

The demand for Home Rule appeared again after the 1910 general elections (January and December). As a result of these elections, the Home Rulers under Redmond held the balance of power in Parliament between the Liberals and Conservatives. With the passage of the Parliament Act, in 1911, the House of Lords veto on law also came to an end. From 1912, it was no longer possible for the House of Lords to stop Home Rule. It could only delay it for two years. As a result, Unionists in Ireland began to resist Home Rule with demonstrations and armed resistance. The Ulster Volunteer Force (UVF) was created in 1912. The UVF comprised 100,000 armed men. In 1913, nationalists formed the Irish Volunteers to defend Home Rule. By 1914, Britain faced the prospect of civil war in Ireland between two armed **paramilitary** groups.

Paramilitary: Similar to an army in that they use weapons and dress and behave like soldiers, but not the official army of the country.

Although Home Rule was passed in 1914 – and met the wishes of most of the Home Rulers – it was postponed until the end of the First World War. Redmond supported the decision to postpone Home Rule. He also supported the First World War policy of the British. However, a significant minority of opinion within the Irish Volunteers felt strongly that fighting for Irish freedom was more important than fighting for Belgian freedom. While many in the North supported the War enthusiastically, many in the South did not. Opposition to the War culminated with the Easter Rising, in 1916.

Nine counties in Ireland in 1921

This was organised by the Irish Republican Brotherhood, but also included other nationalist groups. The declaration of Irish independence, which was posted on the front of the General Post Office (GPO) in Dublin contained the names of Patrick Pearse, Thomas McDonagh, Thomas Clarke, Sean MacDiarmid, James Connolly, Eamonn Caennt and Joseph Plunkett.

The rebellion started on Easter Sunday 1916. However, it was badly organised and most of the promised German help failed to arrive. The British Army quickly suppressed it, even though there was clearly some sympathy for the 'rebels' among Irish people.

As was often the case, strong action by the Irish led to rapid concession by the British. Lloyd George, the British Prime Minister, started to negotiate a Home Rule Settlement shortly after 16 'rebel' leaders had been executed. These included the signatories of the Declaration of Independence. They had not died in vain. The Irish Convention of 1917–18 contained representatives of most Irish political groups. However, it made no progress towards a political settlement that would satisfy Nationalists and Unionists. Unionists demanded that the six counties of North-East Ireland should remain part of the UK.

The general election in December 1918 proved to be a turning point in Irish history. Sinn Fein won 73 out of the 105 Irish seats (the Ulster Unionists won 26), and simply opted out of the United Kingdom. They set up their own separate parliament in Dublin and their own government with Eamon de Valera as President.

Guerrilla war: A conflict fought between armies, usually an unofficial armed group (the guerrillas) against an official army.

Dail Government: The 'illegal' government set up in Dublin after the 1918 general election.

Passive resistance to British rule soon turned to armed conflict by the summer of 1919. From 1919 to the summer of 1921, a **guerrilla war** developed in southern Ireland between British forces and Irish Volunteers known as the Irish Republican Army (the IRA). Although technically under the control of Cathal Brugha, the real power behind the IRA campaign was Michael Collins, Minister of Finance in the **Dail Government**.

Dominion status: A country becomes independent, and rules itself, but retains the British monarchy as formal Head of State. This status was similar to that of Canada.

The Anglo–Irish War (1919–21) was particularly brutal. Lloyd George tried to bring about peace with a Home Rule solution with the Government of Ireland Act of 1920. This aimed to create separate Home Rule parliaments for both the North and the South, but the Republicans in the South rejected it. The war continued until June 1921, when a ceasefire was agreed and treaty negotiations between Republicans and the British Government began. In December 1921, the Irish Republican delegation, under a threat made by Lloyd George of renewed war, signed the Anglo–Irish Treaty. In the Treaty, the Irish accepted a status far removed from an independent Republic. Instead, they accepted **dominion status** within the British Empire, as the Irish Free State. This decision was to split the Republican movement and cause civil war in the Irish Free State between 1922 and 1923. An issue that caused little debate in the Treaty and in the split that led to civil war was the partition of Ireland. The Irish negotiators believed a boundary commission set up under the Treaty would give so much of North-East Ireland to the Free State that partition would not be possible. When the Boundary Commission reported in 1925, it ensured that the six north-eastern counties (Antrim, Down, Armagh, Tyrone, Fermanagh and Londonderry) stayed outside the Free State as Northern Ireland.

The four provinces of Ireland in 1921

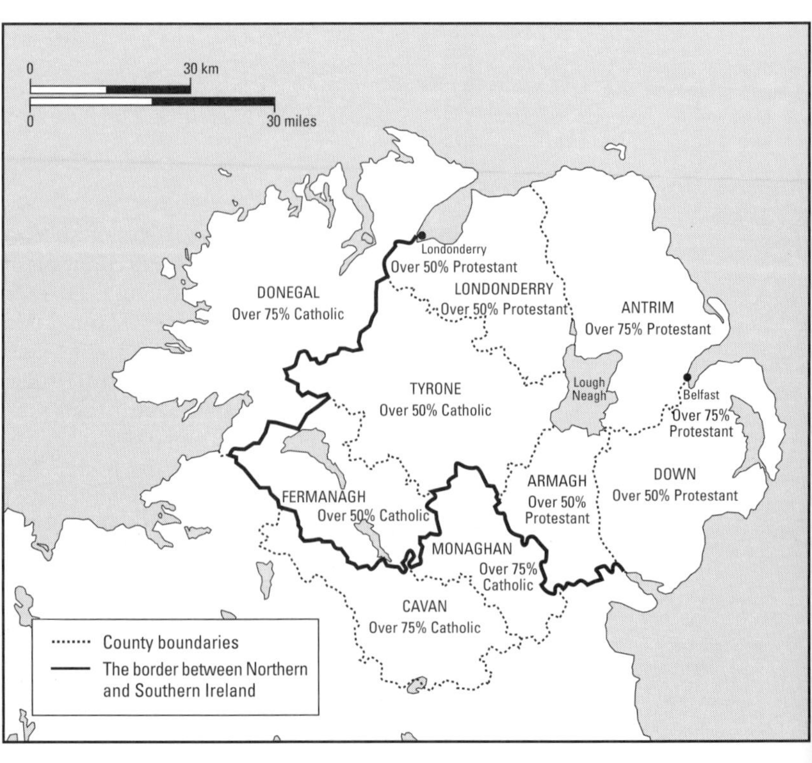

1. How far did opposition to the Union of Britain and Ireland change between 1798 and 1921?

2. Why were some forms of opposition to Union more successful than others (1798–1921)?

5.2 Theme 2: Who supported the Union?

5.2.1 Why did religion become a major issue in Anglo-Irish politics in the 19th century?
5.2.2 Why did Unionism grow in strength after 1870?
5.2.3 What role did the Unionists play in the crisis of 1912–1914?

Key Issues

- *Who were the Ulster Unionists?*
- *What were the strengths and weaknesses of the Unionist movement?*
- *Assess the nature and extent of Ulster Unionism.*

5.2.1 Why did religion become a major issue in Anglo-Irish politics in the 19th century?

When England moved away from the Roman Catholic Church in the 16th century, Ireland did not. It remained a strongly Roman Catholic country. Protestantism became the religion of the 'alien' British rulers, and the religion of the landed classes, as the 16th and 17th centuries progressed. In the North, mainly in Ulster, much land was removed from Catholics by force. It was given to Protestants from Scotland and England. Those Protestants in the North were also able to gain considerable security of tenure for their land, something that was not allowed to Catholics in the South.

Penal laws: Laws that discriminated against Roman Catholics, forbidding them from holding key offices, for example.

The **penal laws** also meant that Catholics were excluded from the vote, from sitting in the Irish Parliament in Dublin, and from any post of importance in the government or in the legal system. In addition, Roman Catholics had to pay a tax (the tithe) to support the Protestant Church in Ireland. It was hardly surprising that, by 1800, not only was there a strong resentment of Protestants by Catholics, but there was also a strong desire by the Protestants to retain their privileged position.

In the course of the late 18th and early 19th centuries, some of the restrictions on Roman Catholics were removed. They were allowed to vote, and then to stand for Parliament. The deep antagonism between the two religions remained. It was only among highly educated people that there was tolerance and cooperation between the religions. For the most part, there was a deep and mutual loathing.

Protestants formed about 25% of the total population of Ireland, but nearly 60% of the population of the North where they were concentrated. They owned the bulk of the land. Most of the industry of Ireland was in the North as well. It was also in Protestant hands. The 'haves' were Protestant and the 'have nots' tended to be Catholic. Even the famine hit the Catholics of the South much harder than the Protestants in the North.

5.2.2 Why did Unionism grow in strength after 1870?

Unionism: The belief that Ireland had to remain part of the United Kingdom, ruled from London.

Obviously, the Protestants of Ireland viewed the erosion of their privileged position, with emancipation and so on, with concern. When Home Rule, which for them meant Catholic rule from Dublin, became a serious possibility in the 1870s, Ulster **Unionism** (or Orange Movement) became a strong and organised force in the North. It then started to play an important part in British politics.

Hatred of Roman Catholicism and a strong dislike of Fenian violence were important factors in the growth of organised Ulster Unionism. There was also a strong element of rich versus poor in it. The Protestants in the North were very conscious that much of their wealth was dependent on the economic and political link with mainland Britain being maintained. The South may have suffered economically from Union, but the North gained. Many in the North were deeply worried by the land war and the activities of the Land League in the 1870s, and this added to their deep insecurity and sense of fear. Irish nationalists made no attempt to calm the fears of the Protestants, often making it clear that Home Rule would be an opportunity to settle old religious and economic scores.

Ulster Protestants made few attempts to convince Southern Catholics of their willingness to compromise and conciliate, and mutual loathing was the order of the day. The commentator who called it 'tribal warfare' between Catholic and Protestant was not far from the truth.

The rise of the Home Rule Movement in Ireland, the growth of a Home Rule Party in the House of Commons, the election of 16 committed nationalists in Ulster in 1886, and Gladstone's first Home Rule Bill, brought Unionism to a real crisis. The Unionists were aware that they might soon be ruled from Dublin and they would be a minority religion. They also feared that the intolerance with which they treated their Catholic neighbours would happen to them.

In 1886, the Protestants in the North formed the Loyalist Anti-Repeal Union, determined to oppose the march to Home Rule. They got strong support in England from the rising Tory star, Lord Randolph Churchill, who sensed that Ulster Unionism could be a powerful political weapon to use against the Liberals, as he played the '**Orange** Card'. Like many later Conservatives, Churchill's intentions were more to help the Conservatives and to damage the Liberals, than to bring any Irish 'problem' to an end. Just as Liberals underestimated the strength of Irish nationalism, Conservatives failed to realise the explosive potential of Ulster Unionism and the lengths to which the Unionists would go to prevent Home Rule. They encouraged a force which they were unable to restrain within sensible boundaries.

Orange: The colour associated with the Protestant cause. It came from the Dutch royal family of Wilhelm III who won the battle of the Boyne, in 1690, against the Catholic James II.

Unionists' fears subsided after the failure of Gladstone's two Home Rule Bills, but the strength of Unionist feeling did not die. Conservative programmes to ease the economic situation in the South were viewed with hostility in the North and Conservative suggestions for devolution just deepened the Unionist suspicions that the Conservatives were using Ulster for their own political ends.

5.2.3 What role did the Unionists play in the crisis of 1912–1914?

In 1905, the Ulster Unionist Council was formed. It was created after Sir Anthony MacDonnell, a civil servant in Dublin, tried to put forward a plan for **devolution** for Ireland. At last, the Protestants in the North had a well-organised and disciplined organisation, which could campaign effectively for their objective of remaining an integral part of the United Kingdom. It was led by James Craig (1871–1940), a man of extreme views and considerable organisational ability. The other key leader of the Unionists was Sir Edward Carson (1854–1935), an outstanding public speaker, but also one prepared to arouse real anger amongst the Unionists and encourage extremist militant behaviour.

Devolution: A form of home rule, which encourages as much local government as possible, pushing decision making away from the capital to the localities.

When the Liberals introduced the Third Home Rule Bill in 1912, Craig and Carson had behind them a powerful and organised pressure group determined to resist, at all costs, what was seen as a threat to their religion,

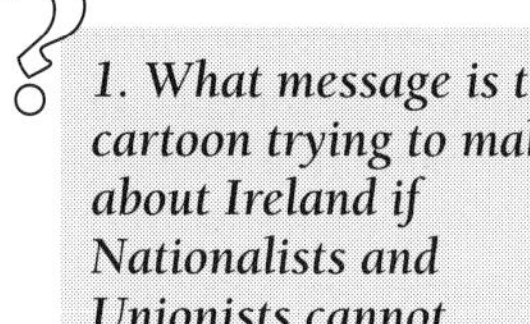

1. What message is the cartoon trying to make about Ireland if Nationalists and Unionists cannot agree?

2. How useful is this cartoon as evidence of the Ulster Crisis of 1912–14?

Punch cartoon, 15 April 1914, entitled 'The Fight for the Banner'. John Bull (background left) represents Britain. The person of the left of the banner is John Redmond, leader of the Irish Nationalists. On the right is Sir Edward Carson, leader of the Irish Unionists. John Bull is saying to Redmond and Carson: 'This tires me. Why can't you carry it between you? Neither of you can carry it alone.'

status, wealth and values. Two hundred and fifty thousand Ulstermen signed the Solemn League and Covenant – a commitment to retain the union, by force if need be. Huge protest marches of over 100,000 Ulstermen were features of the years before 1914, when Home Rule would come into force. In addition, the Ulster Volunteer Force (UVF) was created in 1912. The UVF was an illegal organisation, determined to use force to prevent Home Rule. In 1914, it was involved in gun running on a large scale from Germany, and illegally armed many of its members.

The UVF was openly encouraged by Conservatives, led by former British Army officers, and advised by ex-Generals of the British Army. Official endorsement seemed to be given to armed rebellion, against the wish of Parliament.

The Conservatives, with their determination to wreck the Liberal Government by fair means or foul, must take a degree of responsibility for the likelihood of civil war in Ireland with their incitement of the Unionists. The incompetence of the British Government was seen over the Curragh Mutiny, when they appeared to tolerate the refusal of British Army officers with family links to Ulster to obey orders they did not like. Those orders might include using force to enforce Home Rule.

Unionism was put on ice in 1914, with the declaration of war. Most of the Unionist volunteers joined up and fought. It was in fact the 36th (Ulster) Division that suffered the worst casualties in the carnage of the first day of the battle of the Somme.

1. To what extent was the rise of Unionism in Ireland a reaction to the growth of Irish Nationalism?

2. How would you account for the changing fortunes of the Protestant ascendancy in Ireland in the period 1798–1921?

3. Why were the Ulster Unionists unable to prevent Home Rule for the South?

Unionists were, of course, appalled by the 'treason' of the Easter Rising in Dublin in 1916. But, in a way, it helped towards a peaceful solution of the Irish problem in 1922, when North and South separated. Protestant Ulstermen had no wish to be united, even under British rule, with those who seemed to ally with the Germans in the South.

There was no way the Ulstermen could prevent Home Rule. Irish nationalism was far too powerful a force for them to fight on their own, if the British Government stopped trying to prevent it. All they could attain was to keep the North in British hands, using their close links with the Conservative Party and their willingness to fight and cause a serious civil war as key cards. British public opinion was used to fighting wars against those who wished to stop being a British possession. However, it would not tolerate a war against those who wanted to stay.

5.3 Theme 3: Change and continuity in the attitude of British governments and parties

5.3.1 Why, and with what results, did Ireland become an ever more divisive issue in British politics, 1798–1922?
5.3.2 What was the impact of Ireland on British politics – from Union to the 1830s?
5.3.3 What impact did Ireland have on British politics from the Famine to 1900?
5.3.4 What impact did Ireland have on British politics, 1906–1922?

Key Issues

- *Did the British Government adopt a consistent attitude to Ireland in this period?*
- *What was the impact of Ireland on the politics of the UK during this period?*
- *How, and why, did attitudes towards Irish Home Rule change in this period?*

5.3.1 Why, and with what results, did Ireland become an ever more divisive issue in British politics, 1798–1922?

Throughout the period between 1798 and 1922, Ireland was a central and usually highly divisive issue in British politics. Ireland cost the English taxpayers millions and thousands of lives were lost. It led to the exclusion from public gaze and ministerial attention of many other important issues. It was always in the headlines, but few ever really analysed why. There was always the assumption that Ireland as an integral part of the UK was of benefit to all. When the possibility of independence for Ireland was raised, few in England could envisage that idea as an acceptable concept.

The same idea had been evident when the United Kingdom 'lost' the American colonies, but to the surprise of many, both the UK and the USA flourished when separated. The UK seemed able to give almost complete independence to Canada, New Zealand and Australia in the 19th century, but not to Ireland. Perhaps it was too close to home, and therefore might be of value to 'enemies'; or possibly the arrogant English felt that although the Irish may not have wanted 'English' rule, they needed it for their own good.

The fact that many leading politicians in the UK owned land in Ireland may have encouraged a proprietary attitude by some. The Marquis of Lansdowne, for example, a key figure in the Conservative Party and its leader in the House of Lords at the time of the crisis over the Third Home Rule Bill (1912–14), owned large estates in County Kerry, and derived considerable income from them. So did many other Conservative peers who felt it necessary to throw out Gladstone's Second Home Rule Bill 'in order to preserve the integrity of the Empire', rather than save their own financial interests.

5.3.2 *What was the impact of Ireland on British politics – from Union to the 1830s?*

Autonomy: The control or government of a country, organisation or group by itself, rather than by others.

Union, in 1800, was highly controversial. Not only did many in Ireland oppose it as they felt that it would damage Irish interests and reduce what little **autonomy** they had under the old Irish Parliament, but it was also strongly opposed in England. Many in England disliked the extensive use of patronage by Castlereagh and Cornwallis. Commercial interests, always strongly represented in the House of Commons, felt that giving equality to Ireland might damage English commerce. Peers resented the arrival of Irishmen, and many saw it as a concession to both force and Catholicism.

When the second part of the 'deal' – the ending of discrimination against Roman Catholics – was attempted, the King refused. Pitt then felt obliged to resign as he had committed himself to giving the Roman Catholics in Ireland equality with the Protestants. Within months of what had been seen as the solution to the Irish 'problem', it had claimed its first major English political victim – an exceptionally able Prime Minister.

Once the Napoleonic Wars were over, Ireland returned to play a serious role in politics in London. Many issues divided Liverpool's Cabinet between 1812 and 1826, but the bitterest division came over whether Roman Catholics should be allowed to take a seat in the House of Commons. The penal laws were still in existence and there was a deep degree of religious intolerance against Roman Catholics going back to the age of Elizabeth and the Gunpowder Plot of James I. In the eyes of many, Roman Catholicism was seen as the religion of traitors.

After providing a constant source of friction within the Cabinet for more than a decade, the issue of Catholics entering Parliament came to a head in 1828. Wellington and Peel were forced to give in to force. This led to the destruction of the old Tory Party and the rise of the new Conservative Party. Ireland also played a large part in the fact that the Tory Government managed to lose the election of 1830. O'Connell formed a small, but quite powerful, group in the Commons. This led to further reforms for Ireland, which continued to divide English politics.

The tithe wars of the 1830s divided the Whig Government, as the more 'liberal' members were not so enthusiastic for coercion as were the more conservative 'Whigs'. The latter prevailed, and the Irish Coercion Act of 1833 gave the State huge police powers. In 1834, it was a dispute over the Anglican Church in Ireland that led to a major government split. The Prime Minister, Grey, resigned over the issue. Not for the last time was Ireland to be the downfall of a major English politician.

Grey was replaced by Peel, whose Government collapsed in 1835 when the Whigs, Radicals and, of course, the Irish MPs joined together to bring it down. Irish support was critical to the Whigs until 1840. This meant that the Whigs had to take on Irish former issues, such as the Poor Law and education in Ireland, which they would have preferred to avoid as it meant upsetting the more conservative Whigs.

Even the arrival of Peel with a majority Conservative Government, in 1841, did not end Ireland as a divisive issue in British politics. Ireland became an even more important issue. Peel's reform programme for Catholic education, landlord/tenant relations and the franchise was hated by the right of his own party. William Maynooth split his own party and led to the resignation of one of his key ministers, Gladstone.

Peel's Irish reforms are seen as failures. They did not calm Ireland. Also, they led to the split of his party, and his party was out of office until 1874. The Famine led to the repeal of the Corn Laws and massive political disruption. It set the scene for the fragmented politics of the 1846–68 period. Ireland had divided and disrupted British politics on a huge scale, from Union to the Famine.

5.3.3 What impact did Ireland have on British politics from the Famine to 1900?

In the years after the Famine, until 1865, Ireland appeared 'quiet' as far as London was concerned, and was ignored. However, the huge resentment that had built up in Ireland over the Union and the Famine was to place it firmly back on the political agenda. The Fenians used violence from 1865 to 1867. From 1870, Isaac Butt used parliamentary means. Also, Gladstone's decision to 'pacify' meant that Ireland was to dominate British political life from the mid-1860s until 1921. The failure to 'pacify' Ireland then has led to problems up to this day. Ireland was to have a huge impact from 1868 onwards, making and breaking governments, parties and reputations.

The Gladstone Administration of 1868–1874

Ireland played a significant role in Gladstone's Administration. Although much of the work confirmed Gladstone's 'liberalism', it had important side-effects. Many people in Ireland felt that Gladstone was doing too little, too late. In England, people felt he was doing too much. Gladstone's Church Act upset the Anglican Church and those on the right of his party saw his Land Act as an attack on property rights. Unionism as a powerful political, social and religious force came into being at this time, largely inspired by Gladstone's actions. The Whigs, the more conservative elements in the Liberal party, started to view the Prime Minister as a dangerous radical. They looked towards the Conservative Party as their natural home.

Gladstone's Ballot Act created Irish nationalism as a powerful parliamentary force in the election of 1874. To cap it all, Gladstone's Government was defeated in the House of Commons over the Irish Universities Bill in 1873. He split his party over this issue of supporting 'Catholic' education, and resigned after a motion of 'no confidence' in the Commons over it. Gladstone may have started his Administration with a 'mission to pacify' Ireland, but he not only failed, but also injected a lethal ingredient into British politics.

Disraeli's 1874–80 Administration did not concern itself with Irish issues. Perhaps it should have done, as by 1880 the mixture of Irish nationalism and the Land League was forcing Ireland back on to the British Government's agenda.

Much of Gladstone's Second Administration (1880–85) was dominated by Ireland. The Prime Minister was forced to both coerce and appease Ireland with a tough Coercion Act, the arrest of Parnell, and the passing of the Second Land Act, which again worried the more conservative members of the Liberal Party. His policy on Ireland led to a drift to the Conservatives. After the horror of the Phoenix Park murders, with the killing of the Chief Secretary in cold blood in Dublin, Gladstone's Government collapsed again in 1885, leaving Parnell and the Irish Home Rule Party holding the balance of power in the Commons.

Convinced that Home Rule was the only solution, Gladstone put through his first Home Rule Bill in 1886. This failed, splitting his own party and driving its most talented member, Joseph Chamberlain, into the Conservative Party. This became known as the Conservative and Unionist Party as a result.

English politics was dancing to an Irish tune. Churchill and the 'Orange' card introduced a degree of fanaticism into politics, where consensus and courtesy were replaced by passion and illegality.

The Conservative policy to Ireland in the 1886–92 period was simple. Having won the election largely because of the Liberal implosion over Ireland, the Conservatives largely gave in. After Liberal election victory in 1892, Gladstone introduced his second Home Rule Bill. Although it cleared the Commons, the Lords rejected it and this unconstitutional measure was a precursor of the greater constitutional crisis over the role of the Lords, in 1909. Once again, Ireland had been the causative factor of a major crisis in England.

The Conservative reaction in the post-1894 period demonstrates the remarkable pragmatism of that party. On one hand, there was the ruthless repression of 'Bloody Balfour'; on the other, more radical land reform at a cost to the British taxpayer unimaginable to the Liberals.

London ignored the growth of Irish nationalism in the South. There was neither understanding nor wish to understand. It was a totally reactive policy.

5.3.4 What impact did Ireland have on British politics, 1906–1922?

With the Liberal electoral victory in 1906, Irish aspiration was aroused. However, it was not matched by a favourable Liberal response. An awareness of the Lords' likely reaction was a key factor. After the 1910 elections, the Irish Home Rule Party held the balance of power in the Commons, so they had to be appeased. Needing their support in order to defeat the Lords, Herbert Asquith promised, and then introduced, a Home Rule Bill. Part of the bitter opposition to reforming the Lords lay in the knowledge that Irish Home Rule would follow.

Passage through the Commons was bitter. With senior conservative politicians in London openly inciting the Unionists to armed rebellion, and the King to unconstitutional action, Ireland continued to play a highly damaging role in British politics.

The mismanagement by Asquith of the whole Irish crisis worsened the situation. The problem of the North and the South would not go away, and a 'wait and see' policy was not what Ireland needed. Asquith allowed a situation to arise over the Curragh Mutiny in which officers in the Army were more or less allowed to dictate policy to the politicians. He had to dismiss his Secretary of State for War, Seeley, over the crisis.

The First World War eased the Irish problem temporarily, but it failed to go away. The Easter Rising returned it to the forefront. Again, there were bitter disputes between those in London who wished to coerce and punish, and those who wished to appease. Whether to introduce conscription into Ireland also provoked serious disunity in London and Dublin. Compelling Irishmen to fight for the freedom of others was not easy.

Black and Tans: Former English soldiers recruited to reinforce the police in Ireland. They could be brutal and often ignored the usual legal methods used by the police.

1. What were the attitudes of the main UK political parties to the Unionists?

2. How far did the policies of the two major political parties in Britain – the Whig-Liberal Party and the Tory-Conservative Party – change towards Ireland between 1798 and 1921?

With Lloyd George dependent on Conservative support to remain in power after 1918, he had to heed the grievances and wishes of the Unionists. The Conservatives would not tolerate Ulster being forced to join the South, so partition was imposed on Lloyd George through English political necessity.

The methods used by the **Black and Tans** brought discredit to the British Government. The way in which Sinn Fein simply set up its own parliament and government in Dublin brought ridicule on London. Although the settlement of 1920–22 was the best that was possible in the circumstances, it was a important cause of the downfall of Lloyd George in 1922. Ireland had claimed yet another political victim.

Once the South gained its independence, the Conservatives proceeded to ignore the North. This proved to be a tragic error, as the Protestants embarked on a ruthless policy of discrimination that was to lay a basis for the trouble that exploded in the 1960s, and last to this day.

5.4 Theme 4: Change and continuity in the Irish economy

5.4.1 What were the causes of the Famine and what impact did it have on the Irish economy and people?

5.4.2 How did the Irish economy develop after the Famine?

Key Issues

- *Which proved to be more difficult for British governments to deal with in Ireland during the period 1798–1921, religious or economic issues?*
- *How successfully did British governments tackle Irish economic problems, 1798–1921?*
- *What role did economic issues play in Anglo-Irish history, 1798–1922?*

Introduction

Subsistence economy: When most of the economic activity is focused on simply growing enough food for the people that produce it and not for sale at market.

The economy of Ireland at the time of the Union was a direct contrast to that of England. There had been major agriculture and industrial change in England in the course of the 18th century. Mainland UK had become highly productive and wealthy. Ireland had not shared in that rapid and profound economic change. It still had a primarily rural system, with only 20% of the population in towns by 1800. Ireland's agriculture was a **subsistence economy** and there was virtually no heavy industry. The domestic/cottage industries, such as weaving and spinning, were devastated by the massive industrial growth in the UK. Denied the markets that the English had easy access to, and with no sophisticated banking system, a poor transport and communications system, and virtually no local energy source, Ireland could not compete.

There was a substantial population growth in the latter part of the 18th and early 19th century, which put a huge strain on Ireland. This was caused by a lowering of the marriage age, as babies and their mothers were more likely to survive if younger and healthier. Health awareness increased and the Irish staple diet, the potato, was not an unhealthy diet.

The population growth caused problems, with no welfare system and no industrial towns to absorb the surplus rural population, as in the UK. Union, it was hoped, would lead to a sharing of the English markets and a sharing in English wealth – but it did not happen. Economic backwardness encouraged political unrest.

Emigration: Leaving your mother country to live in another country, often far away (e.g. America or Canada).

Ireland suffered considerably in the economic downturn after the end of the Napoleonic Wars, in 1815. The serious social and economic division between landlord, tenant and labourer grew; the decline of the cottage industries speeded up and generated even more poverty. The system of land holding discouraged investment in the land, and if a tenant farmer worked to improve land and output, he could find himself being asked for a higher rent as his reward. The tenant farmer was unlikely to get any compensation for improvement to land. So, as long as the rent was paid and the family fed, there seemed little point in trying to generate a profit.

How far does this illustration explain why Irish emigrants became resentful of British rule in Ireland from the 1850s?

Emigration was the only solution for many, but it was often the solution of the youngest and best. Union did not solve any problems for many Irish people. In fact, it could well be seen to have caused more problems. *Laissez faire* was very much the approach adopted by governments in London when it came to social and economic conditions, and they did not change that approach for Ireland. Behind the political and religious events lay great poverty and deprivation.

Drawing from the *Illustrated London News* of May 1851. It shows the cramped conditions on an emigrant ship.

5.4.1 What were the causes of the Famine and what impact did it have on the Irish economy and people?

Emigration in the 1820s and 1830s had not solved Ireland's problems, nor had Ireland shared in the economic progress made in the rest of the UK at that time. Industrial stagnation, land shortage, declining agricultural employment and poor diet were the main features of Irish economic history after 1815. Hungry people supported Daniel O'Connell.

Blight: A form of fungal rot.

Added to this grim scene, came total disaster by 1845. **Blight** struck the potato crop, which was the staple (basic) diet for the vast majority of the Irish people, especially in the Catholic South. With a very poor population, few economic resources, overpopulation and inefficient system of local government, the blight became a tragedy in months. People started to starve, in their thousands.

Overall, the actual aid given by the rest of the UK was limited. The Government in London had no experience in dealing with such a famine. Also, there was a strong tendency in London to assume that the situation was exaggerated. In addition, with the prevailing *laissez-faire* economic ideas, it was not felt to be part of the role of a government to intervene in such matters.

The Government in London appeared to be more concerned with the implications of repealing the Corn Laws. It was also more concerned about the economic interests of British farmers and political pledges given in the election of 1841 than about actually stopping a large number of UK citizens in Ireland starving to death. Britain was possibly the richest country in the world at the time, with vast resources of money and shipping. It had all that was needed to both buy food and to ship it to Ireland and feed those there.

The English Government seemed to devote itself to academic debates on both the causes and the extent of the problem. It discussed whether public works would actually help or not, and should soup be given out by Protestant organisations with a requirement to convert before the food was consumed.

The governments of both Peel (1841–46) and Russell (1846–52) appeared to be particularly concerned to ensure that Irish landowners paid for Irish poverty, and that the English taxpayer would not suffer for Irish profits. A particularly hard winter in 1848–49 simply increased the death rate. It is estimated that over a million died of starvation or related illnesses in Ireland in this period. Possibly a further million emigrated during or immediately after the famine years, which did not end until nearly 1852.

Given the possible resources at the disposal of a British government, it is perhaps remarkable that there was so little resentment expressed against the Union. What the Government in London had done was too little too late. While the biographers of Peel and Russell might see them as able leaders, with their Bank Charter Acts and calm handling of the Chartist disturbances, viewed from an Irish perspective the fact that a million UK citizens died of hunger, they were clearly less than 'able'.

5.4.2 How did the Irish economy develop after the Famine of 1845–1849?

Much like the economic recovery in Britain in the late 1930s, what recovery there was in Ireland was as much in spite of the actions of Government as because of them. There was no initiative at all from London to ensure that the situation was not repeated. If there had been, then perhaps the IRB and the Land League might not have had little support. After the London government's response, or lack of it, to the famine in Ireland, Union was permanently damned in the eyes of the vast majority of Irish people, both educated and otherwise.

Animal husbandry: Careful breeding and management of livestock to get better food and animal products (such as wool).

With fewer people (and therefore a less acute land shortage), and the ending of the Corn Laws, Irish agriculture could develop more easily. Smaller-scale farmers still focused on subsistence, and not profit, but larger-scale ones could start to develop livestock and **animal husbandry** for a profit. With most farm prices up, profits were made. Increased rail networks came to Ireland by the late 1850s, making rapid movement of food to towns much easier. Crop rotation, evident in much of Britain by the 1790s, spread to Ireland particularly after the 1860s, as it was easy to see how a cash crop could be developed. Horse power replaced human power, but agricultural machinery did not arrive on a large scale until the 20th century.

Gladstone's two Land Acts brought more peace to the countryside, but they also made it realistic for the tenant farmer to invest, adapt and, above all, improve. Balfour's Land Purchase Act was also vital. In 1899, a Department of Agriculture was set up in Ireland in order to educate farmers (almost a hundred years after a similar organisation was set up in England). The Wyndham Land Act effectively abolished the landlord class in Ireland. By the end of the period, the vast majority of farmers owned the land they worked, and therefore had a vested interest in both its quality and productivity.

The British Government did play a more central role in this area, between 1881 and 1915. In order for the intentions of the Land Act to be implemented, £86.1 million was paid out, and peace and economic justice come to the Irish countryside. Over 4 million emigrated, between the famine and 1914, and that was important to ease social and economic tension.

Industry largely passed Ireland by, except for Ulster. Towns in the South, such as Dublin and Cork, saw a total contrast with England, with the percentage involved in industry actually dropping in Ireland in the 19th century. Linen – the traditional primary industry in Ulster – dropped in importance in the second part of the 19th century, and was replaced by shipbuilding and engineering. The vast proportion of the heavy industry in the North was under Protestant and Unionist control, and it was common for Catholics to be excluded deliberately from any post other than the completely menial. Not only were there religious, social and landholding differences between Ulster and the rest of Ireland, there were major economic differences there as well. Even the retail sector flourished much more in Belfast than in Dublin.

Entrepreneurs: People willing to take risks by investing in new ideas/plans/techniques in business and industry.

The British Government played no role in the development of industry in Ireland. Railways developed there as **entrepreneurs** felt they could profit from them. The only serious government involvement came in land issues, and that was for political reasons rather than any other. Conservative policy was a reaction to pressure and designed to prevent the perceived evil of Home Rule.

Economic issues played a vital role in Anglo–Irish politics until the 1880s. They fuelled much of the unrest, which occurred both before and after the Famine. Once mass emigration, improved farming and landholding changes had come in, then economic factors were to play a smaller role in fanning the flames of Irish nationalism.

Compared with other factors, such as politics, how important were economic issues in bringing about change in Anglo–Irish relations between 1798 and 1921?

The Great Reform Act of 1832

6.1 How unrepresentative was the electoral system before 1830?
6.2 Why did parliamentary reform become a major issue from 1830?
6.3 What were the main features of the Reform Crisis between 1830 and 1832?
6.4 Historical interpretation: Was Britain on the brink of a revolution in 1830–1832?
6.5 How far did the Reform Act change the electoral system?

Key Issues

- *Why was parliamentary reform such a controversial issue in 1830–32?*
- *How serious was the Reform Bill crisis?*
- *How far did the Reform Act change the British political system?*

Framework of Events

1829–31	Economic distress caused by harvest failure leads to high grain prices and unemployment
1830	January: Formation of Thomas Attwood's political union June: Death of George IV; new King William IV July: Fall of Charles X in France August: Swing Riots take place in southern England November: Collapse of Wellington's ministry marks end of Tory rule Earl Grey becomes Prime Minister of a Whig ministry
1831	March: First Reform Bill proposed by Lord John Russell; defeated by Tories in committee stage; Earl Grey calls an election April: Whigs return to office with an increased majority of 130, committed to reform July: Second Reform Bill is introduced October: Bill is defeated in Lords by a majority of 31; leads to riots in Nottingham, Derby and Bristol. Prominent members of the Lords attacked, including several bishops December: Third Reform Bill is introduced
1832	March: Third Bill passes through the Commons but now faces possibility of defeat in Lords May: Grey asks for the creation of 50 new Whig peers to ensure a majority in Lords. William IV refuses to agree and Grey resigns. Wellington tries for six days to form a Tory ministry but is unable to do so. The King asks Grey to return as Prime Minister. New Whig peers not needed as Tory supporters in Lords abstain June: Third Bill finally becomes law on 4 June. Separate Reform bills for Ireland and Scotland.

Overview

THE period 1830–32 was dominated by the single issue of parliamentary reform, when events allowed the Whigs to take power under their leader, Earl Grey. The process was not a smooth one and the country seemed on the brink of revolution when the Lords rejected the Second Reform Bill in the autumn of 1831.

The reasons why this situation came about have provoked intense debate among historians. Eric Evans believes that the collapse of Tory rule in 1830 allowed the Whig reformers the chance to introduce reform that would otherwise have been denied to them had the Tories stayed in office. The economic crisis that occurred between 1829 and 1831 heightened the tension, but is not now regarded as the main reason why the crisis emerged.

It must be remembered that the Whig Government, under Earl Grey, was not trying to alter the constitution radically. Instead, it was trying to open the vote to the emerging group in society – the middle classes. Grey was convinced that a moderate measure would satisfy respectable property owners and break the alliance that had grown up between the radicals and the middle class. It would be a mistake to regard Grey as a democrat: he was quite clearly an anti-democrat. He told the House of Lords at the height of the crisis in 1832, 'The principle of my reform is, to prevent the necessity for revolution, there is no one more dedicated against annual parliaments, universal suffrage, and the secret ballot than I am.'

The outcome of the Act has also caused as much debate among historians as it did among contemporaries. Some have claimed that the changes marked the beginning of a new era. Equally, there was bitter disappointment, especially among the working class. They accused the Government of betrayal because of the insistence on a £10 property qualification. This sense of betrayal would fuel further demands for radical change through the Chartist movement.

The Tories found the Reform Act equally unacceptable because they regarded electoral change as a revolutionary measure that would upset the natural influence of prosperity and rank. In addition, the Tories claimed that the House of Commons would be at the mercy of public opinion – as Sir Robert Peel argued: 'when you have established the overpowering influence of the people over this House (i.e. the Commons) what other authority in the State can – nay what other authority ought to – control its will or reject its decisions?'

The crisis over reform and the terms of the 1832 Act also changed the influence of the monarchy over politics through the reduction of patronage. It also made the two political parties, the Tories and the Whigs, establish national organisations in order to contest the votes of the new middle classes. Ultimately, the 1832 Act was the starting point for further electoral change as the century would reveal.

6.1 How unrepresentative was the electoral system before 1830?

The main problem facing those campaigning for parliamentary reform at this time was that the system of electing MPs was rooted in history and had changed little since the middle of the 17th century. There were two basic types of constituency: the counties and the boroughs.

The counties

These, as their name suggests, represented the major counties of England, Scotland, Wales and Ireland. In England and Ireland, each county elected two MPs regardless of its size and population. There were some alarming irregularities in the pre-reform Parliament but, according to its supporters, the system worked because interests were more important than numbers. In Wales and Scotland, only one MP was elected for each county and the charge of serious under-representation cannot be ignored. Qualification for voting in the counties was relatively easy to define but was based primarily on the land you owned. Any man (not woman) who owned land or property worth 40 shillings (£2) a year was eligible to vote. This had been the case since 1430 and the relative decline in the value of property meant that the numbers eligible to vote in elections for county seats had steadily increased.

The boroughs

The situation in the borough constituencies was far more confusing. The boroughs were usually the most important towns of each county, as they had been defined in the mid-17th century. Before 1832, most British boroughs had two MPs, whereas in Wales, Scotland and Ireland there was one each. Borough electorates varied enormously: some like Liverpool had over 5,000 members, but some like Old Sarum literally only had a handful.

Rotten boroughs: These were borough constituencies in the pre-reform Parliament, which were very small and used to elect promising young politicians without a contest. The most infamous rotten borough was Old Sarum, which had a population of only 7.

These latter constituencies were known as '**rotten boroughs**'. They were controlled by wealthy members of society, usually aristocrats. They fulfilled

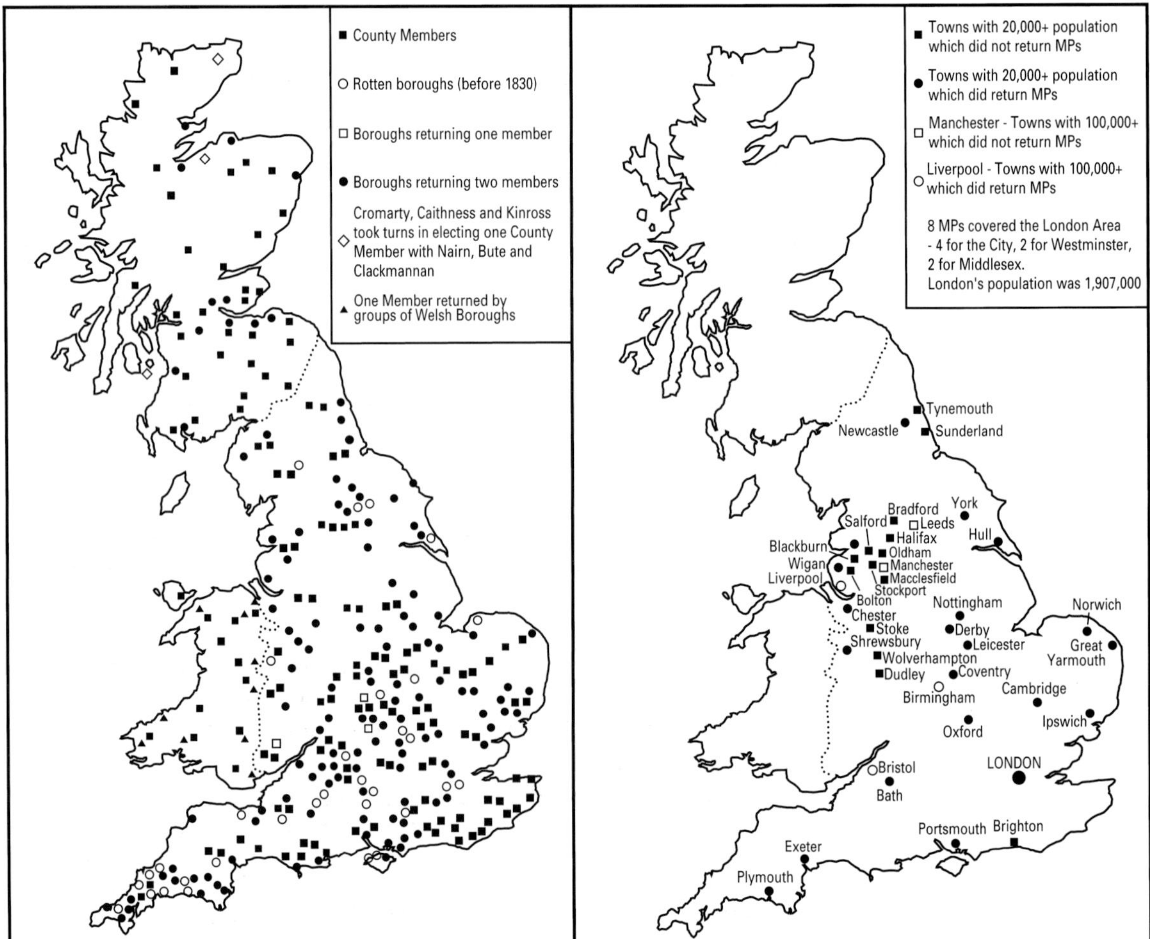

The unreformed electoral system, 1830

The reformed electoral system, 1832

a useful purpose in allowing the election of a promising young MP, but could equally maintain the position of an unpopular member. These rotten boroughs were common: well over 50 English boroughs had fewer than 40 voters, yet each was represented by two MPs. These pre-reform boundaries had been drawn up in the 17th century when Britain was predominantly a rural country, before the industrial revolution had changed the face of the landscape. For example, Birmingham, although a large town, had no MPs because it was not a borough. By 1831, Lancashire with a population of 1.3 million had just 14 MPs, while Cornwall with only 300,000 was represented by 42 MPs.

Was there a demand for change?

Britain was a changing society. As a result of the industrial revolution, the middle classes had been growing in economic prosperity. They now possessed economic power and influence, but lacked the political power associated with representation in Parliament and government. This was especially so during the Liverpool Administration when unpopular legislation, such as the Corn Laws and income tax repeal, seemed to weigh heavily against the consumer in favour of the producer. The political system as it existed tended to discriminate against the middle classes, especially in the borough constituencies where many were denied the vote. Their property rights were evidence of a respectable class of men who could be trusted to receive the vote and not abuse it as many Tories feared the working class would. Political philosophers such as Jeremy Bentham, the utilitarian leader, advocated a reform of Parliament as this would satisfy his maxim that any government existed to provide 'the greatest happiness of the greatest number'.

Who had the right to vote before 1832?

Although ownership of property worth over 40 shillings (£2) gave you the vote in county constituencies, the situation was far less clear-cut in the boroughs. A mixture of ancient privileges and eccentricity dictated who could vote in borough elections. In general there were five main types of borough constituency.

- *Freeman boroughs*
  In this type of borough those who could vote were those who had received or had bought the 'freedom' of the borough. This privilege was then passed on to relatives.

- *Burgage boroughs*
  These tended to be very small constituencies, as only those owning certain certain pieces of land or property (burgage plots) were allowed to vote.

- *Scot and Lot boroughs*
  An easy borough to identify as those male householders who paid local rates were entitled to vote. Electorates tended to vary in size here. An example of this type of borough was Preston in Lancashire.

- *Potwalloper boroughs*
  This type of borough constituency shows the eccentricity of the pre-reform borough electoral system. Here, incredibly, the vote was given to those who owned a house and fireplace on which to boil a pot. Not surprisingly, the electorates tended to be large in these types of constituency. An example of this type of borough was Taunton in Somerset.

What difficulties would the electorate have in deciding who was entitled to vote in a borough constituency?

- *Corporation boroughs*
  Only the corporation or town council were allowed to vote here, so the electorate was very small. Over 90% of this type of borough had fewer than 50 voters.

Critics of this system pointed to the fact that of the 432 borough seats many were prone to electoral corruption. In addition, significant and growing areas of the county had no borough representation at all. As the historian Eric Evans has stated, 'the base of the economy was moving north but none of Manchester, Leeds, Sheffield or Birmingham had a seat in parliament'. Put simply, the North and the Midlands – the centres of the industrial revolution – were heavily under-represented, whilst the South – prominent in the past – was now over-represented in relation to its overall contribution to the wealth of the nation.

Why were elections seen to be unfair?

The modern electoral system takes great care to ensure that every aspect of an election is fair and above accusations of bribery or vote rigging. This was not the case in the early part of the 19th century. The following reasons made the practice of fair elections even more unlikely.

The absence of a secret ballot
Voting in an election today is very much a private affair, conducted in secret by the individual according to his or her conscience. In a 19th-century election, up until 1872, voting was an 'open' affair. Everyone knew the way in which an individual had cast his vote. This, of course, could lead to intimidation because the candidate knew how each person had voted and could bribe or blackmail him to change his mind at the last moment. The tenant, for example, was never free to vote with his conscience because his landlord knew how he voted and might threaten to evict him if he did not follow the landlord's lead.

1. What were the major weaknesses of the unreformed electoral system before 1830?

2. Which weakness do you regard as the most in need of change? Give reasons to support your answer.

Bribery and corruption
Any candidate standing in an election at the time knew that in order to ensure victory he would have to spend exorbitant amounts to win undecided voters over to his side. This was especially true in constituencies with large electorates: open bribery included cash gifts, free beer and, in some cases, the promise of employment. Usually, the election lasted a fortnight and as the episode drew to a close, the money for the undecided voter increased to unrealistic proportions. In the smaller constituencies, the landlord could nominate his candidate in what was usually a non-event as a contest. These 'pocket boroughs' were used as a tool by their owners to sell to the highest bidder and were usually passed down from father to son.

6.2 Why did parliamentary reform become a major issue from 1830?

The collapse of the Tory Government in November 1830

The Tories had consistently refused to extend the vote, arguing that ownership of property rather than number of voters was the hallmark of Britain's successful political system. Of course, the Tories would be the major losers in any redrawing of the political map. Royal support from both George III and George IV strengthened them. Yet, by the end of the decade, there were bitter internal divisions exposed within the Tory Party over the issue of Roman Catholic emancipation. These produced a climate where the Tory Ultras were even willing to support reform in order to annoy Wellington and Peel and to ensure that a wider franchise would reject issues such as emancipation! Had the Tories not split over the religious issue, then the prospect of introducing reform under a Whig government might not have existed.

The revival of the Whigs

Coinciding with the decline of the Tory Party in this period, there was a revival in the fortunes of the Whig Party. The Whigs were far more enthusiastic about the idea of cautious reform, but could hardly be described as democrats themselves. They believed that any change to the existing political system had to be done to preserve its key features, rather than destroy it. As a party, the Whigs were far more in tune with the new forces shaping society and, although many Whig MPs were aristocratic by background, it is also true that a significant number were drawn from the rising middle classes – the major beneficiaries of industrialisation. The Whigs had tried to sponsor reform bills previously, but on three occasions – in 1792, 1793 and 1797 – they had failed, all due to the opposition of George III.

Charles Grey, second Earl Grey (1764–1845)
Grey was one of the leading Whig politicians of the period. A member of an aristocratic Northumbrian family, Grey spent most of his career in opposition, apart from a brief period as Foreign Secretary in 1806–7. Always an advocate of electoral reform, Grey was Prime Minister in 1832 when the first Reform Bill was passed. Following his resignation in 1834, he retired to his Northumbrian estate, where he died in 1845.

The Whig Party had spent the period 1807–30 in opposition, but during the later part of the 1820s had begun to find its political feet. Its leader, Earl Grey, was a known support of moderate reform. He believed that the system had become out of date and the new 'men of property' among the middle classes should be given a say in the running of affairs if the country was to avoid anarchy and chaos. The corruption of the existing political system was arming the radical opponents of the system and detracting from the moderate changes Grey was proposing. The historian John Derry, in an article in *Modern History Review*, claims that Grey 'saw himself as keeping alive the possibility of moderate, practical reform, a safe halfway house between loyalist reaction and radical extremism'.

E.A. Smith goes further by claiming that the motivation behind the Reform Bill was to safeguard the pre-eminence of the aristocracy against the encroachments of royal tyranny. Grey had learnt the lessons of the past when George III had vetoed plans for reform. According to Smith, in an article in *New Perspective*, 'Grey was attempting to restrain the potential violence of a popular uprising and channel moderate opinion into safeguarding existing constitutional safeguards against royal tyranny'. Grey was fortunate in that he was given the opportunity to implement his ideas when the Tory ranks split in 1830.

The fall of Charles X of France in 1830

The issue of reform was also heightened by events across the Channel in France. The restored Bourbon dynasty that had ruled since 1814 had become increasingly unpopular with the people. This was primarily because its king, Charles X, ruled in a heavy-handed manner and had refused to recognise the results of sweeping election gains for the Liberal opposition in 1829. In desperation, Charles issued the Ordinances of St Cloud, which sparked a revolution in the French capital in July 1830. Critics of the system in Britain argued that if the French monarchy had fallen due to a failure to recognise genuine popular electoral grievances, then surely the potential existed in Britain for the same to happen.

Why did the death of George IV help reform?

The death of the reigning monarch in England, in June 1830, raised reform expectations even higher. George IV had not only been, arguably, the country's most unpopular monarch, but was also a staunch opponent of Roman Catholic emancipation and electoral reform. Under the Tories, he had never had to face the prospect of agreeing to the issue of reform, but was forced to agree to demands for emancipation just before his death. The new king, his brother William IV, although not a reforming enthusiast, was sufficiently realistic to appreciate the need to remedy some of the worst excesses of the existing system. Fortunately for the Whigs, the tide of popular opinion was definitely in their favour and the accession of a new monarch required a new election. Pro-reform candidates did well. The existing Tory Prime Minister was forced out of office and a new Whig ministry, under Earl Grey, was created in November 1830.

What do you regard as the most important reason for making parliamentary reform a major political issue between 1830 and 1832? Give reasons to support your answer.

The importance of a political alliance between the middle class and working class

A closer relationship was forged between the middle and working classes between 1829 and 1832. The main catalyst for this was Thomas Attwood, a Birmingham banker who formed the General Political Union to agitate for reform. This 'pressure group' organisation was very successful in raising the profile of the reform issue through rallies and petitions. Its success was assured by its emphasis on peaceful protest. The main aim of cautious reformers like Grey was to try to split this alliance and convince the middle-class elements that their future was assured by support for moderate reform.

6.3 What were the main features of the Reform Crisis between 1830 and 1832?

When Wellington was forced to resign in November 1830, the Whigs, under Earl Grey, were asked to form a government. The country was in no mood for compromise and reform was to be the key political issue. Grey, given the political and economic climate, felt he had to tackle the reform issue. As he said, 'We did not cause the excitement about reform. We found it in full vigour when we came to office.' Indeed, the Whigs were keen to avoid a worse scenario – namely the breakdown of law and order, and revolution.

The question facing the new government was how to find a balance between preserving the traditional system and securing social peace and public order. Grey's instructions to the four-man committee, whose job it was to frame the Bill, summarised his attitude:

> 'A reform of such scope and description as to satisfy all reasonable demands and remove at once, and forever, all rational grounds for complaint from the minds of the intelligent and independent portion of the community.'

In March 1831, Lord John Russell introduced the Bill to the House of Commons amid popular excitement in the country at large. It took 15 months before the Bill was finally passed and illustrated the extent of Tory opposition to it, especially in the House of Lords.

Why was the first Reform Bill defeated?

The first Reform Bill, introduced by Russell, aimed to redistribute 100 rotten and pocket boroughs and give seats to the industrial North and Midlands. Generally, the Commons was alarmed at the proposals, which also included a £10 qualification for voting rights in the boroughs. There had been some discussion on the introduction of a secret ballot, but this was dropped after pressure by members of the aristocracy. Thomas Attwood and the political union welcomed the proposals because they would retain the alliance between the middle and working classes. However, some working-class activists had already seen that the property qualification would mean that most of the working class would not receive the vote.

Referendum: A vote in which the people in a country or area are asked to say whether they agree or disagree with a particular policy.

The first Bill managed to pass its second reading in the Commons by one vote, but was defeated in the committee stage. Grey took the initiative and called a general election in April 1831, which became a national **referendum** on the issue of reform. The result was a triumph for Grey. Although the Tories held on to some of the rotten boroughs, the Whigs increased their support in the counties and were returned with a majority of 130. Grey took this as a signal to proceed with his reform plans and a second bill was duly drawn up.

How does a Bill become an Act?

In Parliament there are different types of legislation:

A Private Bill: This is a proposal for legislation usually put forward by a private individual or company for a specific purpose. For instance, Acts of Parliament permitting the construction of specific turnpike roads, canals and railways began as private bills.

A Private Member's Bill: This is a proposal for legislation put forward by a Member of Parliament who is not a member of the government. The Merchant Shipping Act, 1875, began life as a private member's bill put forward by the MP for Derby, Samuel Plimsoll.

A Public Bill: This is a proposal for reform put forward by the government.

Private Member's Bills and Public Bills follow the same process. They can be introduced either into the House of Commons or the House of Lords.

First reading: an announcement to the House that a proposal for reform will be considered in the near future.

Second reading: the stage when the principle of the proposal is debated and voted on. If defeated in a vote, the proposal is withdrawn.

The Committee stage: the House appoints a committee of members who study the proposal in detail. Amendments and alterations to the proposal can be made at this stage. Once scrutiny of the proposal has been concluded, the Bill is sent back to the full House. This is the most important stage of the process.

Report Stage: the Bill is then reported back to the House where it can be debated and alterations proposed by the whole House.

Third reading: the amended Bill is then 'read' before being sent to the other House of Parliament where it goes through the same procedure. Up to 1911 the House of Lords had the right to veto (reject) Bills proposed by the House of Commons.

Royal assent: once the bill has passed all its stages in the two Houses of Parliament, the monarch must then sign it before it can become law. Technically, the monarch can veto a Bill by not signing it. The last monarch to do so was Queen Anne in 1703 with the Scottish Militia Bill.

Why did the defeat of the second Reform Bill have serious consequences?

A slightly amended Bill was introduced in the summer of 1831 and by September had passed through the Commons and committee stages relatively unscathed, before reaching the House of Lords. The Lords, at this time, was dominated by Tory peers, who were opposed to the idea of changing the electoral system. They regarded the Bill as the first taste of democracy, equating reform of the lower house (the Commons) as a prelude to changes in the upper house (the Lords). Grey, however, realised that if any Bill was to become law it had to pass successfully through the Lords. As their Lordships possessed an absolute veto on any government bill, however large the majority in the Commons, it was obvious that the second measure was destined for the same fate as its predecessor. In October, the Bill was duly defeated by 41 votes.

The introduction of the third Bill, December 1831

The third measure was presented to Parliament in December 1831. By this time, the Whigs' Commons majority had risen to 162, but more importantly the anti-reformers in the Lords now only had a majority of nine. This could only realistically be overcome if William IV were willing to agree to the creation of Whig peers in the upper house to neutralise the Tory influence. It looked as if the Bill would pass relatively easily through the Commons, but it was surprisingly defeated in the committee stage by a Tory amendment in March 1832.

This had the possibility of weakening the Bill, but Grey pressed on only too aware that the creation of new peers was unavoidable. However, he did so rather reluctantly, claiming at the time 'I wish to God it could be avoided'. The King refused to accept Grey's demands because of the many constitutional implications. Almost immediately, in May 1832, Grey resigned.

Why was the 'May Days' crisis of 1832 important?

The country was once again plunged into the depths of potential catastrophe. The King had no alternative but to approach the Duke of Wellington to try to form a Tory ministry. The Duke's opinions on reform were well known and if any reform was passed the public knew it would be severely diluted. The public outcry reached revolutionary intensity once again. Mass demonstrations were organised in Birmingham by the National Union, under Thomas Attwood. In London, Francis Place's political union urged a **run on the banks**, refusal to pay taxes and a proposed takeover of local government. 'To stop the Duke, go for gold' was the rallying cry as strikes and demonstrations gripped the country once again.

Run on the banks: Francis Place encouraged people to close down their bank accounts. As banks keep only a fraction of deposits in the form of cash, such a policy could cause banks to collapse through an inability to meet their debts.

In the event, Wellington's attempts to form a government proved useless. William IV was now prepared to agree to the creation of the new peers to solve a major constitutional crisis. Accordingly, the King asked Grey to form a ministry four days later. Under the most severe public pressure, the anti-reform stance collapsed completely and the threat of the creation of the new peers was enough to convince the Lords they had to give way. Most Tory peers abstained and the Bill was passed on its third reading, by 106 to 22. On 7 June 1832, the Bill received royal approval.

Why do you think it was so difficult to pass the Reform Act of 1832?

6.4 Was Britain on the brink of revolution in 1830–1832?

A CASE STUDY IN HISTORICAL INTERPRETATION

It is usually the case that revolutions occur when political change fails to respond to economic distress. Criticism of any unpopular regime usually has an economic motive, and this was certainly the case in Britain in 1830. The mounting pressure to change an unrepresentative electoral system was given further impetus by a sharp deterioration in the economy.

The crisis was caused by harvest failure, high prices and unemployment that fell most heavily on the agricultural sector and was restricted geographically to the south of the country. The rural unrest started in the summer of 1830, and has been described by the historian Asa Briggs as the 'village labourers' revolt'. The unrest took on many different forms, such as the destruction of threshing machines and the burning of corn. It also had a political slant, expressed in hatred towards tithes and the administration of the **Poor Law**. Gaining momentum through the made-up name of 'Captain Swing', these so-called 'swing riots' lasted for over a year and alarmed the landowners who had always regarded the south-east of England as the most loyal part of the country.

Poor Law: This related to the support of paupers in the community, especially when there was no concept of a welfare state as we have today. Before 1834, each parish was responsible for its own poor. However, after the 1834 Poor Law Amendment Act the system became much harsher.

Magistrates: Officials who act as judges in law courts which deal with less serious crimes or disputes. They decide whether cases are important enough to be passed on to higher courts.

The Whig Government was in no mood to compromise, and dealt with the unrest swiftly and decisively. Lord Melbourne, the Home Secretary, urged **magistrates** to take a hard line: special courts were established to deal with the rioters and, in September 1830, nine labourers were hanged and many more transported abroad. These disturbances were not an attempt to incite a national revolution and many issues were localised and dealt with effectively by the authorities. They were, however, a sharp reminder to those in charge at Westminster that the country could not tolerate any more delay over the main political issues of the day.

The case for

Was this situation the most serious threat a government has had to face in Britain in peacetime? The political crisis over electoral reform created an almost revolutionary climate in Britain in 1830–32. The defeat of the Second Reform Bill by the Lords, in October 1831, caused widespread unrest. The historian E.P. Thompson claims that 'Britain came within an ace of revolution between 1830 and 1832'. There is no doubt that, in the autumn of 1831, this comment may well have been most applicable. Eric Evans suggests that 'Britain was never as close to revolution as in the autumn of 1831'. The public's high expectations had been badly let down by the Lords who were regarded as being completely out of touch with the people's wishes. This defiant gesture by a small grouping provoked an immediate outburst all over the country.

As well as pressure from the Birmingham Political Union, Francis Place made London the centre of opposition to the Lords but not the Whig Government. Elsewhere, there were violent protests throughout the country. Many members of the Lords identified with anti-reform, such as the Duke of Wellington and the Duke of Cumberland, were attacked as mob rule threatened to overrun the country. Furthermore, some Anglican bishops came under attack for their decision to vote against the Bill. Riots spread from the capital and large-scale incidents occurred in Derby and Nottingham. The most serious rioting occurred in Bristol on 29 October, when a violent mob attacked the city centre in what can only be described as a serious breach of public order. The only thing that prevented full-scale revolution at this stage was the Government's desire to proceed with reform. The Whig Government decided not to resign at this very tense time but to carry on with their reform proposals and attempt to direct violent protest into 'safe and legitimate reform'.

The May Days crisis of 1832 again saw the public anger for reform reach the intensity of the previous autumn. Demonstrations in London and Birmingham were especially critical of Wellington's refusal to entertain the idea of reform, but thankfully the Lords gave way and the tension diffused itself.

The case against

The Whig determination to proceed with reform regardless of the public opposition of the Tories and the King must be regarded as the most important reason. Earl Grey was enough of a politician to realise that the defeat of the first two Bills and the public disturbances that followed would increase the desire to proceed with reform. Public opinion was something that he was acutely aware of, but as always his intention was 'reforming to preserve' rather than letting the floodgates open to democracy.

1. Using the evidence, choose two reasons for and against the view that Britain was on the brink of revolution between 1830 and 1832.

2. Using material for both this and previous chapters, why do you think the period 1830–1832 was such a difficult situation for the Whig Government?

The decision in May 1832 to allow the Third Bill through the Lords was a momentous one. The upper house had been a constant brake on any change but their decision to absent themselves deserves some praise, even though they only agreed to the measure because they feared for their own position within the constitution if the disturbances had continued. Moderate reform was more of a safeguard of their position than violent revolution.

The violence of the period also proved too much for the fragile alliance between the middle and working classes. Once the terms of the Act became clear, the artisans under Attwood signified their disapproval of the more radical elements of the working classes. This split in the reform movement made the potential for armed revolution much easier to control. The disappointment of the radicals would be much more acute when the terms were finally approved in the summer of 1832.

6.5 How far did the Reform Act change the electoral system?

The main changes brought about by the 1832 Reform Act can be summarised as follows:

- The same number of seats was retained, at 658.
- 56 boroughs of fewer than 2,000 votes in England were totally disenfranchised.
- 31 small boroughs lost one of their two MPs.
- 22 new two-member constituencies were created (for example, Manchester, Leeds and Birmingham).
- In addition, 20 new single-member constituencies were created.
- Representation of the counties was increased by 61 members to a total of 253.
- Uniform property qualification of £10 in boroughs.
- Scottish electorate increased substantially to 65,000, while Ireland had three times the population of Scotland but less than twice the representation.
- New electorate totalling approximately 813,000 out of a population of 24 million (less than 500,000 before 1832). Electorate increased substantially but still only a small percentage of the population. Now about one in seven males could vote.

- All voters to enlist to qualify for the vote.
- No secret ballot. Landlord intimidation could still occur.

What were Whig motives in passing the reform?

Grey was speaking the truth when he talked of the Bill as an aristocratic measure that was designed primarily to safeguard the country against revolution. As the historian E.A. Smith claims, 'Grey presented reform as a means to restore the old constitution, not to create a new democratic one'. Although the Whigs had on the face of it changed the political map forever, their achievement was limited and would be in need of severe modification at a later date, notably in 1867 and 1884.

How did the electoral changes affect the middle class?

One of the major changes was the enfranchisement of the 'respectable classes' (i.e. those that qualified for the uniform £10 householder franchise). These included small-scale businessmen, shopkeepers and some skilled craftsmen. This had the desired effect of splitting the alliance between the middle classes and the working class.

Contemporary middle-class newspapers such as the *Leeds Mercury* and the *Manchester Guardian* received the news of reform with 'strong emotions of joy and hope'. Yet there was no immediate influx of middle-class MPs into Parliament, as local politics were seen to be far more rewarding than the laborious tasks of central government.

Moreover, most middle-class gentlemen simply could not afford the cost of being a Member of Parliament. There was no salary, and with Parliament sitting for most of the year it was seen as a full-time job. The composition of Parliament, therefore, remained largely unaltered from what it had been before 1832. The aristocracy continued to exert an enormous influence on events at Westminster long after the Act was passed.

Why did the working class feel betrayed by the terms of the Act?

The *Poor Man's Guardian*, a mouthpiece of radicalism, was correct when it claimed in 1832, 'the millions will not stop at shadows but proceed onwards to realities'. The working-class sense of betrayal was deepened by the terms of the 1832 Reform Act. The Whigs made no attempt to deny that the £10 test was designed to exclude the lower classes from the vote. As the National Union of the Working Classes claimed, 'the Bill is a mere trick to strengthen the towering exclusiveness of our blessed constitution'. This sense of disappointment could only lead to demands for further reform and, towards the end of the decade, the Chartist movement was born from the ashes of the Reform Act.

How did reform affect the House of Commons and the Lords?

The profile of the House of Commons, the representative element in the constitution, was strengthened as a result of reform. The crisis revealed the power a determined government possessed, especially when armed with a majority in the Commons and backed by public opinion, to overcome the opposition of nobility and monarchy. As far as the House of Lords was concerned, the abolition of the nomination boroughs (pocket boroughs) reduced the scope for exercising their patronage in choosing representatives in the Commons.

Even so, this over-estimates the impact of the Act on Parliament. The aristocracy and landowning classes continued to have a strong and influential role in affairs. For example, up until 1858 county members had to possess a landed estate of £600. As Robert Stewart claims, in *Party and Politics 1830–52* (1989), 'politics was a money-spending, not a money-making, occupation'. It has been calculated that only 52.5% of elections were actually contested between 1832 and 1867, and the opportunities for corruption may even have increased. Grey's refusal to entertain the idea of a secret ballot meant intimidation still occurred at elections – whole estates being coerced into voting for their landlord.

Why did the Crown's influence decline as a result of the Act?

The Act severely restricted the power the Crown had in influencing events at Westminster. Rotten and pocket boroughs had been a powerful source of royal patronage in the Commons. In addition, the crisis revealed the failure of the monarchy to deliver a majority in Parliament at a time of crisis – William IV was forced to rely on Grey after Wellington's failure to form a ministry in May 1832. Put simply, a ministry could now survive without the support of the Crown and Lords but not without the support of the Commons.

How did the Act promote more effective party organisation?

The reform crisis and the terms of the Act increased the possibility of a two-party system. The Act made provisions for the registration of voters who had to enrol to qualify for, and satisfy, the £10 property qualification. The result was that both Whigs and Tories had to organise themselves on a national basis and be acutely aware of public opinion by way of local party managers. The establishment of the Tory Carlton Club (1832) and the Whig Reform Club (1836) was a further impetus to this trend. Scotland, Wales and Ireland increased their representation, and any contested election in these countries tended to be won by the Whigs, who gradually built up their influence outside the southern counties. Even so, the influence of independent MPs continued to be considerable and in many constituencies local, rather than national, issues tended to dominate.

?

1. What do you regard as the most important consequence of the 1832 Reform Act?

2. Which groups were most pleased and most disappointed by these changes? Give reasons to support your answer.

Why did the 1832 Reform Act lead to demand for future changes?

Perhaps the most important consequence of the 1832 Reform Act was that it prepared the way for further political, social and economic change. It was the first and most important assault on the 18th-century constitution and the starting point on the road to democracy, even though that was not the intention of those who sponsored the Act. The Whigs had regarded it as a final settlement but the trickle of electoral reform eventually became a flood in 1867 and 1884. As historian John Derry claims, 'Earl Grey's Reform was conservative in the best sense of the word as it prepared the way for a century of peaceful political evolution.'

Source-based questions: Great Reform Act 1832

SOURCE A

Such, generally speaking, as the House of Commons is now, such it has been for a long succession of years: it is the most complete representation of the interests of the people, which was ever assembled in any age or any country. It is the only constituent body that ever existed, which comprehends within itself those who can urge the wants and defend the claims of the landed, the commercial, the professional classes of the country: those who are bound to uphold the interests of the lower classes, the rights and liberties of the whole people. It is the very absence of symmetry* in our elective franchises which admits of the introduction to this House of classes so various.

* symmetry = common rights to vote

From a speech by Sir Robert Inglis to the House of Commons, March 1831. Sir Robert Inglis was a strong opponent of reform.

SOURCE B

A criticism of the Pre-Reform Parliament by Cruikshank, 1831. Cruikshank was a leading cartoonist and savage critic of the existing system. The date is important bearing in mind how close it was to the passage of the Reform Act in 1832. 'St Stephens' refers to the House of Commons and the people around the trough are the recipients of the money and corruption from the closed or rotten boroughs (listed on the waterwheel). The whole system is propped up by muskets which suggest it can only be defended forcibly. Sleeping below 'St Stephens' are people unaware of the situation, preferring to sleep through rather than challenge obvious corruption and waste of public money.

SOURCE C

The end of government is the happiness of the people; and I do not conceive that, in a country like this, the happiness of the people can be promoted by a form of government in which the middle classes place no confidence, and which exists only because the middle classes have no organ by which to make their sentiments known.

A speech in the House of Commons, March 1831, by T.B. McCauley, a Whig MP who supported the idea of limited reform.

SOURCE D

27 Feb. Anything which amounts to the formation of a new Constitution I oppose …

2 March We are quite appalled. There is not the remotest chance of such a Bill being passed by this or any House of Commons … This really is a revolution … It is unquestionably a new constitution. The general sentiment is that the measure goes a good deal too far. It is applauded by the Radicals and by some Whigs, but it is very distasteful to a great part of the Whig Party.

3 March The general belief is that the Bill must be thrown out on the second reading. I expect Ministers will then resign and anarchy begin … I feel inclined as a choice of evils to support and even speak out in favour of the Bill.

5 March The measure takes very much with the country.

8 March I still consider the Bill dangerously violent, but apprehend less danger from passing it than rejecting it.

27 March The *chance* of the Bill being carried by the present Parliament is the certainty that it would be carried by the new parliament.

From the diary of John Campbell, 1831. Campbell was a moderate Whig; he was unaware that some modification of the system was needed.

Source-based questions: Great Reform Act 1832

1. Study Source D.

What is meant by 'second reading' in the passage of the 1832 Reform Act?

2. Study Source C.

How reliable is this source as evidence of support for the reform of Parliament?

3. Study Sources B and D.

How far do these sources agree on the weaknesses of Parliament before the passage of the 1832 Reform Act?

4. Study Sources C and D.

How, by use of language and style, do both authors suggest that the reform of Parliament was needed?

5. 'The pressures for the reform of Parliament were both widespread and inevitable.' Using the sources and the rest of this chapter, how far do you agree with this statement?

7 The Whigs, 1833–1841

Key Issues

- *Why was there a need for social and economic reform in the 1830s?*
- *How successful were the Whigs' reforms?*
- *Why did the Whigs fall from power?*

Framework of Events

1830–34	Earl Grey, Prime Minister
1833	Abolition of slavery within the British Empire Althorp's Factory Act First Government Grant for Education
1834	Irish Church Reform Act; Poor Law Amendment Act Earl Grey resigns and Lord Melbourne becomes Prime Minister King William IV dismisses Lord Melbourne over Irish Church reform
1834–35	Peel made Prime Minister of a minority Tory/Conservative government
1835	The Municipal Corporations Act Peel's Ecclesiastical Commission Catholics made magistrates in Ireland; Orange Order suppressed February: Lichfield House Compact April: General Election results in a new Whig government under Lord Melbourne
1836	Marriage Act allowing Nonconformists to be married in their own chapels Tithe Act; Limited Liabilities Company Act The Established Church Act improves the size of dioceses Central Registry of Births, Deaths and Marriages
1837	General Election results in a Whig victory, but with a reduced majority
1838	Pluralities Act relating to the Church of England prohibits more than two livings held by a clergyman
1839	Penny Post legislation announced; passed a year later 'Bedchamber Crisis'
1840	Irish Municipal Reform Act
1841	Defeat in General Election; Peel made Prime Minister of a new Conservative government.

Overview

Benthamites: Followers of Jeremy Bentham who argued that the test of any successful government was its desire to promote 'the greatest happiness of the greatest number'. Many of the Whig reforms were based on this philosophy. (See also 'utilitarian' on page 55.)

Humanitarians: Those members of society who had a genuine interest in improving the welfare of the lower orders. Humanitarian pressure led to the abolition of the slave trade in the British Empire in 1833 and to Althorp's Factory Act of the same year.

Lichfield House Compact: A semi-official alliance agreed in February 1835 between the Whigs, O'Connell's Irish Party and the Radicals. Its purpose was to bring down Peel's minority Tory/Conservative Government and it succeeded in April 1835.

THE Whig period of government between 1830 and 1841 produced much remarkable legislation. The demand for reform came from a number of sources, such as the **Benthamites** and **Humanitarians**, who for a variety of reasons attempted to convince the Whigs that something should be done about known abuses of society in the factories, towns and slavery in the Empire. The controversy is: were the Whigs actually responsible for what happened or were they the prisoners of other people's ideas?

The reforms passed by the Government amount to an impressive package of genuine attempts to counter distress and to improve living standards. The abolition of slavery within the British Empire in 1833 and the reorganisation of town government in the Municipal Corporations Act of 1835 are especially worthy of mention. On the other hand, there was much that was neglected and the reforming initiative was half-baked in certain areas. The Factory Act of 1833 failed to solve the problem of long working hours and the use of child labour in the factories, while the Poor Law Amendment Act of 1834 was used to tighten the system of welfare, leaving those unable to help themselves arguably worse off than before.

There is a clear dividing line after 1835. Prior to that date, the Whigs attempted an ambitious reform programme that aimed to change many elements of society through the direct involvement of the State. The defeat of Peel's minority Tory/Conservative government as a result of the **Lichfield House Compact** led to a new Whig Administration in 1835. The premiership of Lord Melbourne (1835–41) was less spectacular and less energetic.

By 1841, the Whigs had lost their reforming zeal and initiative. They were accused of being manipulated by the Irish party at Westminster, led by Daniel O'Connell. The working class, although unable to vote, had meanwhile found a sense of purpose under the banner of Chartism. Ultimately, the real reason why the Whigs lost the election was that the resurgent Conservatives under Sir Robert Peel had more energy and vitality.

7.1 What were the pressures for reform in 1833?

The Whigs

The 1832 Reform Act showed that peaceful change could be forced on Parliament. It opened the way for a series of reforms that attempted to change the way in which society was run. Historians have argued over the motivation behind these reforms, but there is no doubt that the majority of the Whig Government – firstly under Grey up to 1834 and under Lord Melbourne thereafter – continued to see change as being piecemeal and pragmatic. The 1832 Reform Act was regarded by the Whigs as a final settlement of constitution and was done to preserve, rather than revolutionise, the situation. The reforms that followed must be seen in the same context – they were crumbs from a rich man's table rather than a genuine attempt to reorganise society.

There were a number of genuine Whig radicals, such as Henry Brougham and John Durham, who did not appear in Melbourne's more reactionary ministry after 1835. The Whig motivation for reform came from a belief that the duty of government brought a responsibility to try to improve social problems but, in turn, government expected a certain degree of respect and gratitude. The Whigs had a strong sense of 'reforming to preserve', so a small amount of social change was preferable to the avalanche of revolution. Indeed, as party political lines and organisation became clearer, there is a view that suggests the reforms were openly pro-Whig: the reorganisation of the **municipal corporations** in 1835 being an obvious attack on the Tory stranglehold in this particular area.

Municipal corporations: These were the equivalent of modern-day town councils. They were in need of reform as the councillors were regarded as being corrupt and unaccountable. The Whigs also realised that the municipal corporations were a Tory/Conservative stronghold.

The Whigs, therefore, were reluctant reformers whose public duty required minor reform of obvious abuses but not enough to change the basic features of society or upset their influential supporters in business. What is surprising and ultimately to their discredit is that they knew there were many weaknesses apparent in society at this time, but refused to take advantage of a golden opportunity they had created for themselves. So, by 1841, little or nothing had been done to stop exploitation in the mines, to give one example. If the pressure for reform did not come from the Whigs, who else played a key role?

The Utilitarians/Benthamites

The major force behind the implementation of the reforms of the 1830s was a broad group of politicians, administrators and theorists whose main test of any government was its accountability and efficiency. The maxim 'the greatest happiness of the greatest number' had been coined by the father of utilitarianism, Jeremy Bentham. Benthamites exerted a considerable amount of pressure on the Whig Government to improve the efficiency of government institutions such as the Poor Law, municipal corporations and factory conditions.

Their main administrative innovation was the use of **commissions** and reports to investigate social issues. All the major pieces of legislation mentioned above were anticipated by commissions of investigation and a scientific test was used to measure efficiency. Most of the Whig legislation of the 1830s had a utilitarian undercurrent running through it, the classic example being the New Poor Law of 1834 designed primarily to improve the efficiency of dealing with those in society unable to look after themselves. It would, however, be a mistake to regard the Utilitarians as democrats: they were not. Their prime aim was not to improve the welfare of the working classes but if it happened as a consequence of their reforms they were willing to accept it.

Commissions: Bodies set up by the Whig Government at this time to investigate the idea of change. They were a useful introduction, taking evidence from all classes, and their recommendations became the basis of government policy. Commissions were a favoured tactic of the Utilitarians.

Leading Utilitarians such as Edwin Chadwick (see page 127) and Joseph Parkes were to be found on many of the commissions set up by the Government. There is no question that this influential grouping did have a major impact on the Whig Government in the 1830s.

Robert Owen (1771–1858)
Born in Newtown, South Wales, Owen is famous for the efficient and humanitarian way he ran his factories at New Lanark in Scotland. He proved that better working conditions and shorter hours, combined with good housing and regular education, actually increased rather than decreased production. Owen was also a leading light in the trade union movement and in 1833 founded the Grand National Consolidated Trades Union at the time that the Whig Government was trying to undermine their influence. Not surprisingly, Owen became associated with the Chartist movement but abandoned it after the violence of 1839 and 1842.

The Humanitarians

The Humanitarians were a cross-party group of individuals committed to the improvement of working conditions, especially in the mines and factories. By the 1830s, the full scale of industrialisation had produced horrific working conditions, especially in the textile industries. The Humanitarians demanded basic human rights, such as a maximum ten-hour day for adults and severe penalties for those employers who attempted to exploit children in the workplace. Tories such as Lord Ashley and Sadler could be found alongside known radicals and the future Chartist leader Feargus O'Connor in a concentrated effort to improve the dignity of the oppressed. The model for factories was that run by the Welsh socialist Robert Owen at New Lanark, Scotland. Owen proved that a safe working environment encouraged rather than reduced efficiency and a contented workforce meant a more productive one.

Evangelical movement: The religious revival initiated in the Church of England in the 1830s/1840s to raise spiritual awareness and aiming to win support away from Nonconformist churches.

1. What was the most important influence affecting Whig policy in the 1830s? Give reasons to support your answer.

2. Did these different groupings have a genuine desire to help the poor or were they keen to improve the efficiency of government?

Evangelicals

Closely connected to the humanitarian movement were the Evangelicals. They took a religious and moral interest in social improvement and change. The leading light in the **Evangelical movement** was William Wilberforce, a Tory by political persuasion but with a deep social conscience and a passionate desire to abolish slavery. He drew support across party lines because of the moral certainty of his cause.

That the Whig Government chose to be influenced by these various pressure groups can be interpreted in two ways. On the one hand, that it was the sign of a weak government which was being dictated to by external forces rather than initiating these reforms on its own. This can be used as evidence that the Whigs were cautious reformers who lacked the imagination and creativity to instigate the reforms themselves. On the other hand, the existence of these organisations also shows that the Whigs were willing to listen to advice. The Utilitarians were especially useful as their reports and commissions could be the basis for government policy even if all the groundwork had been completed for the Government by an external body.

7.2 How significant were the reforms on slavery, factory conditions and education?

William Wilberforce (1759–1833)
Entered Parliament in 1780. His Bill for the abolition of the slave trade was passed in 1807. Then, largely through his efforts, slavery was abolished in the British Empire in 1833.

The abolition of slavery in the British Empire, 1833

The Whigs' first major assault on the notion of inequality was the abolition of slavery in the British Empire in 1833. This was the logical step after the abolition of the slave trade in 1807. The main terms of the Act included the freeing of all slaves, although they had to serve an apprenticeship of up to seven years to their former owners. In addition, the Government agreed to pay £20 million to the slave owners in compensation. Although the Whig Colonial Secretary, Lord Stanley, introduced the Emancipation Bill, there is no doubt that the main motivation came from William Wilberforce, a leading Evangelical who had spent his life campaigning against slavery. The obvious attractiveness of the Bill from a humanitarian viewpoint is hardly in doubt, but the Whigs came under criticism from a variety of groups who used self-interest as a convenient way to ignore obvious humanitarian abuses.

There was widespread criticism from those involved in slavery and foreign plantations, such as the port of Liverpool, which lost out as a result of the Act. Abroad, especially in the West Indies, there was a feeling of betrayal and there is no doubt that the 1833 Act pushed up labour costs as former slaves gained their freedom. In the West Indies, the local economy was so heavily reliant on slavery that it experienced a deep recession as a result. In South Africa, the white Boer settlers saw the Act as an attempt to jeopardise their livelihood. They used it as an excuse to move inland in the Great Trek of 1835 to found their own Boer republics free from British control.

Lord Althorp's Factory Act, 1833

If the abolition of slavery was regarded as a moral evil in an international context, then the system of 'industrial slavery' practised in many British factories was a moral evil on the Whigs' own doorstep. The working

Edwin Chadwick (1800–1895)
Born in Manchester in 1800, Chadwick was mostly responsible for drawing up the New Poor Law in 1834. Heavily influenced by Benthamite ideas, Chadwick proved to be an able administrator and was also involved in investigating the condition of public health. His 1842 Report on the Sanitary Condition of the Labouring Poor in 1842 proved to be an important milestone.

conditions in the new industrialised factories were truly appalling. Both adults and children were forced to work long hours in extremely dangerous conditions without any insurance or rights.

The situation had been critical for years. Politicians of all persuasions knew that the system had to be changed, but had little idea how. The real force for change was Lord Ashley (later the Earl of Shaftesbury), another leading Evangelical. Pressure also came from Edwin Chadwick, who called for a royal commission into the conditions of the factories. The commission's recommendations provided the basis of the 1842 Report on the Sanitary Condition of the Labouring Poor. Critics argued that it was heavily weighted in favour of the employers above the wishes of the employees.

Main terms of the Act proposed by Lord Althorp, the Whig Chancellor, in August 1833:

- No child under the age of 9 could be employed in a factory.
- Those children between the ages of 9 and 13 were restricted to an 8-hour day, two of which had to be given to education.
- Older children were restricted to a 12-hour day.
- Four permanent inspectors were appointed to oversee implementation.

Critics also argued that the whole operation was a cosmetic exercise which merely tinkered with the worst excesses of the factory system. Employers ingeniously overcame the major clauses by operating a shift system, which ensured that most adults still worked a 12-hour day. The provision for education, like the appointment of four permanent commissioners, was a good idea in theory, but in practice was totally unmanageable. There were only four commissioners for the whole country and only one for the North of England where new factories were located. Parents used the lack of certification to lie about the ages of their children because their income was vital to any family living on or below the poverty line. In addition, it was generally assumed that the major terms of the Act related almost exclusively to the textile industry and no mention was made of extending the practice to other industries.

However, there is a danger of viewing the Act only from a late 20th-century perspective. The Whigs knew that too much factory legislation could have severe implications for the economy and would lead to a possible reduction in output. It was a sad fact of life that children, at this time, did make a crucial contribution to the workings of the economy and any change would have serious consequences. The Whig ministers were quick to admit that their legislation was never meant to be anything more than a starting point on the road to the removal of exploitation in the workplace.

Government Grant for Education, 1833

The Factory Act had ambitiously stated that those children between the ages of 9 and 13 should be educated for two hours during an eight-hour shift. The principle was welcomed but in reality parents refused to send their children to school if they were better employed in the factory or down the mine, adding to the family income. Today, the idea of state education is well established but, at this time, schooling was the responsibility of two bodies, both religiously inspired. The National Society was funded by the Church of England and the British and Foreign School Society by nonconformist groups. Both the

1. Study the two pictures. What are the major differences in the working conditions between the two sources?

2. 'Lord Althorp's Factory Act of 1833 had solved the problem of dangerous working conditions.' Using the sources and the information from the chapter, how far do you agree with this view?

'Children in a Cotton Factory', painting by T. Onwyn, 1840

Inside a cotton-spinning factory in Britain in the 1840s

1. In which of these areas do you think that Earl Grey's Government made the greatest impact?

2. Can any criticism be made of these reforms? Give reasons to support your answer.

Anglican and the nonconformist organisations received a small amount of money, mainly for the upkeep of school buildings. The initial government grant was £20,000 but this rose to £30,000 and was given by the newly created Education Department of the Privy Council by 1839. Yet again, it would be foolish to expect anything more than these meagre amounts when the idea of state education had yet to be established. Seen in a broader perspective, however, they can be viewed as a modest foundation stone from which more ambitious projects could develop – like many other areas of Whig policy.

7.3 *The New Poor Law of 1834: success or failure?*

A CASE STUDY IN HISTORICAL INTERPRETATION

Existing arrangements

In the late 20th century we take the existence of a modern welfare state as a fundamental right for citizens of a democracy. The situation, however, never evolved naturally and the system for helping the poor in Britain in the 19th century was a concept that had massive political implications. The original Elizabethan Poor Law Acts of 1597 and 1601 had made local parishes responsible for the wellbeing of their own poor, and all members of the parish who owned property contributed to what was known as the poor rate. Another Act in 1662 restricted the practice even further by stipulating that those unable to look after themselves could only receive relief in the parish of their birth. This obviously restricted the mobility of the poor if they wanted to claim relief. The able bodied and idle poor were subject to varying degrees of aid among the country's 15,000 parishes, where payments varied widely. By 1795, the whole system was under strain as unemployment rose.

An attempted solution was the Speenhamland system devised in 1795 (see page 43). Although restricted to central and southern England, it was the first real attempt to confront the challenges of the changing situation. Depending on the size of the family in question and the price of bread, relief payments were to be made from parish poor rates to add to the low wages the applicant already received. Employers realised the benefits of lowering wages because they knew that the outdoor relief would supplement their employees' income. For the first time, one could now work and receive **outdoor relief** in the form of cash payments, as long as you resided in the parish of your birth. Critics argued that the system encouraged idleness because the poor knew that there was always a safety net on which to fall back. This was assuming, of course, that the parish was organised enough to give out regular payments. It would have been to the disgust of those ratepayers who now had to pay ever-increasing amounts to make the system work. By 1830, it has been calculated that parishes were paying £8 million

Outdoor relief: This was the means by which each parish supplemented the low wages of those people eligible for poor relief from the parish poor rates. These payments depended on the size of the applicant's family and the price of bread at that time.

The proposals of the Poor Law Amendment Act 1834:

- Outdoor relief would no longer be provided for able-bodied poor, although in some cases to the infirm/elderly.
- There would be an expansion of the workhouse system for those unable to help themselves. Conditions in these 'Whig Bastilles' would be so unattractive that the poor would have to help themselves rather than enter a workhouse. This was known as the 'less eligibility' concept.
- Parishes would now be grouped into Poor Law Unions to create larger units. The intention was that each of the individual categories of poor (able-bodied, impotent and idle) would be given their own individual workhouse.
- Central control would be regulated through the establishment of a Poor Law Department in Somerset House, London. Three paid commissioners would regulate local provision, but local paid officials (Poor Law Guardians), elected by ratepayers, within each parish would help administer locally.

per annum just on the upkeep of the poor rate. It was obvious that the same new measures were needed primarily to save money on the rates, but also possibly to tackle the causes of poverty.

Edwin Chadwick was the secretary of the commission appointed to investigate the working of the Poor Law. It was expected that the Report would be highly critical of the present arrangements and would at least attempt to demand value for money for the ratepayer. The Report, published in February 1834, provided the basis for the New Poor Law of the same year. The terms were a commentary on what Chadwick and his colleagues described as a waste of ratepayers' money.

Did the Act improve matters?

The working classes and those poorer elements in society found the new terms even more difficult to contemplate than before. No attempt was made by the commissioners to tackle the causes of poverty as it was naturally assumed by them that the system would deter rather than encourage those people from falling on state relief. The abolition of outdoor relief caused much distress throughout the country, especially in industrial areas affected by unemployment. Had it not been for a series of productive harvests and the beginnings of the 'railway age', which tended to create jobs, then the whole situation would have been a lot worse. There is no denying that the Chartist movement drew heavily for its support from those disaffected by the Poor Law Amendment Act of 1834. There was a great deal of anti-poor law agitation, especially in the North of England. Even so, the implementation of the Act was mixed. Outdoor relief continued in many areas, and there were differences in the level of provision. The principle of separate workhouses was never applied rigorously.

Is it possible to defend such a harsh system? There is no doubt that, from the ratepayers' point of view, the Act was a success because the numbers of those in receipt of poor relief dropped dramatically after 1834 and the Act tried to remedy a system in need of reform. The workhouse did seem to deter the unemployed and the administrative apparatus it created paved the way for many significant social changes at a later date. Your viewpoint depends entirely on whether you look at the Act from the point of view of administrative efficiency or its effect on the poor.

The traditional view of the new Poor Law, as expressed by historians such as Elie Halévy, is that the Benthamites under Edwin Chadwick changed British society forever and that the new Poor Law was an important stepping stone in this process. In the 1960s, however, this view was challenged by Mark Blaug. Blaug argued that there was nothing wrong with the workings of the old Poor Law and that much of the evidence presented to the royal commission, of which Chadwick was secretary, had been manipulated. Opinions of the new Poor Law depend, as with so many of the other Whig reforms, on the interpretations of the intentions of those that drew it up. If you take the view that it saved the ratepayer money then you would applaud its achievements. If, on the other hand, you felt that it made the position of the working classes worse you would agree with one opinion that it was one of the most unfair laws of the 19th century.

1. What were the major terms of the New Poor Law of 1834?

2. How far was the New Poor Law a success? Give reasons to support your answer.

Source-based questions: The New Poor Law

SOURCE A

People who never could be made to work have become good labourers, and do not express any dissatisfaction with the measure. In most parishes the moral character of the poor is improving: there is a readiness to be more orderly and well-behaved … The great body of labouring poor throughout the Union have become reconciled to it; the workhouse is held in great dread; cases of bastardy are on the decline.

Report of the Market Harborough Union, 1836. This is a primary source, taken from a report from a Poor Law union newly established by the 1834 Act. Poor Law unions were larger units than the previous parish system and each contained separate work-houses for the able-bodied and idle poor. This is a particularly flattering picture of the work of the new bodies in Leicestershire.

SOURCE B

When the Commissioners went north in 1837 to apply the new act there, they were met by such violent and organised hostility that in many areas the principles of 1834 proved impossible to apply, and outdoor relief continued … Its threatened abolition was regarded as a piece of upper-class vindictiveness [spite] and greed.

A secondary source, taken from The Georgian Century: 1714–1837 *by S.E. Ayling, published in 1966.*

SOURCE C

A contemporary cartoon from Punch *magazine, 1843. The caption makes a play on the phrase 'the milk of human kindness'. In this case, any human kindness is absent; the Poor Law officials are hideously portrayed, one as the Devil. The angel is crying at the separation of a mother from her child at the gates of the dreaded workhouse.*

1. Study Source B and use information from this chapter.

What is meant by 'outdoor relief' in the context of the Poor Law?

2. Study Sources A and B.

How far are the authors of these sources in disagreement as to the effects of the Poor Law?

3. Study Source C.

How useful is this source to an historian in understanding the effects of the Poor Law?

4. 'The benefits of the New Poor Law were outweighed by its negative effects.' Using the sources and the information above, how far do you agree with this view?

7.4 To what extent did the Whig reforms bring major changes to British society?

The Municipal Corporations Act, 1835

The transformation of the borough electoral system in the 1832 Reform Act was seen by the Whigs as the starting point for further reforms in local government. Borough town government was both inefficient and unrepresentative. It was dominated by small groups who tended to elect themselves into positions of power on the town council. They paid lip-service to the idea of social care, and services such as water and public health were virtually ignored. Since unreformed boroughs were dominated by Tory members, the whole attack took on a political slant, but this was disguised in the interests of administrative efficiency. There is no doubt that this area of government needed reform and the Whigs took on the task enthusiastically. In 1833, a royal commission was set up to investigate the problem of municipal or town government. Its main figure was the Benthamite, Joseph Parkes. Known abuses were pinpointed and an Act, passed in September 1835, attempted to solve them.

- The idea of a secret borough was abolished – from now on, all borough councils were to be elected by all adult male ratepayers.
- Those sitting on the council were only to sit for three years – to ensure a healthy turnover, one-third of the councillors were elected on an annual basis.
- There was to be a paid town clerk, together with the idea that accounts should be regulated and scrutinised to avoid corruption.
- Each new council was given the option, but not compelled, to make social improvements.

The measures did help to make borough councils more representative and accountable. In many ways, they laid the foundation for elected local government. However, it was very much a middle-class affair as the Whigs ensured that the working classes were excluded from involvement by restricting the right to vote. Furthermore, the permissive nature of the social improvement requirement meant few councils used their powers to alleviate any of the social distress, public health difficulties and poverty that confronted towns in a new industrial age.

Reform in the Church of England

With many nonconformist supporters within their ranks, the attitude of Whigs to the established Church of England was less heavily influenced by the Anglican establishment than the Tories. Their proposals were quite drastic, amounting to a kind of reform bill for the Church. During Peel's Tory/Conservative ministry of 1834–35, a royal commission had been established to investigate the condition of the Church. When the Whigs returned to office in 1835 under Lord Melbourne, they were willing to implement its proposals.

Dioceses: Administrative units for the Church of England: for practical purposes the country was divided into dioceses, each with its own bishop.

The Established Church Act of 1836 improved the size of **dioceses** and created two new ones, in Manchester and Ripon. In addition, the Church of England gained a permanent body, the Ecclesiastical Commission, which was used to monitor future changes. In the same year, a Bill was introduced to transfer the payment of the hated tithes to a money payment, which was seen as less burdensome. Two years later, in 1838, the Pluralities Act was introduced. This aimed to end a known abuse among the clergy who

William Lamb, Lord Melbourne (1779–1848)
An aristocratic Whig, Melbourne was a member of the House of Commons until 1828 when he moved to the Lords on the death of his father. As Home Secretary, he repressed the Tolpuddle Martyrs but did not oppose the 1832 Reform Act. In 1834, Lord Melbourne became Prime Minister briefly, before being dismissed by the King over Irish Church reform. He became PM again in April 1835 and implemented a number of reforms. A tutor and mentor to the young Queen Victoria, Melbourne resigned in 1839 over the Jamaican constitution but soon returned after the 'Bedchamber crisis'. He was defeated in the 1841 general election by Sir Robert Peel. Melbourne left politics soon after suffering a strike.

worked in more than one parish in order to supplement their income but which resulted in a neglect of their duties and in corruption. The Act limited the number of parishes held by one person to no more than two, which had to be no more than 10 miles apart.

The reforms taken as a package constituted a commonsense response to known loop-holes in the system of church administration. They met with general approval.

Legislation to help nonconformists

Three important Acts were passed in 1836 to help the position of nonconformists in England.

The Marriage Act, 1836
This reform allowed Nonconformists and Roman Catholics to marry in their own churches provided they were properly licensed and a civil registrar was present. In the same year, a civil register of births, marriages and deaths was introduced, thereby breaking the Church of England's monopoly in such matters. The other main consequence of this was that the 1833 Factory Act could now be more strictly enforced, as proof of age could be presented to a potential employer. Also, the monopoly exerted by the Anglicans in university education was partially lifted when a charter was granted to London University as a non-sectarian university.

The Limited Liabilities Company Act, 1836
This reform encouraged investment by private investors through the idea of 'limited liability'. If such a company went bankrupt, the shareholders did not have to pay the full losses. In an age when railway building was increasing at a rapid rate, the measures were just the incentive the industry needed: by 1837, 1,500 kilometres of new track had been laid, and a year later the first railway connecting the new industrial centres of Birmingham and London was ready.

The introduction of the Penny Post, 1840
The postal service before 1840 had been haphazard and inefficient, primarily due to the time it took to transport the letter. Rowland Hill managed to convince the Government that the introduction of a penny stamp for a half-ounce (14g) letter would speed up the whole process dramatically. Hill proved to be correct and the benefits were immediate: the new system was far more efficient than the previous system. Much use was made of this in the Anti-Corn Law League's campaign up to 1846.

1. What were the major features of Lord Melbourne's reforms between 1835 and 1841?

2. 'For a party pledged to reform, the Whigs achieved little in the years 1835 to 1841.' How accurate is this view bearing in mind the reforms outlined above?

Evaluation of the reforms from 1833 to 1841

1 To their critics, the Whigs wasted a glorious opportunity to institute far-reaching social, political and administrative change: known abuses apparent when they took the reins of government in 1830 remained a focus for discontent a decade later. The impetus for change came not from the Whigs themselves, but from individuals such as Ashley, Oastler and Chadwick. The reforms were limited in that they were only prepared to go so far, the 1833 Factory Act being a classic example of this attitude. Indeed, the working classes felt little benefit from the regime; long working hours and the harshness of the new Poor Law offered ready-made propaganda for the new working-class movements such as Chartism. The Whigs' share of the seats in the House of Commons fell from 385 in the 1835 election to 345 in the election of 1837. This was surely a clear sign that the Whig reforms were not as popular with the electorate as they were claimed to be.

2 Yet, Whig supporters argue that the reforms must be seen in context. The

1830s were a momentous decade in terms of social reform, far greater than what had gone on before. The key was the adoption of Benthamite methods, namely the establishment of royal commissions, the appointment of inspectors and central control of finance. The abolition of slavery was an obvious triumph and the first steps on the road to measured state intervention in education and national and local government had been made. Some historians have gone so far as to claim that the reforms themselves amount to an administrative revolution.

7.5 How successfully did the Whigs deal with Irish problems?

Problems in Ireland were one of the major reasons why Wellington's Tory Government was brought down in 1830. The basic problems still remained: that a land-starved peasantry was forced to pay rents to landlords who were often absentee, Protestant *and* English. In addition, the Church of Ireland (the Anglican Church in Ireland) was maintained by these taxes (the tithe) in a country where the majority of the population was Roman Catholic. Thus, when Grey took office in 1830 the situation was already serious. It was made worse by the beginnings of a 'tithe war' a year later. The refusal to pay the tithe was a rejection of established authority. The campaign was brilliantly led by the 'uncrowned king of Ireland', Daniel O'Connell. He preached non-violence and, by 1832, had the support of 40 or so MPs at Westminster committed to the repeal of the Act of Union between Britain and Ireland.

In 1831, the Whig Government introduced a national system of elementary education for Ireland. The Government financed the establishment of a network of schools to provide non-denominational education for 5–11 year olds. Instruction was to be in English. Therefore, Ireland received a national network of elementary schools almost 40 years before England and Wales. In addition, these schools aided the rapid decline in the use of the Irish language during the 19th century.

In 1833, Edward Stanley, the Irish Secretary, introduced a Coercion Act which aimed to stamp out the unrest and to collect the vast arrears of unpaid tithes. The terms of the Act included the banning of meetings unless approved by the Government. Tactfully, the part of the strategy aimed at removing discontent centred on the reform of the Church of Ireland. The authorities calculated that there was too much bureaucracy and a Bill proposed the abolition of 10 dioceses. The hope was that a substantial amount of money would be saved annually – conservative estimates put the figure at around £150,000. The crucial question was what to do with this money? Irish radicals and English nonconformists wanted the money saved to be spent on improving the education and moral welfare of Irish Catholics. Stanley, and members of the Tory/Conservative opposition, wanted the money to go to the Church of Ireland to support clergy suffering as a result of the unpaid tithes. In the event, the Irish Church Temperalities Act (1834) was passed in a watered-down version, much to the disappointment of O'Connell and his supporters. This climbdown led to the resignation of Stanley. A dispute over the renewal of the Coercion Act finally forced Grey's resignation and led to a minority Tory/Conservative Government under Sir Robert Peel. Once again, the Irish issue had brought down the Government.

Where did this leave the Whigs? The new leader, Lord Melbourne, was no radical, nor any more of an enthusiastic supporter of the Irish cause than Grey. Yet he was enough of a realist to appreciate that in order to bring down Peel's Government he would have to cooperate with O'Connell and the radicals. This agreement of February 1835 was known as the Lichfield House Compact

Orange monopoly: The Orange Order was set up in 1795 to safeguard the interests of Irish Protestants, especially in the north of the country. During the Whig decade, all major administrative posts were in Orange/Protestant hands.

1. Which reforms do you regard as being the most successful? Give reasons to support your answer.

2. Why do you think the Whigs' Irish policies were unpopular with the Tory opposition in the period 1833–1841?

(see page 124). It succeeded in returning Lord Melbourne to office, in the same year. Critics argued that the Whigs were now under the control of radical and Irish MPs. Indeed, from 1835, O'Connell agreed to tone down demands for the repeal of the Act of Union. Many legislative initiatives concerning Ireland were vetoed as a result of strong opposition from the House of Lords. However, some advances were made: the **Orange monopoly** was questioned and Catholics made significant advances in the administration of Ireland, for example through the Irish Municipal Reform Act which was passed in 1840. In addition, the Poor Law was extended to Ireland in 1838 and O'Connell was appointed Lord Mayor of Dublin in 1841.

Although there was relative peace in Ireland during the period 1835–41, the Government was subjected to continuing hostile criticism from the Tories who accused the Whig regime of supporting Catholic interests in Ireland. This extract from *The Times* of 1837 was typical: 'Lord Melbourne, who has for these last two years and more been levying open war against, or trickily undermining, the ancient laws, the fundamental institutions, and the Protestant monarchy of Great Britain.' The Irish question would continue to loom large for the remainder of the century, as Robert Peel would find out in 1841–46.

7.6 Why did the Whigs fall from power in 1841?

In the election of July 1841, the Tories/Conservatives under Sir Robert Peel won a majority of seats in the House of Commons, by 367 to 291 against their Whig counterparts. The aim of this section is to ask: why?

A loss of reforming zeal after 1835?

There is a convenient dividing line in understanding the Whig decade in power. Under Earl Grey, the Whig Party seemed to have a definite plan for their reforming programme. Grey passed the Reform Act in 1832 essentially to preserve the main features of the Constitution. His other reforms, such as the Factory Act and the abolition of slavery, showed a reforming zeal that many admired regardless of their political affiliation. Grey's resignation and his replacement by Melbourne signalled a change of direction and a relaxation of the reforming programme. Melbourne had once claimed 'I am for holding the ground already taken but not for occupying new ground rashly' and the flood of reform became a trickle between 1835 and 1841. Important opportunities were lost to improve social conditions in the towns and to further improve working conditions in the factories. The issue of free trade was not resolved and, by 1841, critics argued that the Whigs had simply run out of ideas.

A public relations failure with the electorate?

The Whigs, both under Grey and Melbourne, failed to convince the public of the real effectiveness and meaning of their reform package. The agricultural depression of 1830–31, which resulted in the Swing Riots and severe legislation to punish the offenders, lost the Whigs much support. In addition, the transportation of the Tolpuddle Martyrs to Australia in 1834, for daring to set up their own trade union, lost the Whigs much sympathy – especially among the working classes. Despite their scientific approach to legislation, the Whigs failed to appreciate the causes of discontent. Under Lord Melbourne, the relationship with the Irish minority at Westminster under O'Connell brought allegations that the Whigs were merely in the pay of their masters across the Irish Sea. Also, the legislation after 1835 suggested a strong leaning towards the nonconformists which alienated much mainstream Anglican opinion and again supported the argument that the Whig agenda was not of their own making.

The rise in working-class unrest

There was a strong revival of working-class radicalism during the 1830s, which eventually found expression in Chartist protest, beginning in 1839. The failures of the Reform Act and the obvious unfairness of the new Poor Law in 1834 had convinced many in the working classes that the Whigs were just as bad as, if not worse than, the Tories. The sense of betrayal was deepened by the end of the decade as Britain had sunk into a serious economic crisis and the numbers receiving poor relief had climbed to crisis proportions. Squalor in the cities, inadequate public health arrangements and the threat of unemployment provided useful ammunition for those working-class leaders such as Feargus O'Connor.

The revival of the Conservatives under Robert Peel

When the Whigs had taken office in 1830, the Tory Party had been in complete disarray. They were split from top to bottom over the issue of Roman Catholic emancipation. It seems as if the party, clinging rigidly to its old aristocratic ideas, was destined to remain out of office for a long time. Yet, within a decade, Sir Robert Peel, the new leader of the Conservative Party (as it was now more often known) had transformed the party's image and profile. Peel attempted to broaden the basis of the new party's appeal by winning over the newly enfranchised middle classes, whilst still trying to retain many of the fundamental features of Toryism. The new Conservative philosophy was summarised by the election address Peel gave to the electors of Tamworth in December 1834, claiming that his party was now prepared for 'a careful review of institutions undertaken in a friendly temper, combining with the firm maintenance of established rights, the correction of proved abuses, and the redress of real grievances'. This 'Tamworth Manifesto' was the basis for the changes Peel made to the party in the 1830s.

1. Why had Melbourne's Government become so unpopular by 1841?

2. 'The defeat of the Whigs in 1841 was solely the result of their own mistakes.' How accurate is this view in your opinion?

In addition to a new policy direction, the Party was organised on a national basis and much credit here must be given to F.R. Bonham, the Party's election manager. The Conservatives actually held office under Peel for a brief period in 1834–35, and between 1837 and 1841 a series of promising election results confirmed the public's perception that the resurgent Conservative Party under Peel should be given an opportunity to implement its ambitious social and economic programme. In 1839, following Melbourne's resignation over the suspension of the Jamaican constitution, it seemed as if the Tories would be given an opportunity but Peel's refusal to form a ministry as a result of the 'bedchamber crisis' (see page 140) ensured that Melbourne was recalled.

Sir Robert Peel and the Tory/ Conservative Party, 1830–1846

8.1 How did Peel transform the Conservative Party between 1832 and 1841?
8.2 What were the key features of Peel's social and financial reforms in 1841–1846?
8.3 How successful was Peel's Irish policy in the years 1841–1846?
8.4 Historical interpretation: 'The great betrayer of his Party'. How far does Peel merit this description?
8.5 Whey were the Corn Laws repealed in 1846?
8.6 Why did the political crisis over repeal lead to the collapse of Peel's ministry in 1846?

Key Issues

- *What impact did Sir Robert Peel have on British politics between 1830 and 1846?*
- *What changes did Peel make to the Tory/Conservative Party in this period?*
- *Why did the Conservative Party split in 1846?*

Framework of Events

1830	Tory Party in disarray following passage of Catholic emancipation
1830–32	Peel opposes the Reform Bill during its two-year passage through Parliament
1834	December: Peel's first ministry lasts 100 days until April 1835 'Tamworth Manifesto' issued
1835	April: Peel defeated by the 'Lichfield House Compact'
1839	May: Peel refuses to take office after 'bedchamber question'
1841	August: Peel becomes Prime Minister for a second period
1842	March: First free trade budget April: Mines Act
1843	Daniel O'Connell's Clontarf meeting is banned Devon Commission reports its findings
1844	July: Bank Charter Act, Companies Act August: Factory Act, Irish Colleges Bill
1845	February: Maynooth Grant; Queen's Colleges founded October: Irish Famine begins December: Peel resigns over Corn Laws; returns as Prime Minister
1846	June: Corn Law Repeal introduced Government defeated over Irish Coercion Bill; Peel resigns.

Overview

Sir Robert Peel already had experience of ministerial office before he became leader of the Conservative Party. He had served with distinction in Ireland as Chief Secretary between 1812 and 1818, and had earned the label of an 'enlightened' Tory minister during the period 1821–27. He had also been Home Secretary in Wellington's brief ministry of 1828–30. During his career, he was not only his Party's leading politician but also its most effective parliamentarian.

Sir Robert Peel (1788–1850)

Pollarded: Lacking principles and convictions.

Peel's re-organisation of party structure began with his 'Tamworth Manifesto' of 1834 and continued up to his resignation as Prime Minister in 1846. No area of government escaped his scrutiny as he attempted to liberalise trade, set Ireland on a new course and improve the working and material condition of the lower orders. Norman Gash, Peel's most sympathetic modern biographer, has claimed that he embodied the spirit of the time and 'more than any man was the architect of the Victorian age'.

On the other hand, some historical writing has been critical of his career. G. Kitson-Clark has claimed Peel worked with 'a blurred background, **pollarded** principles and no ardent or extensive ideas'. It is true that he was very unpopular with a large section of his party who accused him of betraying the fundamental ideas of Toryism by undermining the Protestant establishment in Ireland and the protection of the agricultural interest in Parliament. He was also arrogant and aloof which heightened this unpopularity.

Ultimately, an assessment of Peel's career depends on whether you see him as the benefactor of his country or a politician who betrayed party interest on numerous occasions.

He entered Parliament as a Tory in 1809. As Home Secretary (1822–27 and 1828–30), Peel founded the modern police force. In 1829, he introduced Catholic emancipation. After the 1832 Reform Bill was passed, Peel reformed the Tories under the name of the Conservative Party, hoping for middle-class support. Peel was Prime Minister twice (1835–35 and 1841–46). He fell from office in 1846 because the majority of the Conservative Party opposed his repeal of the Corn Laws. Peel and his followers then formed a new party, the Peelites. Most Peelites, including William Gladstone, later joined the Liberals.

8.1 How did Peel transform the Conservative Party between 1832 and 1841?

Why did Peel take over from Wellington?

The Tory Party looked to be in total disarray in 1830 after the passage of Roman Catholic emancipation the previous year. Moreover, the Party was in serious difficulty as a result of the Reform Bill crisis and seemed destined for a long period in the political wilderness. Wellington had resigned as Prime Minister determined that a new leader of the Party should be found. The crushing defeat in the 1832 election, which left the Party with a mere 185 seats, made this even more pressing. The Tories were humiliated and needed to find a way of claiming the middle-class voters, whom the new Reform Act had enfranchised.

The most obvious potential leader of the party in 1832 was Robert Peel, who had already gained valuable ministerial experience in Ireland and in the Home Office. He was undoubtedly the most effective orator among the Tories in the House of Commons, but he was not a popular choice with everyone within his party. The Ultra-Tories found his support for Catholic emancipation unforgivable. Other contemporaries found him difficult to categorise. Daniel O'Connell compared Peel's smile to the gleam on the silver plate of a coffin lid, while Lord Ashley described him as being 'like an iceberg, with a slight thaw on the surface'. Even so, his fellow Tories had little doubt that he was the best man for the job.

Why were the '100 days' such a significant watershed for Peel and his Party?

The Reform Parliament that met in 1833 merely confirmed Peel as the leading spokesman of those opposed to a more general extension of the franchise. By 1834, he had won over any doubters in the Commons and the Lords regarding his suitability. By the time William IV dismissed the Whig Prime Minister Lord Melbourne, in December 1834, and sent for Peel to form his first ministry there had been a remarkable transformation in the fortunes of the Conservative Party.

Although Peel's first ministry was a minority government that only lasted 100 days, until it was finally defeated by the Lichfield House Compact of 1835, Peel showed some vision in church policy and in Irish affairs. He now had a firm grip on his parliamentary party, but above all the experience of his first ministry convinced him that the basis of his party's electoral support had to be extended, although not at the expense of its traditional policies. By the time a fresh election was called in January 1835, Peel had already published what historians now describe as the 'Tamworth Manifesto' (December 1834). Although primarily directed at his constituents in Tamworth, the 'manifesto' emphasised that the new 'Conservative' party accepted the idea of moderate continuing reform, but only of 'proven abuses'. The historian Lord Blake sees this as the main difference between a Tory and a Conservative (*The Conservative Party from Peel to Thatcher*, 1985). The 'Tamworth Manifesto' was seen as a cunning and brilliant attempt to win over the new middle-class electorate and party agents ensured that the message it contained occupied a prominent position in the national press. It proved to be the catalyst for changing the Tory Party into the 'Conservative' Party – a term that was first used for the election of that year.

In what ways was Conservatism different from Toryism?

Peel's new conservative principles owed a great deal to his experiences under the so-called 'Enlightened Tory' period (see page 55). However, much in the new conservatism was retained from the traditional Tory position:

- a defence of the Anglican or 'Established' Church
- a belief in the constitutional privileges of the House of Lords
- the maintenance of law and order
- respect of the role of the monarch and his ministers.

Dogmatic: When you fail to appreciate the value of another person's opinion because of your own biased viewpoint.

The new conservatism, however, was different in the sense that Peel was trying to modernise the Party by making it less narrow and less **dogmatic**. The most important reason for this change was the Reform Act of 1832. Although he had 'been unwilling to open a door which I saw no prospect of being able to close', Peel accepted the changes the Act introduced and began to use them to his advantage. He still insisted that it was a final settlement, and throughout the rest of his career attempted to undermine movements such as Chartism that were committed to further reform. Peel recognised that the middle classes were more important than ever in society and the Party needed to evolve policies that reinforced the traditional but also moved to embrace the new industrial society. As Peel claimed in the 'Tamworth Manifesto', he was in favour of 'combining, with the firm maintenance of established rights, the correction of proven abuses, and the redress of real grievances'. Such ideas were bound to win over men of property and give them a stake in the running of the country. 'Good government' was something that Peel stressed and was a concept that was equally applicable to the new middle-class electorate as to the traditional Tory supporter. Peel regarded the new Conservative Party as a reforming party, rejecting the Ultra-Tory position. As the historian Norman Gash has stated, Peel's aim was to try and 'turn the Tory Party of one particular class into the Conservative Party of the nation'.

The new conservatism also stressed the need to take advantage of the new boundary and constituency changes brought about by the 1832 settlement. The Party now had to be organised on a national basis. As the historian Eric Evans has claimed, 'Peel was among the first to recognise the importance of an extended party organisation in the constituencies'. He encouraged electoral organisation and registration of the newly enfranchised '£10 householders'. Much credit for this reorganisation must also go to F.R. Bonham, the party agent responsible for spreading the new gospel. From 1831, the Carlton Club acted as a prototype Conservative central office. While Peel and his Party remained in opposition until 1841, there was clear evidence of the results of this activity in the election of 1835 where the revived Conservative Party won 273 seats, and again in 1837 when it increased its share of the seats to 313.

What impact did the 'Bedchamber Crisis' of 1839 have on Peel and his Party?

Peel used the time in opposition after the 1835 election to build up gradually his control of the party and to widen its electoral appeal. His policies were based on a desire to undermine the demand to widen the franchise and if necessary support the Whig Government of Lord Melbourne in suppressing unrest in Ireland. The spectacular gains made by the Conservatives in the 1837 general election were a sign that the Party would be able to assume the challenge of government with confidence if an opportunity arose.

In 1839, Lord Melbourne resigned over a crisis concerning the Jamaican constitution. The Whigs were a spent force in terms of ideas and policies. In such a situation, the young Queen Victoria called on Peel to form a ministry. His supporters were delighted that such an opportunity had presented itself at exactly the right time in the new party's development. Peel, aware of the need for a public show of confidence from the young Queen, demanded the removal of some, if not all, of the women holding household posts at Court. These posts were currently held by the wives of leading Whig noblemen and had been the personal appointments of the outgoing Prime Minister, Melbourne. The Queen, who had never liked Peel, refused – primarily as a show of loyalty to Melbourne, the only politician whom she could confide in at that time. As Norman Gash has claimed, her hostility on the issue 'was because she was losing her minister, not her ladies'. In the event, Peel made the correct decision in turning down the opportunity, allowing the final two years of Melbourne's ministry to drift on aimlessly until June 1841, when a successful vote of 'no confidence' was put before the House of Commons.

Why did the Conservative Party win the 1841 election?

There are a number of reasons why the Conservatives were able to secure a majority of 76 seats in the 1841 election. It amounted to a combination of Peel's reorganisation of the party and the weakness of his Whig opponents. The reasons for success have been analysed elsewhere in this book (see Chapter 7), but it is interesting to concentrate on the fact that Peel was elected on a pledge to retain the Corn Laws, despite his own serious misgivings on the issue. Although the Party made gains throughout the country, it remained predominantly rural and English in support. Historians such as Eric Evans and Ian Newbould have questioned the view that Peel was solely responsible for the revival in his Party's fortunes. They argue that the election victory reveals that Peel was elected

1. How did the Conservative Party differ from the Tory Party?

2. 'Peel's victory in the 1841 general election represented a victory for Toryism rather than Conservatism.' Assess the validity of this statement.

on traditional Tory, rather than 'Conservative', values, and the Party made little headway in the areas, especially in the North, which were supposed to provide the basis for Conservative support. In certain areas, such as the largest boroughs, the Conservatives actually lost support. This evidence suggests that the broader base of electoral support that the new Conservatism required failed to convince all of the electorate. They placed their faith in the older values to which they had grown accustomed over a period of time. As Eric Evans has stated, 'The evidence of Peel's leadership of the 1830s suggests that he knew well enough how to revive Party fortunes by an appeal to established Tory values.'

8.2 *What were the key features of Peel's social and financial reforms in 1841–1846?*

Peel's second ministry proved to be one of the most influential periods in the whole of the 19th century. The sheer breadth of the issues he attempted to tackle in this period were a marvel, to both contemporaries and subsequent historians. Social reform, the reorganisation of the nation's finances and an attempt to soothe the tensions in Ireland all played a crucial role in the development of his policy. Yet it was the repeal of the Corn Laws in 1846 that finally led to the collapse of the party and a period of political exile that would last for over 20 years.

Social reform: Why did the Government pass the Mines Act 1842 and the Factory Act 1844?

Peel had shown a genuine sympathy for the plight of the material condition of the lower orders in his early career, and his reforms as Home Secretary in 1829 had tried to address some of their grievances. In 1841, his Government set up a national relief fund campaign and attempted to investigate the appalling conditions of the growing industrial areas of Britain's major cities. The picture of unemployment and deprivation revealed when the results were published in 1842 alarmed Peel and his contemporaries. Peel concluded that any reform package must aim to remove the causes of poverty and hardship, but must also attempt to improve some of the working conditions. Pressure was also exerted on the government by leading individuals campaigning for social reform, such as Lord Ashley (later Lord Shaftesbury). The combination produced two major pieces of social legislation: the Mines Act 1842 and the Factory Act 1844.

- The **1842 Mines Act** was a response to the dangerous working conditions revealed in the report of the Royal Commission Peel had set up. It stated that all children under ten were to be forbidden from working underground. Women were also forbidden to work underground. This seemed to be a commonsense response to a dangerous industry where deaths were commonplace.
- The passage of the **Factory Act in 1844** was largely the work of the Home Secretary, Sir James Graham. It reduced the working hours for those under the age of 13 and recommended safety improvements in factories, such as the fencing of machinery. It has been claimed that Peel was less interested in social reform than his financial policies but this is

an unfair criticism of a genuine attempt to improve the conditions in the mines and the factories.

- The **Railway Act, 1844**, was the work of the President of the Board of Trade, William Gladstone. It aimed to regulate the activities of the new railway companies, whilst safeguarding the interests of the passenger. The Act also instituted the 'parliamentary' train. This required each railway company to put on at least one train per day that stopped at every station on the line.

Financial reform: What were the major changes made between 1841 and 1846?

At the beginning of Peel's second ministry, the country was facing serious economic problems. Exports had fallen sharply, creating an industrial slump. In addition, a series of poor harvests since 1837 had kept bread prices high. As well as causing hardship and misery for the workers, the slump was accompanied by a financial crisis in which many small banks collapsed. In such a climate, the Chartist message seemed to be more popular than ever. Finally, the Whigs had left a deficit of over £2,000,000. Peel was determined to tackle the causes of poverty and came to the simple conclusion that 'We must make this country a cheap country for living, and thus induce people to remain and settle here – enable them to consume more by having more to spend'. The starting point for this was the 1842 Budget, which Peel drew up personally and which was to be remembered as one of the most famous of the whole century. The main focus of the Budget was:

- firstly, the reintroduction of income tax
- secondly, a gradual removal or lowering of **tariffs** on imported goods.

Tariffs: These were the list of duties or customs to be paid on imports and exports. Tariff reform was designed to get rid of these restrictions.

Pence in the pound: Before 1971 British money comprised pounds, shillings and pence. There were 240 pence in one pound; 12 pence in one shilling and 20 shillings in one pound.

The re-introduction of income tax

Peel had made up his mind for some time that he would reintroduce income tax when he returned to power. (It had been abolished in 1816 by Lord Liverpool's Government.) He decided on 7 **pence in the pound** on incomes over £150 per annum. This, he hoped, would not only absorb the Whig deficit but also yield a handsome disposable surplus. Initially, it was planned as a temporary measure of three years but it turned out to be so profitable that Peel persuaded Parliament to renew it for another three years – since then no government has been able to afford to abandon it.

The lowering of tariffs

The logical consequence of re-imposing income tax was reform of the tariff system. Although William Huskisson had removed many tariffs in the 1820s, the Whigs had taken no further action. In 1841, there were still about 1,200 commodities subject to tariffs. Peel was strongly influenced by a group of northern industrialists calling themselves the Manchester School, and came to believe that tariffs were stifling British industry. Their argument was that import duties made raw materials – such as cotton, wool and iron ore – more expensive, thereby keeping production costs too high. Foreign countries therefore resented British tariffs and were less willing to trade than they would otherwise be.

Tariffs, including the duty on imported corn, made imported food more expensive and increased difficulties for the poor. In Peel's mind, removing tariffs would bring down the cost of British goods abroad, increase exports, stimulate industry and provide more jobs. In addition, the cost of living would be cheaper, to the benefit of the working classes. In his Budgets of 1842 and 1843, Peel swept away a large number of the remaining duties, so that after 1845 duties on over 600 articles had been removed completely, and duties on 500 others greatly reduced. For example, items such as raw cotton, meat and potatoes were now free from any import duty.

There was a slight reduction in the import duty on corn, though not enough to satisfy the free-trade advocates of the Anti-Corn Law League. Despite this, Peel was already investigating the possibility of abolishing the hated Corn Laws if it would mean cheaper bread – the staple diet of the majority of the working classes. This was to have enormous political consequences, as the crisis over repeal would reveal in 1846.

Collectively, these measures worked exactly as Peel had hoped: trade revived; exports increased; while the rate of unemployment and prices fell. Britain began to move out of the 'hungry 40s' and into a new golden age of prosperity that lasted until the mid-1870s.

The Bank Charter Act, 1844

Other measures were introduced to improve the shaky financial system. Peel aimed to restore confidence in a system that had suffered four major financial crises since 1819, all of which had been followed by bankruptcies among the country's banks. The main problem was that banks could issue paper banknotes with no limit on the account. If companies got into difficulties, investors lost their money and could not repay the banks. Some banks, having over-issued notes, would then collapse due to insufficient gold reserves to back the paper currency. Peel thus concluded that the economy could only expand if the currency were stable. The aim of the Bank Charter Act was to regulate three rules:

- No new banks were allowed to issue notes.
- Existing banks were limited to their average issue of notes.
- The Bank of England was given greater control over banknote issue, which was linked to bullion reserves and securities.

1. Who gained and who lost as a result of Peel's financial measures?

2. Explain the motivation behind tariff reform between 1841 and 1846.

This measure proved highly successful: it placed a serious restriction on credit and was the starting point for the modern methods used to control an economy, whilst at the same time placing mid-Victorian England on a far surer financial footing than before.

The Companies Act, 1844

The aim of this legislation was to place business and commerce on a surer foundation and to increase public confidence in the honesty of business. The Act insisted that companies should be registered and produce annual accounts. It confirmed the image that all were accountable for their actions in a ministry determined to improve the financial health of the nation.

8.3 How successful was Peel's Irish policy in the years 1841–1846?

More than any other politician of his era, Sir Robert Peel had built up a wealth of experience regarding Irish issues. He had served as Chief Secretary for Ireland (1812–18) and had earned a reputation as a hardline Protestant determined to uphold the interests of the Church of Ireland – the Anglican Church in Ireland. Catholics gave him the unflattering nickname of 'Orange Peel'. He had also come into direct contact with Irish issues when Home Secretary under the Liverpool and Wellington ministries and had been responsible for the passage of Catholic emancipation in 1829 which outraged the ultra-Protestant Tory wing in his party. He was faced with another crisis of Irish origin when he came to power in 1841, namely a movement led by his old enemy, Daniel O'Connell, which aimed to repeal the Act of Union of 1800 (the Act that made Ireland part of the United

Kingdom). Ultimately, Peel's policy towards Ireland aimed to win over moderate Catholic opinion, whilst retaining the key features of the Protestant establishment. His policy again brought accusations that he had betrayed the Party and passed policies that were unacceptable to most Protestants.

How effectively did Peel deal with the Repeal Movement?

Daniel O'Connell, the champion of non-violent Irish Nationalism, was convinced that Peel's election victory in 1841 represented a step backwards in relations between Ireland and Great Britain. There was no love lost between the two men, as the Lichfield House Compact of 1835 had shown, but O'Connell was convinced that mass agitation would succeed in the 1840s as it had done in the 1820s. The Repeal Association, as it became known, campaigned for an end to parliamentary union with Great Britain. It aimed to use the distraction of Chartist agitation and the difficult economic situation of the early years of Peel's ministry to mobilise support in Ireland. Once he had realised the severity of the situation in Ireland, Peel made it quite clear that he was prepared to use force to uphold the Act of Union. The crucial year was 1843, when O'Connell organised a huge meeting at Clontarf to highlight the issue of repeal. Peel's response was the passage of a Coercion Act, which banned the meeting, leading to the arrest of O'Connell on a charge of conspiracy. Unlike the situation in 1829, Peel had kept his resolve, whilst O'Connell had lost his. The resolute government response led to the failure of the Repeal Movement, but it also had two important consequences:

- Peel now resolved to investigate areas where the Government could improve the conditions of the Irish people and investigate possible areas where there could be some compromise over religious issues.
- Irish Nationalism would reject O'Connell's constitutional approach and resort to armed violence to bring about political change.

The Devon Commission, 1843

As part of the attempt to improve relations with Irish Catholics, Peel instructed Lord Devon to investigate the question of land tenure. There were three main problems as far as the Government was concerned:

Leases: Contracts by which the lessor, in this case the aristocracy, gives land to the lessee for a specified period of time.

- **Leases** on land were short and not expected to exceed three lives. This meant that farmers were unlikely to invest in their land because they were uncertain of reaping any long-term benefits and, even if they did so, were not entitled to any compensation after the end of the lease.
- Since the end of the Napoleonic Wars, there had been a continuous depression in agriculture with an accompanying fall in prices. Landlords cruelly countered such developments by cancelling existing leases and drawing up new ones. This meant that tenants had no security and could be evicted and replaced.
- To make matters worse, there was pressure on the land owing to an increasing population. The population of Ireland increased from 5 million to 8.25 million between 1800 and 1845. In such a situation, farm rents were extremely high and many peasants were landless and reliant on their staple diet, the potato.

When the Devon Commission reported its findings in 1843, it recommended limited compensation for those tenants who had carried out improvements. Peel sponsored a bill to the same effect. Despite this, the bill was defeated in the Lords by hardline Protestant peers and self-interested Irish landowners.

The appointment of Heytesbury as Lord Lieutenant of Ireland, July 1844
Although parliamentary union between Britain and Ireland had been created with the Act of Union in 1800, Ireland possessed a separate administration after that date. It was based at Dublin Castle and had responsibilities for departments such as the Poor Law, the Board of Works and Irish Railways. The official head of the Irish administration was the Lord Lieutenant, who was the monarch's official representative in Ireland. He lived in the Vice Regal Lodge in Phoenix Park, Dublin.

Lord Heytesbury followed Peel's policy of granting concessions to Roman Catholics and his view stood in marked contrast to his predecessor, Earl De Grey, who was a supporter of the Protestant Ascendancy in Ireland.

The Irish or Provincial Colleges Bill, 1844
Education, Peel felt, would be the cornerstone of an improved understanding between Protestant and Catholic in Ireland. A non-**sectarian** approach seemed to be the most effective way of bringing about this change. Peel thus proposed to establish three new Queen's Colleges to educate Irishmen regardless of their religious backgrounds. The Ultra Tories within his own party, who saw it as a dangerous precedent, opposed the measure. Catholics were sceptical – O'Connell refused to support the measure in Parliament, while the Catholic authorities in Ireland regarded them as 'Godless Colleges' designed to undermine their influence. Once again, self-interest and bigotry undermined a modest initiative. Despite this, the colleges were established in Belfast, Cork and Galway.

Sectarian: An outlook that was designed to favour one religion over another. In Ireland at the time, it was claimed that Anglican policy was sectarian in that it ignored Catholic wishes.

The Maynooth Grant, 1845
To try to win over moderate Catholic opinion, Peel offered to develop Maynooth College, established in 1797 to train Catholic priests, by giving £30,000 for its rebuilding and increasing its annual grant from the Government. Gaining the loyalty of the priesthood was important because the Catholic clergy were a vital link in educating the peasantry and were also important political spokesmen. Despite opposition, Peel pressed ahead and the Bill was passed even though 149 backbench Tories revolted and voted against it. Moderate Catholic opinion welcomed the initiative, but there was a hostile reaction in England. Peel, said his critics, had performed another major U-turn and, even worse, was threatening the whole basis of Anglican control in Ireland. Relations with the extreme Protestant Tory ultras had now reached an all-time low and hostile petitions flooded in from all areas of the country. Writers in the magazine *Punch* summed up Tory opinion:

> 'How wonderful is Peel
> He changeth with the Time,
> Turning and Twisting like an eel,
> Ascending through the slime'.

Peel's President of the Board of Trade, William Gladstone, resigned from the Government over the Maynooth Grant. When it seemed that things could not possibly get any worse, the Irish potato famine intervened to trigger the sequence of events that led to his fall from power a year later.

The Irish Famine, 1845–1849
There was nothing new about famine in Irish affairs prior to 1845. Indeed, there had been serious harvest failures in 1817, 1822 and 1842, but what made the situation worse after 1846 was that the potato crop had failed in successive years. Even so, potato blight was not restricted to Ireland but spread across Europe. What did this mean in real terms? Firstly, in times of scarcity prices are pushed up beyond the means of most of the peasant population. Secondly, the system of relief was unable to cope with mass starvation and charity had to be given despite existing Poor Law arrangements.

1. How successful were Peel's policies towards Ireland between 1841 and 1846?

2. Why did Peel's measures cause such opposition within his own Party?

3. What were the consequences of the Irish famine in the decision to repeal the Corn Laws in 1846?

Arguably the worst human tragedy of the whole of the 19th century occurred in Ireland and led to the deaths of over one million people and increased the desire for emigration by a further half a million. Peel was confronted with a nightmare scenario: what if the famine lasted another three to four years? He resolved to try and organise a huge relief operation but, at the back of his mind, lay the questions if the situation continued how could the Corn Laws be justified? Peel gave his opinion that the only real remedy for Irish famine was 'the removal of all impediments to the import of all kinds of human food'. What he was saying was quite clear, there had to be total repeal on all foodstuffs. Yet, he knew that this would cause such an outcry among the landowning agricultural interest within his own Party that he was unlikely to survive its consequences. Undeterred, Peel began the greatest gamble of his career.

8.4 *'The great betrayer of his Party'. How far does Peel merit this description?*

A CASE STUDY IN HISTORICAL INTERPRETATION

When considering this question it is worth remembering that the period 1829–46 was a transitional period in British politics, as the political system was moving from one based on loyalty to the Crown to one based on loyalty to Party. Peel, as a politician of the Regency/Hanoverian period, always took the traditional view. The idea of placing the interests of your political party first was a creation of the late 19th century. To make an effective evaluation of the question we must ask what we expect of our political leaders. Are they elected to satisfy the interests of the party they represent or are they responsible for the national interest? Some would argue that the two are incompatible, although Peel attempted at least to ensure they existed side by side.

The case for

The career of Sir Robert Peel, according to his critics, is a catalogue of betrayal and treachery. On numerous occasions during this period he sacrificed the interests of his Party in the pursuit of what he defined as the national interest. They claim the process started in 1829 when, as Home Secretary, he passed the Catholic Emancipation Bill against the wishes of the vast majority of those within his Party. It continued when he remodelled the party in his famous 'Tamworth Manifesto', where he was aiming to widen the basis of his Party's support.

Traditional Tory values – such as the defence of the agricultural interest – were swamped by what the Ultras claimed was a dilution of party principles and a blatant bid for the votes of the newly enfranchised middle classes. While in office between 1841 and 1846, Peel's arrogance led to treachery on a number of key party principles. Firstly, in the 1842 Budget he reintroduced income tax at 7 pence in the pound, a direct betrayal of the 1816 measure that Lord Liverpool had introduced to abolish it. Furthermore, the emphasis on tariff reform, although of benefit to the majority, flooded the country with cheap products that were damaging the landed interest. A series of controversial measures in Ireland in the 1840s, such as the Maynooth Grant of 1845, alarmed the ultra Protestants within his own Party that he was undermining the whole basis of Anglican control in Ireland and with it the fragile unity of the 1800 Act of Union.

1. Is this cartoon in favour or against Peel?

2. What are the dangers of one person dominating a ministry at the expense of his/her Cabinet colleagues?

3. How useful is this cartoon to a historian writing about Peel's ministry 1841–46?

Cartoon from *Punch*, 1845, referring to the number of policies that Peel was attempting to follow at the same time: the Maynooth Grant, free trade and income tax. The pathetic-looking Lord Russell is awestruck at Prime Minister Peel's ability to conduct so many policies simultaneously.

Finally, the greatest act of betrayal occurred in the summer of 1846 when the cornerstone of party policy, the Corn Law, was repealed despite the fact that two-thirds of his own Party voted against it. The historian Eric Evans claims that Peel 'proved himself untrue to their Tory principles on Ireland, on religion, on commerce and, finally and fatally, on the landed interest itself'. Peel's duty, claim his critics, was to look after the duty of his Party first. However, according to historian Ian Newbould, 'he set out to build a party and instead split one, many of the materials of which were not of his making'.

The case against

According to his supporters, Peel realised that the needs of his country were more important than the narrow interests of a minority within his own Party. His intellect and strength of character ensured that his new party adapted successfully to the changing industrial society that was Britain in the 1840s. It was high time that bigoted and outdated views were put to rest and that a new party emerged stronger from the disaster of the Reform crisis. Instead of destroying his Party, Peel recreated one, giving it a sense of purpose and direction that had been so absent under Wellington. All his reforms were intended to uphold the basic features of Conservatism and make the aristocratic landowning faction more popular. His policies on free trade were part of a continuous process that reached a climax with the ultimate triumph of his career, the repeal of the Corn Laws in 1846.

Peel was more concerned with 'good government' and providing the solutions to years of uncertainty and poverty in the lower orders. What was obvious to him was that this had to be based on cheap living conditions and if this meant upsetting the protectionist lobby within his own Party then it was worth taking the risk, despite the obvious consequences. His policy in Ireland was not designed to destroy the Protestant establishment, quite the opposite. His aim was to win over moderate Catholic opinion by making them appreciate the value of 'good government' even more. His wish was to draw moderate opinion away from the extremes of the repeal movement and the violence of later generations of Irish patriots. As the historian Norman Gash has stated, 'What Peel gave the Conservative opposition was national leadership of a kind they were not to see again for another generation ... national leadership is often more effective than party leadership.' Historian Donald Read claims that 'Peel was arguably the best peacetime Prime Minister in British history' and that when he died he 'was the hero equally of the newly enfranchised, propertied middle classes, and of the disenfranchised, propertyless masses'.

1. Did Peel place the needs of his country above those of his Party? Give reasons to support your answer.

2. Which do you think is the most important?

8.5 Why were the Corn Laws repealed in 1846?

What were the major factors that led to the repeal of the Corn Laws in 1846?

1 Peel's gradual conversion

It is clear that after the outbreak of the Irish potato famine Peel realised that Corn Law repeal must follow. This reveals a politician who remained unconvinced by either its value or the desirability of special protection given to the agricultural interest within his own Party.

As early as 1834, Peel had complained to Wilson Crocker that 'agricultural prosperity was interwoven with manufacturing prosperity, and depended more on it than the Corn Laws'. In addition, Peel, who came from a manufacturing background rather than a family with landed interests, thought it unfair that agriculture should be protected solely. Some have gone as far as to say that Peel's failing health produced a desire to retire from politics in 1845–46, and this issue provided a convenient excuse.

2 The aftermath of the outbreak of the Irish Famine

The political consequences of the Irish famine were enormous. Peel realised that a temporary suspension of the Corn Laws in Ireland had to have an effect in Britain. Put simply, the Irish famine merely made up his mind over the question of timing. As Norman Gash claims, 'the Irish famine merely foreclosed the mortgage'. For Peel, it was the condition of England that was a more immediate concern than the condition of Ireland.

3 The success of budgetary and tariff reforms

The obvious success of the 1842 and 1845 budgets convinced Peel that further tariff reform would stimulate industry and reduce unemployment. Thus the attack on the Corn Laws would be a part of a consistent strategy that had been initiated when a **sliding scale** on the Corn Laws had been introduced in 1828. In particular, Peel was concerned with food prices – cheap bread he regarded as the only permanent means of tackling the misery of the masses, which would then improve the social stability of the country. In this light, the repeal of the Corn Laws would be seen as the crowning glory of a consistent strategy.

Sliding scale: A modified form of the Corn Laws introduced in 1828. If British wheat was selling at over 73 shillings (£3.65) a quarter, there would be no tariffs on imports from abroad; but if the price fell, the tariff or duty would be increased. At least this system took into account changing conditions in supply and demand rather than the absolute prohibition of the original Corn Law in 1815.

4 An opportunity to restore confidence in the political system

Despite the opposition of the protectionists within his own Party, who claimed that repeal would lead to cheap grain, Peel believed it would strengthen their position. He claimed that the retention of the Corn Laws was undermining, and not strengthening, the aristocracy – the pillars of Conservative support. Growing public hostility was undermining their position and, therefore, the national interest. Peel claimed that repeal would remove a source of bitter social division and reveal the landed interest as being generous **paternalist** benefactors, not a group out of touch with a new industrial society. Argued from this viewpoint, it was not a measure to undermine the agricultural interest or a question of class betrayal, but a measure that would have benefits for all involved.

Paternalist: Someone who rules or governs his country by well-meaning policies. He rules the country as a father would rule his family (i.e. in their interests).

5 The appeal of the Anti-Corn Law League

The Anti-Corn Law League was a single-issue pressure group founded in Manchester in 1838. It was led by two able politicians, Richard Cobden and John Bright. Both men were leading lights in the 'Manchester School' that had viewed the Corn Laws as the moral evil of society. The Anti-Corn Law League grew mostly in the manufacturing towns. Agitation lay silent in times of relative prosperity and cheap bread, but flared into action when grain prices were high and depression hit the country. The League used religious, humanitarian and economic arguments to support their campaign, copying the tactics of other successful pressure groups. Its propaganda relied initially on petitioning Parliament, but this was abandoned in 1842 as ineffective. Instead, the message was gradually spread by lecturers and by the League's own journal, the Anti-Corn Law circular, which became hugely popular. The latest communication techniques of the Penny Post and the railway were used to spread the message on a nationwide basis.

In a series of high-profile meetings, free traders argued that the industrial revolution had spread to the continental countries and that European agriculturists would take their trade elsewhere if they found the English market too difficult to penetrate and would refuse to trade for British manufactured goods. Cobden and Bright's arguments remained confined to the middle classes, despite Peel's obvious conversion.

As the historian Norman McCord claims, 'the League made a great deal of noise, but it had the part of a chorus which did not play a decisive part in the action: the decisive steps were taken in Parliament'. The League did play a major role in placing the issue of repeal at the forefront of the political agenda, but it cannot take all the credit for the events of 1846. Events in Ireland and Peel's own conversion were far more important.

1. What pressures forced the repeal of the Corn Laws in 1846?

2. How accurate is the view that without the Irish Famines there would have been no repeal of the Corn Laws?

8.6 Why did the crisis over repeal lead to the collapse of Peel's ministry in 1846?

At the height of the Irish famine, in November 1845, Peel told his Cabinet that the Corn Laws must be repealed immediately. He used the excuse that this was the only reasonable way of getting cheap food into Ireland. Peel and his Home Secretary, James Graham, had great difficulty persuading the Cabinet to accept their analysis of the situation.

The protectionist lobby in Parliament and the Cabinet objected to repeal on a number of grounds:

- The removal of the Corn Laws would cause an influx of cheap foreign wheat, which would ruin British agriculture and create mass unemployment in the rural areas.
- Peel was too heavily influenced by the middle-class-dominated Anti-Corn Law League which was suspected of being merely the beginning of a plot to undermine aristocratic influence.
- Peel had been elected in 1841 on a commitment to retain the Corn

Laws. Repeal would not only be a breach of aristocratic confidence, but also a rejection of the electorate's wishes.

Not surprisingly, a majority in the Cabinet opposed Peel's policy and he had no alternative but to resign in December 1845.

Lord John Russell, the Whig leader, was called to form a ministry. He failed to do so because he was known to be a supporter of free trade and because Palmerston demanded the position of Foreign Secretary while his Cabinet colleagues would only allow him to take a post in the Colonial Office. Thus the situation demanded that Peel be recalled and a new ministry created.

Peel's new Repeal Bill was introduced into the Commons in 1846 and aimed to phase out the Corn Laws over a period of three years. There was a fierce debate that lasted five months, during which Peel had to face accusations that he had both betrayed the confidence of his Party and exaggerated the extent of the famine in Ireland. The protectionist case was put forward by Lord George Bentinck and Benjamin Disraeli, who launched savage personal attacks on Peel. Bentinck regarded Peel as 'no better than a common cheat', a man who had indulged in 'wholesale examples of political lying and pledge breaking'. Here, they claimed, was another example of a man who had consistently betrayed his Party as Catholic emancipation, the re-introduction of income tax and the Maynooth Colleges Grant had already revealed.

Despite these attacks, and the fact that two-thirds of his own Party voted against him, the combined Whig/Peelite majority ensured that the Bill was given its third reading and sent to the Lords. Thanks to the support of Wellington in the Upper House, the Bill was soon passed and became law in June 1846. Peel's mission was complete, and rather than the nightmare the protectionists had predicted of England being swamped in foreign grain, repeal proved to be the starting point for 30 years of economic prosperity.

Peel was conscious of the need to try to calm the increasingly difficult situation in Ireland. In the same month, Peel introduced a **Coercion Bill** to the Commons but the protectionist rebels combined with the Whigs and the Irish MPs to defeat it, and with it Peel's Government. It was a rather low-key end to the career of one of the country's greatest politicians, but his departure meant the end of Conservative government for almost 20 years and the division of his party into Conservative and Peelite groupings.

Coercion Bill: Government by force when the situation is so dangerous that normal methods have failed. Force usually implies special powers being given to the Army or the Police.

1. What were the various pressures moving towards the repeal of the Corn Laws in 1846?

2. Briefly summarise the arguments in favour and against repeal.

3. Why do you think repeal split the Conservative Party?

Source-based questions: Peel and the Corn Laws

SOURCE A

I fairly own that I do not see how the repeal of the Corn Law is to afford relief to the distress which we are threatened. I quite understand that if we had never had a Corn Law, it might be argued that we should now have had a larger supply in our warehouses, or that from the encouragement given by a free trade in corn to the growth of it in foreign countries, we should have a larger fund on which to draw for a supply. But I think it next to impossible to show that the abandonment of the law now could materially affect this year's supply, or give us any corn which will not equally reach us under the law as it stands.

From a letter to Sir Robert Peel, 30 November 1845, written by Henry Goulbourn, Chancellor of the Exchequer at the time. The date of this primary source is important because by this time the Prime Minister had admitted to Cabinet colleagues that the repeal of the Corn Laws was inevitable.

SOURCE B

When we complain of the right honorary gentleman [Peel] not treating his party fairly, we speak of the great body of the community whose views they represent.

… I say that it is the first duty of a minister to maintain a balance between the two great branches of national industry … and we should give a preponderance [leading role] to the agricultural branch; this is not in order to pamper the luxury of the owners of land, but it is because our present system is the only security for self-government; the only barrier against that centralising system [in this case, control exercised by one person] which has taken root in other countries. My constituents are not landlords; they are not aristocrats; they are not great capitalists; they are the children of industry and toil; but they believe that their social and political interests are involved in a system by which their rights and liberties have been guaranteed; and I agree with them. I have the same old-fashioned notions …

From speeches by Benjamin Disraeli in the House of Commons during the Repeal debate, February–March 1846. Disraeli was leading spokesman for the Protectionist cause and later became leader of the Conservative Party and Prime Minister.

SOURCE C

A contemporary view of Peel's legacy to the nation from Punch *magazine, 1850.*

---

1. Study Source A.

According to this source what is meant by 'the distress with which we are threatened'?

2. Study Sources A and B.

How far are the authors in agreement as to the reasons why the Corn Laws should be retained?

3. Study Source C.

How reliable is this source as evidence of popular attitudes to the benefits of the repeal of the Corn Laws?

4. Study Source B.

How does Disraeli, by the use of language and style, explain how Peel abandoned the wishes of the agricultural interest?

5. *'Peel's decision to repeal the Corn Laws was popular with all sections of society.' Using the sources and information from this chapter, how far do you agree with this view?*

Chartism

Key Issues

- *Why did a working-class protest movement emerge in the 1830s and 1840s?*
- *How serious was the Chartists' threat to the political system?*
- *Why did Chartism fail?*

9.1 What were the causes of Chartism?
9.2 What was so appealing about the Charter?
9.3 What were the main features of the Chartist movement between 1839 and 1850?
9.4 Historical interpretation: Chartism – political or economic movement?
9.5 Why did the Chartists fail to achieve their aims?

Framework of Events

1832	Reform Act fails to satisfy the working classes who are denied the vote
1834	Poor Law Amendment Act produces a hostile reaction, especially in North of England
1836	London Working Men's Association (LWMA) founded
1837	January: LWMA draws up the six points of the Charter
	May: Birmingham Political Union revived by Thomas Attwood
	November: *Northern Star* first published in Leeds
1838	People's Charter first published
1839	February: General Convention meets in London
	May: Convention moves to Birmingham
	June: First Petition presented to Parliament
	July: Petition rejected by 235 votes to 46
	November: Newport Rising. Severe economic crisis begins
1840	July: National Charter Association (NCA) founded in Manchester
1841	August: Feargus O'Connor released from jail
1842	January: Complete Suffrage Union (CSU) founded in Birmingham
	May: Second Chartist Petition presented to Parliament and rejected by 287 votes to 49
	August: Strikes break out in 23 English counties. Plug Riots. Trade begins to revive
1843	William Lovett abandons the movement
1845	April: Chartist Land Cooperative founded
1846	June: Act passed to repeal the Corn Laws
1848	Third Petition presented to Parliament
1851	National Land Cooperation wound up
1855	Death of Feargus O'Connor.

Overview

William Lovett (1800–1877)

THE Chartist Movement had its origins in the radical tradition that flourished in Britain during the 18th century. It aimed to change the existing post-1832 political settlement to create a fairer system that would meet the political wishes of the working class, as well as the middle class. It was certainly the largest and most important assault by the lower orders on the political establishment during the 19th century and tended to provoke a very hostile reaction, especially in Parliament. The reasons why Chartism developed can be explained partly by the failure of the 1832 Reform Act to satisfy the expectations of those denied the vote, as well as other more immediate causes, such as the introduction of the new Poor Law in 1834. Its impact also fluctuated depending on the economic health of the nation: Chartism was more popular when the dark shadow of unemployment and high prices affected the lives of ordinary working people. Economic slumps in 1837–42 and 1847–48 coincided with large-scale unrest.

There is no doubt that, at its height, Chartism did attract the mass support the 3 million signatures of the Second Petition of 1842 suggest. Yet it still was not able to penetrate the minds of the majority of MPs who rejected several petitions point blank. During the 1840s, it also attempted to widen its appeal through a potential alliance with the other major protest movement of the period, the Anti-Corn Law League. The fact that this alliance collapsed suggests a fundamental difference between those Chartists who looked for a peaceful or '**moral force**' solution and the more extreme '**physical force**' part of the movement. The last major expression of Chartism was in 1846–50, but after the rejection of the Third Petition and a return of prosperity in the 1850s, it seemed that the Chartist message had failed.

'Moral force' Chartism: This was the idea that Chartism could achieve its aims through non-violent, peaceful protest and make closer links with the moderate elements of the middle class. William Lovett was the leading spokesman for this view.

'Physical force' Chartism: These Chartists believed that the only way to change the existing political system was through violence when all other forms of protest had failed. 'Physical force' Chartists were especially prominent in the Newport rising of 1839.

The movement produced many celebrated figures, such as William Lovett and Feargus O'Connor, who attempted to expand Chartist activity into a Land Plan and a more comprehensive education programme for the working classes. This broadened the appeal of the movement, but in the short term Chartism failed to achieve its objectives due primarily to the strength of Peel's Government. To simply dismiss Chartism as a failure would not do justice to the vital lessons working people learnt in organising themselves against what they regarded as an abuse of basic human rights. Over a period of time, all but one of the six points of the Charter were implemented, which may suggest that it was not the complete failure some historians would have us believe.

9.1 What were the causes of Chartism?

Chartism was the world's first working-class movement. It aimed to change the existing political situation in Britain by widening the electoral laws. Historians find it a difficult movement to categorise, primarily because of the fact that it had such varied components and interests. However, in identifying what produced the movement in the 1830s and 1840s a number of factors are now considered vitally important.

1 The disappointment of the 1832 Reform Act

The passage of the 1832 Reform Act was heralded by its supporters as the final settlement of a difficult constitutional issue and one which had averted a potential revolution in Britain. The major beneficiaries were the middle classes who were now given a say in the election of MPs to Parliament. The Act, however, was viewed in a completely different manner by the working classes, who saw the Bill as treachery of the highest order. Many working-class boroughs, such as Middlesex, had been disenfranchised, as well as those with burgage tenants and Scot and Lot taxpayers (see page 111). The working class, without the property qualification that was required to vote, still felt alienated from the political system that was being used as they saw it to undermine their interests. As the historian S.J. Lee claims, in *Aspects of British Political History 1815–1914* (1994) 'the Chartists aimed at removing the cut off point each social class seemed bent on applying against the class immediately below itself'.

2 *The continuing tradition of radical politics*

Since the 18th century, there had always been a strong radical tradition in British politics despite the attempts of Lord Liverpool's Government to crush it between 1815 and 1821. Key figures such as Henry Hunt, William Cobbett and Major Cartwright continued to press their demands for political and economic change. Even the deaths of Hunt and Cobbett in 1835 failed to stop the spread of the radical message, as new leaders such as Feargus O'Connor filled their shoes. The continuity of working-class protest against the inequalities of the political system is a key point to understand in assessing Chartism.

3 *The unstamped press*

Part of this strong radical tradition had always been an emphasis on the written word via a strong, radical press. William Cobbett's *Twopenny Trash* and Thomas Wooler's *Black Dwarf* had been instrumental in creating a climate for educated discussion in the coffee houses of the major industrial centres. The Six Acts of 1819 had attempted to stifle the press by introducing a 'stamp duty'. This pushed up prices and made it very difficult for the radical press, as it existed, to survive. Yet, between 1830 and 1834, hundreds of small political papers were established, such as Hetherington's *Poor Man's Guardian* which was deliberately published 'contrary to the law', failing to carry a stamp or sell at a minimum legal price of 7d (3p). The paper continued to be published despite 'the so-called taxes on knowledge'. This gave the emerging Chartist Movement, through its influential newspapers *Northern Star* and *The Poor Man's Guardian*, a wider audience for their ideas. A network of local agents was already well in place by the time the Chartist message began to widen, and one of Chartism's key subsidiary organisations – the London Working Men's Association – had strong connections with the printing industry.

4 *Opposition to Whig social legislation*

Working-class discontent was increasing because of the effects of the factory system and the operation of the New Poor Law of 1834. In the factories, the long working hours were the subject of numerous campaigns, notably the '10 Hours Movement' which attempted to reduce the workday to ten hours and to keep children out of the factories. Reaction to the New Poor Law was even more marked. The abolition of existing forms of poor relief and their availability only in the dreaded workhouse created the idea that poverty was due to laziness. Ending the current system, it was argued, would force people to look for work, but the Act had completely underestimated the causes of poverty in England and helped fuel the flames of working-class discontent.

The movement against the Poor Law was especially strong in the North of England where depression had hit the textile industry in 1837–38, while technological change had led to the erosion of jobs, wages and the social position of the handloom weavers (an influential group supporting Chartism). It has been estimated that with the rise of mechanised textile factories about 400,000 handloom weavers faced economic ruin. As a result of these pressures, there were inevitable violent incidents, such as in Huddersfield and Bradford where the Poor Law Guardians had to be protected by the local cavalry, and at Todmorden where police constables were attacked and troops called in to restore law and order. By 1837, Feargus O'Connor had established the *Northern Star* in Leeds to campaign for an end to the Poor Law. The movement, although failing to influence the Government, did have an important bearing on future Chartist strategy.

5 Economic origins

To many historians, Chartism was a 'knife and fork question' – that is, it was most closely associated with periods of economic hardship and with the transformation of the British economy through the process of industrialisation. Chartism reached its height during periods of economic depression: the late 1830s, 1842 and 1837–48. This seems to suggest that the appeal of the Charter came from a desire to alter the political system in order to gain economic change. The process of industrialisation also meant that certain trades faced decline with the onset of mechanisation. The most significantly affected group were the handloom weavers. Numbering approximately 400,000 in the early 1840s, this section of the work force faced the prospect of declining wages as new machines were introduced into the textile industry.

As a result, Chartism tended to be strongest in areas undergoing change through industrialisation such as Stockport in Cheshire and the West Riding of Yorkshire.

1. What were the major reasons why Chartism developed as a movement by 1839?

2. Did the movement owe its origins to the circumstances of the 1830s or were there longer-term reasons for its growth?

9.2 What was so appealing about the Charter?

The appeal of the People's Charter

The publication of the Charter, in the spring of 1839, was made by the London Working Men's Association. The six points of the Charter need individual explanation.

- *The vote for all males over 21*
  This had obvious appeal as it stated that all men, regardless of the property they owned, were worthy of a vote in the election of MPs and therefore should have a say in the political affairs of the nation. This was finally introduced in 1918.
- *Secret ballot*
  Many voters had been intimidated by their landlords or employers to vote not according to their conscience but under the threat of eviction. A secret ballot, it was claimed, would take away this pressure. Finally introduced in 1872.
- *Equality of constituency size*
  This was demanded so that each constituency would be the same size. The idea behind it was that regional variations would

disappear and each town and city would have equal representation in Parliament. Even the strongest Chartist supporters, however, were aware of the problems that an increased number of Irish MPs would bring at Westminster. Finally introduced in 1885.

- *No property qualifications for MPs*
  Radicals claimed that the need for a property qualification to enter Parliament prevented many from standing for office. Feargus O'Connor, for example, was disqualified from his seat in 1835 for that precise reason. This was abolished in 1858.
- *Annual Parliaments*
  Originally passed in 1716, the Septennial Act ordered that elections need only take place every seven years but the reform crisis had revealed the system to be outdated as three were held between 1830 and 1832. Annual general elections would be genuinely democratic and give a fairer representation of the people's views because MPs had to face re-election each year. This has never been implemented.
- *Payment of MPs*
  Since all these changes would alter the social composition of MPs at Westminster it was demanded that MPs should be paid and not be reliant on private income, as they had been previously. This was finally passed in 1911.

1. Which of the six points of the Charter do you find the most appealing?

2. Why would the People's Charter have aroused such criticism from a Tory aristocrat?

Give reasons to support your answers.

9.3 What were the main features of the Chartist movement between 1839 and 1850?

Thomas Attwood (1783–1856)

The failure of the Three Petitions

The First Petition, 1839

The unrest and hatred towards the Whig Government of the 1830s obviously had to have some visible form of protest. The London Working Men's Association, formed in 1836, and the revival of Thomas Attwood's Birmingham Political Union in 1837 were at the forefront of the protests. In 1838, Attwood drew up a petition based on the ideas put forward by the People's Charter. During the course of the year, a number of high-profile mass meetings were held that were especially well attended in the North of England. The idea of a petition was not new, but the question emerged of what to do if Parliament rejected it? A national convention was called in London, in 1839, to discuss strategy and to develop the idea of a 'national holiday' or general strike. O'Connor advocated using the threat of physical force (see page 158), but the more moderate members of the leadership, under Lovett, maintained that peaceful methods were more likely to succeed. By May 1839, 1.2 million signatures had been gathered. However, Parliament was in recess as a result of Melbourne's resignation over the Jamaican constitution, so the convention moved to Birmingham where there was continued talk of violence and armed struggle.

For a while it seemed as if popular pressure would force Parliament to make changes as it had in 1832. Yet Parliament showed a greater resolve in

Cartoon from *Punch* published in 1848.

NOT SO *VERY* UNREASONABLE!!! EH?

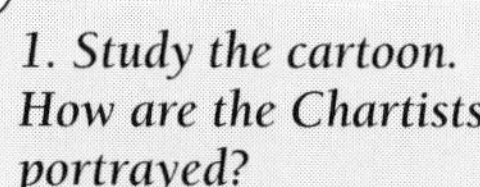

1. Study the cartoon. How are the Chartists portrayed?

2. Do you think the cartoonist is in favour of, or against, the Chartists' message? Give reasons to support your answer.

rejecting the petition by 235 votes to 46. Disappointed by this outcome, the idea of 'a sacred month' of strikes was put forward but the whole episode revealed inherent weaknesses such as a division in the leadership over strategy and a lack of support in Parliament.

The Second Petition, 1842

Despite the failures of 1839, a hard core of Chartists still believed in the vision of a new society based on the six points of the Charter. Although morale was low and many of the leading personalities had been imprisoned, the hard core was determined to continue the fight for what they regarded as 'natural justice'. Economic recession, which had always been a stimulus to political unrest in this period, re-emerged with increasing vigour in 1841–42. Unemployment, low wages and despair were to be the raw materials for a more violent outburst of Chartist activity in 1842. This coincided with the establishment of the second Chartist convention, which met in London in April 1842. It presented Parliament with a new petition containing 3.3 million signatures the following month. The petition was again rejected by 287 votes to 49, despite the lawful, peaceful protest. Once again, the political establishment had held firm and resisted pressure to change the political system.

The Third Petition, 1848

The usual cocktail of ingredients reappeared towards the end of the 1840s to bring the Chartist message to the fore once again. A depression had hit all the major industrial areas and unemployment had risen dramatically. This provoked O'Connor into action once again. In 1847, he was elected as MP for Nottingham and drew up plans for the relaunch of a National Convention and the presentation of a new petition to Parliament. On this occasion, his plans seemed to be more ambitious, as there was talk of a new Republican constitution with O'Connor as President. In addition, the Chartist message was given a sharper focus by the news of a revolution in

France, in February 1848, that overthrew the unpopular government of Louis Philippe. By April 1848, plans were made for a huge open-air rally on Kennington Common, London, which would coincide with a march to present the Third Petition to Parliament.

The whole atmosphere was very tense, but the response of Russell's Government ensured that the whole protest fizzled out. The march on Parliament was banned and only a handful of Chartists were allowed to accompany O'Connor to present the Petition, which was found to contain a disappointing 2 million signatures. Also, the Government had put the defence of the capital in the hands of the ageing Duke of Wellington and created thousands of special constables, including the future Napoleon III of France. Not surprisingly, Parliament rejected the petition by a huge majority. This proved to be the last great upsurge in Chartist support. The circulation of the *Northern Star*, a useful indicator of Chartist support, dropped dramatically and O'Connor was declared insane before he died in 1855.

The use of violence

The Newport Rising, 1839

The failure of the National Convention and the rejection of the First Petition were two of the many reasons why the South Wales valleys rose in revolt at the end of 1839. The area had been a hothouse of industrialisation, especially in the iron and coal industries, but living and working conditions remained appalling, spawning a rich radical and trade unionist tradition.

On 3–4 November 1839, a demonstration was held in Newport, centred on the Westgate Hotel. It degenerated into violence, and soldiers fired on the conspirators. Modern historians such as D.J.V. Jones now accept that the Newport insurrection was not part of a national strategy and was merely part of a local expression of unrest. However, the event did have national consequences. John Frost and Zephania Williams, two of the leading conspirators, were transported abroad for life whilst other leading Chartists, such as Lovett and O'Connor, were arrested and imprisoned. The first period of Chartist activity had been a resounding victory for the authorities.

Plug Riots at Preston, Lancashire, August 1842

Feargus O'Connor (1794–1855)
The most well-known spokesman of the Chartist movement, O'Connor was MP for Cork 1832–35. He was at the forefront of the anti-poor law campaign and this led to his involvement with the Chartist protest. Initially through the *Northern Star* but gradually through his powerful public speaking, O'Connor advocated the 'physical force' element of Chartism and was associated with the failed Land Plan of the 1840s. In 1847, he was elected MP for Nottingham. Always controversial, his career was tragically cut short when he was declared insane in 1852 and died three years later.

1. What kind of splits became apparent in the Chartist movement between 1839 and 1846?

2. Between 1839 and 1846 Chartist activists pursued their political interests in a variety of ways. How might this have

(a) strengthened the movement

(b) weakened it?

3. At what point during this period do you think the movement had the greatest chance of success?

The Plug Riots, 1842

The revival of the Chartist message coincided with a serious outbreak of Chartist unrest in 1842. There were violent protests during the summer months in Staffordshire, Lancashire, Cheshire and Yorkshire, as well as in many other counties in England. Part of this was the so-called Plug Plot (a sabotage campaign to remove the plugs from factory boilers), especially in the North and Midlands. The extent to which Chartists were involved in these activities remains uncertain but the desire to implement the six points of the Charter was a convenient excuse used by many across the country.

The New Charter Association general council meeting in August 1842 was unwittingly forced to approve a general strike to take place on 14 August. Yet many Chartists had reservations and Peel's Government was able to turn the issue on its head by accusing the Chartist leadership of organising a general strike. The violence of 1842 was far worse than 1839, but the authorities had again won the day and ensured that imprisonment and transportation were standard punishment for industrial unrest. By the end of the year, misery, hopelessness and hunger were forcing people back to work and in such a desperate situation support for Chartism levelled off.

Political organisations

Chartism created a number of important political organisations in this period. The most significant of these was the New Charter Association (NCA), founded in Manchester in July 1840. This organisation provided the central organisation that the Chartist movement had previously lacked. According to historian Edward Royle, 'The New Charter Association became the backbone of Chartism for the next 12 years'. The national structure ensured that 'localities' were well represented: by April 1842, there were 401 such organisations with a membership of around 50,000. Increasingly, the NCA began to make tentative links with other campaigning groups, such as the Anti-Corn Law League. The League was predominantly a middle-class organisation and gradually became uneasy about the presence of O'Connor and other 'physical force' Chartists. Indeed, further links were made and the 'moral force' element of the movement increased by the establishment of the Complete Suffrage Union (CSU) in 1842. The CSU had grown out of the Birmingham Political Union and was moderate enough to recognise that cooperation between itself, the NCA and the Anti-Corn Law League was the way forward. Lovett and Lowery were leading members, together with Joseph Sturge and Edward Miall.

Other areas of Chartist activity

Chartism was far more than just a political movement and a number of leading Chartists attempted to widen the appeal of the movement in a number of important areas.

Education

William Lovett, for example, had always been keen to stress the link between Chartism and education. For him, the two were important concepts: political change could not come about without an educated public. Lovett had always been attracted by the non-violent appeal of the movement and had never denied the attraction of closer cooperation with the Anti-Corn Law League. To men like Feargus O'Connor, this was unacceptable and by 1843 personal dislike, as well as division over future policy, had forced Lovett out of the movement.

Christian Chartism and local government

Chartist activity was also prominent in religious circles. In Scotland, the idea of 'Christian Chartism' developed, stressing the link between God and the democratic freedom Chartists demanded. Individuals, such as Joshua Hobson in Leeds and Isaac Ironside in Sheffield, were also prominent in local government affairs.

The Land Plan

Feargus O'Connor was credited with the idea of developing a Chartist Land Plan in this period. The idea was to ease the unemployment situation as well as giving the settlers freedom and self-respect. The establishment of the Chartist Cooperative Land Society in 1845 was based on the following ideas:

- each family was given a 4-acre plot and cottage, paying an annual rent of £1.5s an acre
- Chartists bought shares for £1.6s each.

The whole experiment was a costly failure as the settlers were unused to farming methods and there was talk of financial irregularities. By 1851, the whole land experiment had been wound up in complete failure. However, some of the Chartist land settlements survived, such as Charterville (near Witney, Oxfordshire).

Source-based questions: Feargus O'Connor

SOURCE A

I regard Feargus O'Connor as the chief marplot [troublemaker] of our movement … a man who, by his personal conduct joined to his malignant [destructive] influence in the *Northern Star*, has been the blight of democracy from the first moments he opened his mouth as its professional advocate [spokesman] … By his great professions, by trickery and deceit, he got the aid of the working classes to establish an organ to promulgate [make known] their principles, which he soon converted into an instrument for destroying everything intellectual and moral in our movement … the *Star*, a mere reflex of the nature of its master … By his constant appeals to the selfishness, vanity, and mere animal propensities [feelings] of man, he succeeded in calling up a spirit of hate, intolerance and brute feeling, previously unknown among Reformers.

From The Life and Struggles of William Lovett *by William Lovett, published in 1876. Lovett rejected O'Connor's 'physical force' Chartism, preferring peaceful methods. The two men were great rivals.*

SOURCE B

Of the importance of Feargus O'Connor as a national leader, there can be no question … O'Connor has been seen as the evil genius of the movement. In fact, so far from being the exploiter and distorter of the movement, O'Connor was so much the centre of it that, had the name Chartism not been coined, the radical movement between 1838 and 1848 must surely have been called O'Connorite Radicalism. Remove him and his newspaper and the movement fragments, localises and loses its continuity.

From The Chartists *by Dorothy Thompson, 1984. The author takes a more sympathetic view of O'Connor's ability and writes from a left-wing standpoint.*

SOURCE C

If ever men deserved to be classed among cowards and poltroons [spineless cowards], and to meet with the scorn and derision of mankind, it must be frankly confessed by all readers of Irish history that the kings of Ireland were entitled to that distinction, and none more so than the ancestors of O'Connor.

He showed himself to be either cowardly or treacherous towards those whom he styled his friends. A love of popularity was the besetting [most obvious] sin of the latter [O'Connor]. To win and retain that popularity, with O'Connor all means were justifiable.

From History of the Chartist Movement 1837–1854 *by R.G. Gammage, 1854. This was the first history of Chartism and was heavily biased against O'Connor. However, it is a useful source, drawn from contemporary observations of the leading members of the movement.*

Source-based questions: Feargus O'Connor

SOURCE D

A Punch *cartoon from the 1840s. It compares O'Connor to Titus Annius Milo, a political radical in Rome during the 1st century BC. Like O'Connor, Milo was regarded with great suspicion by the authorities and attempted to use popular protest to change the system. In the cartoon, O'Connor is shown shaking the foundations of Peace and Order (shown by the tree) due to his emphasis on universal suffrage and vote by ballot. The lion symbolises the anger of the British public, whilst Peel and Wellington hide in the tree.*

SOURCE E

No one matched O'Connor in the qualities demanded of a national leader. He was a superb platform speaker with a splendid presence, wonderfully racy and vivid in his language, and wildly funny both on the platform and in his writings. Many historians have seen only his braggadocio [boasting], the … expressions of prophecies and claims that could never be fulfilled. But much more important was the confidence that [he] generated among the poor and downtrodden. It was this crucial belief in the righteousness of the cause, and his ability to communicate it in unequalled terms, that allowed O'Connor to tower above his fellow Chartists.

From 1884 by John Saville, 1987. This secondary source analyses the effectiveness of forces of law during the last revival of the movement.

1. Study Source A.

What is the 'Northern Star' mentioned in the source?

2. How, by his use of language and style, does William Lovett criticise Feargus O'Connor's influence on the Chartist movement?

3. Study Sources A, C and D.

How far are the sources in agreement over their criticism of Feargus O'Connor?

4. Study Source B.

How reliable is this source as evidence of O'Connor's character?

5. 'Feargus O'Connor was vital to the success of the Chartist movement.' Using the information in this chapter and the sources above, how far do you agree with this statement?

9.4 Chartism – political or economic movement?

A CASE STUDY IN HISTORICAL INTERPRETATION

Case for the 'political view'

The view that Chartism represented a politically aware working class figures strongly in the writings of historians Dorothy Thompson and James Epstein. Both argue that the movement had a coherence and organisation that allowed it to withstand the many criticisms of the working classes as incapable of being trusted with the vote. Thompson is especially keen to see the movement as 'the response of a literate and sophisticated working class' who tended to act independently of any economic conditions. This view has recently been supported by John Belchem, who dismisses the view that Chartism was merely a 'knife and fork' question. He argues that:

- the movement was political and not economic;
- based around the six points of the Charter, the movement organised its ideas on an identifiable political grievance, namely the campaign for parliamentary reform;
- this history of political protest can be traced back to the end of the Napoleonic Wars when a prominent radical tradition developed;
- Chartism itself grew out of this tradition and directed itself against anti-working-class political legislation that had been drawn up by the Whigs, such as the new Poor Law of 1834;
- ultimately, 'Chartism cannot be understood by the changes in the trade cycle, by the study of economic statistics and charts of social tension'.

Case for the 'economic view'

The economic motives in the development of the Chartist movement are also plain to see. The historian Edward Royle takes this view, claiming that 'Chartism was fired by economic discontent, not the demand for political rights'. Quite simply, economic depression and unrest helped to create the climate where political change could take place.

There is no question that Chartism grew in strength at precisely the time when the economy was undergoing recession. W.W. Rostow's social tensions theory claims that in times of 'high' tension – 1838–39, 1841–42 and 1847–48 when bread prices were high – Chartist activity was strongest. Yet, in 1843 to 1846, when Peel's ministry was at its most effective, 'low' social tension as a result of cheap bread prices weakened the strength of the Chartist message.

Chartism was strongest in areas where domestic industry was in decline, such as the West Country, and made little progress where the railway boom had soaked up the excess unemployment. This view is supported by Mark Howell who agrees that Chartism was a movement created by the 'impatience engendered by breakfastless tables and fireless grates', whilst Elie Halévy claims that Chartism represented 'the blind revolt of hunger'. It is certainly true that Chartism was more popular when jobs were scarce and bread prices high.

To what extent was Chartism a movement for political rather than economic change?

Ultimately, interpretation depends entirely on whether you see Chartism as 'a knife and fork question' or as a defined political movement. Recent research has tended to see both political and economic components as being interrelated. The historian P. Gregg claims that 'Chartism was a political movement based on economic grievances'. This modern interpretation seems to do most justice to the complexities of this fascinating academic debate.

9.5 Why did the Chartists fail to achieve their aims?

The attitude of Parliament

After the passage of the 1832 Reform Act, Radicals had always hoped for an extension of the vote and the implementation of the six points of the Charter. The common feeling was that popular pressure had forced the Government into change in 1830–32, so why should similar pressure not succeed a number of years later? Yet in spite of these hopes, the parliamentary élite refused on three occasions – in 1839, 1842 and 1848 – to approve the demands of the Charter.

Why did this occur? The establishment felt it had already changed the constitution once and was not prepared to do so again. The organisation of government was small and compact and the same people who ran Parliament controlled both the Church and the Army. In 1834, the Prime Minister, Earl Grey, warned against 'a constant and active pressure from without to the adoption of any measures the strict necessity of which has not been fully proved, and which are not strictly regulated by a careful attention to the settled institutions of the country'. Faced with such an attitude, it was no surprise that the Chartist message failed to influence the majority of those in Parliament and among the nation's establishment.

Divisions among the leadership

Chartism was such a large umbrella organisation that it was bound to arouse different views and ideas regarding its purpose. Initially, the divisions in the movement were kept hidden, but during the 1840s two completely different attitudes emerged.

- 'Moral force' Chartism placed strong emphasis on non-violent protest, educating the working classes and, if necessary, cooperating with middle-class pressure groups such as the Anti-Corn Law League. The leaders of this tradition were William Lovett and Francis Place. The former left the movement in 1843.
- An alternative tradition was 'physical force' Chartism, which supported the idea that an armed struggle was likely and, in some cases, welcome. The Newport Rising of November 1839 and the Plug Riots of the summer of 1842 represent the high point of this tradition.

A third aspect of Chartism was illustrated by the career of Feargus O'Connor who used the threat of violence but who remained within the law during his political career. Through his powerful platform speeches and the messages carried in his *Northern Star* newspaper, he managed to convince the majority of Chartists to follow his lead. It was almost impossible for one movement to contain these alternative traditions.

A personality clash between Lovett and O'Connor added to the divisions and exposed the contradiction of a movement demanding constitutional change having to resort to violence to bring it about.

Regional differences

Chartism was strongest in the North, but weakest in the South. This is a generalisation, but successful revolutions such as the French Revolution of 1789 have shown that control of, and the support of, the capital is vital for success. As S.J. Lee claims, in *Aspects of British Political History*, 'London was merely the stage on which Chartism acted out its major role'. The Chartist movement tended to act in isolation and there were few examples of a coordinated national strategy to undermine the Government. Different areas interpreted Chartism in their own way. The North, under the control of O'Connor, was strongly in favour of physical force, whilst Birmingham was heavily influenced by the Complete Suffrage Union with its close links to 'moral force' Chartism and the Anti-Corn Law League. In Scotland, the Chartist message was spread by the idea of 'Christian Chartism'. Thus, each region had a different agenda and the government was able to divide and rule successfully. In *Chartist Studies* (1963), historian Asa Briggs highlights these regional differences.

Strength of the British State

Both the Whig Government of Melbourne and the Conservative ministry of Peel had few problems in resisting the potential threat of Chartism. Following the 1832 Reform Act, the political system was relatively stable and both the Army and Police were loyal to the Government. The passage of the Rural Police Act in 1839 ensured that a nationwide police force was able to monitor and deal with any outbreak of discontent. In 1848, for example, Russell's Government was highly organised in dealing with the Kennington Common demonstration. It ensured that the capital was well secured by 7,000 soldiers, 4,000 police and 85,000 special constables, with bridges and railway stations guarded. In addition, both Whig and Conservative governments acted swiftly to arrest known troublemakers and to transport them abroad if necessary. The new railway network was also used to transport troops to meet any threat where it existed and telegraph communication could warn authorities of any danger in advance. As Robert Stewart claims, in *Party and Politics 1830–1852* (1989), 'Chartism's fatal weakness was that it had neither parliamentary strength nor the means of gaining it. It had to develop into a revolutionary movement or collapse.'

Lack of middle-class support

The physical force element of Chartism ensured that the majority of the middle classes refused to support Chartism. Despite the efforts of Lovett, the close cooperation that had existed in 1831–32 was conspicuously absent in this period. The middle class now had an organisation of their own, the Anti-Corn Law League, that was prepared to campaign on an issue closer to their hearts than anything Chartism could promote. The League was successful in gaining middle-class support on a single issue. In addition, the middle classes were content with the gains they had made in 1832 and did not want their property subject to the violence of O'Connor and his mob.

1. What do you regard as the most important reasons why Chartism failed?

2. Was its failure due more to its own internal problems or the strength of the authorities?

The success of Peel's reforms

The popularity of Chartism usually coincided with an economic crisis. The factors that helped the Chartist message to spread were countered in a series of far-sighted laws, such as the Mines Act of 1842 and Repeal of the Corn Law in 1846. The mid-Victorian boom had been created and was to continue well into the future. This prosperity was reflected in rising wages and increased food consumption. As living standards improved support for the Chartists declined.

1. What do you regard as the most significant developments in the Chartist movement between 1839 and 1850? Give reasons to support your answer.

2. Using the information in this chapter, do you think the Charter posed a threat to the existing order or was it merely an attempt to redress obvious weaknesses in the system?

Summary

All these reasons stated would seem to suggest that, in the short term, Chartism achieved little. However, is this a fair evaluation of such a complex movement? It is fairer to say that Chartism did achieve a great deal in the long term. All but one of the six points of the Charter had been put into effect by 1918. The establishment of 'annual parliaments' was the only point of the Charter that failed to pass the test of time. Time has proved, however, that any successful government needs at least five years to promote successful legislation and to transform the society it inherits. The lessons learnt from the Chartist struggle were to be of vital importance when the question of the extension of the franchise appeared once again in 1867 and 1884. The rise of the Labour Party has many of its origins and experiences with the Chartist movement. Rather than dismiss the movement, E. Hopkins, in *A Social History of the English Working Classes, 1815–1945* (1979), claims that the Chartists represented 'the most striking and widespread working-class movement for political reform in the 19th century'.

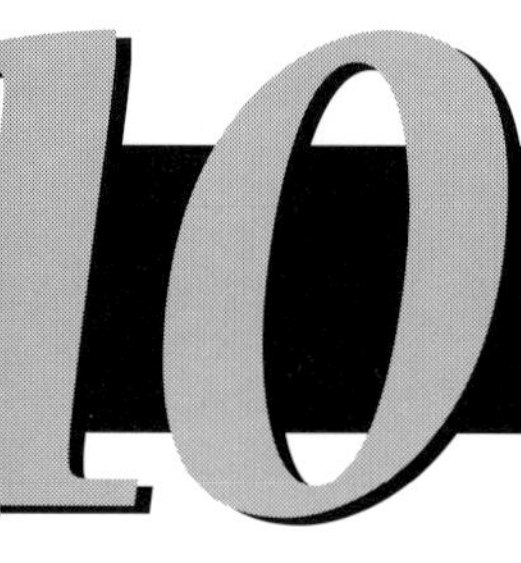

Economic change 1815–1846: the growth of railways

10.1 Why did changes occur to the railway industry between 1815 and 1846?
10.2 What were the key features of railways in the development of the Victorian economy and society between 1815 and 1846?
10.3 Historical interpretation: Has the impact of the railways been exaggerated?

Key Issues

- *What were the most significant developments in the railway industry during this period?*
- *Why was railway growth so important to the development of the Victorian economy in this period?*
- *Did railways change Victorian society in this period?*

Framework of Events

1825	Opening of the Stockton–Darlington Railway in north-east England
1829	Rainhill trials take place for the Liverpool–Manchester Railway
1830	Liverpool–Manchester Railway opens
1837–40	Period of the first 'railway mania' takes place, brought about primarily by an investment boom. This period witnesses the rise of George Hudson as a railway magnate.
1838	Opening of the London–Birmingham Railway
1841	Thomas Cook sells his first excursion ticket
1844	Gladstone's Railway Act lays down the minimum standards for new railway companies to follow
1845–47	Period of the second 'railway mania' begins when at least 4,500 miles of track are laid.

Overview

In an economic sense, the years 1815 to 1846 were dominated by the growth of railways. Few areas of the economy were untouched by the unparalleled speed and dramatic changes brought about by this expansion. Industries such as coal, iron and timber grew on the strength of the railways. The social impact was equally impressive: regional isolation was overcome and the growth of cities such as Birmingham, Manchester and London speeded up. New professions – such as civil engineering, surveying and architecture – responded to the new challenges placed before them. Railways also brought improvements in trade, communications and postal services, and perhaps even the introduction of a standard measure of time across the country (General Standard Time – GST).

Even so, some historians have questioned the impact of the railways and argued that they did not initiate these changes, but were rather a reaction to events already in progress as a result of the Industrial Revolution. To contemporaries, the railways were, more than any other economic development, a symbol of the age.

10.1 Why did changes occur to the railway industry between 1815 and 1846?

Technological change

Coalmining provided the initial stimulus for railway development. Early experiments with railways involving wooden rails and horse-drawn wagons dated back to the 17th century. The first cast-iron rails were laid at Coalbrookdale in 1767, and by 1800 it is estimated that there were over 600 kilometres of track in existence, mostly associated with coalmining activities. Steam power led to new developments in engine construction, pioneered by men such as Richard Trevithick in South Wales and William Hedley in Durham, who designed the steam engine 'Puffing Billy' in 1813.

However, the man most associated with technological change was the Northumbrian engineer, George Stephenson. He revolutionised the railway industry through his vision and insight into mechanical problems. In 1825, he built the first railway to run passenger services: the Stockton–Darlington, with the famous engine 'Locomotion Number One'.

1. Look at the picture. Why is this such a momentous occasion?

2. How reliable is this image in outlining popular enthusiasm for the railways at this time?

The success of the venture encouraged businessmen to look at the new form of transport as an alternative to canals and roads. Canals carried low-value bulk goods but were slow, and freight charges were high. Roads could carry high-value goods that were light in weight, but quantity was limited. The next great railway development was deliberately aimed at breaking the monopoly of the Bridgewater Canal between Manchester and Liverpool. Stephenson's Manchester–Liverpool Railway was a triumph, not only as a financial success but also in its technology (his engine 'The Rocket' reached speeds of 20 miles per hour), and in civil engineering (the viaduct over the

Opening of the Stockton–Darlington Railway, 1825

River Sankey and the crossing of the Chat Moss bog). As the teething problems faced by the early engineers were overcome, more advanced steam engines and stronger wrought-iron rails added to the growth of goods and passengers on the ever-expanding railway system.

The creation of a railway network

The success of these early ventures led to the formation of railway companies to exploit the new developments. The investment opportunities soon proved highly attractive, and the public rushed to buy shares in the new ventures. 'Railway mania' had begun. By 1838, approximately 750 kilometres of new track had been built and a network of lines gradually developed. Whereas before railways had been regionally based, now they began to link different regions. London and Birmingham were connected by 1838, for example. The important industrial areas of South Wales were serviced by the Taff Vale Railway, and there were significant developments in the West Country and Scotland. By the early 1850s, all the major routes had been created, but there remained much scope for consolidation.

Government assistance

Although the railway network was in private hands, and at times development was incoherent and badly planned, in the 1840s the Government began to take an interest in regulating the industry. A powerful parliamentary lobby, led by railway magnates such as George Hudson, pressurised the Government into encouraging more railways. The most important piece of railway legislation was passed in 1844 during Peel's second Ministry under William Gladstone, then President of the Board of Trade. This required:

- the creation of a Railways Board to carry out regular inspection of railway companies and investigate accidents;
- that trains should run at least once a day in each direction along a line, stopping at all stations;
- that to encourage passengers, fares should be no more than a penny a mile.

Increased demand

What were the major changes in the railway industry between 1815 and 1846?

Was the work of individuals more important than other factors in these changes?

Railway development was, in many ways, a response to an increased demand as a result of industrialisation. The most obvious examples occur in the iron and coal industries. Coal was the essential raw material of the Industrial Revolution and railway development grew up in many areas to supply the demand for the substance. Many of the new networks were built originally to improve links with the coalmining industries. Developments in the iron industry proved to be no less important. The discoveries in the iron industry had a spin-off effect on the growth of the railways, such as an increase in demand for railtrack. Improved communications enhanced the development of other industries, such as the cotton industry in north-west England. The building of the Liverpool to Manchester Railway, for example, increased the easy transportation of the raw cotton from the port of Liverpool to the Lancashire textile mills.

10.2 What were the key features of railways in the development of the Victorian economy and society between 1815 and 1846?

The impact of the railways was certainly very significant in the early Victorian age, but the precise role of the railway industry in economic and social growth has recently been subject to intense historical debate (see below). Railways had an effect on most areas of Victorian life, but this was most apparent in the following areas:

- the creation of employment
- reduced journey times
- the growth of towns and cities
- the growth of the professions
- the food and retail industry
- a change in the landscape
- effects on other forms of transport.

The creation of employment

The development of such an important industry was bound to create a huge demand for employment in associated industries. For example, the iron industry grew enormously: by 1840, it has been calculated that rails alone amounted to 15% of total output. As well as stimulating an export boom, it also led to the establishment of new ironworks such as Cyfartha, in south Wales. Coal output increased to meet the demand for steam engines and there were increases in productivity in both the brick and timber industries.

Corporate images: The new railway companies attempted to create a sense of identity by giving employees a uniform to distinguish them from other companies.

In addition, the new industry needed drivers, guards, signalmen, engineers and a host of station staff. **Corporate images** were developed as the new railway companies attempted to assert their new superiority over their local rivals. It was obvious that labourers were needed to build the new lines and although these 'Navvies' (or Navigators) had been heavily involved in the building of canals, it was during the railway age that the term became most common. They acquired a sinister reputation for violence and alcoholism. J.R. Francis, a contemporary, described them in 1851 as 'rude, rugged and uncultivated. Possessed of great animal strength, collected in large numbers, living and working together, they are a class by themselves.' Estimates vary but about 300,000 navvies were employed in the railway industry by 1847. Many had fled Ireland during the Famine and came to England in search of work and a new life. The increase in the number of jobs available had a political consequence in that a large number of the working class found employment and were distracted from the more appealing elements of Chartism (see Chapter 9).

Reduced journey times

The benefits of rail transport were to have a huge effect on journey times. Both the road and canal industries attempted to cut costs and offer attractive packages to travel, but they were unable to match the enormous improvements in travel time that railways provided. The journey between London and York, for example, had taken almost a day and a half by stagecoach. Now it was reduced to eight hours by train. These reduced times led to other important spin-offs. The railways broke down local isolation and created an integrated communication network. Men and women could now travel to and from work by train and leisure-time excursions became commonplace. Thomas Cook the travel agent offered his first holiday excursion ticket in 1841.

1. Compare the two maps. Where does the greatest amount of railway building take place between 1845 and 1852?

2. Can you explain why this area became so densely populated by the railways?

3. How useful are maps to a historian studying the changes brought about by the railway age?

Railway network in 1845

Railway network in 1852

The growth of towns and cities

Some towns were specifically created for the purpose of servicing the new railway industry. Crewe and Swindon, at the beginning of the 20th century, grew from small villages into major railway centres. As well as increasing the size of the cities, railways also changed their physical appearance. The suburbs of the cities increased their middle-class orientation as a result of an improved rail network. On the coast, the railways helped to create the holiday resort. Seaside towns such as Blackpool and Southport grew due to their close connection with the railway industry. The cotton towns of Lancashire also acted as a stimulus to railway growth, as did the coalmining valleys of south Wales.

The growth of the professions

The problems of land ownership and the skilled negotiation needed to conclude complex agreements led to the development of a flourishing legal trade to cater for the demand of the new industries. Lawyers were needed to arbitrate in disputes between interested parties and to take part in sale and conveyancing (process of transferring the legal ownership of land). Accountancy as a profession also developed from the huge sums of money that the new railway boom created. Compensation claims, bankrupt railway companies and mismanagement all helped those employed in this side of the industry. The sheer size of the new railway companies, such as the Great Western Railway, forced those in charge to adopt a new approach to management. This has led some critics to suggest that some railway managers employed an almost military-style attitude to disciplining the workforce.

The food and retail industry

Isambard Kingdom Brunel (1806–1859)
One of the most famous engineers and businessmen of the railway age, he brought a skill and insight to the new technology required for the railway building. Brunel's most famous achievement was the building of the Clifton suspension bridge. Towards the end of his career he became involved in ship design and this led to the building of the steamships the 'Great Western' and the 'Great Eastern'.

Railways were able to transport most food items quickly and safely, so that commodities such as milk could be transported overnight ensuring that it reached its destination in a fresh condition. Other items transported – such as fish, fresh vegetables and other dairy products – ensured that businesses would be able to extend their markets throughout the country and move out of their restricted area. This had an obvious beneficial effect: the retail trade grew to meet the new demand for goods. New shops were opened all over the country, helping to break down local isolation while ensuring that there was never a food shortage confined to a certain area. For the consumer, this meant lower prices and a wider choice. Some groups, such as farmers, initially opposed these developments as they were worried that cheap food would put them out of business, but they were gradually won over when they realised that their own products could be transported further afield.

A change in the landscape

The railway age transformed not only the urban areas but also the old rural environment. Railway architecture, such as viaducts and tunnels, were either an eyesore or a welcome addition to the panorama of the countryside depending on your point of view. Civil engineers such as Isambard Kingdom Brunel made fortunes out of these new developments, but many were opposed to what they regarded as the end of an era. Matthew Arnold, headmaster of Rugby School, regarded the building of a railway station at Rugby in 1839 as being the end of an era. Yet to most people the railway age gave the impression of being a society in transition, moving forward to feed the demands of a new and exciting generation.

The effects on other forms of transport

Railways had an enormous effect on transportation by roads and canals. Stagecoach operators were unable to compete with either the reduction in journey times or the comfort that a modernised railway carriage could provide. Turnpike trusts were forced to raise tolls in their areas, but this led to large-scale protest, especially in south-west Wales where the **'Rebecca' riots** broke out in 1843.

'Rebecca' riots: These took place in rural Carmarthenshire and Cardiganshire in 1843 and were a social protest against an increase in tolls on the turnpike trusts, as well as being part of a protest against an English landowning class. Many of the protesters dressed up as women, hence the term 'Rebecca' riots.

Canals fared little better because railway companies tended to use them as a means of connecting transport links between routes. In some cases, railway companies bought up shares in a canal company for this purpose. Ultimately, railways had an advantage over other forms of transport in moving goods and people cheaply and faster over a wider area of the country. By 1850, long-distance road traffic had disappeared and many canals had become unprofitable enterprises. There was no longer the need for manufacturers to stockpile goods in the winter months, and capital could now be released and used more productively.

Perhaps it is too easy to exaggerate the effect of railways. Canals, for example, continued to carry more freight than the railways for several decades after 1830 and although long-distance road transport virtually disappeared, railways stimulated the growth of short-distance road transport – such as carrying goods and passengers to and from railway stations. Initially, the railways were built on a regional basis and often the gauges were different – usually either seven feet and a quarter inch (214 cm) which was used by the Great Western Railways built by Brunel, or four feet eight and a half inches (143.5 cm) which was the measurement accepted by other rail companies. To make matters even more confusing, Ireland had its own gauge width of five feet three inches (160 cm). Initially, these different measurements caused great difficulty!

Other changes

1. What changes did the railways make to:

(a) the Victorian economy?

(b) Victorian society?

2. What do you regard as being the most significant change that railways made? Give reasons to support your answer.

Railways were in part responsible for the creation of a more literate public. Newspapers printed in London could now be sent by rail directly to different parts of the country so that everybody shared the same news and a new sense of identity. National political campaigns benefited from the fact that politics was transformed by these developments in transport: groups such as the Anti-Corn Law League in the 1840s were especially aware of the positive effects railways could have. The development of the postal service under Rowland Hill was also made easier by the railways. Letters and ideas could now be circulated to all areas of Great Britain and what amounted to a communication revolution had begun. Railways were also regarded as a great source of technological and scientific prestige and confirmed the often assumed view that Britain led the field in scientific advancement. The Great Exhibition of 1851 was as much a celebration of this fact as anything else. Finally, it can be argued that the railways began the British obsession with regular timekeeping on the basis that uniform railway timetables led the change to a common time for all of Britain.

10.3 *Has the impact of the railways been exaggerated?*

A CASE STUDY IN HISTORICAL INTERPRETATION

The case for railways

The case for railways as being the most important economic and social development in the whole of the 19th century is a very strong one. The fact that Britain entered a period of prosperity between 1850 and 1875 is due in no small part to the growth of the railway industry, as well as the other by-products and spin-offs associated with the industry. Social mobility, increased investment opportunities and the movement towards a more urban society are just three. The historian W. Court has argued that 'The level of economic activity in Great Britain during the middle period of the 19th century is unintelligible without reference to the railways'. E.J. Hobsbawm, in *Industry and Empire* (1968), sees the railway booms that occurred in this period as saving **capitalism** by providing investment opportunities and demand for capital goods at a crucial period when the early industrial revolution based on cotton and iron was over. F.R. Crouzet has claimed that 'the railways relaunched the industrial revolution'. M. Freeman has eloquently summarised the social changes by claiming: 'They (the railways) became associated with a fundamental transformation in social thought and attitude. In some senses, they mesmerised society into new codes of life.'

Capitalism: A system based on the theory that possession of capital or money when used in production determines the control of labour.

The case against railways

This view of the railways has recently been challenged by a number of economic historians who, although not wishing to challenge the importance of the railways, wish merely to put the developments into context. B. Mitchell disputes the view that railways led industrial growth. Instead, he argues, they played a supporting role to more important industries such as coalmining. G. Hawke, in *Railways and Economic Growth in England and Wales 1840–1870* (1970), supports Mitchell's ideas by developing the idea of **counter-factual analysis**. By estimating the social saving of the railways – that is, if railways had not existed – he calculated the extra burden placed on road and canals, and concluded that railways only achieved a **social saving** of between 7% and 11%. Thus, transportation by rail was only marginally more efficient than those of traditional methods.

T.R. Gourvish has attempted to combine the two viewpoints by claiming that railways may not have been essential to economic growth. They merely built on existing foundations. Equally, he does not minimise their importance by claiming that 'Railways had a greater influence than any other single innovation before the age of oil and electricity'.

Counter-factual analysis: A term used by economic historians to calculate the effect of something if it has not been present. In this case, the impact on the economy if the railway age had not taken place.

Social saving: Closely connected with 'counter-factual analysis'; put simply, this is the benefit derived from the railway industry. It can be difficult to calculate depending on which evidence you wish to use.

1. Summarise the arguments in favour of and against the importance of railways.

2. Which of these two views seems to be the more appealing? Give reasons to support your answer.

? Source-based questions: The importance of the railways

SOURCE A

Economically the productivity of British industry was now assisted by the best and most inexpensive transport system in the world. In a thousand different ways, from cheap Midlands coal for the London householder to the light reading literature provided by W.H. Smith's station bookstalls, the railways helped to remould [reshape] Victorian society.

From Aristocracy and People, Britain 1815–1865 *by Norman Gash, published in 1987 – a secondary source from a modern history textbook.*

SOURCE B

There were, however, many powerful opponents to the railway companies. Stagecoach proprietors, innkeepers, and horsedealers all saw their livelihood threatened; the canal companies became aware of a powerful competitor. The most potent force of resistance lay simply in the natural conservatism of the country. Trains were considered to be 'dangerous and a nuisance'.

From Nineteenth-Century Britain 1815–1914 *by Anthony Wood, published in 1981 – a secondary source from a modern history textbook.*

SOURCE C

Painting of Paddington Station by William Powell Frith, 1862. It captures the frenzy of a busy London railway station at the height of the railway age.

SOURCE D

Railway development, 1830–1870

	Miles of track open	*Passengers carried (m.)*	*Passenger train receipts (£m.)*	*Freight carried (m. ton)*	*Freight train receipts (£m.)*
1830	98				
1832	166				
1834	298				
1836	403				
1838	743	5.4			
1840	1,498				
1842	1,939				
1844	2,148	25.2	3.4		1.6
1846	3,036	40.2	4.6		2.8
1848	4,982	54.4	5.6		4.2
1850	6,084	67.4	6.5		6.2
1852	6,628	82.8	7.3		7.7
1854	7,157	104.3	9.6		9.7
1856	7,650	121.4	10.6	63.7	11.4
1858	8,354	130.7	10.9	71.9	11.9
1860	9,069	153.5	12.2	88.4	14.2
1862	9,953	170.0	13.0	91.9	14.7
1864	10,995	217.4	14.7	108.5	17.7
1866	11,945	261.2	16.4	121.8	20.1
1869*	13,170	298.6	17.6	n.a.	21.4
1871*	13,388	322.2	18.1	166.5	23.2

Figures for 1868 are seriously deficient; hence statistics have been included for 1869 and 1871.

From The Forging of the Modern State: Early Industrial Britain 1783–1870 *by Eric Evans (Longman), quoting from Mitchell and Deane.*

Source-based questions: The importance of the railways

SOURCE E

The people would be smothered in tunnels, and those that escaped suffocation would be burned in the carriages. Eton College opposed it because it would harm the discipline of the school. A farmer objected because his cows might be killed in passing under an archway. The water in the Thames would be decreased, and the supply to Windsor Castle destroyed.

From A History of the English Railway *by J.R. Francis, 1851*

1. Study Source A.

Explain the phrase 'the railways helped to remould Victorian society'.

2. Study Source D.

What evidence is contained in this source to show the positive impact of the railways on the Victorian economy?

3. Study Sources B and E.

What are the similarities between the sources in their criticism of the impact of the railways?

4. Study Source E.

How does the author, by the use of language and style, suggest that the railways were a backward step for British society?

5. 'The railways had a positive impact on the Victorian economy and society.' Using the sources and the information in this chapter, how far do you agree with this statement?

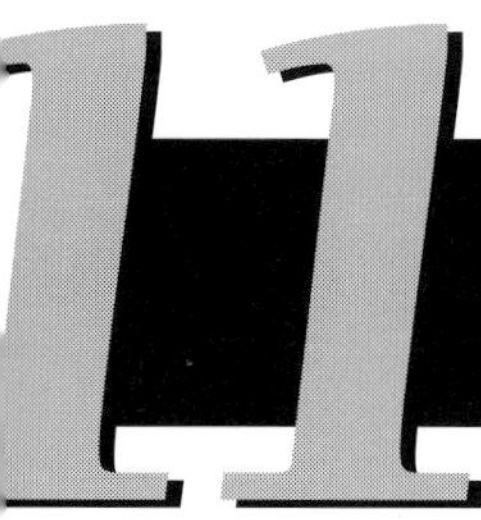

British domestic politics, 1846–1868

11.1 What was the impact of the repeal of the Corn Laws on the British political system?
11.2 How successful was Lord John Russell as Prime Minister 1846–1852?
11.3 Why was the Derby–Disraeli Administration formed in 1852 and what impact did it have?
11.4 How successful was the Whig–Peelite Coalition of Aberdeen in domestic affairs?
11.5 Why did Palmerston dominate this period and what contribution did he make to British domestic politics?
11.6 Historical interpretation: The rise of the Liberal Party
11.7 What impact did Derby, Disraeli and the Conservatives have on British politics in this period?
11.8 How and why was parliamentary reform achieved in 1867?

Key Issues

- *What was the impact of the repeal of the Corn Laws on British politics?*
- *What is the importance of this period for the careers of Gladstone and Disraeli?*
- *Why was there such a degree of political instability in this period?*

Framework of Events

1846	Resignation of Peel; formation of Russell Administration
1847	General election – Bentinck leaves Conservative leadership
1848	Chartist demonstration at Kennington Revolutions in Europe Public Health Act
1851	Resignation of Russell; Palmerston is dismissed; Russell returns
1852	Russell is defeated in Commons General election – no party with clear majority Derby–Disraeli minority government formed; defeated in Commons; Aberdeen Coalition formed
1853	Gladstone's first Budget Palmerston's domestic legislation
1854	Crimean War
1855	Roebuck's Motion and defeat of Aberdeen's Coalition in Commons Palmerston becomes Prime Minister
1856	Peace of Paris – Crimean War ended
1857	General election – Palmerston wins
1858	Palmerston defeated in Commons – resigns
1858–59	Derby–Disraeli minority Administration
1859	Willis' Rooms meeting. Liberal Party formed officially
1860	Cobden Treaty with France
1864	Gladstone's 'Pale of the Constitution' speech
1865	Palmerston's final election victory; death of Palmerston; Russell becomes Prime Minister
1866	Gladstone introduces Reform Bill into the House of Commons Liberal Party splits over Reform Bill Conservative minority Administration formed
1867	Disraeli introduces and passes Reform Act
1868	February: Disraeli becomes Prime Minister November: Liberal election victory December: Gladstone forms first Administration.

Overview

THIS period – 1846 to 1868 – is usually seen as one of marginal significance in British political history, overshadowed by the Administration of Peel which went before, and by the great administrations of Gladstone and Disraeli which came after. There is a feeling that little of importance happened domestically – apart, possibly, from the Second Reform Act at the very end – and that the 'great events' which should be known by students of history happened overseas, such as the Revolutions of 1848 and the Crimean War.

However, the period is of central importance. In contrast to Europe, there was considerable political stability in Britain. There may have been frequent changes of government, but there was a broad and growing acceptance of our constitutional and political system, and a recognition that it provided a framework in which the country could progress and people could prosper.

It was a key formative period in many ways. Political parties began to take on a role and develop along lines that became increasingly recognisable. Politicians learned lessons from the past and rapidly adapted to new circumstances. By the end of this period, a two-party system was there. Politicians and the public both accepted the need for and saw the benefits of so such a system. Britain was moving towards a more representative and democratic system even before the 1867 Reform Act came along to confirm this and to give it recognition. It was still an age where personalities mattered, and it is possible to explain the 'ins' and 'outs' of political events in terms of personal likes and dislikes. The fondness of the Queen and Prince Albert for some politicians, and the great personality clashes – such as those between Gladstone and Disraeli, Russell and Palmerston – often provide the best explanations for events, rather than a split over any great issue. However, issues could split parties, just as Repeal did for the Conservatives in 1846; but on the whole when potentially great issues arose, such as parliamentary reform in 1851, there was the tendency to back down for fear of a repeat of the passions of 1845–46.

This was a formative period for Parliament, government, personalities and parties. It therefore merits careful study as much for what happened as for what did not. It is interesting to see that while many of the standard texts – ranging from the traditional *Age of Reform* by E.L. Woodward (1938), through to Asa Briggs' *Age of Improvement* (1961) – tend to pass briefly over this period. The political biographers – such as Robert Blake (1966) and S. Weintraub (1993) on Disraeli, R. Shannon on Gladstone (1982) and Bourne (1984) and J. Ridley (1970) on Palmerston – place a great emphasis on this very period as a crucial stage in their subjects' career and development. To the social and economic historian, this period is of huge importance, as it is to the historian of Empire and foreign affairs.

This is a period of contrasts. Some historians have seen it as a time of political instability, with minority governments and majority governments being overturned with regularity. Parties had not yet formed into the tightly organised and disciplined bodies they were later to become. Members of Parliament saw themselves more as free agents, rather than party delegates to the House of Commons liable to vote as the Whips told them to. Even though in a comfortable majority between 1855 and 1858, and 1859 and 1865, Palmerston, the Prime Minister, found himself defeated more than a hundred times in the House of Commons. It is also seen as a period of calm and consolidation after the heady events of the late 1840s, and dramatic external events in the Crimea and the war with Russia. For the Liberal Party, it was to be a vital period of evolution. The Conservatives would see it as a period of stagnation and inertia, ending with one of the most remarkable events in 19th-century politics, their Reform Act of 1867.

There were dramatic events overseas (which will be dealt with separately) which frequently overshadowed domestic politics, and at times caused upheaval in government itself. There are no items of legislation, bar the Reform Act of 1867, which dominate specific years, but there are areas of critical evolution that must be noted as without them an understanding of the politics of the late 19th century cannot be attained. Such areas range from local government, through education and public health, to the role of the State, the British Empire and the ever-recurring topic of Ireland. Any would-be historian who tries to leap from the Corn Law crisis of 1846 and the failure of Chartism in 1848 to the heady days of Disraeli and Gladstone of the 1870s, is liable to find they have a woefully incomplete understanding of what happened and why.

11.1 What was the impact of the repeal of the Corn Laws on the British political system?

The impression given by many historians was that the Conservative split over repeal had a devastating impact on the British political system. Certainly, those wishing to see British politics in traditional two-party terms would see the events of 1846 as catastrophic. Whereas, in a broader context, the Conservative split could be seen as more a re-adjustment within a constantly evolving process – along the lines of the Canningites' refusal to serve under Wellington in 1828.

What was the impact of the repeal of the Corn Laws on the Whigs?

John Russell, first Earl Russell (1792–1878)
Russell was Leader of the Commons 1852–55, Foreign Secretary 1859–65 and Prime Minister 1846–52 and 1865–68.

The immediate result of Peel's resignation was that John Russell formed a Whig minority Administration in 1846. (The term 'Liberal' did not come into common use until 1859.) There had been no election since 1841, which Peel and his Conservatives had won. This new Administration was essentially a coalition between the Whigs, Liberals (and the name was being used increasingly), Radicals and Irish. The Whigs tended to be members of the older aristocratic families, with considerable wealth, and were traditionally favourable to reform and to religious toleration.

A definition of a Liberal is more difficult in the context of the 1840s: they tended to come from a different, more middle-class, background than the Whigs; favoured a more active role for government in politics; and their money was more likely to come from industry than land. (The fact that this describes many of the key Peelites, as well as perhaps Peel himself, shows why party divisions became so blurred in this period.)

Radicals are equally difficult to define. They tended to be those who were sympathetic to Chartism or deeply concerned with single issues, such as factory reform or the removal of religious disabilities. Again, the fact that some of the radicals had strong links with some members of the Conservative Party is revealing of the fluid state of English politics. There were other supporters of Russell: ranging from supporters of the Manchester School of free trade economics to reformers of the Edwin Chadwick type. The potential for a split similar to that suffered by the Conservatives in 1846 was just as great. Russell never gloated about the predicament that Peel had

William Gladstone (1809–1898)
Gladstone became a Tory MP in 1832. He was Conservative Minister from 1841 to 1846; Chancellor of the Exchequer 1852–55 and 1859–66; Leader of the Liberal Party from 1867 and Prime Minister 1868–74, 1880–85, 1886 and 1892–94.

found himself in in 1846: he knew it could easily happen to him. There were potential splits in ideology (political ideas), in attitude and over policy, and Russell must be given credit for holding together such a diverse group.

Repeal played an important part in the rise of the Liberals, not only giving them office, but also seeing to their growth as an identifiable and understood group in politics. In addition, there had been a further decline in the influence of the Whigs. The days of the aristocratic Melbourne were over. The job of government was increasingly seen as being to legislate to solve the great issues of the day, and not just to administer. The repeal split was to play a key role in encouraging into the Liberal ranks men of ability, experience and talent, of whom the key was Gladstone. The 'Liberal' element in the party, which had been led by Grey and Melbourne, looked like being marginalised by the excellent administrative and other reforms of Peel in the 1841–46 period. Yet without the 'Liberal' elements the Whig Party could easily have disintegrated, as it alone could not have got an effective coalition going with the Radicals and the Irish. It could be argued that the repeal split played a vital part in the history of the Liberal Party, just as it did with the Conservatives.

What was the impact of Repeal on the Peelites?

There was also now a new group in politics, the Peelites. They had no effective leader as Peel, while remaining in politics, provided no leadership. It might be fair to say that he simply went into a sulk. In addition to Gladstone, there were other able men such as Sir James Graham, who had been Home Secretary under Peel. It was generally agreed that most of the ablest of the Conservative Party under Peel had severed their connection with the rank-and-file of the party, now looking to Lord George Bentinck for leadership (and not getting much). There was no coherent Peelite philosophy. These men had been enthusiastic supporters of Peel's Budgets and legislation of the early 1840s. They were perhaps closer in their basic beliefs to Russell and his Cabinet than to the other Conservatives under Bentinck and Disraeli, even though they sat on the same Opposition benches in the House of Commons.

Most of the Peelites supported the main measures of the Russell Administration of 1846–52, both foreign and domestic. The presence of this able and articulate group of men, slightly adrift in the political river, was to be a major cause of the political instability of the period. There was also tremendous bitterness between the two wings of the Conservative Party. Disraeli was seen as 'traitor to the cause' and the 'burglar of others' intellect' by men who had not long before been members of the same party. Peel was seen as a non-leader who 'had a staff but no army'.

What was the impact of Repeal on the Conservatives?

The Conservative Party was simply unprepared for Repeal and the bitterness that it generated. Peel had offended many of his MPs. He had damaged their income (or so they thought) and their status. Many Conservative MPs and their voters still felt that parties stood for interests, as opposed to policies and principles, and that those interests should not be sacrificed to expediency, however great the emergency. Peel's pragmatism, however necessary it may have been over Repeal, was not popular with many of those who had put him in power.

The rest of the Conservative Party, the rank-and-file, was in a very difficult situation. Protection as an economic issue was in fact dead, but of course many were reluctant to accept that. There was no obvious leader after Bentinck, and he was unsuited to leadership as soon as a divisive issue such as religious toleration appeared. Disraeli was not seen as an alternative as there

Protectionist wing: Those who supported the continuation of the Corn Laws, with the tax on imported corn, designed to protect the interests of the landowning class.

Edward Stanley, 14th Earl of Derby (1799–1869)
Stanley first became a Whig MP in 1820, and was a Whig Minister 1833–34. In 1837 he was elected as a Conservative MP, serving as Prime Minister in 1852 and 1858–59. In 1844, he moved to the House of Lords.

were real doubts about his sincerity and background. The Peelites detested him for his bitter attacks on Peel in 1846, and naturally he was seen as an obstacle to reunification of the Party. There were a growing number of Conservative backbenchers in the **protectionist wing** of the party who were beginning to feel, by 1848, that Disraeli had used them as a stepping stone to further his own ambitions.

There seemed to be no alternative to Disraeli. Those who had served under Peel, but had declined the Peelite label, were too old. Edward Stanley (later Lord Derby), on whom the nominal leadership had fallen, offered Disraeli unofficial leadership of the Commons in 1848, simply not daring to offer him it properly. Disraeli declined, until Stanley did it properly in 1849. The Party was also divided over religious toleration, be it for Jews or Catholics, the former being an area where Disraeli (himself a Jew) naturally preferred to remain silent given the deep-seated prejudices of many of the MPs whose support he badly needed.

By 1850, there was a gradual acceptance of the leadership of Derby and Disraeli. However, within the Party there was still considerable suspicion about the latter, particularly as many protectionist Conservative MPs rightly suspected that Disraeli was looking for a way to abandon protection.

What political changes occurred as a result of the Repeal of the Corn Laws?

How significant an event was the Repeal of the Corn Laws in the history of the Conservative Party in the 19th century?

Conclusion

In simple terms, the Repeal split widened a pre-existing split within the Conservative Party, which was partly personal, partly ideological and partly due to differing attitudes towards the evolving party system. It also played an important, but not to be exaggerated, part in keeping the Conservative Party out of a majority situation until 1874.

The Repeal of the Corn Laws played an important part in reviving and evolving the fortunes of the Liberal element of the old Whig Party, which had been marginalised by Peel in the early 1840s, when he had stolen many of their potential policies. It explains why the Peelites were more ideologically comfortable within the Liberal Party when they eventually got there, and how Gladstone could work quite well with Palmerston and Russell under Aberdeen, and later under Palmerston in the 1860s.

11.2 How successful was Lord John Russell as Prime Minister 1846–1852?

Lord John Russell proved to be an able Prime Minister. He has always been overshadowed by others – be it earlier prime ministers like Peel and Melbourne, or later ones like Palmerston, Gladstone and Disraeli. Even over the time when he was Prime Minister there has tended to be a focus more on the work of his Foreign Secretary, Lord Palmerston. Russell has been seriously underrated. For a start, he was in office for nearly six years, and in a minority situation in the House of Commons for the whole time. A Peelite/Conservative re-unification was always a possibility, and could overthrow him at any time. He was dependent also on maintaining the cooperation of a diverse group of Whigs, Liberals, Radicals and Irish. There were a large number of seriously divisive political issues during his Administration, ranging from the retention of income tax to religious toleration (the Jewish Bill). Many of his Radical supporters wished for major reforms, yet he had deeply conservative elements within his own Party to consider, and too radical an approach might well unite his opponents. To unite the radical and liberal elements in his own Party, ally and work with the Peelites and keep in harmony with the instinctive conservatism of men like Palmerston required very considerable skill.

At the same time, there was not the strong party system of discipline, with

Whips: Chosen MPs who have a responsibility to ensure that other MPs of the same party vote with the party line in Parliament.

its **Whips** and focus on loyalty, which was to emerge later. The tradition of the independent MP – the representative of his constituents and not their delegate – was still strong. Persuasion and a willingness to listen and compromise were needed to get, and keep, a majority in Parliament. Russell had to fight an election in 1847 when, although he managed to improve his parliamentary position, he was still not in a majority (325 Whig/Liberal etc., 226 Conservatives/Protectionists, 105 Peelites).

It should also be remembered that Russell's Administration lasted longer than either its predecessor or quite a few of its successors. He also had the additional complications of a monarch quite determined to assert her influence in both domestic and foreign affairs. Also, Victoria was backed by her able and strong-minded husband. To stay in power for six years and achieve what Russell did was no mean achievement.

What were the main problems facing Russell's Government in the years 1846–1852?

There were also major problems, both domestically and internationally. Chartism was going through its final phases. Russell also had to deal with the events at Kennington in 1848, with the mass petition and the genuine fear that Revolution might come to the streets of London as well as in Europe. Thousands of special constables, ranging from Gladstone to the future Emperor Napoleon III of France, were recruited to deal with the imagined crisis, yet it passed off peacefully. Russell was criticised for taking too 'soft' a line with the Chartists in 1848. No Chartist newspapers were suppressed, for example. Russell felt that if they had real grievances, they had a right to express them. His common sense handling of the Chartists, together with the sensible handling of soldiers by their commanders, was a key factor in the peaceful settlement of events in 1848. In the background, there was the huge turmoil in Europe in 1848, with revolutions affecting many major powers, and Britain was to play a major role in stabilising Europe.

What factors assisted Russell in his retention of power?

Certainly he had some advantages. The opposition remained bitterly divided, not just over protection but also over issues such as religious toleration, which divided the protectionist Conservatives, with Bentinck and Disraeli disagreeing with their own backbenchers. Peel provided no leadership until his death in 1850. Bentinck died in 1848, although he had resigned the 'leadership' earlier. With the death of Bentinck, there was a great reluctance among the protectionist Conservative backbenchers to accept the leadership of Disraeli, as they were beginning to suspect that not only was he considering abandoning protection but that he had cynically manipulated them in his bid for power.

Further reasons for Russell's success and tenure of office came from the able work of Palmerston at the Foreign Office. The growth in prosperity of both agriculture and industry also helped. Russell did not have the background of the 'Hungry 40s' to work with. Sir Charles Wood at the Exchequer provided the sound finance that, naturally, had a great appeal to the Peelites. He had good men, as well as good measures, and the background of peace and prosperity was bound to make his Administration more popular. Also, there was no clear alternative to Russell and his Whigs.

How significant was the domestic work and legislation of Russell between 1846 and 1852?

Russell's background was traditionally Whig, which preferred to administer rather than legislate, and was very much in tune with the *laissez-faire* philosophy of the age (see page 49). This saw the government of the day having a fairly minor role and it being the responsibility of the individual to deal with problems affecting himself and his family. Russell never quite fitted into this traditional mould, and he was more than prepared for his Government to take an active role.

The work of Sir Charles Wood at the Exchequer continued along the lines laid down by Peel in his earlier Budgets, and gained the support of Gladstone. There was to be no return to the situation that Chancellor Baring had left for Peel in 1841 (a huge deficit).

There were to be some important social reforms in this period. Most will be dealt with in more detail later, but it is important to view them as part of the work and achievement of Russell.

What did Russell achieve in Ireland?

In Ireland, Russell inherited a disaster of enormous magnitude. It is estimated that nearly a million died in the 1845–47 period, and there was in addition the huge social and economic dislocation caused by the mass emigration of many of the survivors. The administrative system in Ireland (and in the whole of Britain for that matter) was totally unable to cope with a disaster of this magnitude, and the prevailing *laissez-faire* attitude did not encourage intervention by government.

Peel had brought in two measures to help relieve the famine:

1. The importing of US maize which would be sold cheaply.
2. The provision of public works, such as road building, which would give labourers the money with which to buy this cheap food.

Even though backed up with a lot of charity from England, the plans broke down as there was not the infrastructure to deal with them. Russell gave up the works and allowed outdoor relief on a large scale. Even though it had been a Whig Government in the 1830s that had abolished this type of aid, Russell was more than prepared to put need before political consistency. (It might be noted, however, that of the £7 million spent on Irish relief by the Russell Government, only about 50% was a straight grant, the rest was lent. The loan was never actually repaid. There were limits to an English government's generosity to the Irish!)

Peel's Government had made an attempt to deal with some of the grievances of Irish tenants, and Russell made an attempt in 1848 to introduce a **tenant-right bill** which he hoped would end the terrible system of 'murder on one side: ejection on the other'. However, he could not get it past the Committee stage (see page 115) in Parliament and he lacked the political muscle to move it further; evictions continued by the thousands. Bankrupt landlords got a better deal, and legislation, which came into effect in 1849, helped them. **Coercion** was necessary to deal with the odd attempt to copy the revolutions of 1848 led by Smith O'Brien MP, but he was transported to Australia for his pains. Russell managed to persuade Queen Victoria to visit Ireland in 1849. This was received with enthusiasm in many, but not all, quarters.

Tenant-right bill: A measure designed to give the people who rented land in Ireland greater security of tenure against eviction and increased rents.

Coercion: Term given to government policy – usually involves the removal of civil rights and can include imprisonment without trial.

Further attempts by Russell to deal with the genuine grievances of the Irish tenant failed. He also failed in an attempt to 'make Cork like York' by creating a fourth Secretaryship of State for Ireland, and abolishing the Viceroyalty. This, he hoped, would help greater integration of Ireland into the United Kingdom. He did manage to get in some reforms to the notoriously corrupt electoral system, and increase the electorate in Ireland from 45,000 to 163,000, as well as make a major step with the creation, in 1850, of the non-denominational Queen's University in Belfast. Russell was by no means the last Prime Minister to discover that there were real limits to what an essentially English Cabinet and Parliament would tolerate in the way of 'concessions' to the Irish. The gap between English and Irish attitudes continued to grow, but not for the want of Russell trying.

What important domestic legislation did Russell's Administration pass?

Factory reform

There was progress in other areas, such as factory legislation. The impetus that had developed under Peel, with the Factory Act of 1844, was to continue. Ashley Cooper, who had been the driving force behind much of the early work, had resigned his seat in sympathy with Peel. Leadership of the reform movement passed to John Fielden, who tried hard to get the working hours of women and children reduced to a maximum of ten a day. He was narrowly defeated in 1846, but tried again in 1847, with some sympathetic, but not too overt, support from the Russell Government, and was successful. It did not completely stop all work by women and children for more than ten hours, so another Act was brought in in 1850, known as Grey's Act, which did more to limit such practices. Even that, which had more sympathetic support from Russell, was not perfect. It was not until 1853, under Palmerston as Home Secretary, that a shorter working day for women and children finally arrived.

Russell can be criticised for not doing enough in this respect, and for relying too much on the pressure of such men as John Fielden to protect women and children from exploitation. The principle of *laissez-faire* was decisively broken with these Acts, and they were crucial stepping stones for what was to come later. Russell was quite prepared for his Government and Party to intervene and become involved where necessary. The attitude of the more traditional Whigs, where *laissez-faire* was the rule, was going. Russell's Administration, in contrast perhaps to those of 1830–41, did not have to be goaded by pressure groups into action in the same way.

Anthony Ashley Cooper, 7th Earl of Shaftesbury (1801–1855)
Ashley Cooper became MP in 1826, and Earl in 1851. He was a persistent agitator and pressure group leader for humanitarian and social reform. He became Chairman of the Sanitary Commission on the Crimean War in 1855.

John Fielden (1784–1849)
Radical MP for Oldham. Fielden was a successful manufacturer. He was also known as a benevolent despot.

The Public Health Act, 1848

The other major measure was the Public Health Act of 1848, which will be dealt with in more detail later. In the words of one historian: 'the great clean up effectively began when the central government carried the Act of 1848'. Central government now had the powers, feeble initially, to compel local authorities to act in the vital areas of water supplies and sewage. For the first time, central government took on an initiating role in this key area. It was a major step forward and Russell's Government must be given some credit for it, although much of the work had been done by that outstanding one-man pressure group, Edwin Chadwick.

1. Did Russell achieve more in Ireland than he did in England during his premiership of 1846 to 1852?

2. 'A greatly underrated Prime Minister'. Discuss this view of Russell's premiership of 1846–52.

Conclusion

The Administration might not merit the title of a 'great reforming administration' in the same way that others in the 19th century might, but it was a key formative time. The initial state grant to education had come earlier, but Russell saw to it in this Administration that it was substantially increased. With the Great Exhibition in the background, which was a major achievement in its own right, and little pressure or demand for major reforms, Russell's achievements were not insubstantial.

11.3 Why was the Derby–Disraeli Administration formed in 1852 and what impact did it have?

The seeds of destruction were always present in Russell's Administration. He was always in a potential minority, and was kept in office through the goodwill and support of the Peelites. Russell never had quite the enthusiasm for sound finance and administration, which would have wedded the Peelites closely to his cause; the Peelites also had too many reservations about colleagues like Palmerston to wish for any closer alliance. Although Russell did promote able young men, there were still too many of the traditional Whigs in key positions in his Cabinet. With serious internal problems, such as the demand for major reforms emanating from radicals, there was always an element of borrowed time about his Administration. His Government was defeated on a Private Member's motion (see page 115) in 1851 to reform the franchise, and he resigned, but had to come back in as there was no one else capable of forming an administration. He was defeated in early 1852, when Palmerston and his supporters voted against him on a Militia Bill.

Derby and Disraeli's Government which followed was to have little impact, if any. There was no serious legislation forthcoming in the short session of the spring of 1852. Parliament was dissolved in the early summer and there was a general election.

The results brought no great comfort to any party. The Conservative Government gained 310 seats, the Whigs 270, the Irish about 40 and the Peelites were reduced to about 40. There was still a minority situation with the Peelites and/or the Irish holding the balance of power. The Government was nearly defeated just after the new Parliament opened when an attempt was made to split it over the highly contentious issue of protection, but it was Palmerston who saved them

With Derby seemingly supporting protection in the Lords, and Disraeli coming out against it in the Commons, the Government did not seem set to last, and it did not.

Why was Palmerston dismissed?

The dismissal of Palmerston in 1851 over his premature recognition of the *coup d'état* of Louis Napoleon (later Napoleon III) in France, further weakened Russell's Government, perhaps more than he realised. Napoleon had seized power in France illegally and Palmerston should have waited until the French people had accepted him as their ruler before recognising him officially. The dismissal proved to be an unwise move. Russell was unaware of how popular a figure Palmerston was in Britain. What was more, Russell had alienated both the Irish and the Peelites over the Ecclesiastical Titles Bill in 1851, and his attempts to further the cause of parliamentary reform helped to alienate the more conservative members of his Cabinet. His rather personal style, where personalities seemed to matter more than policies, was not conducive either to the smooth running of government.

On a bill put forward by the Government to improve the militia, as there was yet another scare about the possibility of a French invasion in February 1852, Palmerston voted with the Conservatives. The dispute between the two men was out in the open again. This time Russell was beaten, and resigned. It was widely seen as Palmerston extracting his revenge. As Palmerston himself wrote, after his wife's widely publicised 'victory party', 'I have had my tit-for-tat with John Russell, and I turned him out.' With such an attitude towards party loyalty, Russell's achievement in remaining in power for so long, and achieving so much, is substantial.

The formation of the new Minority Administration

The Conservatives had already been offered office when Russell resigned the previous year (1851) but Stanley had rejected it. He was never enthusiastic about office, much to the despair of the ambitious Disraeli. Derby was still largely in favour of protection, which was a major stumbling block, particularly given the size of the protectionist minority in Parliament.

With such an insecure base, and given the fact that Derby, although he had quite an intellect, was a poor economist with an amateur approach to government, it is hardly surprising that the Administration lasted for so short a period. Derby preferred to spend his time with his beloved horses and racing. He viewed the prevailing passion for statistics and **royal commissions** with great distaste. Other than the fact that he was there, it is hard to see much of a contribution made by him to the evolution of the Conservative Party, or to modern conservatism.

Royal commissions: Investigative bodies picked to examine major problems of state, which report back with recommended solutions. Members were usually men of stature and experience in the relevant areas.

Disraeli as Chancellor of the Exchequer

The key figure in the Administration was Benjamin Disraeli – in office for the first time as Chancellor of the Exchequer (and Leader of the Commons). There was no apprenticeship for him. His own self-confidence and the assurance from Derby 'that they will tell you the figures' (and the flattery that Canning had been in the same situation once) overcame that problem.

Palmerston had been offered the post first, but had declined – an indication of the fluid nature of politics at the time. Only three members of the Government had held office before. It became known as the 'Who? Who?' Administration after the reaction of the ageing, and slightly deaf, Duke of Wellington to the names of the Cabinet as they were read out to him.

Disraeli's Budget of 1852

The final stroke came with Disraeli's first Budget, in December 1852. The background was one of concern about the intentions of France with a fear of invasion and therefore a need to spend more on defence. Disraeli's own backbenchers were looking in suspicion at his attitude to free trade.

It was generally conceded to have been a competent Budget, given the shortage of accurate information coming from the Treasury and Disraeli's own weakness in the area of finance. He wisely conceded that the day of protection was over, but had the wisdom to cut the malt tax which was seen as a gesture designed to benefit the landed interest. Tea duty was cut – in fact, there were several items which would have pleased the strong free-trade lobby. With the growth of free trade, and therefore a reduction of income from import duties and the like, coupled with a growing need to spend on areas such as defence and education, Disraeli had to bring in additional funds from elsewhere. Direct taxation was the answer. He raised the level of income tax, but in such a way that it was only those with comfortable incomes who would suffer. There was also a radical proposal to differentiate between earned and unearned income when it came to assessment for taxation – hardly the sort of idea expected in the Budget of a Conservative. It was generally agreed to have been an impressive performance on Disraeli's part not only in terms of delivery and presentation, but also in his grasp of politics and economics.

The Budget was defeated, to the surprise of many. The key factor in the defeat was Gladstone's intervention. He tried to make out that he had not intended to speak against the Budget, but the evidence suggests that he had been planning his attack on Disraeli for some time.

Any chance of a reconciliation between the two wings of the Conservatives had now disappeared. Revenge for what Disraeli had done to Peel in 1846 had been obtained, and the confusion in British politics was to continue.

1. What were the main events during Derby's short Conservative Administration?

2. Assess the importance of the short Conservative Administration of 1852 on:

(a) the career of Disraeli

(b) the career of Gladstone

(c) the history of the Conservative Party.

3. Why did two governments fall in 1852?

Conclusion

The Conservatives had gained a little from their few months in office: an ability to work together rather better, and the problem of protection had gone. The mistrust of Disraeli was still present among backbenchers, and Derby had not gained any more enthusiasm for power. The Conservative Party still had a long way to go before it could gain the necessary popular, and parliamentary, support for a majority administration. However, Disraeli had now 'arrived' as a key political figure, and a growing number of Conservatives saw no alternative but to continue with him as unofficial leader of the Party.

The Administration failed because, like its predecessors, it lacked a clear base in Parliament and in the country. Until that group of able men – the Peelites – decided that there was no future in the centre ground of politics, there was to be no government with a secure majority.

11.4 How successful was the Whig–Peelite Coalition of Aberdeen in domestic affairs?

With the defeat of the Derby–Disraeli Administration over the Budget, the Government had to resign. With no budget there could be no government. The problem was for the Queen to find another one, and there was a marked lack of enthusiasm among her former ministers of all parties and persuasions to take on the task. The Palace's distaste for Palmerston did not make administration forming easy either.

In the end the Earl of Aberdeen, who had been Peel's Foreign Secretary between 1841 and 1846, was persuaded to form an administration. He was liked, rather than respected, by his colleagues. He could keep the peace, and it was felt that he did not threaten. However, he was not known for his leadership qualities, and when they were needed they were to be found wanting.

It was essentially a coalition between the Peelites and the Whigs. Although the Whigs/Liberals formed the bulk of the support in the House of Commons (they had about 270 seats in the Commons to the Peelites' 40), the Cabinet contained six Peelites to six Whigs. Palmerston was tempted to join the Conservatives in opposition. He resisted the temptation as he needed the ministerial salary. He came in as Home Secretary (the Palace had forbidden his appointment to the Foreign Office). Gladstone got the job he had longed for at the Exchequer and Russell took on the Foreign Office (briefly). Interestingly enough, in the light of later events in the Crimea, the three key 'military' posts went to supposedly efficient and able Peelites: the Duke of Newcastle, James Graham and Sidney Herbert. As Palmerston himself said, 'the Administration contains almost all the men of talent and experience in the House of Commons, except Disraeli'.

The Cabinet got on very well together, personally, although there were several issues that were to cause division, and the good-natured relations were not to survive the stresses of war. Attitude towards coalitions tended to be dominated by Disraeli's famous phrase that 'England does not love coalitions', but there was no alternative to start with given what the electorate had produced in 1852. Contemporaries did not see this mixed Cabinet as unusual. It did produce, both in terms of budgets and legislation, a fair amount of real quality. Also, the point should be made that in later years when coalitions normally come together to win wars, it was war which destroyed this one.

Palmerston at the Home Office

There were two broad areas where Aberdeen's Administration merits serious consideration. On the whole, the history of the period is dominated by the war which broke out with Russia and the problems (and successes) to which the war led. These will be dealt with in Chapter 13.

Lord Palmerston did not view the Home Office as a soft option. He was always a man of energy and determination, and his work in 1853–54 plays an important part in the history of social reform in the 19th century.

- His Factory Act of 1853, while not going as far as some of the more radical reformers wished, was a major step forward in reducing the working hours of women and children, and preventing exploitation there.
- His Smoke Abatement Act in 1853 was an important move in trying to cut down the harm done to the environment by coal and other fumes in towns.
- Palmerston played a key role in making vaccination compulsory against smallpox.
- He offended many vested interests when he stopped the practice of burials in churches on the grounds of health.

As his biographer Ridley says, 'Palmerston's belief in freedom of trade did not extend to tolerating practices which interfered with public health'. He was to play a key part in getting the idea accepted that public health should be administered by boards, staffed by government officials with compulsory powers.

Palmerston also ended transportation as a form of punishment. He played an important part in improving prison conditions, and reducing the maximum sentences that could be imposed on those convicted. He also put through the Reformatory School Bill in 1854 which was designed to keep young offenders out of prison, where they would be exposed to hardened criminals as role models, and attempt to put them back on the straight and narrow. It was a highly productive period for Palmerston, and one in which the public benefited. Palmerston's work at the Home Office (and the other domestic reforms when he was Prime Minister between 1855 and 1865) has often been overshadowed by his work in foreign affairs, but it was of great importance.

Gladstone as Chancellor of the Exchequer, 1852–1855

The other key figure in the domestic side of the coalition was William Gladstone. Not only did he play an important role in gaining support for the Administration by his Budgets, but he also pushed himself forward as one of the dominating figures of contemporary politics. He made a real start in the process of civil service reform and the ending of the patronage system of appointment within the **Civil Service**. His insistence on honesty and efficiency within the whole service started a process of great importance for the administration of the country. His promise to end income tax (which war was, of course, to prevent) by 1860 naturally proved highly popular. Sophisticated knowledge, superb oratory and sheer hard work impressed both Parliament and the public.

Civil Service: All the government departments that administer the affairs of the country and all the people who work in them.

Gladstone was essentially an able and aggressive loner. He made the Chancellor of the Exchequer's job into the most important in the Government, after the Prime Minister. He was very good at mastering the detail of government finance, while at the same time having clear and popular principles on which to base his work. They were to:

- get the Budget into surplus and end deficit financing
- reduce direct taxes
- simplify the whole process of taxation and administration
- develop the whole idea that the administration of the public's money is almost a sacred trust to be administered with total efficiency and honesty.

As Gladstone himself wrote in 1855: 'Finance is, as it were, the stomach of the country from which all the other organs take their tone.' He insisted that his department, the Treasury, stood above all others in importance. His aggressive approach, backed up with great debating skills, mastery of detail, and sheer ability and persistence ensured that, by 1855, both he and his department had gained hugely in status. Gladstone managed to bring upon himself and those he worked with the reputation for sound finance that Peel had gained, and that was of major importance in winning the respect and loyalty of many independent backbench MPs.

His attack on Disraeli's Budget in 1852 had shown his destructive capacity. His own Budget of 1853 showed not only his ability as a speaker and his mastery of detail, but also his ability to get his principles over clearly and to produce a Budget which matched up to them. It was his work on income tax that confirmed him as a front-rank politician.

1. What were the main achievements of the Aberdeen Coalition Government?

2. 'Rightly condemned for its conduct of the Crimean War, the Aberdeen Coalition should be praised for its work at home.' To what extent do you regard this statement as an accurate description of Aberdeen's Government? Use information from this chapter and Chapter 12.

Reasons for the fall of the Coalition

The key reason was the conduct of the war, which will be dealt with in Chapter 12. Aberdeen did not have the ability or personality to hold together such a group of men when under pressure. Public opinion was not getting the quick victory in the war it wished for, and the failings of the military in the conduct of the war were being highlighted daily by the first war correspondent of modern times, W.H. Russell of *The Times*. Tales of the miserable conditions our troops had to live and fight in were read daily in the press. John Russell had resigned over the unwillingness of the Administration to further his ideas on parliamentary reform, and Palmerston, who had succeeded him as Leader of the Commons, did not defend the Government with any vigour. Aberdeen may well have been a consideration here! A motion to set up a Committee of Enquiry into the conduct of the war by the radical MP, Roebuck, in January 1855 was carried, much to Aberdeen's horror, and he resigned. Victoria, having tried to get Derby and several others, had to turn to Palmerston to form a government. Once again, party loyalty had proved too weak, and personal ambitions too strong.

11.5 Why did Palmerston dominate this period and what contribution did he make to British domestic politics?

This can be looked at in two ways. Some would argue that Palmerston was not an exceptionally talented politician and was particularly fortunate in both circumstances and opponents. A background of rising prosperity, a growth in real wages and employment, and a decline in working-class discontent helped. There were few people within or outside of the political system who really wished to destroy the existing social or political system.

'The House of Commons debating the French Treaty of 1860', a mezzotint (a form of engraving) after the painting by J. Philip. Gladstone is on the front bench; Palmerston is speaking.

There were no emerging Karl Marxs in Britain and Chartism was seen largely as a discredited force. Working-class ambitions were not revolutionary, and seemed to find the necessary outlets in education, religion and the slow growth of a moderate trade unionism. There were no threats to him or what he stood for. There was, in fact, more opposition to him within his own party than from anywhere else. The Conservative Party remained a divided force, unhappy with its leadership and without any coherent policies, or even a desire to oppose the administrations of Palmerston. With the support of the monarchy, the press (generally) and being in tune with the times, it might well be argued that Palmerston was Prime Minister by default. There was simply no alternative, and unless Palmerston made a bad error of judgement (which he was to do in 1858), then as long as he did not do too much, he would remain in power.

Critics of this view, or supporters of Palmerston, would argue strongly that in fact he was a politician of real ability. He held together two Ministries, both of which contained a group of individuals who frequently disagreed on major issues such as parliamentary reform, war and peace. He laid the basis of the modern Liberal Party at the meeting at the Willis' Rooms in 1859, which Gladstone was to build on, and which was to dominate politics through to 1914. He ended a dreadful war and made a more than satisfactory peace. He managed to work well with Queen Victoria, who together with her husband – the able and involved Prince Albert – wished to play a role in the government of the country which was not always welcomed by many politicians.

Palmerston brought many able men into government. It was generally agreed that his Administration of 1859–65 was particularly able once he had brought in the former followers of Peel. He managed to blend them into an effective unit, mixing them with the more aristocratic Whigs as well as more radical MPs. At the same time, he found a role in government for the growing number of middle-class businessmen and lawyers who were beginning to make up an increasing percentage of Liberal MPs. Gladstone, at the Exchequer, was to make huge advances in public finance and administrative reform, and he needed support and controlling. Britain moved towards free trade: the Treaty with France in 1860, which was negotiated with his old foe Richard Cobden (the great agitator for the repeal of the Corn Laws), is seen as the highpoint of this movement, and it was done while Palmerston was Prime Minister. He ensured that contentious issues such as divorce reform and the abolition of paper duties were dealt with without his Administration splitting too badly.

He knew how to handle Parliament: he was one of the most impressive debaters of his day when on form. He was well aware of the growing influence of the press: his wife's elegant salon, where the rich and famous were entertained, regularly played host to the editors of *The Times* and *Morning Post*. Journalists were frequent attenders at shooting parties at his country house. Palmerston was well aware that a good relationship with the press (and intelligent briefing and leaking) could win many friends. He knew how to appeal to men of all classes, but particularly those who had the vote. He was a good speaker in public as well as in Parliament. While he can be criticised for failing to tackle some of the major social problems of the day – be they in education or in the dreadful conditions in which many British people lived – he can be defended in that there was no great demand for reform, nor did he have the means to impose such changes on an unwilling population.

Palmerston was an able politician in tune with his time and the voters. He gave them good and cheap government, administered well, and legislated when there was both a need and a demand. Politics is the art of the possible, and Palmerston usually had an excellent grasp of what was possible.

The traditional view is that Palmerston did little throughout both his periods as Prime Minister, and that he was only interested in foreign affairs. There is an element of truth in this. His domestic record contrasts unfavourably with that of Peel between 1841 and 1846, and the later administration of his **protégé**, William Gladstone, between 1868 and 1874. It is also argued that he did more as Home Secretary on the domestic front, between 1852 and 1855, than he attained as Prime Minister.

Protégé: A person who is helped and guided by an older and more experienced person over a period of time. The younger person is often being groomed to take over from the older person at a later date.

Palmerston was known as the 'Tory chief of a radical Cabinet', and this is quite a useful description. However there was no great demand for radical reform, either political or social, whatever may have been a need. He was a traditional Whig in many respects, one who believed the role of the Government was to administer (something which he did very well) and not to legislate unless necessary.

Civil Service reform, 1853–1855

The groundwork for Civil Service reform was laid in this period. The Crimean War had highlighted the inefficiency of a service that gave office to men on grounds of parentage or relations, rather than ability. Palmerston had been instrumental in setting up a Royal Commission in 1853. The Northcote–Trevelyan Report on the Civil Service had appeared while Palmerston was Home Secretary. It recommended entry by competitive examination in order to attract able men to assist Ministers to run the country. Although it was Gladstone who played the key role in actually putting the process into practice – with a lot of support from Palmerston – a radical transformation had been achieved by the time of Palmerston's death in 1865. A group of men, committed to serving the public, were coming into the Civil Service who had the necessary ability to advise Ministers on policy.

Palmerston's domestic legislation

In 1857, the first attempt was made to reform the laws on divorce. Up to this point, divorce was only possible by the House of Lords, seen as the highest court in the land. This was incredibly expensive and only really open to members of the aristocracy and the very rich. This Act made it possible for divorce to be obtained in the ordinary courts. However, the law was still strongly biased in favour of men, for whom adultery was not seen as grounds for divorce by a woman; whereas if a woman 'erred', then this provided grounds for her husband to divorce her.

1. Give reasons why you think Lord Palmerston was such an important political figure in this period.

2. Why was Palmerston made Prime Minister and why was he able to stay in office for so long? (See Chapter 12 on Palmerston's foreign policy in the 1850s and 1860s so that you can make a comparison between his achievements in domestic and foreign affairs.)

Major reforms to companies were undertaken with the Joint Stock Companies Act of 1858. This played a vital role in developing investment in this country, as it limited the liability of the ordinary shareholder. The Companies Act of 1862 laid down precise rules for companies to follow when it came to their accounts and registration. In a country where *laissez faire* was still the prevailing philosophy in business circles, these were important steps forward to protect and encourage ordinary shareholders and to enhance the reputation of British businessmen at home and abroad.

The Offences against the Person Act of 1861 was another important measure that clarified and made many aspects of the criminal law more humane. The state grant to education increased radically while Palmerston was Prime Minister. He was never as enthusiastic as Russell when it came to spending public money on education, but he was prepared to help local authorities that were enthusiastic. Palmerston was concerned about the State taking on too great a financial burden, and he was also well aware that further government involvement in education would also stir up tremendous religious passions (and lose votes).

Palmerston opposed any major attempt to deal with the Irish land question, the root of so much of the Irish 'problem', even though he was an Irish landlord himself. He did let a weak bill through in 1860, which did little to improve the bad relationship between landlord and tenant in Ireland. Palmerston saw the agitation for reform in Ireland as part of a Catholic plot to win power in that country. However, he did much to assist the Lord Lieutenant, Lord Carlisle, to improve the economic conditions in Ireland. One writer has commented that Palmerston temporarily 'solved the Irish Question, not by concessions, but by commonsense'.

11.6 *The rise of the Liberal Party*

A CASE STUDY IN HISTORICAL INTERPRETATION

The 1850s were central to the rise and later dominance of the Liberal Party. The Party shed the 'Whiggish' image of the 1830s and learned the harsh lessons that came with division and defeat. It gained the reputation (partly by absorbing key Peelites such as William Gladstone, Edward Cardwell and Sidney Herbert) of being good at handling public finance and administration, of competence and integrity. It became a progressive party with increasingly popular ideas, and was learning to market them to the electorate. Its foreign policy was popular, and Palmerston ensured that it was well advocated. Its broadly *laissez-faire* policies were in tune with popular temper, but its willingness to undertake reform in areas ranging from education and sanitation, to the Civil Service and eventually Parliament showed its sensitivity to public opinion.

John Stuart Mill (1806–1873)
A philosopher and a Radical, John Stuart Mill was possibly the greatest English thinker of the 19th century. He was a Liberal MP from 1865 to 1868. His key work, *On Liberty*, was published in 1859.

It gained a good electoral base in the boroughs – the growth of towns in the period reduced the Conservative rural vote. The Cabinet and the Parliamentary Party reflected well the political nation and its hopes and ambitions, as well as the diversity of opinions in contemporary society. There were radicals in both the social and political sense in the party, as well as businessmen and lawyers, aristocrats and philosophers – such as John Stuart Mill. Richard Cobden and John Bright, seen as representatives of so much of middle-class England, were both Liberal MPs.

The Liberal Party was not a party that supported democracy, but it was seen by many of the British people at the time of Palmerston's death as being the party of business sense, moral integrity and administrative efficiency, and one which they would vote for. As historian Jonathan Parry puts it, in *The Liberal Party* (1990): 'Order balanced liberty, the State balanced individual activity, the Establishment balanced free thought, national defence balanced good economy and the aristocracy balanced popularity.' The Party had a tremendous appeal, and it won elections.

Some historians, such as Michael Winstanley in *Gladstone and the Liberal Party* (1990), have been more critical of the Party, arguing that it was little more than a series of fragile coalitions in its make-up. They saw the Liberals as undertaking 'a series of shifts and compromises that betrayed liberal impulses devoid of coherent purpose … party labels were useful for what they excluded as much as being guidelines to what was positively included'. There was no evident intention under Palmerston of creating a nationally organised party, with members or conferences. That was to come later under Joseph Chamberlain. As the historian Harold Hanham wrote in 1959: 'The chief characteristic of national party organisation in the 1850s and 1860s was impotence.'

Some feel that the Liberal Party was a result of ambitious men doing deals for selfish reasons in order to get into power and stay there. The Party came together in 1859 to destroy Derby's Government, and for no other reason. The key figures, Palmerston and Russell, were men who worked together as the alternative was opposition. They, given their huge political differences in areas such as parliamentary reform and the role of the State, had no business to be working together.

In some of the more traditional histories of the period – such as Llewellyn Woodward's *Age of Reform* (1938) – it is interesting to note that Gladstone (Chancellor of the Exchequer 1859–66 and Leader of the Commons after Palmerston's death in 1865) tends to get more coverage than Palmerston in domestic matters, and yet he was not in office from 1855 to 1859. What are the reasons for this?

Gladstone refused to take office in 1855. Many would argue that this refusal, together with that of the rest of the key Peelites, was to play a leading part in the political instability of the period. Return to the Conservative Party was not possible in 1855 as Disraeli stood in the way and the memories of his savaging of the 1852 Budget were still strong. Gladstone neither liked nor trusted Palmerston, and disapproved of his foreign policy and his private life.

Gladstone also made several political errors between 1855 and 1859. He failed completely to realise the significance of Palmerston and his hold over the British political scene. The fact that there was no alternative escaped Gladstone, and he was shocked and surprised by Palmerston's victory in the 1857 election. He opposed several key measures supported by the Whig Cabinet in the 1855–58 period, such as the Divorce Bill. Also his lukewarm attitude to Disraeli's Reform Bill would not endear him to Russell and some of the more radical Liberals either. His career looked destined to end unless he was prepared to compromise and join with one of the two re-emerging political groups.

What role did Gladstone play in the formation of the Liberal Party?

There is an interesting difference of views among historians about precisely what led to the formation of the Liberal Party and what was Gladstone's role in it. Some, like Michael Winstanley in *Gladstone and the Liberal Party* (1990), do not see Gladstone's role as a very significant one. They argue that the intention of the main participants in 1859 – such as Russell and Palmerston and some of the Peelites other than Gladstone – was primarily a negative one. It was simply out to defeat Derby and Disraeli. Historian Norman McCord sees it as a much more positive process. He calls it 'a deliberate consolidation of various liberal groups'. G.R. Searle, however, feels that Gladstone played a much more important role, calling it a Radical and

Whig alliance pulled together by Gladstone. His family circumstances (particularly his middle-class and manufacturing background) and personality made him a natural candidate for a key role in such an alliance.

H.C.G. Matthew's major biography of Gladstone (1986) also sees the man playing an important part in the formation of the Liberal Party, but has differing views as to his reasons. Matthew argues that ambition played a part in Gladstone's decision to join up with Palmerston, but that it primarily was 'the hard-headed response of an able politician with a programme of action, to join a Cabinet at the outset of its formation'. Richard Shannon, in his biography of Gladstone (1982), feels that it was Gladstone's attitude towards Italy, which had moved closer to that of Palmerston's, which was vital in enabling Gladstone to feel that he could work with a man of whom he had often disapproved. The fact that public opinion was highly sympathetic towards Palmerston was also a factor in Gladstone's thinking. However much Gladstone was seen to be a man of great principle and above the rough and tumble of daily politics, the historian G. Shannon points out that he was very sensitive to the moods of the public, and this move was partly in response to one. Harold Perkin, in *Origins of Modern English Society* (1969), argues that one of the major reasons behind the formation of the first fully 'Liberal' ministry was that it was a response to growing middle-class pressure for a party that was neither Tory nor Whig, but more a vehicle for their ambitions.

While Palmerston's biographer, J. Ridley (1970), naturally places the greatest emphasis on the key role of his study in forming the Government and Party in 1859, with his personality and experience being the dominant forces, others play down the role of personalities. Jonathan Parry, in one of the most recent studies of the Liberal Party in this period, argues that they had become by 1859 'the natural respectable ruling force in Britain'. He maintains that the unification was a natural process. The fact that they were no longer radical or overwhelmingly Whig, with a good foreign policy and a reputation for sound finance, and striking good 'chords' with the rank-and-file, made them the natural choice of the people.

How able was Gladstone as Chancellor of the Exchequer, 1859–1866, and how important was his work?

It has been argued that in some ways this was the most successful period in Gladstone's political career, and some of his most lasting work was done while Chancellor of the Exchequer. After Palmerston and Russell had agreed to work together in 1859, and a regrouping of politicians had taken place at the Willis' Rooms meeting, Gladstone accepted the latter as the lesser of two evils, and took office as Chancellor of the Exchequer.

His predecessor as Chancellor, Sir George Lewis, was a highly competent administrator, and had left no huge problems. Palmerston tended to leave Gladstone to his own devices where possible, so he had a relatively free hand to form his own policies. Just as Gladstone saw working under Palmerston as an unfortunate necessity if he wished to have a political career, Palmerston was well aware of the value of adding the Peelite reputation for sound finance and good administration to his new Liberal banner.

Gladstone's Budgets of 1859–1865

It was in these key pieces of legislation that Gladstone developed the ideas he had gained earlier, while working under Peel (perhaps the only other 19th-century leader who is remembered for his Budgets). Gladstone laid down certain key principles, which have lasted well into the 20th century. The first was that the administration of public money was almost a sacred trust. Those who had anything to do with its collection, auditing or spending had a major responsibility to the public to ensure that there was no waste or fraud. The second was that economy was a real virtue and government had a primary responsibility to set an example here. Thirdly, he felt that government had a responsibility to take as little money out of taxpayers' pockets as was possible, and his aim was not only to reduce income tax but if possible to abolish it altogether. There was to be economy, efficiency and honesty at all levels, and any evidence of waste was to be eliminated.

Gladstone's first Budget of 1859 set the scene. His ideas were put firmly into practice. Initially he had to raise income tax slightly, but this was to compensate for the loss of revenue that came from the abolition of duties on a wide range of goods. He worked consistently throughout his time as Chancellor to remove almost every duty on imported goods. Britain achieved the nearest it ever got to completely free trade, unrestricted by taxes on imports, under Gladstone. He had completed the work begun by Peel decades before.

In addition, Gladstone worked hard to reduce income tax. He managed to get it down from 9 pence to 6 pence in the pound by the time he left office. He was also able to reduce substantially the number of people who actually had to pay it. Unless a man earned more than £200 a year (more than a skilled working man earned), there was no liability for tax. Gladstone would have liked to have abolished it totally, but realised that unless the country would tolerate radical cuts in defence and other services it was not possible. He was aware it was essentially a fair tax, as the burden fell most on those who could afford to pay, and he ensured that this principle at least was retained.

Getting these Budgets through the Cabinet was never an easy task, as Palmerston and several other key members of the Cabinet were concerned with the poor state of Britain's defence, and were anxious to increase defence spending significantly. On more than one occasion, Gladstone had to go to the point of resignation to attain his goals, but he achieved great success in his attempts to raise public finance to a high level.

Gladstone's reform of the Civil Service

Gladstone's work is also important in several other areas. Perhaps the least publicised is the way he used his position as Chancellor and Head of the Treasury to insist that rigid economy and a war on waste was carried into all other government departments, and that the principles of competitive examination for entry to the higher ranks of the Civil Service was spread to other departments. By the time Gladstone had finished his work in 1866, the British Civil Service was far leaner and more efficient, giving the public a better and cheaper service than it had ever done before.

In addition, he ensured the creation of the Public Accounts Committee of the House of Commons, the first permanent Select Committee of MPs who had the responsibility of monitoring the spending of all the Departments of State. This was central to Gladstone's thinking about public trust and accountability. The Head of every Civil Service Department was to be held responsible to the elected representatives of the British people for every penny spent by their department. This committee has proved to be one of Gladstone's more lasting legacies, and it still meets today to carry out the duties that Gladstone laid down.

Abolition of paper duties, 1861

Excise: A tax levied on internally produced goods, as opposed to those brought in from abroad.

These duties, which were an **excise** on paper, meant that books and newspapers cost more than they needed to. This was frequently called a 'tax on knowledge'. One of the reasons why some of the more right-wing members of Palmerston's Cabinet (and possibly Palmerston himself) were anxious to keep them was because they felt that with no such tax there might be the growth of a revolutionary and cheap press. This could inflame the minds of the working class. What papers there were were comparatively expensive, and not readily available to the poorer members of society. Gladstone first introduced the measure in 1860, but met with a wall of opposition within his own Government, as well as in the House of Lords. The Bill was allowed to drop that year, but Gladstone got his way the following year after he again threatened to resign. There was a compromise in the end, as he did both increase defence spending and raise the income tax slightly for one year to pay for it all. The worst fears of his opponents were not realised, but in the course of time books and magazines did come down in price, and gradually a cheap and popular press developed.

The Cobden Treaty, 1860

This commercial treaty, in addition to Gladstone's Budgets, formed the final part of Britain's move towards free trade. Relations with France had not been good. There had been concerns about France's expansion into Italy, gaining Nice and Savoy, and proposed French developments over a possible Suez Canal were ringing alarm bells for Palmerston and Russell. This was a major reason why they wanted to increase spending on defence in this period. Gladstone agreed with the free trader, Richard Cobden, that an end to any commercial rivalry between Britain and France would be important to easing political and international tension, and Cobden's treaty did just that. Signed in 1860, it reduced substantially the duties which British manufacturers and coalowners had to pay when importing to France. British exports to France were to double in the following decade, while the French were able to export their wines and cognac to Britain at much reduced rates. The tense relationship between the two countries eased, improving balance sheets on both sides at the same time.

?

1. What were Gladstone's main achievements in the years 1855 to 1865?

2. Why do you think the Liberal Party was formed?

11.7 What impact did Derby, Disraeli and the Conservatives have on British politics in this period?

The simple answer to this is 'very little'. It was highly frustrating for Disraeli, anxious to demonstrate his abilities to a wider audience, to remain in opposition throughout much of the period. Derby – idle and able – kept the title of Leader but was unwilling to exercise much leadership. Many of the Party were still highly suspicious of Disraeli, not only for his tactics in 1845–46, but also for the way in which he had abandoned Protection in 1852. Derby and Disraeli had publicly clashed over India in 1853, over the issue of Crown control, and it was seen very much as a disagreement between Disraeli and a right-wing Conservative leader.

Why did the Aberdeen Coalition fall in 1855?

The Aberdeen Coalition fell apart without much prompting from the Conservatives in 1855. Disraeli had backed the war, while criticising its conduct; whereas Derby had remained silent on the whole issue. They were hardly a picture of unity, agreement and energy. What cannot have made relations between the two leaders of the Conservative Party any better was the news in 1854 that Derby was trying to recruit both Palmerston and Gladstone back into the Party. Disraeli was well aware that part of the price for either of those recruits would be his departure from the leadership of the Commons.

When Aberdeen left office in 1855, Derby was offered the premiership, but to Disraeli's fury he declined the post. There was still no Conservative majority in the Commons. Derby demonstrated a similar lack of interest when the committee set up by the House of Commons to look into the conduct by Britain in the Crimean War – to see why so many soldiers had died of wounds and disease – produced a report which was highly critical of many members of Palmerston's Government. (Many of these had, of course,

Punch cartoon of 20 February 1858 entitled 'Dignified Position'

The cartoon refers to the fall of Lord Palmerston's Government over the defeat of the Conspiracy to Murder Bill, 1858. The 'foreign gent' in the cartoon is Emperor Napoleon III of France.

(a) Using information from this chapter, explain how Napoleon III is connected with Palmerston's defeat in 1858.

(b) How useful is this cartoon in explaining the public reaction to Palmerston's defeat in 1858?

been in the Aberdeen Coalition, including Palmerston himself.) Disraeli wished to make political mileage out of it, Derby showed a lack of interest. As Chief Whip Jellify wrote, in October 1855, 'it is impossible to exist without a policy, and still less possible for an Opposition to be of the same policy as the government to which it is opposed'. The Conservatives seemed to stand for nothing, and have no grounds for opposing the Government. As Palmerston was referred to at the time as 'a Conservative Minister working with radical tools', it is hardly surprising that there was little disagreement between the two parties. Palmerston had after all started his career as a Tory.

Why did the Whig/Liberal Party win the election of 1857?

The election of 1857 produced no improvement in Conservative fortunes. Derby's position was referred to as 'invisible' during the campaign. Try as Disraeli could to involve him, and suggest policies such as parliamentary reform, Derby declined. The election confirmed the Liberals in power, again. Disraeli had to wait until they fell out among themselves or made a major error, for his chance of office.

This chance came in 1858, when Palmerston made a rare mistake in misjudging public opinion over the Orsini bomb plot. There had been an attempt on the life of the French Emperor, Napoleon III. It failed, although innocent bystanders died when a bomb was thrown at the French Emperor. It came out that not only was the bomb British-made, but some of the planning had been done in this country. Naturally the French were furious. To pacify them, Palmerston attempted to put through a bill designed to prevent plotting against foreign governments while resident in this country. Public opinion was outraged at these concessions to 'our old enemy', and this was reflected in Parliament in 1858 when Palmerston found himself defeated and he resigned. The passions that he had aroused in the Don Pacifico debate (see page 208) had turned against him.

The second Derby–Disraeli Minority Administration, 1858–1859, and the years which followed

Derby and Disraeli found themselves in power again, with a minority government. They were conscious that they were there reluctantly, and as soon as the Liberals reunited (many usual Liberal supporters had voted against Palmerston in the Commons over the 'Orsini' Bill), they would be out of office.

There was little that this minority government could actually do. They got through a bill that had been designed by the previous administration to alter the relationship with India. The main attempt at change was Disraeli's effort to bring about parliamentary reform, and seize the title of 'reforming party' from the Liberals. Derby showed a little enthusiasm, particularly when it was pointed out that the franchise (vote) might be extended to win more Conservative voters in the **shires.** There were no clear principles behind the Bill – such as an extension of the right to vote to a particular class – but Disraeli managed to get the idea of the Conservative Party as a party which would consider basic reform at least partly accepted by the party and the public. The lack of enthusiasm by the rest of the Cabinet, and the obvious absence of a parliamentary majority (or much public demand for the reform of Parliament) ensured that the Bill had no future.

Shires: The 'Shires' or 'shire counties' are the counties in the central part of England (e.g. Leicester*shire*), which are mainly rural.

With these Bills in mind, and the absence of a majority, the Conservatives got a dissolution of Parliament from Queen Victoria in May 1859. Although there was a small increase in the number of Conservative seats, the Government was still in a minority. When Russell and Palmerston got together, and rallied the Liberals again in June, the Conservative Government resigned.

The experience was useful for the Conservatives. Major issues had been tackled, such as the government of India and parliamentary reform, but there had been open divisions over reform and the removal of discrimination against Jews, so the Conservatives did not stand a great deal higher in the opinion of the public.

Disraeli felt that the years that followed – 1859–66 – represented the lowest point of his career. Derby openly recommended that no attempt be made to challenge Palmerston's dominance. In fact, his instructions to

The two cartoons here deal with Conservative proposals for electoral reform in 1859.

(a) What reasons do you think are given for the failure of the Conservative reform proposals of 1859 in these cartoons?

(b) How useful are these cartoons to a historian writing about the defeat of the Conservative reform proposals in 1859?

Punch cartoon of 21 May 1859 entitled 'The Anglers' Return'. The figure on the left represents the House of Lords and the figure on the right Disraeli, the Conservative leader in the House of Commons.

Punch cartoon of 26 March 1859 entitled 'Great Poaching Affray on the Liberal Preserves'. Disraeli is on the right; the figure on the left, holding the gun, is Lord John Russell, a leading Liberal politician.

GREAT POACHING AFFRAY ON THE LIBERAL PRESERVES.

1. What were the main developments in domestic affairs between 1855 and 1865?

2. 'Wasted years'. Discuss this view of the Conservative Party between 1846 and 1866.

Disraeli in 1860 said that we should 'keep the present men in and resist all temptations to avail ourselves of a casual majority'. In other words, to support the Government and not provoke national disunity. It was a novel view of the role of the Opposition.

There was clearly no Conservative strategy throughout this six-year period, and the attendance of Conservative MPs was invariably low – they had nothing to do. On major issues such as the American Civil War the Conservative Party was divided between support for the North and the South; the latter was the pro-slavery and more conservative side, but with the divisions much deeper on the government side, the simplest action seemed to be to do nothing. The only time the Conservatives appeared in large numbers in the period was to criticise Palmerston's handling of the Danish crisis of 1864, and to oppose a Liberal Reform Bill in 1865, but these were very much the exceptions.

11.8 How and why was parliamentary reform achieved in 1867?

The Reform Act of 1867 was, in many respects, one of the most remarkable events in British politics in the whole 19th century. It is remarkable not only for who passed it, the Conservatives, but also for the way in which it was passed and in the wide-reaching impact it had on British politics and the whole democratic process in Britain. The 1867 Reform Act was referred to, at the time, as a 'leap in the dark'. This was not only because few realised what the implications might be of extending the vote to a propertyless working class in the towns, but also because there was little awareness while the Bill was being passed of how many additional voters would actually get the vote. Even stranger was the fact that although the Conservatives passed the Act while in a minority government, they gave the vote largely to skilled workers in the urban areas, which were traditionally seen as Liberal strongholds. The situation was reversed in 1884, when the Liberal Gladstone extended the same franchise to the rural areas, which were seen as Conservative strongholds. The urban workers who gained the vote in 1867 showed their gratitude to Disraeli for passing the Bill by returning a Liberal government with a substantial majority. It was a curious affair. Why?

Why did parliamentary reform return as a major political issue?

Many historians feel that the key reason was the death of Palmerston, who died in 1865 just after winning yet another election. There had been rumours that he was about to be sued by a young woman for maintenance of an illegitimate child he had recently fathered. Disraeli worked to suppress the rumours on the grounds that if Palmerston could prove his potency at the age of 80, then this would not only increase his popularity, but also make the Conservative attack that he was too old to run the country difficult to sustain.

Palmerston had certainly been no enthusiast for reform, but with the premiership passing to Russell in 1865, he was determined to end his parliamentary career in the way in which he had started it, with the reform of Parliament. Both Liberals and Conservatives had toyed with the idea of parliamentary reform in the previous decade or so, but there had been limited demand for it, and it had been a divisive issue within the two parties. In 1864, Gladstone stated his viewpoint in a speech that included the phrase that he felt that members of the working class, who had demonstrated their worth as citizens, had 'the moral right to come within the pale of the Constitution'. In other words, they should be able to vote. They paid taxes and rates in many cases, and in others quite substantial rents, so were not too removed from the principle of 'property' which had been enshrined in the 1832 Act as the essential requirement for a vote.

With Russell and Gladstone leading the Party, and growing pressure from outside for reform, with a middle-class Reform Union and a more working-class Reform League raising fears that the pressure politics of the Anti-Corn Law League might return, public opinion swung in favour of widening the franchise.

The First Liberal Bill: why did it fail?

Robert Lowe (1811–1892)
Lowe became an MP in 1852; was Junior Minister 1852–55, 1855–58 and 1859–64. He became Chancellor of the Exchequer in 1868, and stayed in office until 1873.

In March 1866, Gladstone introduced a parliamentary reform bill into the Commons. It was not as radical as many had hoped. The right of his Party was alarmed about the unpredictability of the new voters, and there was also hostility from the Conservatives. Disraeli was critical of this Bill as he felt that the aristocracy would suffer and lose their natural leadership of the country. The Bill succeeded in dividing the Liberal Party. Robert Lowe – a brilliant speaker and intellect – led a group of Liberals into the 'No' voting lobby in the House of Commons (with the delighted Conservatives), and succeeded in bringing down his own government.

The Liberals were not sure what they wanted. Many Liberal MPs did want more improving legislation of a social and economic type, and felt that this was the way to get it. Others felt that with the growth in numbers of prosperous working-class men involved in local politics, it was a good idea to give the vote to as many future Liberal voters as possible. There was a feeling also that there was 'an intelligent working man' out there – a sober and responsible citizen who merited the vote.

Russell was involved emotionally, and apart from his desire to get a Bill through, he did not have any clear ideas. Gladstone had very mixed feelings on the subject. He knew that it might help his rise to leadership in the Party if it succeeded, and he felt that some of the potential voters might not only be Liberal, but also sympathetic to his desire for reducing government expenditure. However, he also felt that these new voters might be vulnerable to radical pressures for increased spending by government. Gladstone also felt that such 'dark forces' might threaten both the Lords and the Church. He was no democrat either.

The Bill Gladstone finally came up with was moderate. Neither Russell nor Gladstone had any desire to offend the more conservative Liberal MPs who were known to be concerned about the issue. Between 350,000 and 400,000 men, mainly in urban areas, would get the vote. There would be a limited redistribution of seats to change the grossly unfair allocation of seats in Parliament to actual numbers of voters.

The Conservatives initially led the opposition to it: some on grounds of principle; others, like Disraeli, sensing that reform was in the air (as well as the potential for dividing the Liberal Party), looked more critically at the Bill's details. The strongest opposition came from dissident Liberals, led by Robert Lowe, who felt strongly that this was too great a move towards democracy, that Parliament would become no more than a meeting of delegates from the various classes, and that taxation would increase as would trade union power. Lowe was opposed to the idea of equality he saw as lurking behind the Bill. The Bill was defeated and the Government resigned.

Why did the Conservatives take up the issue of parliamentary reform?

The Conservatives found themselves in a minority government in June 1866, yet again, as the majority grouping had failed to remain united. Derby again led the Government, from the Lords, with Disraeli again as Chancellor and Leader of the Commons. Reform was definitely in the air. A large demonstration in favour took place in Hyde Park, London, within weeks of the Government taking office – known as the Hyde Park riots. They were nothing like as extreme as in 1832 (see page 117), but the demonstrations created enough fears to keep the issue in the forefront of people's minds.

The Conservatives had played a role in resisting Gladstone's fairly modest bill, although Disraeli had been non-committal on the principles behind the Bill, contenting himself with challenging the detail. He had, of course, advocated parliamentary reform on more than one occasion in the past. Some historians – such as Robert Blake and John Walton – feel that Gladstone bowed to pressure from social and economic, as well as political, forces outside Parliament. They argue that democracy was coming, and that to stand in the way would be foolish and risking revolution. Other historians feel that the answer should be looked for within the secret plans of a small political élite at the centre of power. Was Disraeli meekly bowing to the winds of change – or out to 'dish the Whigs'?

There was certainly popular pressure for reform. More than one demonstration produced a crowd of at least 100,000, which worried the organisers as much as it did the Government. There was an additional background of a growing industrial and agricultural depression and a cholera epidemic. Certainly, there was a feeling in political circles that it might be dangerous not to concede, and the Conservatives were not immune to that feeling.

However, some historians saw the issue more in party political terms. Conservatives felt that they could now market themselves not only as the resisters of unwarranted change, but also as the developers of some constitutional progress. Some, including Disraeli himself, were weary of years of opposition, and wanted to be seen as the party of government. It is easy to see the Bill in terms of cynical opportunism on Disraeli's part, but his defenders have argued that this was part of a wider plan to bring about 'Tory Democracy' to Britain. Palmerston had stolen the Conservatives' conservatism, why should the Conservatives not steal the Liberals' liberalism? One biographer of Disraeli, Robert Blake (1966), argues that this was not the case. Disraeli did not believe that the urban working class would vote Conservative, nor did he think in terms of his ability to persuade such a class to do so.

The Liberals were badly split, and would remain so as long as parliamentary reform stayed on the agenda. This would also mean that the Conservatives would remain in office. In addition, Disraeli knew that the Liberal Bill was carefully designed to do maximum damage to the Conservative vote in the constituencies. So with the tide flowing in favour of reform, it seemed to make sense to flow with it and to put forward a bill which might benefit the Conservative Party in terms of votes. Even Derby, tired of opposition or of being a stop-gap premier, was enthusiastic. He surprised all by being prepared to take an initiative, more so than the initially cautious Disraeli. Straight party political gain was probably the dominant factor in the reasons behind the Conservative adoption of a Bill for the reform of Parliament.

Why did the Bill pass, and what changes did the Second Reform Act make?

Faced with such pressure both from above and below (even the Queen was in favour), Disraeli introduced his Bill into the House of Commons in February 1867. This was after the Queen's Speech had offered the reform of Parliament 'without unduly disturbing the balance of power, shall freely extend the elective franchise'. Ministers were not in agreement on either the principles or the details of a bill prior to the Opening of Parliament, and several Ministers were fundamentally opposed to any reform at all. One complained bitterly of 'the error of attempting to frame a Reform Bill in the week previous to its production'. There were widely differing views within the Government of what might be the outcome, in terms of actual voters, of full **household suffrage**, or giving the vote to those who paid rates of more than £5 a year.

Household suffrage: Where the right to vote was given to every male householder.

Disraeli's initial Bill underwent radical change in the Cabinet in the days prior to its formal introduction into Parliament. He had not envisaged full household suffrage in the boroughs, and Peel (son of Sir Robert) had opposed this in the Cabinet. Royal pressure was put on Peel to concede, and he did. The Cabinet insisted on the retention of many 'fancy' franchises, as safeguards – such as giving second votes to those who held savings, or who were graduates, or paid a certain amount in direct taxation. This did not satisfy the more conservative members of the Cabinet, who felt that now there might be a working-class majority in many of the boroughs. After a ten-minute discussion in the Cabinet – barely two hours before Disraeli had to introduce the Bill into the House of Commons – a more limited version was drafted. This did not satisfy many Conservative MPs, so the Cabinet went back to its original, more radical, proposal. Three members of the Cabinet resigned: Cranbourne, Peel and Carnarvon.

Fortunately, with the Liberals bitterly divided, Disraeli got his Bill through the vital second reading in the Commons. Only seven Conservative MPs supported Gladstone's attempt to defeat the Bill, but 45 Liberals voted with the Government and there were 28 important Liberal abstentions. The Bill proceeded to the Committee stage (see page 115). Just as the Bill had been unusual in its creation and remarkable in its drafting stages, the

Committee stage was to follow suit. One key amendment, Grosvenor Hodgkinson's, added nearly half a million voters to the franchise.

The final measure added nearly a million voters, virtually doubling the electorate in size. In towns, working-class voters were now in a majority; while rural constituencies remained, in electoral terms, firmly middle class. 'Fancy franchises' largely died out as the Bill progressed, and there was a degree of redistribution of seats. Towns of 10,000 or less lost one of their two MPs. There was now urban household franchise, with no formal financial qualification. It was fundamentally different to the first draft, and what was remarkable was that Disraeli had managed to carry his Party with him. He had gained their support for this measure. It was a remarkable personal achievement. Cranbourne, the future Lord Salisbury (Prime Minister of Britain in the latter part of the century), called it a 'surrender'. Others referred to it as 'shooting Niagara', but Britain had made a major step forward towards democracy, in an essentially peaceful way. This was to have a major impact on Britain in a huge variety of ways. Robert Lowe said, 'We must now educate our masters' – and the great Education Act of 1870 was to follow. Politicians, in particular such Liberals as Joseph Chamberlain of Birmingham, saw that the future lay in party organisation on a hitherto undreamed-of scale as the route to power. It is more than a coincidence that the next two administrations – those of Gladstone (1868–74) and Disraeli 1874–80) – saw more legislation affecting areas of British life than perhaps any other in the entire century.

1. Why was it so difficult to pass a parliamentary reform bill between 1865 and 1867?

2. What were the main changes brought about by the Second Reform Act of 1867?

3. To what extent did the Second Reform Act bring change to the British political system?

What was the immediate result of the Act?

Once the Bill was through in August 1867, Parliament went into recess and did not reconvene until early 1868. Derby resigned through ill health in February 1868 and Benjamin Disraeli replaced him as Prime Minister. As Disraeli put it, he had reached the 'top of the greasy pole' at last. John Bright, his old foe over the Corn Laws, put it differently: 'it is a triumph of intellect and courage and patience and unscrupulousness employed in the service of a party full of prejudices and selfishness and wanting in brains'. Disraeli was not to enjoy power for long.

Gladstone had replaced Russell as the Liberal leader in 1866, and an election was called, against the wishes of the Queen, in the autumn of 1868. The Liberal majority was increased. The new voters in the towns did not show any gratitude towards their benefactors who had given them the vote. Instead, they voted mainly for the Liberals. Gladstone toured the country giving speeches to mass audiences. He realised that the new voters had to be won over. Disraeli contented himself with one written address and a single speech. He lost.

Source-based questions: The Second Reform Act of 1867

SOURCE A

5 March 1867 … The state of the Reform Question and of the ministry is now more critical than it had been at any former time. There is not, as far as I can judge, much excitement or violence of feeling amongst the people, but a great deal of interest, and on the part of the educated classes, some not inconsiderable apprehension of possible results. The radical newspapers are of course screaming their loudest. *The Times* disapproves of the recent resolutions … but is anxious for a Bill of some sort to pass, and not averse to it being done by the present government.

From Journals and Memoirs *by Lord Derby*

SOURCE B

Commentators have praised Disraeli's brilliant opportunist tactics and, above all, his flexibility. Having formed a temporary alliance with the right wing (Adullamite) Liberals in 1866, to unseat the Liberal Government, he now made common cause with the left-wing, radical element of the Party. He was willing to see borough representation radically reformed rather than allow the bill to be lost. Unlike Lowe, he did not fear the urban masses, and he was unwilling to accept a much larger working-class borough electorate.

From Government and Reform *by Robert Pearce, published in 1994.*

SOURCE C

I think the danger would be less, that the feeling of the larger numbers would be more national, than by giving the vote to a sort of class set aside, looking with suspicion on their superiors, and with disdain on those beneath them. I think you would have a better chance of touching the popular heart, of evoking the national sentiment, by bringing in the great body of these men who occupy houses and fulfil the duties of citizenship by the payment of rates.

Disraeli in the House of Commons, July 1867

SOURCE D

I had to prepare the mind of the country, and to educate – if it be not too arrogant to use such a phrase – to educate our Party. It is a large party and requires its attention to be called to questions of this kind with some pressure. I had to prepare the mind of Parliament and the Country on this question of reform … when you try to settle any great question, there are two considerations which statesmen ought not to forget. First of all, let your plan be founded upon some principle … and let is also be a principle that is in harmony with the manners and customs you are attempting to legislate for.

Disraeli in a speech in autumn 1867, after the Reform Act became law.

---

1. Study Sources B and D.

Explain the meaning, in the context of the 1867 Reform Act, of the following phrases:

(a) 'the right-wing (Adullamite) Liberals'

(b) 'to educate our Party'

2. Study Source C.

What arguments in favour of reform is Disraeli putting forward?

3. Study Sources A and D.

How valuable would these sources be to a historian studying the 1867 Reform Act?

4. Using all the sources and the information in this chapter, explain why the Conservative Government passed a Reform Act in 1867 when it had opposed a milder one in 1866.

12 British foreign policy in the Age of Palmerston: 1846–1868

12.1 Why did Palmerston involve Britain in the affairs of Spain and Portugal?
12.2 How skilful was Palmerston's handling of the revolutions of 1848?
12.3 Why did Palmerston adopt such an aggressive policy towards Greece over Don Pacifico?
12.4 Why was Palmerston dismissed in 1851?
12.5 Historical interpretation: Why did Britain go to war with Russia in the Crimea?
12.6 What were the results of the Crimean War?
12.7 Why was Palmerston involved in the Far East, and what were the results of these involvements?
12.8 Why did Palmerston become involved in the Italian Wars of Unification between 1859 and 1861?
12.9 To what extent was Palmerston's policy during the American Civil War a success?
12.10 How serious a failure were Palmerston's dealings with the Polish Revolt and the Schleswig-Holstein question?

Key Issues

- *How well did Palmerston conduct foreign policy between 1846 and 1851?*
- *Why did Britain fight a war with Russia in the Crimea in 1854–56?*
- *To what extent did Palmerston 'lose his touch' in foreign affairs after 1855?*

Framework of Events

1846	Spanish marriages crisis; Portuguese Civil War
1848	Revolutions in France, German Confederation, Italy and Austria
1850	Haynau Incident; Don Pacifico Affair
1851	December: Palmerston's recognition of Louis Napoleon's *coup d'état* Dismissal of Palmerston
1852	Treaty of London (Schleswig-Holstein Question solved by Great Powers)
1853	Russia occupies Wallachia and Moldavia Turkish Fleet is sunk by Russians at Sinope
1854	Anglo–French Alliance: War begins in March
1855	British army involved fully in Crimea Aberdeen Coalition collapses as a result of conduct of war Palmerston Prime Minister
1856	Peace of Paris ends war with Russia Chinese seize the 'Arrow', Canton bombarded
1858	Capture of Canton
1859	War breaks out in Italy. Russell becomes Foreign Secretary
1860	Capture of Peking. British fleet ensures Garibaldi's successful invasion of mainland Italy from Sicily. Russell Dispatch
1861	American Civil War breaks out. Trent Incident
1862–64	The 'Alabama' affair
1863	Polish revolt against Russia. Start of Schleswig-Holstein problem
1864	Prussia and Austria invade Schleswig-Holstein. Beginning of Danish War
1865	Death of Palmerston after election victory: Russell becomes Prime Minister.

Overview

FOREIGN policy in this period was dominated by Lord Palmerston, who held the office of Foreign Secretary from 1846–51, and Prime Minister from 1855–58 and again from 1859–65. Frequently accused of being no more than a 'gunboat diplomat' (one who used naval force at the slightest opportunity) – indeed of being the originator of gunboat diplomacy – Palmerston was essentially a great **opportunist**, who worked to few long-term objectives or principles. He adapted to changing situations, and dealt with them as they arose, seeking always to further British commercial interests, protect British subjects, and maintain the balance of power on the basis of the 1815 Vienna settlement.

In line with traditional British policy, Palmerston opposed the expansion of Russia and supported the independence of Turkey. He cooperated with, or opposed, foreign governments as suited each situation, forming no lasting alliances with other powers or friendships with foreign statesmen. (As a result, he was distrusted by many of the latter – for example, François Guizot of France and Prince von Metternich of Austria.) Palmerston always intervened to promote peaceful settlements, offering mediation (but never accepting it from others, believing Britain was capable of resolving its own disputes), encouraging **absolutist** governments towards concessions and constitutional reform, but never actively assisting or encouraging rebels. He had no time for **militant nationalism**. Palmerston usually worked on the basis of a strict regard for international law and treaty rights. He achieved his objectives by a mixture of negotiation, persuasion, threats, bluffs, and ultimately force, if the advantage was on Britain's side.

Historians tend to see Palmerston's last period as Prime Minister, between 1855 and 1865, as his twilight years. The worst of the bully in him came out in his dealings with China and Japan. These countries could be seen as 'smaller' than Britain, so Palmerston used Britain's superior force to gain his objectives. With larger nations, such as Prussia and Russia, he could do no more than bluster. Palmerston was seen to have lost his 'touch' with public opinion when he was defeated in the House of Commons over the Orsini affair, in 1858. His ability to live up to his reputation as the able diplomat, shrewd statesman and supporter of liberalism and nationalism were shown to be false in his dealings with Russia over Poland, with Prussia over Schleswig-Holstein, and with both sides in the American Civil War.

Other historians would argue that Palmerston still showed both flair and perception, that his energy was undiminished and his ability to identify what was in Britain's best interests and follow them relentlessly did not falter. It was no coincidence that Britain's exports to all parts of the world continued to increase throughout this period. Business boomed even though his reputation for wisdom may have suffered, and in that sense he did what was expected of him. Palmerston, of course, was not Foreign Secretary during either of his periods as Prime Minister. Lord Clarendon was Foreign Secretary between 1855 and 1858, and Lord John Russell between 1859 and 1865, but both contemporaries and historians assumed that the controlling interest was always Palmerston.

Opportunist: One who deals with, say, social or political problems by practical methods which are adapted to the circumstances of the moment.

Absolutist: A form of government that is undemocratic. Political power is in the hands of one person.

Militant nationalism: The growth and spread of loyalty towards a nation, rather than an individual ruler, with the threat of military force.

François Guizot (1787–1874)
Guizot served the French monarchy from 1814. He was French Prime Minister 1840–48. His right-wing views led to him being sacked in 1848 and sent into exile a year later.

Prince von Metternich (1778–1859)
Metternich was Austrian Foreign Secretary, 1809–48. He was a defender of the Vienna Settlement of 1815.

1. On what principles was Palmerston's foreign policy based?

2. Was Palmerston anything more than a 'gunboat diplomat'? Give reasons to support your answer.

12.1 *Why did Palmerston involve Britain in the affairs of Spain and Portugal?*

There was a long tradition of involvement by Britain and other powers in the affairs of Spain and Portugal. During the Napoleonic Wars, Britain had freed them both from the French. Since then, Britain had intervened to ensure the establishment of theoretically constitutional monarchies in both Spain and Portugal. Palmerston had little interest in being involved in the internal affairs of other countries. Normally, his main concern was to ensure favourable treatment for British merchants and the honouring of both countries' debts to England. However, he could not ignore the French attempt to arrange the marriage of a member of the Bourbon or Orleans families (the royal families of France) to the young Queen Isabella of Spain or her sister. The resulting link between the French and Spanish royal families could lead to a Franco–Spanish alliance with serious implications for balance of power, especially as France was embarking on a new phase of colonial expansion and had recently seized Algeria. As always, Palmerston was following classic British policy. Britain had fought Louis XIV for two decades in the 17th and 18th centuries to prevent such a match. Palmerston encouraged the Spanish queen to marry her liberal cousin, Enrique. However, François Guizot, while going through the motions of negotiating with Palmerston, arranged in secret the marriages of the royal sisters and France's favoured candidates.

Palmerston made an error of judgement: he attempted to rule out the French candidates and assumed the French and Spanish governments would accept this. He was promptly double-crossed by the French who showed the dispatch note from Britain to the Spanish, and took advantage of their anger to get the marriages they wanted. Palmerston had been outwitted.

In Portugal, a civil war broke out between the dictatorial Queen and liberal rebels calling for restoration of constitutional government. Palmerston did not wish to intervene directly, but attempted mediation. He tried to persuade the rebels to stop rebelling, and the Queen to grant concessions and restore constitutional government. He also did his utmost to prevent any other countries getting involved (Spain threatened to intervene) and to encourage moderation on both sides. A settlement was reached at a conference involving Portugal, France, Spain and Britain along lines suggested by Palmerston, although British troops had to be sent to force the rebels to accept it. It was a good illustration of Palmerstonian foreign policy at work: a wish to negotiate, concern for the balance of power and British trade, return to the legitimate ***status quo***, and the use of force when absolutely necessary.

Status quo: Keeping things unchanged.

What does this reveal? Palmerston's determination to maintain the balance of power and follow the principles of British policy, with the traditional suspicion of France's intentions. It shows some sympathy for liberal/constitutional demands, but very little with those who persisted in rebelling against their lawful sovereign. It also shows a desire to restore peace as soon as possible, without anyone else getting involved (best for commerce and the general peace), and in the meantime keep bloodshed to a minimum, and eventually bring about a peaceful solution satisfactory to all parties. Palmerston had no hesitation in using force where it was deemed necessary.

1. What were the problems facing Palmerston in his dealings with Spain and Portugal?

2. Do you regard Palmerston as a success or a failure in his dealings with Spain and Portugal? Give reasons to support your answer.

12.2 How successful was Palmerston's handling of the revolutions of 1848?

In January 1848, an uprising broke out in Sicily and quickly spread to Naples, forcing the king to grant a constitution. (Italy was not a united country at this time, but a collection of separate states – see map on page 71.) Soon after, Paris rose in revolt, forcing Louis Philippe, the French King, and Guizot his Minister, into exile. Revolutions followed in Berlin, where the Prussian King also had to accept a constitution and a liberal government, and in Vienna, leading to the fall of Prince von Metternich's Government and nationalist uprisings in every province of the Austrian Empire. Palmerston could not have much influence on events, as the situation kept changing too quickly for British influence to be brought effectively to bear. As usual he encouraged negotiation, compromise and concessions, disliking revolutions on principle and horrified at the emergence of socialism and other radical ideas. However, he was not sorry to see absolutist governments reluctantly accepting reforms (or to see Metternich and Guizot removed). Palmerston sometimes overreached himself, for the strength of the right-wing/absolutist reaction took events beyond his control.

The February Revolution in France

Pragmatic: Not having any fixed policy or strategy – taking advantage of events as they occur.

Republic: A country whose system of government is based on the idea that every citizen has equal status, so that there is no king or queen and no aristocracy.

In France, the reign of Louis Philippe was brought to an abrupt end and a government consisting of radicals, democrats and a few socialists was established. Palmerston was, at first, supportive. As always he was **pragmatic** – he had never got on with the French monarchy and Anglo–French relations might improve with a **republic**. He established contact with the new government and encouraged it towards moderate policies. Events, however, moved much too fast – the Parisian workers rose and were brutally crushed by General Cavaignac, who then formed a conservative government. Palmerston approved. He had no sympathy whatever for socialist rebels, and wanted to see order restored. When Cavaignac was in turn defeated in elections by Louis Napoleon (with support from socialists), again Palmerston supported the development, although it was directly contrary to the Treaty of Vienna to allow a Bonaparte to sit on the throne of France. There was nothing to be gained by opposing, although Palmerston made efforts to persuade the new regime to tone down its extravagantly nationalist outbursts. Palmerston's overriding pragmatism is clear in all this – he was concerned to see a stable government with which he could do business. Limited attempts were made to safeguard the interests of British subjects, but were not pushed too far – France could not be forced. He was perhaps lucky that other governments, that would normally have taken a stronger line, had more pressing concerns to deal with.

Louis Napoleon (1808–1873)
Louis Napoleon was elected President of France in 1848. He became Emperor of France in 1852, taking the title 'Napoleon III'. He was deposed in 1870. He died at Chislehurst, Kent in January 1873.

The Revolutions in Germany, Austria and Italy

Though in favour of constitutional reform in Austria and the German states, Palmerston gave no encouragement to nationalist movements. Liberal regimes had taken over in Prussia and other German states, and the movement for a united Germany was gathering pace (Germany at that time was actually made up of a large number of separate and independent states). Infected by this new nationalist ardour, the new government of Prussia (one of these 'German' states) attempted to seize the Duchies of Schleswig and Holstein. Palmerston's main concerns were, as usual, to prevent:

- a general European war, as the Austrians were threatening to get involved
- such a serious threat to the balance of power as would be posed by a united Germany or an enlarged Prussia.

Palmerston managed to bring the interested powers together in an international conference. He used his accustomed skill at handling such gatherings to bring about a negotiated settlement of the Schleswig-Holstein question. This was arguably his only outstanding success of the 1848 crisis, soon after which the liberal regime in Prussia fell.

Once the government of Metternich had fallen, in March, widespread rebellion erupted throughout the Austrian territories. Palmerston never wished for the dissolution of the Austrian Empire, since this would create a void into which the Russians might move. He believed Austria should withdraw from Italy (where it had been given large territories at the end of the Napoleonic Wars). This was simply because it appeared that the Austrian position in Italy had become difficult to maintain, following the revolt of Venice and Lombardy and the subsequent intervention of the King of Piedmont-Sardinia. Palmerston argued, quite reasonably given the situation, that Austria should withdraw and consolidate the rest of its Empire if it was to survive. There was no support forthcoming for the Czech or Hungarian revolts (both areas being ruled by the Austrians) – they were within Austria's accepted zone of influence and Austrian withdrawal might lead to Russian expansion.

Palmerston attempted to mediate between Sardinia and Austria to bring about a peaceful end to Austria's presence in Italy, but unfortunately an imperialist reaction took events far beyond his control. First, General Windischgratz crushed the Czechs and the constitutional government in Vienna in quick succession; then the Austrian General Radetzky revived the Austrian army in Italy, defeated the Sardinians and recaptured Austria's possessions of Lombardy and Venice.

Tsar: Title of the emperor of Russia. Also spelled Czar and Tzar. Believed to be shortened form of Caesar (Roman emperor).

Despite Palmerston's protests, the **Tsar** was asked by Austria to send troops to help put down the Hungarians. Palmerston was confined to protesting strongly at the brutality of the suppression, although it was the appearance of Russian forces in Europe that really alarmed him. The new Austrian government was upset by his attempts to interfere, and he emerged as champion of revolutionaries, which had not been his intention. His attempts at conciliation and mediation in the rest of Italy were energetic but generally fruitless. The French and Austrians marched to the aid of the Pope (who was an autocratic territorial ruler as well as a spiritual leader) and crushed the Italian nationalist Guiseppe Garibaldi's valiant but doomed Roman republic in 1849 without reference to Britain. When the King of Naples refused any concessions to his subjects who were asking for greater political freedom, bombarded them in Sicily, and stamped out all opposition, Palmerston was a mere spectator.

1. What problems did the outbreak of revolution across Europe in 1848–49 create for Palmerston?

2. Study the revolutions in France, the German states, Austria and Italy.

(a) In which area do you regard Palmerston as being most successful?

(b) In which area do you regard Palmerston as being least successful?

Give reasons to support your answer.

3. On balance, do you regard Palmerston as more of a success than a failure? Give reasons to support your answer.

Conclusion

Palmerston's reputation as a champion of radicals and revolutionaries was undeserved. He had not wanted the revolutions, and though he supported the granting of constitutional reforms by monarchs, he did not want to see a string of radical republics emerging. He was concerned to prevent events getting out of hand, to avoid a European war resulting from the disorder, and to preserve the existing balance of power as far as possible. Palmerston was not working to any plan, and he dealt with each situation as he found it, or thought he found it. As in the case of Austria and Italy, he could misjudge situations. While he sought to promote the British ideal of compromise between monarch and subjects, he underestimated the capacity of the old regimes to fight for their absolute rights. In the chaos of revolution and reaction, the moral authority of England counted for little, and since he was not prepared to commit forces anywhere, there was very little he could have done that would have made a difference. The balance of power was restored, but Palmerston cannot really take much credit for this.

12.3 Why did Palmerston adopt such an aggressive policy towards the Greek government over Don Pacifico?

This episode is usually referred to as the 'Don Pacifico Affair'. However, there were many factors involved besides the case of this Portuguese Jew with a slightly dubious claim to British citizenship (he had been born in Gibraltar), whose house in Greece was burned down by an anti-Semitic mob in 1847. Bad relations between the British and Greek governments had begun almost immediately on the Greeks gaining independence in 1832, and had continued.

Claiming damages for his damaged property, which the Greek Government declined to pay, Don Pacifico appealed to the British Government. There were, in fact, others in a similar position who were owed money by the Greek Government. Initially, Palmerston ordered a blockade of the Greek coast without consulting his allies, France and Russia, who had guaranteed Greek independence. This was followed by a more extreme blockade of the port of Piraeus, near Athens, and the seizure of a number of Greek merchant ships in 1850. It achieved the intended result in that Don Pacifico was eventually compensated by the Greek Government for about a quarter of the sum he had originally claimed.

1. Assess the significance of the Don Pacifico Affair to Palmerston's career as Foreign Secretary?

2. Should Palmerston be praised or condemned for his actions in the case of Don Pacifico? Give reasons to support your answer.

In one sense this was a success for Palmerston. He had upheld the status of Britain and its citizens (even though this one was a Portuguese money-lender and merchant!). Added to this, Palmerston was to achieve a personal triumph in the House of Commons when he defended himself in a four-and-a-half-hour speech against his critics. He not only outlined his principles, but also stated that he had been defending British citizens against injustice and oppression. He argued that as the Roman citizen of old was able to say *'Civis Romanus sum'* ('I am a citizen of Rome'), and therefore claim the full protection of a mighty empire, a British citizen should be able to say *'Civis Britannicus sum'*, and claim the same degree of protection.

This argument went down well both in Parliament and in the country. Its aggressive nationalism and blatant anti-foreigner appeal struck a responsive note. However, it certainly damaged relations with our former allies in the region – France, Russia and Austria – and gave Palmerston a not unjustified reputation as a bully of smaller nations.

12.4 Why was Palmerston dismissed in 1851?

Russell had not been keen on giving Palmerston the Foreign Office in 1846, but he had no alternative. Palmerston was both popular and experienced, as well as having considerable political ability. Russell needed Palmerston in the Foreign Office more than Palmerston needed the support of Russell. Russell never quite trusted Palmerston's judgement in foreign policy, and he certainly saw him as a potential political rival. Palmerston's able handling of the events of 1848, as well as incidents such as the Don Pacifico Affair, further enhanced his status nationally, and made him virtually irremovable.

However, Palmerston was unpopular with the Queen and her influential husband, Albert. It was partly a personality clash; the Queen strongly disapproved of Palmerston's immoral private life. There had been an unfortunate incident in the late 1830s when Palmerston had been found trying to get into the bedroom of a Royal Lady-in-Waiting at Windsor Castle. There were doubts about how 'accidental' this was. The Queen was not against corresponding with other crowned heads in Europe, such as her uncle Leopold in Belgium, about affairs of state and international relations without consulting her Ministers. Palmerston, too, was not against acting on his own, and failing to consult and inform both the monarch and his Cabinet colleagues as to what he was doing. The precise constitutional role of the monarch was not clear in this respect and Palmerston could have shown more tact in dealing with the Queen. Victoria, on her part, might have shown a greater awareness of where political responsibility lay, and who would be called to account in Parliament in the case of errors.

The Haynau Affair, 1850

The first open clash between Palmerston and the Palace came with the Haynau Affair in 1850. Haynau was an Austrian general who came to Britain on an official visit. He had played a major part in suppressing the popular uprisings against Austrian rule in both Italy and Hungary, and had gained a reputation for brutality towards men and women. When visiting a brewery in South London, Haynau was attacked by a mob and had to be rescued by the police. The Cabinet and the Queen insisted on an apology, which Palmerston grudgingly sent without showing it to them first. The apology indicated clearly that Palmerston felt Haynau got exactly what he deserved, referring to him as a 'great moral criminal'. The Palace was furious about the lack of consultation and tact, which came to a head the following year.

Dismissal over Louis Napoleon's coup d'état, *December 1851*

This arose when in 1851, following revolution and upheaval in France between 1848 and 1851, the nephew of the great Bonaparte himself mounted a *coup d'état* and more or less assumed dictatorial powers. The Palace felt strongly that the former monarch, Louis Philippe, should be restored, naturally having a strong sympathy for fellow monarchs. Russell wanted to stay strictly neutral, as was right and proper in such cases of civil and political unrest in another country. Palmerston, however, fearing that the alternative to Napoleon was a dangerous radicalism of the type that had appeared briefly on the barricades in Paris in 1848, immediately accepted the coup. He gave recognition, without consulting either his Cabinet colleagues or the Palace. A furious Queen Victoria immediately put pressure on Russell to dismiss him. Russell sacked him, fairly sure that the unpopularity of a Bonaparte in Britain would not give Palmerston a good base to appeal to the country from. Palmerston was furious, and took his revenge on Russell early in the following year by voting against him and thus ensuring the collapse of the Russell Administration and the arrival of the first Derby–Disraeli Administration.

Which reasons do you regard as the most important for the dismissal of Palmerston in 1851? Give reasons to support your answer.

The fact was that, although Palmerston was constitutionally wrong in what he did, his action was not forgotten by the successful Bonaparte. Although Anglo-French relations were always to remain tense at times, Louis Napoleon never forgot who had been the first to recognise his claim to authority in France.

12.5 *Why did Britain go to war with Russia in the Crimea?*

A CASE STUDY IN HISTORICAL INTERPRETATION

Opposing the expansion of Russia was classic British policy – a long tradition going back to William Pitt (Prime Minister in the late 18th century) and beyond. There was widespread anti-Russian feeling in Britain. The common view was that Russia was a threat to the safety of Europe, and its expansion, if not checked, might prove unstoppable. If Russia commanded the Straits between the Mediterranean and the Black Sea and Constantinople, it could dominate the Mediterranean. If it moved into Eastern Europe, it could threaten Austria and upset the balance of power. If it expanded in Asia, it could threaten British power in India.

Turkey must be supported, therefore, as an obstacle to this expansion, regardless of the fact that it was a decadent, corrupt and oppressive power, or that the Sultan was incapable of maintaining control of his own territories. Russia not only wanted to expand, in all directions, but was concerned for Orthodox Christians in the Turkish Empire, who were frequently mistreated. (Russia was also part of the Greek Orthodox Church.) After the crushing of the Hungarian revolt, Lajos Kossuth and other Hungarian rebel leaders fled to Turkey. Russia and Austria threatened war if they were not handed over. Such was the determination of Britain to maintain the independence of Turkey, the British ambassador in Constantinople, Stratford Canning, promised British support for the Turks if they defied the Russians and Austrians. Instead of sacking him for exceeding his authority, Palmerston backed him (though the widespread anti-Austrian feeling in Britain at that time played a part in this).

What were the immediate causes of the war?

The Crimean crisis began in 1853, when Palmerston was at the Home Office. Louis Napoleon, anxious to exert French authority abroad, claimed to be the protector of Catholics inside the Turkish Empire, causing Russia to revive its old claim to protect the Greek Orthodox Christians who lived within the Turkish Empire. Both demanded powers that would enable them to enforce these claims within Turkey.

Though this represented a serious threat to the independence of Turkey, the opposition of the British Government was not as strong as might have been expected. It was, in fact, divided – Palmerston and Russell (as well as the public) favoured the traditional policy and vigorous support for Turkey, but Aberdeen and Gladstone were unhappy about supporting a

The Middle East at the time of the Crimean War, 1853–1856

Muslim power that had a tradition of mistreating its Christian subjects. When Ambassador Canning summoned the fleet to the Dardanelles (the usual means of demonstrating support for the Turks), he was overruled for once. After much indecision, the fleet was eventually sent, but this time it merely served to provoke the Tsar into invading the Turkish principalities of Moldavia and Wallachia (roughly modern Romania). He had been threatening to do this for some time, in order to force the Turks to accede to his demands. Meanwhile, the French had changed tack and taken up a violently anti-Russian stance.

The British Government was still divided and hesitant, but a conference of Great Powers was eventually organised in Vienna. It hammered out a compromise, but the Turks, encouraged by Canning, rejected it and attacked the Russians, sending their fleet into the supposedly demilitarised Black Sea. The Russians promptly annihilated the Russian fleet at Sinope. The British public was outraged, but the Government was preoccupied with the dispute about electoral reform over which Palmerston resigned. Eventually, it demanded that Russia leave the principalities, and with the Tsar's refusal the war opened.

The indecisiveness of Aberdeen's Government was a primary cause of the war. The failure to send a clear message to the Russians from the beginning encouraged the latter to take up a position from which they could not back down. The failure to control and restrain either Canning or the Turks led the Sultan (Turkish leader) to believe he could act on his own initiative and be sure of British support. Likewise, little effort was made to restrain or coordinate strategy with Louis Napoleon, whose erratic warmongering kept increasing the temperature of the crisis. It is probably fair to conclude, as most historians do, that it was the absence of Palmerston's firm handling that allowed the situation to deteriorate into war.

Inevitably with so many countries involved, as well as so many major personalities, there has been much debate among historians as to where responsibility should lie for the causes of this war. A.J.P. Taylor, in his masterly analysis of international politics in the middle of the century (*The Struggle for Mastery in Europe*, 1954) saw the war as an early 'cold war', a conflict between East and West. He argues strongly that British concerns about the route to India being safeguarded were irrelevant here. It was a war over European considerations, with the balance of power being the key to the thinking of British politicians. Taylor feels that there were largely selfish motives, in defending Turkey, and that British involvement was a good demonstration of this. The key factor in the final outbreak was the attitude of the French Emperor, Napoleon III. Taylor does allow that British internal politics do play a part, with a weak Aberdeen and Palmerston not being strong enough to let his views dominate.

Others, like George Clayton (*Britain and the Eastern Question*, 1973) argue that Stratford Canning, the British ambassador to Turkey, played the major role. He gave the Turks the impression that the British would always come and help the Turks against the Russians, however much the Turks might provoke the Russians by their poor conduct towards their dependent Christian subjects. Harold Temperly, in his huge study of British foreign policy, argues that Canning's role was insignificant, and that it was British policy, not the French, that led to the war actually starting. Much of the blame, Temperly argues, should be placed at the door of inept British politicians and their willingness to respond too easily to British public opinion. Jonathan Parry argues that it was a direct clash between the British and the Russians over economic interests in the Near East, while Henderson, in his study of Crimean War diplomacy, puts it all down to the blundering of the Tsar of Russia.

Historian Muriel Chamberlain, in a wide-ranging, recent analysis of the

1. What were the causes of the Crimean War?

2. Explain how historians have disagreed over the causes of the war.

causes, accepts some and discards others of the ideas put forward above. She also places a lot of emphasis on the work of Napoleon in the final stages, but argues that the need to defend the route to India (however geographically odd that may seem before the Suez Canal was built) was a major factor in the thinking of the British Government. She is very critical of the role of Aberdeen, and of Russell who was playing too much of a political game at the time. Aberdeen has to accept responsibility for his inept conduct in the last days of peace, and for then trying to conduct a war that he could not really support. Chamberlain also places blame on the forceful role of the press. The press was allowed to lead and not reflect public opinion. This forced the Government into war.

12.6 What were the results of the Crimean War?

When Britain declared war on Russia in 1854, its main concerns were the maintenance of the European balance of power and the need to prevent the Russian navy entering the Mediterranean Sea.

Following the Russian evacuation of Moldavia and Wallachia, the British and French decided to capture the Russian naval base on the Black Sea, Sebastopol. Although this was a sound military objective, the Anglo–French campaign was poorly organised. The campaign did not begin until September 1854, allowing the Russians to fortify the city. The British and French were forced to spend the winter of 1854–55 besieging Sebastopol. This campaign exposed how badly the British Army was organised and supplied. Battles at Balaklava, in October 1854, and Inkerman, in November, showed both the bravery of British troops and the poor quality of their generals.

The Times correspondent William Howard Russell wrote damning newspaper articles about living conditions and bad organisation, which helped to defeat Lord Aberdeen's Government in 1855.

Aberdeen was replaced by Palmerston. Military organisation was improved and Austria, Sweden and Piedmont-Sardinia joined the side of Britain and France. In 1855, Sebastopol fell, mainly to an assault by French troops. In Paris the following year, the peace treaty between Russia and the Allies was signed.

The Crimean War brought about many changes. The war had the first 'on the spot' war correspondent in W.H. Russell. It was also the war that saw Florence Nightingale make her reputation as a nurse, laying the foundations of modern British nursing, at the British military hospital at Scutari, near Constantinople.

In international terms, Britain achieved its major objectives. The European balance of power was maintained. Neither Russia nor Turkey was allowed a fleet in the Black Sea, thereby removing any potential naval threat to Britain in the Mediterranean. The Turks promised to improve the treatment of Christians within their Empire. In addition, Moldavia and Wallachia were given independence but were not allowed to unite. Russia lost southern Bessarabia (see map on page 210).

However, the war had other far-reaching consequences. Austria's decision to side with Britain and France against Russia split the Holy Alliance. In the years after 1856, the lack of Russian involvement in European affairs was an important reason behind the Austrian defeat in Italy by France in 1859 and by Prussia in the Seven Weeks' War of 1866. It would be true to say that the split in the Holy Alliance helped to reshape central Europe.

Although Britain was successful, many of its gains proved short-lived. Moldavia and Wallachia united in 1858 and became the kingdom of Romania in 1861. The Sultan's promise to improve the treatment of his

1. What changes were made by Britain's involvement in the Crimean War?

2. Do you regard Britain's involvement in the Crimean War as having been successful? Give reasons to support your answer.

Christian subjects was not implemented. Most important of all, the demilitarisation of the Black Sea came to an end in 1870, when at the height of the Franco–Prussian War, Russia declared that it was no longer bound by the Treaty of Paris of 1856. The Crimean War brought a lull in the Eastern Question. The issue again brought Europe into crisis and war in the 1875–78 period.

12.7 Why was Palmerston involved in the Far East, and what were the results of these involvements?

The Second Chinese War was, in many respects, a repeat of a problem that he had dealt with earlier in the century. There was a growing friction between the Chinese authorities and the British for a variety of reasons. The British hated the Chinese. The growing opium trade from the East India Company further fuelled Chinese dislike of foreigners. Not unnaturally, the Chinese Government resented what they saw as an intrusion into the private lives of their citizens, and this, coupled with the growing expansion of Christian missionaries into China, did not incline them to be sympathetic to foreigners.

What sparked the crisis in 1856 was the 'Arrow' affair. This ship, sailing in Chinese waters, was registered as British. It was commanded by an Ulsterman (who was not, in fact, a seaman at all). In reality, the ship was

Punch cartoon of 4 September 1858, entitled 'A Little Tea Party'. Britannia (personification of Britain) is saying 'A Little more gunpowder, Mr China?' Mr China rep[lies, 'O-N-Tan-ke-Mum.'

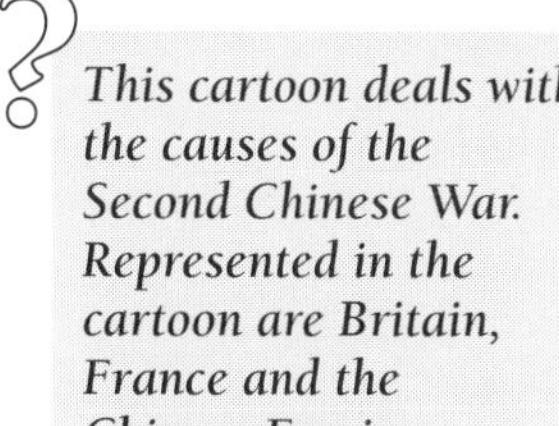

This cartoon deals with the causes of the Second Chinese War. Represented in the cartoon are Britain, France and the Chinese Empire.

(a) What reason do you think is given for the start of the war?

(b) How reliable is this cartoon for the causes of the Second Chinese War?

owned by a local pirate who made his living raiding Chinese ships. When the ship was arrested by Chinese authorities (as it happened just after its British registration had expired), the local British Consul, William Parkes, demanded the release of the ship, commander and crew, as well as a full apology. Not surprisingly, the Chinese refused – law and moral right were perhaps on their side. But the local British authorities were not satisfied, and virtually went to war with the Chinese, without consulting London in the first place. The Chinese, in the end, agreed to release the crew (who were not British) and their commander, but declined the requested apology.

Palmerston, even though the local British authorities had not consulted him, felt it was necessary to back them fully. He was aware that they did not have moral right on their side, but he felt it was vital to uphold British prestige in the region. It was also a good opportunity to force the Chinese to open up the whole of their country to British trade and end any restrictions on the free flow of British goods (and opium).

Palmerston was strongly criticised in both the Commons and the Lords for his conduct. He was defeated in the Commons by 16 votes on a Motion of Censure led by John Bright. In the election of 1857, where the 'Arrow' incident featured prominently, the Liberals won with their largest majority since 1832, and Palmerston had the satisfaction of seeing Bright lose his seat.

The war with China continued after Palmerston regained office, and it was pushed to a successful conclusion under the Conservatives – the final episode being a march to Peking in 1860 and the burning of the Summer Palace of the Emperor of China. The Chinese sued for peace and conceded to the demands of the British. Trade with the Chinese interior was now permitted, the British could send representatives to the capital itself, more ports opened to trade with foreigners, and the opium trade could develop. The morality of the issue could be debated. Palmerston had taken on, admittedly by default, a war with a weaker nation and had used greater force to ensure his objectives. Naturally, merchants and businessmen were delighted – a vast new area was opened up to British trade. British prestige in that part of the world inevitably grew. In one sense, Palmerston was doing what he was paid by the taxpayer to do, but in another he had weakened the moral authority of this country and lives had been lost in the pursuit of hard cash.

Japan 1863–1864

Much the same happened in the case of Japan in 1863–64. This incident should be seen as similar in many ways to both the 'Arrow' and Don Pacifico affairs. In the course of a minor internal conflict in Japan, in Kagoshima, a British citizen and two of his Japanese employees were killed. The Japanese authorities did not quickly meet the demand for compensation, so a naval bombardment by the British Navy followed in which over 1,400 Japanese died.

Palmerston summed up his attitude in a letter to Russell in October 1864, writing:

> 'I am inclined to think that our relations with Japan are going through the usual and unavoidable stages of the intercourse of strong and civilised nations with weaker and less civilised ones. First – agreement for trade; next, breach of engagement, injustice and outrage – then redress demanded and refused – then reparation enforced by hostility. Then temporary acquiescence, then renewed endeavours to break engagements, then successful display of superior strength, and then at last peaceful and settled commercial intercourse advantageous to both parties.'

The accuracy of the last clause can be debated!

1. What were the main issues facing Palmerston in his policy towards the Far East?

2. Was Palmerston more than a 'commercially minded bully' in his policies towards China and Japan in this period?

12.8 Why did Palmerston become involved in the Italian Wars of Unification between 1859 and 1861?

In many respects, Italy is an excellent example to illustrate the many features of Palmerstonian foreign policy. His attitude to liberalism and nationalism, the balance of power, British strategic and commercial interests, and his relationship with the great powers of Europe are all revealed here. Russell had views of his own, and Palmerston was actually a restraining influence to Russell's dislike of autocratic Popes and tyrants. Palmerston's pragmatism was needed to balance the attractive, but unrealistic, policy of Russell.

Palmerston had always looked sympathetically at the nationalistic and liberal aspirations in Italy, primarily as he saw them as barriers to a more radical explosion in an area in which Britain had both commercial and strategic interests. He had never liked the Austrian method of rule in northern Italy (which tended to be ruthless and autocratic), but he saw the Austrians as a restraining force to both the French and other radical forces in Italy.

Italy was still a divided and occupied country in 1859 when the Prime Minister of the northern state of Piedmont-Sardinia, Count Cavour, invaded the Austrian possessions in north Italy, with French assistance.

Palmerston was in a dilemma as he had no wish to see French influence further extended into Italy, and he was well aware that Napoleon might well extract a territorial price in Italy for his aid. It was British influence that ensured that, after initial defeats by the French and Italians, the Austrians were prevented from moving more troops into northern Italy and prolonging the war. As a result, Piedmont-Sardinia was extended substantially across Northern Italy and down towards the Papal States in the centre of Italy.

1. What aspects of British foreign policy were at stake during the Italian Wars of Unification between 1859 and 1861?

2. What actions did the British Government take to protect British interests in Italy during this period?

3. How successful was British foreign policy towards Italy in 1859–61?

The crisis deepened further in 1860 when the popular Italian solder, Giuseppe Garibaldi, led an invasion force to Sicily to overthrow the brutal regime of the King of Naples and Sicily (then an independent sovereign state). It was the Navy which ensured Garibaldi's safe arrival in Sicily. Then, when he crossed the Straits of Messina later in the year to 'liberate' Naples and much of central Italy and bring it into the Piedmontese fold, it was the British Navy which ensured their safe passage across the Straits. This had been vital to the final unification of Italy into one single nation under a constitutional monarch. What was interesting was that Russell and Gladstone pressed Palmerston into this course of action. Russell issued a dispatch warning France against any further intervention. It was Palmerston who, of course, got the credit as the supporter of liberalism and nationalism, but it was his fears of French influence in Italy and his innate caution which had been the overriding features in his thinking.

However, it has been seen as his last great success, even though it did owe a lot to Russell. Britain was owed a debt of gratitude by the new united state of Italy, trade would increase on favoured nation terms, and an ally in the strategically important Mediterranean was gained.

12.9 To what extent was Palmerston's policy during the American Civil War a success?

Palmerston had never been sympathetic towards the United States of America. Memories of the War of 1812 were still there, when Britain fought the United States at the same time as Napoleonic France. Opinion within his own party was divided when a civil war broke out in 1861 between the North, led by the democratically elected Abraham Lincoln, and the breakaway States of the

South who feared that slavery might be abolished and their prosperity destroyed by an industrialised North.

Palmerston disliked the Northern States, seeing them as essentially democratic, which they were. He was both an aristocrat and a snob in this respect, and he was secretly (but not too secretly) pleased to see the initial defeat of the Northern army by the South at the Battle of Bull Run, in July 1861. The fact that he was supposed to have been a champion of the anti-slavery movement himself is frequently forgotten. There were several occasions during the war when Palmerston made sure that material that could be used to damage the North and put the South in a better light was leaked to the editors of *The Times* and *Morning Post*. He was also concerned that Canada might be under threat from the North.

Palmerston's early recognition of the South as a belligerent (this did not mean he recognised them as an independent sovereign state as they wished) did not endear him to the North; nor did the fact that he allowed Southern representatives into Britain.

Two incidents pushed Anglo–American relations to crisis point. The first was when two Southern agents, James Mason and John Slidell (both slave owners!) were sent to London by the Southern President, Jefferson Davis, to gain support. They were arrested on the high seas by the Northern navy while on a British ship, the 'Trent'. This caused uproar in London and the two nations came close to war over a minor matter. It was perhaps the last piece of work by Prince Albert before his death to put pressure on the British Government to 'cool it' with the United States. However, it is worth noting that it was after this incident, with the supposedly more 'liberal' Gladstone and Russell pressing for recognition of the South as an independent state, that Palmerston preached caution and prevented recognition.

The 'Alabama' Affair, 1862–1864

Relations with the Northern States worsened during the 'Alabama' affair. The (Northern) American ambassador to London, John Adams, rightly suspected that a ship, being built in a British shipyard (Lairds of Birkenhead), was destined to serve the South as a commerce raider. It was a breach of international law to allow this to happen. However, when Adams warned the British Government of what was happening, Russell's response was so slow that the ship was able to sail and do a huge amount of damage to Northern shipping. Between 1862 and 1864, the 'Alabama' and other British-built raiders sank or captured 57 Northern ships. The North protested furiously and demanded compensation, but Russell and Palmerston refused to compensate them or to allow the matter to go to **arbitration**. It was not until 1872–73 that Gladstone sorted the issue out, and paid compensation. The whole affair badly damaged Anglo–American relations.

Arbitration: A process whereby a neutral referee imposes a decision on both parties in a dispute.

By the end of 1863, when the North was clearly winning and the Proclamation against Slavery had been issued by the Northern States, public opinion in Britain swung behind the Northern States and the British Government slowly followed suit. Given the issues at stake in the United States, the closeness to war over 'Trent', and the behaviour of the British Government over the 'Alabama', it was an episode in the history of British foreign policy where no credit can be claimed by any politicians, least of all by such experienced men as Palmerston and Russell.

1. What were the main problems facing Palmerston during the American Civil War?

2. Does Palmerston's handling of foreign policy during the American Civil War suggest that 'he had lost his touch'? Give reasons to support your answer.

12.10 *How serious a failure were Palmerston's dealings with the Polish Revolt and the Schleswig-Holstein Question?*

Even more damaging to the reputations of Palmerston and Russell was their response to the outbreak of a revolution against Russian rule in Poland in 1863. Partitioned in the previous century by the Russians, Austrian and Prussians, the Poles directed their bid for freedom against a highly oppressive Russian rule, and appealed for foreign help. They had revolted once before, in 1830–32. The Prussians gave full support to the Russian army's brutal repression.

Palmerston, together with the French, did indicate that they might well assist the Poles, through putting pressure on the Russians. It was unlikely that Palmerston actually had any intention of assisting the Poles with military aid. The Crimean War and its consequences were too fresh in people's minds to want a repeat. Palmerston had serious misgivings about acting in concert with the French as he felt that they had acquisitive motives and he always saw them as the potential trouble makers of Europe. However, Palmerston's vague promises encouraged the Poles to resist perhaps longer than they might otherwise have done, and their revolt was repressed with maximum and well-publicised barbarity. Britain had no means by which they could actually assist the Poles. The Tsar knew it, and openly ignored British pressure. The British Navy was ineffectual in such circumstances and we had no army capable of acting in this situation. It was a public humiliation and demonstrated all too clearly that our support for liberal and nationalistic movements only applied in very select circumstances. Palmerston could realistically have helped the Poles during the Crimean War, but he chose not to, and there was no way in which he would, or could, do it a decade later.

The Danes and the Prussians: 1863–1864

Many would argue that Palmerston's last major involvement in foreign affairs was his most humiliating, and the best evidence that he had 'lost his touch' in his later years. He was certainly outmanoeuvred by Otto von Bismarck, the Prussian Chancellor, who was a wily diplomat and had an absolute clarity of purpose.

Bismarck's main aim was to expand Prussia from its position of one of the major German powers (Germany, like Italy until 1860, was made up of a number of different states), into the dominant north German state, equal in status to Ansovia in the German Confederation. Bismarck wanted initially to gain influence over the two Danish duchies of Schleswig and Holstein, which formed part of the border between Denmark and north Germany. Bismarck wanted the duchies to ensure his northern border. He also wanted the port of Kiel.

Bismarck's preparations were superb. He ensured that the Danes were completely in the wrong diplomatically and had broken the Treaty of London of 1852 (which had been guaranteed by Britain among other powers), which dealt with the future of these two duchies. The Danish king had attempted to incorporate Schleswig into the Danish kingdom in 1863. Bismarck made sure that Russia and Austria were supportive (he had openly backed the Russians against the Poles and was calling in the favour) and that France was uninterested. He knew Palmerston was bound to be suspicious of working closely with the French, whom he suspected of having an interest in expanding into the Rhineland.

Palmerston promised the Danes, publicly, that they would be supported in the event of a war with the Prussians. They were not supported at all. They fought alone, and Palmerston had to endure not only international

1. Why were the Polish Revolt and the Schleswig-Holstein Question regarded as important European issues in the early 1860s?

2. On what grounds can British foreign policy towards the Polish Revolt and the Schleswig-Holstein Question be criticised?

3. To what extent can Palmerston be regarded as a failure in his handling of British foreign policy in the years 1859 to 1861?

(You will need to consult the sections above on the Italian Wars of Unification and the American Civil War, as well as the section on the Polish Revolt and Schleswig-Holstein.)

humiliation but also a defeat in the House of Lords on the issue and only a narrow success in the Commons. He had supported a state that was in the wrong, as the Danish King had broken an international agreement and his bluff had been called. Palmerston had failed to realise the intentions of Bismarck and the rise of Prussia, and its implications for the whole balance of power in Europe. He had lost his touch.

Conclusion

Examples of the flaws in Palmerstonian policy tend to abound in his last period in office. These range from the short-sightedness of the Treaty of Paris of 1856, the crude methods used to advance British trade in the Far East, to the ineptitude of his dealings with the Americans and the Prussians. Only Italy seems to be a bright spot. There were no major wars and trade boomed, and he was also Prime Minister with many other responsibilities. Certainly, there are no achievements in there which can be seen to rival that of Belgium in the 1830s, or Castlereagh's at Vienna in 1815.

Source-based questions: Palmerston's foreign policy

SOURCE A

'I hold with respect to alliances, that England is a Power sufficiently strong, sufficiently powerful, to steer her own carcinoid [cancer], not to tie herself to an unnecessary appendage to the policy of any other government. I hold that the real policy of England – apart from questions which involve her own particular interests, political or commercial – is to be the champion of justice and right, pursuing that course with moderation and prudence ... We have no eternal allies, and we have no perpetual enemies.'

Lord Palmerston, speaking in the House of Commons, March 1848

SOURCE B

'I cannot regret the expulsion of the Austrians from Italy ... Her rule was hateful to the Italians, and has long been maintained only by an expenditure of money and an exertion of military effort ... I should wish to see the whole of northern Italy united into one kingdom ... such an arrangement would be most conducive to the peace of Europe.'

Lord Palmerston to the King of the Belgians, June 1848

SOURCE C

I am very Austrian north of the Alps, but very anti-Austrian south of the Alps. The Austrians have no business in Italy, and they are a public nuisance. They govern their own provinces ill, and are the props and encouragers of bad government in all the other states of the Peninsula ... but a war to drive the Austrians out of Italy would infallibly succeed in its immediate object, but it might and probably would lead to consequences much to be deplored ...

From a letter by Lord Palmerston to Lord Granville, January 1859. Both were Liberal politicians in opposition at the time.

SOURCE D

Despite his benevolence towards Italian unification and his early enthusiasm for Greek independence, Palmerston was no believer in nationalism – that central cause of 19th-century progressives. Disraeli accused Palmerston of being a convert to 'the sentimental principle of nationality', but this is impossible to substantiate; 'the policxy of Palmerston was not based upon sentimental considerations of nationalism but upon the enduring principles of the "balance of power"', asserts A.J.P. Taylor.

From Foreign Affairs *by D.R. Ward, published in 1972.*

---

1. Explain what is meant, in the context of Palmerstonian foreign policy, the following phrases or sentences in the Sources above:

(a) the 'balance of power' (Source D)

(b) 'props and encouragers of bad government in all the other states of the Peninsula' (Source C).

2. Study Source A.

Explain, in your own words, the main ideas that Palmerston argued were the central principles of British foreign policy.

3. Study Sources A and B.

How useful are these sources to a historian writing about British foreign policy in this period?

4. Using the sources and information from this chapter, how effectively did Palmerston deal with Italian affairs?

13 A mid-Victorian boom? Economic and social history 1846–1868

Key Issues

- *Was it a period of real boom – a Golden Age – in British farming?*
- *Was it also a Golden Age for British industry?*
- *Did a mid-Victorian boom bring about major economic and social change?*

Agriculture
13.1 What was the impact of the repeal of the Corn Laws?
13.2 What were the main developments in agriculture in this period?
13.3 Was it a period of boom for British farming?

Industry
13.4 Why was it such a period of growth for British industry?
13.5 How important were the railways to Great Britain?

Social history
13.6 What was done to improve education?
13.7 In what ways did public health and living conditions improve in this period?
13.8 Did the treatment of, and attitude towards, women change in this period?
13.9 Historical interpretation: The development of the trade unions, 1846–1868, and their impact

Framework of Events

1846	State aid to education expanded
1847	Ten Hours Act
1848	Public Health Act
1849	Bedford College, London (for women) created
1850	Factory Act
1856	Education Department created
1859	Divorce Act
1861	Newcastle Royal Commission on Education
1862	Lowe's 'Revised Code' for Education published
1864	Clarendon Royal Commission on Public Schools
1866	Sanitation Act
	Sheffield Outrages
1867	Hornby *versus* Close Court Case
1868	Formation of the TUC.

Agriculture: overview

Real wages: What can be bought with money wages taking into account inflation (general increase in the price of goods and services).

THE devastation that many feared would hit British farming after the repeal of the Corn Laws did not happen. Foreign corn did not flood onto the British markets. The price of corn, that critical factor in the lives of so many citizens who lived on the breadline (poverty line), remained static, more or less, throughout the period. However, an era of cheap food did not arrive either. Rising **real wages**, caused mainly by an industrial boom, were the key element in the stabilisation of wheat prices. There were steady increases in other agricultural prices, mainly livestock based, throughout the period 1846–68.

It was a period of progress in agriculture. Techniques improved in a variety of areas, ranging from drainage to the use of specialist fertilisers. Machinery started to make an impact on farms – if only on the larger farms. Foreign competition did not arrive on a large scale, harvests were good and the growth of the rail system brought advantages to farmers who could transport more perishable produce to markets quickly. It was seen by many as a 'Golden Age' of British farming.

However, it was not all a bright picture. The treatment of agricultural workers was still dreadful. Many of the changes and improvements did not affect the large number of small farms. Huge threshing machines were only usable on large farms, and there was a risk that many farms were becoming over-capitalised. In other words, too much money was being pumped in and there was too small a return on it. The ease with which farming fell into deep **depression** in the decades following this period is indicative that perhaps some of the prosperity was superficial and not deep rooted.

Depression: A time of great reduction in the activity of a country's industries or economy, which causes a lot of unemployment and poverty.

13.1 *What was the impact of the repeal of the Corn Laws?*

The simple answer is 'not much'. The concern about the damaging impact that the repeal of the Corn Laws might have had may have resulted in many farmers looking at their methods and management for improvements in order to compensate for possible damage. Wheat prices did drop briefly between 1848 and 1852, but not by enough to seriously concern even those against repeal, and it was an asset to have the basic food prices drop in a time of social unrest. In fact, the world prices of wheat rose to British levels in the few years after Repeal.

Rise in agricultural prices

Other agricultural prices rose, some quite rapidly, which more than compensated the farmer for the slight fall in wheat prices. The size of the landed interest in the House of Commons fell slightly, but still about 50% of its members were directly involved in the management of farming land in 1868. It should be noted that any legislation that may have directly or indirectly helped farmers – such as cheap government loans for improvement or proper compensation for the arrival of the railway – had an easy passage in Parliament, both in the Commons and in the Lords.

There was a gradual decline in the power of the landed interest, but it was very small in this period. The Protectionists' case vanished easily, and Benjamin Disraeli was aware that his backbenchers had not been reduced to poverty when the Conservatives abandoned protection in 1852. There was no great world stockpile of wheat ready to be rushed in to undercut British grown wheat – Europe was, in fact, short of wheat – and there was not yet the means of transportation available to ship the cheaper American wheat to Britain. The Crimean War was later to hold up Russian supplies as well. The anticipated destruction of British farming simply did not happen. The propaganda of those against repeal of the Corn Laws was proved to be inaccurate.

Why did the repeal of the Corn Laws, in 1846, not lead to major problems in British agriculture?

13.2 What were the main developments in agriculture in this period?

Husbandry: Management of land and livestock.

Capital investment: Spending large sums of money on new equipment or on improving land in the hope that it would result in increased profits.

Guano: Bird droppings from islands in the Pacific Ocean – high in nitrogen and potash, so good fertiliser.

How far did British agriculture change in the years 1846 to 1868?

A major survey of agriculture by Caird in 1850–51 showed a lot of backward **husbandry**, and many cases where bad landlords and poor agents had neglected to develop and improve. In some areas, there was pioneering work and an effective use of land and science. The main point about this period was that neglect declined and effective use spread. It was also an age of real **capital investment** in agriculture.

The graduates of the new Royal Agricultural College at Cirencester (founded in 1845) came out onto the job market, and ideas from the Rothamstead Agricultural Research Station (founded in 1843) began to spread as well. Membership of the Royal Agricultural Society (founded in 1838) grew and blossomed under royal support. There was a growth in professional standards among the agents who managed the great estates for their aristocratic owners.

There was a huge increase in drainage projects, always expensive, to improve both the quality of land and the amount of land that was cultivated. In this period, in the region of £20 million were spent on draining over 4 million acres of land. There was a growth of technical efficiency: some have called it another Agricultural Revolution, with much more intensive farming designed to produce a much higher output per acre. There was real development in the use of fertilisers (including imported ones like **guano**) and a lot of thought went into the correct feeding of animals and the way in which land was used and crops rotated. Machinery, such as the steam-driven threshing machines, appeared on the larger farms.

There was also a greater awareness of the needs of the market place, and the speed with which farmers adapted to the arrival of the railways was impressive. Cattle were shifted to market quickly without the need for long-distance droves which weakened them and reduced their weight and price. The Vale of Evesham, in central England, adapted rapidly to the provision of fruit and vegetables for the London markets.

13.3 Was it a period of boom for British farming?

1. Study the chart on agricultural prices from 1851 to 1870.

What information does the data show about the price of agricultural goods during this period?

2. Using the information in this section, is there any evidence to suggest that British agriculture was prosperous in the years 1846–68? Give reasons to support your answer.

'Boom' is probably too strong. There was stability in the price of wheat and other prices rose steadily, but not spectacularly (see the chart below).

	1851–1855	1856–1860	1861–1865	1866–1870
Wheat	103	98	87	100
Barley	82	98	86	101
Oats	90	87	87	101
Beef	77	85	87	94
Mutton	80	88	93	93
Cheese	75	86	84	102
Milk	65	84	82	89

(These are index numbers; 1840 is the base year with a value of 100. Therefore, wheat in 1851–1855 at 103 is 3% above the 1840 price.)

The best growth in prices lay in livestock-related areas. A steady increase in major elements of farming production was bound to have a good impact on farmers generally. As real wages rose nationally, and in particularly in urban areas, and with a growing middle class spending an increasing proportion of their income on quality food, there was certain to be an increase in demand for meat, all types of dairy produce, and of course wool.

Rural depopulation could be absorbed by the growing demand for labour in the towns and factories, so the problems caused by mechanisation and the switch to livestock-based farming (which used less labour than the more labour-intensive crops) was not too noticeable. Also, the huge drainage works absorbed a lot of labour. The great urban demand for milk, which rail could meet, also led to a shift in the use of the labour force to milking and transportation. With excellent market conditions and a growing population, and rail making access to towns easy, prices rose steadily in most parts of farming produce (20%–50%). So when a severe depression came in the 1870s this period was looked back on as a period of prosperity.

What were the main weaknesses in British agriculture?

On the surface all looked well, but there were problems. The agricultural labourer was still badly treated, and there was to be no serious improvement in their pay, working or living conditions until trade unions developed later in the century.

There was still a great deal of conservatism in farming. Commentators noted the survival of a large number of very small farms. At the beginning of this period, over 20% of the cultivated acreage consisted of units of under 100 acres (40 hectares) and there is little evidence of much change throughout the period. The farms really suited to the age of 'high farming', with its new investment, new methods and machinery were those over 300 acres and they were less than 30% of the total number of farms. The majority of farms were not suited to the new age, and in many cases it passed them by.

There was a huge amount of investment, especially on drainage, but there was often a poor return on money invested. The Duke of Northumberland spent over £500,000 on improvements in this period and never got more than a 2% return on his capital. A lot of this new investment went into producing more land for wheat cultivation, or improving it, and when serious competition in the form of cheap wheat did come in from abroad, much of the investment was obviously wasted.

There was still insecurity of tenure for tenant farmers who, by and large, cultivated the smaller farms, and therefore they had little need to improve the quality of the land or their methods. The situation was not confined to the Irish tenant farmer, and a Parliament dominated by large-scale landowners, many of whom got most of their income from their tenant farmers, was unlikely to support any major changes. Landlords liked to keep leases short because, in the age before the secret ballot, they liked to influence their tenants' voting behaviour. If the tenant farmers voted contrary to their landlords' wishes they could be easily evicted, and frequently were.

Is there a strong case to suggest that agricultural prosperity faced major problems? Give reasons to support your answer.

Much of what happened in the period of 'high farming' was a misdirection of resources, and when the prices dropped later there was either a poor or a very low return on investment. This led to a reluctance to invest in the future.

The system of farming had become too dependent on growing markets and rising prices, and was unable to rid itself of the need to grow wheat. Farming was still dependent on the weather, and heavy rainfall in the early 1860s caused major problems and showed the limitation of the 'boom'. Much of the 'boom' was dependent on outside factors over which neither Britain nor its farmers had any control. When circumstances changed, like a fall in internal demand or a major improvement in the means of transportation of foreign wheat, then the system showed how prone it was to catching cold.

Industry

13.4 Why was it such a period of growth for British industry?

The 1850s and 1860s are always seen as the high point in the growth and development of the British economy. Britain reached the peak of its industrial might. One of the reasons for Britain's success was the complete absence of any serious rivals, either in Europe or elsewhere. Other reasons for economic success were a good banking system, a superb geographical position to exploit, a tradition of international trade, an excellent transportation network and a growing home market. Given those advantages – and the list could be extended to include a plentiful supply of coal and a cheap labour force – it might be argued that it would be difficult not to succeed.

As with agriculture, warning signs could be seen:

- A lack of investment in new technologies.
- A decline in **entrepreneurship**.
- A poor educational system.
- A growing social divide between those who generated the wealth and jobs, and the political and social élite who wished to have less and less to do with 'trade', and who failed to understand its needs and its role in the creation of wealth.

Entrepreneurship: A willingness to take risks and invest in new ideas/plans/techniques in business and industry.

Palmerston, for all his many failings, knew what was the basis of his electorate's wealth.

Viewed from almost any angle, this was a period of boom. The 'feel good' factor was evident wherever you looked. The 'Great Exhibition' in London at the beginning of the period demonstrated the ingenuity and longstanding success of British industry. It was a period of continuing optimism. There was a continuous property boom, which used large amounts of labour. In any town or city – ranging from Aberdeen to Glasgow, Leamington Spa to London – can be found big housing developments from the 1850s and 1860s onwards.

Prices rose steadily. Real wages grew, as did investment and production. Whatever statistics are seen, they seem to point to solid and healthy growth – be they in imports or exports, railway investment or industrial output.

A variety of factors explain the steady rise in prices. Those who support the **quantity theory of money** point to the increase in gold supply (there were discoveries in California in 1848 and Australia in 1852 – and the bulk of it ended up in the vaults of the Bank of England). The Bank cut its interest rates and increased lending; cheap money is always an asset to the property developer or to the investor. The rise in public demand seems to be the primary reason. The impact of new gold overseas stimulated the demand for British manufactured goods, as did wars such as the Crimean in the 1850s and the American Civil War of the early 1860s. **Reasonably inelastic supply and increased demand** was bound to have a healthy impact on prices from the British point of view.

Quantity theory of money: Prices are influenced by the amount of money in circulation. Prices will increase if more money is on circulation.

Reasonably inelastic supply and increased demand: There was not much increase in production – yet demand for British goods increased.

Exports showed a steady growth: they were worth £53 million in 1845, £122 million in 1857 and £136 million in 1860, and they continued to grow in the 1860s. Britain made a great deal of money in opening up and developing industries in other countries. In fact, it was perhaps an error to assist the industrialisation of countries that were later to become our rivals.

British capital, machinery and skills were vital in developing the railway

1. In what ways did British Industry grow and develop in the years 1846 to 1868?

2. Why did prices rise in this period?

3. Using the information in this section, is there any evidence to suggest that the prosperity of British industry might be short-lived?

networks of many other countries. At one stage in the early 1860s, Brassey, the English contractor, had railway building contracts on five separate continents. In the period 1846–68, between 20% and 25% of world trade was British.

	1850	**1870**
Exports	£83	£244
Imports	£103	£303
Deficit	£20	£59
Invisible earnings*	£31	£112
Surplus	£11	£53

* money from shipping, insurance, banking and finance

British trade between 1850 and 1870 (figures in £ million)

13.5 How important were the railways to Great Britain?

Railways supported, but did not lead, economic growth. The level of investment throughout the period was huge, about £18 million per annum by the late 1860s. Railways had a big impact on other areas of the economy, ranging from the increased demand for coal and labour to the development of the London Stock Exchange (and provincial stock exchanges) and the regulation of companies. There was growth in the **capital market**. Many people who had never invested before did so with railways, and with its huge capital costs it encouraged the banks to look favourably at large-scale capital lending which was to prove vital for the later development of British industry.

Capital market: Where it is possible for the investor to place savings and earn a profit on that investment; and where the entrepreneur can raise large sums of money for expansion.

Railways as employers

The industry employed large amounts of labour. Although there were peaks and troughs, it could go as high as 250,000 (in 1847), but dip as low as 40,000 in some years. Inevitably, those employed spent their money on items such as clothing and housing which was a factor in the steady increase in domestic demand that helped the rest of British industry. Not only were labourers needed, but the demand for bankers, lawyers, engineers and surveyors grew as well.

The demand the railways had for iron and steel was huge. It also encouraged technological development in the iron industry. With a steady increase in demand at home, then overseas markets could be developed. It was this that was vital for the growth of the South Wales iron and steel industry. The demand for coal grew, and so did the services required from the mechanical and civil engineers. The miles of track available went from 6,000 miles in 1850 to 13,500 miles by the late 1860s. Building, maintaining and operating it required a big labour force, both skilled and unskilled. Every mile of track needed more than 300 tons of iron. The lower transport cost helped other industries, and played a vital role in the development of others, both industrial and rural. The huge fruit and vegetable industry around the Vale of Evesham in central England grew rapidly as the produce could be inside the major cities within hours, and the effect of such produce on the diet and health of citydwellers was bound to be beneficial. Such competition also forced other forms of transport to cut their costs, so both producer and consumer were bound to benefit.

Obviously, the canal operator (and investor), and the owners of coaching inns would suffer, and they did. Coastal shipping was also hit as the amount of freight on trains went from 17 million tonnes in 1846 to 115 million tonnes in 1865. Some of that was traffic generated by the speed and flexibility of the railway system, but some was bound to come from the canal, the coach and the ship. Agriculture was helped, new industrial sites set up to produce iron and steel for the railways, and coal could be easily brought in to help make it.

Suburb: Area of a town or city not close to the centre, where people who work in the centre often live.

The **suburb** became a feature of the city. Railway towns like Crewe and Swindon grew, and the working class became mobile as there was at last a cheap form of transport other than walking. The railway was part of the maturing process in Britain's industrialisation. It did not have the impact on the nation that early industrialisation had in the late 18th century, it was part of a broader growth process in the mid-19th century.

1. What changes took place in the railway industry at this time?

2. How important were railways to British industry in this period? Give reasons to support your answer.

The growth of the railway was largely unchecked throughout the period. There was regulation in an earlier Act of 1844, but little thereafter, in spite of concerns about safety and company concentration. There was a royal commission in 1865, which reported in 1868, recommending few changes. With over 200 MPs and peers involved in railways in some way, as directors and so on, there was little likelihood of demand or desire to reform.

Print of 'The Workmen's Train': Metropolitan Line station in London

Conclusion

A major factor in the growth of the British economy was the absence of real competition in the areas where Britain made its money, in railways, coal, iron, steel, and above all textiles. There was also the possible misapprehension that the 'boom' was primarily caused by free trade.

Workhouses: The only way a poor person could get state benefits was by entering a locally run building, where food and shelter was provided in return for work.

There was too great a dependence on single industries, textiles for example. When the American Civil war broke out, and the supply of the vital raw material – cotton – dried up, Lancashire was devastated and the **workhouses** could not cope. Countries which were to be future rivals – the USA, Germany and France – were involved in wars, from which

Britain benefited. Although in other key industries, such as coal, the picture looks better – with output rising consistently throughout this period, and mechanisation increasing (mainly as women and children could not work underground) – the output per man did not increase greatly. There was little or no investment in areas such as coal cutting. It was still done by a man with a pick.

Vital inventions by Henry Bessemer were made in steel manufacturing in 1856, and a product of real quality produced by 1858 in Sheffield, but it took a long time for the long-term benefits of steel to be known. The age of steel came to Britain later than it should have done if it wished to remain at the forefront of world industry. Industry may have been maturing, but it was also ageing, and there was a complacency and a reluctance to change in Britain. There was too great a dependence on world trade, and what had happened to a large slice of industry during the American Civil war should have warned many about the dependency on a few staple industries which were losing their technological edge.

'A mid-Victorian boom.' Using the information so far in this chapter, do you think this is an accurate description of the British economy in the years 1846–1868? (Mention both agriculture and industry)

Social history: overview

THE years 1846 to 1868 were not a period of any dramatic changes in the social history of Britain. The earlier decades had seen great changes, with the New Poor Law, the first effective Factory Acts, the first grant to education and measures taken to stop some of the worst exploitation of women in the workplace. The decades following this period were also to see fundamental changes in all of these areas.

This period can best be seen as part of a learning process. There was a growing belief on the part of governments, Parliament, and the country as a whole that the day of *laissez-faire* was over. It was realised by more and more that people living in vast cities were simply unable to provide for themselves in the spirit of the 1830s, that society had to take some responsibility for its citizens and how they lived and worked. It was very much the age of the Royal Commission, where able groups of men examined the problems in a scientific way and laid bare some of the worst failings of society. These commissions also made positive recommendations for governments to act upon. It was the custom for governments to pass major laws in response to Royal Commission recommendations.

The size and scale of the social problems were made very clear, and there were recommendations on how citizens could live longer and be more productive. Increasingly, people looked to government for the solutions. They were not really forthcoming in this period. The public were not interested in parliamentary reform until the very end of the period. There was no mass working-class agitation for better conditions. Not only were the older generation of politicians, such as Palmerston (but not perhaps Russell), against state intervention into the lives of the citizen or local government, but so also were the rising generation, such as Gladstone, both on grounds of practical politics and ideology. As a result, there are not many Acts to learn in this period!

13.6 What was done to improve education?

Although no major legislative changes took place in this period, it is an important formative time between the first state grant to education in the 1830s to the legislation of the 1870s which made education for all children both free and compulsory.

Russell was always an enthusiastic supporter of educational improvement. It was he who not only got the legislation through in 1846 which changed the basis of the state grant to education, but also played an important part in raising the level of state funding to £1.3 million by 1862. He was also a strong supporter of a Bill in 1850 to make local authorities play a more active role in education. Opposition from the Churches prevented it from becoming law.

Sir James Kay-Shuttleworth (1804–1871)
James Kay-Shuttleworth was a doctor. He became a Poor Law Commissioner and then Secretary of Education. He served on the Committee of the Privy Council (1839–49) and was a key figure in the development of public education in Britain.

A lot of the money was spent on teacher education. In the decade between 1855 and 1865, over 12,000 men and women trained as teachers. Russell wanted more, and ensured that local government had the power to raise additional funding if they so wished to improve the quality of both schools and teachers in their areas. Few did, and this further reinforced the need for central pressure and funding to get a decent education for the nation's children. The key figure in this early teacher education programme was James Kay-Shuttleworth who, in the end, felt the scheme of better teacher education was a failure, as too little was done both in terms of quality and quantity. In one sense he was right, but the failure of the scheme to bring about radical change further reinforced the point that it would take a major initiative by central government before much was achieved in education.

A separate Education Department, under the Privy Council, was set up in 1856, partly to ensure more effective control of what state funding there was, but also to ensure that the money was better targeted. A Royal Commission in 1861, chaired by the Duke of Newcastle, proposed a national scheme of education administered by central government. However, it broke down under pressure from **religious dissenters**. Newcastle's time was not wasted, as much of his Commission's thinking was included in later legislation.

Religious dissenters: Those who were not members of the Church of England. Usually used to refer to Protestants such as Methodists and Baptists.

However, under the guidance of Robert Lowe, who was later to split the Liberal Government over parliamentary reform, there were major administrative changes in the early 1860s with effective targeting of public money. Between 1863 and 1869, over a thousand new schools were created with over 300,000 pupils in them. This laid an excellent basis for the legislation of 1870, and made it actually possible to implement it. Lowe may have cut spending on education, but he pushed up standards of basic literacy and improved attendance at schools. The methods he advocated, in the 'Revised Code' of 1862, possibly damaged the quality of teaching. Lowe was a great enthusiast for rote learning, but the system was at least partly prepared for the great changes and expansion to come.

There was a slow growth of the urban grammar school towards the end of the period, but they did not really start to flourish until later. They were initially fee-paying and therefore only open to those from a wealthy background. The public schools continued to grow, producing in theory the Christian gentlemen hoped for by Thomas Arnold, the headmaster of Rugby School in the 19th century. Clarendon's Royal Commission in 1864 criticised the public schools for their emphasis on Classics and their encouragement of 'idleness', but no action was taken. Given the number of ex-public-school pupils in the Cabinet, this is perhaps hardly surprising.

The bulk of educational provision was still left to voluntary provision – the dame school, the charitable schools and others, so heavily criticised by Charles Dickens. The Inspectorate, set up in the 1830s, also criticised the quality of education offered by the voluntary, and largely church, sector. These criticisms, like the Newcastle and Clarendon Commissions, played a role in persuading public and government opinion towards the inevitable step of state intervention.

There was a small growth in higher education provision: Oxford and Cambridge opened their doors to those who were not Anglicans in the 1850s and the few other universities, such as London, did increase in numbers. Overall, the progress was small and it was not until the great boom in the northern universities later in the century that the numbers of graduates increased significantly. Scotland was different, with its four great universities – St Andrews, Aberdeen, Glasgow and Edinburgh – producing a higher number of graduates per head of population than England and Wales. Hence a much greater number of Scottish teachers were graduates and the general quality of primary and secondary education was much higher.

There are three main reasons for the comparative lack of real progress in education in this period: religion, cost and social. Sheer apathy may have played a part as well, but that is more difficult to quantify.

Religion was probably the biggest reason for lack of progress. The Anglican Church, losing its worshippers to both the Nonconformist chapels and to a growing **secularisation**, wished to have a monopoly on education. That way it would influence the rising generation.

Secularisation: Unwillingness to see Church matters as particularly important.

Nonconformists opposed this fundamentally, as well as opposing the obvious solution of having a non-denominational system where the religious education of the child was left to the parent and the Church on a Sunday. It was the bitter opposition of the Churches to a major Bill in 1850, to provide a free primary education by Local Authorities, that warned politicians that education was a 'hornet's nest' not worth stirring. Thus progress had to be made through more subtle administrative methods, rather than by legislation.

The second reason is simple, and that was cost. As most taxpayers were not prepared to accept that a proportion of their tax should go to the education of other people's children, it was virtually impossible for either local or central government to justify the raising of sufficient taxation to pay for a national system of education.

As most taxpayers could afford to pay for whatever education they required for their own children (only the rich paid much tax then), to raise the millions necessary for a properly funded system of the type recommended by the Duke of Newcastle was out of the question. There were limits to the proportion of their incomes that taxpayers were prepared to contribute to the national good, and there was no great wish on the part of government to extract it for this, or any other public service such as the provision of clean water.

The third reason is best described as 'social'. Some people felt strongly that the poor should not be educated at all. It would give them ideas above their 'station' and would not provide employers with a supply of cheap manual labour. Others felt that the lower classes should only get a basic education, severely practical, with a strong element of social control in it, where their place in life was made clear. There were further debates about whether the children of the working classes might come into contact with 'contaminating' literature in schools, and perhaps it was an idea to keep them illiterate after all.

Similar debates, it might be remembered, had occurred when Gladstone tried to abolish the paper duties which would lead to cheaper newspapers. Education inspectors summed it up in one of their many damning reports on the system of education in this period when they wrote that 'there is an inveterate prejudice that education in any higher sense is a privilege annexed to a definite social position'. They went on to point out, in the same report, that what was available for the middle class and above was focused mainly on the Classics, and was expensive, inefficient and only for boys.

The period's main importance lies in convincing all that there was a problem and that the State, both nationally and locally, had to solve it.

1. What were the main changes in education in the years 1846 to 1868?

2. To what extent can the Government be blamed for the slow progress in the provision of education?

13.7 In what ways did public health and living conditions improve in this period?

Cholera: A serious and often fatal disease that affects the digestive organs. Drinking infected water or eating infected food causes it.

Tuberculosis: A serious infectious disease that affects the lungs and other parts of the body.

The simple answer to this question is 'not a lot' overall. There was some very slow progress in most places, but in a few areas a great deal was done. The fact that the period both started and ended with **cholera** epidemics, and cholera is a disease resulting from urban squalor, is indicative of this. **Tuberculosis** – also a disease of poverty and squalor – actually rose in numbers in this period, in spite of a growth in real wages generally. It is not a period to be proud of in the history of welfare.

The reasons for the Public Health Act of 1848

There was one major piece of legislation: the Public Health Act of 1848. Chartism, the need to do 'something' for the poor, and the dreadful evidence of the 1842 Royal Commission in which Edwin Chadwick had shown what life was like for the urban poor – all played a part in putting pressure on the Government to act. Chadwick recommended what was needed to solve the problems of the dreadful mortality in towns. Peel's reluctance to intervene and the constant recurrence of cholera (it was estimated that over 90,000 died in the cholera epidemic of 1848–49) also played a part in the Whigs' acting when they did.

Local authorities – with rare exceptions such as Liverpool – would not act on their own initiative, as powerful local interests, with national political connections, were hostile to any centralisation by London. Also, few people wished to see an increase in local taxation, which would be inevitable if proper water supplies and sewage disposal were to be undertaken. If there was to be change it would have to come from central government. What also hindered efforts was that the local authority had to get legislative backing from Parliament to obtain the powers necessary to raise the relevant money and to undertake the work of slum improvement. This was expensive in itself, before any actual work started.

The 1848 Public Health Act

A whole range of pressures led to this Act, including pressure from the main author of the 1842 Royal Commission, Edwin Chadwick. The main terms of the Act were as follows:

- Local authorities were given the power to set up Local Health Boards, supervised by a Central Board in London, led as it turned out by the forceful, but tactless Edwin Chadwick. The general principles behind the Act were similar to those governing the Poor Law.
- The Central Board had the power to create local boards once 10% of the inhabitants had petitioned for one. The Central Board could compel the Local Authority to set up a local board when the death rate in that area rose above 23 per 1,000 in a year.
- The Central Board was given virtually no powers to make the Local Boards act, and few in the end were set up. Towns like Leicester, which took on the Act fully and really worked to provide both clean water and 'nuisance' disposal, found their **rates** going up from 9d in the £ to 2 shillings 3d [11p]. This was not an example that many other locally elected people wished to follow.

Rates: Local taxed based on property values.

Implications of the 1848 Public Health Act

Edwin Chadwick made himself very unpopular with his attacks on those who governed towns (many of whom happened to return Liberal MPs). A

Children playing in London slums, mid19th century

a result, the powers of the Central Board were removed in 1854 and it was broken up in 1858. There was a limit to what the *laissez-faire* principles of the age would stand, or politicians would accept from their constituents in the form of regular complaints about the methods of Chadwick or the possible costs of 'improvement'.

However, by 1864 over 400 towns had taken up these powers, stirred perhaps by the continuing outbreaks of cholera (over 10,000 Londoners died in 1866 alone) and the fact that the death rate in cities was still well above 20 per 1,000 per annum. Some pioneering authorities, such as Manchester and Liverpool, had shown what was possible with enterprise and with huge reservoirs leading to an excellent supply of high-quality water. These examples, coupled with a growing public pressure (and

Punch cartoon, 14 June 1859, entitled 'The London Bathing Season'

THE LONDON BATHING SEASON.

1. What message is this cartoon attempting to convey about the level of pollution in the River Thames?

2. How useful to a historian is this cartoon on the issue of public health in mid-Victorian Britain?

possibly also with the death of the more conservative Palmerston), led to the Sanitation Act of 1866 which was to make further real progress in this vital area for public health.

The Sanitation Act, 1866
This Act gave government the power to insist on all local authorities employing sanitary inspectors with powers to insist on the removal of 'nuisances', the provision of sewers and a clean water supply. Further legislation passed by both the Gladstone and Disraeli Administrations built on the 1866 Sanitation Act, and led to a gradual decrease in the death rate by the end of the century. It was a slow process.

Working conditions

As far as working conditions were concerned, there are only two pieces of legislation of note in this period: the Ten Hours Act of 1847 and the Factory Act of 1850. These should be seen as part of a wider campaign, which started with the Factory Act of 1833.

The Ten Hours Act, 1847
Chartism played a large part in the fact that the first Act was passed without amendment in 1847. It was introduced by John Fielden, a Radical MP, to a background of well-organised petitions, demonstrations and marches. It was another campaigner in this area, Richard Oastler, who played an important part in the organisation of the extra-parliamentary pressure.

Peel had opposed such a measure earlier, but was out of office. Sympathetic (right wing and protectionist) Tory MPs could now quite happily vote for it, and perhaps at the same time undermine the profits of Liberal manufacturers who were supposed to be benefiting so much from the abolition of the Corn Laws. A trade depression, which reduced demand, may have also played a part in the unusual lack of protest by the manufacturing lobby. The Ten Hours Act limited the working hours of women and young persons under 18 to 10 hours, but it was still possible for men to be worked for 12.

The 1850 Act further restricted women's and children's hours in textile factories, insisted on proper breaks for meals, and reduced Saturday working. Again it needs stressing that these Acts only applied to the larger textile factories, and were not extended to cover other types of factory until 1867.

There was improvement in this area, but of a limited nature in a small number of industries. It was the rise in real wages that did more to assist the improved standard of living and the quality of life in this period.

1. In what ways did public health and working conditions change in the years 1846 to 1868?

2. 'The governments from 1846 to 1868 did very little to improve living and working conditions.' How far do you agree with this statement?

13.8 Did the treatment of, and attitude towards, women change in this period?

Again, the general answer to the question is 'No'. What legislation there was which affected women specifically – such as the Divorce Act of 1857 and the Contagious Diseases Acts of 1864 and 1866 – could be seen as setbacks, and good indicators of the best of Victorian double standards.

The Divorce (1857) and Contagious Diseases Acts (1866–1867)
The 1857 Divorce Act made divorce easier for the very rich, but still made it difficult for a woman to divorce her husband. The husband, however, could divorce his wife for reasons which did not apply to her. The Contagious Diseases Acts, caused by growing fears about the spread of sexually transmitted diseases among servicemen and Britain's subsequent lack of military preparedness, gave the State the power to detain women who had such

diseases, as well as insisting on regular inspection of prostitutes. The Acts did not require the inspection of men who used the prostitutes and who might be the actual spreaders of disease, nor could the men be detained. *Laissez-faire* might be coming to an end, but more quickly for women than men. The legal status of women, where they were effectively the property of their fathers or husbands, did not alter throughout the period.

Women's employment opportunities

The opportunities available outside marriage and the home possibly even deteriorated for most women throughout the period. There was a huge growth in domestic service, as the size of the middle class grew. By the middle of this period, getting on for half the female workforce was in domestic service. In this work, low wages and long hours were the norm. Women were much cheaper than male servants.

The percentage of women taking on unskilled work in factories grew. They were also the lowest paid in the country in home working, ranging from lace to nail making, where in both cases the wages were well below subsistence level for a single person. Factory Acts did not cover home-workers. Prostitution, the last refuge for desperate women, increased throughout the period. It was not a good time to be a poor woman.

The death rate for women in childbirth grew as well, with puerperal fever spreading rapidly, caused by the lack of hygiene on the part of male doctors who were playing a larger part in the delivery of babies. Even the discovery of anaesthetics for use in childbirth in 1847 did not spread widely, in spite of royal patronage, as many male doctors felt it was unnatural for women to use such an aid.

Women's education

Although there were some educational improvements for women, not many were that helpful. As one major Anglican Educational Society wrote in 1861, 'we have no desire to make girls like little Newtons or little Captain Cooks', and urged that the focus of a women's education should be on mending shirts. Lowe's Revised Code of 1862 placed even more emphasis on the teaching of purely 'domestic' subjects to girls.

What improvements were there?

There were signs of change, but they have to be looked for. The Factory Acts of 1847 and 1850 played an important part in reducing the hours that women and children could work, but they only concerned large textile mills. It was not until 1867 that the Conservatives introduced legislation that extended this principle to a huge range of other industries.

For working-class girls there was little education available except that provided by factories under the terms of the Factory Acts, or by the workhouses. Much of that was poor quality, and tended to focus on training girls in a purely domestic role. What helped the growth of female literacy in this period, and it did grow, were Church Sunday Schools. However, the churches added their own social values to their '3 Rs', and altering the status of women was not one of them.

It was in the education of middle-class girls that there was positive improvement. Some of the education provided for girls outside the home was little more than a finishing school type, where deportment and the management of servants were the primary items on the curriculum.

However, in 1850, Frances Buss founded the North London Collegiate School for girls – a non-denominational, purely academic school, which took the new examinations set by the Oxford and Cambridge Board. Similar

1. How did women's position in society change in the years 1846 to 1868?

2. 'Do you think there was an improvement in the position of women in Britain in this period? Give reasons to support your answer.

schools were set up by nonconformists in several provincial cities, which were praised by the Taunton Royal Commission in 1868 for the quality of the academic training provided. It was the pupils from these schools who passed on to the Queen's College in London (set up in 1848), to train women in education and social work, or to Bedford College (set up in London in 1849 by women for women). It was the products of these higher education establishments who led the way in the major advances in women's education in the latter part of the 19th century.

13.9 *The development of the trade unions, 1846–1868, and their impact*

A CASE STUDY IN HISTORICAL INTERPRETATION

There is a lot of debate about the nature and extent of trade union development in this period, as well as about the reasons behind the development of trade unions and the link between this development and working-class movements generally. Some historians have argued that there was a pendulum effect, going from working-class focus on political action – such as Chartism – and then swinging back to union-based action to improve pay and conditions. Much the same cycle has been suggested for later in the century when mass unionism developed in the 1890s, and then moved to political action with the growth of the Labour Party in the early years of the 20th century.

Gradual growth of unionism, 1846–1868

This period is seen as a key period of 'union' development. There may have been a link with the trade cycle as well, with real wages rising and unemployment not being at high levels. Given this useful background, then there was scope for union activity, as it tended to be in times of hardship and falling real wages that the hungry working class looked to political action to ease their lot.

What historians agree about is that British unionism in the mid-19th century was not motivated by any strong political views. The ideas of Karl Marx or even our own less radical and more socialist Robert Owen struck no deep chords in union members. They did not want to change society much. They only wanted to improve their pay and working conditions, and ensure employment and a degree of care in times of sickness and in old age. More than one radical complained in the late 1860s about the difficulty of getting the unions involved in the agitation for an increase in the franchise.

New Model Unionism

There have been suggestions that there was a 'New Model' unionism in this period. The novelty being in the formation of unions based on skilled men, who largely accepted the capitalist *status quo*, and who were keen on centralised administration of the union and ensuring welfare-type benefits for their members. They were also opposed to mass membership for the unskilled and were hostile to the strike process, and possibly embarrassed by the links with violence and mass agitation which Chartism had given to working-class movements.

The current view – held by historians such as A. Musson and E.W.H. Hunt – is that there is no great watershed in the development of trade unions in

Britain in the middle of the 19th century. There was just a development process and a strengthening of processes which had been developing since the beginning of the whole process of industrialisation, when men started to work in factories in large numbers for the first time.

There had been attempts to centralise the organisation of unions before, in the 1820s and 1830s, and the Penny Post and the railway now made it easier. There was an increasing demand for skilled men, with recognised qualifications, and both employer and employee could benefit from this. Unions now placed far more emphasis on membership being restricted to properly apprenticed craftsmen. This ensured employment, status and good pay for the members. The unions tended also to put more emphasis on comparatively large membership fees, with a range of 'friendly' society benefits for their members, such as sick pay and pensions for widows and orphans. They wanted the 'closed shop', where only members of the union might work in a factory or site, and were narrow and sectionalist in their approach. They were interested in their members and not in the working class in general or the future of their industry in the long term.

Industrial relations in the period

There is no evidence that the 'new' unions of the period adopted an unusually peaceful attitude to industrial relations. They were prepared to strike and did so, but they saw the strike weapon as a necessary evil and used it with care. Employers with full order books were more prepared to negotiate with their workforce as large profits were at risk.

Chartism may have failed in the sense that none of the points were achieved, but it and the revolutions of 1848 in Europe were a warning to the wealthy that the working class had some muscle. There was also a greater willingness by the unions to conciliate and look for a peaceful solution. With no welfare state to protect workers and their families, going on strike was not a decision to be taken lightly as they might well go hungry. The executives of the skilled unions were increasingly exercising better control of their members, and their members were seeing evidence that unity and discussion led to beneficial settlements for all.

Growth of national unions

There were several developments of importance in this period. The first was the increasing centralisation of individual unions, such as the Amalgamated Society of Engineers (ASE) under William Allen or the carpenters under Robert Applegarth. They had strong central leadership, tight administration and a good welfare system for their members. In addition, there was a growing tendency towards the end of the period for the union leaders to meet. Although joint action was still a long way down the line, they were beginning to be part of a growing **pressure group** which was to have a significant effect on politics and the economy. Union leaders were learning that legislation to improve conditions was possible if approached correctly. The National Miners Association, led by MacDonald, was able to persuade Parliament to put through the Coal Mines Regulation Act of 1860 which improved working conditions in the mines.

Pressure group: A political organisation which wishes to influence political decision making but does not wish to gain political power. (See also page 19.)

The Sheffield Outrages (1866) and Hornby versus *Close Case (1867)*

It was at the end of the period that the most significant developments took place. The first was an incident in Sheffield in 1866, known as the 'Sheffield Outrages', where explosives were used as a means of union discipline, which resulted in an innocent citizen being killed. The aim had been to persuade individuals to accept union leadership. Naturally, the incident aroused widespread concern about the role of trade unions and their methods.

This was followed by a decision by the House of Lords in a legal case known as Hornby *versus* Close. The unions discovered, to their horror, that their funds which had been put aside for welfare purposes (or for any other purpose) were not protected by the law from union officials who absconded with them. The decision also cast doubt on the whole status of unions and their relationship with the law.

These two events led to a royal commission on unions, which was to report later. This led to the vital legislation of 1871 and 1875 (see Chapter 15).

The formation of the TUC, 1868

The other direct effect of these events (and growing unemployment was to play a part as well) was the decision to institute the Trades Union Congress in 1868. This was not a federation of trades, but an annual conference of all unions, which agreed to look at not just sectional issues, but political and social ones as well. It met for the first time in June 1868. It was to have a major influence on British political, social and economic history. The first meeting had 34 delegates representing 118,000 members. It discussed a wide range of issues, including housing and education, as well as the legal status of trade unions. The working class was beginning to realise that it had muscle, particularly as a growing number of union members had been enfranchised by the Parliamentary Reform Act of 1867.

1. What were the main developments in British trade unionism between 1846 and 1868?

2. Why do you think historians have differed in their views on the growth of trade unionism in this period?

Conclusion

The dramatic events of British trade union history may be seen to have happened later, with the growth of mass membership and the formation of the Labour Party. However, the gradual growth of moderate working-class organisations, more concerned with the Master and Servant Law than with Karl Marx, with sick pay than socialism, was of enormous significance for the future development of British history.

? Source-based questions: The impact of the railways in the 19th century

SOURCE A

It is all too easy to underestimate the role of the railways in the Victorian economy. Railways were more than a technologically superior mode of transport which reduced costs and facilitated the speedier, more reliable movement of passengers and freight. They were also a major industry in their own right, and the first example of large-scale enterprise in the United Kingdom. Their promotion and construction in the 40 years after 1830 had important linkage effects in several industries ... and helped to transform financial institutions and the habits of savers.

From Railways and the British Economy *by T.R. Gouvish, published in 1970*

SOURCE B

Permanent employment by the railway companies

Year	Employees
1850	56,000
1856	100,000
1875	250,000
1890	350,000
1910	600,000

Canal charges per ton, Hull to Manchester

	Before railways	*After railways*
Corn	120p	65p
Cotton	152p	100p
Manufactured goods	225p	120p

Statistics from Railways – a New Age

SOURCE C

... the bulk of the half a million third-class passengers who are carried on this railway in the course of a year are strictly the working classes ... in one respect a remarkable use has been made of the facilities afforded by railway communication. On the occasion of several strikes, when there was a press of work, bodies of workmen have been engaged in London and carried to Manchester ...

From the Official Report from the Officers of the Railway Department to the President of the Board of Trade, *1842*

SOURCE D

The travelling is cheaper, safer and easier. A great deal of traffic, which used to go by other roads now comes by railway; both time and money are saved ... locomotives travel in safety after dark. The rate of carriage goods is 10s [50p] a ton; by canal it used to be 15s [75p] per ton ... More persons now travel to their own business ... coal pits have been sunk, and manufactures now established on the line ... it is found advantageous for the carriage of milk and garden produce.

From the Annual Register *of 1842: a semi-official publication*

Study Source A.

1. Explain the meaning of the following phrases in the context of the advantages of railways:

(a) 'a major industry in their own right'

(b) 'first example of large-scale enterprise'.

2. What disadvantages are mentioned in Sources A–D about the impact of the railway in the 19th century?

3. How useful is Source B to a historian writing in the early 21st century?

4. Study all the sources above and use the information from this chapter. Do the sources explain fully the benefits brought by railways? Give reasons to support your answer.

From Poor Law to Welfare State, 1830–1948

Key Issues

- *How did attitudes to the poor change, 1830–1948?*
- *In what ways did State provision for the poor change, 1830–1948?*
- *Why did reform take place so slowly?*

14.1 Why was there opposition to the unreformed Poor Law?
14.2 What did the 1832 Poor Law Commission recommend?
14.3 What were the results of the Poor Law Amendment Act?
14.4 How did policy change in the later part of the 19th century?
14.5 How did Beveridge lay the foundations of a new type of State action?
14.6 Why was effective factory reform so difficult to achieve?
14.7 What efforts were made to improve public health?
14.8 How did housing policy change, 1866–1946?
14.9 What were the effects of government intervention in education?

Framework of Events

1802	Health and Morals of Apprentices Act
1832	Poor Law Commission
1833	Althorp's Act
	First Government Grant to Education
1834	Poor Law Amendment Act
1835	Municipal Corporations Act
1837	Compulsory registration of births introduced
1842	Mines and Collieries Act
	Chadwick's Report on sanitary conditions of labouring population of Great Britain
1844	Factory Act
1847	Poor Law Act; Second Factory Act
1848	Public Health Act
1850	Another Factory Act
1858	Disappearance of General Board of Health
1862	Revised Code introduced by Robert Lowe
1866	Sanitary Act
1868	Torrens Act
1870	Forster's Education Reform Bill
1875	Public Health Act; Artisans' Dwellings Act
1878	Further Factory Act
1890	Housing of the Working Classes Act
1902	Balfour/Morant Education Act
1908	Old Age Pensions
1911	First National Insurance Act
1918	Fisher's Education Act
1919	Addison Act
1924	Wheatley Act
1930	Slum Clearance Act
1942	Beveridge Report
1944	Butler's Education Act
1946	Second National Insurance Act; New Towns Act
1948	National Assistance; National Health Service
1951	Some NHS charges introduced.

Overview

Collectivist: Opposite to *laissez faire*; describes the belief that government intervention in social and economic affairs can be of benefit to society.

DID governments steadily respond, in a humanitarian way, to the exposure of appalling conditions, as argued by historians such as Oliver MacDonagh? Public opinion, it is said, forced a remarkable change in making the State face its responsibilities to protect the poor. The State made a **collectivist** response by stepping in to help the weakest members of society.

On the other hand, was the growing trend towards collectivism restrained by *laissez-faire* values? The historian Dicey argues that it was these values which emphasised the activities of the free, competitive market at the expense of those who required state protection. In this model, state intervention was held back by a prevailing attitude to 'let things alone'.

In a sense, the study of social reform during the 19th century was the result of the stresses between these sets of forces: *laissez faire* and collectivism. Often, it was a case of two steps forward, and one pace back – both at a local and national level.

Much depended on individuals and radical pressure groups. There was not only a reluctance to spend ratepayers' money, but also doubts about the capacity of administrative structures to support change.

14.1 Why was there opposition to the unreformed Poor Law?

The 'old' Poor Law which existed at the beginning of the 19th century was based on the Elizabethan Poor Law Acts of 1597–98 and 1601. These Acts had made each parish responsible for its poor by collecting a poor rate. The belief persisted that poverty was the result of laziness and that a proper living could only be made through hard work. Beggars and vagrants were to be severely punished. It was acknowledged that the sick and aged could not look after themselves, hence poor-houses were built for them. In addition, outdoor relief (sometimes money, but often food) was provided for individuals who could not work through no fault of their own.

Levels of poverty continued to rise and the system for supporting the poor was disorganised and out of date. Action was clearly needed in the 1790s when distress and disturbances resulted from poor harvests and increases in prices because of the war with revolutionary France. The most famous response to this alarming situation was from the magistrates of Speenhamland in Berkshire, in 1795. Relief from the rates was added to wages according to a sliding scale depending on the size of a labourer's family and the price of bread. At least this system avoided the worst examples of starvation; and it suited the employers who were spared social disruption and who managed to keep a pool of cheap labour.

However, the 1830s saw the case being made for a complete overhaul of the way industrial society dealt with their poor. By then the 'Swing' riots of 1830–31 revealed rural discontent. Speenhamland and its local variations had 'tied' farm labourers to their parishes. Population movement to urban areas, where there was demand for workers, was suppressed. The rural poor had become dependent on their form of poor relief, which was seen as heavy-handed and paternalistic. It was reliant on handouts and charity, which sapped dignity and initiative. Inevitably, employers kept wages low as the heavy financial burden was passed to the rates. Twenty per cent of national expenditure was spent on the poor. In 1832, it amounted to £7 million when it had only been £1½ in 1776.

Why did the Poor Law need reforming by the early 1830s?

14.2 What did the 1832 Poor Law Commission recommend?

In 1832, the 26 members of the Poor Law Commission set out to investigate the operation of the Poor Law system. Among its members were those such as Edwin Chadwick who adopted the views of Jeremy Bentham, that everything had to be subjected to the test of utilitarianism. Did the Poor Law, as it existed, provide 'the greatest good of the greatest number' (Bentham), or could it be more efficient? Were the poor actively seeking work (which in turn would lead to prosperity and the happiness of many), or were they being demoralised by relying on public charity?

There was also an acceptance that the complete abolition of outdoor relief was impossible, although that aim was strongly canvassed. The young, the sick, the old and the disabled would have to be supported. This was the beginning of that 'collectivist' view which would become more apparent as the 20th century approached. It was a collectivism that acknowledged that society and the State would need to intervene to defend those who could not support themselves.

When the report was published in 1834, its moral tone was clear. Employers were helping to keep wages artificially low so that they would be made up from the rates. The free labour market was being upset and the labouring poor were becoming sluggish.

The 'Principles of 1834' were set out by the Commission, and they became the Poor Law Amendment Act.

- 'Less eligibility' applied to those workhouses that had to be built for the able-bodied who could not find employment. Conditions had to be worse in the workhouse than for the poorest workers outside it. In other words, they were less eligible for decent conditions. Here was Bentham's influence – encouraging workers back to work at the first opportunity.
- The 'Workhouse Test' was to test if a pauper was sufficiently in need by seeing if the individual would accept a place in a workhouse. Hence outdoor relief was forbidden (except for the old and sick) and the only place to receive it was in a workhouse. Refuse the offer of relief and the pauper would fail the test.
- Finally, parishes were to be grouped into unions to build workhouses. A Board of Guardians would be elected by ratepayers to control a workhouse. In an effort to ensure the uniform application of the system, to replace the inefficiency and corruption that preceded it, a national administration would be created. There would be three Poor Law Commissioners in London, with Chadwick as Secretary. Twelve Assistant Commissioners would inspect the operation of what was the Poor Law Amendment Act. It set forward the intention of a centralised, national system with the Commissioners independently trying to ensure the uniform application of the rules.

What were the main differences between the old Poor Law and the recommendations of the Poor Law Report?

14.3 What were the results of the Poor Law Amendment Act?

On the face of it, the Poor Law Commissioners could take some satisfaction from the savings made and the reduction of corruption. Outdoor relief appeared more limited as the poor rate which cost over £6 million in 1833–4 fell by over £1 million over the next ten years.

In other aspects, the Poor Law Amendment Act failed to achieve its aims. Even Chadwick had to admit that some of his hopes had been dashed. Separate workhouses – for the young, aged and sick – were never built.

'General' workhouses were constructed, often overcrowded and disease ridden. A variety of standards was applied to the provision of relief from locality to locality, much against the intentions of the 1832 Commissioners.

The belief that the moral lot of paupers would improve if they found work, was never likely to amount to much. The poor of industrial districts hated the workhouse. Their full horror became apparent during the 1837 Great Depression and the 'Hungry 40s'. **Trade cycles** created conditions in northern towns over which no one had much control. It was here where anti-Poor Law agitation erupted into violence against the guardians. There were attacks on workhouses. Poverty occurred through no fault of the individual. If there was no work to be had, the workhouse deterrent meant nothing. Crucially, the provision of out-relief had to continue to the able-bodied. In Sheffield, this accounted for much of the increase in Poor Law costs, from £12,000 in 1837 to £55,000 in 1843. The harshness of the Act attracted fierce comment, and condemnation. Workhouses were characterised as 'Bastilles', where inmates were exposed to harsh discipline, poor standards of diet, and dangerous or pointless tasks such as oakum picking and bone crushing. Families were separated, and meals were taken in silence. Charles Dickens' portrayal of conditions in *Oliver Twist* stands alongside the Scandal of the Andover Workhouse, where inmates were forced to chew animal bones to relieve their starvation. Although the Guardians had mismanaged affairs, they had kept to the spirit of the Act. The 1847 Poor Law Act replaced the Commissioners with a Minister who was responsible to the Government and Parliament. However, little changed.

Trade cycles: The changes in economic condition from boom, through recession to depression (slump), recovery and then a return to boom.

Why was there opposition to the Poor Law Amendment Act across Britain, but especially in the North of England?

The Poor Law continued to be applied, although it is clear that many of its original principles had been undermined in practice. Workers, meanwhile, turned to Chartism for an improvement in their conditions of life.

14.4 How did policy change in the later part of the 19th century?

From the 1860s, new attitudes to social welfare slowly began to accompany the growth of **democracy** and the acceptance that the State had a broader responsibility for the individual. Progress was slow and difficult. Old habits and attitudes persisted even when the inadequacy of the old Poor Law had

Democracy: A system of running organisations, businesses, government etc. in which each member is entitled to vote and participate in management decisions.

Poor Law Hospital

been demonstrated. Concessions to the sick and aged amounted to little, and were often given grudgingly. They went alongside the acceptance of a more 'collectivist' outlook, which underpinned the setting up of the Local Government Board in 1871. The two decades that followed witnessed the introduction of compulsory elementary education, the spread of a public health service, royal commissions on housing, changes in the franchise and the rise of mass trade unionism.

After 1867, a change of heart about the treatment of the sick came with plans to start building pauper hospitals. However, alongside it came a campaign to reduce the numbers claiming outdoor relief, in the hope that private charity might fill the gap. Despite the 1870 Depression, the numbers of people receiving out-relief fell by one-third. People wanted to avoid the workhouse at all costs.

Meanwhile, the public was being made aware of the extent of poverty in the midst of plenty. Reports from Charles Booth and Seebohm Rowntree, and books such as Sims' *Horrible London* and Mearn's *The Bitter Cry of Outcast London*, shocked the public and exposed the gaps in provision. It may have been true that workhouse conditions were improving – in 1892, men were provided with tobacco and, in 1894, women were allowed tea to mash themselves. This was tinkering with the discredited principles of 'less eligibility'. In 1909, the Poor Law Commission reported that 'the great principle of 1834 is not adequate to the new position'.

Why did attitudes towards poverty change between 1834 and 1900?

The 'new position' was social reform agenda of the new Liberal Governments (1905–15) and the necessity to deal with the 'Two Nations' poverty of Edwardian England.

What was 'New Liberalism' and to what extent did the Liberals lay the foundations of the Welfare State?

After 1908, a remarkable period of social legislation laid down some important welfare reforms, including old age pensions and National Insurance. The reason for these reforms and their impact are discussed in detail in Chapter 23.

14.5 How did Beveridge lay the foundations of a new type of State action?

The Second World War exposed not only the patchy nature of welfare coverage but also the degrading nature of a system which, in the 1930s, had been based on **means testing**. State handouts were based on need rather than, as William Beveridge foresaw, universal entitlement. Beveridge was Master of University College, Oxford. He was asked, in 1940, to examine current provision against a background of evacuation, wartime crisis and a huge expansion of government controls.

Means testing: Before a person could receive welfare payments a survey was made of their wealth. Only those who were extremely poor received welfare payments. The means test was regarded by the poor as a humiliating survey.

Before the Second World War, welfare was:

- kept to a bare minimum
- given as charity to the destitute and helpless
- calculated on what a family earned
- humiliating and linked to the hated Poor Law
- designed to prevent people 'sponging' off the State and to make them find work.

During the Second World War, 'welfare' came to mean:

- something to be given as a right for all people
- that children from well-off and poor homes would get what they needed
- that assistance was given without means testing
- that there should be no second-class citizens
- something which the whole country would contribute to, by helping those who were in need through no fault of their own.

The hospital service was typical. This had relied on voluntary and local authority hospitals. It was totally inadequate for wartime conditions, and required the creation of a centrally funded emergency hospital service. Amid the wartime spirit, Beveridge aimed for a complete range of health and welfare services that looked after people 'from the cradle to the grave'.

Beveridge's vision was to eliminate what he called the 'five giants': 'Want, Disease, Ignorance, Squalor and Idleness'. The Beveridge Report was an immediate success, promising a comprehensive social policy.

The Beveridge Report 1942

- It recommended an insurance scheme: benefits would be paid out as everybody's right in return for contributions paid in while people were working.
- Universality: all would pay a single weekly contribution by buying a stamp and sticking it on an insurance card. Rich and poor would pool their payments so there would be something for everyone.
- Benefits would guarantee a basic minimum income at times of sickness, disability, unemployment and throughout old age.
- There would be no means test.
- It suggested grants for 'normal incidents of life' which needed extra money: maternity grants and funeral grants.
- Contributions were shared between state, employer and employee.
- Family allowances would prevent extra children pushing families below the poverty level even when a wage was coming in. A falling birth rate underlined the importance of encouraging larger families. Family allowances was the first of the social reforms to be introduced, in 1945.

The National Insurance Act of 1946 put many of Beveridge's proposals into operation. For those still in financial difficulties, National Assistance was introduced in 1948. This was not dependent on a 'means test' of other members of your family, but on your own needs.

Central to all this was the creation of the National Health Service (NHS). The historian Peter Calvocoress called this 'perhaps the most beneficial reform ever enacted in England'.

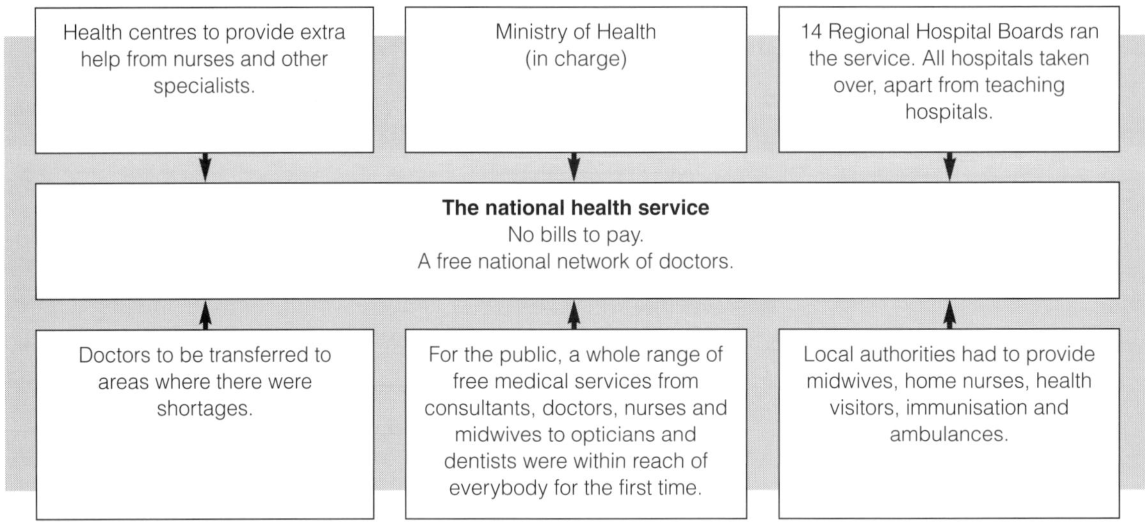

What is the meaning of the term 'Welfare State'?

How did the State provision for the poor change with the introduction of the Welfare State?

Did the Welfare State bring about a 'revolution' in the provision of welfare, housing and education in Britain? Explain your answer.

How successfully had the Labour Government dealt with the issues raised in the Beveridge Report?

It was a remarkable achievement, completed on a massive scale and in the face of opposition from the doctors who opposed being part of a vast State system. They still wanted to 'sell' their skills to private patients.

Aneurin Bevan, Minister of Health and Housing, was able to compromise sufficiently to allow doctors some private pay patients and beds in hospitals. Despite these difficulties, the NHS came into being on the first 'free day', 5 July 1948.

The new service was soon in difficulties. The expense of running a free service was apparent almost immediately. Costs rose, yet Britain also wanted to hold onto its status as a nuclear power. In 1951, charges had to be introduced. Certain groups of people were asked to pay part of the cost of dentures, spectacles and prescriptions. Taxation increased and it looked like a retreat from Labour's 'New Jerusalem'.

Historians remain divided about the Labour Government's postwar reform programme. Kenneth Morgan attests to its success, calling it one of the 'most effective' of all Labour Governments, 'unique in its legislative vitality'. Clement Attlee and his ministers had achieved something close to a revolution.

Other historians, such as Correlli Barnett, claim that 1945 marked a point in which decline can be seen both industrially and on the world stage. He refers to a working class becoming unhealthily dependent on 'state maternalism' – sometimes called the 'nanny state'.

Neither extreme can adequately explain the remarkable impact of these reforms, and the new role of the State from which there would be no retreat.

14.6 Why was effective factory reform so difficult to achieve?

Despite the bleak realities of life in pre-industrial England, it seems that agricultural and cottage workers were extremely dissatisfied with the working conditions in the new factories. If the domestic system had brought long working hours and poor living conditions, factories brought a loss of control over their lives and an integration with the pace of machines. The way of life in a factory was alien to working people and it was necessary for owners to enforce factory discipline on a labour force unwilling to conform. Initially, the family might impose discipline where it was able to work together. However, owners were not inclined to consider conditions of employment when concentrating on the growth of their enterprise. There was pressure to take children too young and to sub-contract the imposition of discipline to foremen and managers, rather than family groups. Technical advances were mainly responsible for this collapsing kinship system. Richard Robert's automatic mules meant that an adult spinner needed nine young assistants, not a family working together.

Workers were losing control of their lives. The worst expression of this was the cruelty and exploitation suffered by children. Reformers were at work, both in the 1802 Health and Morals of Apprentices Act and in 1819, to limit child labour. Little was achieved, as there was no proper system of inspection or enforcement.

Nevertheless, there were forward-looking groups who pushed on. Progress was slow as supporters of reform were diverse and therefore disorganised. There were pioneering owners, such as Robert Owen and John Fielden. Benthamite Edwin Chadwick was soon involved, as well as representatives of both agricultural and industrial interests in sections of the Whig and Tory Parties. Both parties were divided among themselves on the issue of factory reform. Men such Richard Oastler, the steward of a landed estate, joined with northern clergymen to attack the savage treatment of young children and employers who took no paternalistic interest in their workers.

Moral concerns often outweighed humanitarian ones. Evangelical reformers were keen to root out the evils and corruption of industrial society. Select committees and royal commissions again set out to gather evidence as the ground work to legislation. Famously, the Mines Commissioners were shocked to find, in 1842, evidence of half-naked females and males working closely underground. They published, in the Blue Books, what they had intended to find out anyway.

Apostles of *laissez faire* defended the *status quo* and individual liberty, as well as raising the spectre of economic failure if workers' hours were lessened and pay improved. The free-market economists emphasised that individuals should enter into their own contractual arrangements and work to their own best interests. Owners were obsessed by the idea of fixed capital. They had invested in machinery, and output and profit varied according to how long they worked. Employers were in a position of strength given the size of the labour force and the fact that so many women and children were seeking employment. Nor were owners impressed by the argument that good treatment of workers would improve output, despite the example of employers like Robert Owen.

This was all very well for owners. Reformers pointed out that women and children were in no position to determine the nature of the 'free market' contract. By the 1840s, when the worst abuses were publicised, particularly in spinning, there was an acceptance that concessions might be necessary to head off excessive interference in their businesses.

Hence the debate centred on the extent to which the State would step in to protect workers. (The major Acts passed before 1850 are described on the next page.)

What remained to be done after 1850?

There was a rearguard action against further reforms. However, on balance, there was more to be done than had been achieved by 1850.

Textile factories were covered, but conditions in mines remained poor. Workshops were not covered and further Acts were needed to extend protection to the metal trades, printing, bleaching and dyeing, blast furnaces and all small workshops. Dangerous occupations, such as match making, remained unprotected and it was not until 1866 that sanitary regulations were enforced in factories.

The Main Factory Acts

The 1833 Factory Act (Althorp's Act)

- Children aged 9–13 could work up to 9 hours a day and only 48 hours per week.
- Children aged 14–18 could work up to 12 hours a day and 65 hours per week.
- No child could be employed under the age of 9 and children aged 9–11 were to be given 2 hours schooling a day.
- The crucial aspect was the appointment of 4 inspectors, clearly not enough, but the first step towards enforcement.

1837: The compulsory registration of birth

- This was essential if children of working age were to be regulated.

1842: Mines and Collieries Act

Following two reports into mining conditions:

- no women and girls could work underground
- no boys under 10 could work underground
- inspectors were to be appointed in 1843.

1844: Factory Act

- The minimum age for children to start work was lowered to 8.
- Children under 13 could only work 6½ hours a day.
- Women and the young between 13 and 18 could only work a maximum 12-hour day.
- Dangerous machinery was to be fenced.
- The 'Ten Hours Movement' regarded the Act as unsatisfactory. Men like Oastler, Fielden, Stephens (the Chartist leader) and Tory Lord Ashley had campaigned for a Ten Hours Bill ever since the first one failed in 1831. Fielden tried again in 1847.

The 1847 Factory Act

- Restricted the hours of woman and young people to 10 hours a day.
- Nothing so far had limited the hours of men. It had been hoped that, as children's hours fell then it would be necessary to limit the running of machines so that men's hours would fall too. Not so. Owners got round this by using teams of children in relays. Hence the 1850 Act was passed.

The 1850 Factory Act

- Established a uniform working day.
- Woman and the young were to work between 6 a.m. and 6 p.m. or between 7 a.m. and 7 p.m.
- There would be 1½ hours for meals.
- Work on Saturday would cease at 2 p.m.

1. What were the main obstacles to the introduction of factory reform?

2. What do you regard as the most important factory reform passed between 1819 and 1878? Give reasons for your answer.

The gang system of itinerant women agricultural labourers was not regulated until 1867, while the shocking use of chimney boys was not outlawed until 1875.

The Act of 1878 codified over 100 different Acts, applying standards to all factories and workshops.

- No children could be employed under 10.
- Women's hours were a maximum of 56½ in textiles and 60 hours in other factories.

Men continued to be neglected, and nothing had been done to regulate the 'sweated trades'. Even by the end of the century, most workers remained unprotected, exploited and in danger.

14.7 What efforts were made to improve public health?

The pace of urbanisation was startling. In 1800, only 25% of the population lived in towns. By the end of the century, the figure was 75%. Between 1801 and 1851, when death rates were at their highest, the population doubled from 10.5 million to 20.8 million.

Houses were built at enormous speed. They were unplanned and insanitary, with no thought of the health of occupants. An unregulated free-market economy produced housing, which had a catastrophic effect on the lifespan of their inhabitants. In 1842, labourers in Manchester had an average age of death of only 17 years of age. This was unsurprising in overcrowded, insanitary back-to-backs where there was neither clean water nor the means of disposing of sewage. Regular visitations of cholera – in 1831, 1848, 1853 and 1866 – highlighted the dreadful mortality rates, especially since the disease visited all classes, not just slum dwellers. Lack of knowledge about disease was only part of the problem. True, doctors had little success in curing people. Medical science had not yet discovered that germs cause disease (not until 1864). What was more significant was the lack of interventionist responsibility. *Laissez-faire* attitudes left landlords to do as they wished with their properties. Social prejudice dictated that the poor were weak, feeble and lazy. There was no will to make inroads into public health problems. Henriques refers to apathy and 'the collapse of communal responsibility'. Collectivism had not taken hold and local government was in chaos. Four hundred local improvement acts, passed up to 1845, made hardly any impact.

Who would pay for better drains and improved water supply on the scale required? Certainly not ratepayers. They had no intention of paying for it. Before 1835, there was no single 'system' of local government. The local Boards of Health that had been set up to deal with the cholera epidemic of 1831 were closed down as soon as it was over. In 1835, Parliament set up 178 councils in towns or boroughs with charters, through the Municipal Corporations Act. Male householders could now elect the council to take over from 'Improvement Commissioners' who carried out street cleaning, paving, lighting and water supply. But 13 years later, a third of English towns still had no drainage or street cleaning. Places like Sheffield and Glasgow, which only gained charters to become towns in the 1840s, had to be included in the Act later. It was possible to bring some order out of the confusion of local government, but progress was slow.

The late 1830s and early 1840s saw attempts to capture the public's attention with the scale of the squalor in Britain's slums. The historian S.E. Finer acknowledges that England 'appeared for the first time to get a sense of sight and smell and realise that they were living on a dungheap'.

Gustav Doré's 'Over London by Rail' – a view of London in the 19th century

Having a system of local government did not necessarily lead to reform. The new ratepayers – local members of the middle classes – were committed to individualism, the free market and limited expenditure of their own money. A major shift in such values would be slow in coming, despite the accumulation of evidence about the state of public health. For example, in 1838, Dr Southwood Smith investigated Whitechapel in London. He found 1,400 cases of poverty linked to cases of fever.

Edwin Chadwick, as Secretary to the Poor Law Commissioners from 1834, was very aware of the cost of disease and the consequent wasteful burden on the rates. If the wage-earner fell ill, the family would have to claim poor relief. Chadwick's 'Report on the Sanitary Conditions of the Labouring Population of Great Britain' (1842) brought together evidence from doctors all over the country. It was a bestseller. Significantly, the report was printed under Chadwick's name instead of under the name of the Poor Law Commission. The Commission had recognised that the Report contained findings that could upset ratepayers. Chadwick's obsession with clean water supplies, better drainage and good ventilation (as he blamed disease on harmful smells) would certainly carry a high cost. He wanted a system of small earthenware pipes with water flowing through, to flush out the sewage. However, the confused system of local administration and the inefficiency of the water companies, who could not guarantee supplies, meant that 'sanitary engineering' was unlikely to succeed in the short term. It relied on water pipes being connected to every house and more than two or three hours of supply a day.

It mattered little to the 'Dirty Party' – that groups of MPs who most strongly supported *laissez-faire* principles – that money could actually be saved on Poor Law expenditure if something was done to moderate the spiral of poverty and disease, by cleaning up towns.

Peel set up the royal commissions on 'large towns and populous districts', which published their reports in 1844 and 1845. They showed that little seemed to have been done since the cholera outbreaks of 1831 and 1832. It would take another disastrous outbreak of cholera, in 1848, before anything was done.

The 1848 Public Health Act set up a General Board of Health, in London. It could create local Boards of Health if 10% of the local ratepayers asked for one or where the death rate was above 23 per 1,000 of the population. Local Boards of Health had a wide role to control water supplies, cemeteries, sewage, the paving of streets and their drainage.

However, the reform was only grudgingly passed, almost as a favour rather than as a right. There was widespread suspicion of centralised control because local ratepayers might lose control over their expenditure. The whole principle of the authority of central government to interfere locally was not accepted. Tories could sense the imposition of taxes on rural areas to solve the problems of towns. Here was a national problem to which there was no national consensus about its solution.

The 1848 Act was undermined from the start by opponents. The General Board of Health could not force local action. The local boards could only advise – their powers were entirely permissive. Medical Officers of Health could be appointed, but there was no compulsion. Manchester did not have one until 1868. By 1854, only one-sixth of the population was covered by local Boards of Health. Chadwick, who had sat on the General Board of Health, resigned in the same year. His constant interfering and tactless manner meant that his resignation was greeted with delight. The General Board of Health itself had disappeared by 1858. The strong local forces against centralised reform had won, but only for the time being.

On the one hand, reformers were disappointed at national developments. There is a clear case that really improving public health would remain beyond the Victorians. Mortality rates were slightly higher in the early 1870s than they were in the 1840s. Cholera struck again in 1865 and 1866, and claimed 20,000 lives. Medical officers were frustrated by the fact that different authorities looked after burial grounds, urban sanitation and water supplies. Tuberculosis (TB) thrived in the slums and smallpox still managed to kill 44,000 people in the 1870s.

On the other hand, certain principles had been established for later action. In 1853, the compulsory vaccination of babies against smallpox was introduced. Sanitary engineering had evolved technically and John Simon (Medical Officer of Health in London 1848–55) proved that piped water and effective sewers could make an impact on mortality rates.

A Sanitary Act of 1866 forced local authorities to appoint sanitary inspectors. Parliament was in a position to insist on the removal of 'nuisances' and on the provision of sewers and good water supplies.

In 1868, a Royal Sanitary Commission into the health of towns eventually led to the formation of a Local Government Board in 1871 to oversee local provision. The 1875 Public Health Act was a major step forward and laid the foundations for reduced mortality rates at the turn of the century.

The Public Health Act, 1875

A mass of regulations, introduced over a period of 30 years, were brought into one Act. It contained little that was new but it laid foundations that would last well into the 20th century.

1. Every area had to have a Medical Officer of Health and sanitary inspectors.
2. Councils were given powers to build sewers, drains, public toilets and reservoirs.

1. To what extent was the 1875 Act a 'turning point' in development of public health legislation?

2. Why was there so much opposition to reform, despite the obvious evidence of need?

3. Councils were to ensure that refuse was collected and to control the supply of pure water.
4. Local authorities had the power to disinfect houses where people had caught infectious diseases.

The Government was trying to prevent disease at last. After 1874, doctors also had to sign death certificates showing each cause of death. Eventually, they had to give notification of infectious diseases.

14.8 How did housing policy change, 1866–1946?

The same set of values that held back factory and public health legislation also hindered attempts at improving housing. Not all landlords were obstructive, but many were. Since land lay at the heart of their beliefs, the problem of dealing with slums, which still had a commercial value despite their condition, would be doubly difficult to solve. Compensation would be needed if slums were to be cleared or improved. Who would pay? How much compulsion was required? How far would the private interests of the slum landlord be compromised in the interests of public health, public order and public morality? The need for action was all the more urgent as demand for houses far exceeded supply.

Private charities and individuals such as George Peabody and Octavia Hill did what they could. Hill bought and repaired slum properties, letting them out at profitable rents to families who would take a pride in them. A

Aerial view of Cumbernauld, Scotland

few employers tried to lead the way, such as George Cadbury at Bournville and William Hesketh Lever at Port Sunlight. Such shining examples of model villages made little impact on Britain's gloomy and overcrowded slums. Central government proved as ineffective as ever. In all, 27 housing Acts were passed in the second half of the 19th century. Once again, local ratepayers could delay reform. The lack of proper administrative bodies at local level further slowed down progress.

- In 1866, the Treasury made loans available if local authorities wanted to build houses. Only Liverpool applied.
- In 1868, The Housing (Torrens) Act said that landlords had to keep property in good repair. If repairs were not carried out, the local authority could use their powers and make sure that houses were made good.
- In 1875, the Artisans' Dwellings Act – the work of Disraeli's Home Secretary Richard Cross – gave local authorities even more power. They could clear whole areas of poor housing and re-house people nearby. Landlords were to be paid compensation if their property was pulled down. The Act also laid down the thickness of walls, the size of rooms, the spaces between buildings and standards of sanitation.

However, the Acts may well have shown the State as willing to interfere in property matters, but the powers were hardly used by local authorities. In the 10 years following the 1875 Act, only 11 councils gained permission to pull down slums and only four bothered to replace houses they demolished. Clearly, this made overcrowding worse. Only Birmingham, under Joseph Chamberlain's leadership, made spectacular improvements, but it was the only town of any size to take action.

It was not until the 1890 Act was passed that effective action was taken.

The Housing of the Working Classes Act, 1890

The 1884–85 Royal Commission on the Housing of the Working Classes made alarming reading. The Prince of Wales, Cross, Chadwick and Shaftesbury all played their part in drawing Parliament's attention to squalid housing. This led to the 1890 Act. It stands alongside the 1875 Public Health Act as a major step forward.

1. It brought together into one law a confusing mass of earlier regulations.
2. It strengthened local authority powers to demolish houses.
3. It encouraged them to build single 'council' houses.

Not for the first time, proper solutions seemed to be beyond the Victorians. It would not be until 1919 that the Government actually gave out money to build houses.

Housing policy between the wars, 1919–1939

House building had almost ground to a halt during the First World War. It was apparent, once again, that supply lagged far behind the demand caused by growth in population. The shortfall was around 600,000 houses. Little enough use was being made of the powers given to local authorities to build new houses. When Lloyd George promised returning soldiers 'a country fit for heroes to live in', people remembered it as a promise of 'homes fit for heroes to live in'. Could this promise be kept?

In the summer of 1919, the first postwar Housing and Town Planning Act was passed. It was commonly known as the Addison Act. This Act required local authorities to make good the shortages of houses. The money came from the Treasury, which covered what was spent by local authorities above the total raised by a **penny rate**.

Penny rate: Money raised at local level to pay for welfare.

Government intervention, adding to local rates, was a major step forward and was evidence of its commitment to creating sufficient housing. Council housing had been born, but the Act was overtaken by the 1921 economic crisis and only 170,000 houses were built – not the half a million Addison hoped for. Nevertheless, the historian A.J.P. Taylor points out the change: 'He (Addison) more than any other man established the principle that housing was a social service.'

The Conservative Government of the 1920s targeted money differently – on private builders. They made little contribution to working-class housing. It had to wait for the Wheatley Act of 1924, passed by the Labour Government, to increase the subsidy for rented accommodation and introduce a long-term programme of council house building. Well over half a million were built up to 1939, at a cost to the government of some £4 million per year under the scheme.

The other important development was the Slum Clearance Act of 1930, designed by Arthur Greenwood during the second Labour Government. The aim was not only to demolish slums, but also to re-house the inhabitants. The National Government of the 1930s accepted the first aim but abandoned the second, relying on private builders to make up the gap – often at prices workers could not afford.

New towns – the post-Second World War era

By the end of the Second World War, the housing situation was desperate. Two out of every seven houses had been destroyed or damaged. Quick remedies were needed. Prefabs helped. From 1946 to 1948, 148,000 were built. Bevan, in charge of housing as Minister of Health, turned his attention to more permanent council housing. In the five-year period following the end of the war, 800,000 quality council houses were built. Even so, shortages were worse than ever, because the number of families was growing even faster.

The contribution of private builders was limited. The subsidies available went to local authorities so that new houses went to those who really needed them. Rent restrictions kept rents down. But the shortfall was estimated, at the end of the 1940s, to be anything between one and two million houses.

In line with the post-war Labour Government's liking for State initiative and direct economic planning, the proposals for new towns were certainly ambitious. Under the New Towns Act of 1946, 20 new towns were built. These new communities were meant to relieve pressure on the old inner cities, particularly London. As the population moved, there were incentives to attract industries out to the New Towns – with some success. From the first tentative steps of the early housing acts of the mid-19th century to the completely integrated economic planning and direct intervention embodied in the New Towns Act, public policy seemed to have gone from ineffectual permissiveness to ultimate **Keynesian management**. Later changes in policy by Conservative governments who disliked collectivist responsibility would undermine the direct interventionism of postwar governments. Housing policy once again offers evidence of more continuity than change.

Keynesian management: Economic theory that states that the Government can regulate the levels of unemployment and inflation through the use of direct taxation and government spending, It was followed by British governments from 1944 to 1976.

1. Why were the early housing reforms so ineffective?

2. What do changes in housing policy tell historians about attitudes to the role of the State in social welfare?

14.9 What were the effects of government intervention in education?

The tone of early education reform was also moral. The 1834 Report referred to the need to promote the religious and moral education of the labouring classes.

The voluntary societies who pioneered elementary education were clearly not up to the task. Important individuals and pressure groups pressed the case for secular compulsory education. In 1862, the Revised Code introduced government grants and 'payments by results' – but it did nothing to solve the shortage of schools. The National Education League, founded by Chamberlain in 1869, was one that acknowledged that international competitors such as Prussia appeared to be better schooled and to produce more responsible workmen.

The 1867 widening of the franchise brought more encouragement, although Gladstone had no enthusiasm for education. At least he recognised that some response was necessary to the pressure groups. In 1870, Forster introduced his Education Reform Bill. **Elementary schools** were to be provided everywhere to fill the gaps left by religious and voluntary schools. School Boards would be established which had powers to raise a rate and set up elementary schools if they wished. Grants would continue to voluntary schools. The Cowper-Temple clause allowed parents to withdraw their children from religious lessons. Grants were made to mainly Anglican as well as some Catholic schools but from central government, not from the rates.

Elementary schools: Schools educating students from 5 to 11 years of age.

There were high hopes of improvements in education. However, the 1870 Act was not a miracle cure. Buildings were austere, classes too large and teaching methods too narrow. If education was now seen as a right, not charity, what was on offer was meagre. Complaints about cost surfaced again. Given the compulsory nature of attendance, schools found themselves providing school meals long before they had to do so by law (1906). It was all too apparent that poor children lacked the health and nourishment to engage in schooling. This provides another link to the debate about national efficiency at the turn of the century (page 383). The future of the Empire was at stake and there was concern about the strength of the Army, as Britain was perceived to be lagging behind its major rivals.

Robert Morant had become the driving force at the Board of Education. He was an able and formidable civil servant, who was responsible for the next major piece of legislation. His 1902 Education Act responded to the need to offer something beyond elementary schooling. Efforts by School Boards to create secondary schools from the rates had been ruled illegal. The Boards themselves had run their full life. They had served their purpose in the days when there was no proper pattern of local government. The creation of County Councils, in 1888, provided the required framework. It allowed the new Act to abolish School Boards and transfer responsibilities to 'Local Education Authorities' (LEAs) in the County and Council Boroughs.

LEAs were allowed to set up secondary schools with parents paying modest fees but with scholarships available from elementary school. Rate support was provided, although this caused a damaging political controversy about rate aid for church schools (page 362).

Education provision was integrated with the old grammar schools, which remained largely for the middle classes. Children of labourers still lost out when leaving elementary school. Nevertheless, this was an important step forward. While education still lagged behind Britain's commercial rivals, a new concept of state responsibility was emerging at last. It was a far cry from the principles of 1834. If complete *laissez-faire* policies had ever existed (which is unlikely), this kind of state intervention was on a scale previously not attempted. The ground had been prepared for the greatest changes, which were yet to come.

Which were the most important reasons for the increasing Atate activity in education?

The 1918 Education Act

Lloyd George, given the aspirations of the postwar world, again set out to prove that he was capable of driving radical reform. H.A.L. Fisher was the President of the Board of Evaluation. He planned a remarkable Bill that would fundamentally advance education, by raising the school-leaving age to 14. It promised the possibility of 'day continuation' or part-time education up to 18 – a most important innovation. It extended medical inspections from elementary schools to secondary schools, and promised that no child should be excluded from education if parents could not find fees.

The economic problems of the 1920s frustrated the Act, in particular the idea of education beyond 14. Apathy and a reluctance to spend money continued to hamper progress. The Hadow Report of 1926 made important recommendations about dropping the 'elementary school' label and replacing it with the primary/secondary split at 11. Secondary schools were to be 'grammar' or 'modern' schools. It foresaw the raising of the school-leaving age, which was eventually agreed for September 1939. War put paid to that idea.

The Spens Report of 1938 highlighted the lack of technical education, an interesting piece of thinking which admitted that education had to do more than provide basic training. Instead, it had to adapt to the needs of a technological society.

The Education Act of 1944

Winston Churchill had pointed towards the need for great developments in education as early as March 1943. The gaps in technical education, the weaknesses of current provision as exposed by evacuation and the sacrifices made because of the war effort brought a feeling that more should be expected of education. Schools were not just there to provide cheap labour for industry but as a preparation, said Ernest Bevin, for 'industry, occupation and citizenship'. High-quality education was needed to secure the future in a technically complex world.

The Act was the product of a conservative, R.A Butler. It created a new Ministry of Education and 146 local education authorities. The school-leaving age was raised to 15 and secondary pupils were divided on ability, being sent to grammar, technical or secondary modern schools. Religious education and worship were to be compulsory, albeit with a 'conscience' clause. The reality of secondary education for all had been achieved, through a combination of wartime collectivism and cross-party cooperation and a time when Britain continued to struggle against its wartime enemies. A great advance had been achieved, not only in education but also as part of the postwar Welfare State. The 'Welfare State', as conceived by Labour governments, reflected a spirit of humanitarianism and communal responsibility which seemed so far from the values of society 100 years previously.

1. Choose any ONE government policy, or piece of legislation, passed in the period 1850–1914 which you consider to have been a significant turning point in government attitudes towards the poor. Explain why you think that it was a turning point.

2. 'In the period 1830–1948, governments adopted an increasingly informed and understanding attitude towards the causes of poverty in Britain.'

How far do you agree with this judgement?

3. Why, during the period 1834–1948, did governments come to tackle the social problems caused by urbanisation through State intervention rather than laissez faire*?*

4. Examine the changing problems faced by those who wished to expand the public provision of education between 1833 and 1944.

Gladstone and the Liberal Party, 1868–1894

Key Issues

- *Why was the Liberal Party affected by internal disunity?*
- *How successful was Gladstone as party leader and Prime Minister?*
- *How far did the Liberal Party bring social and political change to Britain?*

GLADSTONIAN LIBERAL PARTY

Gladstone's own ideas
High Church Anglican
Free trader
Cobdenite foreign policy

New Model Unions
Wanted legal recognition of trade unions

Nonconformists
Wanted religious and political equality with Anglicans.
Wanted non-denominational education

Whigs
Aristocrats and landowners

Regional support
Strong support from Wales, Scotland and the South-West.
Strong in Ireland until the appearance of the Irish Home Rule Party

Sectional interests 'faddism'
Pressure groups who supported the Liberal Party:
- United Kingdom Alliance and Band of Hope wanted laws against drinking alcohol
- Land reformers
- Educational reformers (such as the National Education League)
- Liberation Society wanted to disestablish the Church of England

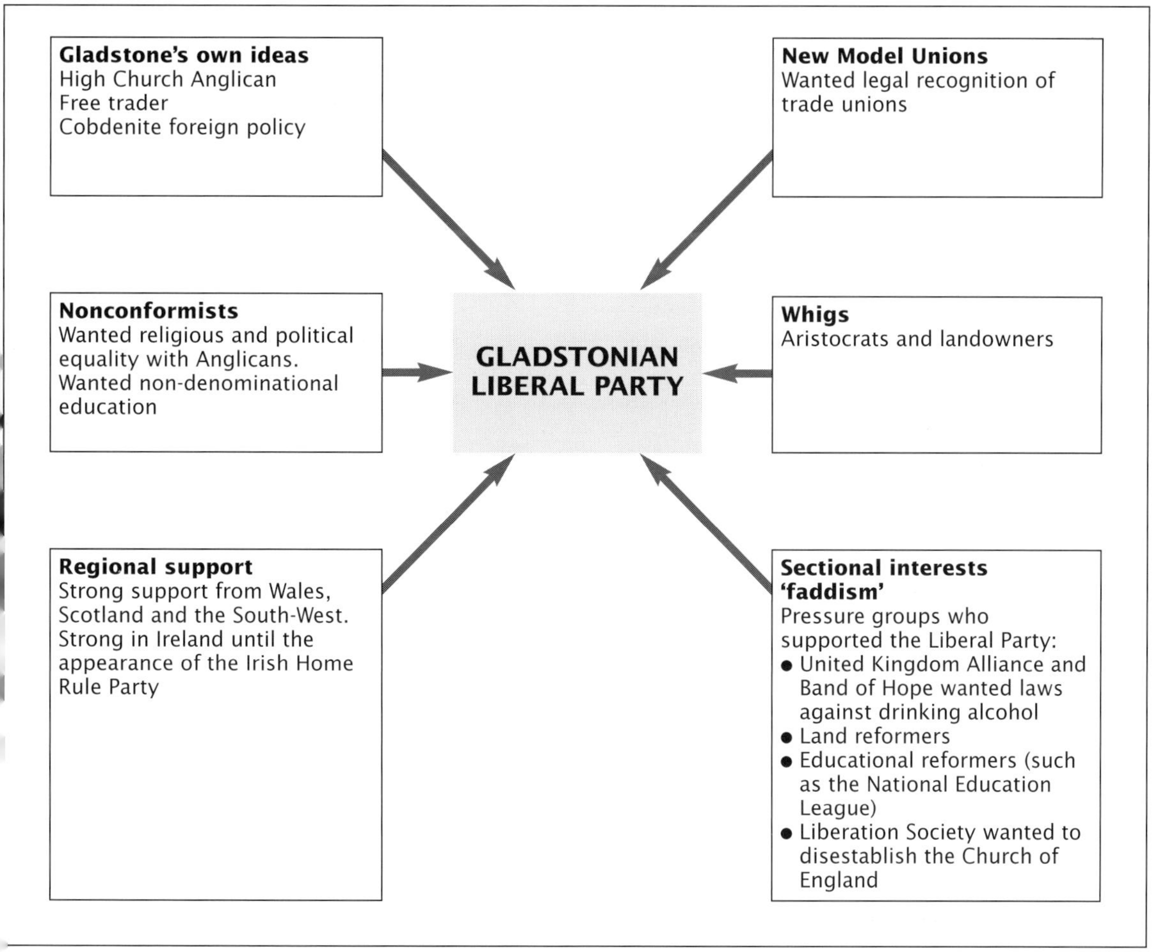

Overview

THE Liberal Party was the dominant political party for most of the period 1868–94. In 1868, 1880, 1886 and 1892 the Liberal Party formed the government, although on the last two occasions with the support of the Irish Home Rule Party.

As the Liberal Party dominated in British politics, so William Ewart Gladstone was the dominant force within the Liberal Party. Indeed, to many of his fellow Liberals Gladstone 'was' the Liberal Party. Gladstone's remarkable political career began in 1832 when he was elected as a right-wing Tory MP. As a minister in Peel's governments of 1835 and 1841–46, he was one of the rising stars of the 'Peelite' Conservative Party. Following the party split on the Corn Laws in 1846 (see Chapter 8), Gladstone became a leading figure in the Peelite faction of the House of Commons. As Chancellor of the Exchequer in the Whig–Peelite coalition of 1852–55, he developed a national reputation for cutting taxes and placing Britain on the road to free trade. In 1859, as a supporter of Italian unification, he joined Palmerston's Liberal Government, thus completing his political journey from right-wing Tory to Liberal.

Gladstone was, undoubtedly, the leading Liberal politician of his era. He supported free trade and, under his leadership, his governments passed many significant reforms which abolished privilege and moved Britain towards a **meritocracy**.

Meritocracy: The idea that the appointment of individuals to positions of authority should be based on ability and qualifications, not upbringing.

High Churchman: A member of the Church of England who supported the Oxford Movement's view that Anglican church services should be similar to the Catholic Church but without recognising the Pope as head of the Christian Church.

He did not, however, always represent the views of his Liberal supporters. As a **High Churchman** and a supporter of the right of the aristocracy to govern, Gladstone led a party where many opposed the privileged position of both the Church of England and the aristocracy. One of the main themes of this period is the potential disunity of the Liberal Party. In 1873–74, and again in 1880–86, the Liberal Party was affected by division within its ranks. Eventually the Party did split, over the issue of Irish Home Rule, into two factions: the Gladstonian Liberals and the Liberal Unionists.

Politics was changing rapidly during this period. In 1867, the franchise had been widened to include the skilled workers in urban areas. In 1872, the secret ballot was introduced and, in 1884, the right to vote was extended to most adult males. Both major parties, the Liberals and Conservatives, developed nationwide party organisations in reaction to the changing circumstances. In the general election campaigns of 1880 and 1885, politicians such as William Gladstone and Joseph Chamberlain campaigned across the country on national issues. The years 1868 to 1894, therefore, represent the foundation of the modern party political system.

Gladstone led the Liberal Party during a period of considerable political change. But he was also a politician of an older generation compared with his major rivals within the Liberal Party: Gladstone was 59 when he became Prime Minister for the first time in 1868. When he retired as Prime Minister, in 1894, he had reached the advanced age of 85. He was often out of step with younger politicians. His main rival for much of this period, Joseph Chamberlain, was a **nonconformist** from Birmingham who possessed a radically different view of which policies the Liberal Party should follow. The disunity within the Liberal Party and the split of 1886 had much to do with the rivalry between Gladstone and Chamberlain.

Nonconformist: A Protestant who is not a member of the Church of England. Examples are Methodists, Quakers and Baptists.

15.1 *What was Gladstonian Liberalism?*

Gladstone led a political party that was itself the product of the changing social and economic conditions taking place in Britain during the 19th century.

In Parliament

The party in Parliament was a mixture of Whigs, Peelites, Liberals and Radicals who had all come together in the period following the split within the Conservative Party in 1846.

- The **Whigs** were members of the British aristocracy who had opposed too much monarchic influence in politics and had passed the Great Reform Bill of 1832. Among active Whigs were some of the largest landowners in the country, such as Lord Hartington (later the 8th Duke of Devonshire). The leading Whigs were members of the House of Lords. However, junior members of the Whig families sat as MPs.
- The **Peelites** were the former followers of Sir Robert Peel who supported free trade. Predominantly from industrial and commercial backgrounds, they included Gladstone among their number.
- **Liberals** were also from industrial and commercial backgrounds, having joined forces with the Whigs in the 1830s and 1840s to support free trade, the freedom of the press and freedom of religion.
- **Radicals** was a term used to describe a wide variety of MPs who wished to see radical change in certain aspects of British society. Some were nonconformists who opposed the privileged position of the Church of England as the **State Church**. Others advocated reform in areas such as education, the laws governing alcohol and land reform.

State Church: The Church of England was recognised as the official religion of England, receiving financial support from the Government.

The issue that finally brought this rather disparate group of politicians together was their combined support for Italian unification and their desire to remove a minority Conservative government under the Earl of Derby. At Willis' tea rooms, on 5 June 1859, the Liberal Party was formally launched as a distinct parliamentary party.

Outside Parliament

The Party received support from a variety of social and economic groups. In his book *The Formation of the Liberal Party 1857 to 1868*, John Vincent identifies three forces which helped to create the party as a nationwide institution.

- First, the rise of political nonconformity and its desire to receive equality of treatment with the Church of England. The Liberation Society, a pressure group led by Edward Miall, called for the removal of the privileged position of the Church of England as the State Church and the preferential treatment enjoyed by Anglicans in institutions such as Oxford and Cambridge universities. Backing from this group explains why the Liberal Party received strong support from areas such as Wales, Scotland and the West Country, where nonconformists were numerous. In addition, until 1868 the Liberal Party received considerable support in Ireland. Thereafter, following the formation of the Home Rule Party, the Liberal Party there went into terminal decline.

New Model Unions: Trade unions that represented skilled workers such as engineers and boilermakers.

- Second, the Party received support from **New Model Unions** which represented the interests of skilled workers such as engineers, carpenters and boilermakers. This social group largely received the vote

Friendly Societies: Independent, non-profit-making organisations providing financial support for members during illness or in death, in return for weekly/monthly subscriptions (e.g. Hearts of Oak Friendly Society).

1. Who were the main supporters of the Gladstonian Liberal Party? Give reasons to support your answer.

2. 'The Gladstonian Liberal Party was made up of a mixture of competing interests.'

Using the information in this section, explain what this statement meant and why it proved to be a major problem for the Liberal Party under Gladstone.

with the passing of the Second Reform Act of 1867. They were also faced with the problem of lack of legal recognition for their trade unions. Many had operated as friendly societies, under the **Friendly Societies** Act of 1855. This meant they could offer their members financial support in the event of sickness or death. However, they could not bargain for wage rises nor strike. In the court case Hornby *versus* Close, 1867, these unions found that their funds were not protected from theft. They, therefore, supported the Liberal Party in the hope that legislation would be introduced to grant them legal protection.

- Finally, Vincent refers to the importance of the rise of provincial newspapers as a means for spreading support for the Liberal Party. With the development of railways and the removal of taxes on newspapers in 1861, the newspaper industry outside London grew rapidly. Newspapers such as the *Manchester Guardian* and the *Leeds Mercury* supported Liberal causes.

These three developments all took place during the mid-Victorian economic boom of 1850–73, when there was a major increase in the size and wealth of the industrial and commercial classes in relation to the aristocracy which owed its wealth and status to agriculture. As a result, the Liberal Party received strong support from urban areas, such as the growing industrial cities of Birmingham, Manchester and Leeds.

Gladstone's views

On top of this background of a political party made up of many different, often competing factions, there are Gladstone's own political views. These were sometimes in tune with the views of the majority of Liberal supporters but, at other times, were at odds with them.

A central key to understanding Gladstone's views is to realise that he was a deeply religious man who believed that his involvement in politics was related directly to his religious beliefs. Much of his stature as a politician was based on his ability to think of political problems as moral issues. His opposition to the Bulgarian Horrors, his opposition to **Beaconsfieldism** in 1879–80, and his campaigns on Irish issues all seemed like religious crusades. Gladstone's moral stance on political issues annoyed many of his political foes. For example, one complained about Gladstone always having the ace of trumps up his sleeve and, particularly, the fact that Gladstone always claimed that God had put it there.

Beaconsfieldism: The name given to Disraeli's foreign and imperial policies, which were seen as costly and aggressive.

In practical terms, Gladstone was a firm supporter of free trade for the whole of his political life. Alongside this was his dislike of government interference in the lives of its citizens. As a result, Gladstone supported **retrenchment**, thereby lowering taxation. This was combined with a constant drive to improve the efficiency of government and other national institutions.

Retrenchment: The policy of keeping government expenditure to a minimum.

The basis of Gladstone's view of the 'minimalist' state was the importance of the individual. Gladstone did not see society as a set of competing economic classes, but of individuals where each should have the opportunity to fulfil their potential. As he stated, 'I will always back the masses against the classes.' This did not mean that Gladstone was a democrat. He was, even by the norms of the time, a social conservative. In 1878, he said to the art critic, John Ruskin, 'I am an out-and-out inequalitarian.' He believed in rule by those individuals in society who had a tradition of service to the State and possessed sufficient wealth to be above the charge of possible corruption. He was, therefore, a supporter of the traditional roles of monarchy and aristocracy.

An overall assessment of the Gladstonian Liberal Party

It is clear that the Gladstonian Liberal Party was a complex political phenomenon. Gladstone himself did not reflect the views of many Liberals. Inside Parliament, a rift grew between Whigs and Radicals that led to the split of 1886. Outside Parliament, the Party comprised a wide variety of competing groups, each in pursuit of its own political aims.

Historians such as D.A. Hamer, in *Liberal Politics in the Age of Gladstone and Rosebery* (1974), and Martin Pugh, in *The Making of Modern British Politics* (1982), have referred to 'faddism' within the Liberal Party: meaning that the Party was susceptible to splits. Even before Gladstone had become Liberal leader, the Party had split over the issue of parliamentary reform when Robert Lowe led the 'Adullamite' faction against Gladstone's electoral bill in 1866.

This problem was to affect the Gladstonian Party throughout the period. When Gladstone retired as Prime Minister, in 1894, the Party had been split into two distinct factions for eight years.

1. Using information contained within the chapter, explain the meaning of 'retrenchment' (bottom left-hand corner of the cartoon).

2. Do you think this cartoon is in support of Gladstone? Give reasons to support your answer.

Punch cartoon, December 1879, entitled 'The Colossus of Words'.

Source-based questions: The social backgrounds of Liberal Party MPs

TABLE A

Background of Liberal MPs (as a percentage)

Interest	1859–74	1892	1914
Land	49.2	8.1	6.0
Business and finance	30.1	44.2	40.0
Law	16.7	24.8	22.0

TABLE B

Backgrounds of Conservative and Liberal MPs in 1892 (as a percentage)

Interest	Liberal	Conservative
Land	8.1	28.5
Business and finance	44.2	25.9
Law	24.8	24.1

1. Study Table A.

In what ways did the backgrounds of Liberal MPs change between 1859 and 1914?

Explain why the changes took place.

2. Study Table B.

How different were the social backgrounds of Liberal and Conservative MPs in 1892?

Explain why these differences existed.

15.2 How successful was Gladstone's First Ministry in bringing social and political change?

Introduction

Gladstone became Prime Minister for the first time in December 1868, when the Liberal Party ousted a minority Conservative government under Benjamin Disraeli, winning a majority of 106 seats over their rivals (Liberals 382; Conservatives 276).

Gladstone's first Cabinet reflected the diverse composition of the Liberal Party. It contained three former Peelites (Gladstone, Cardwell and De Grey), with three Liberals (Childers, Goschen and Bruce) and two Radicals (Lowe and Bright). However, the largest group within the Cabinet was the Whigs, who held seven posts including Foreign Secretary, Irish Secretary and Colonial Secretary. All the Cabinet members belonged to the Church of England, except John Bright who, as a Quaker, was the first nonconformist to hold Cabinet rank.

The government over which Gladstone presided has been described by Michael Bentley, in *The Climax of Liberal Politics* (1987), as 'one of the most energetic and prolific administrations of the 19th century'. In *Gladstone* (1975), E.J. Feuchtwanger stated that 'Gladstonian Liberalism can be defined largely in terms of the reforms accomplished in this period'.

The main principles of Gladstonian Liberalism were clearly present in the reforms passed. Support for free trade, administrative efficiency in government, retrenchment and individual self-expression are all apparent in many of the reforms. Many contemporaries saw the ministry as one that was engaged in an attack on privilege to create a meritocracy.

However, many of the reforms were also aimed at satisfying the political demands of pressure groups associated with the Liberal Party. Education reform (National Education League), trade union reform (New Model Unions), and licensing reform of the liquor trade (United Kingdom Alliance and the Band of Hope Union) highlight a key feature of the Liberal Party: its diversity of support.

We need to ask two questions when assessing the reform programme of Gladstone's First Ministry:

- How far did the reforms bring social and political change?
- Did the reforms satisfy the aspirations of the various pressure groups which supported the Liberal Party?

Irish reform

These reforms and Gladstone's policy towards Ireland are dealt with at length in Chapter 17 (pages 294–311). However, Gladstone did use the slogan 'Justice for Ireland' as his major rallying cry during the 1868 general election to unify the disparate elements of the Liberal Party.

The disestablishment of the Church of Ireland Act in 1869 did possess major features to please Liberal supporters. The Liberation Society, which wished to disestablish the Church of England, saw Irish disestablishment as a first step towards their ultimate goal. Liberals, in general, also saw the Act as removing an obvious Irish grievance. However, many Whigs viewed this attack on the Irish 'Establishment' with deep suspicion. The later Irish Land Act was seen as an attack on the rights of property and helped push the Whigs towards the Conservative Party, where most were to end up after 1886.

The most controversial aspect of Gladstone's Irish policy was his Universities Bill of 1873. This had the uncanny knack of upsetting both conservative Whigs and left-of-centre Radicals. The Government's defeat on the Bill by three votes, in March 1873, forced Gladstone to resign temporarily from office. However, Disraeli's refusal to form another minority Conservative administration forced Gladstone to continue in office for another ten months.

Education reform

The Liberal Ministry's involvement in educational matters covered a wide spectrum.

- In December 1868, it passed the Public Schools Act, which revised the governing bodies of the 'Clarendon' schools such as Eton, Harrow and Winchester. This was followed, in 1869, by the Endowed Schools Act, which aimed to improve secondary education by appointing three commissioners to revise the trust deeds of schools such as Manchester Grammar School. Any further proposals for reorganisation had to be submitted to the Education Department.
- Of greater significance was the University Tests Act, 1871, which dealt with a major nonconformist grievance in higher education. The Act allowed non-Anglicans to take up teaching posts at the universities of Oxford, Cambridge and Durham. It also allowed non-Anglicans to qualify for scholarships and fellowships at these universities.
- By far the most important educational reform, and one that stands out as a milestone in English educational reform, was the Forster Elementary Education Act, 1870. This Act laid the foundations of the English elementary education system. Until 1870, elementary education (children from 5 to 11 years) was carried out in church schools administered by either the Church of England through the National

Society, nonconformists through the British and Foreign School Society or by the Roman Catholic Church. Since 1833, these schools had received some financial assistance from the State. From 1839, a government department supervised expenditure.

Demands for reform came from those, such as industrialists, who feared that Britain's competitive edge in world trade and industry was being damaged by the lack of an effective education system. They pointed to both the USA and Prussia, Britain's two major economic rivals, as states that, by 1870, had introduced free, compulsory, state-funded education at elementary level. It would be an exaggeration to state that the spectacular military successes of the Prussian army in 1866 and 1870 were the prime cause for reform. However, Gladstone stated, in an article in the *Edinburgh Review* in 1870: 'Undoubtedly, the conduct of the campaign, on the German side, has given a marked triumph to the cause of systematic popular education.'

To support a campaign for change along these lines Joseph Chamberlain, a Birmingham industrialist, launched the National Education League in 1869. This pressure group campaigned for free, compulsory, **non-denominational** elementary education. They were opposed by the National Education Union, which wanted to retain education under direct Church control.

Non-denominational: Christian education without a bias towards one type, e.g. Anglican or Catholic. Usually based on Bible reading.

The Act that was eventually passed was a compromise between these two positions. It created what became known as the 'Dual System', whereby elementary education was provided either by Church schools or locally administered State schools, known as Board schools. W.E. Forster, the Vice-President of the Education Department of the Privy Council, who was responsible for the passage of the Bill, declared that he wished to 'complete the voluntary system and fill up the gaps' and 'to cover the country with good schools'.

School Boards were created, elected by ratepayers with the task of creating schools where Church schools did not exist. London was to make up one School Board. These School Boards were given the power to levy local rates to meet part of the cost of Board schools but not Church schools. The rest of the money was provided by central government.

Within Church schools, denominational religious teaching continued. In Board schools, only Bible teaching was permitted. However, if a parent wished to have denominational religious teaching for their child, under the Cowper-Temple clause of the Act, they had the power to remove their children from a Board school to attend religious teaching of their choosing. As a result, religious classes were always timetabled at the end of the school day to allow this practice to take place. Fees were to be paid by parents to Board schools but School Boards could, under Clause 25 of the Act, establish free schools in poor districts. This could mean 'voluntary' or Church schools. The National Education League (NEL) was outraged by this, because they were against any financial support for these schools.

Although the Act had considerable long-term consequences, it fell far short of the aspirations of the National Education League. The League took the unprecedented step of running its own candidates against the Liberals in the 1874 general election. Further legislation in 1876, 1880 and 1891 went a long way to meeting the NEL's aims but to this day the 'Dual System' has survived.

Army reform

The reforms in the Army, made under the direction of Edward Cardwell Minister of War, contained many of the principles underpinning Gladstonian Liberalism: the improvement of efficiency, an attack on privilege and the enhancement of individual self-expression.

The demand for reform came from many quarters. First, there was the memory of British military incompetence during the Crimean War

(1854–56). More recently, the experience of the American Civil War and the successes of the Prussian army in wars against Denmark and Austria during the 1860s meant that the British Army was in dire need of modernisation.

To meet these challenges, Cardwell made the Commander-in-Chief of the Army subordinate to the Minister of War. This was meant to ensure the political control of the Army. Queen Victoria, however, insisted on her son, the Duke of Cambridge, retaining the position of Commander-in-Chief until the 1890s, even though he lacked the qualifications for the post.

- The War Office Act, 1870, divided the War Office into three departments: the Commander-in-Chief, Surveyor-General and Financial Secretary. This was in a bid to improve efficiency.
- Improved efficiency was also the purpose behind two further acts. The Army Enlistment Act, 1870, permitted a three-year enlistment in the army in addition to the normal 12 years. The Army Regulation Act, 1871, increased the size of the Army from 200,000 to 497,000. The country was divided into military districts, usually a county, each with a central barracks, to encourage recruitment. Authority for the militia was transferred from the Lord Lieutenant of a county to the War Office.
- To bring the British Army into line with other modern forces such as France, Prussia and the USA, a new breech-loading infantry rifle – the Martini-Henry – was introduced to replace the muzzle-loading Enfield rifle musket.
- In an attack on privilege, the most controversial aspect of Cardwell's reforms was the abolition of the purchase of commissions. In future, promotion within the officer class was to be based on merit only. This proposal met such fierce opposition in the House of Lords that it was introduced by royal warrant, not Act of Parliament, in July 1871.

Another area of controversy was the decision to withdraw British troops from the self-governing colonies, in particular Canada and New Zealand. Gladstone believed that these colonies would only be truly self-governing if they looked after their own defence. This decision created considerable opposition in Canada, which feared US invasion and had experienced the Red River Revolt in 1867, and from New Zealand, where the Maori Wars were in progress. Benjamin Disraeli, the Conservative leader, even went so far as to claim that this proposal was part of a Gladstonian plot to dismember the British Empire.

Civil Service reform

As another aspect of the promotion of a meritocracy, in June 1870 the Government, by Order-in-Council, made all public posts within the Home Civil Service open to competition through public examination. This completed work begun by the Northcote-Trevelyan reforms of 1854. However, the Diplomatic and Foreign Civil Service were exempt.

Licensing reform

Under pressure from the United Kingdom Alliance and the Band of Hope Union, the Home Secretary H.A. Bruce introduced the Licensing Act of 1872. This gave Justices of the Peace (JPs) the right to grant licences to publicans, to fix opening and closing hours and to check on the adulteration of beer. The Act disappointed the two Liberal pressure groups who felt it was too lenient. However, the Act did upset the brewing interests and the 'drinking masses'. As the historian R.C.K. Ensor states, the Act saw 'a positive and permanent shift of the publicans and brewers to the Tory Party'.

Electoral reform

Hustings: Political activities such as speeches that take place in the period just before an election.

In 1872, the Government implemented one of the Chartists' six points with the passage of the Ballot Act. The reform was introduced by W.E. Forster. It declared that voting in elections should be by secret ballot and that candidates should no longer be nominated at the **hustings**. Although this enhanced the right of voters to cast their votes without intimidation, it did not end electoral malpractice. In 1883, the second Gladstone Administration had to pass the Corrupt and Illegal Practices Act.

Trade union reform

An important pressure group, which supported the Liberal Party in the 1868 election, had been the New Model Unions. They were keen to gain legal recognition following the Hornby *versus* Close case of 1867. The Trade Union Act, 1871, gave trade unions the legal protection they wanted.

Gladstone also wanted 'to prevent violence and, in all economic matters, for the law to take no part'. The Liberal Government therefore passed the Criminal Law Amendment Act, also in 1871, which aimed to prevent violence in strikes by making intimidation illegal. However, in the Gas Stokers' Case of December 1872, the judge, Justice Brett, declared that trade unionists could be charged for intimidation under the law of conspiracy, while JPs interpreted the term 'intimidation' very widely to include such actions as dirty looks at strikebreakers.

This legislation and its interpretation in the courts caused great resentment among trade unionists. By November 1873, the Liberal Cabinet had come to the conclusion that a reform of the law was required. It agreed to a proposal similar to that eventually passed by the Conservative Government as the Conspiracy and Protection of Property Act, 1875.

The Supreme Court of Judicature Act, 1873

This legislation was the work of the Lord Chancellor, Lord Selborne. It established one Supreme Court, divided into the High Court and the Court of Appeal. The courts of Queen's Bench, Common Pleas, Exchequer, Chancery, Admiralty, Probate (Wills), and Divorce, which had all been independent of each other, were to become three divisions of the High Court (Queen's Bench, Chancery and Admiralty, Probate and Divorce [wills, wives and wrecks]).

This Act was part of Gladstone's attempt to streamline institutions and to introduce administrative efficiency. However, Selborne's attempt to abolish double appeals was not successful and in 1876 appeals were allowed to the House of Lords.

Local government reform

One of Disraeli's last acts as Prime Minister, in 1868, was to set up a royal commission on sanitary matters. It reported in 1871 and recommended 'that the present fragmentary and confused Sanitary Law should be made uniform'. As a result, the Government passed the Local Government Act in 1871, which reorganised health administration under a Minister for Local Government.

In 1872, another act – the Public Health Act – established the Urban and Rural Sanitary Authorities responsible for public health in local areas. These were the forerunners of Urban and Rural District Councils.

Summary

Gladstone's First Administration was certainly responsible for wide-ranging reforms. Legislation such as the Local Government Act, the Supreme Court

1. Use the information on pages 260–264 to list those reforms which helped to move Britain towards a meritocracy. Then list those reforms aimed at pleasing a pressure group associated with the Liberal Party.

2. On balance, do you think the Gladstone Ministry was more concerned with creating a meritocracy than supporting the demands of Liberal pressure groups?

Give reasons to support your answer.

of Judicature Act, the Forster Elementary Education Act and Cardwell's Army reforms were all significant in improving the efficiency of the nation's institutions.

The Ballot Act went a considerable way to ensuring freedom of choice at elections. The Trade Union Act allowed trade unions to operate legally, while the Criminal Law Amendment Act attempted to allow those who still wished to work during an industrial dispute to go to work unmolested. Much of the legislation also bore the mark of pressure group demands for reform, such as the Universities Test Act, the Licensing Act, the Forster Education Act and the Trade Union Act.

However, the ministry is regarded as a landmark in the attack on privilege and the promotion of a meritocracy. The Irish Church Act, the abolition of purchase of army commissions, the Universities Test Act and the open competition for Home Civil Service posts all contributed to making Gladstone's First Administration a great reforming ministry. As E.J. Feuchtwanger states, in *Gladstone 1874 to 1898* (1995): 'In terms of legislative achievement the Government was to become one of the greatest of the 19th century and by far the most important of the four governments of which he was head.'

15.3 Why did the Liberal Party lose the 1874 general election?

Given E.J. Feuchtwanger's verdict of Gladstone's First Ministry, why did the Liberals lose the 1874 general election so convincingly, winning only 242 seats to 352 for the Conservatives?

Disraeli's leadership of the Conservative Party

At the time, many Liberals believed the pattern of politics of the previous 25 years would re-occur, with Liberal governments followed by a minority Conservative government for a short period. Disraeli signalled his unwillingness to follow this path when he declined office, in March 1873, after Gladstone had resigned over the Irish Universities Bill.

Tactically, Disraeli's refusal to take office allowed the Liberal Government to disintegrate between March 1873 and February 1874. By the time Gladstone resigned over a Cabinet disagreement on reducing military expenditure, the Liberals were fighting as much among themselves as against the Conservatives.

In addition, the Conservative Party had undergone considerable reorganisation since 1867. A National Union of Conservative Associations and a Central Office had been created under the guidance of Principal Agent J.E. Gorst. As a result, by 1874 the Conservatives had a highly effective electoral machine. Conservative chances were also enhanced by Disraeli's policy programme outlined in 1872 at Manchester and the Crystal Palace (see Chapter 16).

Alienation of important groups within the Liberal Party

Although the Administration was successful in passing many reforms, it also upset a considerable number of its own supporters. The National Education League was disappointed with the Forster Education Act and put up candidates against official Liberal candidates in the 1874 general election. In the election, 200 out of the 425 Liberal candidates were pledged to repeal

Forster's Act. The United Kingdom Alliance was disappointed with the Licensing Act and the New Model Unions were campaigning against a repeal of the Criminal Law Amendment Act.

Unlike 1868, when Gladstone was able to rally the Liberals with the slogan 'Justice for Ireland', his campaign slogan for 1874 – 'the abolition of income tax' – did not have the same effect.

Alienation of important sections of the electorate

The reforms passed by the Liberals had also upset important groups who could influence the outcome of the election. Landowners were suspicious of the possible impact of the Irish Land Act on property rights. They were able to persuade their tenants to vote Conservative. The Church of England was dismayed by the Irish Church Act and Universities Test Act, and the officer class and landowners by the attacks on privilege, in particular the abolition of the purchase of commissions.

According to Gladstone, the brewing interest also had an influence on the election. Having been forced into second place in a two-member constituency at Greenwich by a Conservative distiller called Boord, he exclaimed that 'we have been borne down in a torrent of gin and beer'. The brewing interest clearly had an influence on the Greenwich election, but its influence nationwide has been exaggerated.

Unpopularity of some policies

One important area of electoral discontent was Gladstone's imperial and foreign policy (see Chapter 18), which was decidedly unpopular. Disraeli exploited disquiet over the 'Alabama' affair and imperial issues to some effect in the election. There were also fears about indirect taxation. In 1871, Robert Lowe, the Chancellor of the Exchequer, unsuccessfully attempted to place an indirect tax of ½d on a packet of matches.

The ministry was also plagued by a number of scandals, including the controversial appointment of Sir Robert Collier to the Privy Council and a Cambridge graduate to the parish of Ewelme, Oxfordshire (a parish reserved for Oxford graduates). However, the most important scandal involved irregularities at the Post Office in the summer of 1873. The scandal led to the dismissal of the Postmaster-General and a Cabinet reshuffle.

The most significant problem was the Irish Universities Bill of 1873, which created such an outcry that it led, temporarily, to Gladstone's removal from office. The ministry never really recovered from this crisis.

1. Which of the reasons for Liberal defeat in 1874 mentioned above were outside Gladstone's immediate control?

2. 'The Liberal Party lost the 1874 general election because it upset sections of the electorate.' Using the evidence contained in this section, do you agree with this statement? Give reasons to support your answer.

The rise of the Home Rule Party in Ireland

Following its formation as the Home Government Association in 1870, the party grew rapidly capturing 58 seats in the 1874 election, mainly at the expense of Irish Liberals.

Summary

Gladstone lost the 1974 general election primarily because of problems within the Liberal Party itself and the alienation of large sections of the electorate. However, Disraeli and the Conservatives exploited Liberal difficulties very effectively.

Source-based questions: The general election of February 1874

SOURCE A

The signs of weakness multiply, and for some time have multiplied, upon the government, in the loss of control over the legislative action of the House of Lords, the diminution of the majority of the House of Commons without its natural compensation in increase of unity and discipline, and the almost unbroken series of defeats in [by]elections in the country.

From a letter from Gladstone to Lord Granville, the Foreign Secretary, 8 January 1874.

SOURCE B

As I sat opposite the Treasury Bench the Ministers reminded me of one of those marine landscapes not very uncommon on the coasts of south America. You behold a range of exhausted volcanoes. Not a flame flickers on a single pallid crest.

From a speech by Disraeli in April 1872 describing the Liberal Cabinet.

SOURCE C

When we look at the poll in the City of London, in Westminster, in Middlesex, in Surrey, in Liverpool, Manchester, Leeds and Sheffield, in the metropolitan boroughs and in the home counties, in all centres of middle-class industry, wealth and cultivation, we see one unmistakable fact, that the trading class, and the comfortable middle class has grown distinctly Conservative. The inference is unmistakable. The effective force of the middle class has grown for a season Conservative. The Conservative Party has become as much the middle-class party as the Liberals used to be.

This, then, appears to us the great lesson of the elections of 1874 that the middle classes have gone over to the enemy bag and baggage.

From 'The Conservative Reaction', published in The Fortnightly Review *after the election of 1874.*

SOURCE D

The underlying cause of the Liberal defeat was the simultaneous loss of working and middle-class voters. The working classes were disappointed because Liberal reform, for all its achievements, had not really changed their lot. The middle classes were alarmed not merely by what the Liberal Party had done, but by events such as the Paris Commune, which seemed to portend threats to all property and security in the future. The alienation of particular groups of Liberal activists meant that the Liberal Party could probably not realise its full voting potential.

From Democracy and Empire: British History 1865 to 1914 *by E.J. Feuchtwanger (1985).*

---

1. Study Source A.

How reliable is this source as an explanation for Liberal defeat in the general election of 1874?

2. Study Source B.

How, by his use of language and style, does Disraeli explain how the Liberal Government had 'run out of steam'?

3. Study Sources C and D.

How far do the sources agree on the reason for Liberal defeat in the 1874 election?

4. Use all the sources and your own knowledge to answer the following question:

'Do these sources provide a full explanation for the Liberal defeat in the 1874 general election?'

Give reasons to support your answer.

15.4 Gladstone and Chamberlain
A CASE STUDY IN HISTORICAL INTERPRETATION

In the history of the Liberal Party between 1868 and 1894 one of the dominant themes was the conflict between William Gladstone and Joseph Chamberlain over who should lead and direct the Party and what role the Government should play in the lives of its citizens. The conflict between the two politicians was a major factor behind the split in the Party over Irish Home Rule in 1886.

Radical Joe?

Gladstone and Chamberlain came from two very different social and political backgrounds. Gladstone was a High Churchman, born in 1809 into a rich Liverpool commercial family. He attended Eton and Oxford. Chamberlain was born in London in 1836. He was a nonconformist (a Unitarian) and did not attend university. Chamberlain made his commercial and political reputation in the West Midlands, centred on Birmingham. He represented a new kind of politician for mid-Victorian politics. Unlike Gladstone, he made his political reputation outside Parliament. Beginning with the Birmingham Liberal **Caucus**, he then founded and led the National Education League. From 1873 to 1876, he was Lord Mayor of Birmingham and was responsible for the complete urban renewal of the city. His use of the power of local city government to transform the water, lighting and housing of Birmingham made him a fervent supporter of the positive benefits of elected local government. In 1884, he put forward his Central Board Scheme, which he believed would solve the 'Irish problem': elected local government was what Ireland required, not Home Rule.

Caucus: A local party organisation made up of active, committed members.

To ensure that the Liberal Party should follow this path, Chamberlain was the driving force behind the creation of the National Liberal Federation of 1877. The aim of this body was to supply effective party organisation throughout the country. More importantly, it would decide Liberal Party policy, thus allowing radicals like Chamberlain to have a major influence on party affairs.

By 1877, it would seem that Chamberlain had laid the foundations for the success of his version of Liberalism. The Liberal organisation in the country was falling into the hands of radical Liberals like himself. After Gladstone's decision to resign the leadership of the Liberal Party in 1875, the Party was led by a Whig aristocrat, Lord Hartington. However, Gladstone's return from political retirement in 1876 to lead the Bulgarian Agitation against Disraeli's Near Eastern policies (see Chapter 18) allowed Gladstone to wrestle back control of the Party. The historian R.T. Shannon, in *Gladstone and the Bulgarian Agitation* (1963), described Gladstone's return from retirement as 'the ruin of radicalism'. It may not have ruined radicalism as such but it did thwart Chamberlain's chances of capturing the Liberal Party.

Although a member of Gladstone's Government from 1880 to 1885, as President of the Board of Trade, Chamberlain spent virtually the entire ministry at odds with the Prime Minister. Gladstone refused to consider Chamberlain's plans for elected county local government. Chamberlain was frustrated at Gladstone's preoccupation with Irish affairs and with what he saw as Gladstone's over-reliance on the Whigs.

In June 1885, in an unprecedented move, Chamberlain published his Radical or 'Unauthorised' Programme in which he stated his own version of radicalism. This included free schools, payment for MPs, **manhood suffrage**, compulsory land purchase to provide farm labourers with smallholdings and allotments, graduated property tax, reform of the House of

Manhood suffrage: The right of all adult males over 21 years to vote in elections.

Lords, triennial parliaments (elected every three years) and the end of the Church of England's role as the State Church. The aim of the programme was nothing less than an attempt to capture the policy-making platform of the Party. As Chamberlain wrote on 7 October 1885 in a letter to a Liberal minister, A.J. Mundella, 'we shall sweep the country with free education and allotments and the Tories will be smashed and the Whigs extinguished'.

While Chamberlain differed from Gladstone on the role of government in society, he also differed markedly on the importance of the British Empire. Chamberlain had been greatly influenced on this subject by a series of lectures in 1882 and 1883 by John Seeley, a noted Cambridge historian, entitled 'The Expansion of England'. Seeley claimed that the main theme of British history since the Norman Conquest had not been the gradual erosion of the power of the monarchy and the creation of parliamentary government. Instead, he said that the main theme of British history had been the creation of the world's largest empire. Seeley also contended that unless the British Empire was strengthened it was likely to lose its world power status to rising states such as the USA and the Russian Empire in the early 20th century. To Chamberlain, Irish Home Rule threatened to split the mother country of the Empire apart. As a result, he was honour bound to oppose it.

Chamberlain was, therefore, both a radical and an imperialist. He was a social imperialist, a politician who advocated widespread social reform at home, in order to strengthen the 'mother country' and support imperial expansion abroad.

'The People's William'?

To many contemporaries, Chamberlain seemed like a politician in a hurry to implement change. Gladstone, on the other hand, was thought to be approaching the end of his political career. Unfortunately for them, many politicians incorrectly predicted Gladstone's retirement. This is not surprising. In 1874, Gladstone was 65 years old. Very few people at that time would have thought Gladstone would still be Prime Minister 20 years later!

Gladstone's retirement from public life seemed to have happened in 1875, when he resigned as Liberal leader. However, he did not resign his seat at Greenwich. What frustrated many of his colleagues was Gladstone's insistence, on a number of occasions, that his involvement in politics was associated with one issue. From 1876 to 1880, it was hostility to Disraeli's foreign and imperial policies. During his Second Ministry, it was Ireland. After 1886, it was Irish Home Rule. Even after he had retired as an MP, Gladstone returned in 1896, at the age of 87, to lead a campaign against Turkish atrocities in Armenia!

To the end of his political career, Gladstone maintained his support for the fundamental principles that had underpinned his commitment to Liberalism since the 1850s: free trade, administrative efficiency, the minimalist state and a peaceful foreign policy ('Peace, Retrenchment and Reform'). Indeed, he resigned as Prime Minister in 1894 in opposition to increases in naval expenditure. Was Gladstone therefore 'the ruin of radicalism', as suggested by R.T. Shannon? Was he the politician who split the Liberal Party over Irish Home Rule in 1886; or did he help unite the Liberal Party and lead it to victory in 1868, 1880, 1886 and 1892?

As a politician who had been involved in the formative stages of the Liberal Party, Gladstone possessed considerable support within the party. In addition to the middle-class supporters of liberalism within the electorate, Gladstone's name was directly linked to the achievement of free trade and the economic boom with which it was associated. From the mid-1860s, he also became associated with the extension of the right to vote to skilled workers. By the time he became Prime Minister, he had already gained a national reputation as a statesman and politician: the 'People's William'. Therefore, whenever Gladstone supported a particular policy his standing in the Party and the country was sufficient to gain mass support.

Gladstone realised, perhaps more than any other politician, the diverse nature of the Liberal Party and its capacity to split into competing groups. Between 1859 and 1895, each Liberal Administration had fallen from power because of internal divisions. To hold the different aspects of the Liberal Party together, Gladstone believed that a single issue, which contained clearly defined Liberal principles, should be used to force unity on the party at election times. In 1868, Gladstone used the rallying cry of 'Justice for Ireland', in 1874 'Abolition of Income Tax', in 1880 'Anti-Beaconsfieldism' (opposition to Conservative foreign policy) and in 1886 and 1892 'Irish Home Rule'. It is true that Gladstone did lead the Party to stunning victories in 1868 and 1880. Yet, in 1886, his decision to support Irish Home Rule split the Liberal Party in two. Although Round Table Conferences took place between the two factions (Gladstonians and Liberal Unionists) in 1887, unity was never restored. After 1895, the Conservatives and Liberal Unionists 'fused' to become the Unionist Party.

Gladstone, Chamberlain and the split of 1886

Which of these differences help to explain why Chamberlain crossed the floor of the House of Commons during the Home Rule debate in 1886 to join 92 of his Liberal colleagues as the Liberal Unionist faction supporting the Conservatives? Chamberlain's decision seems somewhat odd in the sense that most of the Liberal Unionists were the Whigs he had been attacking over the previous decade. Secondly, by crossing the floor (see page 389) he helped split his own radical supporters. Those radicals who became Liberal Unionists were mainly from the West Midlands (Chamberlain's own power base).

Since 1886, historians have produced several explanations for Chamberlain's action. Many cite his personal dislike of Gladstone and his frustration with the Liberal leader over issues such as elected county local government. With the formation of his Third Ministry in 1886, Gladstone had attempted to reduce the ministerial salary of Jesse Collings (Chamberlain's closest political supporter) from £1,500 to £1,200. Others point to Chamberlain's ambition to reach the top in politics by whatever method. With Gladstone coming to an end of his political career, a split in the Liberal Party could speed up this development with Chamberlain eventually taking over as leader of a reunified party.

However, Chamberlain's main reason lay with his belief that Irish Home Rule would split the United Kingdom and damage the Empire at a particularly turbulent period of world history. Chamberlain, in the final analysis, was an imperialist first. His radicalism was as much to do with his fear of the rise of socialism as with a genuine attempt to improve the material wellbeing of the poor. As G. R. Searle notes, in *The Liberal Party, 1886 to 1929* (1992), the formation of the Social Democratic Federation in 1883 as Britain's first Marxist party alarmed Chamberlain as to the prospect of a British party similar to the German SPD threatening the Liberal Party's position. In this sense, he did foresee the threat of a labour party replacing the Liberals.

On the other hand, historians such as A.B. Cooke and J. Vincent, in *The Governing Passion* (1974), see the split on Home Rule as part of a deliberate act by Gladstone to reassert his control of the Liberal Party. By 'ditching' Chamberlain and his immediate following, Gladstone was able to regain control. Although disagreeing with the timing and precise purpose of Gladstone's Irish policy, T.A. Jenkins – in *Gladstone, Whiggism and the Liberal Party* (1988) – believes the Liberal leader's actions are explained by his desire to lead the Party effectively.

1. In what ways did Gladstone and Chamberlain represent different types of Liberal?

2. Using the evidence contained in this section, who do you think was more responsible for causing the split in the Liberal Party in 1886, Gladstone or Chamberlain?

Give reasons to support your answer.

15.5 'A Ministry of Troubles': Gladstone's Second Ministry, 1880–1885

While Gladstone's First Ministry is associated with widespread reform, his Second Ministry is linked with crisis and conflict. Why?

Ireland

When Gladstone came to power, Ireland was in a state of considerable unrest. The Land War between peasants and landlords was in full swing. In Parliament, the Irish Home Rule Party led a campaign of obstruction that disrupted the working of the House of Commons so effectively that the Speaker, Henry Brand, introduced major reforms of procedure, which included the Closure and the Guillotine to bring debate to a vote. From 1880 to 1885, Ireland was in a state of almost permanent crisis.

Imperial and foreign affairs

Between 1880 and 1885, the Government faced serious crises in the Transvaal (1881), Egypt (1882), southern Africa (1884–85), the Sudan (1885) and a major crisis with Russia over Afghanistan, known as the Penjdeh incident (also in 1885 – see Chapter 18).

Gladstone's leadership

When Gladstone became Prime Minister in 1880, he claimed that his main aim was to reverse the costly and aggressive foreign and imperial policies associated with Disraeli's Conservative Government – what he termed 'Beaconsfieldism'. (Disraeli had been made Lord Beaconsfield in 1876.) As R.T. Shannon stated, in *The Crisis of Imperialism* (1976): 'Gladstone looked upon his return to office as a temporary expedient, a duty imposed on him to restore the natural and legitimate pre-1874 order but not obliging him to stay on after this had been achieved.'

Gladstone had no clear view of what he wanted to achieve as Prime Minister beyond this limited aim. Many Liberals thought he might take the opportunity of the 50th anniversary of his entry into Parliament, 1882, as a suitable time to retire. Instead, he continued as Prime Minister. As a result, the Government lacked firm leadership and direction, allowing divisions within the Liberal Party to surface. This worked to Gladstone's advantage. As H. Matthew notes, in *Gladstone* (1995), by suggesting that he intended to retire in the near future, Gladstone could always delay consideration of any major problem which required a long-term solution.

The conflict between Whig and Radical

The division between aristocratic Whig and Radical came to a head during the ministry. Gladstone upset the Radicals by filling his Cabinet with Whigs. There were nine Whigs compared with three Radicals (Bright, Chamberlain and Dilke). Whig representation in the Cabinet far outweighed their numerical support within the Party. Gladstone believed he was balancing the various factions of liberalism. Instead, he helped cause resentment among the Radical faction.

For most of the period, it seemed as though civil war had broken out between these two groups. Whigs favoured repression in Ireland, while the Radicals wanted reconciliation. When Gladstone introduced his Compensation for Disturbance Bill, in 1880, 60 Whig peers voted with the opposition. In imperial affairs, the Whigs were generally in favour of expansion of the Empire while the Radicals were against, although Chamberlain did support the acquisition of territory in southern Africa in 1885.

The crisis came to a head following Chamberlain's publication of the

Radical Programme in 1885. So, by the time Gladstone announced his support for Irish Home Rule in 1886, it was not surprising that a large number of Whigs were willing to desert Gladstone to form the Liberal Unionist faction.

The Bradlaugh Case

Charles Bradlaugh, an avowed atheist, was elected as Liberal MP for Northampton in 1880. He refused to take the religious oath which was necessary if he wished to sit in the House of Commons. The Evidence Amendment Acts of 1869 and 1870 and the Parliamentary Oaths Act, 1866, gave Bradlaugh the right to refuse. However, this right was refused by the Speaker after consultation with the Clerk of the House, Erskine May. A select committee was established. It rejected Bradlaugh's claim by the casting vote of the chairman. Bradlaugh stood for Parliament for Northampton on two further occasions, was re-elected and then refused entry to the Commons. Finally, in 1885, he was allowed to take his seat.

The reason this relatively minor issue caused so many problems for the Gladstone Administration was that it was used by a small group within the Conservative Party to launch attacks on the Conservative leadership in the House of Commons. Since the death of Disraeli, the Conservative Party had been led by Lord Salisbury in the Lords and Sir Stafford Northcote in the Commons. A group of young Conservative MPs, known as the 'Fourth Party' [The Liberals, Conservatives and Irish were the other three], comprising Randolph Churchill, Drummond Wolff, John Gorst and Arthur Balfour (Salisbury's nephew), were dissatisfied with Northcote's inability to exploit the ministry's problems for the benefit of the Conservatives. Although their opposition was not directed at Gladstone, their activities did disrupt Commons proceedings whenever Bradlaugh's case was discussed.

What were the achievements of Gladstone's Second Ministry?

- **Dealing with the Agricultural Depression**

  When Gladstone came to power, the country was in the grip of a major agricultural depression that had begun in the mid-1870s (see page 332). Pressure groups such as the Farmers' Alliance had hoped the Liberals would provide some security for tenant farmers against eviction.

  The Liberals did pass a number of reforms to aid tenant farmers. The Abolition of the Malt Tax, 1880, repealed the malt tax and replaced it with a tax on beer. This eased the tax burden on farmers who had to pay a tax on malted barley. The Ground Game Act, 1880, allowed tenant farmers to shoot hares and rabbits as a supplement to their diet. In 1883, the Agricultural Holdings Act made Disraeli's permissive legislation of 1875 compulsory. This gave tenant farmers extra security of tenure.

- **Irish reform (see Chapter 17)**

  The Administration passed the Land Act of 1881, which gave tenant farmers the three 'Fs' of free sale, fair rent and fixity of tenure. However, the most successful aspect of government policy was coercion from 1880–83, which helped to bring the Land War to an end.

- **Parliamentary reform**

  A major aim of radicals within the Party was the extension of the right to vote. Between 1883 and 1885, the Liberal Government passed three Acts making significant changes to the electoral system. These stand, along with the 1832 and 1867 Reform Bills, as milestones on the road towards parliamentary democracy.

In 1880, in spite of the Ballot Act of 1872, serious electoral corruption was uncovered which led the Government to pass the Corrupt and Illegal Practices Act in 1883. It laid down rigid rules for the conduct of parliamentary elections, including a strict limit on expenses by candidates and heavy penalties for bribery and intimidation of voters.

The most significant Act was the Representation of the People Act, 1884, which extended the right to vote. Approximately 2.6 million new voters were added to the electoral roll, increasing it from 3.1 million in 1883 to 5.7 million in 1885. The Act also applied to the entire United Kingdom, unlike in 1832 and 1867 when three separate reform bills had to be passed for England, Ireland and Scotland. In specific terms, it still defined the right to vote on property qualification but this was made the same for both borough (town) and county constituencies. However, there still remained seven ways of qualifying for the vote.

It would be an exaggeration to say that the Act gave the vote to all adult males. As the historian Neal Blewett points out, in *Peers, Parties and the People* (1972), about 40% of the adult male population remained without the vote until 1918. However, the Act did have a big impact on Ireland where the electorate grew from 220,000 to 740,000, helping the Irish Home Rule Party to gain over 75% of the Irish seats in the 1885 election (85 out of 103).

The proposals also caused considerable unease among Conservatives who believed the electoral changes would benefit the Liberals. As a result, Lord Salisbury opposed the Bill unless a separate bill to redistribute constituencies accompanied it.

A Redistribution of Seats Act followed, and was passed in May 1885, a month before the fall of the Government. Multi-member constituencies, like Gladstone's old seat at Greenwich, were phased out and the principle of constituencies with equal numbers of voters was introduced. This meant constituencies were much smaller, covering areas with either distinctly working-class electors (West Ham North or Woolwich) or areas with middle-class voters (Ealing, Kingston and Wandsworth). Boundary Commissioners were appointed to maintain equality between seats and to redistribute seats when the movement of population occurred.

These three acts were a considerable change to the electoral system. As H.J. Hanham states, in *The Reformed Electoral System in Great Britain, 1832 to 1914* (1968): 'The whole system of election had to be created afresh. The parties had to create new divisional associations and divisional office, to find new candidates, to help get new registers ready and generally to begin things anew.'

1. What were the main problems facing Gladstone in domestic affairs during his Second Ministry?

2. Which reform passed by Gladstone's Second Ministry do you regard as the most important?

For both questions, give reasons to support your answer.

Other reforms

The Liberals were also active in other areas. The Burials Act, 1880, was designed to please nonconformists who were now allowed to bury their dead in parish churchyards without any religious service. The Mundella Education Act, 1880, made elementary education compulsory and created the position of truancy officer to enforce attendance.

The Employers' Liability Act, 1880, was the first act to provide financial compensation of workers injured at work. In 1882, the Women's Property Act gave married women legal protection for their property. Before that date, on marrying, the husband gained legal possession of all his wife's property.

15.6 What impact did Gladstone have on late Victorian politics?

Protectionism: Policy of placing taxes on imported goods.

In *Gladstone 1874–1898* (1995), H. Matthew states that 'It is not difficult to see the latter part of Gladstone's public life as a failure: religion on the wane, the free-trade order giving way to militarism and **protectionism**, Britain bloated by imperial expansions, Home Rule unachieved, the Liberal Party divided.'

Is this an accurate assessment of Gladstone's career after 1868? It does seem to be rather harsh. Gladstone had been Prime Minister on four occasions. During his time in power, he had led governments that had done much to destroy the Anglican/landowning monopoly of political power. He passed a large number of reforms during his First Ministry, which attacked privilege and helped to establish a meritocracy. His Cabinets were the first to contain nonconformists (Bright in 1868 and Chamberlain in 1880) and a Catholic (Lord Ripon in 1886). In 1883 to 1886, he passed electoral reform which moved Britain closer towards manhood suffrage. Just at the time when he left office, in 1894, the Liberal Government passed the Parish Councils Act which extended elected local government down to village level in the counties.

On the other hand, Gladstone's decision to support Irish Home Rule split the Liberal Party in two and led to 20 years of Conservative domination of British politics.

Yet, as T.A. Jenkins suggests in *Gladstone, Whiggism and the Liberal Party* (1988), Gladstone's leadership may have split the Party in 1886 but it was also a major factor in holding the diverse elements of liberalism together in the years 1868 to 1886. As a politician who appealed to Radicals and Whigs alike, Gladstone had the unique ability of holding the Party together, winning power in 1868 and 1880. Gladstone deliberately balanced Whiggism and Radicalism, as shown in his choice of Cabinet Ministers in 1880. It could be said that without Gladstone the Liberal Party would not have stayed united for so long! Following his resignation as party leader in 1894, the Party was led, in turn, by Lord Rosebery (1894–96), William Harcourt (1896–98) and Sir Henry Campbell-Bannerman (1898–1908). None of them had the ability to lead and unify the Party as Gladstone had done before 1886.

As for Gladstone's ideas, free trade remained the central feature of economic policy until the First World War. It was the main reason for the Liberals' landslide success of 1906. Gladstone's support for the minimalist state survived until the rise of New Liberalism after 1908. However, Liberal support for Irish Home Rule remained a difficult and unpopular policy to defend.

The historian E.J. Feuchtwanger wrote in 1975: 'Gladstone was a towering figure in the Victorian age. The shape and the content of politics would have been quite different without him. Towards the end of his long public life there was a sense in which he had outlived himself, but the values he championed with such fervour have perennial validity.'

The Conservative Party of Disraeli and Salisbury, 1868–1895

16.1 Was Disraeli the founder of the modern Conservative Party?
16.2 To what extent did Disraeli's Second Ministry, 1874–1880, bring social and political change to Britain?
16.3 Why did the Conservatives lose the 1880 election?
16.4 Historical interpretation: Gladstone and Disraeli compared
16.5 How successful was Salisbury in domestic affairs between 1885 and 1892?
16.6 What impact did Disraeli and Salisbury have on late Victorian politics?

Key Issues

- *What contribution did Disraeli make to the development of the Conservative Party?*
- *To what extent did the Conservatives bring social and political change to Britain?*
- *Why were the Conservatives the dominant political party after 1886?*

Framework of Events

1867	Formation of National Union of Conservative and Constitutional Associations
1868	February: Disraeli succeeds 14th Earl of Derby as Conservative leader and Prime Minister after 29 years as MP
1870	Formation of Conservative Central Office
1872	January/February: Conservative meetings at Burghley House in a bid to replace Disraeli with 15th Earl of Derby 3 April: Speech at the Free Trade Hall, Manchester 24 June: Speech at the Crystal Palace, London. These speeches outline the main principles of Disraelian Conservatism.
1873	March: Disraeli refuses to form minority Conservative government following fall of the Gladstone Government over the Irish Universities Bill
1874	First Conservative leader to win a general election since Peel in 1841 Factory Act, Public Worship Regulation Act
1875	Public Health Act, Artisans Dwellings Act, Sale of Food and Drugs Act Conspiracy and Protection of Property Act, Employers and Workmen Act July: Beginning of Near Eastern Crisis November: Disraeli purchases shares in Suez Canal Company
1876	Merchant Shipping Act, Education Act, Enclosure Act August: Disraeli becomes the Earl of Beaconsfield
1877	Outbreak of Russo–Turkish War Start of agricultural depression
1878	Carnarvon and Derby resign from Cabinet over British policy in the Near Eastern Crisis Factory and Workshops Act, Epping Forest Act July: Treaty of Berlin Gorst resigns as Principal Agent – replaced by W.B. Skene Great Depression worsens with rise in unemployment
1879	Start of Land War in Ireland Crises in Zululand (southern Africa) and Afghanistan Gladstone's first Midlothian campaign

1880	March: Disraeli loses general election
1881	19 April: Disraeli dies. Leadership of Party assumed by Salisbury and Northcote
1882–84	Fourth Party attacks on Northcote's leadership
1883	Primrose League is formed
1884	Capt. Middleton becomes Principal Agent, coordinates Conservative organisation
1885	Salisbury forms First Ministry after June general election
1886	Crisis over Home Rule, Liberal Party splits and Salisbury wins general election to form his Second Ministry
1887	Randolph Churchill resigns as Chancellor of the Exchequer, thereby removing a major challenger to Salisbury's leadership
1888	County Councils Act
1892	Liberals form government with Irish Home Rule Party support
1895	Conservatives win election and Salisbury forms Third Ministry.

Overview

THE history of the Conservative Party between 1868 and 1895 is one of a major political institution adapting to change. This change took many forms. In the period 1850–73, there was considerable economic growth, in particular in manufacturing and commerce (see Chapter 13), but from 1873 to 1896 economic growth began to slow down with contemporaries calling the period the Great Depression (see Chapter 19).

There was also considerable social change. The population grew from 28.9 million in 1861 to 37.7 million in 1891. This was accompanied by a major shift in population from the countryside to towns. Between 1861 and 1901, the number of towns in England and Wales with populations over 50,000 rose from 37 to 75, and the proportion of the population living in urban areas rose from 36% to 45%.

After the passage of the 1867 Reform Act, the electorate increased by 1 million, with the vote being extended to skilled workers in urban areas. In 1884, the right to vote was extended further, by approximately 2 million, to include a majority of adult males.

All these changes affected the Conservative Party. Firstly, the Party had been seen, in particular after 1846, as the party of landowners. With the widening of the franchise and the social and economic transformation of Britain, the political, social and economic position of landowners came under threat.

Secondly, if the Conservative Party wished to remain a major political force it needed to widen its political appeal beyond the landowning classes who, after 1867 and 1884, were making up a smaller proportion of the electorate. Although the largest party in Britain from 1846 to 1859, the Conservatives had always been outvoted by a combination of Whigs, Liberals and Radicals. Between 1846 and 1868, although the Party had formed the government on three occasions (1851–52, 1858–59 and 1866–68), it had been in a minority.

Between 1868 and 1902, the Party was led by two very different personalities. Benjamin Disraeli was party leader from February 1868 until his death in 1881. Disraeli stands out as a unique character in 19th-century politics. He did not attend a public school or go to university. He was from a Jewish background, although he was a member of the Church of England. His wealth came from writing popular

Anti-Semitism: Against Jews or the Jewish religion (Judaism).

novels and from having married a rich widow. Unlike Robert Peel, who represented the factory-owning class, or Lord Salisbury, who represented the landowning class, Disraeli's position within the Party was based on his own talents as a parliamentary debater and orator. He was the classic outsider at a time when **anti-Semitism**, both in the Party and the country, was high.

Lord Salisbury led the Party from Disraeli's death (initially with Sir Stafford Northcote, 1881–85) until his own retirement in 1902. Although not as flamboyant as Disraeli, he can be regarded as the most successful leading politician of the century. A member of the Cecil family, who had been Elizabeth I's chief ministers, he strongly reflected the right of the aristocracy to rule, and was the last Prime Minister to govern from the House of Lords. He won four of the six general elections he fought – in 1885, 1886, 1895 and 1900. In 1885, he was only out of office for seven months.

By 1895, the Conservative Party, under these two leaders, had transformed its party organisation and broadened its electoral support to include important sections of the middle class (Villa Toryism). It had also changed from being a party that had formed brief minority governments into the dominant political party in Britain.

16.1 *Was Disraeli the founder of the modern Conservative Party?*

Of all the leaders of the 19th-century Conservative Party, Disraeli is the only one still regularly quoted by senior Conservative politicians. As John Walton wrote in his article in *History Review* 'Disraeli: Myth and Reality', 'no other politician has such an enduring popular aura; no other statesman can be relied on to influence the attitudes of voters a century or more beyond the grave'.

So, to what extent can Disraeli be regarded as the founder of the modern Conservative Party?

The case for

Party organisation

If a modern Conservative returned to the 1870s, he or she would recognise much of the party organisation and structure that had been established during Disraeli's leadership. The Party established organisations in response to the need to win votes from the new electorate following the passage of the 1867 Reform Act. A 'National Union of Conservative and Constitutional Associations' was founded in November 1867. Lord Blake, a leading historian of the Conservative Party, has called this 'the first centralised mass organisation to be formed by a British political party'. In 1870, J.E. Gorst was appointed the Party's Principal Agent and started to organise working men's associations and clubs, and registration societies. In the same year, Conservative Central Office was created, under the guidance of C.J. Keith-Falconer who worked closely with Gorst. From 1872 onwards, Central Office and the National Union were closely linked through a common headquarters and Gorst's position as agent and honorary secretary of the National Union.

This new organisation was an important factor behind the Conservatives' general election success in 1874 – its first since 1841. Sixty-five of the 74 Conservative gains in England and Wales occurred under the direction of active local associations.

Policy

In the period before Disraeli's leadership, the Conservative Party was known as a 'Little England' party, because of its opposition to furthering British interests abroad. After the famous policy speeches at Manchester and Crystal Palace in 1872, Disraeli firmly associated the Conservative Party with defence of the British Empire and British interests around the world. Since then, the Conservatives have been identified as the patriotic party.

More controversially, Disraeli is associated with the idea of 'One Nation' Conservatism, whereby the Party is thought to represent the interests of all the electorate rather than just one section of it. Some historians, such as P.R. Ghosh, claim a direct link between Disraeli's policies in government and the social comments on the idea of two nations – rich and poor – which he made in his novels of the 1840s, most notably *Sybil*. Other historians, however, such as Paul Smith, believe that Disraeli's policy of 'elevating the condition of the people' which he made in his 1872 speeches was of a more recent origin.

The idea of 'One Nation' Conservatism is closely linked to the belief that Disraeli was a supporter of 'Tory Democracy' – the idea that the Party was committed to aiding the poor and underprivileged of society. The social reforms of Disraeli's Second Ministry that dealt with a wide range of issues, such as factory reform, housing, public health and trade union reform, all seem to support this view.

This view of Disraeli, and his role in the Party's history, was first put forward forcibly by Lord Randolph Churchill during the mid-1880s and was supported by the Primrose League founded in Disraeli's memory. This important Conservative organisation was established in November 1883 and named after Disraeli's favourite flower. With slogans such as 'True Union of the Classes', its members regarded Disraeli as their inspiration. By 1891 the League's membership exceeded 1 million and by 1912, 2 million.

The case against

Disraeli's own views

Disraeli did not believe that the policy and organisational changes made under his leadership meant he was creating a new party. In 1880, he wrote to Lord Lytton stating 'they [the Tory Party] have existed for more than a century and a half as an organised political connection and having survived the loss of the American colonies, the first Napoleon and Lord Grey's Reform Act, they must not be snuffed out'.

Throughout his political life, Disraeli believed he was maintaining a long political tradition, not changing it. He always believed that he should defend the aristocratic and monarchic traditions of the country. In this respect, his support for a parliamentary reform act in 1867 and of social reforms were more to do with winning support for a party that defended this principle than anything new.

The views of historians

Although P.R. Ghosh argues, in *Style and Substance in Disraelian Social Reform* (1987), that Disraeli's Second Ministry (1874–80) marked the real beginning of a lasting Conservative willingness to pursue policies of social reform through legislation, most historians tend to play down Disraeli's commitment to social and economic change. Bruce Coleman, in *Conservatism and the Conservative Party in Nineteenth-Century Britain* (1988), states that 'Disraeli, like other Conservatives, had seized the plentiful opportunities offered by Gladstone's First Ministry, but he did little to reshape Conservatism significantly in either thought or policy. In so many respects it is the continuity and traditionalism of Disraeli's ministry that stands out, not any new departure.'

1. In what ways did the organisation and policies of the Conservative Party change after 1868?

2. Which of the two cases mentioned above – 'for' and 'against' – do you find most convincing? Give reasons to support your answer.

The Conservative Party was simply adjusting naturally to the post-Palmerstonian situation and reasserting its traditional commitment to stability and security both at home and abroad, in contrast to what the Liberals seemed to offer. This view is echoed by John Walton who regards Disraeli's skills in presentation, through speeches and style, as a greater contribution to the development of the Party than his changes in policy. In this sense, Disraeli is more like a modern politician than a politician associated with a particular set of policies. He was prepared to adopt the policies necessary in order to win power so that he could preserve the privileged position of the monarchy, the aristocracy and the Church of England.

As John Vincent noted in his short biography of Disraeli, in *Modern History Review*, in 1975: 'He left the Tory Party very much as he found it. Below the surface, changes were taking place that were to turn the Tories from the "country party" of the squires into the Party of business, the residential suburbs and the genteel south-east.'

16.2 To what extent did Disraeli's Second Ministry, 1874–1880, bring social and political change to Britain?

Introduction

Disraeli's First Ministry had lasted from February to November 1868. He had succeeded the 14th Earl of Derby as party leader. During that ministry, the parliamentary reform acts for Ireland and Scotland and a Corrupt Practices Act were passed. Public executions were also abolished, mainly because of loss of life among the crowd at the execution of a **Fenian**, and a royal commission into sanitary laws was set up.

Fenian: A member of an Irish revolutionary movement formed among Irish immigrants in the USA in 1858 by James Stephens. The movement spread to Ireland in 1865. The name was derived from the *Fianna*, the legendary Irish heroes. The Fenians were largely responsible for awakening Gladstone to the urgency of the Irish problem.

Although he had arrived 'at the top of the greasy pole' of politics late in life, at 64, Disraeli was not safe from challenge as party leader. In 1872, at Burghley House, a group of leading Conservatives attempted to replace him with the 15th Earl of Derby. It was only because of Derby's reluctance that this challenge was not successful.

Disraeli's Cabinet on the formation of his Government in 1974 was the smallest between 1832 and 1916, with only 12 members. It was dominated by members of the aristocracy, with Lord Derby at the Foreign Office, Lord Carnarvon at the Colonial Office and Lord Salisbury at the India Office. In terms of domestic reform, the most important members were Richard Cross, the Home Secretary, George Sclater-Booth, President of the Local Government Board and Lord Sandon as Vice-President of the Privy Council.

According to Cross, the Home Secretary, Disraeli had no clear legislative programme on coming to office. E.J. Feuchtwanger, in *Democracy and Empire: British History 1865 to 1914* (1985) states: 'Not only was Disraeli disinclined and ill-equipped to hatch such a design, he knew that his victory owed much to a desire in the country for a quiet life.' Indeed, Disraeli had written to Cross: 'We came in on the principle of not harassing the country.'

How significant were Disraeli's domestic reforms?

Factory reform

In the 1874 general election, many Conservative candidates, particularly in Lancashire and Yorkshire, had openly supported the Nine Hours Movement pressure group. The 1874 Factory Act failed to meet the full demands of the Nine Hours Movement, although it did reduce the hours workers were forced to do in a day to 10 hours, allowing for a half-day on Saturday. This had a major impact on the development of team sports, such as football and rugby. Cross also set up a royal commission into factories. This led to the 1878 Factory and Workshops Act, which brought both factories and workshops under general government inspection.

Housing reform

The Artisans' Dwelling Act, 1875, was regarded as one of the most important Acts of the administration. It allowed local authorities to impose the compulsory purchase of slums deemed unhealthy and to oversee their replacement with planned housing. This was to be financed with government loans at low interest, but the houses were built by private enterprise. Disraeli referred to it as 'our chief measure'.

However, the Torrens Act of 1868, passed by the Liberals, would have covered similar ground if it had not been blocked by the House of Lords. The 1875 Act was also heavily influenced by pressure from the Charity Organisation Society and was supported by the Liberal Party. In addition, the Act was so hedged around with restrictions and so expensive to implement that it was little used. In 1879, Cross had to introduce an amending act to deal with the burden of excessive compensation costs, and even then the legislation proved largely ineffective. Apart from the celebrated case of Joseph Chamberlain in Birmingham, by 1881 only 10 out of 87 English and Welsh towns had taken any action under the Act.

Public health reform

George Sclater-Booth, whose exclusion from the Cabinet may suggest the low priority Disraeli gave to public health reforms, was responsible for the passage of the Public Health Act, 1875. This brought all previous legislation dealing with the subject under one Act. It also established a system of powers and checks on sewage and draining, public lavatories and cellar dwellings. The Sale of Food and Drugs Act, 1875, emerged from a report by a select committee of the House of Commons and laid down regulations about the adulteration of food. Its impact was reduced by the failure to compel local authorities to appoint analysts to assess adulteration. Similarly, the Rivers Pollution Act, 1875, failed to offer an adequate definition of pollution or ways of punishing polluters once these were identified.

Trade union reform

The Criminal Law Amendment Act, 1871, had aroused considerable opposition from the New Model Unions. The Liberals had already decided to change this legislation before they lost office. On coming to power the Conservatives passed the Conspiracy and Protection of Property Act, 1875, which allowed peaceful picketing.

The Conservatives also planned to introduce a Master and Servant Act, but this gave way to the Employers and Workmen Act, 1875. This Act recognised the relationship of employer and employee in a mature capitalist economy. It was the result of a royal commission set up by Richard Cross. The Act accepted that breaches of contract by employers and workmen should be treated as offences under civil law. Prior to the Act, employers could be tried under civil law and if found guilty were liable to a fine, whereas workmen could be tried under the Criminal Law, where, if found guilty, they could face both a fine and imprisonment.

As a result of this legislation, Disraeli declared that he had 'satisfactorily settled the position of labour for a generation'. Alexander MacDonald, a trade unionist, Liberal MP and member of the 1875 Royal Commission, was moved to declare that 'the Conservatives had done more for the working classes in six years than the Liberals had done in 50'. However, the historian Bruce Coleman believes that 'the considerations which persuaded Cross and Disraeli to take a major step in the reform of labour law seem to have been largely ones of electoral expediency'.

Education reform
Lord Sandon's Education Act, 1876, increased pressure on working-class parents to send their children to school by setting up School Attendance Committees. The motivation for such reform came from the Church of England whose schools, particularly in rural areas, were short of both pupils and income due to the competition from Board Schools, set up under the Forster Act of 1870.

Economic reforms
In 1874, the Chancellor of the Exchequer, Sir Stafford Northcote, reduced income tax, abolished duties on sugar and extended grants in aid for local authority expenditure on police and asylums. The following year, he established a Sinking Fund (see page 30) to reduce the National Debt. However, income tax was raised later in the ministry to meet the expense of the agricultural depression and colonial wars in South Africa.

In 1875, the Government passed the Friendly Societies Act, based on the findings of a royal commission set up by the Liberals. The Act attempted to establish the registration of societies and to improve their financial stability without involving any responsibility for the Government.

In the following year, the Merchant Shipping Act was passed, also based, in part, on the findings of a royal commission that had been set up by the Liberals in 1873. The driving force behind this legislation was the Liberal MP for Derby, Samuel Plimsoll. Intense pressure from shipping interests made the Conservatives reluctant legislators. Their Unseaworthy Ships Act, 1875, failed to produce any real change. Even the use of maximum load lines set out in the Merchant Shipping Act was not made compulsory.

Agricultural reforms
From 1875, British agriculture entered a period of depression (see Chapter 19). However, with the Conservative Party heavily influenced by the landlord interest, limited assistance was made to the rural community.

The Agricultural Holdings Act, 1875, was a measure supported enthusiastically by Disraeli. It was intended to extend to farmers in England something of the protection given to their Irish counterparts by the 1870 Land Act ensuring compensation for improvements. However, the Act was permissive, with landlords' rights preserved.

The Enclosures Act, 1876, helped to protect the remaining areas of common land, while an act of 1878 saved Epping Forest (north-east of London) from destruction.

In Ireland, by 1879, the agricultural depression had resulted in the outbreak of the Land War. Unlike Gladstone, Disraeli made no effort to solve Irish economic problems. However, in 1878, an Intermediate Education Act was passed giving schools the right to receive surplus funds created by the Irish Church Act, 1869. In the same year, the Irish Secretary, Lord Lowther, passed an Act creating the Royal University of Ireland.

By 1880, much of Great Britain and Ireland were suffering the adverse effects of a succession of wet summers and falling prices for agricultural goods. Yet the Disraeli Government did virtually nothing to alleviate the problem.

Licensing reform
In response to the opposition from brewers and distillers to the Bruce Licensing Act, 1872, the Conservatives passed the Intoxicating Liquors Act, 1874. However, in some areas, the Act curtailed licensing hours even further and, in the end, pleased nobody.

Religious matters
Perhaps the most controversial legislation by the Conservative ministry was the Public Worship Regulation Act, 1874. Even before Disraeli took office,

Anglo-Catholicism: This was a movement within the Church of England which began at the University of Oxford in the 1830s and 1840s. Led by John Henry Newman, the 'Oxford Movement' – while denying the Pope's authority over the Church of England – wished to adopt Roman Catholic religious practices.

the Archbishop of Canterbury, Archibald Tait, was planning a campaign against 'ritualism' in the Church of England. This was the practice of adopting Roman Catholic forms of worship associated with the rise of '**Anglo-Catholicism**' within the Anglican Church. It was introduced by Tait in the House of Lords as a Private Member's bill, but received government backing. Although supported by the Queen, it outraged Anglo-Catholics in the Cabinet such as Hardy, Carnarvon and, above all, Salisbury. It helped to deepen the splits within the Anglican Church.

1. Which of the reforms passed by Disraeli's Second Ministry do you regard as the most successful in bringing either political or social change to Britain?

Give reasons to support your answer.

2. 'On balance, Disraeli's ministry cannot be regarded as a reforming administration.'

Using the information in this section, how far do you agree with this statement?

Summary

The reforms of Disraeli's Second Ministry have received a 'mixed press' from historians. Some historians, such as P.R. Ghosh, believe the changes to be very significant; others, such as Paul Smith and Bruce Coleman, take a more sceptical position. Overall, a number of features emerge.

- Firstly, many of the reforms were continuations of work begun by the preceding Liberal Government. Alterations to the laws on picketing, the law on friendly societies and merchant shipping law were all set in train by the Liberals. In addition, many other Acts, such as the Artisans' Dwellings Act, received Liberal support.
- Secondly, the Government introduced legislation to aid its supporters, such as the Education Act and Public Worship Act to defend the Church of England. Although the country was facing the effects of an agricultural depression after 1875, little was done to aid the farming community at the expense of the aristocracy.
- Finally, much of the legislation was permissive in character. Without compulsion, statutes such as the Agricultural Holdings Act, the Artisans' Dwellings Act and the Merchant Shipping Act, had a very limited impact. As historians P. Norton and A. Aughey, in *Conservatives and Conservatism* (1981), state, 'the reforms gave "self-help" an institutionalised push offering no opposition to established orthodoxies about the sanctity of property and the role of the state in the economy'.

Source-based questions: The Conservative Party

SOURCE A

'Gentlemen, I have referred to what I look upon as the first object of the Tory Party – namely, to maintain the institutions of the country, and reviewing what has occurred, and referring to the present temper of the times upon these subjects, I think the Tory Party, or, as I will venture to call it, the National Party, has everything to encourage it. Gentlemen, there is another and second great object of the Tory Party. If the first is to maintain the institutions of the country, the second is, in my opinion, to uphold the Empire of England. Gentlemen, another great object of the Tory Party, and one not inferior to the maintenance of the Empire, or the upholding of our institutions, is the elevation of the condition of the people.

From Disraeli's speech at the Crystal Palace, 24 June 1872.

SOURCE B

If the Tory Party is to continue to exist as a power in the State, it must become a popular party. The days are past when an exclusive class, however great its ability, wealth and energy, can command a majority of the electorate. The liberties and interests of the people at large are the only things which it is now possible to conserve: the rights of property, the Established Church, the House of Lords, and the Crown itself must be defended on the grounds that they are institutions necessary to the preservation of civil and religious liberties and securities for personal freedom. Unfortunately for Conservatism, its leaders belong solely to one class; they are a clique composed of members of the aristocracy.

From 'Conservative disorganisation', published in The Fortnightly Review, *1882*

SOURCE C

In 1865 the Conservatives' strength lay in England where 221 of their 294 MPs held seats, particularly in counties and small boroughs. Their representation even in counties was threatened by urban expansion. Yet their perilously narrow electoral base was to be modified in three ways. First, the Liberal hold on Scotland strengthened slightly, and on Wales greatly, while in Ireland the Home Rulers mopped up 80% of the seats after 1874. In this way the Conservative position as the English party was considerably accentuated. Second, the Liberals extended their base in the counties following the 1884 franchise reform. Thus, whereas in 1868 Conservatives had won 115 out of 154 English county seats, in 1885 they held only 105 out of 239; counties had become a key element in an overall Liberal majority. Conservatives were saved only by their growing support in large boroughs and suburban seats, which reached a climax in 1900 when they took 177 English boroughs as against 162 English counties.

From The Making of Modern British Politics 1867 to 1939 *by Martin Pugh, published in 1982.*

---

1. Study Sources A and B.

With reference to both sources, and to information contained within this chapter, explain the meaning of the two highlighted terms as they applied to Britain in the third quarter of the 19th century.

(a) 'the elevation of the condition of the people' (Source A)

(b) 'the Established Church' (Source B).

2. Study Source B.

How useful is this source to a historian writing about the Conservative Party in the 1870s?

3. Study Sources A and B.

How far are the authors of these sources in agreement on the aims of the Conservative Party?

4. Study all three sources and use information contained in this chapter.

To what extent had the Conservative Party become the 'National Party', as mentioned by Disraeli in Source A, in the years 1868 to 1895?

16.3 Why did the Conservatives lose the 1880 election?

In 1880, the Conservatives lost most of the seats newly won in 1874. Losses occurred in all types of constituency in all parts of the United Kingdom. Even Lancashire, where the Conservatives had made major gains in 1874, saw a swing to the Liberals. In all, the Conservative Party lost 100 seats. With a total of only 238 in the new House of Commons, the performance was worse than 1868 and the Conservatives were even in a minority in English seats. So why had the Party performed so badly?

The timing of the general election

A.B. Forwood, the leader of the Liverpool Conservatives, had advised Disraeli to call a general election immediately after the foreign policy triumph of the Treaty of Berlin, in 1878 (see Chapter 18). Instead, Disraeli continued in power, choosing to call the election in March 1880 after some favourable by-election results. These results proved to be misleading. In Liverpool, the Conservatives held a seat that the Liberals thought they might win. However, the Liberal share of the vote increased. In Southwark, London, the Conservatives won because the Liberal vote was split between a radical and a moderate.

Party organisation

The Liberal Party organisation had improved greatly since 1874. In 1877, Joseph Chamberlain had helped to establish the National Liberal Federation (NLF), giving the Party a national organisation for the first time. By the time of the 1880 general election, over 100 local Liberal organisations were affiliated to the NLF. Under the secretaryship of Francis Schnadhorst, the Liberal Party was able to fight an effective campaign.

In contrast, the Conservative Party organisation had deteriorated. Gorst had resigned as Principal Agent in March 1878. He was replaced by W.B. Skene, who proved to be entirely unsuitable for the post. During the campaign, he was criticised for his incompetence and he resigned shortly after the defeat.

Disraeli's election campaign

Like the party organisation, Disraeli's election campaign was far from effective. Due to ill-health he had been elevated to the peerage, as the Earl of Beaconsfield, in 1876.

As a peer, he followed the custom that peers should not campaign in elections. His only involvement in the campaign was an attempt to make the problems in Ireland an election issue. In his place, the Leader of the Conservatives in the Commons, Sir Stafford Northcote, proved no match for the Liberal front bench team in electioneering.

Little was said on either side about future legislation. The Liberals suggested they might change land property law, which would attract the farming vote. The Farmers' Alliance, a pressure group of tenant farmers linked to the Liberal Party, was active in many rural constituencies and received pledges of support for almost 60 candidates, all of them Liberals.

The agricultural depression

From 1877 onwards, the country suffered a major agricultural depression (see Chapter 19). The import of cheap North American grain had led to a fall in corn prices, while a partial potato famine had caused major problems in Ireland (see Chapter 17).

The Conservatives lost 25 English county seats, reflecting the effects of the depression. Disraeli noted, 'Hard times, as far as I can recollect, has been our foe and certainly it is the cause of our downfall.'

The effects of the depression led to the formation of the Farmers' Alliance, in 1879, which campaigned against the Conservatives and was a major reason for the loss of at least 19 seats.

The 'Great Depression'

From 1873, like most other European economies, the rate of growth in the British economy slowed down – what contemporaries referred to as the 'Great Depression' (see Chapter 19). In Britain, the depression led to a fall in real wages. Real wages fell by 5% between 1873 and 1879. The average level of unemployment rose from 1%–2% in 1871–74 to 6%–8% in 1878 and 11.4% in 1879. Although the Great Depression was not the result of Conservative policies, the Government suffered adversely at the polls because of its impact.

Imperial issues

In his two Midlothian campaigns of 1879 and 1880, Gladstone concentrated his attack on the Conservatives by criticising Disraeli's imperial policy (see Chapter 18). He attacked 'Beaconsfieldism', which he regarded as an aggressive and expensive foreign and imperial policy that was not in Britain's interest. Gladstone criticised the terms of the Treaty of Berlin because Disraeli had committed Britain to the defence of Turkey's Asiatic territory. He also attacked the foreign wars in Afghanistan and southern Africa, which he called pointless and barbarous.

1. Of the reasons mentioned above which one can be regarded as a political reason and which one can be regarded as economic?

2. Which of the reasons mentioned above do you think was the most important in causing the Conservative defeat at the 1880 general election? Give reasons to support your answer.

Rise in taxation

Although Northcote had been able to reduce income tax in 1874, the wars in Afghanistan and southern Africa had led to a rise in expenditure. This forced the Government to increase income tax from 2 pence in the pound (£) in 1874 to 5 pence in the pound in 1880. (See Glossary on page 142.)

The absence of 'sectionalism' in the Liberal Party

Unlike the period 1873–74, the Liberal Party had overcome the problem of internal disunity by 1880. Nonconformists, who had deserted the Party over educational issues in 1874, supported Gladstone's attack on Beaconsfieldism. Trade unionists who had disliked the Criminal Law Amendment Act, 1871, were now satisfied with the Conservative trade union laws and, rather ironically, returned to support the Liberals.

16.4 Gladstone and Disraeli compared

A CASE STUDY IN HISTORICAL INTERPRETATION

Introduction

In British parliamentary history it would be difficult to find a more intense rivalry than that which developed between Disraeli and Gladstone. Disraeli referred to Gladstone as 'AV' (arch villain).

They first became opponents during the debate on the repeal of the Corn Laws, in 1845–46, when Gladstone supported Peel and Disraeli agricultural protection.

Following the Conservative split, Gladstone became a Peelite and Disraeli became the leading protectionist spokesman in the Commons.

Benjamin Disraeli (1804–1881)
Disraeli was a Tory MP from 1837. He became Conservative Leader of the Commons in 1851; was Chancellor of the Exchequer 1852, 1858–59; and became Prime Minister in 1867.

During the short-lived Conservative Ministry of 1851–52, it was Gladstone's attack on Disraeli's budget that led to the fall of the government. Following the fall of the Whig–Peelite coalition in 1855, the Earl of Derby approached Gladstone with the offer of the post of Chancellor of the Exchequer in a Conservative government. Gladstone declined the job because he refused to serve in any government containing Disraeli. The rivalry intensified during the reform debates of 1866–67 and during the Liberal Ministry of 1868–74. Perhaps the height of their rivalry came over foreign and imperial policy, between 1876 and 1880, with the Gladstone-led Bulgarian Agitation and his Midlothian campaigns.

Did Gladstone and Disraeli differ on policy or were they merely rivals for power?

	Gladstone	***Disraeli***
The role of the State	Gladstone believed the idea of the 'minimalist' state, keeping government intervention to a minimum. His support for '*laissez-faire*' policies covered trade, taxation and the role of government in society. Forster's Education Act, 1870, the Local Government Act, 1871, and the Licensing Act, 1872, all emphasise the importance of local decision making.	In a study of the domestic legislation of 1874–80 it is clear that Disraeli also supported a *laissez-faire* attitude to government regulation. Much of the legislation passed was permissive in character (e.g. the Artisans' Dwellings Act, 1875). The idea that Disraeli championed the cause of social improvement, in direct contrast to Gladstone, is difficult to support.
Taxation	Throughout his career, Gladstone tried to reduce taxation, cut public spending (retrenchment) and restrict defence spending. During his periods as Chancellor of the Exchequer, 1852–55 and 1859–65, there was a major reduction in taxes, in particular indirect taxes such as customs duties, paving the way for Britain to become a free trade nation. In the 1874 general election, he campaigned for the abolition of income tax.	Disraeli was Chancellor of the Exchequer in 1851–52 and again in 1858–59. He lacked Gladstone's expertise in finance but did believe in the importance of low taxation. His appointment, in 1874, of Sir Stafford Northcote to the Treasury and the retrenchment-minded G. Gathorne-Hardy to the War Office reinforce this view. Although his Second Ministry is noted for imperial expansion in southern Africa and Afghanistan, Disraeli was against both wars and abhorred the costs. His refusal to provide relief to those suffering distress during the agricultural depression after 1877 was due, in part, to his fear of raising taxation.
Trade	Throughout his political life – from his role as President of the Board of Trade in 1841–45 until his death – Gladstone was an advocate of free trade. His period at the Treasury in the 1850s and 1860s was a major factor in making Britain a free trade nation by 1865.	Disraeli rose to political prominence during the Corn Law debates of 1845–46 as a major defender of agricultural protection. However, following the defeat of his 1852 budget Disraeli, like the rest of the Conservative Party, abandoned protection and adopted free trade. Yet, during the agricultural depression in 1877, Disraeli did toy with the idea of re-imposing import taxes on grain.

	Gladstone	*Disraeli*
The Church of England	Although the leader of a party with a strong nonconformist element, Gladstone was a devout Anglican. He supported the branch of the Church of England known as Anglo-Catholicism, which supported the use of Roman Catholic style services. Religion was a central feature of Gladstone's life. He began his political career believing that the foundation stone of society should be the close link between the State and the Church of England, as stated in his 1838 book, *The State and its Relations with the Church*. In his later political life, however, he moved away from the idea of a State-supported Church. He was responsible for the passage of the Irish Church Disestablishment Act, 1869, and other legislation which helped remove the Anglican Church's privileged position in society.	In his speeches in 1872 at Manchester and the Crystal Palace, Disraeli emphasised his support for the Church of England. He opposed the Irish Church Disestablishment Act, 1869, and the University Tests Act, 1871, on religious grounds. During his Second Ministry, Sandon's Education Act, 1876, was designed specifically to aid the Church of England. However, Disraeli supported Archbishop Archibald Tait's attacks on ritualism (the name given to Anglo-Catholic religious practices) which was the aim behind the Public Worship Regulation Act of 1874. Also, unlike Gladstone, Disraeli always supported the position of the Church of England as the State Church.

1. How are Gladstone and Disraeli portrayed in this cartoon?

2. How reliable is this cartoon in its depiction of Gladstone and Disraeli?

Punch cartoon, August 1878, entitled 'A Bad Example'. Dr Punch (headmaster) is saying: 'What's all this? You, the two head boys of the school, throwing mud! You ought to be ashamed of yourselves!'

	Gladstone	Disraeli
The role of the aristocracy	Although head of a radical party, Gladstone believed in the natural governing right of the aristocracy. In his Cabinets of 1868–74 and 1880–85, he chose Whig aristocrats in numbers which far outweighed their numerical importance in the Party as a whole. However, towards the end of his political life, in 1893–94 Gladstone began campaigning for a reduction in the political power of the House of Lords.	In his 1872 speeches, Disraeli defended the position of the House of Lords and the role of the aristocracy in politics. In the 1867 Reform Act, Disraeli attempted to protect the power of Tory squires in rural constituencies with the maintenance of the 1832 freeholder franchise and the over-representation of county compared to borough seats. During his Second Ministry, although many social reforms were passed, none of them threatened the political or economic position of property or landed wealth.
Ireland	For most of his political career after 1868, Gladstone was associated with this issue (see Chapter 17). There has been much controversy about Gladstone's motives in Irish policy, but it is clear he spent considerable time on the issue and passed several significant reforms.	In contrast, Disraeli never visited Ireland and avoided the issue for much of his political career. In 1844, he referred to Ireland as having 'the worst executive in the world' but did nothing to alter it when he was in power in 1851–52, 1858–59 and 1866–68. During his First Ministry, in 1868, he was involved in subduing the Fenian movement and during Gladstone's First Ministry he defended the Anglican Church in Ireland and Irish landowners. In his own Second Ministry, the position of Irish Secretary was not given Cabinet rank, but Sir Michael Hicks-Beach and Lord Lowther, the Irish Secretaries, did pass some minor reforms (see Chapter 17) even though they did not deal with the land issue. Although he made an attempt to make Ireland an issue in the 1880 election, Disraeli had little positive involvement in Irish affairs. During the 1880 election, he described Home Rule as 'scarcely less disastrous than pestilence and famine'.
Foreign policy	There are considerable differences between Gladstone and Disraeli on foreign policy (see Chapter 18). Gladstone believed in using the Concert of Europe to maintain European peace. He supported the arbitration of international disputes such as the 'Alabama' Award and the Penjdeh incident. He also opposed an aggressive foreign policy, which was likely to increase government spending.	Disraeli strongly criticised Gladstone's foreign policy in 1872 and, according to the historian Richard Shannon, 'took up the mantle of **neo-Palmerstonianism**'. During his Second Ministry, he followed an active foreign policy during the Near Eastern Crisis of 1875–78.

Neo-Palmerstonianism: Following an aggressive foreign policy to defend Britain's interest, in the manner of Lord Palmerston.

	Gladstone	*Disraeli*
Imperial policy	During his First Ministry, Gladstone, and his Colonial Secretary to 1870, Lord Granville, were accused of trying to dismantle the British Empire. The withdrawal of British troops from New Zealand in 1869, the granting of self-government to Cape Colony in 1871 and the attempted sale of Gambia to France were all seen as part of this process. During his Second Ministry, however, Gladstone's Government invaded and occupied Egypt in 1882 and participated in the partition of west and southern Africa. These policies seem contradictory. Gladstone believed in 'freedom and voluntaryism' in imperial relations. Throughout his career he tried to create an association of self-governing nations held together by a common allegiance to the monarchy and a common language, history and tradition. This was to be limited to colonies that were governed by whites, such as Canada, the Austrialian colonies, New Zealand and Cape Colony. Gladstone's most important statement on the Empire came in September 1878, in 'England's Mission', an article in the periodical *Nineteenth Century*. Gladstone stated that Britain had a civilising mission to spread the benefits of English civilisation throughout the world. In this respect, British rule in India and Africa was for the benefits of the native inhabitants because Britain provided sound administration and enlightened government. He was, supposedly, opposed to aggressive, expansionist policies to enlarge the Empire. Hence his opposition to Beaconsfieldism in 1876 to 1880.	There has been debate about Disraeli's sincerity in imperial matters. However, since S.R. Stembridge's 'Disraeli and the Millstones' in the *Journal of British Studies* (1965) and F. Harcourt's 'Disraeli's Imperialism' in the *Historical Journal* (1981), it has now become accepted that he had consistent views about the importance of the Empire throughout his career. Although he showed little interest in Canada, the Australian colonies and New Zealand, the Empire, to Disraeli, was the commercial and military basis of Britain's claim to be a world power. At the centre of the Empire was India. He used troops from the British Indian Army in Abyssinia in 1867–68 and in Malta in 1878, during the Near Eastern Crisis. In contrast to Gladstone, Disraeli saw the Empire as a military machine. This helps explain why the Near Eastern Crisis was so important to Disraeli because of its impact on the sea route to India through the Suez Canal. Although in favour of a powerful Empire, Disraeli was not always in favour of imperial expansion. He opposed the war with the Zulus in 1879 and the conflict in Afghanistan. The fact that aggressive policies occurred during his Ministry was due to personal weakness by Disraeli not design.

1. Using the information contained above, write down those areas of policy where Gladstone and Disraeli were in general agreement.

2. Then write down where you think they disagreed.

3. Then explain how far you think this is an accurate assessment of Gladstone and Disraeli.

1. In what ways does this portrayal of Gladstone and Disraeli differ from the Punch *cartoon of 1878 (see page 287)?*

2. Hercules represents the British electorate in the general election campaign of 1880.

What choice does he face when choosing between Gladstone and Disraeli in the election?

Explain your answer.

Punch cartoon, 1880, entitled 'The Choice of Hercules'.

16.5 How successful was Salisbury in domestic affairs between 1885 and 1892?

Robert Arthur Talbot Gascoyne-Cecil, third Marquis of Salisbury (1830–1903)

Following Disraeli's death, the leadership of the Conservative Party passe to Lord Salisbury in the Lords and Sir Stafford Northcote in the Commons Throughout Gladstone's Second Ministry, Northcote's leadership wa criticised heavily by the group of Conservative backbench MPs known a the Fourth Party. By the time of the general election of 1885, Salisbury wa regarded as leader.

During Salisbury's period as Conservative leader, the Party became th dominant force in British politics and passed many significant reforms. Why

The Liberal split of 1886

The Home Rule crisis brought the Liberal dominance of mid-Victoria politics, which had lasted from 1859 to 1886, to an end. The crisis led t the creation of the Liberal Unionist Party, which supported th Conservatives throughout the period 1886–95. Led by Lord Hartingto this party contained a large number of Whigs and a group of radicals closely associated with Joseph Chamberlain.

Villa Toryism

There was a marked increase in middle-class support for the Conservative Party. The commercial classes, who had formed one of the pillars of Gladstonian Liberalism, were becoming disillusioned with many of the radical causes put forward by pressure groups associated with the Liberal Party, such as nonconformists and land reformers.

As middle-class suburbs developed around Victorian cities, the Conservatives began to win seats in urban areas. This trend was enhanced by the redistribution of seats in 1885, which created single-member constituencies.

Conservative Party organisation

The formation and popularity of the Primrose League after 1883 and the development of Conservative working men's clubs helped spread the electoral support for the Party. With the appointment of Captain Middleton as Principal Party Agent and his coordination of Conservative organisation after 1884, the Party gained an effective electioneering machine.

Imperialism

The Conservatives became associated with the main issues of the day, most notably imperial expansion. Although there was an influential group within the Liberal Party called the Liberal Imperialists, the Liberals were generally against the growth of the Empire.

'Angels in Marble': working-class Toryism

Although trade unionists supported the Liberal Party, the newly enfranchised voters of 1867 and 1884 had a significant pro-Conservative element. These groups were prominent in areas with large Irish Catholic minorities, such as northern Ireland, Lancashire and central Scotland. The anti-Catholic elements in these areas tended to vote Conservative. Towns with a large military and naval presence, such as Portsmouth, were attracted by the Party's policy on defence spending, while the Liberal Party's attachment to licensing reform meant a large proportion of the 'drinking masses' voted Conservative.

Finally, although the secret ballot had been introduced in 1872, the politics of deference (voting on the advice of your social superiors) continued to exist. Tenants on large estates and those in domestic service were most affected by this.

Domestic reforms, 1885–1892

- **Ireland** (see Chapter 17)

  Under the guidance of the Irish Secretary, A.J. Balfour, a policy of land purchase and coercion helped bring order to the Irish countryside through a policy termed 'Constructive Unionism ' or 'Killing Home Rule through Kindness'.

- **Labour reform**

  Against the background of the agricultural depression and high unemployment, which led to the Trafalgar Square Riots of 1887, the Salisbury Government passed a number of reforms. The Working Class Dwellings Act, 1885, extended the power of local authorities to remove slums. This was extended by the Housing of the Working Classes Act, 1890. The Labourers' Allotment Act, 1887, allowed labourers to achieve 'manly independence' by allowing local authorities to provide land for allotments. This was extended with the Small Holdings Act, 1892, where small plots of land were made available for agricultural labourers. The Mines Regulation Act, 1887, extended government regulation of the coalmining industry.

- **Education reform**

  The 1891 Education Act abolished school fees and was mainly due to the work of Joseph Chamberlain.

- **Local government reform**

  The most significant Act passed in this period was the County Councils Act, 1888. This extended the householder franchise from the towns to the countryside, creating 62 county councils directly elected by the ratepayers. Although a significant piece of legislation, its main aim was to pre-empt the Liberals introducing a more radical measure in the future. Considerable power was still left in the hands of JPs.

1. In what ways did Salisbury's Administration bring about social and political change?

2. Using the information in this section, how far was Salisbury's success as Prime Minister due to the split in the Liberal Party?

Summary

Although the legislative record for the period 1886–94 is slight compared with its immediate Liberal and Conservative predecessors, the changes brought about were not inconsiderable. Most benefited the farming community, not surprising as the Conservatives were the traditional party of the landowner. However, several reforms also benefited the farm labourer. To emphasise the priority given to farming matters a Board of Agriculture was established, in 1889, with a minister at its head.

16.6 *What impact did Disraeli and Salisbury have on late Victorian politics?*

Perhaps the biggest change in British politics in the period 1868 to 1895 was the revival in the fortunes of the Conservative Party. Much credit for this development has been given to Disraeli. Although historians such as Bruce Coleman believe Disraeli's contribution to this process has been exaggerated, Disraeli did play a major role. His policy speeches of 1872 laid the foundation for Conservative policy for the rest of the century. Perhaps more important was the myth of Disraeli, put forward by Randolph Churchill and the Primrose League, as the supporter of 'One Nation' Conservatism. It would seem that Disraeli's impact on the Conservative Party was greater after his death than during his lifetime.

Lord Salisbury, in terms of winning elections and length of time as Conservative leader, was more successful than Disraeli. However, his long-term impact on the Conservative Party was not as great as Disraeli's. According to Salisbury's biographer, Robert Taylor, 'it was Irish Home Rule that made Salisbury'. The split in the Liberal Party enabled Salisbury to occupy the centre ground in British politics. He became 'the safe pair of hands' on the ship of state which helped attract a large number of middle-class voters. By the time of his retirement from politics, in 1902, the Conservatives had become the party of the majority of the middle class.

Salisbury was also a very capable politician. Robert Taylor states that 'Far more than Disraeli, and even Gladstone, Salisbury was a shrewd, though unwilling, practitioner of the arts of party management'.

Under Salisbury's leadership party organisation was used effectively to

1. Who do you regard as the more successful as Conservative leader, Disraeli or Salisbury?

Give reasons to support your answer.

win new middle-class supporters through the Primrose League and working-class supporters through Conservative working men's clubs.

To become undisputed Conservative leader, Salisbury had to first overcome Sir Stafford Northcote. This he had achieved, partly through the actions of the 'Fourth Party', by 1885. Salisbury was fortunate to see the removal of the potential rivalry of the Party's rising star, Lord Randolph Churchill, in 1887, when the latter resigned from the post of Chancellor of the Exchequer on a minor matter. From 1887 to 1902, Salisbury was able to lead the Party without a clear rival.

Ireland and British politics, 1868–1894

Key Issues

- *Why was Ireland a major political issue in British politics in these years?*
- *How successful were British politicians in dealing with Irish problems?*
- *What impact did Ireland have on the British political system?*

Framework of Events

1801	Act of Union creating the United Kingdom of Great Britain and Ireland. Ireland loses its separate Parliament and is rewarded with 105 seats at Westminster
1829	Catholic emancipation, allowing Catholics to become MPs
1845–49	The Great Irish Potato Famine: 1 million Irish people die of disease and malnutrition and over 1.5 million emigrate, mainly to Britain and North America
1858	Foundation in USA of Fenian Brotherhood, committed to creation of an independent Irish Republic by violent means
1865–67	'The Fenian Outrages' – attempted uprising in Ireland; attempted invasion of Canada from the United States; terrorist attacks in England at Clerkenwell, London and Chester
1868	Gladstone wins the General Election, committed to the policy of 'pacifying Ireland'
1869	Irish Church Disestablishment Act
1870	Irish Land Act Protection of Property Act [coercion] Fenian prisoners released
1872	Ballot Act
1873	Irish Universities Bill
1875	Parnell enters Parliament as MP for Meath
1876	Irish 'obstruction' begins at Westminster
1879	'The New Departure' with Parnell linking the Irish-Americans in Clan Na Gael, the Land League and the Home Rule Party
1880	Gladstone wins General Election Parnell replaces William Shaw as leader of Home Rule Party
1881	The Second Land Act
1882	The 'Kilmainham Treaty' The Phoenix Park Murders Formation of National League by Parnell
1884	Third Parliamentary Reform Act increases the Irish electorate fourfold
1885	Gladstone loses election. Home Rule Party holds balance of power

1886	Gladstone converts to Home Rule
	Salisbury loses office
	First Home Rule Bill fails due to split in Liberal Party
1887	'Bloody Balfour', Crimes Act and Plan of Campaign
	Land Purchase Act
1887–89	'Parnellism and Crime' scandal
1890	Parnell forced to resign from leadership of Irish Home Rule Party. Party splits into pro- and anti-Parnellite factions
1891	Land Purchase Act
	Parnell dies
1892	Gladstone wins office with Irish Home Rule support
1893	Second Irish Home Rule Bill passes House of Commons but is defeated in House of Lords
1894	Gladstone retires from politics.

Using the information contained within this chapter, do you think north-east Ireland had little or no land war activism and the west of Ireland had the most land war activism? Give reasons to support your answer.

Ireland at the time of the Land War, 1879–1882

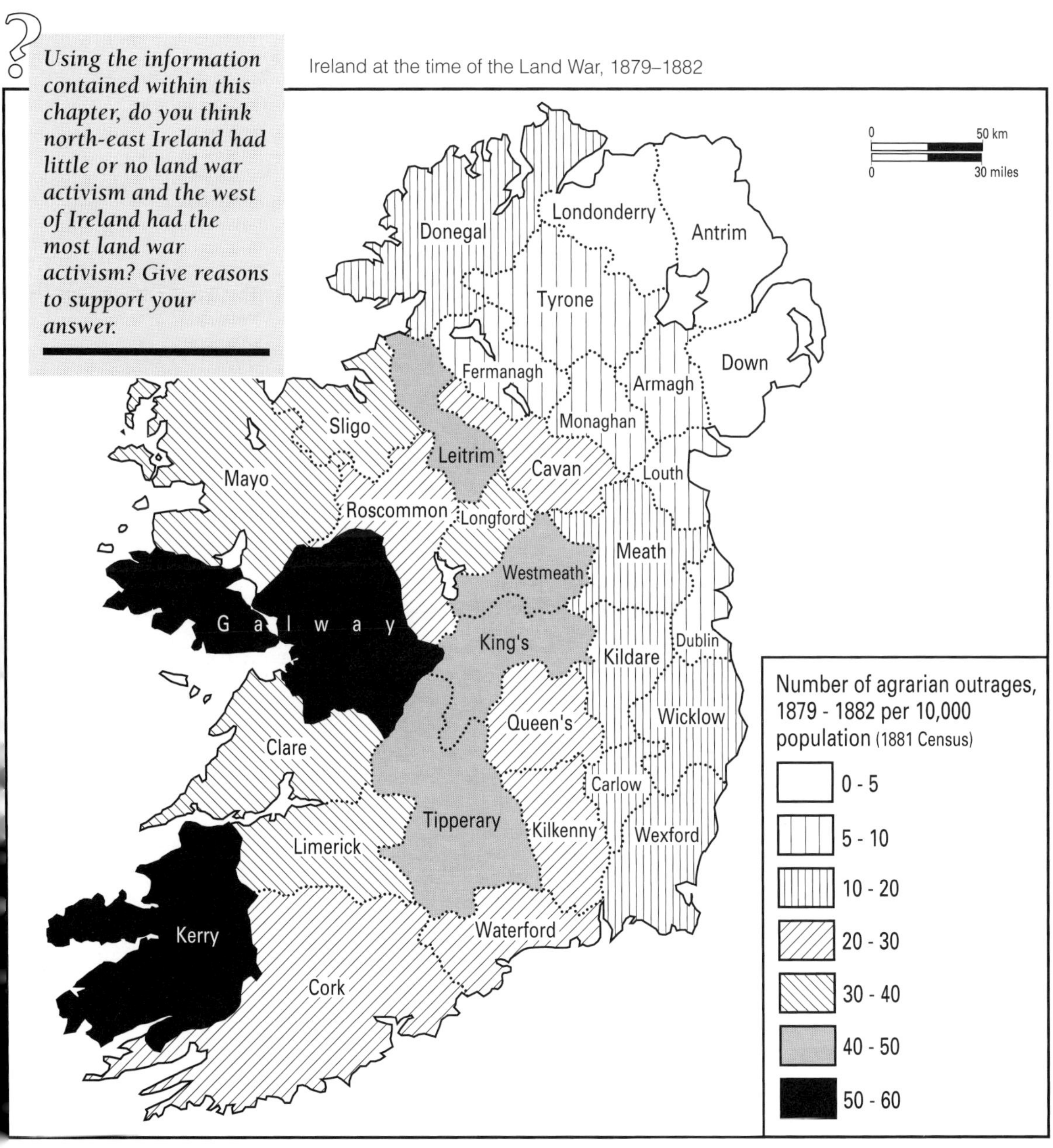

Overview

Of all the issues in British politics in the years 1868–94, Ireland proved to be the most controversial and far-reaching in its effects. Ireland was a major issue during Gladstone's first two ministries (1868–74 and 1880–85). In both ministries, Irish issues caused deep divisions in the Liberal Party. Once Gladstone had converted to the idea of Irish Home Rule in 1886, the Liberal Party split on the issue, paving the way for almost 20 years of Conservative dominance in British politics.

The 'Irish Question' involved four interrelated problems: religion, land tenure, law and order, and the political relationship between Britain and Ireland. Ultimately, after 1886, the last problem – in the form of Home Rule versus maintaining the union between Britain and Ireland – became the dominant aspect.

In 1868, Ireland was part of the United Kingdom of Great Britain and Ireland, as created by the Act of Union of 1800. As a result of that Act, Ireland had lost its own Parliament which had been dominated by the **Anglo-Irish Ascendancy**. In its place, Ireland was given 105 MPs at Westminster and a limited number of places in the House of Lords. On the other hand, the administration of Ireland, in part, continued to be based in Ireland, at Dublin Castle. Departments such as the Board of Works, Education and the Poor Law were based there. In charge of the Irish Administration was the Chief Secretary who usually held a post in the British Cabinet. The monarchy was represented in Ireland by the Lord Lieutenant, who resided in the Vice-Regal Lodge in Dublin.

Anglo-Irish Ascendancy: The social class who dominated Irish society. It comprised members of the Church of Ireland who were the main landowners and who dominated professions such as the law and the armed forces.

Between 1868 and 1894, the Irish problem was most closely associated with one British politician, William Gladstone. In all four of his ministries (1868–74, 1880–85, 1886 and 1892–94) Ireland was a dominant, if not *the* dominant issue. Since the 19th century, there has been considerable controversy among historians over Gladstone's motives for his Irish policies. Some historians, such as J. Hammond in *Gladstone and the Irish Nation* (1938), saw his policies as a genuine attempt to address Irish grievances. Others, such as D.A. Hamer in *Liberal Politics in the Age of Gladstone and Rosebery* (1972) and A.B. Cooke and J. Vincent in *The Governing Passion* (1974), have seen Gladstone pursuing policies that had more to do with ensuring Liberal Party unity and his position as Liberal leader than anything directly to do with solving Irish problems. The whole issue of Home Rule is a major area for studying alternative historical interpretations of one of the 19th century's most controversial issues.

An important factor in making Irish affairs occupy centre stage in British politics was the appearance of a new third force in party politics, the Irish Home Rule Party. Founded in 1870 as the Home Government Association the Party, from 1880 under the leadership of Charles Stewart Parnell, played a major role in ensuring Irish affairs were at the top of the political agenda. Throughout the 1880s, Parnell played a central role in British politics, particularly in 1885–86 when he had considerable influence over the creation of the Salisbury Conservative Government in 1885 and the Gladstone Government of 1886.

By 1894, the issue of Ireland in British politics had split the Liberal Party into two camps, Liberals and Liberal Unionists. It had seen the rise and, after 1890, the rapid fall in political stature of Parnell. The Irish issue had also realigned British politics on a pro- and anti-Home Rule basis for a future generation.

17.1 Why did Gladstone want to 'pacify Ireland'?

By 1868 Ireland, apart from the north-east area around Belfast, had not experienced an 'industrial revolution'. Most of the population lived in rural areas. In the west of Ireland, subsistence agriculture predominated. Between 1845 and 1849, the country had experienced a disastrous potato famine which had resulted in the deaths of approximately 1 million people and forced a further 1.5 million to emigrate, mainly to Britain, the USA and Canada. For the rest of the century, Ireland experienced a decline in population due to mass emigration. The population fell from 8 million in 1841 to 5 million in 1901. At times, rural areas were affected by unrest between the peasant population (through secret organisations known generally as Ribbonmen), and the landowning classes, the most influential of whom were English or Anglo-Irish nobility. By 1868, the rights of peasants who rented land – tenant right – was a major political issue.

In religion, Ireland was predominantly Roman Catholic (about 80%). Another 10% were nonconformists, situated mainly in north-east Ulster. The remaining population, 690,000 out of 5,700,000 according to the Census of 1861, were Anglicans, members of the Church of Ireland. This was the Established or State Church. This meant that it was supported by the tithe, a tax paid by the whole population, that its bishops were appointed by the monarch and it was controlled by Parliament. Some Church of Ireland bishops also had the right to sit in the House of Lords. This situation caused considerable resentment among both Catholics and nonconformists. This had mainly taken the form of opposition to the tithe. Although this problem had been solved, in part, by an Act of 1836 the established position of a church that was followed by only 10% of the population still caused considerable resentment.

The issues of land and religion both helped fuel Irish separatism. In 1858, the Fenian Brotherhood had been established in the USA with the aim of creating an independent Irish Republic by violent means. Between 1865 and 1868, a series of 'Fenian Outrages' occurred, including an attempted invasion of Canada from the USA (31 May 1866), an attempted uprising in Ireland (March 1867) and terrorist attacks in England at Chester (February 1867), Manchester (September 1867) and in Clerkenwell, London (December 1867).

How successful was Gladstone in dealing with Irish matters, 1868–1874?

Gladstone's aims

In November 1868, Gladstone had fought and won the general election under the slogan of 'Justice for Ireland'. The aim of his Irish policy was simple: 'our purpose and duty is to endeavour to draw a line between the Fenians and the people of Ireland, and make the people of Ireland indisposed to cross it'. He proceeded to introduce a series of proposals designed to encourage the majority of the Irish to accept the union of Britain and Ireland.

The Church Disestablishment Act, 1869

In 1869, the Liberal Government passed the Disestablishment of the Church of Ireland Act. Drafted by Gladstone himself, the Act ended the Church of Ireland's special status as a state church from 1 January 1871. Ecclesiastical courts were abolished and Anglican bishops had to be elected by **diocesan synods**. The property of the Church (valued at £16 million) was confiscated and £5 million was given as compensation to the Church, with £9 million being given to the Poor Law Board for poor relief. In addition, the government grant to the Roman Catholic college for training priests at Maynooth and the grant to nonconformists (the *Regium Donum*) were also abolished.

Diocesan synod: A diocese is an administrative area of the Church over which a bishop has control. A synod is a church assembly where representatives of the parishes within a diocese meet to discuss Church matters.

The proposal aroused strong opposition. Conservatives and Irish Anglicans believed it would weaken the Protestant Supremacy, the union of Church and State, and the rights of property. Benjamin Disraeli, the Conservative Party leader, declared that: 'We have legalised confiscation, we have consecrated sacrilege, we have condoned treason, we have destroyed churches.' Opposition in the House of Lords seemed likely to lead to a constitutional crisis, but the intervention of Queen Victoria ensured that, after minor amendment, the Act was given the Royal Assent on 26 July 1869.

Nevertheless, the Act did remove a major grievance and can be justly regarded as, perhaps, the most successful of Gladstone's Irish policies. The Act also raised hopes among nonconformist Liberals of the Liberation Society who saw it as the first step towards the disestablishment of the Church of England.

The Land Act, 1870

Another major aspect of Gladstone's attempt 'to pacify Ireland' was the Land Act of 1870. Many Irish farmers were 'tenants-at-will', subject to six months' notice, without any right to compensation for any improvements they might have made to the land. In the northern province of Ulster, a land custom (Ulster tenant right) allowed for compensation and the ability of a tenant to sell on his 'interest' in the property, a separate payment from that received by the landowner in rent. During the 1850s and 1860s, an Irish pressure group – the Irish Tenant League – advocated that tenants should benefit from the '3 Fs': free sale, fair rent and fixity of tenure. The Independent Irish Party supported this aim at Westminster in the 1850s.

To avoid setting any precedents for changing property rights elsewhere in the United Kingdom, Gladstone accepted the suggestion of George Campbell, a former judge in British India. This was to use the tradition of Ulster tenant right as the basis of land legislation. On 15 February 1870, the Land Act duly became law. Ulster custom was extended to the rest of Ireland, given the force of law, ensuring tenants compensation for improvements on eviction for any reason other than non-payment of rent. The 'John Bright' clauses of the Act allowed land purchase by tenants through a government grant of two-thirds of the price.

The Act enraged landowners who saw it as a challenge to property rights. It also fell far short of the '3 Fs' demanded by the Irish Tenant League. The amount of compensation depended upon the size of the farm and could not be more than £250. Fair rent was to be decided by magistrates (JPs) who were, invariably, landowners. From the onset of the agricultural depression in Ireland after 1877, evictions for non-payment of rent became commonplace, particularly in the West. This led to the Land War.

There was also a plan to include government support for the development of Irish railways and economic development for the Irish peasantry, but this was abandoned.

Coercion

The aim of the Church and Land Acts was to bring peace to Ireland and to reduce support for the Fenians. To further this aim, Gladstone released the remaining Fenian prisoners in 1870. With these measures Gladstone hoped that he would be able to prevent any disorder in Ireland where the Habeas Corpus Act was suspended four times between 1866 and 1868. However, due to rural disturbances in Ireland the Liberals found it necessary to introduce coercion. The Peace Preservation Act, in April 1870, and the Westmeath Act, in 1871, strengthened the authority of magistrates to arrest and detain persons suspected of disorder.

Irish Universities Bill, 1873

Unfortunately, the most conspicuous failure in Gladstone's Irish policy was the Irish Universities Bill of 1873, which led, temporarily, to the fall of his Government. Before 1873, Irish university education was limited to Trinity College, Dublin (an Anglican university, founded in 1591, although Catholics could attend from 1794) and the Queen's colleges of Dublin, Belfast and Cork, founded in 1845, by Sir Robert Peel. The Catholic Church objected to Peel's 'godless colleges' because of the lack of religious teaching. They demanded a Catholic university.

In February 1873, Gladstone proposed that the University of Dublin should be separated from Trinity College which, together with the Queen's colleges and a Catholic university, would provide university education. To avoid controversy, religion, philosophy and modern history would not be taught.

The Bill was opposed by supporters of Trinity College. Nonconformists objected to the State endowment of a Catholic university. Catholics opposed what they called 'miseducation'. The Catholic Archbishop of Dublin, Cardinal Cullen, denounced the proposals. Liberals, generally, disliked the 'gagging clauses' against certain subjects.

On 11 March 1873, the Government was defeated by three votes, with only 12 out of 105 Irish MPs voting for the proposal. Gladstone offered his resignation to the Queen, but Disraeli refused to form a minority Conservative administration.

Overall assessment of Gladstone's Irish policy, 1868–1874

Gladstone had removed the most conspicuous example of alien privilege by disestablishing the Church of Ireland. His Land Act was ingenious through its recognition of Irish custom, but it fell far short of what the Catholic bishops and the Tenant Right League felt was necessary. This helped to fuel the rise of the Irish Home Rule Party.

Gladstone was able to gain the release of the Fenian prisoners in December 1870. However, opposition to the creation of a Catholic university was due to the prevalent anti-Catholicism of the period (increased by the announcement of papal infallibility at the First Vatican Council in 1870 and the accusation of clerical interference at elections in the Keogh Judgement of 1872).

Gladstone had hoped to forge closer links with Ireland by establishing a permanent royal residence in Dublin, making the Prince of Wales Viceroy. This was suggested on several occasions between December 1870 and 1872. However, it was opposed by the Queen.

The historian F.S.L. Lyons, in *Ireland Since the Famine* (1971), stated:

> Gladstone's Irish legislation, though a long way short of revolutionary, had a symbolic significance far beyond its immediate effects. It signalled a fresh way of looking at Irish problems. It marked a new harmony between English liberalism and Irish Catholicism. Above all, it gave notice that the Protestant Ascendancy was no longer invulnerable.

1. Religion, land problems and the desire for Irish separatism all affected relations between Britain and Ireland.

Explain how each of these problems made the Irish Question a major problem.

2. Gladstone planned to 'pacify Ireland' when he came to power in 1868. How successful was he in dealing with Irish problems during his First Ministry?

17.2 Why was Ireland a major issue again by 1880?

In contrast to Gladstone, Disraeli and the Conservative Government after 1874 did not place a high priority on Irish affairs. The Chief Secretary for Ireland (Sir Michael Hicks-Beach until 1878 and then William Lowther) did not hold Cabinet rank. There were only minor reforms, such as the 1878 Intermediate Education Act, providing Irish schools with additional funds from the disendowment of the Church of Ireland and the creation of a Royal University of Ireland in 1879.

However, the period is significant because of the rapid rise in political importance of the Irish Home Rule Party and, within that party, of Charles Stewart Parnell.

Why did the Irish Home Rule Party develop so rapidly after 1870?

There had been a number of Irish political groupings at Westminster since the Act of Union, and within the restricted franchise after 1832. During the 1830s and 1840s, 'The Liberator', Daniel O'Connell (see page 90), had led a small group of Irish MPs, never numbering more than 30. In the 1840s, this group advocated the repeal of the Act of Union and the re-establishment of an Irish Parliament in Dublin. In the 1850s, another 'independent' Irish Party was formed to support the right of Irish tenant farmers and to defend the Catholic Church, but without much success.

Then in 1870, Isaac Butt, a Protestant lawyer who had defended Fenian suspects in court, formed the Home Government Association, campaigning for the right of the Irish people to self-government. This included the control of the Irish executive by an Irish Parliament. Originally a rather conservative association, the body quickly developed into a major focus for Irish nationalism. The Home Rule Party, as it became known, gained several seats in by-elections between 1870 and 1874, usually at the expense of Irish Liberals. Following the 1874 general election, the Party returned 57 MPs to Westminster.

Much has been made of the importance of the Ballot Act of 1872 in helping the rise of the Party. The Act clearly helped prevent landlord intimidation of the relatively small Irish electorate. However, support for the Home Rule Party had already begun to gain momentum, fuelled in part by dissatisfaction with the Land Act of 1870. The Ballot Act merely accelerated the growth of electoral support. Although the Party had made considerable electoral gains by 1874, it suffered from lack of unity and Isaac Butt's indecisive leadership.

In 1875, however, following a by-election victory in County Meath, the Home Rule Party discovered a future leader who would transform the fate of Irish nationalism: Charles Stewart Parnell, a Protestant landowner from County Wicklow.

Parnell's rise to power

Filibustering: The technique of using long speeches and delaying tactics to obstruct legislation.

Clan Na Gael: Founded in New York on 20 June 1867 by Jerome Collins and linked to the Fenian Brotherhood. The Supreme Council of the Fenian Brotherhood was recognised by Clan Na Gael as the provisional government of Ireland.

In 1875, a small group within the Home Rule Party, led by former Fenians Joseph Biggar and John O'Connor Power, began deliberately to obstruct and delay business in the House of Commons through **filibustering**. The aim was to highlight Irish grievances in the hope that Disraeli's Conservative Government would introduce Irish reform. It was to this group that Parnell attached himself and where he rose to be a formidable member of the parliamentary party. In 1876, he defended the Fenians who had attacked a prison van in Manchester in 1867 against claims by the Irish Chief Secretary that they were murderers. This helped Parnell forge links with the Fenian Brotherhood (also called the Irish Republican Brotherhood). Later that year, Parnell was chosen to conduct a fund-raising tour among Irish Americans in the USA. He was able to make contact with **Clan Na Gael**, a leading Irish-American group, and its leader, John Devoy. Finally, in 1877, he was chosen as leader of the Home Rule Association of Great Britain. By that date, Parnell had become the 'leader-in-waiting' of the Home Rule Party.

The Land War and the 'New Departure'

As Parnell was rising to political prominence, Irish affairs became a central issue again thanks to a depression in the Irish economy in the 1870s. A

Michael Davitt (1846–1906)
Born in County Mayo, Davitt emigrated to England and was crippled in an industrial accident. He was an early member of the Fenian Brotherhood. Following the failure of the 1867 Fenian rising in Ireland, he became involved in land issues, culminating in the formation of the Land League. Davitt became MP for Meath in 1882.

1. Why did Ireland become a major problem for British politicians in the years 1876–80?

2. Explain why Charles Stewart Parnell became an important figure in Irish politics in the years 1876–80.

succession of wet summers had seen the reappearance of potato blight and famine in parts of western Ireland. The production of potatoes dropped by 75% between 1876 and 1879. Agricultural prices began to fall as a result of the influx of cheap grain from North America. The prices of principal crops declined by £14 million between 1876 and 1879. In Connaught, the poorest and most westerly province of Ireland, matters were made worse by the outbreak of depression in British agriculture with the loss of migrant work on British farms. In these circumstances, landowners began to re-organise their farms into larger units to benefit from lower costs of production. To achieve this, they had to evict tenants. Many of these landowners were Catholic. In 1879, the worst year of the depression, about 1,000 families were evicted, mainly for this reason.

If Parnell became the focus of Irish nationalist hope in the Home Rule Party, Michael Davitt became the focus of Irish tenant hopes in the agricultural depression. At a meeting in Irishtown, County Mayo, on 19 April 1878, Davitt laid the foundations of what was to become the Land League, a well-organised pressure group which defended the interests of Irish tenants. Influenced by the radical ideas of James Finton Lalor, Davitt wished to see the nationalisation of land. With the development of the Land League came the reappearance of crimes against landlords in the Irish countryside by 'Ribbonmen' – the Land War of 1879–82.

It is against this background that a 'New Departure' in Irish nationalist politics occurred in October 1879. With the support of John Devoy and Clan Na Gael in the USA and the Fenians, Davitt and Parnell formed an Irish nationalist alliance. Parnell became President of the Irish National Land League, which called for lower rents and an end to evictions. Shortly after the General Election of 1880, Parnell replaced William Shaw (Butt had died in 1879) as leader of the Home Rule Party. For the first time since Daniel O'Connell's great triumph of Catholic emancipation in the late 1820s, Irish nationalism was united behind an effective, charismatic leader.

17.3 How successfully did Gladstone's Government deal with Ireland between 1880 and 1885?

Introduction

By the time Gladstone took office again in 1880, the rural areas of Ireland were becoming ungovernable. Although Disraeli's Government had set up a royal commission to study Irish problems, little had been done to address the underlying causes.

According to historian John Vincent, the Liberal leader did not have a clear policy towards Ireland in 1880 and had hardly mentioned Ireland in his famous **Midlothian campaigns** (1879–80). Yet during Gladstone's Second Administration, Ireland became the dominant domestic issue.

Midlothian campaigns (1879–80): Political campaigns undertaken by William Gladstone in the 18 months before the 1880 elections. Although they were aimed at winning the Midlothian seat for Gladstone, he used them to launch a nationwide attack on the Disraeli Government – in particular, on issues of foreign policy.

Concession and coercion, 1880–1881

During the period 1880–82, two individuals, apart from Gladstone, played a major role in forging Liberal policy towards Ireland: Parnell and W.E. Forster. In a negative sense, Parnell and the Home Rule Party forced Ireland into the forefront of the political agenda. Through parliamentary obstruction, the Irish brought the House of Commons' business to a standstill. For instance, on 2 February 1881, it took Speaker Brand, on his own authority, to end an Irish filibuster of 41 hours on the Irish Coercion Bill. As a result of Irish obstruction, the rules of debate and voting were changed radically.

The other major influence was Irish Chief Secretary, W.E. Forster (1880–82). Throughout this period, Forster consistently advocated coercion to break the Land League and to end the Land War.

In 1880, Gladstone attempted to pass a Compensation for Disturbance Bill to deal with the issue of eviction, but this was defeated in the House of Lords. In the autumn of 1880, on the advice of Erskine May, Clerk of the House of Commons, Gladstone introduced a new system of Grand Committees into the Commons to deal with English, Scottish and Irish legislation separately. This led to the reorganisation of the Irish government at Dublin Castle.

Forster introduced the most controversial policy following the trial, arrest and acquittal of Land League officials, in October 1880. In February 1881, Parliament passed Forster's Coercion Act [Crimes Act], which became law in March.

In association with the introduction of coercion, Gladstone accepted the recommendations of the Bessborough Commission into Irish land tenure and passed another Land Act in August 1881. This established a land court to fix 'fair rents' for a period of 15 years. In general, during this period of falling prices for agricultural goods, the land court reduced rents by 25% on average. Land Commissioners were also appointed to assist emigration and to advance three-quarters of the purchase money to tenants wishing to buy their farms. Overall, the Land Act gave the Irish peasant the '3 F's. In addition to fair rent, they were assured fixity of tenure and free sale.

The Kilmainham 'Treaty' and the Phoenix Park Murders, 1882

Although the Act helped to redress many of the shortcomings of the 1870 Land Act, Parnell and the Land League still advocated non-payment of rent and boycotted the Land Act, making it inoperable. As a result, in October 1882, Forster had Parnell, John Dillon and other Land League leaders arrested under the Coercion Act and placed in Kilmainham Gaol, Dublin. Forster also declared the Land League 'an illegal and criminal association'. In response, Parnell issued a 'No Rent Manifesto' from prison.

Gladstone, to break what seemed to be deadlock in Ireland, came to an arrangement with Parnell, through an intermediary, Captain O'Shea, in April 1882, without notifying Forster. By the so-called Kilmainham Treaty, Parnell and the other leaders would be released and arrears of rents would be cancelled in return for an assurance from Parnell that the Land War would end. When the 'treaty' was made public, both Forster and the Lord Lieutenant, Lord Cowper, resigned. Both wanted more severe coercion to smash the Land League.

Yet, just at the moment when stability seemed to be returning to Irish affairs, the new Chief Secretary, Lord Frederick Cavendish (a relation of Gladstone), with his Under-Secretary, Burke, were murdered by the Invincibles, a republican organisation, outside the Vice-Regal Lodge in Phoenix Park, Dublin. For a time, Parnell threatened to withdraw from political life.

In response to the crime, the Liberal Government passed a new Coercion Act (The Prevention of Crimes Act) which set up a special tribunal of three judges to try cases without juries. In addition, it gave JPs the authority to detain suspects and declare meetings illegal.

Why did Parnell become the undisputed leader of the Irish national movement by 1885?

During the later years of Gladstone's ministry, Parnell increased his power and influence over the Irish national movement. In October 1882, he reconstituted the Land League as the National League. The emphasis of this organisation was placed on the achievement of Home Rule rather than the nationalisation of land, as advocated by Michael Davitt. The change suggests that Parnell was a moderating, conservative force in nationalist politics. He adopted a political, constitutional path instead of the direct, radical action preferred by Davitt and the Land League.

In 1884, Parnell introduced 'the Pledge' to his party. All Home Rule MPs were now bound to act and vote together in Parliament. This meant that the Irish Party became the most disciplined in the Commons.

In the same year, the Gladstone Government passed the Third Reform Act, which extended the right to vote to labourers. Although this was an important reform in Great Britain, in Ireland it had the effect of enlarging the electorate by a considerable amount. In the general election of 1885, the Irish Party increased its representation to 86 seats – 85 of 105 seats in Ireland and the Scotland Road Division of Liverpool, a constituency with a large Irish immigrant community.

In addition, Parnell's instructions to the Irish Catholic immigrant community in Britain to support the Conservatives is estimated to have cost the Liberals 20 seats. This move was prompted by the suggestion, made by Lord Carnarvon, that the Conservatives might support Home Rule. With the Liberals remaining the largest party but with a reduced majority of 86 seats, Parnell and the Home Rule Party held the balance of power in the House of Commons, creating a truly three-party system.

As F.S.L. Lyons stated, in *Ireland Since the Famine* (1971): 'His [Parnell's] creation of a disciplined, efficient and pledge-bound parliamentary party, … by its performance at Westminster, offered a living proof that Ireland was ripe for self-government.'

1. Explain how Gladstone dealt with Irish problems during his Second Administration.

2. 'He did more harm than good to British–Irish relations.'

How far do you agree with this view of Charles Stewart Parnell in the years 1880–85?

17.4 Why did Gladstone convert to Irish Home Rule in 1886?

A CASE STUDY IN HISTORICAL INTERPRETATION

W.E. Gladstone's decision to 'convert' to the idea of Home Rule for Ireland is, perhaps, the most important political event in the domestic history of Britain in the second half of the 19th century.

Gladstone's conversion split the Liberal Party in 1886 between Gladstonian Liberals (the majority) and Liberal Unionists (93 MPs) led by Lord Hartington (the future Duke of Devonshire) and Joseph Chamberlain. The Liberal Unionists 'crossed' the floor of the House of Commons during the First Home Rule debate and voted with the Conservative opposition, in order to bring down the Gladstone Government. After the 1895 general election, there was a 'merger' of the two parties. It could be argued that from 1846 to 1886 the Whig–Liberal Party dominated British politics. From 1886 to 1905, the Conservatives, with Liberal Unionist support, were the dominant force.

Was Gladstone a genuine Irish reformer?

Since 1886, there has been considerable debate among historians as to why Gladstone took such an important political decision – a decision made more controversial by the manner in which it was announced. Gladstone's son, Herbert, leaked his father's decision to the *Leeds Mercury* in a spectacular newspaper scoop usually referred to as the 'Hawarden Kite', after Gladstone's country home in North Wales.

According to historian J.L. Hammond, in *Gladstone and the Irish Nation*, first published in 1938, Gladstone had decided that Home Rule for Ireland was necessary because it was the logical culmination of his search for a lasting settlement to the problems of British–Irish relations. According to Hammond,

Gladstone had declared in 1868 that his mission was 'to pacify Ireland'. During his First Ministry (1868–74), he attempted to solve religious problems (Church Act, 1869), land problems (Land Act, 1870) and the universities issue (Universities Bill, 1873). These were seen by Hammond as part of a coherent programme to deal with Irish affairs.

When Gladstone returned to office in 1880, he continued the work of his First Ministry with more land reform (Second Land Act, 1881). However, he was 'forced' towards the Home Rule solution by the actions of Parnell and the Home Rule Party during the 1880–85 period. By 1886, Gladstone had come to the conclusion that Home Rule was the only conceivable long-term answer to the Irish Question. This traditionalist view sees Gladstone as a politician with a genuine interest in solving what he saw as legitimate Irish grievances and follows a line of argument common to liberal historians as far back as Gladstone's contemporary biographer, John Morley.

Other historians, however, have seen Gladstone's conversion as part of a general development of a Gladstonian philosophy on nationality and not something unique to Ireland. E.D. Steele, in an article entitled 'Gladstone and Ireland' in *Irish Historical Studies* (1970), suggested that Gladstone's support for national self-determination among white, Christian peoples had begun as far back as 1850 after a visit to liberal friends in the Kingdom of Naples. From that date, he became an ardent supporter of Italian unification. This concept was reinforced by his period as High Commissioner to the Greek-populated Ionian Islands in 1858 where Gladstone was appointed after serious rioting against British rule on the island of Corfu. During his time as High Commissioner, he became convinced that union with Greece was the most effective answer to the problem. In the debate on the future of the British protectorate over the islands, in 1863, Gladstone was the main sponsor for the islands' union with the Greek kingdom.

In 1876–77, this view on national self-determination was taken a stage further with the publication of his pamphlet 'The Bulgarian Horrors and the Question of the East'. In it he advocated the granting of independence to the Balkan peoples of the Ottoman (Turkish) empire.

This view was reinforced, according to historian R.T. Shannon, in *Crisis of Imperialism* (1976), when Gladstone visited the Kingdom of Norway-Sweden in 1883, on a summer holiday. In that kingdom, the Norwegians accepted rule by the Swedish King in return for a large measure of home rule. The stability of the kingdom impressed Gladstone, who then began to see Home Rule as a possible lasting solution to British–Irish relations.

After 1885, Gladstone received positive proof that the Irish people desired Home Rule. Following the Third Reform Act of 1884, the Irish electorate increased fourfold and in the subsequent general election of 1885 the Home Rule Party increased its seats to 86. Only north-east Ulster was against Home Rule. Therefore, by July 1886, Gladstone had clear evidence to support the case for Irish Home Rule.

Perhaps the precise timing of the Home Rule 'conversion', in early 1886, can be explained, in part, by James Loughlin's observations in *Gladstone, Home Rule and the Ulster Question, 1882–1893* (1986). According to Loughlin, a major influence on Gladstone's decision was a report on the Irish situation by James Bryce made after the June general election in 1885, entitled 'Irish Opinions on the Irish Problem'. Gladstone, it must be remembered, had visited Ireland just once – in 1877 – and he had to rely on others for direct information concerning conditions in Ireland. Bryce painted a picture of Ireland on the brink of social breakdown. To Gladstone, there was an immediate need to find a solution to Irish problems. Hence his decision to include a land purchase bill alongside the Home Rule Bill in 1886.

Was Gladstone a cynical party politician?

In contrast to these interpretations, a group of historians have seen Gladstone and Ireland from a completely different perspective. They have seen Gladstone's Irish policy as less to do with a genuine attempt to solve British–Irish relations and more to do with the nature of Liberal party politics.

In *Liberal Politics in the Age of Gladstone and Rosebery* (1972), D.A. Hamer claims that Gladstone had been aware of the fractious, coalition nature of the Liberal Party for some time. During the 1866 debate on parliamentary reform, the Liberal Party had split. Robert Lowe led the 'Adullamite' faction against Lord John Russell's Liberal Government. The effect was to allow Lord Derby to form a Conservative Administration (1866–68) which passed its own parliamentary reform act.

Veto (Latin – 'I forbid'): A negative vote exercised constitutionally by an individual, an institution or a state. It has the effect of automatically defeating the motion against which it is cast.

Once Gladstone became Liberal leader, he recognised the need to find a rallying cry to unite a political party with a tendency to divide into factions. In the general election of 1868, he used the rallying cry of 'Justice for Ireland'; in 1874, he used the abolition of income tax; and, in 1880, it was anti-Beaconsfieldism. By 1885–86, Gladstone had come to the belief that to prevent the Liberal Party from disintegrating he had to find a strong Liberal theme to unite the Party. Irish Home Rule seemed to fit the bill. According to Gladstone, Ireland had preoccupied his 1880–85 Government giving it little time to pass needed reform at home. Gladstone suggested that once the Home Rule obstruction to the railway line had been removed, the Liberal train of reform was free to move forward.

1. What are the arguments put forward above to support the view that Gladstone wanted to solve the Irish problem?

2. What are the arguments put forward to suggest that Gladstone was more interested in keeping the leadership of the Liberal Party than solving the Irish problem?

3. Explain why historians have disagreed over Gladstone's decision to support Irish Home Rule in 1886.

In *The Governing Passion* (1974), A.B. Cooke and J. Vincent take the more cynical view that Gladstone never expected Irish Home Rule to become law. This now seemed likely with the built-in Conservative majority in the House of Lords and their right of **veto**. They believe that Gladstone converted to Home Rule to 'dish the Whigs' and Joseph Chamberlain in order to regain effective control of the Liberal Party. In 1886, Gladstone was 77 years old and had been an MP since 1832. During his Second Ministry, the Liberal Party had been riven with disputes between aristocratic Whigs and Radicals. Gladstone had seemed to be losing control of his Party. In fact, prior to the June 1885 election, Joseph Chamberlain produced his own unofficial 'Radical Programme' as a manifesto for his wing of the Liberal Party. Once Gladstone 'converted' to Irish Home Rule, Chamberlain and the Whigs left the Party to form the Liberal Unionists. After 1886, although the Liberal Party was smaller it remained under the control of Gladstone until his retirement in 1894.

It would seem that Home Rule could be viewed either from the long-term perspective of British–Irish relations or purely from the viewpoint of British party politics where Gladstone's Irish policy was merely a tool in a game of political tactics to win or to keep political power.

17.5 Why was Home Rule so controversial?

Home Rule had a devastating effect on Liberal Party unity. The issue was responsible for the fall of Salisbury's Conservative Government in 1885 and Gladstone's Liberal Government in 1886. Clearly, it raised many important questions for British politicians.

Superficially, it seems hard to believe why the rather modest Home Rule Bill of 1886 created so much controversy. Under the Bill, Irish MPs would no longer sit at Westminster. This was seen as a blessing to those who had experienced Irish obstruction. Britain would also keep control of defence, finance, posts and trade. So why were so many people willing to oppose Home Rule so vociferously?

Opposition to Home Rule

- Perhaps the strongest opposition to Home Rule came from within Ireland. In north-east Ulster, the population was mainly Protestant. They feared control from a Catholic-dominated, Dublin-based parliament. To them, Home Rule meant 'Rome Rule'. In addition, the economy of north-east Ireland had become industrialised during the 19th century, with linen textile production and shipbuilding predominating.

  In many ways, north-east Ireland had more in common, both religiously and economically, with England and Scotland than the rest of Ireland. To the Protestants of Ulster, the Act of Union meant religious freedom and economic prosperity. Aware of these concerns the Conservative politician, Lord Randolph Churchill, visited Belfast in 1886 and his opposition to Home Rule helped to spark off anti-Home Rule rioting there.

- Also, within Ireland, the landowning class and the Protestant Ascendancy were content with the Act of Union. They feared that a Parnellite-dominated Dublin parliament might introduce radical land reform, which might end their privileged position.

- In Britain, a major reason for opposing Home Rule was Home Rule's possible impact on the British Empire. By the mid-1880s, many politicians were beginning to fear that Britain's pre-eminent position as the world's major industrial and imperial nation was coming under threat from nations such as the USA, Germany and Russia. In 1882, John Seeley of Cambridge University delivered a series of lectures entitled 'The Expansion of England', where he suggested that the future of world history lay in the hands of large states such as the USA or Russia. If Britain wished to remain a world power it would have to strengthen its control over the British Empire.

  In this political climate the idea of dividing the mother country, the United Kingdom, through Home Rule was seen to weaken not strengthen the Empire. Many saw Home Rule as merely the first step towards the creation of an independent Irish state. Apart from personal dislike of Gladstone, it was Joseph Chamberlain's desire to safeguard the Empire that led him to be a Liberal Unionist.

1. What were the reasons why Irish Home Rule was opposed?

2. Why was the issue of Irish Home Rule likely to split the Liberal Party in 1886?

Support for Home Rule

- In opposition to this view, Gladstone suggested that Home Rule would bring peace to the Irish countryside, thus ending a major cost to the British taxpayer for law and order.

- It would also remove Irish grievances and, therefore, would strengthen not weaken the Empire.

On balance, opponents of Home Rule were more numerous. In 1886, the First Home Rule Bill was defeated in the House of Commons by 343 to 313 votes.

1. What message is the author of this cartoon trying to make about the opposition to Home Rule within Ireland?

2. How useful is this cartoon to a historian writing about the issue of Irish Home Rule?

Source-based questions: Irish Home Rule

SOURCE A

1. That ... we declare our conviction that it is essentially necessary to the peace and prosperity of Ireland that the right of domestic legislation on all Irish affairs should be restricted to our country.
2. That, in accordance with the ancient and constitutional rights of the Irish nation, we claim the privilege of managing our own affairs by a parliament assembled in Ireland, and composed of the sovereign, the lords and the commons of Ireland.
4. That ... we adopt the principle of federal arrangement ... leaving to the imperial parliament the power of dealing with all questions affecting the imperial crown and government, legislation regarding the colonies ... relations of the empire with foreign states and stability of the empire at large.
8. ... no legislation shall be adopted to establish any religious ascendancy in Ireland.

From the Proceedings of the Home Rule Conference held in Dublin in November 1873.

SOURCE B

Home Rule will send a quickening stir of grateful life through a discontented land, which has long been rent with civil feuds. It will dress the labourer's face with smiles, lift him in the scale of civilisation, imbue him with the true spirit of human toil. It will educate him and enrich him. It will cover the barren rocks with soil; drain the sterile swamps, people the storm-swept gorges of Ireland's grey hills with beneficent activity and enduring peace.

Joseph Cowan, MP for Newcastle-upon-Tyne. From the Debate on the First Home Rule Bill taken from Hansard, *May 1886.*

Source-based questions: Irish Home Rule

SOURCE C

In America federalism has developed because existing states wished to be combined into some kind of national unity. Federalism [here] would necessarily mean the breaking up of the nation in order to form a body of states. The vast majority of the United Kingdom, including a million more of the inhabitants of Ireland, have expressed their will to maintain the Union. Popular government means government in accordance with the will of the majority, and therefore according to the principles of popular government the majority of the United Kingdom have a right to maintain the Union. Their wish is decisive, and ought to terminate the whole agitation in favour of Irish Home Rule.

From England's Case Against Home Rule *by Professor A. Dicey of Oxford University.*

SOURCE D

The core of opposition to the [Home Rule] Bill, and by far the most effective, came from those Liberals who disagreed with Gladstone's policy. It was Mr Trevelyan (Border Burghs) who stressed that the Liberals were not wholly a Home Rule Party. He had resigned from the government because he believed that there could be no intermediate stage between entire separation and imperial control.

From Home Rule and the Irish Question *by Grenfell Morton, published in 1980.*

1. Study Source A.

What were the aims of the Home Rule Party?

2. Using the information contained within this chapter and in the sources, explain the meaning of the two terms highlighted:

(a) 'religious ascendancy' (Source A)

(b) 'federalism' (Source C).

3. Study Source B.

How, by his use of language and style, does Joseph Cowan suggest that Home Rule would be good for Ireland?

4. Study Sources C and D.

How far do these two sources put forward different reasons why Home Rule for Ireland should be opposed?

5. Study all the sources and use your own knowledge.

How far do these sources explain the reasons put forward for and against Irish Home Rule?

17.6 How successful were Conservative policies towards Ireland between 1885 and 1892?

Introduction

A.J. Balfour, the Conservative Irish Chief Secretary 1887–92, stated that 'I shall be as relentless as Cromwell in enforcing obedience to the law, but, at the same time, I shall be as radical as any reformer in redressing grievances.' Balfour did indeed have notable success in both areas.

The Conservatives held power in 1885 and again from 1886 to 1892. They were firmly against Home Rule, but were nevertheless willing to pass reforms which they thought would remove Irish grievances and with them support for Home Rule. Generally called 'Constructive Unionism' or 'Killing Home Rule with Kindness', it combined a policy of land purchase with strong, resolute government.

Land reforms

The policy of land purchase had begun during Salisbury's short ministry in 1885, where the Ashbourne Land Purchase Act allowed tenants an advance of the whole sum needed to buy land, to be repaid over 49 years at 4% interest. In just three years, approximately £5 million was paid out in loans. This Act was followed by further land purchase acts in 1887 and 1891. These increased the amount of money available for tenants to buy their land. By the early 1890s, over £33 million had been made available for land purchase. In these years, the Irish countryside witnessed a quiet revolution as a new class of land proprietor was created.

In addition to land purchase, the Conservatives passed a land act in 1887 that extended the terms of the 1881 Land Act to include 100,000 lease-holders. They also created a new agency, in 1891, called the Congested Districts Board. It aimed to build roads, piers and bridges and to promote local industries in the poorer parts of western Ireland in counties such as Donegal, Mayo, Galway and Kerry, covering an area of 3.5 million acres. In the building of railways alone, 16,000 new jobs were created.

However, Balfour failed to pass an elective local government reform that would have given Ireland county councils along the lines of England and Wales.

Nevertheless, in 1890, when there was a reappearance of the potato blight in western Ireland, Balfour organised an effective relief campaign that prevented the outbreak of famine.

1. How did Balfour plan to bring peace to Ireland?

2. Who do you think was more successful in dealing with Irish problems: Gladstone between 1880 and 1885 or the Conservatives between 1886 and 1892?

Give reasons to support your answer.

The plan of campaign and coercion

Although the Conservatives passed many significant reforms, Lord Salisbury's Government was still affected by land agitation in the form of the Plan of Campaign, which began in 1886. Under the leadership of John Dillon of the Home Rule Party, tenants were encouraged to bargain collectively for fairer rents on certain chosen estates. If a landlord refused, then the tenants would withhold rent, paying instead into an 'estate fund' to help tenants who might be evicted. This was a new phase of the Land War which had been waged between 1879 and 1882. In response, Balfour introduced the Crimes Act in 1887, which was renewed each year until 1890, to allow magistrates to detain persons suspected of agrarian crimes. Balfour even got Monsignor Persico, a senior Catholic priest at the Vatican, to visit Ireland and report back to Pope Leo XIII. In April 1888, the Pope issued a statement condemning the plan of campaign but the Irish Catholic bishops did little to implement it.

17.7 What impact did Parnell and Gladstone have on British–Irish relations?

The fall of Parnell

Perhaps the most sensational aspect of British–Irish relations during the Conservative period of government involved Charles Stewart Parnell. In March 1887, *The Times* published a series of articles entitled 'Parnellism and Crime' which suggested that Parnell had been linked to terrorism such as the Phoenix Park Murders. Although Parnell immediately denounced the claims as untrue, it was not until a special commission set up by the Government investigated the matter in 1888 and 1889 that the matter was resolved. In February 1889, the journalist responsible for the letters, Richard Pigott, admitted under cross-examination that the information against Parnell was false.

No sooner had Parnell survived this storm than he was cited as an adulterer in a divorce case. Although Parnell's liaison with Mrs Katherine O'Shea had existed since 1880, and included the birth of a child, Mrs O'Shea's husband, Captain O'Shea, a Home Rule MP, did not begin divorce proceedings until December 1889. In a period where the public recognition of sexual immorality was seen as a serious matter, the divorce case created a crisis for the Home Rule Party. On 24 November 1890, Gladstone informed the Home Rule Party that unless Parnell resigned as leader he would not be able to maintain Liberal Party support for Home Rule. The following day, in Committee Room 15 of the House of Commons, the Home Rule Party debated Gladstone's ultimatum. The Party split with 45 in favour of Parnell's resignation and 37 against. Although no longer in command of the majority of Home Rule MPs, Parnell returned to Ireland where he fought and lost three by-elections against anti-Parnellites at North Kilkenny, Carlow and North Sligo. Later, in 1891, he contracted pneumonia and died, aged 45, in Brighton on the south coast of England.

Parnell's impact on British–Irish relations

Charles Parnell was known in his own lifetime as 'the uncrowned King of Ireland'. John Dillon, a leading Home Rule MP, stated on 17 February 1886 that Parnell was 'The accredited leader and ambassador of the Irish people'. Parnell stands out as the most influential Irish politician of the period between Daniel O'Connell in the 1820s and 1830s and the Easter Rising of 1916. With the 'New Departure' of 1879 Parnell was able to become undisputed leader of the Irish national movement for over a decade. In that time he was able to make Home Rule a major, if not the major, issue in British politics.

With the passage of the Third Reform Act, 1884, and the introduction of the 'Pledge' among Home Rule candidates, Parnell was able to exert considerable influence in the British party political system. Following the June 1885 election Parnell and his Party held the balance between the Liberal and Conservative parties, creating a true three-party system. Once Gladstone 'converted' to Home Rule, in 1886, Parnell was able to vote out the Conservatives and to support Gladstone's Liberals. However, once Gladstone had become committed to Home Rule, Parnell lost his position as intermediary between the two main parties. From 1886 onwards, the Irish Party was committed to supporting the Liberals.

While some contemporaries may have regarded Parnell's obstructionist tactics at Westminster as the act of an extremist, he was, in fact, a moderating influence on British–Irish relations. Parnell's leadership of the Irish national movement meant that the movement would follow a constitutionalist course rather than the violence of Fenianism. In October 1882, Parnell created the National League from the old Land League and removed Michael Davitt's radical ideas of land nationalisation from its platform. Again in the late 1880s Parnell consistently refused to support openly the Plan of Campaign.

As F.S.L. Lyons notes, in *Ireland Since the Famine* (1971): 'He [Parnell] was not a physical force man, not a separatist, not the leader of any forlorn hope. He was for winning the maximum self-government by the most efficient means and Parliament seemed to him the road by which Ireland could best come at Home Rule.'

Gladstone and Irish affairs: success or failure?

So much has been written about Gladstone and Ireland that a straightforward assessment of his role and his degree of success will, invariably, be debatable. At one extreme of the argument are Liberals such as John Morley who was determined to show Gladstone's commitment to democratic reform. At the other are historians such as John Vincent who, in his 1977 Raleigh Lecture on Gladstone and Ireland, suggested that Gladstone reacted to developments in Ireland on a piecemeal basis without any overall policy. Vincent believed the only consistent and successful Irish policy followed by Gladstone was coercion and repression.

Gladstone did achieve some measure of success in terms of individual aspects of the Irish Question as it existed in late Victorian Britain. In dealing with the religious issue, his Irish Church Act of 1869 – which disestablished the Church of Ireland – did remove a major religious grievance felt by the majority Catholic population. However, with his conversion to Home Rule the thought of a Catholic-dominated Dublin parliament created a Protestant backlash in north-east Ulster that was to cause problems in the future.

In land reform, Gladstone was the first major British politician since Peel to deal with this problem. His Land Acts of 1870 and 1881 laid the foundation for further reforms under the Conservatives in the late 1880s and 1890s. However, his first Land Act, 1870, made little significant change, while his Second Act, in 1881, was virtually stillborn due to the opposition of the Land League. Compared with the Conservative policy of land purchase, Gladstone's efforts were rather modest.

Home Rule will always occupy centre stage in any discussion on Gladstone and Ireland. While Parnell and his Home Rule Party may have pushed for the policy, it was not until Gladstone's conversion to the idea in 1886 that Home Rule became a serious political issue. From 1886 until the First World War, the granting of Home Rule to Ireland became a major Liberal Party policy. In 1886 and again in 1893, Gladstone attempted but failed to pass a Home Rule Bill.

1. In what ways did Parnell influence British policy and the British political system during his career?

2. How successful was Gladstone in dealing with Irish problems during his political career?

Gladstone's conversion to Irish Home Rule led to a major split in the Liberal Party and to a period of Conservative Party dominance in British politics which lasted until the first decade of the next century. As a political issue, Home Rule was very damaging to the Liberal Party in the short term. In terms of Gladstone's own political career, however, there is some debate as to whether Home Rule was all that bad. By 'dishing the Whigs' and Joseph Chamberlain, Gladstone regained control of the Liberal Party at a time when it seemed likely that he would be forced to retire from politics. Home Rule, far from damaging Gladstone's career, placed him at the forefront of Liberal politics for another eight years until his retirement in 1894, not over Ireland, but over expenditure on the Royal Navy.

Foreign and imperial policy, 1868–1895

Key Issues

- *How far did Britain's foreign and imperial policy change in the years 1868 to 1895?*
- *How successful was British foreign and imperial policy?*
- *Why did Britain take part in the New Imperialism?*

18.1 What were the main problems and issues in foreign and imperial policy in 1868?
18.2 How successful was Gladstone's foreign and imperial policy 1868–1874?
18.3 What impact did Disraeli have on foreign and imperial policy?
18.4 Historical interpretation: Why did Britain take part in the partition of Africa?
18.5 What were the foreign and imperial problems facing Gladstone's Second Ministry, 1880–1885?
18.6 To what extent was Britain in a state of 'splendid isolation' between 1885 and 1895?

Framework of Events

1867–68	The Abyssinian Campaign
1870	Franco–Prussian War breaks out
	Revocation of Black Sea Clauses of Treaty of Paris by Russia
1872	'Alabama' Award
	Speeches at Manchester and Crystal Palace: Disraeli puts forward policy of defending the Empire
1873	Ashanti War begins
1874	Annexation of Fiji
1875	Purchase of Suez Canal Shares
	July: Revolt breaks out in Bosnia and Hercegovina against Turkish rule
	December: Andrassy Note
1876	Royal Titles Act
	Lord Lytton becomes Viceroy of India
	April: Bulgarians rebel against Turkish rule
	May: Berlin Memorandum rejected by Britain and Turkey
	July: Reports reach England of Bulgarian horrors
	Reichstadt Agreement
	November: Serbia defeated
	December: Constantinople conference
1877	Transvaal joins British Empire
	April: Russia declares war on Turkey
	May: British warnings to Russia
	July: Siege of Plevna
1878	Second Afghan War
	Zulu War
	January: Russians reach outskirts of Constantinople
	February: British fleets reaches Constantinople
	March: Treaty of San Stefano
	April: Britain mobilises for war. Indian troops sent to Malta
	May–June: British agreements with Austria-Hungary, Russia and Turkey
	July: Congress of Berlin
1879	Third Afghan War
1880	Britain withdraws from Afghanistan
	First Boer War

1881	Treaty of Pretoria with the Transvaal
1882	Invasion of Egypt
1883	Failure of Ilbert Bill in India
1884	Treaty of London with the Transvaal
1885	Creation of Bechuanaland Protectorate
	General Gordon in the Sudan
1885–87	Bulgarian Crisis
1887	Mediterranean Agreements
1889	Naval Defence Act
1890	Heligoland–Zanzibar Agreement with Germany
1893	Franco–Russian Alliance.

Overview

IN 1868, Britain was a world power. Britain had been the first country to undergo an industrial revolution, so by 1868 Britain was seen as the 'workshop of the world'. Over 75% of all the cotton textiles produced in the world came from the Manchester area. In addition, Britain was the financial centre of the world. In London, the Stock Exchange was a centre for investment, the Baltic Exchange for shipping and Lloyd's for insurance.

However, Britain's main claim to world power status was its Empire. The British Empire was the largest in the world, with colonies in every continent except Antarctica. The centre of the Empire, what Disraeli termed 'the jewel in the Crown', was the British Indian Empire.

Europe in 1871

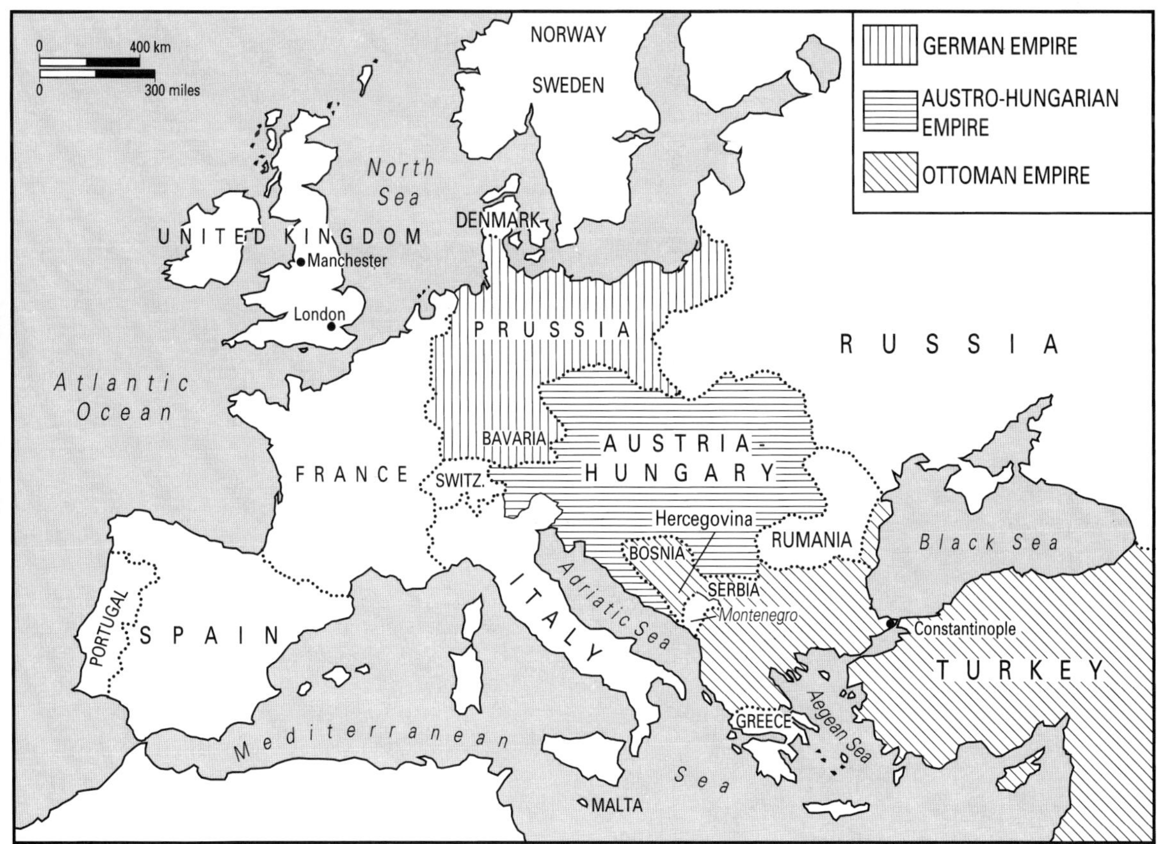

By 1895, Britain's position in the world had changed dramatically. In economic and commercial terms, Britain faced strong rivalry from the United States of America and the German Empire. In terms of imperial possessions, Britain had acquired considerable extra territory, mainly in Africa. In that year, the British Empire covered one-quarter of the globe, containing one-third of the world's population.

In the period 1868–95, Britain came close to war with Russia over the Near Eastern Crisis of 1875–78. Britain did fight a number of colonial wars, in southern Africa against the Zulus in 1878 and the Boers in 1880–81, in Afghanistan in 1878–79 and in Egypt and the Sudan in 1882 and 1885 respectively.

18.1 What were the main problems and issues in foreign and imperial policy in 1868?

As one of the European Great Powers, Britain supported the balance of power that had been created at the Treaty of Vienna in 1815. The only time Britain went to war with another European Great Power between 1815 and 1914 was against Russia in the Crimean War of 1854–56, in order to preserve the balance of power. In 1868, Britain's main commitment in European affairs was to uphold the terms of the Treaty of Paris of 1856, which ended that war. The most important provision of that treaty was that neither the Turkish Empire nor Russia were allowed to keep warships in the Black Sea.

Between 1859 and 1871, however, there was a major transformation in European international relations. Italy became a unified country between 1859 and 1861. More importantly, in 1866, Prussia defeated Austria, and became the dominant German-speaking state. In 1870–71, Prussia then defeated Europe's major military power, France, and created the German Empire. By 1871, the old balance of power of 1814–15 had been altered: Germany was now the continent's main Great Power. Under the influence of the important European statesman of the time, Otto von Bismarck, Chancellor of Germany, an alliance system centred on Germany was created, with the aim of isolating France.

Major changes also took place within the British Empire. In 1867, the British North America Act gave Canada internal self-government. In the course of the second half of the 19th century, other 'white dominions', such as New Zealand, the Australian colonies and Cape Colony, also received self-government.

In 1865, the report of a select committee of the House of Commons recommended a withdrawal from the west African colonies, which were deemed unprofitable. This started a major debate on how the British Empire should develop.

Perhaps the greatest threat to the British Empire came from Russia. Between 1856 and 1870, the Russians conquered the central Asian states of Khiva, Bokhara and Samarkhand. These conquests provided Russia with a border very close to the British Indian Empire. For the rest of the century, Britain attempted to protect India's north-west frontier against possible Russian incursion. This involved both states in trying to gain influence in Afghanistan.

As the historian C.C. Eldridge has stated, Britain 'was both a European state threatened by the menace of continental politics and an imperial power with distant obligations'. Britain's main military force for defending the mother country from invasion, and for protecting the Empire overseas, was the Royal Navy. Since the Battle of Trafalgar in 1805, Britain had been the world's greatest naval power. In the period after 1868, however, British naval power was in decline.

Which of the issues and problems, mentioned above, do you regard as the most important facing Britain in the years 1868 and 1895? Explain your answer.

18.2 How successful was Gladstone's foreign and imperial policy 1868–1874?

Gladstone's views

Gladstone derived his views on foreign and imperial affairs from a number of sources.

- Firstly, he believed in the 'Concert of Europe'. This was the idea that the European Great Powers should act together (in concert) to preserve peace by upholding the balance of power.
- Secondly, he believed war to be both expensive and damaging to trade. He therefore favoured the arbitration of international disputes.
- Thirdly, he believed that British rule over the Empire was a duty and responsibility. Britain had the task of providing efficient administration to the subjects of the Empire. However, when internal self-government was given to colonies Gladstone was of the opinion that they should not have to rely on British military assistance for their internal security.

During his First Ministry, Gladstone, and his Foreign Secretary (after 1870) Lord Granville were heavily criticised by their political opponents for following a foreign and imperial policy, which was against Britain's interests.

The Franco–Prussian War, 1870–71

Prussia's victory over France transformed the balance of power in Europe. However, Gladstone's Government did not intervene directly in the war. The Government received very little criticism for its actions. The main criticism was that Britain did not do enough to stop France declaring war in July 1870.

Once the war had begun, Gladstone's only intervention was to get an agreement from both sides not to invade Belgium, in August 1870. Once the war was over, Lord Granville did intervene to get the war indemnity France had to pay Prussia under the terms of the Treaty of Frankfurt reduced to 5,000 million francs.

The revocation of the Black Sea clauses of the Treaty of Paris

At the height of the Franco–Prussian War, Russia took the opportunity to renounce the section of the Treaty of Paris of 1856 forbidding the Russians to have a fleet in the Black Sea. To Britain, this had been the most important part of the treaty and one of the main reasons why it had fought the Crimean War.

In line with Gladstone's belief in the Concert of Europe, Lord Granville organised an international conference in London, in March 1871, in which all the Great Powers took part. Russia was invited to ask the conference to revoke the Black Sea clauses, and accepted.

The 'Alabama' Award, 1872

This episode was an example of Gladstone's faith in international arbitration. The USA had demanded £9 million in compensation for the damage inflicted on the Union merchant fleet during the American Civil War of 1861–65 by a number of Confederate raiders, the most notable being the 'Alabama'. Britain was accused of breaching its neutrality because many of these raiders had been built at Birkenhead, in Cheshire. In the Treaty of Washington (May 1871), both Britain and the USA agreed to international arbitration in Geneva, Switzerland, to settle the dispute.

In September 1872, the arbitrators awarded the USA damages of £3.25 million (one-third of the original claim).

Although the award ended a long-standing dispute between Britain and the USA, it was deeply unpopular at home. Many believed Britain had not broken its neutrality in the war. In addition, the fact that Britain dropped any claim for damages for the Fenian raid from the USA on Canada in 1866 and gave the USA the right to fish off the coast of Canada, made the award seem like a diplomatic defeat for Britain.

Imperial issues

1. Disraeli heavily criticised Gladstone's handling of foreign and imperial policy.

Write down the areas of policy where you think Disraeli's criticism was valid.

Then write down where you think Gladstone was successful.

2. On balance, was Gladstone a failure in foreign and imperial affairs? Give reasons to support your answer.

Disraeli severely criticised Gladstone's Government on imperial matters, claiming that the Liberal leader wanted to dismantle the British Empire. A number of matters seemed to support Disraeli's claim:

- The decision to withdraw British troops from Canada and New Zealand when these colonies faced internal revolts.
- The decision to offer the Canadian Prime Minister, Alexander Galt, a knighthood, even though Galt was in favour of Canadian independence.
- The announcement, in June 1870, that Britain planned to abandon Gambia in west Africa to France.

Gladstone, on the other hand, believed that white-controlled colonies that had received self-government, such as Canada and New Zealand, should be responsible for their own internal security. He also believed that the British Empire should develop into a group of white self-governing colonies. As part of this plan, Cape Colony was given self-government in 1872.

Also, the Liberals were willing to defend the Empire when problems arose. For instance, in 1873 King Coffee Calcalli of the Ashanti threatened the British West African colony of Gold Coast (now Ghana). The British Government sent a military expedition, which defeated King Coffee in the Ashanti War of 1873–74 and extended British colonial control to include the Ashanti nation.

18.3 What impact did Disraeli have on foreign and imperial policy?

In contrast to Gladstone, Disraeli has been seen as a great defender of the British Empire and British interests abroad. However, the sincerity of Disraeli as an imperialist has been questioned. The Canadian historian, John Morison, stated that Disraeli had no real understanding of the Empire, while R. Koebner and H. Schmidt in their study *Imperialism: The Story and Significance of a Political Word* believed that Disraeli's interest in the Empire was merely a piece of self-advertisement.

This view has been challenged by a number of historians. The most notable was S.R. Stembridge in an article 'Disraeli and the Millstones' (published in 1965) where he pointed to a long-standing interest in Empire throughout Disraeli's career.

Yet Disraeli's foreign and imperial policy has an element of self-advertisement about it. Disraeli, like Palmerston, was able to use foreign and imperial policy to boost his popularity at home. A good example of this was in 1867–68 when he sent 12,000 troops to free some British hostages in Abyssinia. It can also be seen in his handling of the Near Eastern Crisis of 1875–78.

Imperial issues

Contrary to what many contemporaries believed, there was a high degree of continuity between the imperial policies of Gladstone and Disraeli. In his study 'The Imperial Frontier in the Tropics' (1967), W.D. McIntyre noted that in Fiji, the Malay States and west Africa the Conservatives merely carried on policies begun by the Liberals.

The historian C.C. Eldridge goes further by claiming that 'Conservative policy was often the result of a series of uncoordinated developments which did not always meet with Disraeli's personal approval. Disraeli was interested in ideas. He could never be bothered with details. Disraeli never wished to dictate colonial policy. This was left to the Colonial Secretary, Lord Carnarvon.'

As a result, many of the decisions affecting the Empire were made by ministers or officials overseas (men on the spot). In October 1874, Commodore Goodenough annexed Fiji, against the wishes of Lord Carnarvon. In 1874, the Governor of Singapore, Sir Andrew Clarke, was chiefly responsible for establishing British 'residents' in each Malay state. In west Africa, the Conservatives concluded the Ashanti War begun by the Liberals.

The purchase of the Khedive of Egypt's Suez Canal shares, 1875

One area where Disraeli did show initiative was his decision, without gaining Cabinet approval, to buy the Khedive (ruler) of Egypt's share-holding in the Suez Canal Company. Using £4 million acquired from the Rothschild family, Disraeli purchased a 44% share in the operation of the Suez Canal, which had become one of the world's major sea routes since its opening in 1869.

The Royal Titles Act, 1876

On the suggestion of the Queen, Disraeli created the title of Empress of India. The British Indian Empire had been in existence since 1858 and the new title helped to strengthen links with India.

The Confederation of South Africa, 1877

Confederate: To bring a number of states together in a political union.

The main influence on this policy was the Colonial Secretary, Lord Carnarvon. Carnarvon planned to **confederate** the three British colonies of Cape Colony, Natal and Griqualand West with the two Dutch Boer Republics of the Orange Free State and Transvaal. The intention was to strengthen Britain's hold on southern Africa. In 1877, Transvaal agreed to confederate with the British colonies, mainly because of fear of Zulu attacks on its eastern territory.

The Zulu War, 1878

After Carnarvon's departure from the Colonial Office in 1878, the new minister, Sir Michael Hicks-Beach, had no experience of colonial matters and left British policy in southern Africa in the hands of Sir Bartle Frere, the British High Commissioner. It was Frere who decided on a policy of confrontation with the Zulu kingdom, north of Natal. In 1878, this policy led to war, where the British suffered a humiliating defeat at Isandlwana before eventually defeating the Zulus at Ulundi. Disraeli was furious when war broke, but it was too late to prevent it.

The Afghan Wars of 1878 and 1879

Annex: To seize another country, usually by force, and take control of it.

British policy in India was in the hands of the India Secretary, Lord Cranbrook, and the Indian Viceroy, Lord Lytton. They believed the best way to preserve British control in the face of the Russian threat was to **annex** states on the north-west frontier of India. In 1876, Baluchistan was annexed, and in 1878 the decision was taken to install a pro-British ruler in Afghanistan. This led to a British invasion in November 1878. Following the murder of the British agent, Sir Louis Cavagnari, in September 1879, a further British military expedition was made. It was this policy that was criticised heavily by Gladstone in his Midlothian campaigns of 1879 and 1880.

However, as C.C. Eldridge noted, 'once again it had been his [Disraeli's] own weakness as Prime Minister and the blundering of his Secretary of State for India, Lord Cranbrook, that were responsible for the mess. Disraeli's contribution to these events was purely negative: a failure to oversee Cabinet ministers and to control the men on the spot.'

The Near Eastern Crisis, 1875–1878

The crisis which developed in south-eastern Europe (the Balkans) in the mid-1870s was another episode in the **Eastern Question** and proved to be the most serious foreign policy problem faced by the Disraeli Government.

Eastern Question: The international problem created by the belief that the Turkish (Ottoman) Empire was in a state of imminent collapse.

For the first two years, 1875–76, the crisis was limited to a clash between the Turkish Empire and the Christian peoples of the Balkans, most notably the Serbs, Croats and Bulgarians. During this period, the Great Powers attempted to localise the conflict and prevent it turning into a major European war. The Concert of Europe no longer acted as the main diplomatic force in European affairs. In its place was the *Dreikaiserbund* ('Three Emperors' League') of Germany, Russia and Austria-Hungary, established by Bismarck in 1873. From 1875 to 1877, the *Dreikaiserbund* attempted to find a diplomatic solution through discussion, suggestion and advice. It was not until 1877 that Russia decided upon direct action and declared war on Turkey.

The limitations of British policy

During the period 1875 to 1878, British policy towards the crisis was hampered by a number of factors.

- Firstly, there were major disagreements within the Cabinet between Disraeli, who wanted decisive action, and the Foreign Secretary, Lord Derby. Ever since Lord John Russell's humiliation over the Schleswig-Holstein crisis of 1863–64, Derby had been highly reluctant to take an active role in foreign affairs. As Foreign Secretary (then known as Lord Stanley) in the Conservative Government of 1866–68 he had refused to intervene in the Austro–Prussian War of 1866. Likewise, in the early years of the Near Eastern Crisis, Derby did not want to become involved.
- Secondly, Disraeli's main aim, in the early years of the crisis, was to disrupt the *Dreikaiserbund*. Ever since its creation, Disraeli had been suspicious that this league would work against British interests in Europe. Like his mid-century predecessor, Lord Palmerston, Disraeli believed Britain's interests were best served by the preservation of the Turkish Empire and the minimising of Russian influence in the Balkans. In particular, Disraeli followed a traditional policy of trying to prevent Russian warships entering the Mediterranean through the Straits.
- Finally, Disraeli's support for the Turkish government was compromised by the 'Bulgarian Horrors' of 1876, when Turkish troops massacred Bulgarian civilians. This resulted in the anti-Turkish Bulgarian Agitation of 1876, led by Gladstone. With an important section of British public opinion opposed to aiding the Turks, Disraeli's Government found it difficult to intervene on the Turkish side.

The development of British policy, 1875–1876

Following the outbreak of a revolt against Turkish rule in the provinces of Bosnia and Hercegovina, the first major diplomatic attempt to end the crisis came from the Austro-Hungarian Foreign Minister, Count Gyula Andrassy. In the so-called 'Andrassy Note' to the Turkish government, reforms in religion, taxation and landholding were proposed to end the revolt, with a mixed Muslim/Christian commission to supervise the changes.

Disraeli accepted the 'Note' mainly because the Turkish government, Italy and France had accepted it. But he did so with some reluctance. Disraeli believed that he could not let the *Dreikaiserbund* be seen to take the initiative in the crisis. As he stated: 'unless we go out of our way to act with the Northern Powers [*Dreikaiserbund*], they can act without us, which is not agreeable for a state like England'.

Unfortunately, by early 1876 it was clear that the Turks had no intention of implementing the terms of the Andrassy Note. So, on 13 May 1876, the *Dreikaiserbund* produced the Berlin Memorandum, which attempted to arrange a ceasefire in Bosnia and Hercegovina together with the reforms suggested in the Andrassy Note. Disraeli's Government rejected the memorandum, which had the effect of wrecking it. Disraeli made the rejection for several reasons. Firstly, the memorandum was submitted to Britain, for immediate approval, at a weekend. Disraeli believed Britain was being treated 'as if she were Montenegro or Bosnia'. Secondly, Derby was naturally reluctant to follow any fixed policy. However, most importantly, Disraeli wished to prevent the *Dreikaiserbund* from taking the diplomatic initiative. Instead, Britain took an independent line by sending the Royal Navy to Besika Bay. This move infuriated Bismarck and the *Dreikaiserbund* powers, and gave the Turks the hope that they could rely on British support. As a result, the Turkish government rejected the memorandum.

During the first two years of the crisis, Disraeli's attempt to prevent the *Dreikaiserbund* from taking the initiative had prevented a settlement. By the summer of 1876, the Bulgarian Horrors had taken place and the crisis had worsened with the intervention of Serbia and Montenegro on the side of the rebels. This led to a rise of **Panslav** feeling in Russia which the Tsar found it difficult to control. In July 1876, in the Reichstadt Agreement, Austria-Hungary and Russia agreed, in general terms, to divide the Balkans between them. In November, the Russians mobilised 160,000 troops along their Balkan frontier.

Panslav: Movement for the unity of all Slav peoples, under the guidance of Russia.

The Constantinople Conference, 1876–1877

At the end of 1876, Disraeli had become concerned about the deteriorating situation and took the initiative by proposing a conference of Great Powers at Constantinople, the capital of Turkey. Initially, the Conference was successful. All the Great Powers attended and the British representative, Lord Salisbury, worked closely with his Russian counterpart, Count Ignatiev. The Conference agreed on the union of Bosnia and Hercegovina under nominal Turkish rule, an increase in the size of Serbia and Montenegro at Turkey's expense, and self-government for Bulgaria, with the latter divided into two regions.

Unfortunately, the Conference ended prematurely on 20 January 1877 when the Turkish Sultan refused to accept its suggestions. This was due to the military success of Turkey in its war with Serbia and Montenegro. The Russian representative made a last-ditch diplomatic move with the London Protocol of 9 April. When this was rejected by the Sultan, the Russians declared war on Turkey on 24 April. Britain decided to stay neutral but warned the Russians, on 6 May, not to send warships through the Straits.

The Treaties of San Stefano and Berlin, 1878

In 1878, Britain came close to war with Russia. This was due mainly to the Russian military success in the war. Although delayed for several months in besieging Plevna, the Russian army reached Constantinople in January 1878. The Royal Navy was sent to the Sea of Marmora on 23 January and Constantinople itself on 19 February, to prevent a possible Russian attack on the Turkish capital. This British action helped to produce a ceasefire in the war. However, the policy had its cost. Both Derby and Carnarvon resigned from the Cabinet.

The most serious threat of war with Russia came in March, following the publication of the Treaty of San Stefano (see map). This treaty was negotiated for Russia by Ignatiev. As soon as the terms were published, it stirred up opposition throughout Europe – even in Russia itself. Count Shuvalov, the Russian minister, described it as 'the greatest act of stupidity we could have committed'. Britain opposed it for three major reasons. It raised the possibility of allowing Russian warships into the Mediterranean, it disrupted the European balance of power, and it threatened the continued existence of the Turkish Empire.

No sooner had the treaty been published than the Russians, under German pressure, offered to renegotiate it at an international congress in Berlin. Before the congress met, Disraeli made secret agreements with Russia, Austria-Hungary and Turkey to protect British interests. On 30 May, the Russians agreed that the new Bulgarian state should be reduced in size. On 4 June, the Turks agreed to give Cyprus to Britain. In return, Britain offered to protect Turkish Armenia in Asia Minor. On 6 June, the Austro-Hungarians accepted a reduction in the size of Bulgaria in return for their occupation of Bosnia and Hercegovina.

Disraeli and Salisbury were able to achieve many of Britain's aims at the Congress of Berlin. The new state of Bulgaria was reduced in size and Turkey

Using the information contained in the map, explain the differences between the changes made by the Treaty of San Stefano of March 1878 and the Treaty of Berlin, July 1878.

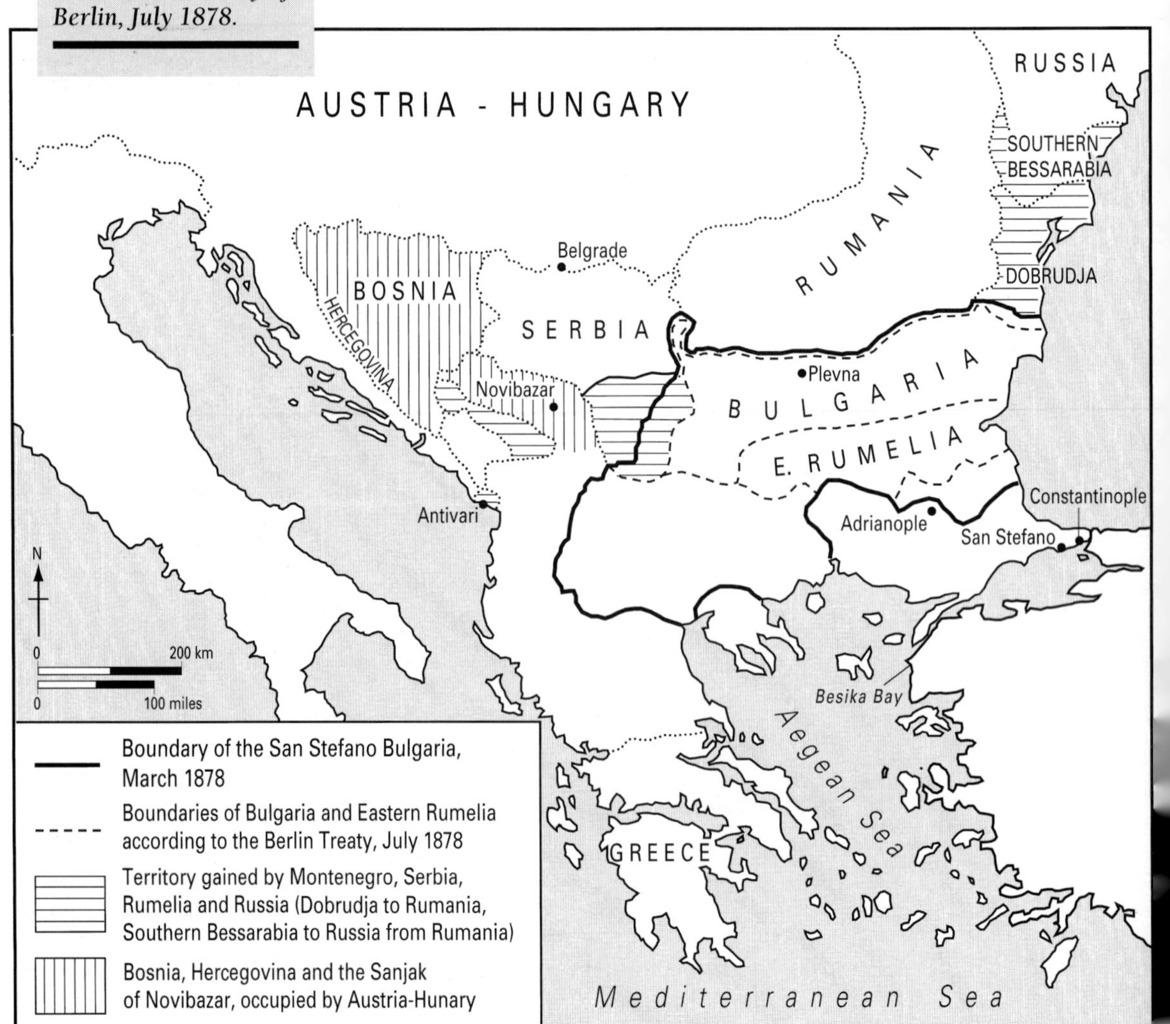

survived as a European power. However, British policy towards the Straits changed. Instead of insisting that they remain closed to warships, Britain accepted that they were an open waterway.

1. Using the information contained in this section, write down those parts of Disraeli's foreign policy that you regard as a success. Then write down those parts of his policy you regard as unsuccessful.

2. On balance, do you regard Disraeli as successful? Give reasons to support your answer.

Summary of Disraeli's policy towards the Near Eastern Crisis

The case against

Disraeli's policy of disrupting the *Dreikaiserbund*, in 1875 and 1876, helped to prolong and deepen the crisis. It was also unpopular in Britain. Once the Russo–Turkish War began, public opinion changed. However, Disraeli's policy of threatening the Russians split the Cabinet and led to the resignation of two ministers. Disraeli brought Britain to the brink of war with Russia without the support of an ally with a large army, and with an obsolete Royal Navy. In the Treaty of Berlin, he had offered to protect Turkey's Asian frontier with Russia without having the military means to achieve it. This was criticised by Gladstone in his Midlothian campaigns.

The case for

Disraeli, at the Congress of Berlin, had re-established Britain's international reputation. His diplomacy had saved the Turkish Empire and preserved the European balance of power. He acquired Cyprus for the Empire. He had achieved these mainly through bluff and the threat of force.

Source-based questions: The Near Eastern Crisis of 1876

SOURCE A

We are always treated as if we had some peculiar alliance with the Turkish Government, as if we were their peculiar friends. We are, it is true, the Allies of the Sultan of Turkey; so is Russia, so is Austria, so is France, and so are others.

What our duty is at this crucial moment is to maintain the Empire of England. Nor will we ever agree to any step, though it may obtain for a moment comparative quiet and a false prosperity, that hazards the existence of the Empire.

From a speech by Disraeli in the House of Commons, 11 August 1876.

SOURCE B

We wished to maintain Turkey as an independent political state. It is very easy to talk of the Ottoman power being at the point of extinction. But when you come practically to examine the question there is no living statesman who has ever offered any practical solution of the difficulties which would occur if the Ottoman Empire were to fall to pieces. One result would be a long and general war, and that alone, I think, is a sufficient reason for endeavouring to maintain the Ottoman Empire.

From a speech by the Earl of Beaconsfield (Disraeli) in the House of Lords, 16 May 1879.

SOURCE C

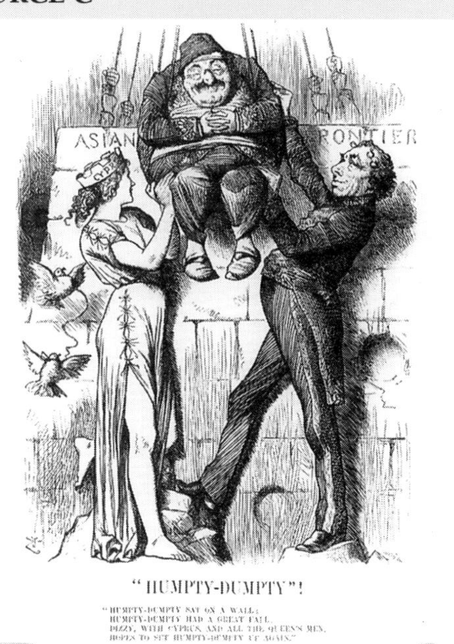

Punch *cartoon, 20 July 1878, entitled 'Humpty-Dumpty'. The verse underneath reads: 'Humpty-Dumpty sat on a wall; Humpty-Dumpty had a great fall; Dizzy with Cyprus, and all the Queen's men, Hopes to set 'Humpty-Dumpty up again.'*

Source-based questions: The Near Eastern Crisis of 1876

SOURCE D

It can be said that Disraeli achieved all his major aims at Berlin. He had preserved some Balkan territory for Turkey, and so Turkey could be expected to act as a barrier to Russian expansion. Certainly Russia was kept out of Constantinople. He had also gained prestige for Britain (and for himself), together with a new possession, Cyprus, which was of strategic value in the eastern Mediterranean. He had avoided war, using only the threat of war to achieve his aims, and had thus forged a successful middle course between hawks and doves in the country.

From Britain and the European Powers 1865 to 1914 *by Robert Pearce, published in 1996. A view on Disraeli's role at the Congress of Berlin, 1878.*

1. Study Source A.

What, according to Disraeli, was the basis of British policy towards the Turkish Empire in 1876?

2. Study Sources B and D.

How far is the view of Disraeli in Source B supported by Robert Pearce's assessment in Source D?

3. Study Sources C and D.

Does this cartoon support or oppose the view of Disraeli's performance at the Congress of Berlin put forward in Source D?

4. Use all the sources and information contained in this chapter.

Do the sources printed above provide an adequate explanation of British policy towards Turkey in the years 1875 to 1878?

Give reasons to support your answer.

18.4 Why did Britain take part in the partition of Africa?

A CASE STUDY IN HISTORICAL INTERPRETATION

Even though Europeans had traded with Africa for centuries, it was not until 1880 that the rapid expansion of European control known as the 'Scramble for Africa' took place. There has been intense debate ever since on why this development took place.

This expansion, and similar colonial expansion in Asia and the Pacific, took Britain by surprise. Gladstone was extremely reluctant to take part. Lord Salisbury, who more than any other British statesman was responsible for colonial enlargement, stated in 1885, 'I do not know exactly the cause of this sudden revolution. But there it is.'

So why did Britain take part?

Investment overseas?

An early explanation came from the British liberal, Joshua Hobson, who produced a book in 1902 called *Imperialism: A Study*. Hobson believed Britain had acquired territory as a base for investment, due to the inequality of incomes between rich and poor in Britain. This created underconsumption of goods and surplus capital to invest and was seen as a malfunction of the capitalist economic system.

Hobson's views were taken a stage further by the founder of Russian communism, Vladimir Lenin, who in 1916 produced *Imperialism: The Highest Stage of Capitalism*. Lenin believed that it was inevitable for capitalis economies to acquire colonies as a guarantee of raw materials and markets for goods.

Neither Hobson nor Lenin, however, had attempted to provide an explanation for the whole partition of Africa. Hobson was trying to explain why Britain became involved in the Second Boer War, while Lenin was trying to explain why the First World War began.

Great Power rivalry

From 1920 to 1961, the main view put forward to explain the partition of Africa was rivalry between the Great Powers. Following the unification of Germany, European states had little opportunity to expand within Europe so they acquired colonies overseas. This was due to several reasons:

- The need to gain prestige was an important factor in French imperialism.
- The belief that Europeans were superior to other races and, therefore, had the right to acquire territory, was called **Social Darwinism**.
- Once the partition began, powers feared missing out on acquiring territory and, therefore, were forced to participate.

Social Darwinism: The belief that human society is based on conflict between racial groups in which certain groups are believed to be superior to others. The superior races were seen to have the right to rule so-called 'inferior' races. Charles Darwin (1809–82) developed the theory of the origin of the human species.

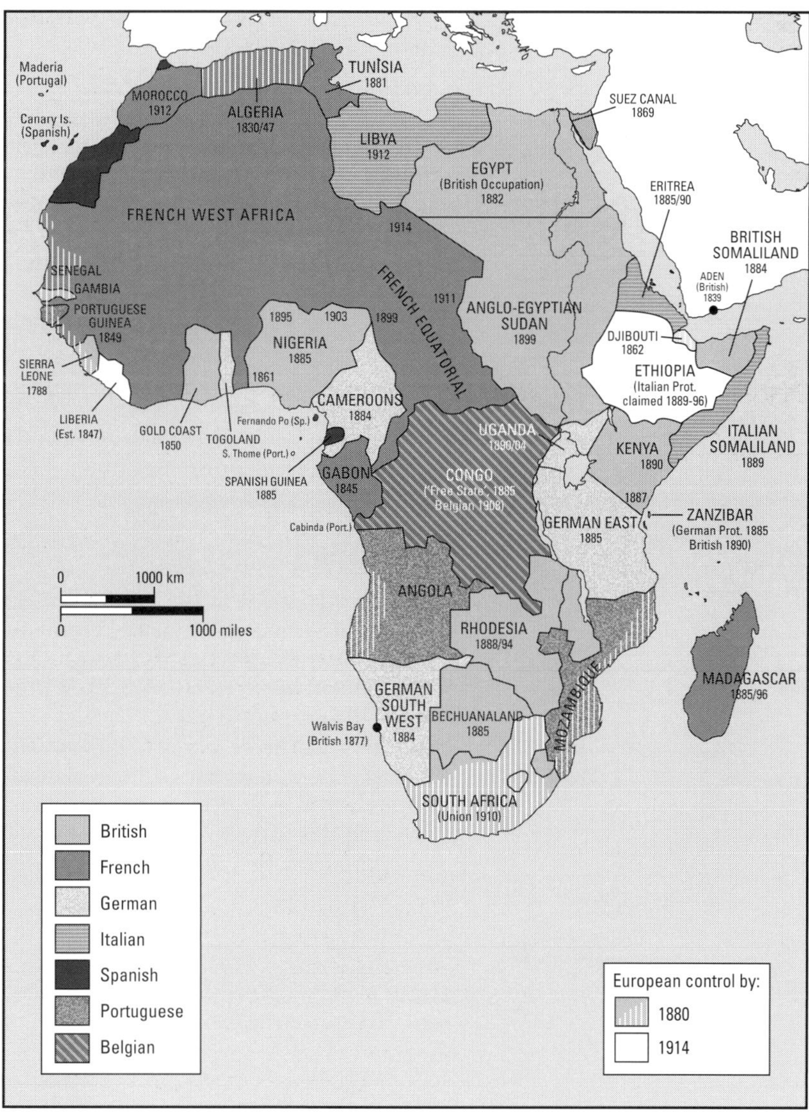

Study the map of the European partition of Africa.

Using information contained in the 'A Case Study in Historical Interpretation' section, give reasons why Britain acquired territory in Africa after 1880 (as marked on the map).

The official mind

In 1961, the most important book on the partition appeared. *Africa and the Victorians* by R. Robinson and J. Gallagher put forward the view that the partition was started by the British invasion of Egypt in 1882. This took place for strategic reasons, to protect the Suez Canal and with it the sea route to India. Robinson and Gallagher saw the protection of the sea routes to India, via the Suez Canal and the Cape of Good Hope, as the prime aim for Britain. They stated, 'without the occupation of Egypt there is no reason to suppose that any international scrambles for Africa either east or west would have begun when they did'.

In 1962, Robinson and Gallagher took their theory a stage further in their contribution to Volume XI of the *New Cambridge Modern History* entitled 'The Partition of Africa'. They stated that Britain had been forced reluctantly to take over African territory because of African resistance to British trade and influence. Britain therefore annexed Egypt and the Sudan, territory in the Gold Coast and Nigeria in west Africa and territory in southern Africa.

The main criticism of Robinson and Gallagher's view was that it failed to take into consideration other reasons for British involvement, such as missionary work and, in particular, economic reasons.

Trade

Several historians of the partition of west Africa, such as John Hargreaves, Colin Newbury and D.K. Fieldhouse, have mentioned the importance of protecting trade as a motive for annexation. The Great Depression in the European economy after 1873 forced states to acquire colonies in order to guarantee raw materials and markets for their goods. Once this process began, other states had to take similar action. Britain had been the major European trading nation in Africa in the 19th century. Faced with French and German colonial expansion, Britain was forced to turn its informal control of an area into a formal colony. Robinson and Gallagher had argued, as far back as 1953, that Britain preferred to have economic rather than political control of an area. This 'informal empire' existed before 1880. Therefore, Britain was forced reluctantly to take part in the partition. Even then, Britain tried to do so 'on the cheap' by declaring protectorates rather than full colonial control. This took place in Nigeria in the 1880s and in Bechuanaland in 1885.

1. Using the information contained in this section and the map, which territories did Britain acquire in the years 1880 to 1895?

2. Using the information contained in this section and the map, which explanation for Britain's involvement in the partition of Africa do you find most convincing? Give reasons to support your answer.

Other theories

Britain's involvement in the partition of East Africa and the occupation of Nyasaland had much to do with helping to abolish the slave trade and with missionary work by David Livingstone. The acquisition of Rhodesia (1886–89) had much to do with Cecil Rhodes' desire to create his own area of colonial control.

However, in *The Theory of Capitalist Imperialism* (1967), D.K. Fieldhouse puts forward the view that 'the historian should begin by studying as fully as possible the general forces operating within Europe and in other parts of the world, and then study each particular case of annexation as a special problem, and, finally, come to some conclusion about why colonisation took place in each case'.

Britain's involvement in the partition of north Africa, with the acquisition of Egypt and the Sudan, had different causes than Britain's involvement in the partition of east, west and southern Africa.

18.5 *What were the foreign and imperial problems facing Gladstone's Second Ministry, 1880–1885?*

Gladstone returned to power in 1880 to reverse what he saw as the aggressive and costly foreign and imperial policies of Disraeli. In the Midlothian campaigns of 1879–80 (see page 301), he virtually committed himself to restoring the independence of the Transvaal and withdrawing from Cyprus, Asia Minor and Afghanistan. Yet, during his ministry, Britain invaded and occupied Egypt and acquired extensive territories in west and southern Africa.

Also, during his Second Ministry, the Liberal Cabinet split on the issue of foreign and imperial policy. Broadly speaking, moderate Liberals stood for the consolidation of Empire. The Whigs, on the other hand, desired expansion. Issues such as the Transvaal and Egypt saw radicals and moderates opposing Whigs. However, over southern Africa, the Whigs received support from two Radicals, Joseph Chamberlain and Sir Charles Dilke, who had heavily criticised the Whigs over Ireland and domestic issues.

The Transvaal and the First Boer War

On achieving office, Gladstone decided to keep Sir Bartle Frere as High Commissioner in South Africa and to continue British rule of the Transvaal because he wished to pursue Carnarvon's policy of confederation. In December 1880, however, the Transvaalers rose in armed revolt and a general Boer rebellion across southern Africa seemed likely. The issue split the Cabinet between Whig and Radical. In February 1881, at Majuba Hill in Natal, the Boers defeated British forces under the Governor of Natal, Sir George Colley.

At the Convention of Pretoria in August 1881, Transvaal was granted internal self-government but Britain retained control over Transvaal foreign policy, known as 'suzerainty'. This meant that Britain had no direct control of the Transvaal but was still responsible for it. In 1884, in the Treaty of London, Anglo-Transvaal relations were placed on a formal footing. However, suzerainty was not mentioned. After 1884 Britain still believed it controlled Transvaal foreign policy while the Transvaal believed it was completely independent. This confusion helped create the conflict which led to the Second Boer War in 1899.

Afghanistan

In 1880, Gladstone intended withdrawing from Afghanistan. However, the new Indian Viceroy, Lord Ripon, believed withdrawal could lead to a breakdown in law and order, and possible Russian intervention. A compromise was reached whereby Britain accepted responsibility for Afghanistan's defence: another example of responsibility without control.

In 1884, the Russians annexed Merv in northern Afghanistan. In March 1885, Russian and Afghan troops clashed at Pendjeh and the Gladstone Government was called upon to meet its guarantee of Afghan independence. Gladstone diffused the situation by submitting the matter to international arbitration.

The Turkish Empire

Gladstone succeeded in dropping the Conservative plan of defending Turkey's Asian border with Russia. British 'military' consuls were withdrawn to be replaced by civilian ones.

After a brief demonstration of force by the Royal Navy off the eastern Balkans, a conference of ambassadors met in London in 1880, which persuaded Turkey to hand over the province of Thessaly to Greece. This was the only example of Gladstone's use of the Concert of Europe during his ministry.

Egypt, 1882–1885

Britain had vital interests in Egypt, both in investments and in the Suez Canal. In 1876, the Khedive of Egypt was declared bankrupt and a Public Debt Commission was created to look after the interests of foreign investors. However, when this arrangement failed, in 1878, two ministers – one British and one French – were appointed to run the financial side of the Egyptian government.

Under the Law of Liquidation of July 1880, the six major European powers were given 66% of Egypt's revenue to pay off its foreign debt. This not surprisingly, sparked off a nationalist reaction which led to a revolt led by an army officer, Arabi Pasha, at the end of 1881.

Gladstone had hoped for joint action by Britain and France to suppress the revolt, but the plans failed for a number of reasons. The French government went through a period of instability in 1881 and 1882. At first, Prime Minister Léon Gambetta wanted joint action with Britain, but he fell from power on 27 January 1882. In May 1882, a joint naval demonstration at Alexandria was planned, but the French failure to involve Turkey meant that it was ineffective and only sparked off anti-western riots in the city on 11 and 12 June. On 11 July, Admiral Seymour, in charge of the British naval force, misinterpreted his instructions and bombarded Alexandria.

The British now faced a complete breakdown of law and order in Egypt so on 20 July Gladstone reluctantly agreed to send a military expedition to restore order, thereby protecting British investments and the Suez Canal. Gladstone had hoped for a 'rescue and retire' expedition. However, once the British had entered Egypt they found it almost impossible to leave without sparking off another breakdown in law and order.

Under Lord Dufferin, the British decided to put Egypt on a sound financial footing. In December 1884, Britain attempted to negotiate an international loan. However, at the London Conference of March 1885, the European powers failed to agree and Britain was forced to remain in control of Egypt – a situation which lasted until 1922.

The Sudan, 1883–1885

The Sudan was a possession of Egypt. In 1881, Mohammed Ahmad (the Mahdi) started a fundamentalist Muslim *jihad* ('holy war') against the Egyptians and westerners. In November 1883, he destroyed an Anglo-Egyptian army and threatened the Egyptian presence in the Sudan. Instead of withdrawing, the Cabinet sent General Gordon to the Sudanese capital Khartoum.

This proved to be a disastrous choice. Gordon was unwilling to withdraw yet the Liberal Government was unwilling to send him military aid. Finally at the end of December 1884, the Government sent a relief force which arrived at Khartoum on 23 February 1885, two days after Gordon had been killed by Mahdist troops who had taken the city. Gordon's death caused uproar in Britain and the episode proved an electoral liability in the June 1885 general election.

The Berlin West Africa Conference and the Scramble for Africa, 1884–1885

For most of the century, Britain had informal control over much of west Africa. In the 1880s, however, France and then Germany began to take formal control of west African territory. In 1884, representatives of 15 nations gathered in Berlin at Bismarck's invitation to decide on who should control west Africa. Gladstone was forced to abandon British informal control in areas such as Cameroon, Togoland and the Congo basin in favour of Germany, France and King Leopold II of Belgium.

Elsewhere in Africa, Britain was on the defensive. In 1884, the Germans claimed control over south-west Africa and the east coast of Africa near Zanzibar. In 1885, the Government took control of the Bechuanaland Protectorate in order to prevent a common border between the Transvaal and German-controlled south-west Africa.

1. Using the information contained within this section, write down those aspects of Gladstone's foreign and imperial policy you regard as successful. Then write down those aspects of his policy that you regard as a failure.

2. On balance, was Gladstone successful in foreign and imperial affairs during his Second Administration? Give reasons to support your answer.

3. During his Second Ministry Gladstone has been described as a 'reluctant imperialist'.

Using the information contained above, how far do you agree with this view?

India

On his return to office, Gladstone replaced Lord Lytton with Lord Ripon as Viceroy of India. Instead of trying to protect British rule in India through acquiring territory on the north-west frontier, Ripon attempted to win support from the western-educated Indian élite. In 1883, he put forward the Ilbert Bill which planned to allow Indian magistrates the right to sit in judgement on whites. This sparked off widespread white opposition and resulted in the Bill being withdrawn. The result was that Ripon upset both whites and educated Indians. One consequence was the creation of the Indian National Congress in 1885 by educated Indians to fight for Indian rights.

An assessment of Gladstone's foreign and imperial policy

In 1880, Gladstone hoped to use the Concert of Europe and friendship with France to ensure European peace and to further British interests. Unfortunately, he completely underestimated the impact of Bismarck's diplomatic revolution. The Dual Alliance with Austria-Hungary (1879), the renewal of the *Dreikaiserbund* (1881) and the Triple Alliance (1882) had led to the isolation of France and the end of the Concert of Europe.

The invasion of Egypt in 1882 soured Anglo–French relations for a generation and upset Turkey and Italy. Gladstone's commitment to Afghanistan led to direct confrontation with Russia in 1885. In Africa, Gladstone proved to be a reluctant imperialist, reacting to events rather than controlling them.

Gladstone was ill-served by his Foreign Secretary, Lord Granville, whose illness and financial problems affected his performance. Foreign and imperial affairs also helped widen the gap between Whig and Radical within the Liberal Party.

18.6 To what extent was Britain in a state of 'splendid isolation' between 1885 and 1895?

On 26 February 1896, the First Lord of the Admiralty, George Goschen, stated: 'Our isolation, if isolation it be, was self-imposed. It arose out of our unwillingness to take part in Bismarck's system. Why are we isolated? We are isolated because we will not promise things which possibly we might be unwilling to perform.'

Ever since that time, politicians and historians have referred to Britain's international position in the late 19th century as one of 'splendid isolation'. How far is this description accurate? Isolation in the context mentioned by Goschen refers to Britain's decision not to be involved in the European alliance system of the late 19th century. In 1879, Germany signed a formal defensive alliance with Austria-Hungary (the Dual Alliance). This was expanded to include Italy in 1882 (the Triple Alliance, or Triplice). Between

1892 and 1894, France and Russia signed a formal defensive alliance (the Franco–Russian Alliance). By 1895, therefore, Britain was the only European Great Power not involved in a formal alliance.

However, in the 1880s, Britain's fear of Russian naval ambitions towards the Mediterranean had led to the signing of the Mediterranean agreements of May and December 1887 with Austria-Hungary and Italy. Although negotiated by Lord Salisbury, they were not followed by Gladstone (Prime Minister 1892–94) or Lord Rosebery (Prime Minister 1894–95). When Salisbury returned to office in 1895, he did not revive the agreements. In 1889, Bismarck tried to persuade Salisbury to make Britain an associate member of the Triple Alliance, but Salisbury refused.

Of the two alliance systems in existence by 1895, the one that seemed to be the greater threat to Britain was the Franco–Russian Alliance. Diplomatic relations between Britain and France had been strained since Britain's invasion of Egypt in 1882. These relations were made worse by Anglo–French colonial rivalry in west Africa. Russia was also seen as a threat to Britain's international position. This threat was seen at the Straits, in Central Asia, in Afghanistan and, by 1895, in the Far East and in northern China. When Britain passed the **Naval Defence Act** in 1889, the Government had France and Russia in mind.

Naval Defence Act, 1889: This Act set the limit on the size of the Royal Navy. From 1889, the Navy was to be at least as large as the next two largest navies in the world combined.

Several contemporaries were pleased Britain had not become involved in formal defensive alliances in Europe. They regarded Britain's isolation as 'splendid' because they felt Britain was above involvement in European politics. It was also based on the belief that Britain was sufficiently powerful not to require permanent allies. Perhaps the main reason was the fact that Britain's foreign policy interests were outside Europe. Therefore, on occasion, Britain did sign treaties with European states to protect the British Empire. In 1885, the Gladstone Government signed the West Africa Act, in Berlin, with France, Germany and other European powers over colonial boundaries in west Africa. In 1890, in the Heligoland–Zanzibar Agreement, Britain settled colonial claims with Germany over east Africa.

1. What does the historical term 'splendid isolation' mean when applied to Britain?

2. Explain why Britain was described as being in a state of 'splendid isolation' in foreign affairs.

Conclusion

During the period 1868–95, Britain's international position came under increasing threat. In India, Britain was threatened by the expansion of Russia into Central Asia. In Africa, Britain's informal empire was threatened by the colonial claims of countries such as France and Germany. This development helped to provoke the European Partition of Africa. By 1895, however, Britain still possessed the largest colonial empire in the world while the Royal Navy was still seen as 'ruling the waves'. Although a major European war almost took place over the Eastern Question, in 1878, the period was generally one of stability. This was due in large measure to Bismarck's skilful diplomacy.

Social and economic change, 1868–1896

Key Issues

- *In what ways did the size, structure and location of population change?*
- *To what extent did Britain experience economic depression from the 1870s to the 1890s?*
- *How far did trade unionism change between 1868 and 1896?*

19.1 What were the main features of British population structure in 1868?
19.2 How far had the population structure changed by 1891?
19.3 Historical interpretation: How far did British industry and trade suffer a 'Great Depression' between 1873 and 1896?
19.4 What were the causes of the agricultural depression?
19.5 Why did New Unionism develop during the 1880s?

Framework of Events

1867	Hornby *versus* Close court case raises doubts about legal protection for trade unions
1867	Siemens and Martin invent open hearth furnace, which increases output of steel
1868	First Trades Union Congress in Manchester
1871	Trades Union Act gives unions legal recognition
1872	Formation of National Agricultural Union by Joseph Arch
1873	Beginning of 'Great Depression'
1875	Start of depression in agriculture
1879	Richmond Commission on Agriculture
1886	Royal Commission on the Depression of Industry and Trade
1888	Matchgirls' strike at Bryant and May's factory in East London. Start of New Unionism
1889	Great London Dock Strike
1890	Formation of Shipping Federation, the employers' response to New Unionism
1894	Royal Commission on Agriculture
1896	End of the 'Great Depression'.

Overview

In 1868, Britain was still regarded as 'the workshop of the world'. Britain was the world leader in the manufacture of textiles, shipbuilding and coal production. In finance, the City of London was the centre for world investment funds and insurance. Yet, as Britain approached the last quarter of the 19th century, this dominance in economic and financial matters was coming under attack. The

United States of America experienced a period of rapid economic growth following the end of its civil war in 1865. Similar economic growth also occurred in Germany which, like the USA, had become a serious rival to Britain as the world's greatest manufacturing and trading nation.

It was during this period of increasing international economic competition that Britain began to experience major problems in both industry and agriculture. Starting in 1873, the rate of economic growth in Britain, in common with many other European states, began to slow down. There were fears of overproduction. Many contemporaries described this development as the 'Great Depression'. In the same decade, British agriculture faced serious problems associated with poor weather and increased foreign competition.

This period of economic change was also associated with major changes in the organisation and membership of trade unions. In 1868, the New Model Unions, representing the interests of skilled workers (artisans) such as engineers and carpenters, were the dominant form of labour organisation. By the end of the 1880s, however, New Unionism had appeared. These 'new' unions started to organise unskilled and casual workers outside the New Model Union structure, such as dockers, gas workers and women involved in match manufacture.

In what ways did Britain experience major social and economic change in the period 1868–96?

By the closing decade of the century, Britain had lost its dominant position in the world economy. Industrial relations had changed dramatically and British politicians had begun to question the foundation stone of British economic policy since the 1840s: free trade.

19.1 What were the main features of British population structure in 1868?

The main source of information about the size, structure and location of the British population was the censuses of 1861 and 1871. In the 'General Report' on the 1871 Census, it was announced that since the beginning of Queen Victoria's reign an additional 5.9 million had been added to her subjects in the United Kingdom.

By 1871, a new trend had become apparent. There was a major movement from the countryside to towns. In most cases, this internal migration was over short distances, except when it involved the Irish. While Britain was experiencing the social and economic changes associated with industrialisation during the late 18th and 19th centuries, Ireland remained a predominantly agricultural economy with a large number of landless peasants (see Chapter 17 on Ireland). Following the Great Famine of 1845–49, large numbers of Irish men and women emigrated, many to the USA. Throughout the last half of the 19th century, Ireland was the only region of the United Kingdom to experience a decline in population.

Although population continued to grow rapidly, the death rate was still high. The main cause of death among men was 'consumption' (tuberculosis), and for adult women it was childbirth. In spite of public health legislation, the new industrial towns contained areas of poor housing and inadequate sanitation which also contributed to poor health.

TABLE 1 Population recorded in the census, 1861 and 1871

Date	England and Wales	United Kingdom
1861	20,000,000	28,900,000
1871	22,700,000	31,500,000

1. Using the information contained here, describe the main features of the population of England and the United Kingdom between 1861 and 1871.

2. Study Table 4. Explain why you think men outnumbered women in agriculture and mining, and why women outnumbered men in domestic service.

TABLE 2 Births and deaths, 1861 and 1871

	Births per thousand	Deaths per thousand
1861	35.8	22.6
1871	35.7	22.0

TABLE 3 Net gain or loss by migration in England (in 000s)

	London	Other towns	Colliery districts	Rural areas
1851–61	+244	+272	+103	–743
1861–71	+262	+271	+91	–683

TABLE 4 The distribution of employment, 1871 Census

	Male	Female	Total
Agriculture	1,350,000	85,000	1,435,000
Mining	371,000	6,000	377,000
Manufacturing	2,089,000	1,269,000	3,358,000
Domestic service	196,000	1,488,000	1,684,000

Razor-grinders at work, Sheffield, 1866

19.2 How far had the population structure changed by 1891?

Between the censuses of 1871 and 1891, Britain experienced a 'Great Depression' in industry and trade and a major depression in agriculture. In Ireland, the depression in agriculture was very serious, involving a partial famine in 1877 and the outbreak of the 'Land War' in 1879. During this period, the overall population continued to grow. While birth rates remained high in towns, there was a decline in the birth rate in rural areas. In 1871, the birth rate in rural areas had been 32.0 per thousand. This had dropped to 29.5 per thousand by 1891. The main cause of this decline was the emigration of young men and women either to towns or overseas.

Over the same 20-year period, there was a decline in the marriage rate. By 1891, people were getting married later while the proportion of married people within the population also declined.

TABLE 5 Population recorded in the census

Date	England and Wales	United Kingdom
1871	22,700,000	31,500,000
1881	26,000,000	34,700,000
1891	29,000,000	37,700,000

TABLE 6 Births and deaths, 1871–95

	Births per thousand	Deaths per thousand
1871	35.7	22.0
1881–85	33.5	19.4
1886–90	31.4	18.9
1891–95	30.5	18.7

TABLE 7 Net gain or loss by migration in England (in 000s)

	London	Other towns	Colliery districts	Rural areas
1861–71	+262	+271	+91	–683
1871–81	+307	+297	+84	–837
1881–91	+169	–31	+90	–845

Study the information contained in Tables 5–8.

To what extent had the trends in population, apparent in 1871, changed by 1891?

Give reasons to support your answer.

TABLE 8 The distribution of employment, 1891 Census

	Male	Female	Total
Agriculture	1,141,000	51,000	1,192,000
Mining	559,000	5,000	564,000
Manufacturing	2,609,000	1,530,000	4,139,000
Domestic service	359,000	1,632,000	1,991,000

19.3 *How far did British industry and trade suffer a 'Great Depression' between 1873 and 1896?*

A CASE STUDY IN HISTORICAL INTERPRETATION

During the period 1850–73, the British economy experienced what has been called the 'mid-Victorian boom'. The economy grew, on average, by 3% per year. Railway construction increased from 9,500 km of track in 1850 to 22,000 km by 1875. In foreign trade, Britain's major export industries (cotton, textiles and coal) performed well. The value of cotton cloth produced rose from £46 million in 1851 to £105 million in 1875, while coal production increased from 60 million tonnes in 1855 to 109 million tonnes by 1870.

From 1873, however, the British economy began to slow down. Unemployment rose. On the eve of the 'Great Depression', in 1872, unemployment was a mere 1%. By 1879, it had risen to 11.4% and was still over 10% in the year of the Home Rule crisis of 1886. So, it would appear, the British economy was suffering from a depression. But how far is this an accurate description of this period of British economic history?

The case for

In *The Great Victorian Boom, 1850–1873* (1975), R.A. Church stated: 'The "Great Depression" was derived from the Royal Commission on the Depression of Trade and Industry in 1886, which offered an opportunity for merchant and manufacturers to ventilate their concern over foreign competition.' It seems clear that contemporaries thought Britain was facing a depression in trade and industry. In 1879, *The Economist* described that year as 'one of the most sunless and cheerless of the century' while, in 1884, the Conservative politician, Lord Randolph Churchill, described Britain's trade being affected by 'a mortal disease'.

There is some evidence to support these views. During the mid-Victorian boom, Britain's export performance was aided by the policy of free trade. After 1873, however, many European countries and the USA abandoned free trade and began imposing taxes on imported goods (tariffs). Italy abandoned free trade in 1878, followed by Germany in 1879, France in 1882 and, finally, the USA in 1883, which raised its tariffs even higher in 1890. The onset of economic protection made it increasingly difficult to export goods to these countries.

In addition, Britain faced increasing competition, in particular from the USA and Germany. Study the information in Table 9 to see how Britain's world lead in steel production had come to an end by the 1890s.

TABLE 9 ***Steel production as a percentage of world production***

	United Kingdom	USA	Germany
1875–79	35.9	26.0	16.6
1880–84	32.7	28.4	17.7
1885–89	31.8	31.4	17.8
1890–94	24.6	33.7	21.4

Not only did Britain face competition in export markets, but the prices of industrial goods fell between 1873 and 1896. Between 1871 and 1896, the price of coal and textiles dropped by over 30%.

It would seem the term 'Great Depression' has some validity after all.

The case against

Although the rate of growth in the British economy did slow down in the last quarter of the 19th century it would be difficult to describe what happened as an economic depression. In 1969, the historian S.B. Saul wrote *The Myth of the Great Depression* in which he pointed out that, although there was a serious lowering of business confidence, it would be wrong to state that the whole economy was in depression. Throughout the period, the economy continued to grow. In 1896, Britain was still one of the world's leading economic powers.

While steel production and metal manufacturing faced increasingly serious competition from the USA and Germany, other industries continued to prosper. For instance, coal output during the 1880s rose by 23.5%, much of it exported.

Study the case for and against the idea that the British economy faced a 'Great Depression' between 1873 and 1896.

Which case do you find more convincing?

Give reasons to support your answer.

Also, Britain was not the only European economy to undergo a slowdown in economic growth. Both Germany and the USA faced similar problems. This was one of the reasons why both these economies introduced taxes on imported goods.

If falling prices were seen as a problem for businessmen, they had the opposite effect for the working classes. Falling prices for industrial and agricultural goods during the period of the 'Great Depression' led to a rise in real wages.

Therefore, although Britain did suffer some economic problems in the years 1873 to 1896, these did not affect the whole economy. As Saul stated, although 'we are far from a full understanding of all the problems ... this at least is clear: the sooner the "Great Depression" is banished from literature, the better'.

19.4 What were the causes of the agricultural depression?

While historians debate whether or not trade and industry faced an economic depression in the years 1873–96, there is strong evidence that agriculture faced serious economic problems during this period. According to the findings of the Richmond Commission on Agriculture, which reported in 1882, the root cause of the problem was a succession of bad harvests. This was due mainly to abnormally high rainfall between 1875 and 1879, which affected wheat and cereal farming.

Almost at the same time, British cereal farmers were facing increased competition from cereal imports, in particular from North America. From the 1870s to the turn of the century, wheat prices followed a downward trend. The rise in North American imports was, in part, due to the development of new prairie lands in the west. It was also due to the steep fall in transportation costs. The cost of carrying a quarter ton of wheat from Chicago to Liverpool fell from 11 shillings (55p) in 1869 to 4s 3d (21p) by 1892. One result was the decline in the acreage in Britain planted with wheat from a peak of 3.6 million acres in 1869 to only 1.3 million in 1904. This was matched by a rise in land given over to raising livestock.

In Germany, when farmers had been faced by the import of cheap Russian grain, the government had introduced tariffs to protect German cereal production. However, government protection for British cereal farmers had come to an end with the repeal of the Corn Laws in 1846. As both the Liberal and Conservative parties were committed to free trade, little was done in the way of government intervention to aid the farming community. (See Chapter 15 on Gladstone and the Liberals.)

Although cereal farming had particular problems, changes in technology had an impact on other sectors of the agricultural economy. In 1882, the

Market gardening: Growing food such as tomatoes, cabbages etc. for a local urban market.

Home Counties: The counties surrounding London; Essex, Middlesex, Kent and Surrey.

first refrigerated cargo of mutton arrived from New Zealand. By the end of the century, the development of canning factories and refrigerated shipping led to the import of meat from Argentina and Australia as well as New Zealand. Almost one-third of meat sold in Britain was imported by 1895.

Not all sectors of the agricultural economy faced depression, however. With the growth of towns **market gardening** grew in popularity, particularly in the **Home Counties**, while the fall in food prices saw the real wages of agricultural workers increase.

Study the causes of the agricultural depression mentioned above.

Which causes do you regard as:

(a) short-term causes

(b) long-term causes?

Give reasons to support your answer.

19.5 Why did New Unionism develop in the 1880s?

In 1868, the first meeting of the Trades Union Congress (TUC) took place in Manchester, attended by 34 delegates representing 100,000 trade unionists. The unions involved in the foundation of this national organisation were New Model Unions. These unions had developed since 1851 and were 'modelled' on the aims and organisation of the Amalgamated Society of Engineers. They all possessed similar characteristics. They had a permanent full-time staff, high subscription rates and offered their members benefits such as funeral expenses and pensions. Membership was limited to **skilled workers**. In addition, strikes were to be held only after consultation with permanent full-time staff, with a ban on unofficial strikes altogether.

Skilled workers: Workers who have passed an apprenticeship to become skilled in a specific craft or job such as plumber, carpenter, boilermaker.

In spite of this moderate stance, trade unions in 1868 were still not legally recognised. It took Gladstone's Liberal Government to offer full legal recognition with the Trade Union Act of 1871. Four years later, Disraeli's Conservative Government permitted peaceful **picketing** during strikes (The Conspiracy and Protection of Property Act).

Picketing: Standing outside a factory or workplace trying to prevent people from going to work.

Even with legal recognition, trade unionism was limited to a small minority of the workforce. By 1888, trade unions had approximately 750,000 members, representing about 10% of all adult male workers in the economy.

The rise of the new unions

Within four years, however, the nature of British trade unionism had changed radically. Between 1889 and 1891, trade union membership doubled. Of greater importance was the change in both aims and organisation of new unions formed at this time.

These 'new' unions were more politically orientated and, in many cases, led by socialists. Unlike the leaders of the New Model Unions, the leaders of the 'new unions' wanted fundamental changes made in the distribution of wealth and income within British society in favour of the low paid. For example, Annie Besant, the leader of the matchgirls' strike of 1888, was a member of a socialist party, the Social Democratic Federation, and the

Fabian Society. Will Thorne, the leader of the London Gasworkers in their strike in March 1889, was also a member of the Social Democratic Federation.

In addition, the new unions were recruited from unskilled, casual workers and not the skilled artisans associated with the New Model Unions. They were also called 'general unions' because they were open to anyone within an industry, regardless of their job. Workers such as women workers in the Bryant and May match factory in East London, gasworkers and dockers had never been unionised before. These were some of the most poorly paid workers in the country, enduring difficult and unpleasant working conditions. Unlike the members of the New Model Unions, these workers could pay only small subscriptions – which were used mainly as a strike fund rather than to provide benefits.

The first strike involving these 'new unions' to capture public attention took place in the summer of 1888, at the Bryant and May match factory. The women were earning, on average, five shillings (25p) for a 70—hour week. The strike was successful and a matchgirls' union was formed the following year with 800 members.

The year was to be more significant for the development of 'New Unionism'. In March 1889, the Gas Workers' and General Labourers' Union was created and by the end of the year had 20,000 members. Of greater importance was the Great London Dock Strike, which began on 14 August and lasted five weeks. By the end of the second week over 100,000 workers were on strike. The dockers, led by Ben Tillett and Tom Mann, demanded a minimum wage of 6d per hour. They received considerable support from within Britain, including that of Cardinal Manning. They also received financial support of £30,000 from dockers in Australia. After five weeks the employers gave in to the dockers' demands. In the same year, a seamen's union and the General Railwayworkers' Union were also formed.

Although some historians have seen 1889 as a turning point for the

1. The two cartoons depict the London Dock Strike of 1889. In what ways are they different in their opinions of the strikers? Explain your answer.

2. 'These cartoons are unreliable sources of information on the London Dock Strike, but are nevertheless useful to a historian.' How far do you agree with this view?

3. Which do you think is more useful to a historian writing about the London Dock Strike, the photograph or the two cartoons? Give reasons to support your answer.

FACE TO FACE!

THE GUINEA-FOWL THAT LAYS THE GOLDEN EGGS.

Two cartoons from *Punch*, dated 7 and 14 September 1889

Photograph of a procession through London in support of the London dockers' strike, 1889

development of British trade unionism, the strike victories of 1888–89 were of limited success. During the 1890s, the employers began fight back. In 1890, the Shipping Federation was created to help break the hold of the Dockers' Union. In 1893, the National Free Labour Association was able to provide **blackleg** labour to the Federation and other employers. As a result, membership of the Dockers' Union fell from 56,000 in 1890 to 23,000 by 1892. The success of the employers in the docks was matched by similar developments in the cotton and coalmining industries. If 1888–91 was a period of rapid growth for trade unions, the 1890s proved to be a period of retreat.

Blackleg: term given to workers who were not union members and were employed during strikes.

Source-based questions: The New Unionism

SOURCE A

Born in slums, driven to work while still children, undersized because underfed, oppressed because helpless, flung aside as soon as worked out, who cares if they die or go on the streets provided that Bryant and May shareholders get their 23%.

From an article in the newspapers entitled 'White Slavery in London' published in 1888, by Annie Besant, leader of the East London Matchgirls' Strike at Bryant and May's factory.

SOURCE B

The Dock Strike was the most famous action during this period, but it was not the only successful one. The matchgirls had shown the way. Will Thorne launched his National Union of Gas Workers and General Labourers early in 1889, and won a battle with the gas companies for an eight-hour day. The membership of Havelock Wilson's Seamen's and Firemen's Union shot up to 65,000. Friedrich Engels, the old Communist and partner of Karl Marx, hoped that the British revolution had arrived at last. He wrote, 'The masses are on the move and there is no holding them.'

From The Illustrated London News, *7 September 1889.*

SOURCE C

In the years 1889–91 total trade union membership doubled. This was a remarkable expansion, although possibly not an unprecedented one. The tendency for trade union membership to expand in sudden dramatic bursts is well known, and the upsurge of 1889–91 had been preceded by similar expansions in 1833–5 and 1872–4. Historians have long sought to explain this uneven pattern of trade union growth, and a whole range of theories have been advanced. It seems reasonable to suggest, however, that socialism was not a cause of the upheaval of 1889. The great union expansion coincided with the period of high employment running from 1889 to 1891. In an overstocked labour market it was only in times of exceptionally high employment that the mass of workers possessed any bargaining power.

From British Trade Unions 1875–1933 *by John Lovell, published in 1977.*

1. Study Source A.

How, by her use of language and style, does Annie Besant emphasise her support for the striking matchgirls?

2. Study Sources B and C.

How far do these sources differ in their explanation of the rise in union membership in the period 1889 to 1891?

3. Study all the Sources and use information contained within this chapter.

Do the sources above provide enough information to explain the rapid growth in trade union membership in the years 1888 to 1891?

Give reasons to support your answer.

20 The era of Conservative domination and the rise of Labour, 1895–1906

20.1 To what extent were the Liberals in decline in the 1890s?
20.2 The origins of Labour representation in Parliament: what difficulties did the early pioneers face?
20.3 Salisbury's Third and Fourth Administrations, 1895–1902: was there any prospect of further reform?
20.4 How serious were the problems faced by Balfour's Government, 1902–1905?
20.5 How successfully did Balfour deal with these problems up to 1905?
20.6 Historical interpretation: Why did the Liberals win a landslide victory in January 1906?

Key Issues

- *Why did the Conservatives, rather than the Liberals, form the governments between 1895 and 1903?*
- *Why did a distinct Labour Party develop during these years?*
- *Why did the Conservatives suffer a crushing defeat in the January 1906 general election?*

Framework of Events

1895	General election returns Salisbury to power with a large majority Coalition between Conservatives and Liberal Unionists
1897	Workmen's Compensation Act Queen Victoria's Diamond Jubilee
1898	Campbell-Bannerman appointed Liberal leader
1899	The Boer War starts
1900	'Khaki' election returns Salisbury to power Labour Representation Committee is formed
1901	Queen Victoria's death; Edward VII becomes King The Taff Vale Judgement
1902	Balfour succeeds Salisbury as Prime Minister Education Act Treaty of Vereeniging ends the Boer War
1903	Tariff reform campaign starts Lib–Lab pact Suffragette WSPU set up
1904	The Report of the Inter-Departmental Committee on Physical Deterioration
1905	Balfour resigns; Campbell-Bannerman calls a general election
1906	January: General Election and Liberal landslide victory Labour Representation Committee renamed the Labour Party.

Overview

Conservative: Technically called the Unionist Party after the Liberal Unionists joined the Conservative Party in 1895.

It is tempting to see politics at the turn of the 20th century as a time of transition from the Victorian age, which closed with the ascendancy of the **Conservative** Party, led by Lord Salisbury up until 1902 (the last time the country was run by an aristocrat from the House of Lords), to the Edwardian age which began with such a sense of uncertainty about the future. Working-class movements and labour representation in Parliament reflected new forces at work in a Britain that felt threatened by international economic rivalry. Our position as 'workshop of the world' was no longer secure and concerns about the 'state of the nation' and 'national efficiency' were growing, particularly since it had proved so difficult to win the South African War against the Boers. The Suffragettes had been formed in 1903 although, as yet, there were only hints of their most militant campaigning.

This chapter ends with an astonishing Liberal election victory in 1906, which brought to an end Balfour's Conservative Government of 1902–05. Contemporaries may have felt unease about what was to come, but there were important elements of continuity as well as change throughout the period. The development of 'labour' was by no means certain, while the Conservative Party remained steadfastly in the hands of the '**Hotel Cecil**'. Many areas of the British economy continued to lead the world, although demands for reform to alleviate the effects of industrial society were growing. Under the Conservatives, however, social reform would not be a prominent feature of government. Why then did they occupy so dominant a position over domestic politics?

'Hotel Cecil': The nickname originated from Salisbury's 1900 Government, which contained many of his relations, including his nephew Arthur Balfour (who later became Prime Minister).

20.1 To what extent were the Liberals in decline in the 1890s?

In the 1895 general election, the Conservatives won 341 seats. When added to the 80 Liberal Unionist MPs, Lord Salisbury had secured a huge majority in the House of Commons. How serious was the collapse in Liberal fortunes? The seeds of Liberal decline were clear during their last Government because of the following:

- Their reliance on the support of the Irish Home Rule Party.
- The division in the party once the Marquis of Hartington and Joseph Chamberlain had led the Liberal Unionists across the floor of the House of Commons to join the Conservatives.
- The defeat of the 1893 Home Rule Bill which left them without a major cause to pursue.
- The results of the 1895 election which revealed their reliance on Welsh and Scottish votes, as they failed to gain a majority in England. Even worse was a failure to increase their share of the working class vote.
- Their prominent figures – Lewis Harcourt, John Morley and Lord Rosebery – who conducted petty quarrels and divergent policies which failed to keep the Party together.

Unity was never an easy matter as the Party consisted of many disparate elements. Gladstone had kept things together, but now there was generous scope for squabbling and in-fighting. Rosebery resigned in 1896, only to be replaced by Harcourt who also failed to give a firm sense of direction to the Party; witness his feeble attempts to discredit Chamberlain for his part in the Jameson Raid in 1896. Harcourt limped on until 1898, when Sir Henry Campbell-Bannerman replaced him. Campbell-Bannerman was solid, uninspiring, largely unknown outside Liberal circles and dwarfed by powerful Conservative figures such as Joseph Chamberlain and Lord Salisbury.

Was it clear to the voters what the Liberals stood for? The historian D.A. Hamer notes that once Home Rule had moved more into the background, 'Sectionalism re-emerged, rampant and uncontrollable'. Another historian, Paul Adelman, in *Gladstone, Disraeli and Later Victorian Politics*

'Faddism': Many Liberals had their own sectional 'fads' or favourite causes, such as temperance reform (limiting the sale of alcohol) or disestablishment (depriving the Church of its connection with the State).

(1983), refers to this 'reversion to "**faddism**", with each Liberal section pursuing its own hare oblivious to the rest of the field'. What was it to be – temperance, land reform, Welsh disestablishment, or Liberal imperialism? The new strand here was Liberal imperialism which had its supporters like Lord Rosebery who wished to develop the Empire, without recourse to aggressive flag waving, and social reform at home.

The problem was that little of this cut much ice with working-class voters in the cities – the Liberals' loss of power in London and other major cities shows this. More recent research by John Vincent and D. Fraser has suggested that the Liberals should have addressed matters of closer interest to the working man – jobs and wages, not flag waving or controlling licensing hours. Local Liberal associations also contributed to the arguments in favour of an independent labour representation in Parliament by turning their backs on candidates from working-class backgrounds – Keir Hardie is a case in point. Men like him were losing faith in the Liberals.

Even more serious, in the short term, was the loss of leadership and money when the Unionists left in 1886. The Party had been unable to fight the Conservatives in 114 seats – not a situation they had been in at the previous election. In 1900, even more Conservatives were unopposed – a source of embarrassment made worse by the Liberal's opposition to the Boer War, which enabled the Conservatives to label many of them pro-Boer. There is, then, a strong case for saying that Lord Salisbury's ascendancy was the electorate's response to the absence of a credible alternative to the Conservatives.

One interpretation is that Liberalism was also being undermined by existing social trends which made their decline inevitable. This view regards the 1906 Liberal victory as merely a temporary, if spectacular, revolt against the Conservative/Unionist alliance. Crudely speaking, the middle classes were drifting to the Conservatives. Representatives of commerce were joining the landowning party, making the dividing line between these two economic groups increasingly blurred, as each invested in the other's interests. Many landowners, for example, were helping to develop railways, shipping and mining. The Conservatives were beginning to represent the fears of substantial elements of the propertied classes who had much to lose if Radical Liberals pandered to **militant trade unionism** or Irish nationalism. An expanding lower middle class – such as junior managers, white collar staff, foremen artisans who wished to protect their salaries and better houses in the suburbs, away from the slums – looked to the Unionists to guard their new status. This was 'villa Toryism' and it adds weight to historian J.P. Cornford's view that class increasingly decided voting patterns. In rural areas, the Anglican clergy and gentry continued to maintain their grip – but 'villa' Tories in the boroughs tipped the scales.

Militant trade unionism: Extreme and sometimes violent workers' action taken against capitalism.

There is also a widely accepted view that Conservative organisation, run by Aretas Akers-Douglas and Captain R.W.E. Middleton, was very efficient. Most seats were fought, the number of party agents multiplied in the constituencies, while plural voting (property owners, businessmen, university graduates) running at 7% of the total vote is generally reckoned to have helped the Conservatives.

The 1884 Reform Act also disadvantaged working-class voters – possibly up to 4 million. The registration system required 12 months in a tenancy before a person could vote. Since working men changed jobs and houses more often, they tended to disenfranchise themselves; anyway, they had weaker habits of political allegiance to any party. If the working class was inclined to apathy as far as political (as opposed to industrial) action was concerned, it made it more difficult for the Liberals to exploit their potential voting support.

The Redistribution of Seats Act of 1885 did much to help 'villa Toryism'.

The Act divided voters into roughly equal constituencies with single members to represent them. Salisbury's hand behind this reform ensured that when the new boundaries were drawn, Conservative voters in the towns would not be swamped. It enabled middle-class suburbs to elect Conservative members. As a result, towns like Sheffield, Glasgow and Manchester were returning Tory MPs. The historian Martin Pugh highlights, in *The Evolution of the British Electoral System, 1832–1987* (1988), the powerful work done by the Primrose League. This was a Conservative social organisation that drew in these middle-class voters to a range of entertainments such as concerts, fêtes, shows and weekend tours. Such 'popular' activities helped to integrate people into the beliefs of the Party, adding to a groundswell of supporters. It helped to spread myths about the reforms passed by the Party. Leaflets such as 'What the Conservatives have done for the British people' effectively spread the message, although the reality lacked substance.

1. What changes took place that enabled the Conservatives to increase their number of MPs?

2. Which was the most important factor in explaining the Conservative ascendancy after 1895? Give reasons to support your answer.

What is more difficult to explain is the support the Conservatives gained from sections of the working class – so-called 'slum Toryism'. Was it the patriotic appeal of Empire, Queen Victoria's jubilees and tales of imperial glory which appealed to the working class? The 'Khaki' election of 1900, called during the Boer War, returned 402 Conservatives and only 184 Liberal MPs to Westminster. The anti-war 'Little Englanders' among the Liberals compromised any chances they might have had, as they split with Rosebery's Liberal Imperialists who were in favour of the war. Such chaos rebounded in Salisbury's favour, and the timing of this election so early during the war must have made an impact of sorts. However, historian H. Pelling challenges the view that the Empire made any lasting impression on a working class more interested in material wellbeing – represented by jobs, prices and wages. If this is the case, then clearly the Liberal Party had little to offer.

Was there a groundswell of support for a new party that might give the working man a voice in Parliament? What progress did 'labour representation' make into the late Victorian political system?

20.2 The origins of Labour representation in Parliament: what difficulties did the early pioneers face?

There was nothing inevitable about the origins and growth of a party that spoke up specifically for the interests of the working class. It grew out of a series of false starts and strangely 'incompatible elements', which came together in the 1880s and 1890s. From its beginnings, socialists found it difficult to decide what methods might be employed to achieve their aims. Competing voices called, at one extreme for a radical socialist programme which aimed for collective ownership of the means of production, distribution and exchange. At the other extreme was a more pragmatic programme that set its sights on getting broad agreement in Parliament for a number of limited, practical approaches to improve working conditions. These tensions were apparent as the early activists took their first steps towards political organisation.

The Social Democratic Foundation (SDF) was formed by H.M. Hyndman, a Cambridge-educated stockbroker and **Marxist**, in 1884. He used the Labour Party mainly to spread revolutionary socialist ideas, although his high-handed and increasingly violent tactics employed when organising demonstrations by the unemployed in London (1886–87) led to quarrels between its prominent members. For instance, H.H. Champion, the editor of a socialist newspaper, *Justice*, was to leave at this time, as did John Burns and Tom Mann. These small groups of the Left were prone to self-destructive internal dissension. Nevertheless, the SDF was a potent force in London, drawing young activists into the movement.

Marxist: Belief in the ideas of Karl Marx, author of *Das Kapital*, often called the manifesto of Communism.

The other important group, formed in 1884, was the Fabians – middle-class intellectuals such as George Bernard Shaw and Sydney and Beatrice Webb. The Fabians supported the virtues of state and municipal socialism, often called 'Gas and Water' socialism, introduced gradually, to moderate the evils of capitalism and usher in a socialist state. They were not alone in opposing the call for a new party to represent labour; they believed the best way forward was for their ideas to 'permeate' the leadership of existing parties. Some historians, such as P. Thompson and Eric Hobsbawm, dismiss claims that the Fabians had any lasting influence. Paul Adelman, in *The Rise of the Labour Party 1880–1945* (1986), gives them credit for being 'successful propagandists for the ideas of "evolutionary socialism"'. He does add, though, that there were fewer than 2,000 socialists in Britain by 1889, and many of them were middle class.

The 1880s also saw the rise of the 'new unions', and the expansion of the right to vote in 1884. How far either of these developments helped the socialist groups is difficult to say. The complexities of the 1884 Reform Act regularly meant that 40% of the male population was unable to vote. It is true that nine working men had been elected to the House of Commons by 1886. As 'Lib–Labs', they shared the views of the old leadership of the Trades Union Council (TUC) in speaking for workers' interests whilst remaining resolute supporters of the Liberal Party. Henry Broadhurst was typical of this group.

Keir Hardie (1856–1915)
Hardie was a miner, nonconformist and founder of the Scottish Labour Party. He was the first 'Labour' MP, representing West Ham South in East London in 1892.

James Keir Hardie, however, was not. He was a miner who worked tirelessly to encourage his fellow workers to vote Liberal, but who came to realise the need for a separate voice in Parliament for working men. In 1888, Hardie polled 614 votes at the Mid-Lanarkshire election, standing as an independent labour candidate. In 1892, he and two other independent labour candidates, John Burns and J.H. Wilson, were elected to Parliament. Hardie's victory at West Ham South (London) was far from his Scottish heartland and proved that working-class voters could be tempted away from the Liberals and Conservatives. The leadership of the trade unions was unconvinced. Despite the success of new unionism in organising unskilled workers, winning the dockers' and the matchgirls' strikes of 1889, their impact was short-lived. In the 1890s, employers began to undermine all unionised labour but the numbers in 'new' unions slumped badly to less than 10% of total union membership. For the time being, the TUC was content, unlike Hardie, to keep the faith with Gladstone.

Why was the Independent Labour Party formed in 1893?

Hardie succeeded in bringing different socialist groups into some kind of 'alliance'. In January 1893, the Independent Labour Party (ILP) was formed at a conference in Bradford, attended by 120 delegates, including socialists from labour clubs, the SDF and Fabians. It drew on grassroots support from a number of regions:

- From Bradford, where prolonged, violent strikes against the Liberal factory owners of the Manningham Mills who were trying to cut wages, led to the establishment of the Bradford Labour Union.
- From Hardie's own Scotland, where the opposition to Irish Home Rule had sapped Liberal strength.
- From Lancashire, where energetic working-class Toryism in certain areas had made it difficult for the Liberals, who were often identified as the mill owners, to make electoral headway.
- In Manchester, where Robert Blatchford had started a popular weekly socialist newspaper, *The Clarion*, while in 1892 the Manchester and Salford ILP was formed.

The ILP proclaimed the socialist principle of collective ownership of the economy. In attempting to maintain as broad appeal as possible, the word 'socialist' was omitted from the title. Instead the 'Independent Labour Party' was chosen and, as historian David Howell notes, the balance was struck with having Labour in the title while trying to pursue distinctly socialist goals.

The ILP rapidly grew in popularity, with 35,000 members by 1895. It followed in the fairly liberal tradition of British trade union activity with none of the overtones of class warfare and revolutionary violence found on the continent. Activists were often ex-Liberals, such as Ramsay MacDonald who had a background in this 'reformist' tradition. Another strand in the ILP was nonconformity. Philip Snowden, then a young Yorkshire ILP worker, wrote in his autobiography that the new party 'derived its inspiration far more from the Sermon on the Mount than from the teachings of the economists'. Clive Behagg, a historian writing in *Years of Expansion, Britain 1815–1914*, agreed that 'many of its leaders were more familiar with the Bible than with Marx'.

Could the ILP develop a wide appeal, at a time when the Liberal Government of 1892–95 seemed to be giving up the ghost? Apparently not. In 1895, the ILP lost in all 28 constituencies where it had candidates. Keir Hardie also lost his seat, leaving the ILP with no representation in the Commons. In the absence of any finance worth speaking of, much now depended on the extent of trade union support – without a firm basis from established working-class organisations. The future looked bleak. Many of the leaders of the older unions, for instance the miners and craft associations, continued to oppose the ILP. However, the adoption by the TUC of central socialist ideas, such as the demand for an eight-hour working day, showed how socialism was slowly infiltrating the trade union movement. Burns and J.H. Wilson were elected onto the Parliamentary Committee of the TUC. The 'old guard' tried to stem the tide. They had no time for the more provocative aspects of the socialist programme and the introduction of the **block vote** system was partly a response to fears that 'dangerous', minority elements might come to dominate the Parliamentary Committee.

Block vote: A delegate would cast votes, which were equivalent to the numbers of members in the trade union he represented.

However, by the end of the 1890s, significant shifts in trade union attitudes were taking place. There was dissatisfaction with the Liberals. They were clearly riddled with factionalism and seemed unenthusiastic about reforms such as the eight-hour day. Local Liberal associations were reluctant to adopt working-class candidates, as at Attercliffe in Yorkshire in 1894. Industrial competition led to a number of long-drawn-out disputes (e.g. the great engineering lockout of 1897) with employers who were extending working hours, using new machines to force redundancies, and drawing on non-union labour to avoid the 'closed shop'. Even the old established craft unions were under attack, making their leaders reconsider their views. In 1899, an Appeal Court ruling (Lyons *versus* Wilkins) limited unions' rights to picket peacefully. Against this managerial and legal onslaught, and with the Liberals offering policies such as Disestablishment and Temperance reform, it dawned on trade union leaders that independent labour parliamentary representation might have its advantages. Similarly, ILP leaders, Hardie, MacDonald, Snowden and Glasier too were recognising the realities of the situation – a deal with the unions might bring progress.

When the TUC met in 1899, the Amalgamated Society of Railway Servants, which was itself fighting against employers who refused to recognise the union, called for a conference to help improve representation for labour in Parliament. The resolution was only passed by 546,000 votes to 434,000, but it was sufficient. When the Conference met in 1900, the SDF, Fabians, ILP and 67 trade unions were represented. A Labour Representation Committee (LRC) was set up with an executive committee consisting of each socialist group but with the trade union members in the majority. The LRC, on Hardie's insistence, set out general aims rather than anything specific such as the cherished 'collective ownership', much to the SDF's anger, and they withdrew as a result.

In 1900, the LRC won only two seats in Parliament: Keir Hardie and Robert Bell (of the Railway Servants' union). There were eight 'Lib–Labs'. Once again, money was insufficient to support candidates during elections. Hardie knew that more dynamic trade union support was the only hope. It would be the Taff Vale Case (see page 347) which cemented the bond between unions and the new party, boosting the number of unions who supported the LRC (affiliations) by 168 between the start of 1901 and the end of 1903. It was quite plain that the Conservative Government would not reverse the House of Lords judgement, while Paul Adelman notes that the Liberals 'were either unenthusiastic for, or pessimistic about the outcome of, a new trade union Bill'. Hence the unions swung their support behind the LRC. Membership rose to about 850,000 and annual revenue had grown to £5,000 by 1903, which helped to finance elections and to pay existing MPs.

1. What were the aims of:

(a) the Social Democratic Federation

(b) the Fabians

(c) the Independent Labour Party?

2. How far was the period after the Taff Vale Case (1901–06) the turning point for the rise of the Labour Representation Committee?

The LRC was now engaged in negotiations with the Liberal Chief Whip, Herbert Gladstone, to form an electoral pact. When it came to such matters as education and imperialism, the LRC and parts of the Liberal Party did tend to think along similar lines. Also, there was a danger of splitting the vote between LRC and Liberal candidates; for example at Lanark in 1901, when this very scenario enabled the Conservative to win. For both parties, precious party funds might be saved. The Liberals could see that they might win some working-class seats, while the LRC would certainly boost their numbers in Parliament. Hence, in certain constituencies, the Liberals would not oppose the LRC candidate, in return for support for the Liberals in Parliament. By 1905, they had agreed to support each other's candidates. For some LRC leaders, it seemed a logical development; others who still nursed their dream of a vigorous socialist programme, such as the SDF, were more uncomfortable. It neatly illustrates the internal dissensions which continued to thrive within the new party.

Despite this, the January 1906 general election saw 29 LRC MPs returned to Parliament. A month later, when they took their seats, they did so as members of the renamed Labour Party.

20.3 Salisbury's Third and Fourth Administrations, 1895–1902: was there any prospect of further reform?

During his Third (1895–1900) and Fourth (1900–1902) Administrations, Salisbury achieved little in domestic affairs. Costs – that is, taxes and rates – were to be kept down. Chamberlain did have schemes for reform, such as the introduction of old age pensions, but he was increasingly drawn into the world of the Colonial Office. Indeed the Boer War brought plans for domestic reform to a grinding halt. Perhaps the Conservatives were fortunate that the economy was doing better and standards of living were rising. An Agricultural Ratings Bill lowered rates for farmers. There were isolated reforms in Ireland, such as the Land Act (1896) which increased the process of selling land to tenants. County Councils were introduced there in 1898 (see Chapter 22).

Perhaps the two major pieces of legislation which Salisbury was persuaded to support in 1897 were:

- An Education Act which increased the State funding for Voluntary (Church) schools.

- A Workmen's Compensation Act which made employers liable to pay their employees compensation if they suffered an injury because of their work.

Chamberlain was able to squeeze some money out of the Treasury for some colonial reforms (see Chapter 21), but otherwise the *status quo* was defended with success.

Do you agree that Salisbury achieved little of lasting importance? Give reasons to support your answer.

The 'Khaki' election of 1900, as stated earlier, returned a massive Conservative majority. However, Salisbury was ill and not entirely at ease with those around him. He waited for the new King, Edward VII, to be crowned and then retired leaving the premiership in the hands of his nephew, Arthur Balfour. Salisbury had probably achieved what he had set out to do – limit reform, defend the interests of the landed classes and steer Britain safely through a difficult period when the Empire was growing apace and numerous agreements had to be reached to dissipate colonial tensions.

Would things change a great deal under Arthur Balfour?

20.4 How serious were the problems faced by Balfour's Government, 1902–1905?

Was Britain still in the ascendant?

Signs of decline alarmed contemporaries. There are many references to 'the condition of England' and 'national efficiency' in the literature of the period. There are numerous strands to the debate. Was it because Britain felt itself isolated in a hostile world (see Chapter 21)? Or was it because Britain's economic lead over its rivals was being lost (see Chapter 26)? Whether or not historians agree on the extent of a 'great depression' in industry and agriculture is beside the point. Contemporaries believed it and their perceptions were underpinned by a series of shocking investigations into poverty which appeared from the 1880s onwards. Charles Booth's massive study, the *Life and Labour of the People in London* (completed in 1903), found one-third of the population barely existing below the poverty line. His findings filled 17 volumes in all, meticulously detailing families who were poor not because they were lazy and feckless, but because of the size of their families. Seebohm Rowntree's study in York, *Poverty: A Study of Town Life* (published in 1899), came to similar conclusions. Unemployment or illness and old age were not the major causes of poverty. At the heart of the problem lay large families, low wages and the death of the main household wage-earner. These were 'scientific' studies, meant to inform rather than dramatise. Other titles, such as *Horrible London*, *The Bitter Cry of Outcast London*, or William Booth's *In Darkest England*, told much the same story. Social degradation, starvation, disease and poverty existed in the heart of Britain's cities.

How could British workers compete with those abroad? How could a country which sought to 'civilise' Africa turn its back on the awful reality which existed at home? They argued that the general health of the country should have been better. The picture of child health was particularly alarming. Infant mortality was as high as 202 deaths per 1,000 births reported in Sheffield, in 1901. Little wonder that a committee was set up in 1903 to investigate why so many volunteers during the Boer War were rejected because of their poor physical condition. In 1900, of 11,000 volunteers in Manchester, 8,000 were deemed unfit to carry a rifle and undertake training.

Here was a rising tide of social pity that demanded collectivist action – state involvement to lessen the extreme effects of the free market economy. Would Balfour's Cabinet respond to the challenge?

Balfour's Premiership: why have his personal qualities been criticised?

Arthur Balfour seemed to be his uncle's 'natural successor', sharing many of his assumptions – he was cautious, suspicious of change, social reform and the 'masses'. There was no doubting his intellect or his awareness of the major issues facing the country in terms of 'national efficiency'. His ministry had its successes; but despite these, Balfour has been roundly criticised. Rich, cultured, aristocratic and aloof, his wit may have been appreciated in 'society' but to others he appeared uninterested, even bored with the tedium of government business. David Lloyd George was provoked to compare him to 'the scent on a pocket handkerchief'. Robert Blake, in *The Conservative Party from Peel to Thatcher* (1991), accuses Balfour of failing to recognise social changes taking place among the electorate, arguing that 'he made insufficient allowance for the unreason of the masses'. Austen Chamberlain realised that, 'He has no comprehension of the habits of his countrymen and no idea how things strike them'. Perhaps he was 'too clever, too cool' (Robert Blake).

Balfour's book *A defence of philosophical doubt* is cited as evidence that the new Prime Minister was more interested in intellectual games than putting his considerable abilities into government action which might address 'the condition of England'. There was no greater contrast than with Joseph Chamberlain who, despite a press campaign on his behalf, was never a real threat to Balfour becoming Prime Minister. Chamberlain knew that, as the leader of a small group of Liberal Unionists who had recently joined the Conservative Party, as well as being non-Anglican, he had little chance of the leadership, but he was willing to join the Cabinet. There must have been times when he was frustrated by a government which lacked drive and direction.

1. What problems faced Britain during Balfour's Administrations?

2. How far do you agree that Balfour was ill-equipped to deal with Britain's problems?

This is the critical view of Balfour and if the impending disaster which was to befall the Conservative Party is anything to go by, then much of it is justified. In Balfour's favour, however, one of his Government's earliest pieces of legislation was designed to improve educational standards, widely believed to be inferior to those, say, in Germany and one of the root causes of what was perceived as 'national decline'. There were other achievements but these were overshadowed by a succession of mishandled problems.

20.5 How successfully did Balfour deal with these problems up to 1905?

The Taff Vale Case, 1901

Trade unionists, not for the first time, felt that their legal rights were again under attack. In the 1890s, the Quinn *versus* Leathem case meant that anyone who organised a strike could be liable to civil action by the employer. Then in 1901, before Balfour had become Prime Minister, the House of Lords, acting as the final Court of Appeal, made their judgement in the Taff Vale Case. In 1900, there had been a strike against the Taff Vale Railway Company in South Wales. The Company took the union, the Amalgamated Society of Railway Servants, to court and won; the union had to pay £23,000 damages. The wider implications were clear: no union could strike without fear of being ruined when sued for damages.

Balfour's Cabinet preferred to set up a royal commission rather than reverse the Taff Vale judgement in law. The Labour Representation Committee (LRC) was a major beneficiary because of the boost to trade union affiliations to the new party (see page 344). It was not a coincidence that the political levy began in 1903. In the same year, the LRC came to an agreement with Herbert Gladstone, the Liberal Chief Whip: the LRC was allocated 35 constituencies where they could campaign for the anti-Conservative vote without the presence of a Liberal candidate too. In return, the LRC would not stand against Liberal candidates anywhere else in England and Wales. The arrangement continued right up to the First World War, and must have played a significant part in increasing the size of the Liberal landslide in 1906.

Balfour's record of helping the unemployed also proved inadequate. The Unemployed Workmen Act, passed in 1905, helped the urban unemployed find work through labour exchanges set up by local Distress Committees. These committees had no funds from the State that it could distribute as emergency relief. They were forced to rely on private charity for that. Once again, the Unionists appeared callous when faced with real need. Hence Robert Blake's view that 'Balfour was singularly insensitive to any save the most predictable reactions of the working class'.

Education

The 1902 Education Act, most commentators agree, was a considerable achievement as it established a new framework for secondary schools that would remain in place until the Butler Act of 1944. Unfortunately, the political storm it caused has been said to have eroded the Government's electoral position – but to what extent?

The Act dealt with the clear inadequacy of secondary school provision. The 1870 Act established provision from the rates for only elementary schools, but many **School Boards** were using their money to provide advanced courses for more senior pupils. In 1901, a case was successfully brought against the London School Board for providing this 'secondary' education. Robert Morant, a civil servant at the Board of Education, knew urgent action was required by the State to take responsibility for elementary and secondary education.

School Boards: Set up in 1870, these committees were elected by ratepayers to build and run elementary schools.

The 1902 Education Act

- The old School Boards were abolished.
- Local Education Authorities (LEAs) took over responsibilities for elementary and secondary education.
- Education was able to expand and Church schools (which were struggling through lack of funds) were to receive financial support from the rates for teachers' pay and education of a unified standard, while the Anglicans and Catholics provided the buildings.
- The numbers of schools and pupils in grant-aided secondary schools quickly increased (from 94,000 in 1905 to 200,000 by 1914) and many LEA grammar schools were developed to provide education for those with ability. Whether the academic education they provided was what Britain needed, given the shortage of graduate technicians, is debatable.

It was this final aspect which is held to have undermined some of the Government's popularity. Not unexpectedly, nonconformists hated what they said was 'Rome on the rates', as they had been looking forward to a time when Church school education might wither away. Nonconformists were now ferociously determined to use the Liberal Party to oppose the strengthening of the Anglican Church's position. Why did Balfour support the Act? Was it a way of dealing with 'national efficiency'? Was it a rational response to the fears that Britain was falling behind industrially because it was failing to provide quality technical education – as argued by K. Young, in *Arthur James Balfour* (1963)? For Robert Blake it was another one of Balfour's 'blind spots' – his failure to grasp the indignation the measure would cause. He soon faced a nonconformist revolt: 7,000 prosecutions of people who refused to pay their rates in 1903. Dr Clifford, a Baptist, helped to organise the opposition to the Act and it was in Wales where the battle raged most bitterly, particularly where nonconformists had to send their children to the only available school, which might be run by the Church. None of this made much sense as taxation had for many years been used to keep some denominational schools going – but in a way, because the subsidies were paid from rates, the impact on a locality was more obvious.

Whether or not the Act played a big part in losing the Conservatives electoral support is open to question. What is not open to question is the way it galvanised the flagging Liberals into a more united and dynamic force. Joseph Chamberlain realised a political mistake had been made as life had been breathed into a Liberal Party which had suffered from ineffectual leadership and divisions over the Boer War. The Act did much to heal the rift between pro-Boers such as David Lloyd George and Liberal imperialists like Herbert Asquith. Liberal energies seemed to be renewed in response to Balfour's persistent contribution to the misfortunes of his own party.

As a postscript, the Government produced a promising Licensing Act in 1904, which attempted to reduce the number of public houses in areas where they weren't needed. Once again, this constructive piece of legislation was used by nonconformists to castigate the Government for introducing a levy on the industry so that the brewers could receive adequate compensation for any losses they suffered.

Chinese slavery, 1902–1904

'Chinese slavery' proved to be another minefield which Balfour could have taken the trouble to avoid. With a little forethought, the Government might have recognised that the decision to send thousands of Chinese labourers to South Africa would provoke an outcry, which would undermine their electoral popularity. The British High Commissioner, Lord Milner, urgently wished to press ahead with rebuilding the economy of South Africa in the wake of the Boer War. The gold mines needed labour and these Chinese labourers were thought to be the answer. Milner's plan had been overruled once by Chamberlain who was more alive to the likelihood of a hostile public reaction. But in 1903 Chamberlain was not in the Cabinet, so Milner's plan was sanctioned. Coming so soon after Britain's embarrassment over the conduct of the Boer War, people were reminded of the 'concentration camp' mentality and 'methods of barbarism' (see pages 365), when the Chinese workers were herded into labour camps. Not only were living conditions appalling (Milner was alleged to have agreed to flogging the Chinese as a punishment), but the close proximity of so many men struck many people as morally wrong as it might lead to 'nameless practices' – a lurid phrase which reflected nonconformist indignation. There was another more practical reason for white working-class anger: jobs were at stake and Chinese migrant labour was closing off any scope for white emigration to South Africa.

There was a sense of over-reaction here – the Liberals did protest too much, and their sense of outrage was somewhat overdone for political advantage – something that Campbell-Bannerman acknowledged when he withdrew the use of the word 'slavery'. By then the damage had been done

The cartoon shows a rich Transvaal gold mine owner in the foreground. In the background are Chinese coolies working behind barbed wire.

(a) What message is the cartoonist attempting to convey about the reasons for the wealth of gold mine owners?

(b) Using information contained within this chapter, explain how the issue of Chinese labour in South African mines affected the popularity of the Conservative Government and the career of Lord Milner, the British administrator of the Transvaal.

and working men, who had clearly voted for the Unionists in large numbers at the two previous elections, were warned by their unions that this was how the Government intended to solve labour shortages. Could the same happen in Britain? The Government, so they claimed, had scant regard for the dignity of labour. Some of the indignation, though, sounded artificial and it is difficult to know how much damage was done. Historian L.C.B. Seaman argues that the Conservative defeat which came in 1906 'cannot be explained solely on rational grounds. Discontent with 20 years of Tory rule was deep-seated but incoherent … in the prevailing atmosphere of disillusionment after the Boer War, the public mind was more impressed by the issue of "Chinese slavery" …'

Combine this with reactions to the Taff Vale Case and it becomes easier to understand how the Government lost the support of the working class.

Joseph Chamberlain and tariff reform, 1903–1905

The worst was yet to come. Following the end of the Boer War, Joseph Chamberlain needed to breathe life into his career; the difficulty of defeating the Boers, the Education Bill and a string of poor by-election results (including the loss of North Leeds) exposed a flagging party. His solution was dramatic – tariff reform, based on **retaliatory tariffs**, **selective import controls** and **imperial preference**. It was a solution that proved to be an electoral disaster.

Retaliatory tariffs: Import taxes placed on goods from a country which itself had imposed tariffs on goods entering its country.

Selective import controls: Tariffs at a lower rate than goods from the Colonies.

Imperial preference: Trade between the Colonies, such as food, to be given preference because it would attract lower tariffs compared with trade with the rest of the world.

Chamberlain intended to challenge the orthodoxy of free trade, which had been an article of faith for both the Liberals and the Unionists for so long. Supporters of free trade were in no doubt that it meant cheap imports of food and raw materials. They had a point as Britain relied on a greater proportion of food imports from outside the Empire than within it. Supporters of tariff reform claimed that a number of countries – including major competitors such as Germany and the USA – had introduced protective tariffs, enabling their economies to expand, while Britain's was slowing down. Some protection, they argued, would give a boost to home industries. Again, such a case was difficult to sustain as it was based on assertion rather than firm evidence. Chamberlain made enthusiastic claims, such as the three-quarters of a million extra jobs which would be created, while the stronger economy would generate more taxes for the introduction of old age pensions.

The arguments were not just about economics. Imperial preference would bind the Empire more closely together by favouring imperial trade, thus giving further impetus to the imperial idea. After the false starts of Chamberlain's proposals for an imperial free trade area (*Zollverein* – customs union) and *Kriegsverein* (an imperial navy had been suggested) at the Colonial Conferences of 1897 and 1902, imperial preference was greeted more warmly. The Premiers of Australia, New Zealand and Canada could see the advantage of protecting their fledgling industries and having lower rates of duty with Britain.

However, on his return from South Africa, where he had been engaged in postwar reconstruction, Chamberlain encountered obstruction from C.T. Ritchie, the Chancellor of the Exchequer. Ritchie's plans for the forthcoming budget, far from introducing further tariffs, were to abolish the existing duty on corn and thereby re-assert free trade. Balfour was not inclined to overrule Ritchie who had threatened to resign on the issue. Chamberlain, exhausted from his trip, was in no mood to fight. His biographer, Julian Amery, called this 'a fatal mistake'.

Chamberlain may have conceded, but it was only temporary. His speech arguing for preferential tariffs with the Colonies and questioning the benefits of free trade, delivered on 15 May 1903 in Birmingham, rocked the Party to its foundations. With characteristic fervour, Chamberlain's appeal to patriotic and imperial sentiments was clear: 'The Empire is in its infancy. Now is the time when we can mould that Empire.' But it was the economic case that drew most fire and if it was meant to incite opposition from within the Party, in particular from Liberal Unionists, it succeeded. By July, a Free Food League had been formed. Three dangerous factions began to divide the Conservatives: '**Whole Hoggers**', '**Free Fooders**' and '**Balfourites**'. Salisbury's son, Lord Hugh Cecil, organised a group of free traders, who became known as 'Hughligans'. Winston Churchill defected to the Liberals.

'**Whole Hoggers**': Chamberlain's supporters who favoured tariff reform.

'**Free Fooders**': Supporters of free trade.

'**Balfourites**': These Conservatives who backed the Prime Minister.

Balfour used his considerable skills to hide the split in their ranks, but matters had gone too far. Balfour might well have been personally sympathetic to tariffs, although perhaps limited to retaliatory duties and certainly not yet. His attempts to sit on the fence merely provoked ridicule as the split deepened. Chamberlain's Tariff Reform League directed the national campaign and with tensions becoming unbearable in the Cabinet, he resigned in September to take his arguments to the people. Balfour quietly agreed this was the best way out, especially if he was to keep the Liberal Unionists and the Conservatives together. Chamberlain agreed. It looked like another appeal for popular support over the heads of the Government. He had done the same in 1886 over Home Rule. Did he nurse any hopes of becoming leader? He probably understood that many Conservatives continued to be suspicious of him, hence his attempt to draw on his personal popularity among the voters. It would be unrealistic to think that Chamberlain had abandoned his hope of ever becoming Prime Minister. If Balfour called an election then it might well be 'Joe's victory'. A defeat might mean the end of Balfour, and Chamberlain could dispute the leadership.

Chamberlain's resignation was soon followed by another, much to Balfour's irritation. Lord Hartington, now the Duke of Devonshire, resigned in October 1903. He was a leading Liberal Unionist and Free Trader and his departure served to underline the deepening crisis. It also served to invigorate the Liberal Party, by uniting them in a zealous cause after so many years when they 'had been hopelessly divided on all the main political issues. This is quite an achievement for any campaign.' (Robert Blake)

Would food be dearer? Asquith was able to rouse Labour and the working class by raising the spectre of expensive food – the legendary 'little loaf' of

How useful is this poster to a historian studying why the Liberals won the 1906 general election?

A party election poster of 1906 attacking the Conservatives.

Chamberlain's making, compared with the Liberal 'large loaf'. There was considerable doubt as to whether the Conservatives were so keen on spending the alleged benefits of tariff reform on social reform, as Chamberlain said they were. Their record so far was unimpressive in trying to help those disadvantaged sections of society. This all helped to cement the electoral pact with Labour and did immense harm, which not even Chamberlain could reverse.

Balfour did his best to stagger on, putting off an election he thought he might lose and refusing to give his complete backing to Chamberlain's views. Joseph Chamberlain wanted an election hoping that the Liberals might self-destruct over Home Rule.

1. Why did

(a) the Taff Vale Case

(b) the Education Act, 1902

cause problems for Balfour's Government?

2. Put forward a set of ideas for and against the introduction of tariff reform in Britain.

3. Which set of arguments do you find most convincing? Give reasons to support your answer.

4. How far was Balfour responsible for the Conservative election defeat of January 1906?

What did the voters think? It appeared that the more they heard, the less they liked. It was difficult to break the link between free trade and prosperity, which had served Britain so well for decades. It did not help that Chamberlain was never a wholehearted protectionist; he merely sought to give some temporary respite to the British economy.

Nevertheless, Chamberlain was convinced the case had been won in the Party, quoting only 27 MPs who might be called Free Traders. The strains were too great and when Balfour detected the whiff of Liberal internal dissension over Ireland (Rosebery made a speech criticising Home Rule), he took the chance to resign in December 1905. Balfour had convinced himself that divisions between the Liberal imperialists of the Liberal League and the Radicals might make it difficult for Campbell-Bannerman to form a government. Indeed, there was a plot of sorts. Three Liberal imperialists – Asquith, Grey and Haldane – had met at Grey's Scottish fishing lodge where they agreed to a compact. All three would not join the government unless Campbell-Bannerman ('C-B') went to the House of Lords and Asquith became Leader of the Commons. 'C-B' was having none of it; his offer to Asquith of the Exchequer was enough to break up the conspiracy and the others were to succumb to the lure of office and personal advancement too.

Campbell-Bannerman called an election for January 1906. The results were sensational. The Unionists were reduced to 157, the Liberals rose to 377. This gave the Liberals a huge majority, even bigger when their political allies were counted in – something of the order of 350 seats. While the Government did introduce some sensible legislation in the fields of education, licensing laws and Irish land reform (see page 369), it was to no avail.

20.6 Why did the Liberals win a landslide victory in January 1906?

A CASE STUDY IN HISTORICAL INTERPRETATION

The scale of the Liberal victory in 1906 continues to be the focus of debate. The overwhelming impression was that the Conservatives had been in power too long. Given 'Balfour's propensity to stir up a hornets' nest by his ... methods of dealing with longstanding problems' (E.J. Feuchtwanger), the Conservatives looked not only like a party divided but also like one which seemed to misjudge the mood of the country and its own policies. The Liberals, on the other hand, appeared united and re-invigorated by a return to some of its traditional causes – primarily free trade, which proved to be the central feature of the election campaign.

What conclusions can be drawn from an analysis of the results?

The Conservatives slumped from the 402 seats won in 1900 to 157, its smallest number since 1832. The Liberals, however, increased from 184 to 377 (or 401 counting the 24 'Lib–Labs'). This reversal appears less dramatic when votes are taken into account. The Liberals gained just under 50%, compared with 43% for their opponents. Historians K.W.W. Aitkin and Robert Blake maintain that the number of votes per opposed candidate for the Conservatives was much the same in 1900 as in 1906; whereas there was a 25% increase in the Liberal vote. This 'suggests ... that the turnover of seats was not caused by a mass conversion from Conservatism to Liberalism but because a large number of people who had abstained in 1900 were stirred to vote for the Liberals – or – if one prefers it – against the Conservatives five and a half years later' (from Robert Blake's *The Conservative Party from Peel to Thatcher*). Recent analysis of Yorkshire constituencies adds weight to the view that an increased Liberal vote could have exaggerated effects because in many seats the winning margin was quite small in terms of numbers of votes. The **'first-past-the-post'** system translated into seemingly large gains of seats (for further discussion of this, see Simon Lemieux's article listed in 'Further Reading' on page 440).

'First-past-the-post': This electoral system, borrowed from horseracing, describes the situation where the candidate who gains the largest number of votes wins the election. Thus, someone would win in an election if they received 10,000 votes even if rivals all had 9,999 votes each.

What was the state of the Conservative Party and did it contribute to its own defeat?

Captain Richard Middleton had effectively oiled the Conservative Party machine up until 1903. His departure marked a decline in organisation, which undermined the Party's ability to fight an effective campaign. The historian E.J. Feuchtwanger has calculated that 27 Liberals were elected unopposed in 1906; whereas in 1900 the boot was on the other foot, when 143 Conservatives were elected unopposed. He also points out that 100 Conservative MPs retired, which probably meant a loss of 'personal' votes.

More serious was the loss of working-class support in once solid Conservative areas, such as Lancashire, London and the South-East. Why? The failure to reverse the Taff Vale decision was not the only issue. Chinese slavery and the 'small loaf' contributed to the conclusion that the Conservatives were unsympathetic towards working people, especially since the Government had been reluctant to introduce effective measures of social reform to alleviate living and working conditions. The historian Duncan Watts suggests that there was a momentum to the anti-government election swing. Since voting went on for three weeks, news of early swings to the Liberals in Lancashire spread elsewhere, which may have added further impetus to changes in voting.

Disenchantment with the Conservatives was apparent among the middle class too. Was this the effects of the Boer War and Chinese slavery which so badly tarnished the imperial dream? With the Conservatives so divided over tariff reform there seemed no objection to voting with the Liberals, who for once had managed to heal their differences. Neither was Home Rule such a prominent issue, so there could be no objections to voting Liberal on that score. Robert Blake argues that these factors partly explain how the Liberals were winning the central ground. His evidence for this was the drift of intellectual support (at the Universities) away from the Conservatives towards the Liberals.

Did the Liberals convince the voters that they should support a new party programme?

This is unlikely, as their programme was largely traditional. Opposition to food taxes, support for free trade, repeal of the Education Act of 1902 to please nonconformists, repeal of the Licensing Act of 1904 to satisfy the temperance lobby and the reversal of the Taff Vale judgement to please trade unionists. It was the usual message, but it did allow the temperance and nonconformist wings of the party to unite and present a vigorous front. Perhaps, then, it was this resurgence which did the trick rather than the substance of what was said. The Liberal programme on social reform, for example on old age pensions, was vague and there was no sign of that great wave of reform which began in 1908.

Did the Liberals rouse nonconformist support? Not especially, as H. Pelling discovered larger swings to the Liberals in areas outside the traditional nonconformist heartland. However, opposition to the 1902 Education Act certainly provided an opportunity for the Liberal Party to come together in the face of their opponents.

1. Why have historians disagreed over the reasons why the Liberals won the 1906 election?

2. Do you agree that the Liberal victory of 1906 was a 'landslide' in name only?

And what of the Labour Party?

The electoral pact with the LRC had been a success and it helped to establish Labour as a third force to undermine the Conservatives in key working-class seats.

L.C.B. Seaman targets the key issues when noting that 'The Liberals swept into power with sectarian prejudices on their Right flank, an angry trade union movement on their Left flank, and with their Centre marching triumphantly into the future behind the [free trade] ghosts of Cobden and Bright'.

Source-based questions: The rise of the Labour Party

SOURCE A

The ILP starts from the assumption that the worker should be as free industrially and economically as he is supposed to be politically … The men who are to achieve … reforms must be under no obligation whatever to either the landlord or the capitalist, or to any party or organisation representing these interests. Suppose, for the sake of argument, that 20 members would be returned to Parliament who were nominally Labour Members but who owed their election to a compromise with the Liberals, what would the effect be upon their action in the House of Commons? When questions affecting the interests of property were at stake, or when they desired to take action to compel social legislation of a drastic character, the threat would always be hanging over them that unless they… maintained party discipline they would be opposed. I have no desire to hold the seat on sufferance … I cannot agree to compromise my independence of action in even the slightest degree.

Keir Hardie commenting on the relationship between the ILP and the Liberal Party. Taken from Stewart J. Keir Hardie *by William Stewart, published in 1925.*

Source-based questions: The rise of the Labour Party

SOURCE B

… the LRC scored a string of by-election victories – at Clitheroe in 1902, and Woolwich and Barnard Castle in 1903. The significance of these developments has been much debated. It can be argued that the establishment of the LRC … was a vital staging post in the ideological as well as the organisational disengagement of the Labour movement from the tradition of Lib–Labism and that it represented a decisive move towards a more class-based system of 'industrial' politics in which the Liberal and Labour parties were bound to compete ever more fiercely for working-class votes. Conversely, it is possible to minimise the extent of the change that has occurred and to stress the basis for continuing cooperation between the two parties which were rooted in a common radical heritage. Despite the LRC's formal declaration of independence at its Newcastle conference of 1903, Liberal and Labour politicians were in agreement on most of the general political questions of the day. They were united in the 1900s by their opposition to the Unionist government and, insofar as they offered distinctive programmes to the electorate, their differences could be seen as complementary rather than competitive in their appeal. This last point is supported by the successful working of the secret electoral pact made between the Liberal chief whip, Herbert Gladstone, and the LRC secretary, MacDonald, in 1903 …

From The Edwardian Crisis, Britain 1901–1914 *by David Powell, published in 1996. The extract explains the historical strands that were the foundation of the Lib–Lab Pact of 1903.*

SOURCE C

To the Electors –
This election is to decide whether or not Labour is to be fairly represented in Parliament.
The Trade Unions ask the same liberty as capital enjoys. They are refused.
The aged poor are neglected.
The slums remain.
Shopkeepers and traders are overburdened with rates and taxation, whilst increasing land values, which should relieve the taxpayer, go to people who have not earned them.
Wars are fought to make the rich richer, and underfed school children are still neglected.
Chinese Labour is defended because it enriches the mine owners.
The unemployed ask for work, the Government gives them a worthless Act …
Protection, as experience shows, is no remedy for poverty and unemployment.
You have it in your power to see that Parliament carries out your wishes.

From the Labour election manifesto of 1906.

---

1. Study Sources A and B.

How different are these sources in the views they express about the relationship between the Liberal Party and representation of labour in Parliament?

2. Study Source C.

How does the language and tone of Source C reflect the Labour Party's attempt to maintain a broad appeal?

Use the Sources and information contained within this chapter to answer the next two questions.

3. Was the electoral pact between the Liberals and the LRC the most important reason why the LRC was so much more successful at the 1906 election? Explain your answer.

4. Was the MacDonald/Gladstone electoral pact of 1903 the most important reason for the Liberal election victory of 1906?

Joseph Chamberlain and the Empire, 1895–1905

Key Issues

- *How was the Empire changing at this time?*
- *How successful was Joseph Chamberlain's work at the Colonial Office?*
- *What was Chamberlain's impact on domestic politics, 1895–1905?*

21.1 What were the motives behind Chamberlain's 'imperial vision'?
21.2 How successful were Chamberlain's imperial reforms?
21.3 What were the origins of the tension between the Boers and the British in South Africa?
21.4 How far was Chamberlain involved in the Jameson Raid conspiracy?
21.5 Historical interpretation: How far was Chamberlain responsible for the outbreak of the Boer War?
21.6 Why did it take Britain so long to conclude the Boer War?
21.7 How significant was Chamberlain's role in tariff and imperial reform after 1895?

Framework of Events

1895	Chamberlain becomes Colonial Secretary
	The Jameson Raid
1897	Queen Victoria's Diamond Jubilee; Colonial Conference; Milner becomes High Commissioner in South Africa
1899	May: Bloemfontein Conference
	October: Boer War begins
1900	South Africa: Relief of Mafeking, Kimberley and Ladysmith; start of a war of attrition
	Australian Federation Act
1902	Colonial Conference; Peace of Vereeniging ends Boer War
1903	Chamberlain's speech promises tariff reform; his resignation from Balfour Government
1905	Balfour resigns from Conservative Government; Campbell-Bannerman forms a Liberal Cabinet and calls an election for January 1906
1910	Union of South Africa comes into existence.

Overview

BEFORE the 1870s, Britain had been reluctant to establish formal constitutiona links with that informal collection of colonies, dependencies, strategic posi tions and areas of influence that later formed 'the Empire'. Britain wa content to trade and act, incidentally, as a 'civilising' force. Self-government was th preferred model: in 1867, Canada had formed a federation of provinces; from 1872 Cape Colony had self-government, while Australia and New Zealand were als beginning to run their own affairs. Direct control was viewed with suspicion, as would involve considerable military expenditure on defence given the potential fo confrontation wherever Britain rubbed shoulders with other powers around the globe.

Only India was the exception to this view. Its affairs were directed from the India Office from 1858, rather than from the Colonial Office. Its commercial and strategic importance gave India a special status. Many British administrators received their first training there, before being sent to regulate the affairs of the sub-continent.

Nevertheless, imperialists such as Charles Dilke and Lord Rosebery were making an impact. Sir John Seeley's lectures on the 'Expansion of England' (1882–83) spread the imperial idea: 'Great' Britain occupied a prominent place on a global scale. However, that pre-eminent position might be under threat from Russia and the USA unless the Empire was moulded into a more effective political, military and economic unit. His patriotic zeal reflected mid-Victorian confidence in its 11 colonies on which 'the sun never sets'. The 'Scramble for Africa' (see Chapter 18) is further evidence of the change of mood.

Joseph Chamberlain caught this imperial sentiment. The town of Birmingham had seen his form of municipal radicalism: Corporation Street, housing improvement schemes and the successful administration of gas and water supplies showed what this dynamic businessman could achieve at a local level. He would bring the same practical approach to the Empire.

Harry Browne's study, *Joseph Chamberlain, Radical and Imperialist* (1974), refers to Chamberlain's 'great gifts, of personality, of intellect, his oratory ...'. Opinions about Chamberlain have tended to be polarised. There was no mistaking the people of Birmingham's affection and regard for this energetic and charismatic figure. However, he has been accused of being too overbearing, too keen on his own schemes without regard for the opposition. It can be difficult for any politician to deny the accusation of being an ambitious careerist. In Chamberlain's case, his nickname 'Juggler Joe' has left him with the reputation of being an opportunist.

Historiography: Views of historians.

'The right man at the right time.' How far does this statement fit Joseph Chamberlain's qualities during this early period when Britain's attitude to 'Empire' was changing?

Some of the **historiography** confirms this unflattering portrait. A.J.P. Taylor has argued that 'Chamberlain's great energies were successful only in destruction ... he was unscrupulous in his means ...'. Richard Jay's verdict that Chamberlain was a 'misfit ... inept in his handling of men and political tactics at important points in his life' is echoed by Duncan Watts who notes that 'he was not a team player'. Certainly Chamberlain's behaviour during the investigation into the failed Jameson Raid left him open to suspicion.

Nevertheless, Chamberlain had his achievements, although they are not as great as they should have been given his remarkable abilities. After 1895, he threw his weight behind the imperial idea. His efforts, though, would eventually lead to war in South Africa and a catastrophic division in the Unionist Party over tariff reform, which contributed to their 1906 election defeat.

21.1 What were the motives behind Chamberlain's 'imperial vision'?

In 1895, Joseph Chamberlain became Colonial Secretary in Salisbury's Government. A more senior Cabinet post may have been offered to him, but this was the one he preferred. He seized the opportunity to execute his imperial vision with the same enthusiasm, drive and overbearing force that he used to such effect in Birmingham. However, now he had a wider canvas, on which he might 'forge a closer union' between the colonies and Britain, welding together the diverse collection of territories 'to create an Empire –

greater and more potent for peace than any that history has yet known ...' (Joseph Chamberlain).

The economic advantages of developing the Empire were prominent in Chamberlain's speeches. Many shared his businessman's concerns – a loss of confidence in the British economy. The 'mid-Victorian boom' appeared to have given way to a cycle of slumps during the last quarter of the 19th century. Contemporaries perhaps exaggerated their fears that industry and agriculture were in terminal decline. In the face of foreign competition, a series of trade depressions during which profits fell and unemployment rose were punctuated by all too brief recoveries. Historians, too, used to speak of 'The Great Depression' (see Chapter 19). However, while this is no longer justified as the outlook was not entirely bleak, there was a genuine feeling among businessmen in depressed areas that something needed to be done. With a population in the colonies and dependencies estimated at 54 million, the market for British goods was huge. There would be a boost to British manufacturing, and to employment both here and in the colonies.

The USA, as well as Britain's leading competitors in Europe such as Germany and France, had already imposed tariffs on British goods to protect their own industries. Many organisations, such as the National Fair Trade League, understood perfectly how trade and food production could be transferred from 'protective foreign nations who refuse to give us their custom in return, to our own colonies ...'. In Chamberlain's heartland, the appearance of German-made manufactures was a visible reminder of how Britain was losing ground.

As the historian A.J.P. Taylor noted, the lack of precise information at the time meant Chamberlain was not in a position to reconsider some of these claims. With British trade, in 1900, running at £711 million with the rest of the world and £237 million with the colonies, the case for the Empire was not overwhelming. Undeterred, 'Radical Joe' could recognise how a revitalised economy could then finance social reform, and tackle the appalling extent of poverty which recent surveys such as Booth's (see Chapter 20) had vividly exposed.

How far was the imperial dream dependent on economic arguments? Lord Salisbury, always cautious and certainly suspicious of Chamberlain's rhetoric, recognised commercial benefits but played the defence card strongly. With the German and French Empires expanding rapidly, the defence of British interests in Egypt (Suez), South Africa and India demanded attention in a world in which Britain was finding itself increasingly isolated.

1. Having studied the motives behind Chamberlain's imperialist ideas, pick out the motives which are:

(a) social

(b) moral

(c) racial

(d) economic.

2. Which of these different types of motive was the most important? Give reasons to support your answer.

Chamberlain understood this very well, but his imperial sentiments went much deeper. They encompassed moral and racial imperatives. The Empire was a force for good, a 'civilising influence', and Britain had a duty to share what Rudyard Kipling popularly referred to as 'the White Man's burden'. This was linked to the 'Anglo-Saxon race which is infallibly destined to be the predominant force in the future history and civilisation of the world'. It would be wrong, within the context of the time, to accuse Chamberlain of losing any sense of social justice. Measures were taken to encourage native development and to eliminate practices such as slavery and human sacrifice. At home, his beliefs took on a powerful aspect of 'social imperialism'. The profits of Empire would help reduce poverty at home, particularly among the aged, providing a link between Chamberlain's foreign ambitions and his domestic radicalism. However, such was Chamberlain's excessive relish to advance his vision that critics were given ample opportunities to swipe at the way in which he advanced himself. He was never one to be modest about his work or to shun publicity. Not everyone shared 'Joe's' enthusiasm.

21.2 How successful were Chamberlain's imperial reforms?

Federal: Where states band together to form a union but retain some form of self-government – as in a federation of Australian colonies.

Constructive work was completed despite a lukewarm attitude to Chamberlain's imperial mission. Salisbury, never at ease with his Colonial Secretary although willing to accept his abilities, could have been more supportive. The Treasury stuck by the old Gladstonian virtue of thrifty government. Neither did Chamberlain's schemes receive rapturous approval by the Colonial premiers themselves. They assembled in London, in 1897, to mark Queen Victoria's Diamond Jubilee. At the Colonial Conference, Chamberlain must have thought that his ideas for a *Zollverein* (Customs union) and an Imperial Council might have gained greater favour. Ultimately, he looked forward to the formation of an imperial **federal** parliament drawing representatives from every corner of the Empire. But his audience drew back from imperial integration on this scale. Colonial premiers suspected that this might mean more interference from London, as well as the prospect of paying towards the costs of Imperial defence. They were content with things as they were – a loose grouping with few precise ties. Chamberlain made little headway except a commitment to hold colonial conferences in the future.

Nevertheless, he carried on. The dream of an imperial federation would collapse unless each colony spoke with one voice. In 1900, Chamberlain played a part in encouraging the six Australian colonies to join together into one federation. It was an important step.

Echoes of Birmingham drew Chamberlain into matters related to public health. Patrick Manson was appointed Medical Adviser to the Colonial Office and investigations were encouraged into the tsetse fly and one of Africa's most virulent diseases, sleeping sickness. The research drew parallels with symptoms discovered in cattle and this led to a breakthrough in treatment. The Treasury was persuaded to part with some public funds and, in 1899, a School of Tropical Medicine in London was set up. A similar school was set up in Liverpool with support from Ronald Ross who had worked tirelessly to find that malaria was carried by mosquitoes. Ross was to complete some practical work – in Sierra Leone, for instance, where marshes were drained, thereby depriving mosquitoes of their breeding habitats. Further botanical research was funded at Kew, where Dr Morris was able to provide useful advice to peasant farmers in the West Indies.

1. What hindered Chamberlain's plans for reforming the Empire?

2. What reforms did Chamberlain make, in imperial affairs, between 1895 and 1903?

A royal commission reported in 1897 that the economic livelihood of the West Indies, which relied heavily on sugar exports, was in dire straits. This was largely because Europe had been stimulating its sugar beet production. Even if new crops could be developed, communications were difficult. Subsidies helped to support regular steamer services between the West Indies and Canada and Britain, while an agricultural department gave advice on how to diversify into the fruit trade. Peasants were helped to own their land and fruit exports rose significantly. These advances were steady and constructive. Could the same be said of events in South Africa?

21.3 What were the origins of the tension between the Boers and the British in South Africa?

In any study of Chamberlain at the Colonial Office, the spotlight falls on his handling of affairs in South Africa. The Cape had been occupied in 1806 and was in a crucial position on the sea route to India. Even after the opening of the Suez Canal, the mineral wealth offered the prospects of fortunes to be made. British interests brought conflict with the descendants of the first Dutch settlers, the Boers. Their 'treks' northwards away from the Cape were an attempt to escape from British influence and to preserve their culture and

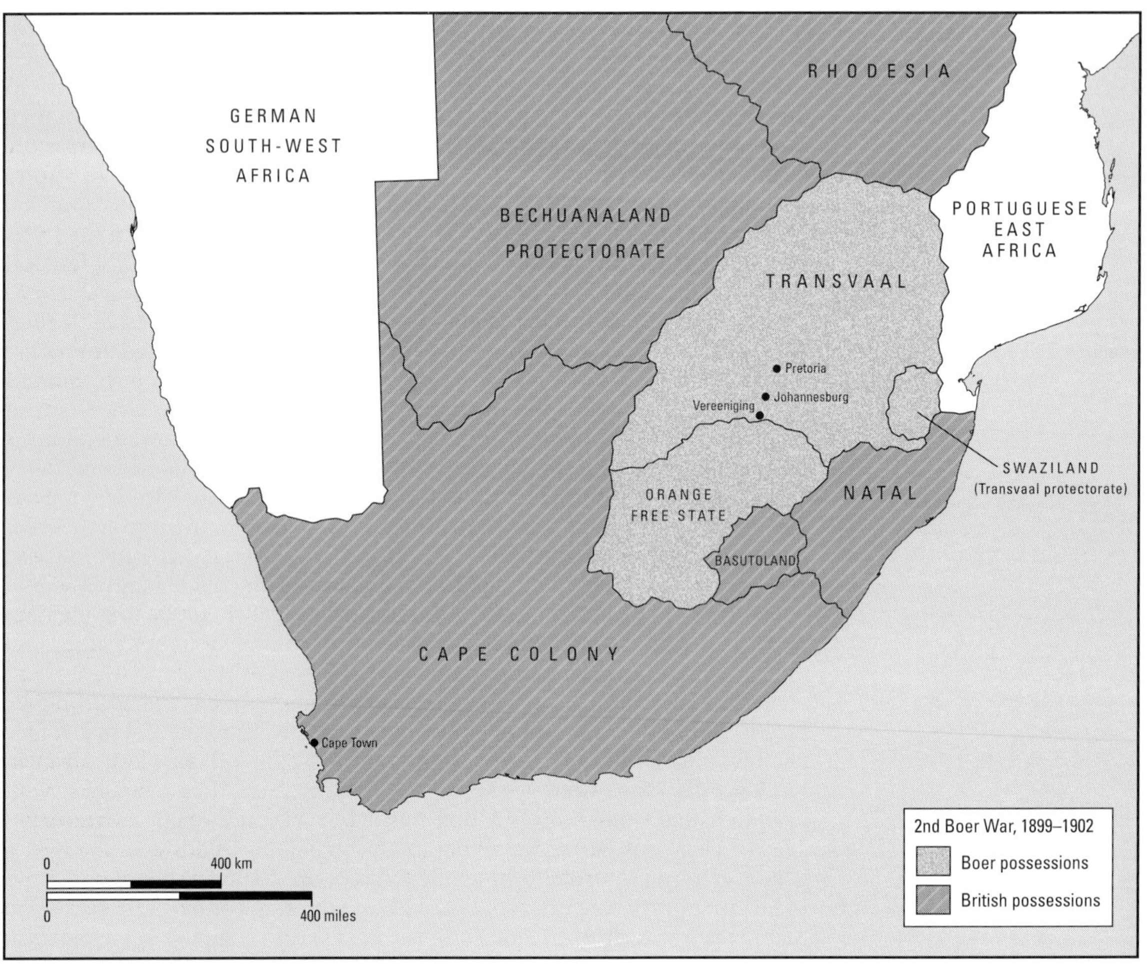

The partition of Africa on the eve of the Boer War

church. At first, their fiercely independent spirit paid off and they gained recognition in the 1850s for two Boer republics, the Transvaal and Orange Free State. They would not find it easy to shake free of the British, who themselves had expanded northwards from Cape Colony and into Natal and Basutoland, effectively cutting off the Boers from the sea and encircling them. Lord Carnarvon, Disraeli's Colonial Secretary, did have plans to incorporate the Transvaal into a South African confederation as part of the British Empire.

Events then took a surprising turn. Notwithstanding the obvious ill-feeling between the two, the Boers were forced to call on British assistance when facing a double threat: one from bankruptcy; the other, potentially more injurious, was a Zulu uprising. In 1877, the Transvaal was annexed and Britain, not without a little difficulty, overcame the Zulus.

With the Zulu threat gone, the tensions between the Boers and the British surfaced again. Gladstone had criticised Disraeli's policy in South Africa, but before he could take action news of a Boer revolt reached London. This successful Boer rising at Majuba Hill, in 1881, pushed Gladstone to accede to Boer demands to regain their independence. This was duly granted at the Pretoria Convention of 1881. Friction between the two sides continued, though, because the Convention had insisted that the Boers accept British **suzerainty** over the Transvaal. What this actually meant was not clear, as suzerainty implied nominal British control or sovereignty over an 'independent' Transvaal. So, another treaty, signed in London (1884) granted self-rule to the Transvaal in all matters except foreign relations. The Boers ruefully agreed – their links with Britain's European rivals, such as Germany, were heavily circumscribed.

Suzerainty: A sovereign or a state having control over another state's external (foreign) affairs.

However, matters were transformed by the 1884 gold rush in the Transvaal. Its wealth enticed men from outside (the Boers called them 'Uitlanders') who had the technological skill to exploit the Transvaal's huge mineral resources. The Boers were caught in a dilemma. They were farmers, not miners, who wished to defend their way of life, but felt swamped by the foreigners. For example, Johannesburg grew rapidly into a town of 50,000 – 44,000 of whom were Uitlanders.

The mining companies exercised remarkable powers. Cecil Rhodes was a central figure in pressing for the extension of British control in South Africa. He had failed to find gold in Rhodesia to the north, and his attention was turning to the Transvaal. As Prime Minister of Cape Colony after 1887, he was attempting to make his fortune from mining diamonds and gold. His British South Africa Company had land, minerals and a private army. Rhodes' vision of a dramatic extension of British power from 'Cape to Cairo' would take the colony a step nearer to conflict with the Boers who blocked his path.

1. Explain how British–Boer relations developed between 1806 and 1887.

2. Which reasons do you regard as the most important in bringing about a worsening in British–Boer relations from 1806 to 1887? Give reasons to support your answer.

Chamberlain's excuse for intervention in the Transvaal was that the Uitlanders were being treated harshly by the Boers. They seemed on the verge of revolt due to heavy taxes, no votes and no rights. Chamberlain admitted to Salisbury that there might be a rising and if it was successful 'it ought to turn to our advantage'. However, a satisfactory explanation of Chamberlain's part in subsequent events – a raid on the Transvaal – has never been given.

21.4 How far was Chamberlain involved in the Jameson Raid conspiracy?

Dr Starr Jameson was an agent for Cecil Rhodes. In December 1895, he planned to take 400–500 volunteer horsemen from the Bechuanaland Protectorate and ride to Johannesburg to join an expected rising against the Boers. Presumably, the intention was that a government more to Rhodes' liking would be installed.

However, there was no uprising in the Transvaal. Jameson might have thought twice about executing the plan, but he carried on. Forty miles from Johannesburg, the volunteers were surrounded, easily captured and Jameson was imprisoned.

Who was to blame for the debacle? How much did Chamberlain know about the Raid? What were the results of its failure? Not surprisingly, the Boers blamed the British, accusing them of being untrustworthy. They began to buy armaments in the expectation of further hostilities. A telegram from the German Kaiser, Wilhelm II, congratulated the Boers and President Kruger for defeating the raid unassisted. Such was the anger in Britain against the Germans, who had presumed they could interfere in colonial affairs, that the Royal Navy took to sea until conciliatory noises came from Berlin. In Britain, the shrill voices of Empire were noticeably quieter – for the moment.

The key question rested on Chamberlain's possible guilt. Was he involved? Did he know about the raid? Could he have stopped it? Would

Chamberlain survive politically? A select committee of the House of Commons made its enquiries and reported in May 1897, without having had access to vital telegrams that passed between Rhodes and Chamberlain.

Kruger Telegram: A telegram from Kaiser Wilhelm II of Germany to President Kruger of the Transvaal, in 1896. It congratulated Kruger on the defeat of the Jameson Raid. It caused considerable hostility towards Germany from Britain.

Given the antipathy towards the Boers and the emotions stirred by the **Kruger Telegram**, it was likely that Chamberlain's denials might be accepted. 'I say to the best of my knowledge and belief that everybody, that Mr Rhodes, that the Chartered Company and the High Commissioners were all equally ignorant of the intentions and actions of Dr Jameson.' Chamberlain's enemies found this less than candid. Nevertheless, Chamberlain was cleared and the finger of blame was pointed at Rhodes.

Historians have disagreed about the Committee's conclusions. Biographer J.L. Garvin agreed that Chamberlain had 'not a shadow of complicity with the Raid'. However, historian Harry Browne quotes two South African historians, J.S. Marais and Jean van der Poel, who don't agree. The latter's reference to Chamberlain's 'official ignorance and private sympathy' points to his knowledge of the Raid, which he did nothing to stop. Indeed, there is evidence of some connivance from the Colonial Office, which, prior to the Raid, sanctioned the transfer of Pitsani, a strip of territory in Bechuanaland, to Rhodes' British South Africa Company. Pitsani was closer to Johannesburg and it was from here that the Raid was launched. Why did the Select Committee not make more of this at the time? Perhaps A.J.P. Taylor's accusation that Chamberlain might blackmail the British South Africa Company is valid – Rhodes was on the spot and could be forced to accept full responsibility.

What evidence points to Chamberlain's involvement in the Jameson Raid?

Chamberlain, smarting from having to defend himself, hardened his views towards the Boers. Indeed, both sides seemed less interested in healing the quarrel.

21.5 *How far was Chamberlain responsible for the outbreak of the Boer War?*

A CASE STUDY IN HISTORICAL INTERPRETATION

Why did war with the Boers break out four years after the Jameson Raid? The historian J.A. Hobson, in *The War in South Africa* (1900), blamed gold. The riches of the Transvaal were tempting. Some historians find that unconvincing. Existing British gold reserves were strong, as was trade and investment with the Transvaal. An alternative view is that the Cabinet continued to be more concerned with strategic considerations – the Cape Town naval base had to be secure if ever Suez was endangered. Was the Cape secure though, given the Boers' anti-British sympathies?

The view of J.S. Marais and I.R. Smith is that the main troublemaker was Sir Alfred Milner. He became High Commissioner in 1897 (see below) and he aggressively pushed his demands that the Uitlanders should be given a vote to the point where war became inevitable. He was the 'man on the spot', and able to influence events directly. In a way, though, Milner knew that to demand a vote for Uitlanders was only a means to an end – the heart of the matter was British supremacy in South Africa. As Milner said, 'is British paramountcy to be vindicated or let slide?'.

A. Porter disagrees (*The Origins of the South African War*, 1980). He says that Chamberlain's attitude remains the key. Basically, he demanded rights for the Uitlanders. More significantly, there was much talk of a federal empire in the 1890s – and a more united South Africa, which included the Boer states, would advance his imperial vision. Chamberlain aimed to convince the British electorate of the importance of imperialism. He hoped that an issue such as the rights of Uitlanders might win the sympathy of the voters. Realising the strategic importance of the Cape and the economic potential in the Transvaal, Chamberlain regarded Boer independence over their internal affairs as unsatisfactory because it undermined British control. As the Transvaal grew more prosperous than Cape Colony, the Boers became confident enough to challenge the British.

Chamberlain looked around for more men who would adopt a more robust position. The British High Commissioner, Robinson, was replaced (at the insistence of the Colonial Secretary) by Sir Alfred Milner in August 1897. Chamberlain could have had no doubts about Milner's approach. He was certainly suspicious of Boer intent and policy now bristled with talk of 'a great day of reckoning' with Kruger. In a sense, though, Chamberlain miscalculated as Kruger could match Milner for his stubbornness. The Boer point of view seemed clear; they had no intention of surrendering their independence and being swamped by the British. Events seemed to be moving too quickly, given Britain's weak military position in South Africa.

The stakes were raised in December 1898. A Boer policeman who shot an English worker was acquitted. In the ensuing storm of protest, Milner petitioned the Cabinet. Chamberlain wavered confusingly between talk of sending an ultimatum and talk of seeking peace. Perhaps he hoped something might come from a conference held at Bloemfontein, in June 1899, between Milner and Kruger. All final attempts to persuade Kruger to grant some voting rights to Uitlanders failed. Time had almost run out, despite a cautious Salisbury who much preferred a policy of drifting 'downstream, occasionally putting in a boathook to avoid a collision' (as Churchill claimed). However, the Cabinet did allow the situation to develop and must share some of the blame. For Chamberlain, it had now become a question of who would issue an ultimatum first; whoever did so, would be regarded as the aggressor.

Why have historians disagreed about the reasons for the outbreak of the South African (Boer War) of 1899–1902?

It came in October 1899. Kruger demanded the withdrawal of British troops from the border with the Transvaal. The challenge was accepted. Milner admitted that it was he who had forced the pace: 'I precipitated a crisis which was inevitable before it was altogether too late.' There were surprisingly few voices raised against what became known as 'Joe's war'. Lloyd George considered it 'senseless' and, not for the first time, drew attention to the way that Chamberlain had seized opportunities to boost profits: 'The more the empire expands, the more the Chamberlain's contract.' Militarily, the 'collision' would not be a happy one for the British.

21.6 *Why did it take so long for Britain to conclude the Boer War?*

The war can be divided into three distinct phases:

- the Boer advances in 1899
- Britain's victory during the conventional war of 1900
- the guerrilla war which lasted from 1900 until 1902.

One reason why the war was prolonged was that the first phase went well for the Boers. Their horsemen operated effectively from the first day, 12 October 1899. Natal and Cape Colony were invaded and three major British towns were besieged: Mafeking, Kimberley and Ladysmith. In the first few weeks, the British had only 13,000 troops and many of these were under siege and hence out of action. The 10–15 December became known as 'Black Week' because it was marked by the defeat of the British Commander, Sir Redvers Buller, at Colenso. Indeed, Buller seemed to have no answer to the Boer fortifications, trench systems and superior rifle fire. Even when reinforcements arrived, they were spread too thinly in vain attempts to lift the sieges of the three towns. Buller had to go.

His replacements were able men who gave the campaign a semblance of intelligent direction. During this second phase, Lord Roberts was in overall command, accompanied by Lord Kitchener of Khartoum. Overwhelming superiority of numbers meant that the Boers were forced back on all fronts. Kitchener was able to give his troops more freedom of movement by organising horse-drawn wagons to maintain supplies. The Boers had, up to this point, correctly predicted that their enemy would stick to the railway routes. However, the British were suddenly more mobile, helping them to relieve Kimberley and capture 4,000 Boer fighters. On hearing the news, the Boers round Ladysmith pulled back so Buller was able to retake the town. In 1900, Roberts and Kitchener continued northwards, relieving Mafeking, occupying Bloemfontein and annexing the Orange Free State. Turning east, Johannesburg fell and, by September, the Transvaal was annexed. The Boers were defeated – or so it seemed.

Large contingents of troops were unable to occupy and effectively control a huge area of territory against an enemy that attacked in small, mobile groups before melting back into the landscape. So it was in South Africa; despite continual British reinforcements, there were sufficiently large numbers of Boer 'commandos' left to obstruct British communications. The Boer chain of command, operating 'on the hoof', remained intact with Schalk Burger as Vice-President of a country which was supposed to have been annexed, and General Louis Botha coordinating strategy.

The British proved unequal to the task of preventing the commando raids. The new tactics adopted by Roberts and later Kitchener, who was given command after Roberts had left, invited censure and reproach. Some Boers had returned to their farms after taking an oath to stay out of the war. Intimidated by Boer commandos, many farmers were pressed back into action. Roberts reacted by burning their farms and herding civilians into camps. Initially, these camps were supposed to protect those who wished to preserve their neutrality, but the military soon extended their use and the infamous 'concentration camp' was born.

In 1901, Jan Smuts penetrated British lines and led a raid that almost reached Cape Town, leading to a Boer revolt there. Kitchener responded with the 'blockhouse system'. This would prevent the Boers' mobility by

British cartoon of a Boer rejecting the olive branch offered by an angel of peace. The person on the right represents the Boer army; the figure on the left represents the Angel of Peace.

1. What message is the cartoon attempting to convey about the reasons for British involvement in the Boer War?

2. Using information from this chapter, about the causes of the war, how accurate is the cartoon? Give reasons to support your answer.

littering the occupied lands with fortified pillboxes and mile upon mile of barbed wire. Thousands of civilians were concentrated in a total of 60 camps, where disease was rife. The army was ill-equipped for running the camps. Estimates vary, but out of a possible population of just over 200,000 it is reckoned that between 20,000 and 40,000 men, women and children died. The physical damage to these incorporated lands was enormous; the further damage to Britain's reputation was dire. Typical was a French cartoon which showed a British soldier kicking a pregnant prisoner. Campbell-Bannerman, the Liberal leader, described the use of camps as 'methods of barbarism'.

Relations between Kitchener and Milner, meanwhile, had reached breaking point. The former was preoccupied with finding a military solution to bring things to a conclusion. The cost of maintaining 250,000 men was crippling and the actions of the army in the field fuelled Boer indignation. Summary execution by firing squad took place for a range of offences, such as rebellion, arson and the murder of non-whites. Kitchener had been using thousands of non-whites as drivers, scouts, messengers and general labourers – this was no longer just a white-man's war.

The civilian authorities clashed with the Army and criticised Kitchener for ignoring his plans to rebuild the economy, for which there were no available resources. They also argued about how to end the war. Milner had no intention of negotiating. The Boers would be broken and only unconditional surrender would do. Kitchener just wanted an end to it – by talks or by force.

In the end, British strategy ground down the Boers. Their lands were being devastated and commandos were slowly hunted down and deprived of assistance. However, it was the British Government who offered talks first. In the end a divided Boer population accepted the terms of the Treaty of Vereeniging.

How far did the peace signed at Vereeniging represent a British victory?

John Morley, a leading Liberal politician, had warned Chamberlain before the war that 'it will bring you no glory'. Apart from the opening stages of the war, this verdict proved valid. The Conservatives won the 'Khaki' election of 1900 convincingly, when things were going well. Historian J.A. Hobson argued that patriotic enthusiasm was widespread as men rushed to join up for the cause. Chamberlain campaigned prominently and the voices of those who found fault were drowned out. David Lloyd George, for example, was dubbed 'pro-Boer' after discovering that it was unwise to speak in 'Brummagem Joe's' own backyard as he had to be smuggled out of town in secret.

However, the mood had changed during the final 18 months of the war. Historians have found it difficult to assess how far popular nationalism waned when it became clear that the Army had found it so difficult to press home its numerical advantage. It became part of the country's soul-searching about 'national efficiency' and the 'condition of England', exposing a vulnerability about our global economic position and sense of isolation. Bemoaning the poor state of recruits for the Army, the Government set up the Physical Deterioration Committee to investigate how Britain's economic power was being undermined. The further embarrassment of the 'concentration camps' seemed to tarnish the imperial ideal, albeit briefly. Twenty-two thousand British soldiers and 7,000 Boer fighters had died, in addition to well over 10,000 blacks and those who had perished from disease in the camps.

The negotiations took three months to complete and, although the annexation of the Transvaal and Orange Free State meant that the Boers became British subjects, the concessions they gained were not insignificant. Boer farmers received compensation for damage caused by the 'scorched-earth policy', and the Afrikaaner language was to survive in schools and in the legal system. The Boers successfully fought to deny political rights to blacks, dashing their hopes and thereby laying the foundations of the blacks' separate status. On 31 May 1902, it was all agreed and the Peace of Vereeniging was signed.

1. What factors helped the Boers to prolong the war?

2. 'The Boer War should never have been fought and was nothing more than an embarrassment for the British.' How far do you agree with this interpretation?

In the longer term, Milner failed to revive South Africa's flagging economy. The Treasury ended subsidies in 1903 and Milner's (in hindsight) desperate decision to call in Chinese workers to solve the shortage of labour in the mines caused yet another furore in Britain. He resigned in 1905.

Joseph Chamberlain tried his best to heal the wounds when he claimed 'We are one nation under one flag', but it was the Liberals who granted home rule to the Transvaal and Orange Free State in 1906. The 1909 South Africa Act led to the birth of the Union of South Africa in 1910. As G.H. le May noted, the Boers could claim they had not been defeated and 'the spirit of Afrikaaner nationalism was unbroken'.

21.7 How significant was Chamberlain's role in tariff and imperial reform after 1895?

Chamberlain's decision to campaign for tariff reform would have profound consequences, principally for the Conservative Party (these are explained in detail in Chapter 20). The scheme was based on imperial preference, so that the colonies could trade more cheaply with each other at the expense of goods from outside the Empire on which higher tariffs were placed. Not only were the voters unconvinced about the benefits of imperial preference, but also the Liberal Party was able to mount a vigorous and apparently united campaign in defence of free trade and cheaper food, symbolised by the 'large Liberal loaf'. It contributed to the landslide Liberal victory of 1906, although Chamberlain retained his seat quite easily. He returned to the House of Commons as Leader of the Opposition because Balfour had lost his seat. In letters of 14 February – the so-called 'Valentine Compact' – Balfour's agreement to continue to pursue tariff reform was secured and some of the differences between the two men were papered over. Chamberlain was, nevertheless, exhausted and, in July 1906, he suffered a major stroke which left him partially paralysed. It was a mark of the esteem in which he was held when Birmingham re-elected him unopposed in 1910.

While some of his main achievements relate to his 'Brummagem' days as Mayor and municipal leader, Chamberlain's career after 1895 remains chequered. He accomplished some useful colonial reforms and the idea of Empire had been advanced. Australia had shown its commitment by sending troops to fight against the Boers. It is true that South Africa had been united, eventually, and Chamberlain visited the colony after the peace in the spirit of reconciliation. While it had always been his intention to develop both British and native interests, at heart he wished to improve the standards of living in Britain. Imperial preference, as a means of protecting home industries, had merit. So perhaps there is a case for agreeing that it wasn't the policies which mattered in the long term, rather his 'style and methods'. Why?

Chamberlain, despite his protests, must take responsibility for not stopping the Jameson Raid. It caused permanent hostility with the Boers and contributed to war. His choice of Milner was provocative, although Chamberlain may well have sought a more cautious approach. The war itself tarnished the imperial vision, while ideas of an imperial federation made little headway because of the indifference of the Colonial Premiers.

What do you regard as Chamberlain's main achievement after 1895? Give reasons to support your answer.

It is likely, though, that the most enduring memory is of a politician who, for the second time, resigned from a government to wage a campaign over the heads of his party leader. He had done it in 1886; he did it again in 1903. The headstrong appeal to the public seems ill-judged as they never fully accepted the arguments in favour of abandoning free trade, which was so strongly associated with Britain's prosperity. He could have stayed in the Government, fought his corner. After all, Ritchie had gone and there was a healthy working Conservative majority. Chamberlain's departure from the Cabinet and subsequent campaigning split the Conservatives and ruined their electoral chances in 1906. To divide a party once may be forgiven; to repeat the exercise with another party implies the triumph of arrogance over good sense. It also reflects the remarkable impact of a man who, nevertheless, could have contributed so much more.

Source-based questions: Joseph Chamberlain

SOURCE A

'... before the end of this present century we may find our fellow subjects beyond the sea as numerous as we are at home. I want you to look forward. Now is the time you can exert influence. Do you wish that if these ten millions become 40 millions they shall still be closely, intimately, affectionately, united to you, or do you contemplate the possibility of their being separated, going off each in his own direction, under a separate flag? Think what it means to your power and influence as a country; think what it means to your position among the nations of the world; think what it means to your trade and commerce ... The influence of the Empire is the thing I think most about, and that influence, I believe, will always be used for the peace and civilisation of the world.
But the question of trade and commerce is of the greatest importance. I hear it stated ... by those whom I describe as "Little Englanders" ... that our trade with those countries [colonies] is much less than our trade with foreign countries ... and therefore we should cultivate the trade with foreigners, and that we can safely disregard the trade with our children.
That is not my conclusion ... I say that it is the business of British tradesmen to do everything they can to keep the trade of the Colonies with Great Britain, to increase the trade and promote it, even if in doing so we lessen the trade with our foreign competitors.'

Joseph Chamberlain, speaking in Birmingham, 15 May 1903.

SOURCE B

On the political right, he is remembered primarily as an Imperialist statesman ... His dream of welding the areas of the Empire under one 'Supreme and Imperial Parliament', and the close links he favoured in defence and commerce, never materialised. However, his views caught the mood of late-Victorian Imperialism as an expression of British patriotic feeling.
His interest in Imperialism was largely inspired by a conviction that there were opportunities for manufacturers and their employees within the Empire. This search for economic advantage is a theme running through his policies towards the African continent as well as the older colonies of Canada, Australia and New Zealand. Tariff reform was designed to assist British businessmen as they strove to compete with foreign manufacturers, and to provide work for those who currently lacked it.

From Joseph Chamberlain and the Challenge of Radicalism, *by Duncan Watts, published in 1992.*

SOURCE C

It was all very well for you and me to know, as we did, what a tremendous issue was behind such questions as franchise and alien immigration; but the public did not. They could not see that the things we were contending for were worth a big war, nor were they particularly pleased with the clients on whose behalf we appeared to be acting. There was too much 'money bags' about the whole business to be agreeable to any of us.

Chamberlain writing to Milner in December 1889 about the reasons for the start of the Boer War.

1. Study Source A.

What does this source tell a historian about Chamberlain's imperial vision?

2. How far does Source A support the interpretation in Source B about Chamberlain's motives for developing the Empire?

3. How useful is Source C in explaining the reasons why the Boer War started?

4. Use the sources and information from this chapter. Why did Joseph Chamberlain regard the Empire as such an important political issue in the years after 1895?

Ireland and British politics, 1895–1922

Key Issues

- *Why was Irish Home Rule a major political issue in the years before the First World War?*
- *How close was Ireland to civil war in the years 1912–14?*
- *How far did the Easter Rising of 1916 affect Anglo–Irish relations?*

22.1 How successful were the Conservatives in dealing with the Irish Question, 1895–1905?
22.2 To what extent did Irish nationalism change in the years before 1914?
22.3 Why did Irish Home Rule become a major political issue after 1911?
22.4 Why did Ulster oppose Irish Home Rule so strongly?
22.5 Historical interpretation: Who was most responsible for the Ulster Crisis of 1912–1914?
22.6 To what extent was the Easter Rising a defeat or a victory for Irish nationalism?
22.7 Why was Ireland partitioned between 1920 and 1921?

Framework of Events

1893	Gaelic League is formed
1898	Local Government Act
1905	Ulster Unionist Council and Sinn Fein formed
1906	Liberal election victory
1912	Home Rule Bill introduced to Parliament
1912	Unionist volunteers begin to organise themselves into Ulster Volunteer Force
	Covenant Day and signing of 'Solemn League and Covenant' in Ulster
1913	Nationalist Irish Volunteers formed in the south
1914	'Mutiny' at the Curragh
	Home Rule Bill passed and six northern counties excluded
1916	Easter Rising in Dublin
1918	Sinn Fein victories in the Coupon Election
1919–21	Anglo–Irish War
1920	Government of Ireland Act creates two parliaments in Ireland – one in the six counties becomes Northern Ireland. The Act did not come into operation for 26 'southern' counties.
1921	Anglo–Irish Treaty: Dominion status given to 'southern' Ireland, which becomes the Irish Free State
1922	Irish Free State comes into being.

Overview

THE case made by some British historians argues that the British electorate showed little interest in the 'Irish problem' and, after 1895, it seemed that many MPs were willing to follow suit. Up until the passage of the 1911 Parliament Act, which limited the powers of the Conservative majority in the

House of Lords, there was no realistic chance of the passage of a Bill that would give Ireland any form of Home Rule. As soon as the Act was passed, Home Rule became a possibility. British politicians returned to the question of Home Rule but found that the Protestant minority in the north of Ireland would never submit to nationalist rule from Dublin. Events from 1912 to 1914 proved that Ireland was again a dominant issue and of central importance to the British political parties. The Liberal Government failed to deal with what turned into a rebellion by Protestant Ulster which almost plunged Ireland into civil war had it not been for the outbreak of world war in 1914. It was identified by historian George Dangerfield (see Chapter 23) as one of three rebellions which marked 'The Strange Death of Liberal England'. By 1914, it not only marked the stubborn defiance of Ulster, but also the rise of Sinn Fein as a nationalist force – a polarisation of politics which ended any hope of a united Ireland and a reconciliation of religious and political differences there. Why did this happen?

22.1 How successful were the Conservatives in dealing with the Irish Question, 1895–1905?

Was the Irish question 'off the agenda' in 1895? Lord Salisbury's Government (1895–1902) and later Arthur Balfour's (1902–05) had no intention of introducing Home Rule. They had other preoccupations: Empire, defence, Europe and the 'Condition of England'.

Policy remained steadfast. 'Bloody' Balfour's 1887 Crimes Act (see Chapter 17) still gave the Government wide and severe powers against rural agitators. However, there were developments. Salisbury and Balfour knew well enough that the inequalities in land ownership would bedevil Ireland; a small number of Anglo-Irish Protestant landlords who owned vast estates deprived the large number of Catholic peasant tenant farmers of land as well as security of tenure. So, in 1896, Balfour encouraged more tenants to buy land from their owners under a scheme that had started in 1885. The policy of 'killing Home Rule with kindness' might satisfy a long-standing cause of Catholic complaint as well as give landlords generous terms for surrendering their land.

What do you regard as the most successful policy introduced by the Conservatives between 1895 and 1905? Give reasons to support your answer.

This process accelerated dramatically when George Wyndham, the Chief Secretary for Ireland, passed The Land Act of 1903. It provided extra money from the Government in the form of loans. Landlords were paid generously and in cash for releasing all their land so tenants could buy it. The peasants could now become proprietors, borrowing at low rates of interest with 68 years to pay. By 1909, over 300,000 out of 500,000 tenant farmers were purchasing land, which is proof of the scheme's success. In addition, 2 million acres of additional land were acquired and divided among the peasant farmers. Meanwhile, the Government supported efforts to improve standards of farming and encouraged these small producers to join together and sell their produce in cooperatives. There was little doubt that these farmers reaped the benefits of the end of landlordism. Such 'pacification' did blunt the attacks from those who saw land as a continuing grievance.

22.2 To what extent did Irish Nationalism change in the years before 1914?

As a political force, the Irish Home Rule Party remained split between pro- and anti-Parnellite factions. This division lasted until 1900, when the party reunited under the leadership of John Redmond (leader of the Parnellite faction) and his deputy John Dillon (who led the anti-Parnellite faction)

(a) What message does the cartoon suggest will be the effect on Belfast of the introduction of Home Rule for Ireland?

(b) How useful to a historian is this cartoon as evidence of the Protestant reaction to Home Rule within Ireland?

Postcard entitled 'Belfast under Home Rule: making a site for the statue of King John of Ireland'

Nationalism, though, was beginning to take different forms. Initially, these were not political; the establishment of a Gaelic League in 1893 encouraged the revival of the Gaelic language, so central to the survival of the culture. The Gaelic Athletic Association was set up to support Irish sports at the expense of anglicised ones such as cricket or tennis. It may be difficult to assess the effects of this 'new nationalism', but it was no accident that the 1890s witnessed the emergence of several writers who argued for the separation of Ireland from Britain. Examples include the socialist and republican James Connolly, and Arthur Griffith who published his own paper, the *United Irishman*, in 1898 to put forward his idea of 'Sinn Fein' ('Ourselves'). Griffith went on, in 1907, to translate these ideas into a political movement and organisation of the same name, aiming for a form of 'dualism' in Anglo–Irish relations, modelled on Austria-Hungary.

In retrospect, these were ominous signs of future activity. As the Government tried to tackle the land problem, reports of constitutional changes showed more erratic progress. On the one hand, the 1898 Local Government Act enabled new county councils to be elected, further loosening the hold of rural landlords in agricultural areas. A scheme devised in 1904 and 1905 by Sir Anthony MacDonnell, a civil servant, planned to devolve some domestic powers, such as finance, from London to an Irish Council. It was met with such howls of protest from Ulster Unionists that it had to be withdrawn. Although MacDonnell was the prime culprit, George Wyndham was forced to resign and it led to organised opposition from Ulster. In 1905, an Ulster Unionist Council was formed in Belfast to represent and shape the views of opinion in the Protestant north.

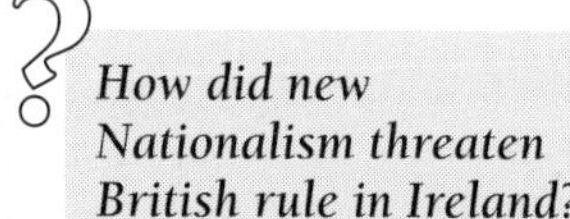

How did new Nationalism threaten British rule in Ireland?

22.3 Why did Irish Home Rule become a major political issue after 1911?

Did party advantage determine the behaviour of the Liberals and Unionists? In 1906, the Liberals won 401 seats (377 Liberals and 24 'Lib–Labs') and a landslide victory. They were still the party of Home Rule, but there was a lack of urgency, with little need for Irish Nationalist support in the Commons. Both Henry Campbell-Bannerman and, later, Herbert Asquith made no secret of their opinion that they had other matters commanding their attention – primarily social reform and the associated problem of how to deal with the Conservative majority in the House of Lords which insisted on sinking Liberal legislation. Indeed, until the Lords veto had been dealt with, there was no prospect of ever passing a Home Rule Bill. Campbell-Bannerman had made no promises to the Irish, save that he favoured a 'step-by-step' approach that might be less harmful to the Party. Gladstone's twin failures in 1886 and 1893 had left their mark, as did subsequent electoral defeats.

The one early attempt at reform – an Irish Councils Bill in 1907, which proposed to devolve some internal affairs to Dublin – made no headway and was abandoned in the face of considerable opposition. The Chief Secretary to Ireland, Augustine Birrell, was not the man for the job and must bear some responsibility when subsequent events went out of control.

Events in 1909 and 1910 put a different complexion on the Irish problem. The budget crisis resulted in a confrontation with the House of Lords. The results of the two elections fought in 1910 about the issue of their Lordships' veto over the Commons' legislation left the Liberals suddenly reliant on Irish nationalist support. In December, the figures stood at Liberals 272, Unionists 272, Irish Nationalists 84 and Labour 42. John Redmond, the leader of the Irish Nationalists in Parliament, could see the prospect of Irish affairs coming to the fore. So far he had been frustrated by lack of progress as this intelligent, moderate man's resolve to achieve change through democratic, constitutional processes had been tested. It was difficult for Redmond to 'keep the faith' with Parliament, given the growth of 'new' more militant Irish nationalism in the 1890s. Redmond had to be seen to be getting results. However, with the prospect of a Parliament Bill receiving the royal assent, the Lords would only be able to delay Irish Home Rule for two years.

Asquith had not spoken out for Redmond's case, so it is tempting to argue that Asquith's dependence on Irish (and Labour's) support during the passage of the Parliament Bill persuaded the Liberals now to put more energy into Home Rule. Redmond did threaten that 'it will be impossible for us to support Liberal candidates in England' and that this withdrawal of Irish voters 'would certainly mean the loss of many seats'. Conservatives agreed. They were not slow to accuse Redmond of making a 'corrupt bargain', the sole aim of which was to keep Asquith in power. This was a pact they would come to despise as it contributed to the loss of their ability to shape events from the Lords regardless of the wishes of the electorate. Indeed this 'bargain', which they regarded as an abuse of the wishes of British voters, became the justification for some of the Unionists' more irresponsible tactics in 1912 and 1913.

Not all writers agree that Asquith was so dependent on Redmond and the view that the Liberals acted purely out of political opportunism has been challenged. Patricia Jalland's view is that the Liberals could survive without the Nationalists in Parliament, so their adoption of Home Rule was part of a historical 'long-standing commitment' to the cause. In part, it is the case that the Liberals not only had Labour support, but also might count on Redmond not voting with the opposition. Redmond knew the only chance of progress was with the Liberals, which made his threats sound a little emptier than he no doubt intended. Whatever the arguments, Asquith did go ahead with proposals for Home Rule.

In April 1912, he introduced his Home Rule Bill.

1. Explain why Asquith was willing to introduce a Home Rule Bill after 1911.

2. How far had John Redmond's position been strengthened by 1912?

The Home Rule Bill

This provided for an Irish parliament which had the facility to pass some limited laws of its own. However, final authority, particularly over finance, defence and foreign affairs was retained at Westminster, in the imperial parliament to which Ireland could send 42 MPs. Ulster would then come under the jurisdiction of the new Dublin Parliament. Although this was a moderate proposal, the reaction of the north was predictable – they loathed it.

22.4 *Why did Ulster oppose Irish Home Rule so strongly?*

The separate identity of Ulster had its roots in the 17th century, when James I and his son Charles I granted large estates of confiscated land to English and Scottish Protestants. These 'plantations' marked out Ulster from the rest of Ireland, which was largely Catholic. There was unlikely to be much common ground between the south's allegiance to Rome and the Presbyterian north with its angry rantings against anything Catholic.

Such divisions became ingrained after The Glorious Revolution of 1688 when James II fled to Ireland and carried on the fight against Protestant William III. William's defeat of James' Catholic forces at the battle of the Boyne, in 1690, continues to cast its shadow over Ireland today. It was a defining moment that cemented the bonds of loyalty between the Protestants, who were concentrated in the northern provinces, and Britain.

Economic trends underlined this as Belfast developed into a manufacturing and trading centre, which saw its future prosperity in commerce with rapidly industrialising Britain rather than the poor, agricultural south. The thought of an antagonistic Dublin government under Home Rule ruling all Ireland, which might use tariffs against British competition, angered Belfast's shipbuilders and linen manufacturers. This would be a Dublin government that would be dominated by nationalists.

Neither was there any prospect of religious tolerance. There had been a steady influx of Catholics from the south, who migrated north during the 19th century in search of jobs and wages. But the religious divisions in the north stirred John Morley, the Liberal politician, to comment on the 'spirit of bigotry and violence for which a parallel can hardly be found … in Western Europe'. It was Parnell's Nationalism and Gladstone's conversion to Home Rule through the introduction of his 1886 and 1893 Bills which provoked defensive measures from Ulster's Protestants. They recognised the need to defend the union from Nationalist Catholics, claiming that 'Home rule is Rome rule'. The legacy of William III was kept alive by the Orange Order, which pledged itself to the union. Unionist clubs sprang up to feed other organisations such as the Ulster Defence Union or the Loyalist Anti-Repeal Union. Lord Randolph Churchill, the Conservative MP, opposed Gladstone's 1886 attempt at Home Rule. In a move that he calculated would do his personal ambitions no harm, Churchill visited Belfast and declared that 'Ulster will fight, and Ulster will be right'.

Gladstone's 1886 Bill also caused his Ulster MPs to abandon the Liberals (see Chapter 23) and join the Conservatives who were ready to embrace the Ulster unionist viewpoint. The new alliance of Conservatives and Liberal Unionists won a majority of constituencies in the north in the 1886 election. Any more attempts at Home Rule would be unable to ignore Ulster's voice. After the defeat of the 1893 Home Rule Bill and the subsequent triumph of the Conservative-Unionists, Irish voices were more muted. Ulstermen relaxed. The Nationalists waited for better times; perhaps after the publication of the Home Rule Bill?

1. What do you regard as the main reason why many Ulstermen opposed Home Rule? Give reasons to support your answer.

2. What evidence might support the view that the 1912 Home Rule Bill stood little chance of success?

22.5 *Who was most responsible for the Ulster Crisis of 1912–1914?*

A CASE STUDY IN HISTORICAL INTERPRETATION

Asquith's failure to treat Ulster as a separate case was, in part, a result of his lack of understanding of the problem and an unwillingness to accept how serious Ulster's opposition might become. Nevertheless, the signs were clear. In September 1911, 50,000 Ulstermen were told by Sir Edward Carson that Home Rule was a conspiracy and that, if it were passed, then they would have to take over the 'government of the Protestant provinces'.

Sir Edward Carson (1854–1935)
Carson trained as a lawyer. His powerful leadership of the Irish Unionists involved getting more than 250,000 Protestants to sign a covenant declaring undying opposition to Home Rule. Carson also set up the Ulster Volunteer Force, in 1913. During the First World War, he served as Attorney General and, later, as a member of Lloyd George's War Cabinet.

Carson was Liberal Unionist MP for Dublin University. His skills were recognised on becoming the Solicitor-General firstly for Ireland, then for England. He was a strong personality, committed to the Union, and so determined to organise resistance to the Bill that some historians have speculated on how far Carson was willing to go. Would he have resisted the Government by force to ensure Ulster's exclusion? Nicholas Mansergh and J.C. Beckett argue that he may well have done so, although both Robert Blake and Graham Dangerfield see Carson as a lawyer and constitutionalist who would probably shrink from open insurrection.

The same cannot be said of Captain James Craig, MP, who was keen to implement his well-laid plans for Ulster's self-government (through the Ulster Unionist Council) and ultimately armed resistance.

- In 1912, there was clear evidence that Protestant volunteers were being drilled and trained in what became the Ulster Volunteer Force. It may have lacked arms but certainly not organisation, as its Commanding Officer was Lieutenant-General Sir George Richardson who had served in India before retiring from the British Army.
- Both Craig and Carson were present when 100,000 Ulstermen marched in military formation through Balmoral (part of Belfast) a day or so before Asquith rose in the House of Commons to introduce his Bill.
- In September 1912, 'Covenant Day' was marked by more parades and demonstrations and the signing of the 'Solemn League and Covenant' by, in the end, just short of half a million men and women. It proclaimed them 'loyal subjects of his Glorious Majesty King George V', who would use 'all means necessary to defeat the present conspiracy to set up a home rule parliament in Ireland. And in the event of such a Parliament being forced upon us we further and mutually pledge ourselves to refuse to recognise its authority.'
- To that end the Ulster Unionist Council continued to make contingency plans to run the province's government if Home Rule was passed. Finance seemed no problem as the Anglo-Scottish landowners and the businessmen of Belfast contributed freely to the campaign.

All this activity continued under the gaze of Asquith's Government, which signally failed to take any firm action against Ulster's leaders.

What was happening in Parliament?

Andrew Bonar Law (1858–1923)
Born in Canada, Bonar Law made his fortune in Scotland as a banker and iron-merchant before entering Parliament in 1900. He was elected Leader of the Opposition in 1911, before becoming Colonial Secretary in Asquith's coalition government (1915–16). He was Chancellor of the Exchequer (1916–19) and Lord Privy Seal (1919–21) in Lloyd George's coalition. He was asked to form a Conservative Cabinet in 1922, but had to resign on health grounds.

It was in Parliament that the Ulstermen were receiving fierce support from the Unionists. Their leader since 1911, Andrew Bonar Law, had grown up in Ulster where he would have listened to the sermons delivered by his father who was a Presbyterian minister. He understood Carson's views and lent his support. Bonar Law stood with Carson at Balmoral in April 1912, taking up the cause with enthusiasm. Three months later at Blenheim Palace, home of the Duke of Marlborough, Bonar Law apparently supported the use of any means to resist the forcible inclusion of Ulstermen in a single Ireland: '… if an attempt were made to deprive these (Ulster)men of their birthright – as part of a corrupt parliamentary bargain – they would be justified in resisting such an attempt by all means in their power, including force … if such an attempt is made, I can imagine no length of resistance to which Ulster can go in which I should not be prepared to support them'. Was this an irresponsible call for armed resistance?

To Bonar Law's defenders, it was entirely just to encourage disobedience and insurrection when the Government seemed intent on sweeping aside the civil rights of a minority. This was a minority that was part of the Empire and wished to maintain their constitutional position as loyal citizens of the

King. During one of the debates, Bonar Law asked MPs if they believed that 'any Prime Minister could give orders to shoot down men whose only crime is that they refuse to be driven out of our community and deprived of the privilege of British citizenship?' Bonar Law's background also reflects a real commitment to the Union.

To Bonar Law's detractors, however, his was a reckless approach which reflected the impotence felt by Unionists after the passage of the Parliament Act now they could only use the Lords to delay legislation. Any strategy was justified if it would bring about a general election they believed they could win on the issue of defending the Empire and the union. Some historians, such as Professor Buckland, also recognise that as Ulster was the Home Rule Bill's '**Achilles heel**', there was much political advantage to be gained from attacking Asquith's inadequate response to the Ulster problem; political opportunism governed the Party's response.

Achilles heel: The weakest spot. Achilles was a Greek hero whose right ankle bone was damaged by fire. It was replaced by one taken from a giant who was a particularly fast runner. Achilles became a fast runner but his right heel was always his weak point. A different version of the myth tells of Achilles' mother, Thetis, dipping him into the river Styx to make him invulnerable. Only his heel, which she held him by, remained vulnerable.

If Bonar Law's 'Grammar of Anarchy', as Asquith called it, has much to answer for, then so do the Liberal leaders for their slow response. In June 1912, an attempt to amend the Bill by excluding four of the Ulster counties came to nothing. Historian K.W. Aikin claims that 'a favourable opportunity was lost', and the crisis deepened. In the House of Commons, Asquith found it difficult to make himself heard as each side traded insults. Indeed, the Prime Minister seemed incapable of grasping how dangerous the situation was. Historians such as Robert Blake generally agree that Asquith's profound respect for, and faith in, the constitution meant that he found it difficult to come to terms with the ferocity of the opposition both inside and outside Parliament. The Budget crisis was evidence of that. Then, as now, Asquith looked for a settlement that might be achieved through established parliamentary channels.

Did he share Redmond's view that Carson was bluffing? Unfortunately, Asquith never looked like dealing with the Ulster threat – all he offered was a policy of 'wait and see'. It failed to give any direction or purpose to government actions. Jenkins, Asquith's biographer, argues that since there was precious little prospect of finding an answer to the Ulster problem in 1912, there was merit in giving time for passions to cool. Certainly, there was no sign of compromise in Parliament. Carson wanted all Ireland, not just Ulster, to remain inside the Empire. Redmond was aware that Sinn Fein extremists would never accept a clause which excluded Ulster from a united Ireland – a view shared by Joe Devlin, leader of the Ancient Order of Hibernians and the Nationalists in the north.

In the event, 'wait and see' made matters worse. The Ulster Volunteer Force (UVF) continued to march and drill. If it indeed was an illegal organisation, then nothing was done to stop their preparations. By January 1913, the Bill had concluded its passage through the Commons only to be rejected by the Lords in an ill-tempered and hostile atmosphere.

More in hope than expectation, King George V was dragged into the crisis when Bonar Law suggested that he should veto the Home Rule Bill and call an election. Party leaders visited Balmoral during September 1913 to listen to the King's anxieties about the threat of Ulster violence and pleas for compromise. As a result, there were talks between the party leaders. Oddly, it was Carson who seemed more willing to accept a settlement; but his insistence that Ulster be defined as the nine northern counties, at least three of which had Catholic majorities, meant that Redmond would reject the proposal. Asquith could not afford to ignore this; neither could Bonar Law ignore the diehards in his own Party who would fight to the last in defence of the Union.

Meanwhile events were moving into a more dangerous phase. Dublin History Professor John MacNeill had long campaigned for a Nationalist force to be formed in the south. In November 1913, the Catholic Irish

Volunteers were set up with 200,000 men in support. Aiken notes that it was set up 'neither to fight for Home Rule nor to fight the Ulster Volunteers'. Potentially, it could be seen as another paramilitary force that could arm itself like the UVF; in which case, it was a step closer towards civil war.

Would the British Army be in a position to stop civil war, if it broke out?

How serious was the 'Mutiny' at the Curragh?

The position of the British Army in Ulster was now called into question as many of its officers were Ulstermen. Field Marshal Frederick Roberts, a respected figure, had his roots in Ulster. So did the Director of Military Operations at the War Office, General Henry Wilson, who managed to keep Bonar Law informed, behind the scenes, of the Army's plans. Would they suppress their countrymen if Home Rule was forced upon them? There was talk among Conservatives that the Annual Army Act should be amended to prevent the Army being used in such a way, against Ulster, unless a general election had taken place. This was dangerous, if not irresponsible, talk and Arthur Balfour warned Bonar Law that others may draw 'a perilous moral from the precedent'. At a time of social unrest led by **Suffragettes** and trade unions, as well as a perilous foreign situation, could Army discipline be relied upon?

Suffragettes: The name given to women who took an active, militant view towards the campaign for votes for women. Activities such as assaults on politicians and burning mailboxes were intended to highlight their case. The most notable Suffragettes were the Pankhursts. Suffragettes were a separate group from the Suffragists – who also wanted votes for women but aimed to achieve this through peaceful persuasion not direct action.

In March 1914, rumours spread that the UVF might try to seize arms. This prompted Churchill and Seeley, the Secretary of State for War, to order reinforcements into key positions in the north to protect munitions dumps. These operations and Churchill's decision to move destroyers to a position just off the coast, followed by a speech in which he said that he thought it was time to 'put these matters to the proof', made the Government's posture appear provocative. Seeley, displaying remarkable lack of judgement, apparently told the Commander-in-Chief in Ireland, General Sir Arthur Paget, that any officer who had a home in Ulster could 'disappear' from duty when the troops were being moved north and deployed. However, anyone else who stayed only to refuse to obey orders would be dismissed. Paget should never have reported this arrangement to his officers. He nevertheless did so, and in such a way that, on 20 March 1914, another Ulsterman, General Sir Hubert Gough, told Paget that he and 57 cavalry officers would resign rather than fight in Ulster. This was a 'mutiny' of sorts and could hardly have come at a worse time.

The way the crisis was handled exposed even more incompetence. Asquith had to abandon the military operations, admitting that it would lead to strikes among about half of the officers in the army. Gough and the others were told to report to the War Office – where they met Seeley and Sir John French. Gough was able to extract assurances that the Army would not be used to crush Ulster's political opposition to the Home Rule Bill.

Asquith faced a barrage of protest. Gough's lack of allegiance had been rewarded rather than punished and there was widespread bitterness from those officers who had maintained their loyalty. Seeley and French were forced to resign and Asquith took over the War Office himself. As if to set the seal on such an embarrassing incident, the UVF had armed itself within weeks. In a highly successful operation, which took place between 24 and 25 April, 35,000 rifles and millions of rounds of ammunition were landed at Larne and distributed without the Government getting to know about it. In these circumstances it is difficult to defend such a catalogue of errors from the Government which had let things drift, from the Army High Command and particularly from the Unionists who had done so much to encourage a climate of disobedience. Historians are undecided as to whether a military solution might have forced Carson to back down; such a solution was now beyond the Government's grasp.

1. Which of the following do you regard as most responsible for the Ulster Crisis of 1912–14?

(a) Herbert Asquith, the Prime Minister

(b) Sir Edward Carson

(c) Andrew Bonar Law.

Give reasons to support your answer.

2. Why do you think historians have disagreed over who was most responsible for the Ulster Crisis of 1912–14?

Nevertheless, Asquith was still discussing with Lloyd George the possibility of changing the Home Rule Bill. His Amending Bill would allow the people of any county in Ulster to vote in favour of exclusion from Home Rule for a period of six years. Carson fumed, calling it 'a stay of execution for six years'. The House of Lords rejected it and inserted a clause, which would permanently exclude all of Ulster. This would never be acceptable to the Government but they persevered. A conference held at Buckingham Palace on 21 July 1914 brought the party leaders together. No agreement was reached on the exact area of Ulster to be excluded and the Conference broke up before they could even talk about the issue of how long Ulster might be left out of Home Rule. The Amending Bill had to be dropped.

Within two days, the danger of armed violence seemed to increase when the Nationalists tried to smuggle in arms of their own at Howth, near Dublin. This time, unlike at Larne, the police stepped in – a point not lost on the Irish Volunteers. The British troops returned to Dublin via Bachelor's Walk where trouble broke out; three Volunteers were killed and over 30 wounded.

Had Asquith let things drift deliberately? If so, the combination of 'wait and see', which relied on the Parties arriving at an unlikely consensus, and diehard Unionist resistance encouraged by Bonar Law, had brought Ireland to the brink of civil war. An altogether different war now intervened.

22.6 *To what extent was the Easter Rising a defeat or a victory for Irish nationalism?*

On 4 August 1914, Britain declared war on Germany. The Home Rule Bill was passed and became law, although it would not be put into effect until the war had ended. John Redmond, leader of the Home Rule Party, was pleased as everybody's expectations were that they would not have to wait too long – after all, the troops would be 'home for Christmas'. In this context, Redmond's patriotic call to arms was not too costly; the nationalist Irish Volunteers would prove their loyalty and would defend Ireland from

Dublin during the Easter Rising, 1916

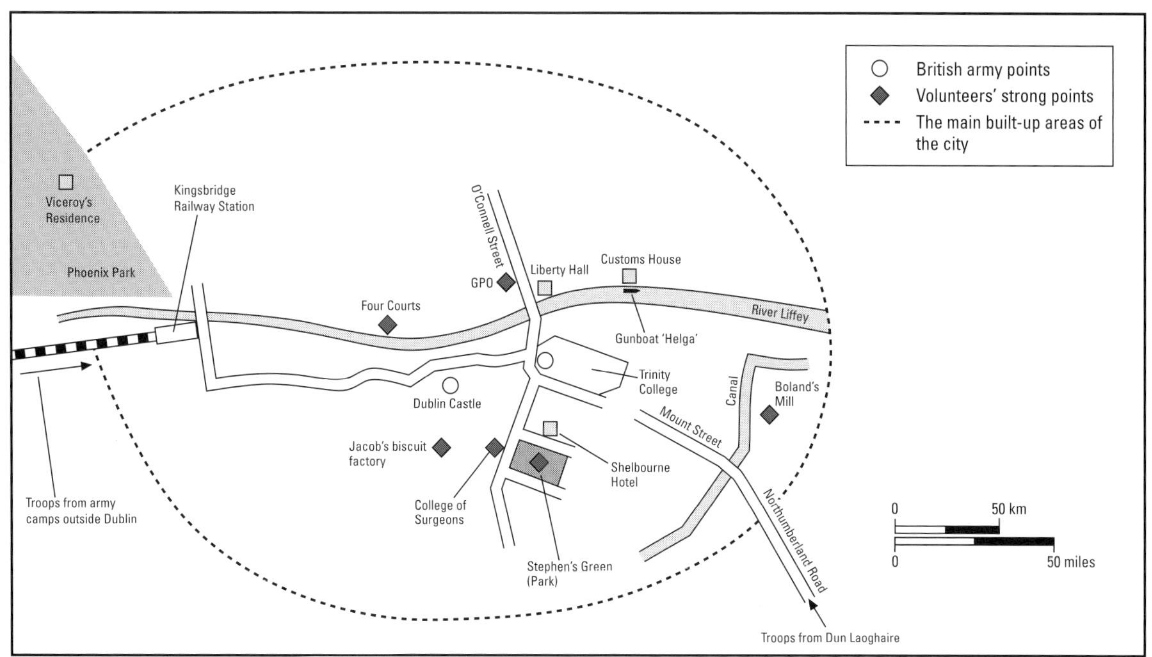

The scene in the General Post Office, Sackville Street, Dublin, 23 April 1916

Does the photograph above reflect the level of destruction caused to Dublin by the Easter Rising?

Give reasons to support your answer.

German attack. He even suggested that 'it would be a disgrace if young Ireland confined their efforts to remaining at home to defend the shores of Ireland from an unlikely invasion ...', so they might fight 'wherever the firing line extends ...'. Certainly, 169,000 volunteers supported Redmond, but not all Nationalists were as enthusiastic, as it was becoming obvious that Allied offensives were stuck in the mud of Flanders.

How long, then, would Home Rule be delayed? There were suspicions that Carson (who joined the Cabinet in 1915) and the men of Ulster (who were allowed to create the Ulster Division) were receiving special treatment. More extreme nationalists saw the chance to exploit Britain's wartime weakness and a breakaway group of 11,000 men, led by John MacNeill, formed themselves into the Irish Volunteers. The rest stayed loyal to Redmond and now called themselves the National Volunteers.

Professor MacNeill was a knowledgeable and enthusiastic campaigner for Gaelic rights and an independent Ireland. However, he found himself overshadowed by more extreme elements who disliked the war and who were willing to die for the revolutionary cause. Some members of the Irish Republican Brotherhood encouraged sacrifice, the symbolic spilling of blood. James Connolly, who placed his Irish Citizen Army at the disposal of the revolution, asked if Ireland would ever be a free nation under the Home Rule Bill. If a free nation was one which could control all its domestic and foreign affairs, then the answer was 'no, most emphatically NO!' Nothing but complete separation would please the extreme nationalists.

Patrick Pearse (see Source A on page 382) prepared plans for a rising. In all, seven men signed the Proclamation of an Irish Republic: Patrick Pearse, James Connolly, Thomas Clarke, Thomas McDonagh, Sean McDermott, Joseph Plunkett and Eamonn Caennt. These plans were drawn up in so much secrecy that Professor MacNeill did not get wind of them, as he disapproved of what they were doing. MacNeill countermanded Pearse's order for a muster of Volunteers on Easter Sunday, the day before the rising began. Sir Roger Casement, once a British Consular official and fervent Irish nationalist, was sent to gain support and arms from Germany. His shipment was prevented from landing and he was captured, only to be hanged later for treason. Nevertheless, the rising was to go ahead, without any real chance of success.

Easter Monday, 23 April 1916, was chosen. It was a quiet day and 1,600 rebels entered Dublin, occupying the General Post Office and other key buildings. Pearse declared a new Irish republic had been born. If this was the case, it would be short-lived. The rebels were not only outnumbered by the Police and the Army, but also no one came to their aid. MacNeill prevented Volunteers from outside Dublin taking part. The general public in Dublin itself looked on with indifference or disapproval. British reinforcements did the rest. On 29 April, amid scenes of devastation, the Irish rebels surrendered. They had lost 450 men dead, with 2,500 wounded. One Dubliner (quoted in G. Morton's *The Irish Question*) called this Easter Rising a 'piece of criminal folly'. Another suggested that 'exclusion of Ulster seems to me to be the only hope for an ultimately united Ireland'. These were hopeful signs that the extremists would be condemned and a settlement might be accepted which left out Ulster.

However, once again the Government mishandled and misread the situation. The anti-republican sentiments were let slip by taking oppressive measures, including **martial law** and thousands of arrests. The British had decided to punish this act of treason with repression. General Maxwell executed 16 leaders of the rising. He also introduced martial law. Stories of torture and beatings began to circulate, which infuriated the Catholic south and contributed to an anti-British backlash. Irish folklore had already begun to turn the leaders of the Rising into martyrs. Even across the Atlantic, there was hostility among Irish-Americans against the imprisonment of 75 of the rebels who carried US passports.

Martial law: Military law when applied to civilians. Normal civil rights are suspended, allowing the Government to arrest individuals and detain them without trial. Suspects could be tried by military court (without a jury) and given the death penalty if found guilty.

Asquith was, yet again, stirred into attempting a negotiated settlement. Lloyd George's solution was Home Rule for the south with exclusion for the six northern counties. Redmond and even Carson approved, but other Unionists and Sinn Fein did not. Historians generally point the finger at the Unionists for blocking this proposal. Whoever was to blame, it delivered two fatal blows: one was to Redmond who lost the initiative to Republicans who now took on the title of Sinn Fein, after the Rising; the other was to any realistic chance of a constitutional settlement. As F.S. Lyons noted, 'the whole constitutional movement was the chief casualty of 1916'. Further proof of this was the failure of more talks in 1917, at the Convention held at Trinity College. This time, Republicans boycotted the Convention and the Ulster Unionists refused to consider any compromise associated with Home Rule.

Sinn Fein, meanwhile, was celebrating four by-election victories, including one by Eamon de Valera who was to become the President of the Irish Republic as well as the head of the Irish Volunteers – a significant concentration of power. Sinn Fein clubs and a membership fast approaching a quarter of a million showed how far they had come from the tiny group which had taken part in the Easter Rising.

In 1918, the Government fared no better. Final German offensives on the Western Front exposed a severe shortage of soldiers and forced the extension of conscription to Ireland after a two-year gap. The Government had been warned about the consequences. Sure enough the protests from all quarters, including trade unions (who organised a one-day strike) and the Catholic Church, were so powerful that the scheme was dropped. The south

1. What results can you give for the military failure of the Easter Rising?

2. In what sense can the Easter Rising be seen as a victory for Irish nationalism?

3. Why did the more extreme nationalists of Sinn Fein replace the Irish Home Rule Party as the main representatives of Irish nationalism by the end of 1918?

clearly regarded the Imperial war as something that no longer concerned them. The arrest of some Sinn Fein MPs made no difference.

If confirmation was needed of Sinn Fein's prominent position in Irish politics, then it came in the coupon election of 1918, when they won 73 seats having previously held only seven. Of these 73, 26 were unopposed and another 34 were serving prison sentences. All refused to take their seats at Westminster. The old Irish Party collapsed from 86 seats to six, and four of those were in Ulster. Redmond did not witness this debacle as he had died several months earlier – his Party and the moderate approach had clearly failed, which added to his own sense of disappointment. The Unionists themselves gained 26 seats; the message from Ulster remained the same. A settlement was as far off as ever. The physical separation of Westminster from Sinn Fein, who took up their seats in their own Republican Parliament (the Dail) in Dublin in January 1919, reinforced the suspicion that the south was going its own way.

22.7 *Why was Ireland partitioned between 1920 and 1921?*

Subsequent events showed how quickly a circle of revolutionary violence was swallowing Ireland. The Irish Republican Army, which had been formed from the Irish Volunteers, came under the talented military direction of Michael Collins who had fought in the Easter Rising. Violence escalated alarmingly, with attacks on property and policemen. The British Government replied by using ex-soldiers called Black and Tans, who were poorly trained and ill disciplined. They matched the IRA's tactics of intimidation, terror and senseless brutality. During this Anglo–Irish War (1919–21), not only were the existing civil authorities being replaced by Sinn Fein government but also martial law was in widespread use.

Was there any hope of a constitutional settlement? The Government of Ireland Act of 1920 gave separate parliaments and governments to the six Protestant counties of the north and to the 26 counties of the south. However, each would have limited internal powers, akin to those proposed in 1914, with considerable authority retained at Westminster's Imperial Parliament. In the subsequent elections, overwhelming victories by Unionists in Ulster and Sinn Fein in the south signalled rejection of the Act. It never stood a chance of working, and terrorist action continued unabated. So did the talks, driven by Lloyd George's determination to find a settlement. He stuck to the task, and agreement was reached by the end of 1921. The Irish Free State, comprising the southern counties, would gain self-governing dominion status (like Canada); while Ulster would be given the right to drop out of the Free State and remain in the Union. The Nationalists were bitterly divided but eventually agreed and this formed the basis of the 1922 constitution.

Was the partition of Ireland an inevitable product of earlier events?

Source-based questions: The Irish Question

SOURCE A

In the name of God and of the dead generations from which she receives her old tradition of nationhood, Ireland, through us, summons her children to her flag and strikes for her freedom … supported by her exiled children in America and by gallant allies in Europe … We declare the right of the people of Ireland to the ownership of Ireland and to the unfettered control of Irish destinies, to be sovereign … we hereby proclaim the Irish Republic as a Sovereign Independent State, and we pledge our lives and the lives of our comrades in arms to the cause of its freedom … The Republic guarantees religious and civil liberty, equal rights and equal opportunities to all its citizens … oblivious of the differences carefully fostered by an alien Government, which have divided a minority from the majority in the past …

The declaration of Irish independence, which was read out by Patrick Pearse during the Easter Rising of 1916.

SOURCE B

I admit they are wrong; I know they were wrong; but they fought a clean fight, and they fought with superb bravery and skill … As a matter of fact the great bulk of the population were not favourable to the insurrection, and the insurgents themselves, who had confidently counted on a rising of the people in their support, were absolutely disappointed. They got no popular support whatsoever. What is happening is that thousands of people in Dublin, who ten days ago were bitterly opposed to the whole of the Sinn Fein movement and to the rebellion, are now becoming infuriated against the Government on account of these executions …

We who speak for the vast majority of the Irish people, we who have risked a great deal to win the people to your side in this great crisis of your Empire's history – we, I think, were entitled to be consulted before this bloody course of executions was entered upon in Ireland.

The consequences of the Easter Rising of 1916. This extract is from a speech made in the House of Commons by John Dillon, a Nationalist MP, in May 1916.

SOURCE C

Protestant opposition to 'Rome rule' was not eradicated [by the Easter Rising]. If anything, it had been reinforced by the republican 'Easter Rising' in Dublin in 1916 and the violent struggles which followed it. For the Protestants, the rising was proof positive of the treachery of the Catholics who had waited until Britain was occupied in a bloody struggle for democracy and freedom, and then attacked from the rear.

From The Religion and Politics of Paisleyism: God Save Ulster *by S. Bruce, published in 1986.*

---

1. Study Sources A and B.

What do these sources reveal about the different approaches to the Irish Question from the Irish nationalists?

2. Study Source C.

This source argues that Protestants would see the Easter Rising as an act of 'treachery'. How would the writer of Source A deny that interpretation of events?

3. 'It was the way the British Government dealt with the Rising rather than the Easter Rising itself which was a "piece of criminal folly".' Use Sources B and C and your reading to explain if you agree with this view.

23 The Liberals in power, 1905–1915

Key Issues

- *Why and how far did the Liberals lay the foundations of the Welfare State?*
- *How far was the political crisis of 1909–11 a turning point in British history?*
- *To what extent had 'Liberal England' been undermined by a succession of pre-war crises?*

23.1 What difficulties did the Liberal Government face under Campbell-Bannerman?
23.2 To what extent did 'New Liberalism influence government policy?
23.3 How far did the Liberals' social reforms lay the foundations of a Welfare State?
23.4 Why did the House of Lords' rejection of the 1909 Budget cause a poliyical crisis between 1909 and 1911?
23.5 How successful were the Liberals in dealing with the political crises between 1909 and 1911?
23.6 How influential was the Suffragette movement in the years 1909–1914?
23.7 How successful was the Government in dealing with industrial unrest in the years 1910–1914?
23.8 Historical interpretation: The 'Strange Death of Liberal England'

Framework of Events

1905	December: Balfour's Conservative Government resigns
1906	January: Liberal victory at the general election Workmen's Compensation Act; Trade Disputes Act; School Meals Act Introduction of free medical inspection for schoolchildren
1908	Asquith becomes Prime Minister Old Age Pensions Act
1909	The People's Budget rejected by House of Lords Osborne Judgement
1910	General elections; constitutional crisis over powers of House of Lords; rise in militant trade union activity
1911	Parliament Act; National Insurance Act; Suffragette and trade union militancy Balfour's resignation; Bonar Law becomes Conservative leader
1912	Irish Home Rule Bill passes Commons, vetoed by Lords (became law in September 1914); Ulster Covenant; coalminers' strike
1913	Trade Union Act; Cat and Mouse Act; Home Rule Bill rejected; Triple Alliance of unions formed
1914	Decline in trade union violence; Triple Union Industrial Alliance formed; Home Rule Act passed but implementation delayed
1915	Asquith forms a National Government with Conservatives and Labour.

Overview

WHAT was the nature of the Liberal Party after their dramatic victory in the general election of January 1906? The figures suggested that the Party could sweep all before it:

Liberal MPs: 400, including 24 Lib–Labs
Conservative and Unionist MPs: 157
Irish Nationalists: 83
Labour MPs: 29.

Temperance: The campaign to limit and then prevent the sale of alcoholic drink; associated with the pressure groups The Band of Hope Union and the United Kingdom Alliance.

The Cabinet headed by Sir Henry Campbell-Bannerman ('C-B') was not without talent. Its members had different opinions about the best way forward, but 'C-B' did manage to hold things together relatively successfully. The victory provided a majority of 130, which was even larger once political allies, such as the Irish Nationalists and Labour, were included. However, things were not as they seemed – there was little hint of that remarkable torrent of legislative reform which was to come after 1908. Few Liberal candidates had made specific references to social reform in their election addresses, although some had made vague references to the importance of introducing old age pensions. Instead, traditional Liberal ideas took their place at the head of the queue – such as ending the Church of England's hold on education, **temperance**, free trade, help for the unemployed, land reform, and perhaps some remedial help for the trade unions which were still paralysed by the Taff Vale judgement (see Chapter 19). Anyone attempting to identify a grand design of social reform would look in vain.

In many respects, it was 'business as usual'. Herbert Asquith, the new Chancellor of the Exchequer, kept the Treasury content with proposals for lower taxation and reduced expenditure. This was in line with old Gladstonian virtues of economies in government and *laissez-faire* individualism. Campbell-Bannerman was cautious, which may well have frustrated Radical Liberals and Labour members who were seeking more in the way of reform. John Burns, the first working man to take a Cabinet post – at the Local Government Board – was disappointing. Even someone who was recognised as a radical, David Lloyd George at the Board of Trade, had not yet seized the moment to take up progressive measures. These would come later, after 1908, during a remarkable period of social and constitutional legislation, which not only laid down some vital welfare reforms but also limited the powers of the House of Lords.

23.1 What difficulties did the Liberal Government face under Campbell-Bannerman?

Denominational schools: Those schools administered by a specific religious group such as the Church of England or Roman Catholic Church.

The new government's early legislation soon ran into difficulties. In 1906, an Education Bill which had in its sights Balfour's 1902 Act (see page 348) proposed that **denominational schools** should be taken into local authority hands and that the amount of religious instruction which could take place should be limited. The attack on the established Church of England would please nonconformists, but it failed to please their Lordships in the House of Lords. The Liberals discovered that the inbuilt Conservative majority in the House of Lords would again sabotage their programme – that of the newly elected government. It was a trial of strength which not only wrecked the Education Bill, but also two further bills. The Plural Voting Bill of 1906, designed to stop property owners voting several times, and the Licensing Bill, which aimed to limit the number of public houses (to satisfy pledges made to the temperance lobby), both fell in the Lords. The impression of a weak government which was beginning to stall or, as one contemporary put it, just 'ploughing the sands', is only countered by some worthy, if unspectacular (as far as the voters were concerned), measures to help children and workers.

The Trades Disputes Act of 1906 was a priority, given the call from Labour MPs for a reversal of the Taff Vale judgement. Campbell-Bannerman took an interesting line; faced with a cautious Liberal Bill, or a Labour Bill which would give the trade unions much more legal protection than they had enjoyed in the past, he chose the latter. The Act was passed and trade unions were made immune from having to pay compensation for damages caused by a strike. It was an important step which enshrined in law rights which were retained for over half a century. It was also a Bill that their Lordships were expected to reject, but did not, especially when there were so many working men's votes at stake. The Home Office, under Herbert Gladstone, rather surprisingly introduced some useful measures. Again, it was Labour influence which pressed for the Workmen's Compensation Act (1906). Employers would pay compensation not only when workmen suffered injury because of their work, but also for any diseases contracted through their employment. Payments would be made after only one week off work, instead of two. Mining MPs brought pressure to bear on the Government, who introduced a modest measure reducing miners' hours to eight and a half a day.

National Efficiency: A political view, popular among some politicians between 1899 and 1914, that is Britain was to maintain its position as a leading world power it had to improve the health and wellbeing of the British population.

The debate about **National Efficiency** continued following the 1904 report of the Interdepartmental Committee on Physical Deterioration, which had shocked the nation with reports of underfed children. A Labour MP introduced school meals, with government backing. The Education (Provision of School Meals) Act of 1906 did run into opposition from those who recognised that the State was taking a significant step forward in its provision. True, the scheme was voluntary, but critics saw it as 'socialism on the rates', and something parents should be responsible for anyway. Authorities only slowly introduced meals. The 1914 figure of 31,000 children receiving school meals sounds less impressive when it is remembered that only half the education authorities provided them at all. A further measure, in 1907, enabled medical inspections of elementary school children. Again it was not compulsory, but Sir Robert Morant, Permanent Secretary to the Board of Education, deserves credit for framing the legislation. Three-quarters of local authorities were providing medical treatment by 1914, and were clearly more active in this area.

For young lawbreakers, probation was introduced in 1907 to avoid their confinement with adult offenders. The Children's Act of 1908 went further. It brought numerous statutes together, banned prison for children under 14, introduced borstals for those under 16, and introduced special juvenile courts.

David Lloyd George, at the Board of Trade, was showing signs of initiating reform. His Merchant Shipping Act (1906) improved conditions of work for merchant seamen. He then managed to pour oil on troubled waters when he settled a threatened national railwaymen's strike.

The electors were unimpressed by the Liberal record as well as the trade depression which was beginning to make itself felt in industry. By-elections began to run against the Government. Ten were lost in 1907 and 1908, including Colne Valley, a Liberal stronghold snatched by an extreme socialist, Victor Grayson. Perhaps old age pensions would revive Liberal

1. What do you regard as the most important reform passed by the Liberals between 1905 and 1908? Give reasons to support your answer.

2. What reasons can you give for the electorate's disappointment with the 1905–08 Liberal Government? Explain your answer.

fortunes. A proposal to introduce this was long overdue, but had been delayed until the 1908 Budget. Asquith was preparing the measure when Campbell-Bannerman had a heart attack.

At 56 years of age, Asquith became Prime Minister of a talented Cabinet that, in the next three years, passed some remarkably successful legislation. Not that there were any signs of this in early 1908, when unemployment was rising, Labour allies were annoyed at the lack of progress on social reform and the naval arms race threatened the Budget surplus which was earmarked for pensions. Neither would the House of Lords look upon Asquith with any favour. Liberal legislation might again grind to a halt in the Unionist-dominated House of Lords.

23.2 To what extent did 'New Liberalism' influence government policy?

'New Liberalism' was beginning to have a slow, if gradual, impact on sections of the Liberal Party, which was preparing the ground for its programme of social legislation – a programme which called for more government intervention to protect the weak, poorer elements of society. Mr Gladstone would not have approved. His *laissez-faire* attitude might have placed the emphasis on self-help and minimal government interference, but even moderate Liberals had recognised the need for more government action.

- The 'condition of England' question (see Chapter 21) had made this more urgent. The decline in national efficiency had cast doubt on Britain's ability to maintain its position in the world.
- William Booth and Seebohm Rowntree had exposed and redefined the extent of poverty. They had shown that family size, low wages, unemployment, illness and old age, and the death of the family's wage earner were to blame for poverty – rather than lax working-class morality such as drunkenness and laziness. If adverse social and economic conditions were the root cause then there was a radical case for the State to provide a 'safety net' – a basic minimum benchmark of assistance.
- The poor state of industrial workers and army recruits made some Liberals wonder how Britain would compete effectively with the USA or Germany.
- The difficulties faced defeating the Boers in 1899 to 1902 (see Chapter 21) had led Lloyd George to comment: 'The country that spent 250 millions to avenge an insult levelled at her pride by an old Dutch farmer is not ashamed to see her children walking the streets hungry and in rags.'
- In hindsight, the 'Great Depression' was perhaps not as severe as was once thought. However, it certainly undermined people's confidence at the time. It was no longer apparent that continued economic growth could solve the problem of poverty without more intervention from the State.
- Public awareness of the trend to a more **collectivist** approach was growing after the passage of new measures such as the 1905 Unemployed Workmen Act (see page 348).

Collectivist: Opposite to *laissez faire*; describes the belief that government intervention in social and economic affairs can be of benefit to society.

- Then there was the effect of having so many more MPs from the ranks of the working class – 53 in the 1906 Parliament. Were they so important in forcing the pace of change? Was the Liberals' response to the threat from the Left merely opportunistic? Historian Duncan Tanner (1994) has argued that 'Liberal theorists were developing their case for intervention long before the formation of the Labour Party in 1900. Very little (Liberal) legislation stemmed directly from labour pressure', although he admits that there were exceptions – trade union reform, school meals and payment of MPs. Nevertheless, the very existence of the Labour group must have crystallised the thoughts of Liberal reformers and 'Old Liberal' doubters alike – especially since there were vital working-class votes to be won. How might the Liberal Party adapt its traditional views and accommodate the rising expectations of the working class? Could 'Old Liberalism' adapt to the conditions of the age? Was 'new' Liberalism the answer?

'New Liberalism'

'New Liberalism' grew out of an intellectual tradition marked out by the teachings of Oxford philosopher T.H. Green, whose ideas were developed by L.T. Hobhouse and J. Hobson in the 1880s and 1890s. In 1893, the first meeting of the Rainbow Circle brought Hobson, radical Herbert Samuel (later a Cabinet Minister) and a number of prominent Fabian Socialists together. Government, they said, should take collective action to establish a national minimum standard of living. The arguments carefully built on traditional Liberal values of individualism. If people were impoverished, through no fault of their own, individual self-reliance was undermined. However, if the Government stepped in to guarantee a minimum standard of living, then the individual would be able to prosper. T.H. Green's idealism expressed it as the 'liberation of the powers of all men equally for contributions to a common good'. The Welsh nonconformist tradition brought a helping of social pity and a sense of Christian mission. The fruits of this activism could be seen when contemporaries spoke of 'municipal socialism'; local authorities were taking the initiative in education, sanitation, public health, poor relief – indeed a whole range of expanding services. There was, however, nothing remotely socialist in the programme of the young Liberals. If the socialists aimed to take over the wealth of the country, the Liberals wished to use that wealth to 'promote measures for ameliorating the conditions of life for the multitude' (Lloyd George).

Reforming 'New Liberals' could see the evolution of traditional party values. Nevertheless, tensions between the 'New' and the 'Old' Liberals remained. Were their differences ones of principle or strategy? Probably both. If the reformers stood for interventionism and a national minimum standard, they also stood for graduated taxation as a means to achieve it. Although still on a modest scale, taxation was seen as a way to shift wealth from the rich towards the poor.

The Cabinet, in 1908, remained unconvinced about the new course. Traditional Liberal values were still strong. However, the tide was turning. L.T. Hobhouse was campaigning strongly for 'collective action'; while, in 1909, J. Hobson wrote that **Gladstonian Liberalism** had been replaced by a new 'commitment to a task which certainly involves a new conception of the State in its relation to the individual life and to private enterprise'. In other words, the emphasis on individualism and limited state interference was shifting towards more state activity so that people had 'equal opportunities for self-development'. Also in 1909, Lloyd George and Herbert Samuel began to argue for state intervention to protect individuals from the effects of unemployment, old age and sickness. Reviving the poor

Gladstonian Liberalism: Its principles were self-help, economies in government, minimal state interference and free trade.

1. How did 'New Liberalism' differ from traditional Gladstonian Liberalism?

2. Which group was more supportive of New Liberal ideas, members of the Liberal Cabinet or grassroots Liberal supporters? Give reasons to support your answer.

might stimulate business – such interests were close to Liberal hearts. Old Liberal individualism was changing its spots. However, the real influence of New Liberalism would not become apparent until Lloyd George and Churchill were in Asquith's Cabinet.

Lloyd George's career, by any standards remarkable, coincides with these shifts in the Party. His historiography characterises him either as a social reformer and opponent of privilege or as a self-seeking opportunist who spoke of reform and used it to advance his career. Elements of both can be identified. His nonconformist energy would soon be harnessed to the crusading cause of radical reform, although there is little doubt that he recognised the political opportunities that presented themselves. At the same time, he made it more acceptable for the Liberal Party to embark on a new course. By 1909, the doubters in the Party were eclipsed – for the moment.

23.3 *How far did the Liberals' social reforms lay the foundations of a Welfare State?*

For mothers and children ...

1906: The Education (Provision of School Meals) Act
1907: Notification of Births Act
Medical inspections of all elementary schoolchildren
1908: The Children's Act

For the old ...

1908: The Old Age Pensions Act introduced a non-contributory scheme, providing 5 shillings a week as a right to those over 70 years of age (7 shillings and 6d to married couples) as long as income did not exceed £31 a year. The full sum was only for those not earning more than £21 a year; between £21 and £31, pensions were on a decreasing sliding scale. The scheme, enacted through the 1909 Budget, cost between £8 million and £10 million.

For the sick and injured ...

1906: The Workmen's Compensation Act forced employers to pay compensation to workers injured at work through accidents and related ailments.

1911: Part 1 of the National Insurance Act provided a payment of 10 shillings a week for a person who was off work because of illness. This lasted for 26 weeks, after which a disablement payment of 5 shillings a week was made. Treatment and medicines would be given free to the insured person but not to his family. A single maternity benefit of £1 10 shillings was paid on the birth of each child.

Who was to pay? For all workers earning up to £160 a year, the State would provide 2d, the employer 3d and the employee 4d – in this way it was claimed that the employee received 9d for 4d on an insurance principle – not charity. Low payments could lead to high benefit, given the balance of the insured risk.

For those out of work …

1905: The Liberal Government renewed the Unemployed Workmen Act. Distress Committees could be set up with grants to help provide work for the unemployed.

1909: a young civil servant, William Beveridge, inaugurated a plan for a national system of Labour Exchanges. By February 1910, 83 were open, and by 1913 this had risen to 430.

1911: Part 2 of the National Insurance Act helped about 2.5 million men in industries where the risk of unemployment was highest, e.g. shipbuilding, construction and engineering. An unemployed person received 7 shillings a week for a maximum of 15 weeks, as long as they had paid enough into the scheme beforehand. In context, the payments were quite low; they were a 'lifebelt' which might be added to any savings people might have.

And for the workers …

1906: Trades Disputes Act reversed the Taff Vale decision.

1908: Miners were to work a maximum of an eight-and-a-half-hour day.

1909: Trade Boards provided some protection for exploited workers in sweated trades, such as tailoring or box making. The Act enabled Trade Boards to fix minimum wages and maximum hours and for inspectors to report employers (who could be fined) who ignored the rulings.

1911: Shops Act granted a weekly half-day's holiday for shopworkers.

1913: Trade Union Act reversed the Osborne Judgement (which prevented members of unions from subsidising the Labour Party) by allowing unions, from a special political fund, to be used to support the Labour Party. People could opt out of the scheme if they chose not to make political payments of this sort.

Was this the 'foundation of a Welfare State'?

Definitions of the Welfare State vary from author to author. Some see it as a loose collection of social, medical and educational services provided by the State. Others see it as a comprehensive attempt not only to provide welfare but also to redistribute income, thereby serving the cause of social justice. By either definition, the Liberals fell short of providing a coherent welfare package – they muddled through, introducing changes which were modest by our standards. Such comparisons, though, are taken out of the context in which politicians found themselves at the turn of the century. A start had been made in the 1890s to establish a local structure of administration which proved invaluable as the Liberals studied other models of provision, mainly from Germany, and then started to make piecemeal reforms. All that Liberalism aimed for at this stage was to provide a basic minimum; it was always going to be a programme limited in its scope. On introducing old age pensions, Churchill declared that they never wished to take the 'toiler to dry land'. They sought only to 'strap a lifebelt around him'.

Whole areas remained unreformed – for example, housing was in short supply, and the dreaded workhouses would continue to have an influence for a number of years to come. Old age pensions and national insurance failed to go far enough. Pensions were not generous and not universal. Numerous people were left outside the scheme, such as ex-convicts and those who had not found employment for some time. The old, however, could emerge from the stigma of the Poor Law and a bold step had been taken. There is no reason to think that the statement 'God bless Lloyd George', recorded by Flora Thompson in *Lark Rise to Candleford*, was not widely shared. The achievement of passing the National Insurance Bills should not be underestimated either. Doctors had been dissatisfied with their level of remuneration, and insurance companies and friendly societies felt that their business was being threatened.

Labour Members of Parliament felt things did not go far enough and they had to be offered the payment of MPs before they swung in behind Lloyd George. Some workers felt that the exclusion of their families was unfair, although others resented the loss of 4d a week. Education continued to fall behind standards on the continent, particularly in Germany. For example, the amount spent on British universities lagged way behind German counterparts. Lloyd George and Churchill, the two moving forces, had been careful not to offend the wing of the Liberal Party which still held Gladstonian values. It is true that the extent of increased State, rather than local, interference was a new route for Liberals to take, but their view of collectivism involved the **insurance principle**. Recent research tends to imply that 'new' Liberalism had made inroads throughout the Party, but not as much as was once thought. Many rank-and-file members were true to traditional Liberal ideas.

Insurance principle: A form of self-help with State assistance to offset the worst effects of unemployment, sickness and old age.

Despite the lack of a long-term plan to fight poverty and despite the caution enshrined in the measures introduced, Liberalism was more dynamic and radical in reform than it had ever been. Many important principles had been established – a greater role for the State; the use of taxation and heavy expenditure to provide a basic minimum and help individuals to realise their potential. It is difficult to criticise the Liberals, who were making *ad hoc* (improvised) reforms to deal with specific problems, for reasons of both political gain and humanitarian concern. The Welfare State, with its commitment to Beveridge-style care 'from the cradle to the grave', is a much later concept. It should not be used to assess a Liberal programme, which never had anything as extensive as that in mind. Nevertheless, these early faltering steps were crucial to the later evolution of welfare services and the social service state. Churchill marked his satisfaction by writing: 'Beginnings are usually hard … but ten years hence all these bickerings will have been forgotten … We shall wonder how we ever could have got on without it, and a younger generation … will thank us for the grand achievement.' B.B. Gilbert explained the nature of this achievement, in *The Evolution of National Insurance*: 'They took British society into an entirely new field of activity, and although by no means solving the problem of the condition of the people, they settled the lines upon which the eventual solution would be found.'

1. Which group do you think benefited most from Liberal reforms:

(a) mothers and chiildren

(b) the old

(c) the sick

(d) the unemployed?

2. How far did the Liberal social reforms of 1906–14 lay the foundations of a 'Welfare State'?

23.4 Why did the House of Lords' rejection of the 1909 Budget cause a political crisis between 1909 and 1911?

When Herbert Asquith became Prime Minister in April 1908, Lloyd George replaced him as Chancellor of the Exchequer, while Winston Churchill, who had **crossed the floor** of the House of Commons in 1903, occupied the Board of Trade. Both Ministers were prominent in a government remarkable for its vigour and pace of reform. Asquith tended to preside over this reforming Cabinet, rather than set matters in motion. It is generally accepted that he gave support, and helped to deal with administrative business with an extraordinary efficiency.

Crossed the floor: Moved from one side of the House of Commons to the opposite side. In this instance, Churchill left the Conservatives to join the Liberals, on the opposition side in the House of Commons.

The Liberals faced a number of costly social and defensive problems. Old age pensions were a priority. 'Before this generation has passed away we shall have advanced a great step towards that time when poverty and wretchedness and human degradation which always follow in its camp will be as remote to the people of this country as the wolves which once infested its forests' (Lloyd George). But how would it be paid for?

Another concern was the German naval threat. Efforts to disarm at The Hague in 1907 had failed as was all too apparent when the Germans passed their Naval Law amendment in 1908. The race to meet this challenge by building a new generation of **Dreadnoughts** was given some urgency when George Wyndham, an opposition MP, coined the phrase which caught the popular imagination: 'We want eight and we won't wait.' This alone would cost £15 million.

Dreadnoughts: A type of battleship, first launched by Britain in 1906, which was more heavily armed and armoured than previous types. Its launch helped to intensify the naval race between Britain and Germany.

So much depended on the success of the Chancellor's 'People's Budget' in 1909 – or what Lloyd George sometimes preferred to call his 'war budget' to fight poverty and squalor. However, Liberal legislation was vulnerable to the inbuilt Conservative majority in the House of Lords. Despite the Liberal view that an unelected House of Lords was undermining the democratically elected government, Balfour was not going to ignore the veto he had over government legislation. His often-quoted words confirmed that 'the great Unionist Party should still control, whether in power or opposition, the destinies of this great Empire'. Lloyd George replied by accusing the House of Lords of being 'Mr Balfour's poodle', although this should not suggest that the Unionists could act with any feeling of agreement. Racked by internal strife over tariff reform, they were able to agree that the new Budget and old age pensions were threats to an individual's rights over his or her own property. Would their Lordships veto the Budget? Custom suggested that the passage of money bills should not be interrupted.

Why did the Lords reject the Budget?

The Budget

The measures proposed would certainly, in Lloyd George's own words, 'hit the rich'.

- Income tax was increased from one shilling (1s) to 1s 2d for those earning over £3,000 a year.
- A new supertax of 6d in the £ was imposed on those earning over £5,000 a year. Combined, these taxes might only affect about 25,000 people in Britain, presumably few of them Liberal middle-income supporters.
- Increased duties were placed on spirits, tobacco, petrol; while a new road fund licence was introduced – some have regarded these as taxes targeted on the wealthy.
- However, the measures which proved to be most contentious related to increased death duties and the ownership of land; taxes which the moral wing of the Liberal Party had for long regarded would penalise income which had not been 'earned'. Workers laboured on the land or under it to create the wealth – the landowner merely spent the profits of other people's toil.
- This included a 20% tax on the amount by which land had risen in value and half a penny in the £ on the increased value of land on which minerals were mined.
- These land taxes would require surveys of land ownership – literally, an intrusion into an individual's property holdings. Calculations were to show that the tax yield would be modest; the psychological impact on the propertied classes, however, was dramatic.

Philanthropist: A person who works for the benefit of others.

1. Why was the People's Budget introduced in 1909?

2. 'Hero or villain'. Which of these descriptions most suits Lloyd George during the debate over the People's Budget of 1909? Give reasons to support your answer.

- Predictably, the Conservatives hated it. The Budget was defeated in the Lords by 350 votes to 75.

Historians have disagreed about Lloyd George's motives. Did he use the Budget to incite their Lordships so he could then diminish their powers, or did the drama unfold entirely by accident? It seems unlikely that the Chancellor engineered the Budget crisis and its outcome – such foresight might even have been beyond Lloyd George's control.

Was the budget inflated to guarantee its rejection? Again unlikely, as the costs of rearmament and pensions gave the Treasury some cause for concern. However, the possibility of the Lords rejecting the Budget must have occurred to the Chancellor. When they did so, he was alive to the possibilities. He grasped the moment to portray himself as a **philanthropist** – in a famous *Punch* cartoon Lloyd George was the highwayman, ready to hold up the rich with the words 'I'll make 'em pity the aged poor'.

23.5 *How successful were the Liberals in dealing with the political crises between 1909 and 1911?*

The significance of the Budget had gone beyond finance – the issue was now constitutional. The House of Lords had departed from established practice and rejected a money bill, but the next step the Government might take was not entirely clear. Asquith was cautious, Lloyd George less so, especially since by-election results seemed to indicate that an attack on the House of Lords might not be too unpopular. But if the powers of the Upper House were to be clipped, then how? Should a general election be called to place the activities of their Lordships in full public glare? For Asquith, this seemed a good moment to go to the country as the Conservatives were in something of a dilemma. Tory Lords did their case no good at all – for instance, the Duke of Beaufort was reported to have said that he would have liked to see Churchill and Lloyd George 'in the middle of 20 couple of

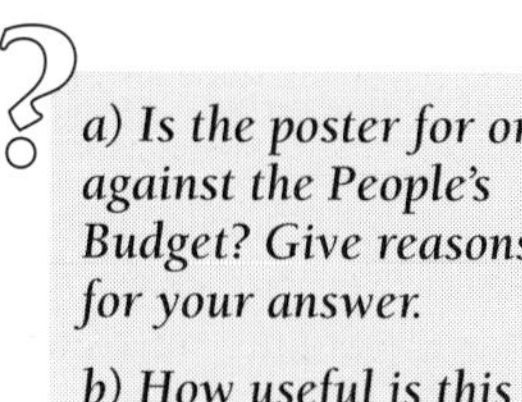

a) Is the poster for or against the People's Budget? Give reasons for your answer.

b) How useful is this poster to a historian as evidence of the public's view of the 1910 People's Budget?

Conservative election poster of 1910

doghounds'. If Balfour allowed the Budget to pass, it would look like surrender to the voters. And the tariff reformers, who were in no mood to surrender, would have probably split the Party. Reject the Budget, as they had decided to, and they stood accused not only of refusing to pay for Dreadnoughts and pensions but also of unconstitutional behaviour. Lloyd George seized on this: 'The question will be asked whether 500 men … should override the judgement – the deliberate judgement of millions of people who are engaged in the industry which makes the wealth of the country. Who made 10,000 people owners of the soil, and the rest of us trespassers in the land of our birth …?'

A general election was called for January 1910. In a very high turn-out of 87%, the result was close:

Liberals: 275
Unionists: 273.

The Irish on 82 and Labour with 40 gave Asquith his hold on power. John Redmond, the leader of the Irish Home Rule Party, had played his card powerfully, insisting that the Lords' veto should be scrapped, opening the way for a Home Rule Bill. The extent to which this 'no veto, no budget' threat was a real one is the subject of some controversy (see Chapter 26). For the time being, Redmond did support Asquith unconditionally – he had little choice.

The election also revealed that the growing tide of Labour gains had been stemmed. None of this was much comfort to the Cabinet, which was wavering and indecisive. Asquith gave no lead and it was at least two months before sufficient confidence had returned and the decision was made to proceed with a Parliament Bill.

- This would prevent the House of Lords from rejecting or changing a money bill.
- Other bills could only be delayed, becoming law if passed by the House of Commons three times (effectively a 'temporary' veto for two years).
- Parliaments were cut from seven years to five.

How would the Bill pass through the Upper House, as the Conservatives would be bound to reject it? Much depended on the attitude of the King. Asquith told the House that he would ask him to create sufficient Liberal peers to allow the Bill through. This would overwhelm the Unionist majority in the Lords. In the meantime, the Budget was pushed through the Commons and was grudgingly passed by the Upper House.

The progress of the attack on the Lords was suddenly halted by the death of King Edward VII, in May 1910. It placed the new King, George V, in a difficult position as he was reluctant to be involved in such a drastic political step so early in his reign.

The summer brought attempts at compromise. A Constitutional Conference brought the political leaders together. Nothing came of it. There was no escaping the stormy backdrop – the Budget, the Lords' veto, but most of all, Home Rule.

As the end of 1910 approached, the King did agree, in secret negotiations, that he would create sufficient Liberal peers, assuming that the contents of the Parliament Bill were put to the voters. The second general election of 1910 took place in December and produced similar results:

Liberals 272
Unionists 272
Irish Nationalists 84
Labour 42.

Attention turned to Balfour and Lansdowne, who now faced yet another uncomfortable choice – allow the Bill through and watch their powers be eroded or force the Government to ask the King to create about 250 extra Liberal peers. The Unionist position could hardly be described as harmonious; tensions continued to exist between those for tariff reform and those in the Party who were sceptical about its appeal to the voters. Once the King's agreement to create Liberal peers had become widely known, the quarrelling among Unionists about how to deal with this erupted. On one side were the 'ditchers' who were willing to flex their muscles and oppose every part of the Parliament Bill – one writer characterised them as 'addicts of political machismo' (E.J. Feuchtwanger). They assumed that the Government would not carry out their threat and press the King into action. Facing them, were the '**hedgers**' who argued that if the Bill was passed then at least they would have some delaying powers left.

'Hedgers': They believed that the Government should give in because further opposition might mean the creation of so many Liberal peers that there would be a Liberal majority in the Lords, enabling the passage of at least Home Rule and anything else Asquith saw fit to put forward.

On 24 July, when Asquith told the Commons that the Bill would return to the Lords, there was such a barrage of abuse that he could not make himself heard for half an hour. Nevertheless, when the Bill reached the Lords for the last time, in August 1911, it scraped through by 131 votes to 114. The 'hedgers', who were boosted by the presence of the Anglican Church (in the form of 13 archbishops and bishops), had prevailed by voting with the Liberal peers – the Unionist dominance of the Lords remained intact but with only the power of delay. The Act proved to be a milestone for the Liberals and for the democratically elected Commons, although it had taken considerable effort, especially on Asquith's part. He had stuck to his task with determination and great political skill. If the Cabinet had sufficient energy left, the Liberal programme of reform and Home Rule could now be implemented. But it would be wrong to assume that a golden age of legislation and reform was about to dawn. 'Events' were to sap the Government as it faced turbulence from trade unions, Suffragettes and Ireland. For the Unionists, the three election failures to regain lost ground, particularly among the working classes, also exposed weaknesses in organisation as well as leadership. Balfour was no longer making the running and it was no accident that the slogan 'BMG' ('Balfour must go') was first heard among the tariff reform wing of the Party. In November 1911, Balfour decided to go, rather than wait to be pushed.

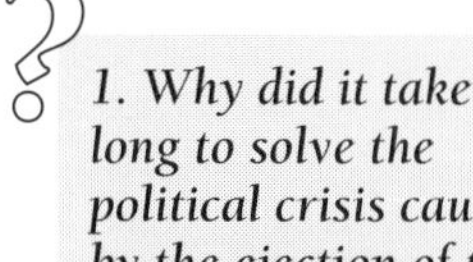

1. Why did it take so long to solve the political crisis caused by the ejection of the 1909 Budget?

2. How far were both the Liberal and Conservative Parties weakened by the constitutional crisis of 1909–11?

23.6 How influential was the Suffragette movement in the years 1905–1914?

The campaign for the vote for women was only one element of a wider movement which saw the cause of women's emancipation slowly advance at this time (see Chapter 26). Hard-won legal rights had already been gained; women could vote in local elections and made valuable contributions on School Boards and as Poor Law Guardians. The next step, the campaigners thought, would be to enfranchise them in national elections. In 1867, John Stuart Mill had inserted an amendment into the Reform Act, which gave the vote to female householders. It was rejected. So many moderate activists began to establish local suffrage societies, coordinated by the National Union of Women's Suffrage Societies and campaigning for change by constitutional means.

When a Bill, introduced in 1897, also came to nothing, it was apparent to some women that more direct action was required. Recent evidence has shown that, in fact, the quiet work of the societies had convinced many people of the legitimacy of their claim for the suffrage. Historians have the advantage of hindsight – others at the time were not so convinced, hence the following trend towards a more militant approach. In 1903, after working for some years in the ILP in Manchester, Mrs Emmeline Pankhurst formed The Women's Social and Political Union (WSPU). This initially small group caught the public's attention when Christabel, one of Mrs Pankhurst's daughters, along with Annie Kenney, heckled Sir Edward Grey at an election meeting in 1905. They were both arrested and Christabel found herself in prison for refusing to pay the fine. Donations and support grew, mainly from upper- and middle-class women. In one sense, their initial financial contributions were valuable, although the failure to draw on wider working-class support hindered the WSPU's progress. Eventually, so did the Suffragettes' militant tactics, with which not all women agreed – in particular, the Suffragists who continued to use constitutional methods right up to 1914.

Liberal politicians were an obvious target. Here was an issue that the Liberals could support – political reform, espousing the rights of individuals, attacking injustices and disqualifications? However, Campbell-Bannerman's only achievement in this area was to pass the Qualification of Women Act (1907) which enabled women to serve on county and borough councils. WSPU militancy rose.

- Churchill was horsewhipped.
- Asquith had his doorbell rung constantly.
- Women chained themselves to railings, set fire to pillarboxes and slashed pictures in the National Gallery.
- Politicians were interrupted at public meetings when speeches were heckled and banners were unfurled.
- Police and courts overreacted and when Suffragettes refused to pay fines, opting for prison instead, they started the tactic of hunger striking.
- The Government's tactics were heavy-handed – resorting to 'force feeding' to keep the women alive did nothing to enhance Liberal reputations.

The year 1910 started with a truce; so far the WSPU had brought their campaign to a point where an all-party group actually considered introducing what became known as a Conciliation Bill. This might have given a vote to female householders and those who qualified by occupation. It was never likely to succeed as Asquith was determined to oppose women's suffrage at all costs. Indeed, in 1911, Asquith was planning to introduce a Franchise Bill to extend male suffrage further and a Plural Voting Bill to stop a practice that so advantaged the Conservatives. It has been said that there was an intention that the Franchise Bill might be amended later to allow the female franchise. This seems unlikely given Asquith's attitude. He had been singled out for particular abuse – house windows broken, clothes torn; there was even a suggestion that his person was in danger. When the Speaker of the House ruled, in January 1913, that an amendment of the Franchise Bill could not be allowed as it would change it too much, Asquith wrote, 'The Speaker's *coup d'état* has bowled over the women for this session – a great relief'. His contribution to the failure of Suffragette militancy is of central importance.

The Government's response

Time had run out. It all coincided with a considerable increase in Suffragette violence, which in turn must have hardened attitudes against them. There is evidence that their tactics alienated men and moderate women who had grown tired of extremism and hysteria. These tactics included arson attacks, as well as the death of Emily Davison at Derby Day in 1913, when she threw herself under the King's horse. Arrests meant hunger strikes to which the Government's answer was the 'Cat and Mouse' Act (the Prisoners' Temporary Discharge for Ill-Health Act), which allowed prisoners to be released and then re-arrested when they had recovered.

Christabel Pankhurst had been forced to flee the country and she tried to organise the campaign from Paris. Her book *The Great Scourge and How to End It*, an anti-male tract, tended to play into the hands of critics who could make out that the WSPU had lost all sense of proportion. There was much talk that women were too emotional, that they would lose their charm, that they suffered from numerous physical weaknesses – critics said that Suffragette behaviour confirmed how unreasonable they could be. Suffragettes were accused of abandoning lawful protest at a time when the rule of law was already being undermined – by the unions and in Ireland.

Indeed, the WSPU lost the sympathy of those who should have been its allies; the Liberal Party was the best chance they had and many Liberal politicians who were sympathetic at first (such as Lloyd George) discovered they too were under attack. Some women were profoundly anti-Suffragette; evidence, for example, the formation of the Women's National Anti-Suffrage League as early as 1908 – it was never as potent a force as the Pankhursts' group but it hinted at a body of critical opinion against it. It included Mrs Fawcett, leading Suffragist and President of the National Union of Women's Suffrage Societies, who claimed that the WSPU had done more harm than good. Mrs Fawcett's organisation had grown steadily from a membership of 6,000 in 1907 to 50,000 in 1913. Historian Martin Pugh notes that this growth was a reaction to the militancy of the WSPU and it was probably 'the one positive contribution of the Pankhursts to winning the vote'. Pugh hints that the Pankhursts' role has been much exaggerated but they did have an amazing ability to publicise themselves and their activities.

Most commentators are agreed that the Liberal Government's response to the Suffragettes also lies at the heart of the crisis. The Government which stood for social reform and justice was seen to be acting in an oppressive un-Liberal manner. What a contrast between the 'softly, softly' approach in Ireland and the forcible feeding of hunger strikers. As the historian L.C.B. Seaman comments:

> The attitude of the Government to middle-class Englishwomen demanding the right to vote, and reacting with violence to the Government's provocative and pointless delay, provides a sinister comment on the persistent Liberal claim to stand for a higher morality than other political parties. The Prisoners' Temporary Discharge for Ill-Health Act ('Cat and Mouse' Act) came strangely from a government which a few years before had been grieved so sorely by the hardships suffered by Boer women and children, and by Chinese coolies in the Transvaal.

1. How important in the campaign for women's political rights was the Women's Social and Political Union?

2. Did the Suffragettes provide a major political threat to the Liberal Government in the years before the outbreak of war in 1914?

Asquith, who had an unshakeable belief in constitutional processes, thus stands accused of forcing the WSPU into militant resistance outside the law. There were opportunities to pass legislation, all scuppered by the Prime Minister. In these circumstances, repeated efforts to introduce Private Member's Bills (in 1908, 1909 and 1913) were doomed. Asquith apparently believed that granting the vote to women on the same basis as men, under the property qualification rules, would mean that these would be better-off Conservative voters, thereby damaging Liberal fortunes. Asquith had no way of knowing if this was true. When war broke out in 1914, women were still without the vote – like the problems posed by union militancy, it was yet another issue that the Liberal Government had failed to settle.

23.7 *How successful was the Government in dealing with industrial unrest in the years 1910–1914?*

Along with Ireland and the Suffragettes, a period of bitter industrial unrest threatened the foundations of society and contributed to the end of liberalism, so it has been claimed. Socialist historians have attempted to identify worsening class conflict that manifested itself in the increasing number of violent strikes, which took place after 1908. They argue that the legal position of unions was threatened, especially after the Taff Vale case of 1902 – as was the rights of unionists to contribute to the Labour Party and have the voice of the working man heard in Parliament. According to left-wing theorists, this was the forerunner of the General Strike, which would challenge the Government and usher in a new form of society.

There is little evidence to support such claims. Much of it was either wishful thinking by comrades elsewhere, such as Vladimir Lenin who was observing events from afar or alarmists like the Mayor of Liverpool who asked that warships be stationed in the River Mersey during the Liverpool dock strike of 1911.

However, there was no doubting the ferocity and intensity of the wave of strikes with which the Government had to deal, although there is little evidence that class war was about to break out which would destroy Edwardian England.

Campbell-Bannerman's Cabinet had already taken steps to reverse the Taff Vale judgement (see page 347) and the years up to 1907 were remarkably quiet when compared with what followed. During that period, somewhere between 1.5 and 4 million days were lost each year through strikes. The figure jumped to over 10 million in 1908 and to 41 million by 1912. The catalogue of serious strikes began in July 1910. A railway workers' strike lasted four days, followed by cotton workers and boilermakers. The worst outbreak was in South Wales where a simmering resentment boiled over into a riot in Tonypandy and at least one death. Winston Churchill sent troops to restore order; his reputation in the Welsh Valleys never really recovered from this. The dispute lasted ten months with victory for the owners who had resorted to using 'blackleg' miners.

The next year was no better. In June 1911, the sailors' and firemen's union went on strike and this led to 'sympathetic' strikes in the docks. Initially, this was unofficial but the National Transport Workers' Federation, formed in 1910 by Tom Mann, organised further disruption in the ports. The worst violence took place in Liverpool where two men were killed in clashes with troops. A national railway strike led to more deaths and Asquith only managed to head off a national strike when Lloyd George was brought in to handle the negotiations. He brought about a settlement by using the spectre of war against Germany to get the men back to work. The railwaymen gained much of what they set out to achieve and their unionised membership tripled between 1911 and 1914.

Three aspects of these disputes illustrate how organised unionisation still had a long way to go.

1. A common cause of the strikes was the refusal of employers to recognise the unions.
2. There was a remarkable degree of hostility shown to union leaders by their rank-and-file members; the latter were more militant than their leaders who tried to come to agreements with employers.
3. The Government was already showing how ready it was to intervene in disruptive disputes. At a time when there were no bargaining mechanisms, Liberals had to abandon *laissez-faire* principles in favour

of helping employers and their men reach pragmatic settlements. It did not happen enough.

In 1912, the National Union of Railwaymen (NUR) was formed from three existing unions and this confirmed the move towards the creation of larger organisations. At the same time, the scale of stoppages also rose spectacularly – and alarmingly for the Government. The battleground moved to the mines where a million coal workers, by far the largest number so far, went on strike in support of their demand of a national minimum wage. The strike went on for three weeks before Asquith introduced a Bill that established a statutory minimum wage fixed by new District Boards, although it failed to satisfy union demands. The dispute was called off when a ballot of members fell short of the number needed to continue the stoppage. Not that there was any peace, because the dockers walked out next in London. This strike never gained any momentum, though, as the rest of the country declined to lend its support.

1. Why did Britain have so many industrial disputes between 1910 and 1914?

2. How far was union militancy the product of a 'Syndicalist' revolt?

Ireland was not immune from union militancy, which must have added to the sense of crisis there. James Larkin, through the Irish Transport and General Workers' Union, organised transport strikes – the worst of which took place in Dublin in 1913. In the same year, the Triple Alliance was formed, comprising the Miners' Federation of Great Britain, the NUR and the Transport Workers' Federation. It looked like a formidable grouping of unions. Potentially, the Triple Alliance could organise stoppages that, if coordinated, would severely disrupt industry and the country. Was a general strike more of a possibility at the end of 1913 and the beginning of 1914? To answer this question, it is important to look at the causes of union militancy.

What lay behind the industrial unrest?

Syndicalism: Ideas that had spread from France which encouraged unions to combine in 'sympathetic strikes', supporting each other with direct action not only to win improved wages and conditions but also to undermine capitalism and governments so that a revolutionary state based on socialist principles might be set up.

Was it the influence of **syndicalism**? Or was this period of strikes a response to prevailing economic conditions?

The syndicalist argument, which can be found in the writings of Cole, Halévy and Postgate, is partly based on an assessment of the impact of ideas – the ideas of Syndicalists such as Georges Sorel in France and Daniel de Leon from the USA. It does seem that important individuals were convinced by their arguments. One of the most famous was Thomas Mann, a key figure in the 1889 Dock Strike in London and the founder of the Transport Workers' Federation. He published a journal called the *Industrial Syndicalist*, as well as forming an Education League to spread Marxist ideas. The movement managed to gain supporters in Ireland, with James Larkin, and in South Wales, where those miners who had been to Ruskin College Oxford (a seat of learning for working-class men) had been influenced by syndicalism. Groups such as the Central Labour College and the Plebs League spread the word and it was not a coincidence that it was in South Wales where 'The Miners' Next Step' was published. It called for one national union to call 'irritation' strikes so that profits would fall, enabling workers to take over all industries.

American syndicalists were particularly enthusiastic to see the creation of larger unions and the Triple Alliance of 1914 was seen as evidence of their influence.

On closer examination, many of these claims appear flawed. Syndicalism made few inroads into rank-and-file membership, which was more influenced by traditional liberal ideas and by economic conditions. 'The Miners' Next Step' of 1912 was followed in 1913 by a sharp decline in the number of days lost to strike action – down from 41 million to 10 million days. Things were equally subdued in 1914. Was this the expected revolution?

Tom Mann had not managed to gain nationwide support for the 1912 docks strike which had ended in failure. His claims of a rising tide of union violence leading to a general strike looked fragile. Neither did the Triple Alliance look too threatening despite the impact of mass, combined action. Its leaders were principally motivated not by thoughts of a general strike but by more practical ends. They wanted to strengthen their hand when bargaining for higher wages. They had strict rules for balloting members before a strike took place, probably in an attempt to prevent unofficial stoppages and so keep a grip on members. It is worth remembering that the militancy of union members was not always shared by the leaders, so the strikers fought them as much as the employers.

What other factors might explain the surge of union activity?

The 1906 Trades Disputes Act must have given unions the confidence to strike without the fear of being liable for damages. It could hardly be said to have provoked the militancy that exploded four years later. Might disappointment with the Labour Party be a factor? There is evidence that Labour was able to maintain its level of support although it was not in a position to make spectacular progress in Parliament or at the polls at the expense of the Liberals. It was seen as the junior partner of the Liberals, as a pressure group that had done solid, if not radical, reforming work. The Labour Party had lost a few seats in the 1910 elections, but this hardly constituted a disaster.

However, the impressions recorded by contemporaries was of a party which contributed little to the Liberal programme of reform except to vote for their legislation in the House of Commons. Ben Tillett wrote a pamphlet in 1908 called 'Is the Parliamentary Labour Party a Failure?' Labour seemed to be still searching for radical policies that would match those of the Liberals. The National Insurance Act was one case where Lloyd George was able to win over Labour's allies, namely the trade unions, and involve them in the operation of the Act. The historian Carl Brand concluded that Labour found itself 'dependent upon the Liberals, dissatisfied with its achievements, unsure of its aims, and apparently in decline'.

It is unlikely, however, that the industrial unrest was directed against the Labour Party, for two important reasons. Firstly, trade union members were more concerned about wages keeping pace with rising prices; secondly, the number of trade union affiliations to Labour rose by 50% between 1906 and 1914. The miners had affiliated in 1909, deserting the Liberals. Labour might have been demoralised inside Parliament but support continued to rise for the Party outside Parliament (see also page 400 for Labour's success in local elections).

Was the Liberal Government to blame?

The Liberal Government was accused, for example, of not taking quick enough action to reverse the Osborne Judgement, which was certainly an embarrassment. Osborne, the secretary of the Amalgamated Society of Railway Servants, took his union to court for using part of his union fees to fund the Labour Party. This was called the 'political levy'. When the case reached the courts of the House of Lords in 1909, the levy was declared illegal. It effectively prevented trade unions contributing to Labour Party funds and election expenses – a situation not reversed until 1913. There was a feeling that the establishment was determined to undermine the Labour Party and the situation was made worse because MPs received no salary. This certainly had a disproportionate effect on working-class MPs and it was not until 1911 that Lloyd George granted all MPs a salary of £400. As the law had been turned on organised labour yet again, union activists were willing to turn to more extreme measures.

The George Dangerfield thesis – 'The Strange Death of Liberal England', published in 1935 – takes the view that the Government's failure to deal effectively with the industrial unrest is more proof that liberalism had been sapped of its strength and ability to cope with the pressures of class politics. This is now widely seen as an exaggeration of the Government's difficulties. It is true that, at times, the Government appeared uncertain and its response heavy-handed – hardly surprising given that unrest on this scale was a new phenomenon. Using troops against strikers was certainly inflammatory. But constructive work was done too. Lloyd George and Sir George Askwith were effective conciliators and, apart from passing a range of legislation to establish minimum wages and limit hours of work, the Government put in place mechanisms to settle disputes such as an industrial council and arbitration. If Liberalism was suffering a 'strange death', it seemed to have a remarkable amount of life left in it.

A far more convincing argument for the industrial unrest lies in economic factors. After 1909, wage rates were not keeping pace with rising prices. Inflation put workers into a position where they would have to defend their standard of living, at a time when people were concerned that Britain's economic supremacy was being challenged by powerful competitors overseas. Price inflation seems to have been worse in 1911 and 1912, coinciding with the period when wages fell most sharply behind the cost of living. Figures also show that it was manual workers who did particularly badly, earning a shrinking proportion of the national income. This is mirrored by the fact that those unions which were under pressure to defend wage rates were those who represented unskilled and low-paid manual workers.

1. Why did people at the time think syndicalism was a major cause of industrial unrest?

2. How far was the Great Labour Unrest of 1910–14 the result of the Liberal Government's failure to deal with Britain's problems before 1914?

Two sets of statistics require further explanation. A trade boom after 1910 soaked up the unemployed, and jobless totals fell from 8% before this date to 3% after it. Union membership also jumped from 2.5 million in 1910 to 4 million in 1914. The historian Pelling drew the conclusion that strike-breakers were in short supply as there were fewer unemployed, giving the rank-and-file more confidence to take action against their employers.

The current balance of opinion certainly favours these economic factors more than the 'political conspiracy' theories. Contemporaries were certainly alarmed by the unrest after 1910, just as they were sure that relative calm had broken out by 1914.

23.8 *The 'Strange Death of Liberal England'*

A CASE STUDY IN HISTORICAL INTERPRETATION

What was the condition of Liberalism at the point when the First World War broke out? In 'The Strange Death of Liberal England', George Dangerfield argued that Liberal decline could be traced to the period 1910–14 when a series of crises over the House of Lords, union militancy, women's suffrage and Irish Home Rule came together. They revealed a party which was unable to cope with, and adapt to, pre-war politics. Indeed, the decline of the Liberals was the inevitable consequence of the failure of the Party to alter views and articles of faith which were rooted in a different age.

Some historians have developed these views further. The 1906 election victory was regarded as a temporary revolt against years of Unionist rule; by 1910, with the loss of over 100 seats and a dependence on the Irish Nationalists to keep them in power, support was ebbing away. Asquith and his colleagues were, it is argued, unsuited to deal with challenges to the stability of the State and the Constitution. The Prime Minister, always a constitutionalist, was never able to understand the attacks made during the Home Rule or House of Lords crises.

Socialist historians such as Pelling claim that the problems created by union violence show that the Liberals were out of sympathy with the working class. In time, Labour would supplant the Liberals. Matthew, McKibbon and Kay show that, at local level, Labour was better organised and was making progress. In Leeds, for example, 14 Labour seats outnumbered the Liberals' 12. Labour was similarly successful in London County Council elections. Trade union membership was growing rapidly and it would give the Labour Party a politically aware base of support. The *Daily Herald* newspaper was founded in 1911 to spread and support the Labour message. Although the parliamentary party did struggle at this time, there is plenty of evidence of the vitality of the Party elsewhere.

A case has been made that 'new Liberalism' was making an impact with working-class voters. Peter Clarke's studies of Lancashire in 1971 found that Liberal social welfare was giving the Party a 'social democratic' face and a new appeal. Lloyd George's dynamism was the sign of a revitalised party that was holding Labour at bay. In 12 by-elections between 1910 and 1914, Labour failed to win one seat and lost three to the Liberals. It suggests a working-class base of support for the Liberals.

This view has not gone unchallenged. Pelling found that parts of the Liberal social welfare package failed to find favour with working-class voters. In 1986, Bernstein argued that even Liberals in particular regional areas were not as committed to 'new Liberalism' as they were to traditional articles of faith. He comments: 'Neither the new liberalism nor Liberal policies of social reform represented a fundamental re-orientation of the Liberal Party so that it could represent the interests of the working class rather than those of middle-class Nonconformists.' In a new study, G.R. Searle also questions whether the Liberal Party's reliance on business for finance fatally undermined its ability to appeal to the working class as a social democratic reforming party.

Duncan Tanner, taking a more balanced view, claims that neither side was making significant progress. 'A study of the Liberal reforms does not suggest that the Party was on the verge of collapse, but neither does it suggest that new Liberalism had effected its complete recovery.' As for Labour, it seemed unable to make inroads into Liberal support, remaining the 'junior partner' but with much potential. Had war not intervened, a new Lib–Lab pact was likely, enabling each to continue to draw on both middle-class and working-class support.

The last word should go to Trevor Wilson. In *The Downfall of the Liberal Party* (published in 1966), Wilson found that in 1914 the Liberals were showing strong signs of continued reform. But then it 'was involved in an encounter with a rampant omnibus (the First World War) which mounted the pavement and ran him over'. The war then led to a fatal split in the Party (1916–17), between the Lloyd George wing and Asquith's supporters. As Wilson comments, 'All that is known is that at one moment he was up and walking and at the next he was flat on his back, never to rise again; and in the interval he had been run over by a bus.'

If the war did the damage, were there signs of good health in 1914? On the one hand, Simon Lemieux believes that the Liberals in 1914 'cannot be given a clean bill of health; many worrying signs were there'. On the other hand, the worst of union militancy was over. The Suffragettes may have attracted considerable publicity but were hardly a threat to the foundations of the State. The House of Lords had been tamed by the Parliament Act.

Ireland (see Chapter 22) had defeated the best efforts of politicians in the 19th century, but the Irish Problem became more acute after 1911 when Home Rule from Dublin was a real possibility. This led to the Ulster

1. Study the sections on the crisis with the House of Lords, the Suffragettes and the Great Labour Unrest in this chapter and the Ulster Crisis in Chapter 22.

What evidence is there to suggest that Britain faced a major social and political crisis in the years 1910–14?

2. Why do you think historians have offered different explanations for the social and political crises of the period 1910–14?

Give reasons to support your answer.

revolt as loyalists pledged that they would never submit to such a move. It brought Ireland to the brink of civil war. George Dangerfield drew on Asquith's failure to resolve this as evidence of disintegration of Liberalism as a political force. There are certainly valid arguments for criticising the policy of 'wait and see' and the policy of drift that contributed to the arming of Ulster and eventually of the Nationalist side. However, it is unreasonable to blame Asquith solely for not solving a complex and long-standing historical problem.

Had the Liberals 'run out of steam'?

Despite tensions between 'old' Liberals and 'new', Lloyd George was planning new initiatives. They included land reform, a minimum wage for agricultural labourers, security for tenants, and better rural housing. The war came and not too much changed. Voluntary recruitment swelled the Army, and emergency measures were taken, such as control of the railways and the Defence of the Realm Act. The Government ended its term in May 1915 after completing a spectacular period of legislation. This was hardly a sign of decline and defeatism.

Source-based questions: The Liberals, 1905–1915

SOURCE A

'I have one word for the Liberals. I can tell them what will make this ILP movement a great and sweeping force in this country – a force that will sweep away Liberalism amongst other things. If at the end of an average term of office it were found that a Liberal Parliament had done nothing to cope seriously with the social condition of people, to remove the national degradation of slums and widespread poverty and destitution in a land glittering with wealth ... then would a real cry arise in this land for a new party, and many of us here in this room would join in that cry. But if a Liberal Government tackle the landlords, and the brewers, and the peers ... then, the Independent Labour Party will call in vain upon the working men of Britain to desert Liberalism that is so gallantly fighting to rid the land of the wrongs that have oppressed those who labour in it.'

Lloyd George's speech in Cardiff in 1906 about the need for social reform.

SOURCE B

To many among the fathers of modern Liberalism, government action was something to be detested. They held, as we hold, that the first and final object of the State is to develop the capacities and raise the standard of living of its citizens; but they held also that the best way to do this was for the State to do as little as possible. Three causes combined to convert Liberalism from the principle of State abstention. The State's legislation was more competent and laws of regulation neither lessened prosperity nor weakened self-reliance as was foretold. It was realised that the conditions of society were so bad that to tolerate them longer was impossible, and that *laissez-faire* was not likely to bring the cure. And it was realised that extensions of law need not imply diminution of freedom, but on the contrary would often enlarge freedom.

Adapted from Herbert Samuel's writings in 1909.

SOURCE C

The outbreak of war in 1914 found the Welfare State in its infancy. The Poor Law was still the basis for the treatment of poverty, and unemployment benefits were low and limited in time. Treatment for ill-health, outside the Poor Law, was given to the worker and not to his family, and little was done for hospitals ... In the wider sense of welfare, education was compulsory only up to the age of 14 ... Housing still lagged behind even basic necessity, and social reform of all kinds was still inhibited by the old *laissez-faire* suspicion of state interference and still governed by the convenient permissive idea. Palliatives, rather than the radical programmes of reform, had been applied. Yet this kind of balance sheet tends to obscure real, if limited, achievement.

From The Shaping of the Welfare State *by R.C. Birch, published in 1974.*

---

1. Study Source A.

How useful is this to a historian studying the aims of the Liberal Party in 1906?

2. How far do Sources A and B agree about the reasons why the Government was taking a more active role in social welfare?

3. Study Sources B and C.

Explain how far the Liberal Government had laid the foundations of the Welfare State by 1914.

24 Britain and the origins of the First World War, 1898–1914

Key Issues

- *Was Britain's policy one of 'splendid isolation' at the end of the 19th century?*
- *Why, and to what extent, did Britain's relations with France and Russia change – was there a 'diplomatic revolution'?*
- *How far, and why, did relations with Germany deteriorate up to the middle of 1914?*

24.1 How 'isolated' was Britain in 1898?
24.2 To what extent did Lord Lansdowne alter British foreign policy?
24.3 Was there a 'diplomatic revolution' between 1902 and 1905?
24.4 Britain's 'New Order'? How far had international relations changed after the signing of the Entente Cordiale?
24.5 Historical interpretation: How justified are criticisms of Sir Edward Grey's handling of foreign policy?
24.6 Why did Britain go to war in 1914?

Framework of Events

1895	The Kruger Telegram
1896	Armenian massacres
1897	Mediterranean Agreements (Austria-Hungary, Italy, Britain) not renewed
1898	Fashoda
	The First German Naval Law
	Kaiser Wilhelm II's visit to Turkey
	Russia sends warships to Port Arthur
1899–1902	The Boer War
1900	Boxer Rebellion in China
	Second German Naval Law
	Lord Lansdowne succeeds Lord Salisbury as British Foreign Secretary
1901	Hay–Pauncefote Treaty (Britain and USA)
1902	Anglo-Japanese Alliance
1904	Russo-Japanese War; Dogger Bank incident.
	Entente Cordiale
1905	First Moroccan Crisis
	Cawder–Fisher Naval reforms
	Sir Edward Grey becomes Foreign Secretary
1906	The Algeçiras Conference
	'HMS Dreadnought' launched
1907	Anglo-Russian Convention; Hague Disarmament Conference
	Haldane's Army reforms
1908	Acceleration of British naval building programme
1909	Anglo-German naval scare leads to campaign for more Dreadnoughts
1911	Agadir Crisis
1912	First Balkan War. Naval agreement between Britain and France
1913	Second Balkan War
1914	June: Sarajevo assassination
	28 July: Austria-Hungary declares war on Serbia
	30 July: Russia mobilises its armies
	31 July: German ultimatum to Russia demanding a stop to mobilisation
	1 August: Germany declares war on Russia

3 August: Germany declares war on France
4 August: German troops enter Belgium; Britain declares war on Germany.

Overview

THE mid-1890s was a period of profound unease for Britain. Lord Salisbury was back at the Foreign Office, in June 1895. Historians who once associated him with a policy of 'splendid isolation', now question the nature of this 'isolation' and whether indeed there was a deliberate attempt by Salisbury to avoid entanglements with other powers. Foster, leader of the Canadian Parliament, first stated that 'The Great Mother Empire stands splendidly isolated in Europe' – a phrase eagerly taken up by Joseph Chamberlain to signify a smug satisfaction with Imperial Britain's global power. However, while it is true that Salisbury was unwilling to commit Britain to alliances which he felt the Government might not be able to honour, he would never have accepted the presumption that Britain's position in the world was 'splendid'. On the contrary, Salisbury was well aware that Britain stood alone in a world where there was ample potential for quarrels and worsening relations with our European neighbours.

- In South Africa, Britain argued with Boers who had German backing. The Kruger Telegram following the Jameson Raid (see page 361) was sent by the German Kaiser, Wilhelm II, to congratulate the Boers for defeating this attempted 'invasion' by a British armed force. The arrival of a German cruiser in nearby Delagoa Bay also provoked anger in Britain – sufficiently so for a Royal Navy battle squadron to be sent to force the withdrawal of the German ship – which it did. Anglo–German relations did appear brittle.
- Relations with France continued to deteriorate over the Nile, where both countries had interests.
- France's ally, Russia, continued to muscle its way into northern China for trade – another area where there were considerable British interests – and into Persia to the north of India, for warm-water ports. Russian warships had been kept out of the Straits and the eastern Mediterranean for the time being, but for how long?
- Events in Turkey merely confirmed the disintegration of the Ottoman Empire, from which Russia and Germany might expect to benefit. British policy remained constant – to keep open trade routes via the Suez at any cost. However, when the Turks carried out massacres of Christian Armenians in 1894 and 1896, Britain pressed for reforms from the Sultan in cooperation with other powers, especially Russia. Nothing came of it and the British Admiralty wondered if the Royal Navy was now strong enough to force its way through the Straits – hence the appeal for a joint naval action with Russia against the Sultan.
- Austria-Hungary took this, correctly, as a sign that Salisbury was less interested in the traditional anti-Russian policy in the Balkans; hence the Mediterranean

Agreement (between Austria, Italy and Britain) was not renewed in 1897. When Kaiser Wilhelm II visited Constantinople in 1898, with Turkey drifting towards the German sphere of influence, it seemed to confirm Britain's sense of isolation and exposure in a hostile world.

24.1 How 'isolated' was Britain in 1898?

The answer is, possibly, 'superficially'. Some historians draw the conclusion that there is evidence that Britain was isolated. Nevertheless, there were signs, as E.J. Feuchtwanger notes, of 'a movement to bring British capabilities and commitments into a more realistic relationship in a period of growing international rivalry'. It is possible to find other examples, apart from the Armenian massacres crisis (1896), where Salisbury's secrecy in conducting diplomacy gave the impression of isolation when in reality he pursued the idea of the Concert of Europe (see Chapter 4). A study of a number of agreements showed that isolation, in its literal sense, was a myth. Certainly its usage as a term seems to have emerged not at the time but only after the First World War, in W.H. Dawson's review of Salisbury's foreign policy (published in 1923). Britain did make international agreements, though firm commitments with other countries in military alliances that might drag Britain into a war were avoided. Goschen, the First Lord of the Admiralty, remarked 'we will not promise things which possibly we may be unwilling to perform'.

How did relations with the USA change?

Monroe Doctrine: Statement made by President James Monroe in 1823 that the continent of America was independent and the European powers could not consider re-colonising it. An attack on these independent states could be viewed as an attack on the USA.

Here, agreements that settled points of dispute were regularly concluded – the USA was a starting point. In 1895, the USA intervened in a frontier dispute between British Guiana and Venezuela. The Americans followed the **Monroe Doctrine**, in its original sense. They regarded the Americas – North and South – as an area where the USA might legitimately interfere to maintain its peace and security. This had evolved. Theodore Roosevelt later summed up the position neatly when he said that the USA was 'an international police power' for the American continent. President Grover Cleveland must have been thinking along similar lines when he demanded that this frontier dispute be submitted to arbitration.

Different writers give different interpretations of British reactions to this. Quoting the Junior Minister who said 'we expect the French to hate us … but the Americans, No!', the crisis can be seen as another revelation of British weakness, especially since the Cabinet agreed to arbitration in an attempt to curry favour with the Americans. On the other hand, writers such as M.C. Morgan find little sense of panic in London and certainly none from Salisbury, who used the incident to improve relations with the USA in a part of the world which was not as vital to British interests as those elsewhere. In the end, the results of arbitration (1899) were favourable to Britain. This finding of a middle course was underlined during the Spanish–American War of 1898, when Britain remained neutral but sympathetic to the USA. When bases on Cuba were ceded to the USA, it meant the withdrawal of British warships from the West Indies. Was this a sign that the Royal Navy's day in the Caribbean had gone or was it evidence of a new 'realism' which concentrated our resources where they were needed?

Lord Lansdowne (Foreign Secretary 1900–1905) was content to build on this developing friendship when the Hay–Pauncefote Treaty of 1901 decided the future of the Panama Canal. The negotiations between John Hay (US Secretary of State) and Pauncefote (British Ambassador in Washington) had not been without their difficulties, but the final agreement was reasonable, given the circumstances. In exchange for US control of the canal, Britain would have freedom of access to it, and there would be no change in the ownership of the land through which the canal passed. US power in the area was not to be denied, but here were the beginnings of that so-called 'special relationship' of which later generations were to speak.

Why did a crisis develop over Fashoda in 1898?

It was to prove less easy to settle points of irritation and argument elsewhere, particularly in West Africa and the Nile Valley. In the vicinity of the River Niger, the British Royal Niger Company led by Sir George Goldie was moving inland, setting up trading posts at the expense of the French. By 1898, after simmering for years, it became clear that this point of conflict had to be resolved. A settlement of sorts was reached when the Crown Colony of Nigeria was established with control exercised through native rulers. France was able to secure some concessions at a later date. No sooner was this matter put to one side, than a stand-off occurred between French and British forces at Fashoda, on the Upper Nile. The British may have controlled Egypt but France's hopes of securing a foothold in the Sudan remained alive. In June 1896, French forces under Captain Marchand received instructions to begin an advance from the Congo east towards the headwaters of the Nile.

Little did he know that Kitchener was painstakingly moving up the Nile Valley with similar objectives. Kitchener's route to the Sudan inevitably led him to Khartoum, into the path of a Dervish army. On 2 September 1898, at

French view of the Fashoda Crisis, 1898. 'What big teeth you have,' says France's Republican Red Riding Hood. 'All the better to eat your biscuit,' replies Albion (England).

Omdurman, the British shattered a Dervish force and captured Kalifa (son of the Mahdi). Within days, Kitchener received news that Captain Marchand and a handful of French soldiers, with some native troops from Senegal, were camped on the Upper Nile at Fashoda. Wasting no time and in no mood to back down, Kitchener confronted Marchand on 19 September. The French, who were outnumbered on the ground, were in no position to argue – it was their turn to be 'isolated' as no other European power lifted a finger to help them – British naval superiority saw to that. The crisis moved to London and Paris where emotions may have run high, but Salisbury's success was never in doubt.

On 4 March, Marchand withdrew from Fashoda and according to the Anglo–French Convention of 1899, Britain confirmed its control of the Nile, so vital to the security of Egypt. It was agreed that the French area of influence lay to the west of the watershed between the River Nile and River Congo. This settlement confirmed the fluidity of Salisbury's approach. It never ruled out the possibility of reaching agreements with other nations, but it was an approach which drew criticism from others in the Cabinet such as Chamberlain, who looked for a more active, aggressive policy. It was becoming apparent that Salisbury, now in the twilight of his career, was being eclipsed by more strident voices.

Why were relations with Germany deteriorating?

Rampant imperialism found its expression in South Africa. It also advertised the glee with which the world greeted Britain's difficulties during the Boer War. Given the Kaiser's meddlesome support for the Boer cause (see Chapter 21), Chamberlain persistently promoted the idea of an Anglo–German alliance between 1898 and 1901. In 1898, both powers agreed a joint loan to Portugal with a secret clause that should Portugal lose control of its African colonies, Britain and Germany would share the land between them. Whether this had any long-term significance is doubtful, especially since Salisbury wanted Portuguese cooperation to stop supplies being shipped to the Boers through Delagoa Bay and so promised what help he could to protect Portugal's more southerly colonies.

Anyway, the idea of progressing to a full Anglo–German alliance was against Salisbury's better judgement – he recognised the dangers it might bring. He could see how German anxiety about Russia and France might drag Britain into a continental war with France. He accepted Balfour's view that the Franco–Russian alliance had significantly altered the balance of power in Europe, so why should Britain help the Kaiser to defend his interests in Europe? If Britain did join the Triple Alliance, then who would get the better bargain – perhaps Germany? Salisbury, maintaining his stand against such entanglements, could see there was no future in the negotiations. The Boer War certainly raised the spectre of Europe's hostility towards British methods – such as the 'concentration camps', the initial military incompetence – but in the final analysis, British naval power and the normal state of rivalry between the European powers meant that intervention against Britain was never a real possibility.

Nevertheless, Chamberlain, the Colonial Secretary, persevered with talks with Germany. When Salisbury returned, after an illness, he signalled that further efforts would prove fruitless because Germany 'will never stand by us against Russia; but is always inclined to curry favour with Russia by throwing us over'.

South Africa was not the only area where Germany tried to exploit Britain's unenviable reputation. In China, Manchu control was in decline and Russia used almost reckless attempts to gain warm-water ports, such as Port Arthur, and 'leases' of land to develop their trade. This was an area of

1. How did Britain's relations with the following countries change in the years 1895–1900?

(a) The United States of America

(b) France

(c) Germany.

2. Was there any evidence of more continuity than change in foreign policy in the years 1895–1900?

particular commercial significance to Britain. However, the impression given by Salisbury's 'seeming no-policy' (a phrase used by G.M. Young, 1936) was that Britain might allow Russia some opportunities to extend its influence in Northern China as long as it did not mean dismemberment of the country.

Germany's 'lease' of Kiao-chow in 1897 and Russia's despatch of warships to Port Arthur in 1898, to force China to grant its 'lease' to them, aggravated the situation still further. Initially, Britain sent a naval squadron to signal a determination to stop the dismemberment of China. Salisbury still attached importance to negotiation. However, a rising in Peking against foreign diplomats, in 1900, by the Boxers (or Society of Righteous Harmonious Fists) showed the volatility of events in China. The Kaiser demanded a joint relief force, which Britain eventually joined after signing the Anglo–German China Agreement. As agreements go, this merely advertised the gap between the two powers; Britain wished to maintain the 'open door', Germany wanted to compete with British traders in the Yangtze Valley.

In November 1900, Salisbury retired from the Foreign Office. His place was taken by the Fifth Marquis of Lansdowne who had been an experienced Secretary of State for War and was acutely aware of the dangers of Britain's isolation.

24.2 To what extent did Lord Lansdowne alter British foreign policy?

Was there a turning point in foreign policy? Did policies change from concluding agreements to concluding alliances? Initially, no; negotiations with Germany and Russia continued fitfully throughout 1901. The differences again proved too wide and the Foreign Office looked elsewhere for common ground. The Hay–Pauncefote Agreement (1901) was a notable success. However, some historians have claimed that the Anglo–Japanese Alliance of 1902 marked the 'end of isolation', if indeed such a deliberate policy ever existed.

The Foreign Office recognised that Japan wished to penetrate and to develop some interests in Manchuria and Korea, bringing it into direct conflict with Russia. It also recognised how British and Japanese interests coincided; both aimed for an 'open door' on Chinese trade, while a Far Eastern ally would strengthen British naval power which was spread far too thinly. If the Admiralty was keen to maintain the 'two power' superiority, the support of the Japanese navy would give Britain a decisive lead over France and Russia and would allow the Admiralty to concentrate its efforts in the Channel.

Lord Lansdowne and Selborne, the First Lord of the Admiralty, both intended to maintain the *status quo* in China and Korea, and the alliance was concluded in 1902. In one sense, its focus was defensive:

- If Britain or Japan was faced by a single enemy, the other ally would remain neutral.
- If either was attacked by two enemies, the other promised to intervene militarily. Britain was assured of support in the unlikely event of the French and Russian fleets coordinating strategy.

For Japan, however, the alliance had offensive overtones. Balfour recognised, in 1903, that Japan might regard itself as 'a match for Russia'. Certainly, Japan would never have considered war against Russia without the alliance. The existence of the alliance made it a possibility. It is dangerous for historians to conclude that subsequent events constitute the results of an earlier set of circumstances. In this case, it is tempting to make a causal link between the alliance and the Japanese attack on the Russian base at Port Arthur in 1904. The world was astonished at the speed and completeness of the Japanese victories on land at Mukden and at sea at Tsushima, in 1905. As a postscript, in the subsequent peace negotiations, Britain renewed the Japanese alliance before the due date and for another ten years. This time, each ally would intervene and help the other if attacked by only one enemy.

1. What were Lord Lansdowne's aims in foreign policy?

2. Why was the Anglo–Japanese alliance of 1902 regarded as an important change in British foreign policy?

How significant though was the original treaty? Did it mean that Lansdowne had taken a 'new course'? Lansdowne thought so and so did some members of the Cabinet, such as Hicks-Beach who claimed that Salisbury's policies had been altered irrevocably. Some historians agree; Harold Temperley and Lillian Penson (quoted in M.C. Morgan's *Foreign Affairs, 1886–1914*) called it 'revolutionary', as it would 'inaugurate a new age' in which Britain's Far Eastern alliance would mean worsening relations with Russia in Europe. C.P. Gooch said it meant that 'England ceased to follow the policy of splendid isolation which had been its course for so many years'. A.J.P. Taylor is less sure about this, making out the case that far from ending isolation 'it confirmed it. Isolation meant aloofness from the European Balance of Power; and this was now more possible than before.' An ally in the East had made Britain feel more secure in Europe and, therefore, more likely to avoid European entanglements. Perhaps subsequent events might prove more significant.

24.3 Was there a 'diplomatic revolution' between 1902 and 1905?

Whatever the scepticism about the Anglo–Japanese Alliance, there is a case for arguing that there was a 'diplomatic revolution' which reshaped and stood existing relationships on their heads. Why?

There seemed no relief from quarrels with Russia and Germany. Balfour became preoccupied with the Russian threat to India, although there was no shortage of places elsewhere on Foreign Office maps which were potential flashpoints with the Tsar's government: Afghanistan, Persia, Tibet, not to mention China. Lord Curzon, the Indian viceroy, wanted troops to move against the Russians to the north; but Lansdowne and Balfour still preferred conciliation to confrontation.

Meanwhile, the Kaiser was keen on linking the German capital, Berlin, with Baghdad as he looked towards an alliance with Turkey at the expense of British influence in the eastern Mediterranean. German investment in the Berlin–Baghdad railway incited considerable hostility in the British press – sufficient to prevent Lansdowne from proposing that Britain should jointly invest in the railway. By 1902, though, there was widespread realisation, even on Chamberlain's part, that a German alliance was now out of the question. Selborne was warning that the expansion of the German fleet could only have one aim – to threaten Britain – as any antagonisms between the Germans and the Franco–Russian alliance would be settled on land.

What was the Entente Cordiale, 1904?

Progress was made in a different direction – a 'diplomatic revolution' in Britain's relations with France. Personalities played their part. Always willing to exploit a rich seam of charm when required, Edward VII's state visit to Paris in 1903 was a startling success. Within days, hostile crowds – who shouted '*Vivent les Boers*' on his arrival – apparently became anglophiles by the time of his departure, more likely to shout '*Vive le Roi*'. Perhaps more long-term impact was made by the French ambassador in England, who was keen to settle a range of quarrels and who found key figures in the Foreign Office willing to listen. Bertie, the Assistant Under-Secretary, noted: 'If we are certain of France, no one can have designs upon us'.

Changing international circumstances in the Far East played a part in making France and Britain look at their policies. By 1903, Japan was no longer willing to stand by quietly as Russian troops were making no effort to leave Manchuria (it was under Russian occupation since the Boxer Rebellion). If there was the possibility of a confrontation between Russia and Japan (see above) then might their respective allies, France and Britain, become involved? The scenario was beginning to concentrate minds in Paris and London.

Then there was the question of Morocco, where a revolt in 1902 threatened the Sultan and his capital, Fez. France was more inclined to see Morocco as its sphere of influence. When Lord Lansdowne met Paul Delcasse following the return visit of French President Emile Loubet to London in July 1903, lengthy talks stumbled towards some kind of agreement about Morocco's future as well as that other source of irritation, Egypt. The outbreak of the Russo–Japanese War, in February 1904, gave the talks a sense of urgency. It was no coincidence that the Anglo–French agreement was concluded in April 1904. Never meaning to be an alliance, this was an **Entente Cordiale**, which aimed to settle points of conflict. At its heart was French recognition of British control in Egypt, while Britain, in return, secretly agreed to partition Morocco. Should the Sultan of Morocco's power collapse, then France would become the dominant influence (with the exception of northern Morocco, opposite Gibraltar, which would go to Spain).

Entente Cordiale: A friendly agreement between two countries.

Interpretations differ about the consequences of the Entente. Balfour and Lansdowne saw wide ramifications; even the possibility, albeit remote at the time, of coming to an agreement with Russia. In October 1904, the Russian Baltic Fleet had sunk some British trawlers at Dogger Bank in the North Sea thinking they were Japanese warships. The Russians offered compensation and the Fleet went on its way, only to be sunk months later at Tsushima by the Japanese. It marked the end of the Russian interest in the Far East and, therefore, offered the opportunity of less menacing relations with Britain. Meanwhile, the German fleet had become the third largest in the world. The Entente Cordiale was never intended to be a threat to Germany, although it certainly made Britain feel more secure.

Did the Entente Cordiale amount to a 'revolution' in diplomatic affairs? E.J. Feuchtwanger, in *Democracy and Empire: Britain 1865–1914* (1985), comments that 'the Entente Cordiale was the result not of a major initiative but pragmatic and tentative responses to changing realities'. Hardly dramatic then, although in the longer term, the significance of the Entente in initiating further changes in the web of European diplomacy seems clear. How might military planners respond to these events?

How was British strategic planning changing?

The Boer War had exposed the inadequacies of Cabinet control over defence and military strategy. What had caused most consternation was the failure of the Army and Navy to coordinate planning – something to which Salisbury and others before him had paid scant attention. Balfour, however, made the positive step of establishing the Committee of Imperial Defence, in 1902. He chaired it and it quickly developed its work from matters of defence to forward planning – and that now meant the possibility of war against Germany. So did the naval reforms started by First Lords of the Admiralty: Selborne, Cawdor, then Fisher. Old ships were scrapped, and the widely scattered fleet consolidated itself under the Atlantic Command (Gibraltar), the Mediterranean Command (Malta) and the Channel Command. There was also a revolution in ship design, with the launch of the first Dreadnought in 1906. Its design, firepower, size and speed rendered all other battleships out of date. The Germans immediately replied by building their own. Lloyd George, along with the other Radical Liberals, was quick to accuse the Government of starting the arms race by creating a ship which no one else had and which Britain, with its naval superiority, did not need. Eight Dreadnoughts were to be built by 1907, and they would now be a constantly irritating factor in Anglo–German relations.

1. Explain how Anglo–French relations changed in the years 1900–1905.

2. Was the Entente Cordiale of 1904 'a revolution' in diplomatic affairs? Give reasons to support your answer.

3. How far had Britain's role in international affairs changed between 1900 and 1905?

24.4 Britain's 'New Order'? How far had international relations changed after the signing of the Entente Cordiale?

How far things had changed would quickly become apparent. Count Bernhard von Bülow (German Imperial Chancellor) and the Kaiser could see no advantages for Germany in this new arrangement between Britain and France, although their response was ill defined and partly motivated by injured pride. The Kaiser intended to put the Entente partners under pressure; it mattered little what precisely might happen as a result of his visit to Tangier in 1905, he merely 'speculated on some undefined success' (A.J.P. Taylor). If Germany hoped to break the Entente (not an entirely remote possibility given recent Anglo–French relations), then the effort failed. Indeed, it had the opposite effect. While in Tangiers, Wilhelm II made a speech asserting two things:

- the independence of the Sultan of Morocco
- that German honour was at stake in an area where they had some interests – interests which were being ignored.

Such an aggressive stance had a sub-plot – von Bülow made no secret of the intention to end Delcasse's career. What strengthened the German hand was the uncertainty that accompanied a change of government in Britain. Balfour and Lansdowne's tenure of office was about to end. In the dying embers of the Conservative Government, Britain stood firmly behind France. That was all very well, but the new Liberal Government of December 1905 brought a new man to the Foreign Office – Edward Grey. Could the French be sure of British support? It was impossible to conceal the anti-imperialist group within the Liberal Party. 'Little Englanders' were vociferous in the Cabinet, arguing that defence expenditure was better diverted towards social reform at home.

Grey was to be the central figure in foreign affairs up to the outbreak of war in 1914. Historians often comment on the nature of a Foreign Office which jealously regarded its work as the preserve of its officials – public school, Oxbridge and drawn from a narrow social élite. This was not an area of Whitehall noted for open debate, although Grey proved to be the ideal minister. True, he was a social reformer at home but his Whig background and thoughtful, sound approach had fashioned a man whom the Foreign

Office could trust. Grey set about convincing the French that continuity of policy had been maintained; the French would have his backing, although not at the price of deliberately antagonising Germany. Perhaps the French were looking for something tangible from Grey, who went so far as to sanction unofficial military conversations between Paris and London. These discussions, which assumed the possibility of transporting British troops across the Channel to assist the Belgian and French armies if attacked, were kept secret until 1911 – a point on which Grey has faced some criticism.

Might the Entente Cordiale become an Anglo–French military alliance?

Would Grey consent to a shift towards an alliance? Cambon, the French ambassador in London, felt things could not be left as they were as he was convinced that the Kaiser was intent on a confrontation. French nerves were strained, although for the time being they had to be satisfied with Grey's assurances of diplomatic support as he pulled back from the possibility of firmer military guarantees. There are grounds for agreeing with Grey, who felt that a military alliance could not have been kept secret; indeed such an alliance might split the country. Liberal neutralists and disarmers had been active in the early years of the Government, contenting themselves with Henry Campbell-Bannerman's assurances that the Army would be reduced and that positive action would arise from the second Hague Conference of 1907 (not that the Germans had any intention of agreeing to disarmament). These elements in the Party remained strong. There was no reason to imagine that Grey was being dishonest in resisting a French alliance. He was able to show that even in 1914, a divided Cabinet only finally agreed to enter the war because Belgium had been invaded and Britain was a guarantor of that country's neutrality under the Treaty of London (1839). Grey always argued that any attempt to join the war any earlier on the side of the French would have meant 'a divided Government, a divided parliament, a divided country'.

Nevertheless, military conversations – however bland and non-committal they are – can only have any meaning if an enemy is identified and strategic plans are devised to deal with that threat. It was self-evident that Germany was the enemy and the British Expeditionary Force would be landed on the continent in a deployment that would help them to defend the Belgians and the left flank of the French army. Such military conversations were bound to come out into the open eventually. When they did so, in 1911, Grey was still left in no doubt that Britain had made no commitments. Therefore, the French had to be satisfied with Grey's assurances of diplomatic support. Metternich, the German ambassador, was told that Britain would not abandon France and that the Entente was popular with the British public.

The Algeçiras Conference, 1906: what was its significance?

The crisis passed. Delcasse was forced to resign, and the Germans were able to insist on an international conference to discuss the future of Morocco. It was held at Algeçiras, Spain, in January 1906 and gave the Kaiser and von Bülow scope to make further mischief. It did not turn out as they imagined; for all their hectoring, the Germans found themselves isolated as the USA, Britain and Italy (revealing cracks in the Triple Alliance) supported France. Only Austria-Hungary and Morocco spoke up for the Kaiser. It was sufficient to reassure the French, and the Entente emerged from this first trial much stronger. Grey had proved reliable and constant and, although the Sultan remained in Morocco, joint French and Spanish policing consolidated what the Entente had agreed.

How and why were relations with Russia changing at this time?

Russia was coming to recognise the desirability of an understanding with Britain. Although Grey was enthusiastic, he knew he would face criticism from the radicals in his own Party, as well as from Labour MPs who would rage at the mention of Tsardom, and the energetic methods used by the autocratic state against fellow workers. Circumstances helped. Russia was turning away from the Far East after the disasters at the hands of the Japanese in 1905. Izvolsky, the Russian Foreign Minister, found himself being approached not only by Grey but also by the Germans who were still looking for an alliance with Russia to undermine their alliance with France.

The Anglo–Russian Convention of 1907 was signed on the same basis as the Entente Cordiale: it aimed to settle points of dispute only. Military arrangements were not under consideration. Arguments about Persia proved difficult but, in the end, the area was divided into three spheres of influence: the northern part for Russia, the southern part (next to India and Afghanistan) for Britain with a neutral buffer area in between. Tibet was to remain independent and Russia recognised that Afghanistan was to be in the British sphere. The Convention was a limited agreement, a point that was brought home to the Russians when Britain failed to support its attempt, in 1908, to open up the Straits to its warships. This has not stopped historians recognising the emergence of a 'Triple Entente' of Britain, France and Russia. As yet, it had little substance. What had more substance was Russia's renewed interest in the Mediterranean and Slav nationalism in the Balkans – future events would show this to be an unwelcome development.

1. How did Britain's relations with France and Russia change between 1905 and 1907?

2. What evidence of there to suggest a fear of Germany was a major aspect of British foreign policy by 1907?

3. Do you think the deterioration in Anglo–German relations was inevitable? Give reasons to support your answer.

24.5 How justified are criticisms of Sir Edward Grey's handling of British foreign policy?

A CASE STUDY IN HISTORICAL INTERPRETATION

Grey's policies attracted some controversy in the literature of the period.

- On the one hand, he is criticised for not doing more to convert the 'Triple Entente', insofar as one existed, into a Triple Alliance. Sir Arthur Nicolson, Grey's Permanent Under-Secretary, did press for this. The argument takes the line that a firm alliance would have made Germany think twice about adopting such an aggressive attitude in the years leading up to war. This view does assume that Grey could have persuaded the Cabinet and Parliament in favour of an alliance of France, Russia and Britain – something he clearly thought was not feasible. Anyway, Grey was unconvinced that forming a rival alliance would make war less likely. France and Russia – confident of British support – might have been encouraged to attack Germany. Alternatively, Germany might well have thought that the best way to escape what it claimed was encirclement would be to put the Schlieffen Plan into operation. This military strategy avoided the dangers of a two-front war by attacking France swiftly and then turning to defeat Russia.
- On the other hand, Grey has been criticised for continually attempting to settle disputes with Germany. Indeed, some progress was eventually made on colonial matters. Did a policy that tried to maintain peace by negotiation merely encourage German aggression?
- For some, isolation would have been a better route. An important pro-German group in Cabinet, which included Harcourt, the Colonial Secretary, pressed hard for non-involvement, as did high-ranking civil servants in the Foreign Office. Opposed to entanglements of any form,

they even disliked references made by Grey to the 'Triple Entente' (a point made by E.J. Feuchtwanger). The historian Zara Steiner, though, has shown that Grey followed his own course. In the context of a growing German threat, Grey had continued his predecessors' policies of reaching agreements wherever hostilities seemed imminent. With France, it was in Egypt and the Upper Nile. With Russia, there had been real dangers in the Far East and Afghanistan. Britain could not have stood by as Germany attempted to recreate an alliance with Russia. That would have exposed the vulnerability in Britain's global position.

- In conclusion, Grey was trying to steer a middle path between over-commitment and supporting France and Russia against German domination of the continent. This position was summed up by A.J.P. Taylor, who emphasises Grey's extraordinary concern to maintain the European balance of power. Many of the twists and turns in Grey's policy can be explained by reference to this.

Whatever the arguments, Grey who was not anti-German saw sense in looking for some kind of understanding with the Kaiser; this was no easy task given the rather gloomy state of Anglo–German relations. Germany was determined to play a world role and find its 'place in the sun'. The associated naval rivalry, according to A.J. Marder (*From the Dreadnought to Scapa Flow*, published in 1961), lay at the heart of the problem. Much has been written recently, particularly by Paul Kennedy (in *The Rise of German Antagonism*, published in 1980), about German economic competition – widely regarded as unfair and, therefore, an important source of irritation. German tariffs on British goods were greeted with hostility and there were accusations that their steel was being dumped in Britain at subsidised prices. However, the picture is much more complex than this. In the period 1890–1913, British imports from Germany trebled and British exports to Germany doubled. The trade between the two was of an unrivalled magnitude and Germany increasingly purchased raw materials from the British Empire and 'invisibles' (banking, insurance services) from the City of London. The two competitors seemed inextricably linked, although these obvious signs of healthy Anglo–German commerce did little to diminish suspicions of the Kaiser's motives. The impression which contemporaries shared was of two great Empires locked on a collision course (something which no doubt appealed to Social Darwinists who believed in the 'survival of the fittest') and it was an impression which found its way into the press and into the stuff of popular fiction.

But, were there signs that Britain was responding to the threat?

How did the Naval Race affect Anglo–German relations?

The German Naval Laws of 1898 and 1900 had forced the British into action, eventually; but was this being sustained? Apparently not. Campbell-Bannerman and many radicals in the Liberal Party were seeking to transfer moneys into domestic reform and Dreadnoughts were twice cut from the lists, in 1906 and again in 1907. This **unilateral** demonstration to reduce tension from the arms race cut no ice with the Germans who responded by expanding their programme. They looked to be eating into Britain's lead, and when Edward VII met the Kaiser in 1908, the German attitude was identical to that taken at the Hague Disarmament Conference a year earlier – naval disarmament was not open for discussion.

Unilateral: A decision made on one's own.

Radical Liberals, who had notable support from David Lloyd George and Winston Churchill, continued to press in Parliament for more arms reductions on the grounds that there was little immediate chance of war and re-armament was undermining social reform at home. McKenna (the new

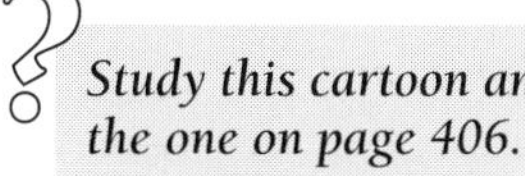

Study this cartoon and the one on page 406.

1. Are these cartoons pro-British or anti-British in tone? Give reasons to support your answer.

2. Using information contained within this chapter, explain why each cartoon may have been published.

German cartoon, 1908, showing Edward VII barring the way to the German navy.

First Lord of the Admiralty) and Grey both appreciated that sea power was the basis of British power in the world. Their case was assisted by George Wyndham's 1909 slogan 'We want eight and we won't wait', which caused something of a frenzy and effectively caught the public mood. This demand for more Dreadnoughts was provoked by rumours circulating in the British press that Germany was accelerating its Dreadnought building programme. After a period of deafening silence, Admiral Tirpitz admitted that he would have 13 Dreadnoughts by 1912 and orders had been placed for two more (thereby surpassing British totals). Newspaper editors were quick to point out that the German government and its figures could not be trusted, so even Lloyd George and Churchill had to admit that more action was needed. Hence, the provision in the People's Budget of 1909 and the promise of four more plus a further four if Germany pushed the arms race further.

How did British politicians and the British press react to the German naval building programme?

In 1910, Grey persisted with talks with Germany. It was typical of his efforts to settle points of difference between them, just as had happened with France and Russia. Hopes of reaching any agreement to halt the arms race faded on Germany's insistence that the price of stopping further naval building was a promise of Britain's neutrality. Britain's agreements with France and Russia ruled that out, especially if Germany provoked war with France.

How serious was the Agadir Crisis of 1911?

Unlike in 1905, the balance of opinion inside the Foreign Office and Cabinet had swung towards taking a more uncompromising stand against German efforts to interfere in Moroccan affairs. In March 1911, French troops occupied Fez. Germany once again saw the chance to advertise its global power and perhaps cause sufficient mischief to undermine the Entente. The Kaiser disapproved of the French action and, on 1 July, a German warship ('The Panther') appeared at Agadir, a port on Morocco's Atlantic coast.

The balance of power was at stake, which Grey had so carefully constructed. If France needed support it would get it. If Grey could warn Germany off, bolster France and avoid making any firm commitments to either side, all well and good. Grey was also concerned about two other pressures:

- British public opinion disapproved of German naval interference so close to Gibraltar.
- Radical Liberals fumed about the immorality of bringing Europe to the brink of war when domestic politics were in turmoil.

Nevertheless, Grey offered both stick and carrot – firmness tempered by the offer of compensation. For the latter, he made it clear that France should offer Germany something, although to claim the whole of the French Congo seemed excessive. Firmness came in the form of Lloyd George who, with Grey's approval, made a speech on 21 July at the Mansion House in London. The message was uncompromising – a clear warning was issued that Britain's honour was at stake.

> 'If a situation were to be forced upon us in which peace could only be preserved by the surrender of the great and beneficent position Britain has won by centuries of heroism and achievement, by allowing herself to be treated, where her interests were vitally affected, as if she were of no account in the Cabinet of nations, then I say emphatically that peace at that price would be a humiliation intolerable for a great country like ours to endure.'

It certainly made an impact. The traditional view, attributed to G.M. Trevelyan, is that the speech was anti-German and in the short term provoked so much resentment in Germany that it nearly caused war. But, in the long term, such a strong line led to a peaceful settlement of the crisis. Alternative views point out that German anger found its expression in a law to build three more Dreadnoughts and persistent demands for compensation. Indeed, the crisis rumbled on until Germany received a slice of the French Congo. Grey was so alarmed that military conversations took a further step. In 1912, a secret Anglo–French naval agreement altered significantly the relationship between the two navies. Much of the French navy was recalled to Toulon and the Mediterranean, leaving Britain to defend the North Sea and, presumably, France's Atlantic coast. Yet again the Cabinet and Churchill were at pains to inform the French that none of this officially meant an unconditional military commitment. France, however, must have been sure of Britain to take this bold step. The reality, despite the denials, appeared to be that Britain was strengthening the Entente. In 1914, there was even evidence of naval conversations between Britain and Russia.

Military planning remained haphazard as it was never fully debated by Cabinet. The Committee of Imperial Defence aimed to harmonise naval and army strategies, although there was little progress. The Army pressed ahead with an expeditionary force of six divisions (150,000 men), while the Navy concentrated its attention on battleships and planning coastal raids. Richard Haldane at the War Office was more effective. He created an Imperial General Staff to direct campaigns and organise mobilisation, completed army reorganisation and formed the Officer Training Corps which supplied young officers during the Great War. Most important of all, Haldane formed the Territorial Army into an effective reserve force. All this was done quickly and with savings on the military budget.

Grey never abandoned negotiations with Germany. His middle course, to maintain a fragile balance of power, meant sending Haldane (Secretary of State for War) to Germany in 1912. Nothing came of this except for some colonial agreements about the Berlin–Baghdad Railway and the future of Portugal's African colonies. At the heart of the problem, forever unresolved, was the naval race. Despite this, relations were cordial – it was almost the calm before the storm.

1. Why did the Agadir Crisis of 1911 make Anglo–German relations worse?

2. 'By 1912 Britain was committed to supporting France in the event of war.' How far do you agree?

24.6 Why did Britain go to war in 1914?

1. What actions did Sir Edward Grey take during the July Crisis of 1914?

2. 'By 1912, Britain was committed to supporting France in the event of war.' How far do you agree?

Study the whole of Chapter 24.

1. Explain the reasons why Britain declared war on Germany in August 1914. You will need to study the changes in Anglo–German and Anglo–French relations from 1898 to 1914.

2. What do you regard as the most important reason why Britain declared war in 1914? Give reasons to support your answer.

As war broke out in 1914, Edward Grey was deemed to have failed in maintaining the 'Concert of Europe'. Any assessment of this needs to start with the European events that led to the outbreak of war. The Balkans had been fomenting since 1912, when the Balkan League of Serbia, Bulgaria, Greece and Montenegro had attacked Turkey in the first war, rapidly followed by a second which broke out because Bulgaria was dissatisfied with the spoils it received. The results were an angry Bulgaria and a much-enlarged Serbia whose vigorous nationalism would prove a threat to the Austrian Empire. In hindsight, the dangers were clear. Austria-Hungary felt Serbia should be silenced as nationalism would destroy Franz Josef's Empire, and Vienna was getting assurances of support from the Kaiser. If Austria-Hungary crushed Serbia, Russia would certainly become involved as the defender of Slav nationalism and Germany would seize the moment to attack Russia, which it saw as a growing threat. There was still no feeling of panic even when Franz Ferdinand (the heir to the Austrian throne) was assassinated in Sarajevo, on 28 June 1914. There was an attitude of 'why should a shooting halfway across Europe cause concern to the British when there was the possibility of an Irish civil war on the doorstep?'

Perhaps the mood changed in the Foreign Office when, on 23 July, Austria sent an ultimatum to Serbia. No one would have thought so on the floor of the House of Commons when Lloyd George claimed that relations with Germany were so very good. Grey was trying to encourage the Powers to attend a conference in London, to no avail.

28 July	Austria declares war on Serbia
30 July	Russia mobilises its armies
31 July	German ultimatum to Russia demanding a stop to mobilisation
1 August	Germany declares war on Russia.

What was Grey to do? As a public policy, Grey repeated that the Government had made no commitment to France's defence. However, Grey's secretive approach to the Entente's military conversations was probably perceived by the French as some sort of commitment. *The Times* debated what might happen if France's coast was attacked and wondered 'if the word honour should be erased from the English language'. On 1 August, the Cabinet was still wavering, repeating its 'no commitment' position. But the tide was turning towards involvement. What sealed it was the German request that troops should be given passage through Belgium. Belgium refused and Grey, under some strain, told the House of Commons on 3 August that not only Belgian independence was at stake, but also the future of Europe which might be under the domination of one power. That would be an intolerable position for Britain. On 4 August, an ultimatum was sent to Germany and in the end only two members of the Cabinet resigned. Morley and Burns argued that Britain would have a free hand if no military conversations with France and Russia had taken place.

Others said that Grey should have been more resolute and decisive – a firm alliance would have deterred Germany. However, Germany was undeterred from invading Belgium and Grey would have found it difficult to swing the Cabinet and public behind him if he had attempted an Anglo–French alliance. As it was, the decision was taken out of his hands by the attack on Belgian neutrality. It enabled Grey, as he said, 'to bring the country into it [the war] unitedly'. Had there ever been a real alternative to the way Grey had conducted Britain's foreign policy?

Source-based questions: The outbreak of war – Britain's position

SOURCE A

Happily I am quite clear in my mind as to what is right and wrong. (1) We have no obligation to France or Russia to give them military or naval help. (2) The dispatch of the Expeditionary Force to help France at this moment is out of the question and would serve no object. (3) We must not forget the ties created by our long-standing and intimate friendship with France. (4) It is against British interests that France should be wiped out as a Great Power. (5) We cannot allow Germany to use the Channel as a hostile base. (6) We have no obligation to Belgium to prevent it being utilised and absorbed by Germany.

Herbert Asquith, writing on 2 August 1914.

SOURCE B

The British Government was technically uncommitted. It had friends, but no allies. Grey felt that he was committed to France, but tried to avoid saying so. He waited for his hand to be forced. On 30 July, he refused to give Russia any promise of support. On 1 August, he even suggested that Great Britain would stay neutral if France were not attacked – though it is uncertain whether he meant what he said. On 2 August, [the Liberal Cabinet] resolved that they would not allow the German fleet to enter the Channel and attack the French ports. This was not decision for war. It was a decision for armed neutrality. The British Government had one worry. It was determined to protect the neutrality of Belgium.

A.J.P. Taylor in an article 'War by Timetable' (published in 1966 in History of the Twentieth Century*).*

1. Study Source A.

How useful is this source in trying to understand why Britain went to war in August 1914?

2. Study Source B.

To what extent does Source B support what Source A says about Britain's commitments in 1914? Explain your answer.

25 The political, social and economic impact of the First World War, 1914–1918

Key Issues

- *What was the impact of the First World War on political parties?*
- *How did the First World War lead to a change in the role of the State?*
- *Was the First World War a turning point in British history?*

25.1 Historical interpretation: How far did the war and coalition government affect the political parties?
25.2 How far did the State increase its role in the economic life of Britain?
25.3 What impact did the State have in mobilising the human resources of Britain?
25.4 What efforts were made to finance the war and plan for reconstruction?

Framework of Events

1914	Kitchener becomes Minister of War Defence of the Realm Act State control of the railways
1915	Asquith forms a coalition government; Lloyd George is made Minister of Munitions Lord Derby's recruiting scheme Treasury Agreements with unions
1916	Lloyd George becomes Prime Minister Shipping controls set up Conscription is introduced
1917	Food Controller is appointed Rationing is introduced Industrial unrest Ministry of Reconstruction is created
1918	Education Act; Representation of the People Act Armistice.

Overview

HERBERT Asquith's deficiencies as a wartime leader were quickly placed under the microscope by the ever-increasing demands of hostilities. The wave of patriotism that greeted the start of the war was translated, politically, into all-party support as the Conservatives, Irish Home Rule Party and most of the Labour Party responded within days of the outbreak of hostilities.

Asquith's appointment of Lord Kitchener as Secretary of State for War did nothing to give firm direction or better organisation to the war effort. Kitchener had gained his reputation as an effective colonial commander and had shown formidable strategic skills in South Africa and the Sudan. At the War Office, however, Kitchener was out of his depth. Years of soldiering had not prepared him for the task of coordinating a large department, organising supplies and war materials, or even having his decisions questioned by Cabinet colleagues. But, like some of his colleagues, he too clung to old methods. His reference to tanks as 'pretty mechanical toys', which would have little impact on the war, illustrates his lack of ideas. It should be added that this did not make him particularly different from those around him. Margot Asquith, wife of the Prime Minister, made the judgement that Kitchener was not much more than 'a great poster'.

Asquith, on the other hand, may have possessed a lawyer's ability to debate the merits of an argument and come to a logical judgement, but circumstances demanded more of a sense of urgency to cut through the torpor.

Kitchener and Asquith attempted to operate in an existing Liberal Cabinet of 20 members; but there was a sense of drift, which frustrated Lloyd George. By the autumn of 1914, Lloyd George was complaining about difficulties with the supply of munitions to the Front. Sir John French also complained about the shell shortage, although he is suspected of using this as an excuse for his poor leadership.

On 15 May 1915, *The Times* printed a telegram from their war correspondent, Colonel Repington. It read: 'the want of an unlimited supply of high explosive shells was a fatal bar to our success'. The same day, the Government was shaken by the resignation of Sir John Fisher (First Sea Lord), who cited the Gallipoli fiasco and the way he had been overruled by Churchill as the main reasons for 'calling it a day'. There was the unmistakable whiff of crisis in the air. In the absence of any good news from the Front, it was difficult to dispel the view that there was a tide of events running against Asquith's Government.

1. What actions did Asquith take after the outbreak of war in 1914 to help the British war effort?

2. Why was a coalition government formed in May 1915?

Asquith took the one way out that he knew would undermine Conservative opposition; he invited the Conservative Party to join the government. In May 1915, a coalition was formed and the last Liberal Government had come to an end. Andrew Bonar Law went to the Colonial Office, when he really wanted to be Chancellor, and Arthur Balfour succeeded Winston Churchill at the Admiralty. Churchill became Chancellor of the Duchy of Lancaster, which was his price for the stalled Gallipoli campaign. Lloyd George made the crucial move to the Ministry of Munitions, where his energy and determination were needed to boost production and to engage a reluctant and uncooperative War Office.

25.1 How far did the war and coalition government affect the political parties?

A CASE STUDY IN HISTORICAL INTERPRETATION

Lloyd George may well have given impetus to munitions production, but central direction of the war was still muddled. Decisions were made so slowly that Sir Maurice Hankey – who had been Secretary of the Imperial Defence Committee and was secretary of an unofficial war committee from November 1915 onwards – was moved to exclaim that the Constitution should be suspended and a **dictator** appointed. He was impatient with the size of the committee (it had nine members), with the fact that final decisions still lay with Cabinet, and that no one seemed to have 'access to all the necessary information on which plans were to be based'. Nobody really

Dictator: A ruler who has complete power in a country, especially power which was obtained by force.

liked the Coalition Cabinet. The Liberals felt betrayed by the intrigue which had let the Conservatives into government, while the Conservatives felt that they had been deceived into joining a government which was seen to be making little headway in the war.

Events in 1916 were no better – the Easter Rising (see Chapter 22), Kut, the Somme, the German U-boat campaign – on top of which political storm clouds were gathering as Liberal sensitivities were injured by the ever-expanding tentacles of government control. The battle over **conscription**, in early 1916, showed reluctant Liberal attitudes at their worst. Twenty-seven Liberals voted against the Conscription Bill and the Home Secretary, Sir John Simon, resigned. At least three other Cabinet Liberals threatened to do the same, fearing the dangers to individual liberty posed by a 'dictatorial' State. Gladstonian liberal attitudes were seemingly being sacrificed to 'Prussian' values.

Conscription: Officially making people in a particular country join the Army, Navy or Air Force.

At least Kitchener was on his way to Russia, in July, enabling Lloyd George to become Minister of War. Rejecting President Wilson's suggestion of American mediation, Lloyd George allowed himself to be convinced that a final 'knock-out blow' was needed against Germany. However, in his view, it required a more energetic approach than Asquith was providing. At the end of 1916, Lloyd George organised a campaign with Bonar Law and Edward Carson for a small War Committee to take over the running of the war effort. Lloyd George would be its chairman. In the intrigue and double-dealing that followed, nobody could escape accusations of treachery, not even the eventual victim, Asquith.

On 3 December 1916, Asquith apparently agreed to the Committee proposal, although he would have final control over policy. *The Times* then published an article the next day, which criticised Asquith, saying that he was being pushed to the sidelines on war policy. Asquith assumed Lloyd George was behind this and announced that the War Committee would not be chaired by Lloyd George but by himself.

Lloyd George resigned and the Conservatives said that they would no longer serve in the Cabinet. A meeting of party leaders held on 6 December at Buckingham Palace recognised that Bonar Law was the natural successor to Asquith. It was Asquith who made the next decisive step. He said that he would not join a government led by the Conservative leader.

By the following day, though, Lloyd George had managed to form a government that the Conservatives agreed to join. Asquith and all the Liberal Ministers resigned and none of them found themselves back in government. They promised support to the Government but loyalty to Asquith. The ensuing feuding between Asquith and Lloyd George divided and destroyed the Liberal Party. It also placed the Prime Minister's destiny in the hands of the Conservatives. Despite Lloyd George's apparently powerful position at the head of the coalition, he could not guarantee to have carried the Liberal Party with him (many considered him a traitor) and the Conservatives tolerated him, exploiting his popularity but never really trusting him. Lloyd George had built his support on shifting sands.

Along with Arthur Henderson (Labour), Lloyd George formed a small War Cabinet made up of Bonar Law, Lord Curzon and Alfred Milner. This was a most important change to the rather chaotic working practices of government. Sir Maurice Hankey became the first Cabinet Secretary ever appointed and he instituted proper records of decisions taken so that these could be communicated to the relevant departments. As the historian L.C.B. Seaman notes, 'It is strange to recall with what lordly amateurism the politicians had hitherto controlled the nation's affairs'.

Punch cartoon, 13 December 1916, entitled 'A Non-Party Mandate'. John Bull is saying: 'I don't care who leads the country so long as he leads it to victory.'

John Bull represents Britain in this cartoon.

1. What reasons are given in the cartoon to explain the formation of the Lloyd George Coalition Government of December 1916?

2. Using information in this chapter, how far does this cartoon explain the reasons for the formation of the Lloyd George Coalition Government?

The decline of the Liberal Party

A fatal blow had been delivered to the Liberal Party. It has been the subject of much debate. Chapter 23 explored the possibility that the Liberal Party had failed to adapt to Edwardian class-based politics and that the 'Strange Death of Liberal England' was already apparent before the First World War broke out. Historian Trevor Wilson argued, in *The Downfall of the Liberal Party, 1914–35* (1966), from a different standpoint. He claimed that Liberalism was still sound in 1914, but then it was knocked down by a 'rampant omnibus' – the war – from which it never recovered. In the December 1910 election, the Liberals had 272 MPs; in 1918, after the 'Coupon election', Asquith's section of the party had 28 MPs, while Lloyd George's had 133. Why did the Liberal Party decline? Was there an acceleration of processes at work before the war? Was it due to the actions of leading Liberals during the war? Or, as Trevor Wilson emphasises, is there a case for arguing that the long-held ideals of Liberalism were incompatible with the conduct of the war?

Firstly, let us examine the record of the Liberal leadership. Lloyd George was traditionally cast as the villain; here was the self-seeking opportunist who was behind the intrigues that made him leader of the coalition with the Conservatives. As historian Martin Pugh notes, in *The First World War in British History* (1995), recent verdicts have been less harsh: 'In the early years of the war, Lloyd George's conspicuous success at Munitions was an asset to the Liberals when under attack over the handling of the war. It is now clear that he did not plot to deprive Asquith of the premiership.' Pugh goes on to argue that Asquith should take more of the blame by neglecting Bonar Law and for refusing to serve in the wartime coalition. By 1918, it was too late; Lloyd George fought the election with the Conservatives and 526 government MPs, endorsed by the 'Coupon' signed by Bonar Law and Lloyd George, had been returned. The division in Liberal ranks had been underlined.

Secondly, is there evidence that the Liberals were uneasy with their interventionist role during the war (see sections 25.2–25.4)? On the one hand, the Liberals' welfare reforms before the war had showed a willingness to shift away from *laissez-faire* policies. Why should more State action bother them? On the other hand, some Liberals such as Arthur Ponsonby were uncomfortable with how the State was threatening civil liberties through the Defence of the Realm Act and, particularly, the introduction of conscription. Ponsonby, like others, joined the Union of Democratic Control, which had been formed at the start of the war to bring about peace by negotiation. Historian A.J.P. Taylor does point out that these views won support at first from middle-class intellectuals and the Independent Labour Party (ILP). It is doubtful, then, if such concerns about the undermining of truly Liberal values really concerned the rank-and-file in the country. Instead, patriotism and a feeling that the sacrifices already made should not be squandered were more powerful emotions.

On balance, the division between Asquith and Lloyd George, confirmed by the 1918 election, was to prove more decisive.

Other divisions?

It was not the only division that took place though. In 1915, Labour MP Arthur Henderson joined the Government as President of the Board of Education but with a particular brief covering industrial relations. This did much to enhance Labour's standing in the country. However, in 1917, Henderson was convinced that Labour Party delegates should attend a peace conference organised by socialists in Stockholm. The Cabinet was furious and Henderson was forced to resign. His departure had two major effects.

- It ended the 'Lib–Lab' electoral pact which had contributed so effectively to several Conservative general election defeats before the war. Now the Conservatives could engage themselves in straight fights with a divided opposition made up of Liberal and Labour candidates, rather than just one opponent. It helped their chances at the ballot box enormously.
- Henderson set about severing links with the Liberals by reforming Labour as a fully-fledged independent party. There were a number of factors that helped this process. Full employment during the war increased the power and membership of trade unions; they rose from 4 million in 1914 to 6 million in 1918. Labour was bound to derive extra support and funds from this expansion. Membership of government gave them not only credibility but also the confidence to strike out on their own. The Representation of the People Act of 1918 – which gave universal male suffrage to those over 21 and to women over 30 – increased the number of voters from 8 million to just under 22 million – it is true that many of these new electors were women. However, many were working-class men and possibly Labour voters, but the extent of this continues to be the matter of debate.

Henderson, meanwhile, was busy improving the organisation of the ILP. Branches were set up in many more constituencies; there was a drive to boost membership and to select more candidates. A new National Executive Committee of 23 members was to be elected by annual conference and by the block vote system, giving more influence to the larger unions. A new socialist programme, 'Labour and the New Social Order', was adopted. The policies it contained, such as state control of industry (Clause Four) and a minimum wage, enabled Labour to fill the gap left by Radical Liberals in many parts of the country. In 1918, just short of 400 Labour candidates stood for Parliament, whereas in December 1910 the figure was just short of 80. In all, 61 Labour MPs were elected in the 1918 election – not a huge increase, but this was the 'Coupon' election and patriotic loyalty to Lloyd George was decisive. However, their share of the vote increased from 7% in 1910 to 22% – the foundations had been laid; in 1922, Labour secured 142 seats.

In Ireland, foundations of a different sort had been not laid but undermined. John Redmond, the leader of the Irish Home Rule Party, found that the start of the war prevented the implementation of the 1914 Home Rule Act. Then events during the war, particularly the influence of Conservatives in the Coalition (who would be certain to oppose Home Rule) and the violent nationalist uprising in Dublin at Easter 1916, led to the rapid growth in support for Sinn Fein. In 1918, Sinn Fein won 73 seats, while Redmond held on to only six (see Chapter 22). The upheaval on the political scene was complete. Was there a similar upheaval in the relationship between State and society?

If contemporary evidence is to be believed, Lloyd George was adept at large-scale organisation as well as showing great resolve to mobilise the resources of the nation. Under him, state control and direction moved ahead at unprecedented speed and into new areas of control.

1. In what ways did the period 1915–18 see a change in the fortunes of political parties in Britain and Ireland?

2. Why have historians disagreed over the reasons for problems in the Liberal Party during the war?

3. Hero or villain. Which of these best describes Lloyd George's role in domestic affairs during the First World War? Give reasons to support your answer.

25.2 How far did the State increase its role in the economic life of Britain?

The defence of the realm

The Government faced the huge task of mobilising the resources of the State to meet the demands of a conflict, the scale of which was so completely outside Lloyd George's previous experience. Throughout the war, piecemeal measures were taken at particular times to meet specific emergencies – these occurred in two distinct phases. Firstly, under Asquith, government interference was more limited. But Lloyd George rapidly expanded the government apparatus after December 1916, transforming the State's involvement beyond recognition.

The problems they faced were enormous: how to mobilise manpower, how to maintain resources for the Army and how to feed the population. And it had to be paid for, preferably avoiding national bankruptcy.

The Defence of the Realm Acts laid the basis of government interference. The first one, in August 1914, gave the Cabinet the power to 'issue regulations as to the powers and duties of the Admiralty and Army Council, and other persons acting on their behalf, for securing the public safety and defence of the realm'. Later Acts gave wide powers beyond economic control into such areas as censorship and control of the press.

Mobilising the economic resources of the State

From the outset of the war, rapid action was taken to place the railways under government control. A Railway Executive Committee, made up of the ten General Managers of the larger companies, would run the system. The government approach to shareholders was followed elsewhere – the profits were fixed at their 1913 rates, while the 130 companies affected would share the profits from a pool. Central direction allowed the rapid movement of troops and war materials between regions.

Jute: This was needed for sandbags.

Flax: Used to make tents.

Essential commodities had to be guaranteed and not only were reserves of wheat built up but meat was purchased overseas in bulk. By 1916, the Government was buying the entire Indian **jute** crop and the Russian **flax** crop. In Britain, measures were taken to guarantee wool supplies for blankets and uniforms. The majority of imported sugar came from Central Europe and a royal commission was established in 1914 to oversee supplies.

Historian Sidney Pollard notes how government purchasing was hampered by a continuing faith in a market economy, as well as in the cycle of supply and demand. Habits were difficult to shift; it was only slowly accepted that government intervention on such a scale would drastically alter normal trading conditions. Government demand for certain goods would so upset prices that their control was essential.

The alleged shell shortage in 1915 brought about an extension of control from Lloyd George's Ministry of Munitions. Lloyd George gathered new people around him, like Eric Geddes, selected from business rather than the Civil Service. They also had to set about finding skilled workers to swell the labour force. The Treasury Agreement of 1915, which was later contained in the Munitions of War Act, laid down an agreement with the unions. In return for guaranteed good wage levels and profits linked to the 1913 level, the unions gave up the right to strike in favour of arbitration. The Government also persuaded the unions to agree to 'dilution' (the use of semi-skilled or unskilled men and women in skilled positions), while restrictive practices would be put aside until the end of the war when they would be restored.

Armaments: Weapons and military equipment.

The Ministry then extended its controls to the supply of raw materials required in the production of **armaments**. The success of these measures was clear: between May 1915 and July 1916, shell production rose from 20,000 a month to 1,000,000. By 1918, the Ministry had 65,000 staff to administer production and supply. None of this avoided tensions and strife within associated industries.

Food supplies (apart from sugar) were generally satisfactory until the end of 1916 when U-boats were taking their toll. What was done? The civilian population was particularly sensitive to price rises and profiteering, but it

A munitions poster, April 1917

took some time; indeed until July 1917, when the prices of meat, sugar and wheat were fixed. By then a Food Controller had been appointed to ensure that food was distributed fairly.

The Board of Agriculture assisted in boosting productivity and thereby reducing the reliance on imports. Prisoners of war and the Women's Land Army provided extra labour; tractors and fertilisers were distributed and mechanisation of farming forged ahead. Pasture was converted to arable, such as wheat and potatoes, so much so that, by 1918, 3 million more acres [1.2 million hectares] of arable were under cultivation. Calculations were based on how many people 100 acres of land could feed; only nine if given over to meat production, but 415 people if it grew potatoes. Hence some foodstuffs were never in short supply – such as potatoes and bread. Bread prices were kept low through subsidies. Rationing only became necessary at the end of 1917 when Lord Rhondda, the Food Controller, introduced rationing in tea, cheese, bacon, butter, margarine and meat.

The threat of shortages often led to hoarding – more dangerous than U-boats to food supplies. There was much talk of only weeks' supply of wheat and sugar left in the country in 1917, but the reality here was very different from the starvation which was rife in Germany because of the effects of the British blockade on German ports.

Wartime controls only seemed to have worked in the short term; in the longer term, they were lifted by 1922. There was a pattern of old habits returning which was repeated elsewhere.

In industry, despite losses of manpower, production was maintained and considerable advances were made in engineering, scientific research and in the rationalisation of production. New industries were created, but it was in shipbuilding where difficulties were experienced meeting demand. Persistent U-boat activity led to the formation of a Shipping Control Committee and the appointment of a Shipping Controller to divert imports towards essential items. A Controller of the Navy was placed in charge of construction and the requisitioning of nearly all merchant ships. By 1917, building capacity had been enlarged (here and abroad, especially in the USA). Helped by expanding steel production, as well as the convoy system, building outstripped losses.

Coal supplies were maintained despite mass enlistment into local 'pals' battalions, such as those in Barnsley or Accrington. Tight government controls were needed to maintain output and, more importantly, to keep prices down. By the middle of the war, central government dictated to the old managers who ran the pits. In 1917 and 1918, national wage agreements tried to keep wages rising with the cost of living, in an attempt to avoid industrial action. Profits were again fixed at pre-war levels, but a Coal Controller claimed most of the excess profits in taxes.

Sidney Pollard comments on how the war taught the Government much about central planning and organisation of national resources; railways were more integrated, supplies of steel and coal were rationalised to meet need, resources were used more efficiently – there was even talk of a 'national grid' for electricity supply. It was a world apart from 1913. Collectivism, evident before the war, had been given its head.

25.3 *What impact did the State have in mobilising the human resources of Britain?*

The Armed Forces

Initially, volunteers responded to the call to arms. By 1915, recruiting figures were tailing off. In October 1915, Lord Derby, who had become Director of Recruiting, introduced The Derby Scheme, by which all men between 18 and 41 would be asked to place their names on a voluntary register. Single men would be enlisted first and, if that proved insufficient, married men would follow. The scheme did not work, as bachelors failed to register; neither did it adequately differentiate between men in essential and non-essential occupations. To fill the gap and to provide more cannon fodder for an army that was looking ahead to one more 'big push' (this time on the Somme as it turned out), in January 1916 all single men between 18 and 41 were conscripted. In May, the decision was taken to extend this to married men.

The distribution of manpower was not without political danger. Conscription was opposed by some Liberal MPs. Asquith survived the crisis, albeit temporarily.

In May 1918, General Sir Frederick Maurice accused Lloyd George of misleading the House of Commons. The Prime Minister had said that troops had not been kept back in England and that the numbers in the reserve sectors of the Western Front were greater at the beginning of 1918 than a year earlier. Asquith seized on this, but to no effect. Lloyd George had, in fact, misquoted the figures but the ex-Liberal leader was unable to make capital out of it. It proved to be a temporary moment of embarrassment, but it underlined that Lloyd George's hold on power was not as firm as it might be especially since he relied on Conservative support to maintain his position in the House of Commons.

The impact of war on the labour force

To imagine that trade union members sacrificed all thoughts of industrial action as they patriotically placed their might behind the war effort is an over-simplification. Shortages of labour were apparent by 1915. Not only had enlistment drained industry of crucial workers, but also the apparatus of exemptions from military service was not put in place until it was too late. Women were soon drafted in. The Treasury Agreement of 1915 allowed for dilution, where unskilled women (and men) were allowed to fill vacancies left by skilled workers. In all, women's employment increased from 3 million in 1914 to 5 million in 1918. Many came from domestic service to which they never returned, but 1.5 million were new workers.

In the short term, women's employment in factories sharply declined after the war when men reclaimed their previous employment. However, in the long term, some occupations came to be monopolised by women after the war, particularly shops, hotels and offices. One million more people drew salaries after the war than before it; some of these were professional men, but women in white-collar jobs contributed significantly to the increase.

Wage rates during the war barely kept pace with rises in the cost of living and workers had to rely on piece-rates or overtime to keep up with price inflation. Trade unions had given up their right to strike and TUC leaders had begun to develop a working relationship with some government departments as part of the war effort. That did not mean there was no discontent among the rank-and-file. South Wales miners went on strike in 1915 and there was trouble among engineering workers of the Clyde. In general, though, serious trouble was avoided until 1917. War weariness by then had combined with anger at price rises, black marketeering and food shortages. The rich still seemed able to buy luxuries. Dilution angered skilled men; they not only witnessed unskilled people just minding machines, which undermined generations of craft skills, but also had to accept fixed wage rates when unskilled workers were able to earn more because they were paid on piece-rates. By 1917, dilution was being applied to all trades without restriction. If a craft worker wished to change jobs, he could not do so unless he received a leaving certificate from his employer. Conscription was badly handled; men who had exemption certificates were sent to France and then had to be recalled – the dignity of labour appeared threatened on all fronts.

Shop stewards: Shopfloor trade union activists who played an important role in local organisation for their members.

Days lost to strikes rose from 2.5 million in 1916 to just short of 6 million in 1918. For instance, Coventry, Sheffield and Manchester were all hit by strikes in the engineering industry in May 1917. Ironically, trade union membership doubled to 8 million by 1919. Rank-and-file members who felt vulnerable turned to **shop stewards** to defend their interests. At a local level, they spoke for the workers, established factory works committees, intervened in disputes and took an active role during unrest. Some had a syndicalist background; those in the munitions industry were particularly important because it was here that industrial recruitment had taken place on a vast scale and where the problems were greatest. Shop stewards played key parts in the strikes on the Clyde in 1915 and 1916. In Sheffield, munitions workers withdrew their labour when exempt workers were conscripted. A serious engineering strike in 1917 was sparked off by more extensions of the 'dilution' principle.

1. What changes did the British Government make to improve Britain's chances of fighting the war effectively?

2. How successful were the Government's attempts to mobilise the work force for the war effort?

The Government was suitably alarmed and responded with a commission. The result was that controls on prices and profits were strengthened, key foodstuffs were subsidised, and national wage rates were improved and imposed by arbitration.

25.4 What efforts were made to finance the war and plan for reconstruction?

The cost of prosecuting the war to a conclusion was staggering. One economist put the figure at just under £4 million a day. How would it all be paid for? Principally, by increasing the National Debt. Some of the costs were borne by bank borrowing, although a significant amount was raised by taxation. Income tax rose from 9d (less than 4p) in the £ in 1914 to 6 shillings (72p) in 1918. Death duties rose sharply and excess profits taxes were imposed on a range of goods. It did contribute to the inflationary spiral and, given the unrest in key industries, some thought was given to reconstruction. In 1916, a new Ministry of Pensions planned to provide benefits to widows and those disabled in the fighting. Dr Addison's Ministry of Reconstruction (1917) prepared measures, inadequate by later standards, to improve health provision and build 'homes fit for heroes to live in'. Herbert Fisher's Education Act of 1918 raised the school-leaving age to 14 and planned to expand tertiary education.

Most dramatically, the Representation of the People Act extended the vote to women over 30 and to men over 21. It was the most democratic reform of the franchise so far and it became part of the mythology of the First World War that the granting of the vote was reward for women's contribution to the war effort. If women had established parity, why were so many displaced by men reclaiming their jobs in industry when the war was over? Had attitudes to women really changed? The historian Martin Pugh argues not; it was still felt that their place was in the home, just as before the war.

1. What methods were used by the Government to raise revenue for the war effort?

2. What changes were made by the Representation of the People Act, 1918?

3. Why do you think women over 30 were given the vote in 1918?

What politicians really wanted to do was to enfranchise more men; the inclusion of so many women, probably over 8 million, was not considered to be a great advantage to any particular party, so there seemed no point in resisting their demands. Pugh argues that confining the vote to women over 30, who were more likely to be married housewives, would add stability to a society which had lost a whole generation of men. Hence, Pugh argues, women were enfranchised by politicians who 'felt satisfied it was safe to do so'. Gail Braybon also argues that for many women things had not changed significantly:

> One can recognise the devastating emotional ... consequences of the First World War, and note the dramatic effect of war work on women's skills, self-confidence and income, yet still be aware that for millions of women life offered limited opportunities for employment, combined with low pay and household drudgery, before, during and after the war.

Historians continue to debate the extent of the impact of the First World War. Did it mark a break with the past or did it accelerate trends that were clearly identifiable in the era before 1914? In the final reckoning, a whole generation had been lost – around 700,000 members of the armed forces. Few families escaped the sense of loss. The 'Great War for Civilisation' would cast its shadow over generations to come.

1. Study the whole of Chapter 25.

2. What do you regard as the most significant change to occur within Britain as a result of the First World War? Give reasons to support your answer.

Source-based questions: Impact of the First World War

SOURCE A

Government regulations have to be suspended during the war because they are inapplicable in a time of emergency. The same thing applies to many trade union regulations and practices … I should like to call attention to those rules which had been set up, for very good reasons, to make it difficult for unskilled men to claim the position and rights of men who have had training … If all the skilled engineers in this country were turned on to produce what is required, if you brought back from the Front every engineer who had been recruited, if you worked them to the utmost limits of human endurance, you have not enough labour even then to produce all we are going to ask you to produce during the next few months. Therefore we must appeal to the patriotism of the unions to relax these particular rules … to enable us to turn out the necessary munitions of war to win a real and speedy triumph.

From a speech made in Liverpool on 14 June 1915 by Lloyd George, in which he asked for the support of workers and trade unions for munitions manufacturing.

SOURCE B

The chloroforming pill of patriotism is failing in its power to drug the mind and consciousness of the worker. The chains of slavery are being welded tighter upon us … The ruling classes are over-reaching themselves in their hurry to enslave us … Comrades, I appeal to you to rouse your union to protect the liberties of its members. An industrial truce was entered into by our leaders behind our backs … Away with the industrial truce! We must not stand by and allow the workers to be exploited and our liberties taken away.

A.J. Cook, a miners' leader, April 1916. Quoted in Britain: Industrial Relations and the Economy 1900–1939 *by Robert Pearce, published in 1993.*

SOURCE C

Industrial unrest worried the Government enormously in 1917 and 1918. The Bolshevik revolution in Russia seemed to give a fillip to revolutionary groups in Britain … There were rumours of a possible general strike, and a workers' soviet was set up in Glasgow, before its leader was sentenced to five years' imprisonment with hard labour. A.J. Cook was also prosecuted, in March 1918, for preaching revolution. Nevertheless, despite these fears and isolated incidents, enough was done by the end of the war to remove grievances and so to blunt the edge of militancy.

From Britain: Industrial Relations and the Economy 1900–1939 *by Robert Pearce (1993).*

---

1. Study Source A.

How does this source help historians to understand the crisis in munitions production during 1915?

3. Study Sources A and B.

How do Sources A and B differ in their views of industrial relations? Explain your answer.

3. 'The First World War had only a limited impact on industrial relations.' Is there sufficient evidence in Sources A, B and C to prove the accuracy of this statement? Explain your answer.

British economy and society, 1896–1914: challenged and transformed?

26.1 Was there a problem with the British economy?
26.2 Historical interpretation: Why did Britain lose its position as the world's major economic power?
26.3 To what extent had the role of women changed within British society by 1914?

Key Issues

- *How far was Britain's position as the world's major trading nation challenged at the turn of the 20th century and in the years leading up to the First World War?*
- *Why did economic growth slow down at this time?*
- *To what extent did the role of women change within British society by 1914?*

Overview: the aftermath of 'The Great Depression'?

By 1900, Britain's unrivalled and dominant position as the 'workshop of the world' was apparently slipping. How serious was the problem? How gloomy were contemporary views of the condition of the economy as the 20th century dawned? As you read in Chapter 19, anxieties about the British economy had been growing since 1870. Some historians regarded the cycle of slumps and brief recoveries which ended in 1896 as 'The Great Depression', a description which has been re-assessed more recently. Regardless of the debate between historians about the myth of a 'depression', contemporaries' confidence in continuing strong growth had been shaken. Unemployment and ruined profits raised the spectre that other nations, particularly the USA and Germany, were catching up and successfully competing with Britain. While there is evidence that these concerns were exaggerated, questions were being asked, such as 'Were the "staple" industries – textiles, coal, iron, steel and ship-building – still able to maintain their grip on world markets?'

Books with titles such as *Made in Germany* and *American Invaders* were widely read. They seemed to reflect a gloomy reaction to a wider debate about 'National Efficiency' and **physical deterioration**, sometimes also referred to as 'physical degeneration'. It was not only the three-year struggle to defeat a small group of Dutch farmers in the Boer Republics, it also included the realisation of shocking inequalities in wealth in Britain: of glittering wealth amid appalling poverty as defined by Seebohm Rowntree, William Booth and Mearns. Was the British work force, many of whom had failed to meet the physical standard required to join the Army, capable of competing on an equal footing with apparently more productive and better trained workers in the USA and Germany? Those British observers who travelled abroad to see things for themselves were not confident that it could.

Physical deterioration: This refers to concerns about the possible genetic decline in the British race, touched on by Social Darwinists (see page323).

26.1 Was there a problem with the British economy?

Contemporaries might trust their judgement, but they would have been hard pressed to prove that British growth was slowing down, as many economic statistics at the end of the 19th century were either non-existent or hopelessly inaccurate. Conclusions based on their available data were at best impressionistic.

Was Britain's wealth on the rise?

On the face of it, Britain's wealth continued to rise.

- Between 1900 and 1913, Gross Domestic Product (GDP) – a measure of what goods were being made and what services were provided – rose by about 1.7% a year.
- Coalmining expanded from 223 million tons in 1900 to a bumper figure of 287 million tons in 1913.
- In shipbuilding, Britain still built about 60% of the world's merchant ships throughout the period 1900–1914.
- Staple industries continued to sell strongly abroad, particularly textiles, and they amounted to 66% of all British exports, 1911–13. New industries were appearing. They reflected technological advances in, for example, chemicals, rubber, oil refining, cars, fertilisers, soap, aircraft and electrical engineering.
- The figures for foreign investment were staggering by any standard – approximately £50 million in 1901, rising to £200 million a year between 1911 and 1913. Capital assets abroad were probably around £2.8 billion.
- While it was the case that the balance of trade was in the red, with imports growing apace and exceeding exports by about £1,500 million a year, the massive profits earned by the City of London for banking, insurance and shipping ('invisible earnings') boosted the balance well into profit.

Hence the signs were of a buoyant economy which was continuing to grow.

Was growth slowing down?

So what was happening, and why? Were competitors abroad catching up? If yes, how quickly were they catching up? Was British industry as up to date as it should be or were foreign methods and organisation of manufacturing more productive? Indications were of a 'retardation of growth' – a slowing down rather than an absolute decline. The warning signs should not have misled anyone into thinking that the British economy was performing strongly.

According to Professor Feinstein, the USA, France, Germany, Sweden and Japan all achieved growth rates in productivity which were about twice those achieved in Britain. Indeed the drop in output per worker was the most alarming feature of British manufacturing (see table).

In 1870, Britain produced about one-third of the world's manufactured goods; by 1913, that had dropped to 14%. Britain's place at the top had been taken by the USA (35%) and Germany (16%). A note of caution might point out that these figures mask differences between particular industries. Some of the newer industries, as well as one well-established industry, shipbuilding, continued to progress. But the country relied excessively on the other old staple industries. Coal, textiles, iron, steel and engineering contributed to

Growth of volume of UK exports, 1830–1913

(annual percentage growth rates)

	1830–57	*1857–73*	*1873–99*	*1899–1913*
Total exports	5.6	3.1	1.9	3.0
Exports of manufactures	5.6	3.1	1.6	2.7
of which				
Cotton textiles	5.1	3.0	1.7	1.6
Other textiles	5.7	3.1	–0.4	1.5
Metals, machinery etc.	6.7	2.3	2.9	3.4
Exports of coal	10.1	3.8	4.8	4.2
Exports less imports of manufactures	5.7	2.4	0.6	2.9

50% of all output in 1907 and employed 25% of the work force. New industries – such as electrical manufactures, rayon production, chemicals and scientific equipment – contributed to only 6.5% of all output and employed 5.2% of the work force. Further, this concentration was deepening; between 1905 and 1907, 95 new cotton mills were opened, but all used conventional equipment. Past habits died hard; old industries were slow to modernise and were sometimes starved of capital. The economic historian Sydney Pollard claims that 'only 8% of coal was cut mechanically in 1913, and even less was mechanically conveyed underground; in the use of electricity, concrete, even steel, Britain's pits seemed backward …'. There had never been so many men employed in the pits, which explains increased output as well as lower productivity per miner.

American textile manufacturers widely used electricity to run more modern machines, which used the latest spindles, hence cutting running costs. The opposite was true of many of Lancashire's cotton mills. Faster growth elsewhere meant Britain was surpassed in the steel industry; by 1913, the USA produced 13 million tons, Germany 7 million tons and Britain 5 million tons. In his study of the steel industry, Temin found very slow adoption of larger, cheaper and more efficient steel processes, while producers clung on far too long to pig iron production instead of changing to steel. In shipping, British builders continued to use steam turbines instead of changing to oil-fired ones. So often British inventors had come up with new processes which were then developed and adopted abroad. Sydney Pollard makes the point that British skilled craftsmen were second to none; it was the shortage of these skilled workers in countries like America which forced them to develop mass production techniques (Henry Ford's conveyor belt process), as well as flexible management practices. British industrialists seemed less dynamic. Cost-reducing innovations were not being adopted, the value of technical innovations was not widely acknowledged, output in new industries languished, and there was a reluctance to provide sufficient technical and managerial education similar to that found in Germany.

1. In what ways was Britain still a major economic power after 1896?

2. Why did it seem that Britain's position as the world's main economic power was challenged after 1870?

British salesmen were finding their markets at home and abroad being 'invaded'. They must have thought that a real decline was taking shape. However, the evidence supports the view that the British economy did continue to grow, but its spectacular lead over the Americans and Germans was being eroded. This growth was certainly less than that of competitors abroad, hence the conclusion that economic historians have drawn is of a 'slowing', a 'retardation of growth', and only a relative decline when British performance is compared with others. How have historians explained the retardation of growth?

26.2 *Why did Britain lose its position as the world's major economic power?*

A CASE STUDY IN HISTORICAL INTERPRETATION

Early start thesis

The 'early start thesis' places those who industrialise first at a disadvantage because Britain would be committed to techniques and processes that were outdated. Latecomers then adopt the latest techniques and rectify mistakes made by the pioneers. Modernisation by British industrialists was made difficult for two reasons:

- Why change practices which have proved successful in the past?
- Changes in one part of a manufacturing process would mean changes elsewhere, and this would prove expensive. For instance, the introduction of automated looms or electricity into the cotton industry would also make it necessary to change the design of weaving sheds.

Critics of this thesis point out that, in the 1860s, the Americans and Germans were using much British equipment, while in the steel industry all three were at roughly the same stage of development. So why did the USA and Germany continue to advance technologically, whereas Britain stuck by older, less efficient processes?

The thesis is weakened further by studies of Britain's shipbuilding industry, which continued to prosper despite its 'early start'. It may be the case that some sections of British industry put their faith in traditional technology, but the thesis fails to explain fully Britain's slowing growth.

Declining demand abroad

Declining demand abroad meant lower British exports because other countries were developing their own manufacturing and raw materials, so Britain was bound to lose its lead. W.A. Lewis wrote, in *Growth and Fluctuations, 1870–1913*: 'The principal reason for the relative stagnation of British industry was that Britain ceased to be the workshop of the world.' Britain's competitors – Germany and the USA – had the technical expertise to exploit their natural resources and so import less from Britain. To make matters worse, Britain persisted with a policy of free trade while others, after the 1880s, imposed tariffs (import duties) on British goods.

Hence, British exports rose by 5.6% between 1830 and 1857, but rose by only 3% between 1899 and 1913.

The historian D.N. McClosky is unconvinced that a drop in demand abroad held back growth, because any drop in exports would have led to unemployment. McClosky found no evidence of a steep rise in the numbers of jobless. It is worth noting that Feinstein counters this, arguing that many people were emigrating from Britain at this time, which would affect the unemployment figures. In summary, it seems that this theory has some merit even if it does not tell the whole story.

What about lost market opportunities?

British manufacturers (for example, of cutlery) concentrated on producing 'aristocratic goods of high individual quality', rather than exploiting a larger mass market which might be supplied with cheaply produced goods from production lines – as did manufacturers in Germany and the USA. This is what the historian S.B. Saul called 'the social depth' of demand. American workers were paid sufficient wages to create more demand. The opposite was true in Britain; low wages depressed home demand and only the upper and middle classes were able to afford the quality goods on offer. Little wonder that Britain relied on its export markets, which were apparently shrinking.

Britain's infrastructure also failed to grow, compared with Germany and the USA, where the growth in factories stimulated the construction industry significantly. Given the larger size of the domestic market in both these countries, as well as their access to cheap, plentiful raw materials, Britain was finding it harder to compete.

Supply side factors

These include poor technical and managerial training, too much investment abroad rather than at home, inferior entrepreneurial skills, and the wasteful use of resources. The last factor exposed particular weaknesses in the British manufacturing economy.

In the USA, the shortage of skilled labour pressured manufacturers (for example, in textiles) to introduce labour saving machinery. In tinplate making, in 1910 the USA was able to make the same amount as in Britain with about one-quarter of the work force. In Britain, the abundance of labour was one reason why manufacturers were slow to introduce new technology. In the mines, why should the owners mechanise when they knew they would never be short of labour? The abundance of fuel had a similar effect. Cheap coal meant there was little effort to introduce technology to cut fuel bills. The Coal Conservation Committee, for example, said the marine steam engine used coal 'with a prodigality which is humiliating'. Oil was more efficient, as was electricity in factories. But owners stubbornly retained their attachment to abundant, cheap coal.

Did too much capital go abroad?

There was evidence that twice as much capital was being invested abroad as was invested at home (1911–13) – a damaging indictment of City financiers which did not help technical innovation on a long-term basis in Britain.

Were entrepreneurs to blame?

The historiographical arguments contain two strands:

- The structure of British industry up to 1914 was dominated by 'smallness' – family-run firms who, according to P. Sargent Florence, were 'reinvesting less of their profit'.
- The early success of British industrialists created 'indolence and apathy', as Burn has shown in his study of the steel industry. The historian D. Landes also referred to the complacency of the sons and grandsons of the founders of family firms, who were more interested in their status as country gentlemen than they were in commerce. He says they 'went through the motions of entrepreneurship between the long weekends'. The decline of the great Tennant chemical works in the late 19th century was attributed to this.

1. What reasons have been given by historians to explain why Britain was losing its position as the world's main economic power?

2. Why do historians disagree about the main reason for Britain's economic decline?

As economic conditions worsened, the easy route to preserve profits was to restrict wages rather than invest in technology, standardised mass production, better management and integrated processes (such as weaving and spinning on the same site) so economies of scale could be achieved. Neither did Britain's scientific training compare favourably with that in Germany.

Perhaps it is easy to criticise entrepreneurs in hindsight. As this review shows, economic historians still find it difficult to explain Britain's slower industrial growth in the lead up to the First World War. How much harder it must have been for entrepreneurs to make sense of the trends at the time.

26.3 To what extent had the role of women changed within British society by 1914?

The historian Louise Black argues the case that a 'new woman' was to be seen by the turn of the 20th century. Who was she? Well, she smoked, played hockey and tennis, went on shopping sprees, used trains and motor cars, and ate out at public restaurants. Almost certainly educated, upper or upper middle class, and single, the 'new woman' shocked Edwardian sensitivities in demanding equal pay, the right to enter the professions, equal rights in marriage and, of course, the vote. David Powell, in *The Edwardian Crisis: Britain 1901–1914* (1996), warns that while this stereotype may have been a 'literary and journalistic creation' there was some truth in it. He writes: 'Contemporaries were aware of the existence of a new generation of women for whom marriage was not necessarily the sole aim of life and who were, through education or employment, throwing off the shackles of a traditional home and upbringing ...'. The progress achieved by women in all areas of Britain's social and economic life was mixed; steps forward were taken in the face of ingrained attitudes which proved harder to change. For many, their lives were little changed from those of their mothers and grandmothers. Indeed, many women saw no reason to challenge the *status quo* as they accepted society's assumptions about their place in it. Other women, however, clearly felt they had far to go before achieving any measure of equality.

Changes were taking place in the world of work, in education, in the law, in public as well as private family life. Above all, though, it was the campaign for women's suffrage which attracted the most attention (see Chapter 23). The Pankhursts' claims that their tactics brought success sooner rather than later are open to question. The WSPU certainly galvanised support, but it also galvanised the opposition which was able to accuse women of being emotionally unbalanced and unfit to take a more active role in society. However, while the Suffragettes created what seemed like an atmosphere of crisis, their work was only part of a larger canvas.

Women, particularly from the middle class, were becoming more involved in politics. Beatrice Webb, for instance, was a leading member of the Fabians (see page 336) although female involvement in national policy and organisation was rare. It was at a local level where things advanced more dramatically. After 1894, women were able to sit on parish and district councils; in 1907, the Qualification of Women Act extended this right to county councils. To add to those who were elected to these bodies, there were hundreds more who sat on School Boards and who served as Poor Law Guardians.

Women at work

At work, class played as significant a part in determining women's employment as did gender. For working-class women, it was true that factory and mill conditions had improved and maximum hours been fixed by statute – just as they had been for men. But it is difficult to accept that any progress had been achieved. Women provided cheap labour for employers and their work was often casual and temporary – for women of childbearing age their health certainly suffered from their annual pregnancies and too rapid a return to long hours of work following the birth. Hence the concern for the nation's health, in which the debate on 'National Efficiency' (see page 384) merely served to emphasise that only unmarried women should seek employment outside the home. Little effort or encouragement was made to help working-class women return to work after adding to the family because society accepted that the 'feminine' role for women was at home, bringing up the children and training their daughters to become, in their turn, mothers and housewives. This attitude so powerfully underpinned Edwardian views of women that it resurfaces continually, even in areas such as education where women had made more progress.

When women did work, it was assumed they would accept roles that did not detract from their 'femininity'. In 1911, 35% – almost all from working-class backgrounds – were in domestic service, although this figure was in decline. The reasons for this are unclear; after 1870, more women had access to education and thereby different types of work in towns, rather than in rural areas. Perhaps there were fewer girls for the 'big house' to draw on. It is not inconceivable that some families could not afford as many servants. Whatever the reasons, unmarried working-class girls were increasingly becoming shop assistants or conforming to stereotypes (cooks, machinists or mill hands), while married women would spend long hours at home dressmaking, childminding or making cardboard boxes.

However, marriage to a skilled working man who could command higher wages brought altogether different social aspirations. Here, a wife could share her husband's pride in the fact that she would not have to 'take in' work and supplement the family income.

Three-quarters of all British women were kept in 'separate spheres' from men. Where they did work together, women were more poorly paid, had poorer chances of promotion and normally completed unskilled tasks. Men were seen as more skilled, adaptable and of managerial status. Even when occupied in the same job, women were paid less. Female clerks received only one-third the pay of male counterparts. Some trade unions disapproved of working women; only 3% of women were unionised compared to 20% for men in 1901.

It was difficult for a poor, single girl to remain 'respectable', and the historiography of women's movements documents how little progress was made to reduce prostitution at this time. The law was much criticised for the hypocritical attitude taken towards punishing the prostitutes when no action was taken against those men who exploited them. Christabel Pankhurst's moral blasts against men as carriers of sexually transmitted diseases (for example in her book *The Great Scourge and How To End It*) provoked hostility and deflected attention away from the campaign to criminalise the procurement of girls for prostitution.

Changes were more apparent for middle-class women by the 1890s. Birth control, while not entirely socially acceptable, was clearly being practised; middle-class women on average had three children compared with the six in working-class families. Superficial analysis might conclude that this released more time for careers or leisure activities. However, middle-class (and upper-class) women were still severely constrained by financial dependence on their father or husband and by stifling social expectations of decorous boredom, then a good marriage, maintaining a position in 'society' by the side of their husband, childbearing and, throughout it all, sexual inhibition. Bertrand Russell, who married his first wife in 1894, commented on how she had been taught to think that 'sex was beastly'.

Opportunities for young, unmarried middle-class women, though, were increasing. Lower-grade work was readily available; women clerks, typists, bookkeepers were in demand. Between 1891 and 1911, the number of women clerks in commerce tripled and 35,000 were employed as telephonists by the GPO (General Post Office; forerunner of British Telecom). Women were taken on as health visitors and even factory inspectors (after 1893). However, it was not untypical that women who became journalists were expected to write about cooking or fashion. Entry into the professions, stubbornly male dominated, would prove harder and relied on expanding educational opportunities.

Education

Certainly, doors were opening. Middle- and upper-class girls attended fee-paying schools or were educated at home. Education for working-class girls in the years after the passage of the 1870 Act gradually became more widespread, and was free and compulsory, although the curriculum reflected society's expectations of adult women's role in society. Universities were accepting women; colleges at both Oxford and Cambridge were established. Women such as Sophia Jex-Blake pioneered access to university medical schools, but it was still difficult to find sufficient places and even more difficult to secure a position in a hospital afterwards.

It is true that there were more dentists, midwives and pharmacists, but progress was slow. In 1881, there were 25 women doctors; by 1901, there were still only 212 (out of a total of 220,000). In 1910, women first took examinations to become chartered accountants. In contrast, 150,000 women teachers dominated the profession in 1891, but at lower rates of pay and with less scope for advancement than men. There were no women solicitors or barristers and only a tiny number had successfully negotiated the selection process for the Civil Service.

The law

Women's legal rights in marriage had made huge strides. They ended the century as the legal equals of their husbands, not just their 'property'. They could keep their own earnings and property – indeed they were free to manage their own property as they saw fit. Having already gained the right to receive maintenance payments, a landmark legal judgement in 1910 also gave divorced women substantial rights over the custody of children. Nevertheless, divorce for women was much more difficult than it was for men. A man only needed to prove adultery by his wife, whereas a wife needed an extra burden of proof, such as cruelty. Equality of treatment was not achieved until 1923.

Despite widening opportunities for women, society's attitudes proved difficult to shift. Married women were still expected to sit by the hearth or their husband's side; 'separate spheres' still determined gender roles. However, pre-war trends were recognisable, especially for younger women – a point which should not be overlooked by those who exaggerate the importance of the First World War in making the dramatic breakthrough by advancing women's position in the economy and society.

Source-based questions: The Suffragettes

(See this chapter and Chapter 23.)

SOURCE A

'We have tried every way. We have presented larger petitions than were ever presented before for any reform; we have succeeded in holding greater public meetings than men have ever had for any reform. We have faced hostile mobs at street corners, because we were told that we could not have that representation for our taxes that men have won unless we converted the whole country to our side. Because we have done this we have been misrepresented, we have been ridiculed ...

Well, sir, that is all I have to say to you. We are not here because we are law-breakers, we are here in our efforts to become law-makers!'

From Mrs Emmeline Pankhurst's speech in front of magistrates in London, 1908.

SOURCE B

The vote was not sought for any practical object, but as a symbol of equality. They were obsessed by an inferiority complex. And similarly upon politics at large their militancy had more effect than their suffragism. The means mattered more than the end ... the WSPU leaders proclaimed, by word and deed, that the way to get results was through violence. Such doctrines are always liable to become popular ...

From England, 1870–1914 *by R.C.K.Ensor, published in 1936.*

SOURCE C

There is a case for saying that by the early 1900s the debate over the general principle of enfranchising women had been largely won. This, however, by no means resolved the problem ... politicians had yet to be convinced that women's suffrage mattered enough to the majority of women to justify devoting scarce parliamentary time to it. Up to a point Mrs Fawcett's non-militants helped to persuade them by mobilising more trade unions behind the cause, and by their shrewd electoral pact with the Labour Party in 1912; this put real pressure on the Asquith Government .... by encouraging a drift of Liberal women towards Labour. In addition, Fawcett's National Union of Women's Suffrage Societies at last began to grow ... from under 6,000 in 1907 to over 50,000 by 1913. Many of the new members were women who had been aroused by suffrage activities; while they did not wish to be involved with militant methods themselves, they felt moved to show their support for the cause in a different way. This was probably the one positive contribution of the Pankhursts to winning the vote.

From Martin Pugh's article 'Votes for Women' (published in Britain 1867–1918 *by the Institute of Contemporary British History, 1994).*

---

1. Study Source A.

How does Mrs Emmeline Pankhurst defend her actions?

2. Study Sources A and B.

Compare the views of a suffragette (Source A) with those of a historian (Source B). Which gives the more reliable account to a historian studying the reasons for Suffragette violence? Give reasons to support your answer.

3. 'The impact of the Suffragettes on society before the First World War has been exaggerated.' Use the sources and your reading to explain whether you agree with this statement.

Further Reading

CHAPTER 2 William Pitt the Younger, 1783–1801

Articles

'Pitt the Younger' by Graham Goodlad in the *Modern History Review* Vol. 13 No. 3 (February 2002)

Texts designed for AS and A2 level students

William Pitt the Younger by Eric Evans (Routledge, Lancaster pamphlets 1999)

The Younger Pitt by Michael Duffy (Longman, Profiles in Power 2000)

Politics in the Age of Fox, Pitt and Liverpool by John Derry (Macmillan, British History in Perspective series 1990)

British Radicalism and the French Revolution 1789–1815 by H.T. Dickinson (Blackwell, 1985)

Chapter 3 The Tory Party, 1815–1830

Articles

In *Modern History Review*:

'English Radicalism before the Chartists' by J.R. Dinwiddy (November 1990)

'"Liberal" and "High" Tories in the age of Lord Liverpool' by G. Goodlad (November 1995)

'The Premiership of Lord Liverpool' by Eric Evans (April 1990)

'Catholic Emancipation' by W. Hindle (April 1995)

Also in *History Review* (formerly *History Sixth*):

'Lord Liverpool – the unobtrusive Prime Minister' by John Derry (20 December 1994)

Texts designed for AS and A2 level students

Britain before the Reform Act: Politics and Society 1815–1832 by Eric Evans (Longman, Seminar Studies series, 1989)

Tories, Conservatives and Unionists 1815–1914 by Duncan Watts (Hodder and Stoughton, Access to A Level series, 1994)

Regency *England: The Age of Lord Liverpool* by John Plowright (Routledge, Lancaster Pamphlets, 1996)

Aspects of British Political History 1815–1914 by S.J. Lee (Routledge, 1994)

More advanced reading

Aristocracy and People: Britain 1815–1865 by Norman Gash (Edward Arnold, 1987)

The Forging of the Modern State – Early Industrial Britain 1783–1867 by Eric Evans (Longman, 1983)

Chapter 4 British foreign policy, 1815–1846

Articles

'Europe after Napoleon – Castlereagh's Foreign Policy' by John Derry in *Modern History Review* (February 1993)

'Canning and the Pittite tradition' by J. Derry in *History Review* No. 24 (March 1996)

Texts designed for AS and A2 level students

Britain before the Reform Act: Politics and Society 1815–32 by Eric Evans (Longman, Seminar Studies series, 1989)

Regency England: Lord Liverpool and Reform by John Plowright (Routledge, Lancaster Pamphlets, 1996)

Aspects of British Political History 1815–1914 by S.J. Lee (Routledge, 1994)

More advanced reading

Some excellent biographies of the leading political figures:

Castlereagh by J. Derry (London, 1976)

Canning by W. Hinde (London, 1973)

Lord Palmerston by Muriel Chamberlain (GBC Books, 1987)

'Pax Britannica'? – British Foreign Policy 1789–1914 by Muriel Chamberlain (Longman, 1988)

Foreign Affairs 1815–1865 by D.R. Ward (Collins, 1972)

The Great Powers and the European System 1815–1914 by F.R. Bridge and R. Bullen (Longman, 1980)

Britain and Europe: Pitt to Churchill 1793–1940 by James Joll (A&C Black, 1961)

Chapter 5 Ireland 1798–1921: a thematic study

The Irish Question and British Politics by D.G. Boyce (Macmillan, 1988)

(See also Further Reading for Chapter 17)

Chapter 6 The Great Reform Act of 1832

Articles

'The Great Reform Act Reconsidered' by Eric Evans, *History Sixth* No. 3 (1988)

'An Aristocrat fights the old political order: Political changes probable' by E.A. Smith, *New Perspective* (1995)

Texts designed for AS and A2 level students

The Great Reform Act by Eric Evans (Routledge, Lancaster Pamphlet, 2nd edition 1994)

Britain before the Reform Act: Politics and society 1815–32 by Eric Evans (Longman, Seminar Studies series, 1989)

Democracy and Reform 1815–83 by D.G. Wright (Longman, Seminar Studies series, 1989)

Government and Reform 1815–1918 by Robert Pearce and Roger Stearn (Hodder and Stoughton, Access to A Level series, 1994)

Whigs, Radicals and Liberals by D. Watts (Hodder and Stoughton, Access to A Level series, 1995)

More advanced reading

Aristocracy and People – Britain 1815–65 by Norman Gash (Edward Arnold, 1987)

The Age of Improvement 1763–1867 by Asa Briggs (Longman, 1969)

The Great Reform Act by M. Brock (Oxford University Press, 1973)

Reform or Revolution? A Diary of Reform 1830–1832 by E.A. Smith (Sutton, 1992)

Party and Politics 1830–1852 by Robert Stewart (Macmillan, 1989)

England in the 1830s, A Decade of Reform by G. Finlayson (Edward Arnold, 1969)

Chapter 7 The Whigs, 1833–1841

Articles

'The New Poor Law' by P. Mandler in *Modern History Review*

'The Age of Reform' by N. McCord in *Modern History Review*

'The Myth of the Old Poor Law and the making of the New' in *Journal of Economic History* (1963)

'The Whigs in the Age of Reform, a Positive Reappraisal' by P. Brett in *Modern History Review*

Texts designed for AS and A2 level students

Government and Reform 1815–1918 by Robert Pearce and Roger Stearn (Hodder and Stoughton, Access to A Level series, 1994)

Whigs, Radicals and Liberals by Duncan Watts (Hodder and Stoughton, Access to A Level series, 1995)

Poverty and Welfare 1830–1914 by Ken Warman (Hodder and Stoughton, Access to A Level series)

More advanced reading
Party and Politics by R. Stewart (Macmillan, British History in Perspective series 1989)
The Passing of the Whigs by D. Southgate (Macmillan, 1962)
England in the 1830s, A Decade of Reform by G. Finlayson (Edward Arnold, 1969)
Aristocratic Government in the Age of Reform: Whigs and Liberals, 1830–1852 by P. Mandler (1990)
Decade of Reform: English Politics and Opinion in the 1830s by Alexander Llewellyn (David and Charles, 1972)
Charles, Earl Grey by J.W. Derry (Blackwell, 1992)
Lord Melbourne by P. Ziegler (Collins, 1976)

Chapter 8 Sir Robert Peel and the Tory/Conservative Party, 1830–1846

Articles
In *Modern History Review*:
'Peel and his Party – The Age of Peel Reassessed' by R. Foster
'Sir Robert Peel and the Conservative Party' by Norman Gash
'Ireland 1800–1850' by T. Chapman
Also in *History Review* (formerly *History Sixth*):
'Sir Robert Peel: A suitable case for Reassessment?' by Eric Evans
'Party in the Age of Peel and Palmerston' by R. Stewart
'Peel' by D. Eastwood
For a less than flattering view of Peel's career:
'Peel: A Reappraisal' by A.J. Boyd-Hilton in *Historical Journal* No. 22 (1979)
'Sir Robert Peel and the Conservative Party, 1832–1841: A study in failure?' by I. Newbould, *English Historical Review* (1983)

Texts designed for AS and A2 level students
Tories, Conservatives and Unionists by D. Watts (Hodder and Stoughton, Access to A Level series, 1994)
Peel and the Conservative Party, 1830–1850 by P. Adelman (Longman, Seminar Studies series, 1989)
Sir Robert Peel: Statesmanship, Power and Party by Eric Evans (Routledge, Lancaster Pamphlet, 1994)

More advanced reading
Sir Robert Peel: The Life of Sir Robert Peel after 1830 by Norman Gash (Longman, 1986)
Aristocracy and People 1815–1865 by Norman Gash (Arnold, 1987)
Conservatism and the Conservative Party in Nineteenth-Century Britain by B. Coleman (Arnold, 1988)
The Conservative Party from Peel to Thatcher by Lord Blake (Fontana, 1985)
The Anti-Corn Law League by N. McCord (London, 1948)
Party and Politics 1830–1852 by R. Stewart (Macmillan, 1989)
The Foundation of the Conservative Party 1830–1867 by Robert Stewart (Longman, 1978)

Chapter 9 Chartism

Articles
'The Nature of Chartism' by H. Cunningham in *Modern History Review* (April 1990)
'Taking Chartism seriously' by C. Behagg in *Modern History Review* (April 1994)
'The Origins and Nature of Chartism' by E. Royle in *History Review* (issue 13, 1992)

Texts designed for AS and A2 level students
Chartism by E. Royle (Longman, Seminar Studies series, 1986)
Labour and Reform, Working Class Movements 1815–1914 by C. Behagg (Hodder and Stoughton, Access to A Level series, 1995)

More advanced reading
The Chartist Experience: Studies in Working-class Radicalism and Culture, 1830–60 edited by James Epstein and Dorothy Thompson (Palgrave Macmillan, 1982)
The Chartists by Dorothy Thompson (Temple Smith, 1984)
Chartism and Society edited by F.C. Mather (Batsford, 1980)
The Last Rising: The Newport insurrection of 1839 (Oxford University Press, 1985)
The Lion of Freedom: Feargus O'Connor and the Chartist Movement, 1832–42 by James Epstein (Routledge, 1982)

Chapter 10 Economic change 1815–1846: the growth of railways

Article
'The Age of Steam: Railways in Victorian Britain' by M. Freeman in *Modern History Review* (February 1992)

More advanced reading
Transport in Victorian Britain by David Aldcroft and Michael Freedman (eds) (Manchester University Press, 1988)
Railways and Economic Growth in Britain 1840–1870 by G.R. Hawke (Oxford University Press, 1970)
Capital Formation in the Industrial Revolution by F. Crouzet (ed.) (Methuen, 1972)
Railways and the British Economy, 1830–1914 by T. May (London, 1972)
Industry and Empire: from 1750 to the present day by Eric Hobsbawm (Penguin, 1999)
The Industrial Age: Economy and Society in Britain by Charles More (Longman, 1989)

Chapter 11 British domestic politics, 1846–1868

Articles
In *Modern History Review*:
'Palmerston' by S.J. Lee (March 1996)
'Cobden after the Repeal' by K. Fielden (November 1994)

Texts designed for AS and A2 level students
Conservatives and Unionists by D.C. Watts (Hodder and Stoughton, Access to History series, 1994)
Government and Reform by Robert Pearce (Hodder and Stoughton, Access to History series, 1994)
Democracy and Reform by D.C. Wright (Longman, Seminar Studies series, 1970)
Gladstone and the Liberal Party by Michael Winstanley (Routledge, Lancaster Pamphlets, 1986)

Advanced reading
Gladstone by G. Shannon (Hamish Hamilton, 1982)
Disraeli by I. Machin (Longman, 1995)
The Liberal Party by J. Parry (Yale University Press, 1990)
The Conservative Party from Peel to Churchill by Robert Blake (Penguin, 1982)

Chapter 12 British foreign policy in the Age of Palmerston, 1846–1868

Articles
A particularly good article in *New Perspectives*:
'The Eastern Question' by A.L. Mcfie (September 1996)
A particularly good article in *Modern History Review*:
'Pax Britannica' by Muriel Chamberlain (September 1996)

Text designed for AS and A2 level students
Foreign Affairs by D.R. Ward (Collins, 1982)

Advanced reading
Palmerston by J. Ridley (Constable, 1970)
Palmerston by Muriel Chamberlain (GBC Books, 1987)
The Foreign Policy of Victorian England by K. Bourne (Longman, 1970)

Britain and the Eastern Question by G. Clayton (University of London Press, 1971)

Chapter 13 A mid-Victorian boom? Economic and social history, 1846–1868

Articles

'The New Poor Law' by J. Garrard (*New Perspectives*, March 1997)
'Distress and Reform 1815–1867' by P. Catterall (*Modern History Review*, November 1994)

Texts designed for AS and A2 level students

Labour and Reform by C. Behagg (Hodder and Stoughton, Access to History Series, 1995)
The Rise of British Trade Unionism 1825–1914 by A. Brown (Longman, Seminar Studies series, 1978)
Victorian Social Reform by E.C. Midwinter (Longman, Seminar Studies series, 1982)
The Changing Role of Women 1815–1914 by P. Bartley (Hodder and Stoughton, Access to History series, 1996)
The Great Victorian Boom by R. Church (Macmillan, 'Studies in Economic and Social History' series, 1975)
Laissez Faire and State Intervention in Britain by A.J.P. Taylor (Macmillan, 'Studies in Economic and Social History' series, 1978)

More advanced reading

British Labour History by E.W.H. Hunt (Weidenfeld and Nicolson, 1981)
The British Economy by D. May (Collins, 1972)
Railways and the British Economy by T.R. Gourvish (Macmillan, 1980)
The Making of Social Policy in Britain by K. Jones (Athlone Press, 1991)

CHAPTER 14 From Poor Law to Welfare State, 1830–1948

Texts designed for AS and A2 level students

Laissez-faire and State Intervention in the Nineteenth Century by A.J.P. Taylor (Macmillan 1972)
The Poor Law in Nineteenth-Century England and Wales by A. Digby (Historical Association, 1982)
Endangered Lives. Public Health in Victorian Britain by A. Wohl (Dent, 1983)
Before the Welfare State by U. Henriques (Longman, 1979)
The Coming of the Welfare State by M. Bruce (Batsford, 1968)
Education for the Nation by R. Aldrich (Cassell, 1996)
Education in the Twentieth Century by P. Gosden (Methuen, 1976)
State and Society: A Social and Political History of Britain, 1870–1997 by Martin Pugh (Arnold, 1999)
British Society since 1945 by A. Marwick (Penguin 1996)

More advanced reading

Modern Britain: an Economic and Social History by S. Glynn and A. Booth (Routledge, 1996)
Social Conditions in Britain 1918–39 by S. Constantine (Routledge, 1984)
Class and Cultures. England 1918–51 by R. McKibbin (Oxford University Press, 2000)

Chapter 15 Gladstone and the Liberal Party, 1868–1894

Articles

In *Modern History Review*:
'Gladstone and Liberalism' by Paul Adelman (Vol. 2 No. 3)
'The Man who refused to be Prime Minister' (on Lord Hartington) by Patrick Jackson (Vol. 3 No. 1)
'John the Baptist of Gladstonian Liberalism' (on John Bright) by John Vincent (Vol. 3 No. 2)
'Parliamentary Reform in the 1880s' by M. Pugh (Vol. 4 No. 1)
'Juggler Joe: Radical and Unionist' by D. Watts (Vol. 5 No. 1)

In *History Review* (formerly *History Sixth*):
'Whigs in the Gladstonian Liberal Party' by E.J. Feuchtwanger, No. 7 (Sept. 1990)
'Joseph Chamberlain and the Liberal Unionist Party' by D. Dutton, No. 18 (March 1994)

Texts designed for AS and A2 level students

Gladstone, Disraeli and Later Victorian Politics by P. Adelman (Longman, Seminar Studies series, 2nd edn, 1987)
Joseph Chamberlain, Radical and Imperialist by H. Browne (Longman, Seminar Studies series, 1974)
Joseph Chamberlain and the Challenge of Radicalism by Duncan Watts (Hodder and Stoughton, 1992)
Whigs, Radicals and Liberals 1815 to 1914 by Duncan Watts (Hodder and Stoughton, Access to History series, 1995)
Gladstone and the Liberal Party by M. Winstanley (Routledge, Lancaster Pamphlets, 1990)
Government and Reform 1815 to 1918 by Robert Pearce and Roger Stearn (Hodder and Stoughton, 1994)

More advanced reading

Gladstone 1809 to 1874 by H. Matthew (Oxford University Press, 1988)
Gladstone 1874 to 1898 by H. Matthew (Oxford University Press, 1995)
Democracy and Empire: British History 1865 to 1914 by E.J. Feuchtwanger (Arnold, 1985)
The Making of Modern British Politics 1867 to 1939 by Martin Pugh (Blackwell, 1982)

Chapter 16 The Conservative Party of Disraeli and Salisbury, 1868–1895

Articles

In *Modern History Review*:
'Disraeli: Political Outsider' by Robert Blake (Vol. 1 No. 2)
'Perspectives: Tory Democracy' by Paul Smith and Bruce Coleman (Vol. 1 No. 4)
'Concepts: Conservatism' by Bruce Coleman (Vol. 6 No. 3)
'Lord Salisbury and Late Victorian Conservatism' by Graham Goodlad (Vol. 2 No. 3)

In *History Review* (formerly *History Sixth*):
'Disraeli: Myth and Reality, Policy and Presentation' by John Walton (No. 14, December 1992)

Texts designed for AS and A2 level students

Gladstone, Disraeli and Later Victorian Politics by P. Adelman (Longman, Seminar Studies series, 2nd edn, 1987)
Tories, Conservatives and Unionists 1815 to 1914 by Duncan Watts (Hodder and Stoughton Access to History series, 1994)
Disraeli by John Walton (Routledge, Lancaster Pamphlets, 1990)
Aspects of British Political History 1815–1914 by Stephen Lee (Routledge, 1994)

More advanced reading

Disraeli by Ian Machin (Longman, Profiles in Power, 1995)
Lord Salisbury by Robert Taylor (Allen Lane, 1975)
Democracy and Empire: British History 1865 to 1914 by E.J. Feuchtwanger (Arnold, 1985)
The Conservative Leadership 1832 to 1932 edited by D. Southgate (Macmillan, 1974)
Conservatism and the Conservative Party in the Nineteenth Century by Bruce Coleman (Arnold, 1988)
The Conservative Party from Peel to Thatcher by Robert Blake (Fontana, 1985)
The Making of Modern British Politics 1867 to 1939 by Martin Pugh (Blackwell, 1982)

Chapter 17 Ireland and British politics, 1868–1894

Articles

In *Modern History Review*:

'Britain and Ireland 1880–1921: Searching for the Scapegoat' by Christopher Collins (April 1991)

'Gladstone's Irish Policy: Expediency or High Principle?' by E.J. Feuchtwanger (November 1991)

'Parnell and Home Rule' by Donald MacRaild (February 1993)

Also in *History Review* (formerly *History Sixth*):

'Gladstone and Ireland' by Alan O'Day (March 1990)

'Joseph Chamberlain and the Liberal Unionist Party' by D.J. Dutton (March 1994)

In *The Historian* (Winter 1995) there is an article on Gladstone by Ian Machin.

Texts designed for AS and A2 level students

Great Britain and the Irish Question 1800–1922 by Paul Adelman (Hodder, Access to History Series, 1996)

Home Rule and the Irish Question by Grenfell Morton (Longman, Seminar Studies series, 1980)

More advanced reading

Ireland Since the Famine by F.S.L. Lyons (Weidenfeld, 1971)

Modern Ireland 1600–1972 by R. Foster (Penguin, 1988)

For more advanced reading on Gladstone:

Gladstone 1809–1874 by H.C. Matthew (Oxford University Press, 1988)

Gladstone 1874 to 1898 by H.C. Matthew (Oxford University Press, 1995)

Chapter 18 Foreign and imperial change, 1868–1895

Articles

In *Modern History Review*:

'European Imperialism in the late 19th Century' by Andrew Porter (Vol. 2 No. 4)

'Conflict in the Balkans 1876–1878' by John Morison (Vol. 3 No. 1)

'British Idea of Empire' by Kathryn Tidrick (Vol. 4 No. 1)

Texts designed for AS and A2 level students

The British Empire 1815 to 1914 by F. McDonough (Hodder and Stoughton, Access to History series, 1994)

Britain and the European Power 1865 to 1914 by Robert Pearce (Hodder and Stoughton, Access to History series, 1996)

The Scramble for Africa by Muriel Chamberlain (Longman, Seminar Studies series, 1974)

The Eastern Question, 1774–1923 by A. McFie (Longman, Seminar Studies series, 1989)

The Partition of Africa by J. MacKenzie (Routledge, Lancaster Pamphlets 1983)

Disraeli by J. Walton (Routledge, Lancaster Pamphlets, 1990)

More advanced reading

'Pax Britannica'?: British Foreign Policy 1789–1914 by Muriel Chamberlain (Longman, 1988)

Victorian Imperialism by C.C. Eldridge (Hodder and Stoughton, 1978)

Britain and the Eastern Question by G. Clayton (University of London Press, 1971)

Democracy and Empire by E.J. Feuchtwanger (Arnold, 1985)

Crisis of Imperialism by R. Shannon (Paladin, 1976)

Chapter 19 Social and economic change, 1868–1896

Article

'The Dock Strike of 1889' by Joyce Howson (*Modern History Review*, Vol. 7 No. 3)

Texts designed for AS and A2 level students

Labour and Reform, 1815–1914 by Clive Behagg (Hodder and Stoughton, Access to History series, 1991)

The Economy 1815–1914 by Trevor May (Collins, 1972)

The First Industrial Nation by Peter Mathias (Methuen, 1969)

More advanced reading

The Myth of the Great Depression by S.B. Saul (Macmillan, 1969)

Industry and Empire by Eric Hobsbawm (Penguin, 1969)

British Trade Unions 1875–1933 by John Lovell (Macmillan, 1977)

The Victorian Economy by F. Crouzet (Methuen, 1982)

Chapter 20 The era of Conservative domination and the rise of Labour, 1895–1906

Articles

In *Modern History Review*:

'A Rogue Result' by Simon Lemieux (Vol. 4 No. 2, November 1992)

G.D. Goodlad on Lord Salisbury (February 1996) and a series by Duncan Tanner on the rise of the Labour Party (November 1989, April 1994).

Texts designed for AS and A2 level students

On the Conservative Party:

Tories, Conservatives and Unionists 1815–1914 by Duncan Watts (Hodder and Stoughton, Access to History series, 1994)

Gladstone, Disraeli and Later Victorian Politics by Paul Adelman (Longman, Seminar Studies series, 1983)

As a general text:

Democracy and Empire, Britain 1865–1914 by E.J. Feuchtwanger (Edward Arnold, 1985)

The following provide different interpretations:

The Conservative Party from Peel to Thatcher by Robert Blake (Fontana, 1985)

The Making of Modern British Politics 1867–1939 by Martin Pugh (Basil Blackwell, 1982)

On the Labour Party:

The Rise of the Labour Party 1880–1945 by Paul Adelman (Longman, Seminar Studies series, 1986)

Labour and Reform, Working-Class Movements 1815–1914 by Clive Behagg (Hodder and Stoughton, 1991)

Biography:

Keir Hardie by Kenneth Morgan (Weidenfeld and Nicolson, 1975)

More advanced reading

Party and the Political System in Britain 1867–1914 by J. Belchem (Blackwell, 1990)

The Rise of the Labour Party 1893–1931 by G. Phillips (Routledge, 1992)

Political Change and the Labour Party, 1900–24 by D. Tanner (Cambridge University Press, 1990)

Chapter 21 Joseph Chamberlain and the Empire, 1895–1905

Articles

Two useful articles reprinted in 'Britain 1867–1918', by the Institute of Contemporary British History (Heinemann):

'Juggler Joe: Radical and Unionist' by Duncan Watts

'Brits, Boers and Blacks: The Boer War 1899–1902' by Keith Surridge

Texts designed for AS and A2 level students

Joseph Chamberlain, Radical and Imperialist by Harry Browne (Longman, Seminar Studies, 1974)

Joseph Chamberlain and the Challenge of Radicalism by Duncan Watts (Hodder and Stoughton, 1992)

More advanced reading

The Boer War by T. Pakenham (Weidenfeld and Nicolson, 1979)
The Origins of the South African War by A. Porter (Manchester University Press, 1980)
The Fall of Kruger's Republic by J. Marais (Oxford University Press, 1961)

Chapter 22 Ireland and British politics, 1895–1922

Texts designed for AS and A2 level students

Great Britain and the Irish Question, 1800–1922 by Paul Adelman (Hodder and Stoughton, Access to History series, 1996)
Home Rule and the Irish Question by Grenfell Morton (Longman, Seminar Studies, 1980)

More advanced reading

Ireland since the Famine by F.S.L. Lyons (Fontana, 1973)
The Irish Question 1840–1921 by Nicholas Mansergh (University of Toronto Press, 1965)
Ireland 1780–1914 by S.R. Gibbons (Blackie, 1978)

Two further central texts about Ulster

The Liberals and Ireland. The Ulster Question in British Politics to 1914 by Patricia Jalland (Harvester Press, 1980)
'Irish Unionism' by Patrick Buckland (Historical Association pamphlet, 1973).

Chapter 23 The Liberals in power, 1905–1915

Articles

In *Modern History Review*:
Martin Pugh on votes for women (September 1990)
Ewen Green on the Parliamentary crisis of 1910–1911 (April 1996)
Paul Adelman on the decline of the Liberals (November 1989)
Simon Lemieux on the Liberals 1910–1914 (November 1992)
Duncan Tanner on 'New Liberalism' (November 1990)

Texts designed for AS and A2 level students

The Shaping of the Welfare State by R.C. Birch (Longman, Seminar Studies, 1974)
The Last Years of Liberal England, 1900–1914 by K.W. Aitken (Collins)
The Edwardian Crisis, Britain 1901–1914 by David Powell (Macmillan, 1995)
Lloyd George and the Liberal Dilemma by Michael Lynch (Hodder and Stoughton, 1993)
Democracy and Empire: Britain 1865–1914 by E.J. Feuchtwanger (Edward Arnold, 1985)
Lloyd George – The People's Champion by John Grigg (Methuen, 1978)
See also 'Women's Suffrage in Britain 1867–1928' by Martin Pugh (Historical Association, 1980) and *Electoral reform in War and Peace 1906–1918* by Martin Pugh (Routledge and Kegan Paul)

Chapter 24 Britain and the origins of the First World War, 1898–1914

Texts designed for AS and A2 level students

Foreign Affairs, 1886–1914 by M.C. Morgan (Collins, 1972)
See also *British Foreign Policy, 1870–1914* by Judith Ward (Blackie, 1978)

A useful Historical Association publication is F.R. Bridge, '1914 The Coming of the First World War' (1983) and A.J.P. Taylor's 'The Struggle for Mastery in Modern Europe' can be used selectively.

More advanced reading

The War Plans of the Great Powers 1880–1914 by P.M. Kennedy (ed.) (Allen and Unwin, 1979)
Britain and the Origins of the First World War by Zara Steiner (Macmillan, 1977)
August, 1914 by B.W. Tuchman (Constable, 1962)

Chapter 25 The political, social and economic impact, 1914–1918

Articles

In *Modern History Review*:
A. Marwick on the impact of the Two World Wars (September 1990)
K.O. Morgan on Lloyd George (February 1994)

Texts designed for AS and A2 level students

The Deluge by Arthur Marwick (Bodley Head, 1967)
There is a collection of essays in *The First World War in British History*, edited by S. Constantine, M. Kirby and M.B. Rose (Edward Arnold, 1995).

Impact of war on women and on politics

The Making of Modern British Politics by Martin Pugh (Blackwell, 1982)
Women's Suffrage in Britain, 1867–1928 by Martin Pugh (Historical Association, 1980)
Testament of Youth by Vera Brittan (Gollancz, 1978).

Chapter 26 British economy and society, 1896–1914:

Texts designed for AS and A2 level students

The Changing Role of Women, 1815–1914 by Paula Bartley (Hodder and Stoughton, 1996)
The Edwardian Crisis, 1901–14 by David Powell (Macmillan, 1996) – section on women.

Texts about women's suffrage

Women's Suffrage in Britain, 1867–1928 by Martin Pugh (Historical Association, 1980)
Separate Spheres: the Opposition to Women's Suffrage in Britain by B. Harrison (Croon Helm, 1978)
One Hand Tied Behind Us: The Rise of the Women's Suffrage Movement by J. Liddington and J. Norris (Virago, 1979)

Introductory texts which cover Britain's economic history:

The Industrial Age: Economy and Society in Britain, 1750–1985 by Charles More (Longman, 1989)
Britain: Industrial Relations and the Economy, 1900–1939 by Robert Pearce (Hodder and Stoughton, 1993)

Index

Glossary terms

Profiles

MAIN INDEX